A TREATISE ON

MIND

VOLUME 7

The Constitution of

Shambhala

PART A

General Considerations on Shambhala

Other Titles in the Series

The I Concept

Volume 1: The 'Self' or 'Non-self' in Buddhism

Volume 2: Considerations of Mind - A Buddhist Enquiry

Volume 3: The Buddha-Womb and the Way to Liberation

Cellular Consciousness

Volume 4: Maṇḍalas - Their Nature and Development

Volume 5: An Esoteric Exposition of the Bardo Thödol (Part A)

Volume 5: An Esoteric Exposition of the Bardo Thödol (Part B)

The Way to Shambhala

Volume 6: Meditation and the Initiation Process

Volume 7: The Constitution of Shambhala (Part B and C)

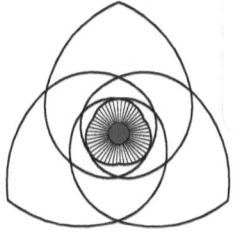

VOLUME SEVEN

The Constitution of

Shambhala

PART A

General Considerations on Shambhala

BODO BALSYS

UNIVERSAL DHARMA
PUBLICATIONS
SYDNEY, AUSTRALIA

ISBN 978-0-9923568-6-6

Revision 4, 2025

Āḥ!

Homage to the Lord of Shambhala.
Inconceivable, inconceivable, beyond thought
Is the bejewelled crown of this most excelled Jina.
He whose Eye has taught many Buddhas.
And who will anoint the myriad,
that in the future lives will come.
As I bow to His Feet my Heart's afire.
Oh, this bliss, this love for my Lord
can barely be borne on my part.
It takes flight as the might of the Dove.
The flight of serene *nirvāṇic* embrace.
The flight of Light so bright.
The flight of Love so active tonight.
The flight of enlightenment for all to come to
their mind's Heart's attire.

Obeisance to the Gurus!
To the Buddhas of the three times.
To the Council of Bodhisattvas, *mahāsattvas*.
To them I pledge allegiance.

Oṁ Hūṁ! Hūṁ! Hūṁ!

Dedication

Thanks to my students, past, present and future, and in particular to those that have helped in the production of this Treatise.

Oṁ

Acknowledgments

Special thanks to Angie O'Sullivan, Kylie Smith,
and Ruth Fitzpatrick
for their efforts in making this
series possible.

Oṁ

Contents

Preface ... xi

1. The Exoteric Myth of Shambhala ... 1
   - The nature of Shambhala ... 1
   - The depiction of Shambhala in the texts ... 4
2. The Meditation Process and Shambhala ... 22
   - The five levels of Shambhala ... 22
   - The first Shambhalic level ... 24
   - The second Shambhalic level ... 37
   - The inverted triangle ... 50
   - A note on the third and fourth Rays ... 55
   - The Christ's department ... 56
   - The Dharmakāya Way ... 67
   - The third, fourth, and fifth Shambhalic levels ... 74
3. The Qualities of the Ashrams ... 81
   - Preamble ... 81
   - The formation of the Ashrams ... 84
   - Ray considerations ... 96
   - The departmental heads and the Hierarchical Heart centre ... 111
   - The Hierarchical twelve-petalled lotus ... 119
   - Further astrological considerations ... 137
4. The first and second Ray Ashrams ... 144
   - The major Hierarchical dispensation ... 144
   - The significance of the Piscean era ... 152
   - The Chohans of the Rays of Mind ... 155
   - Subsidiary Ray considerations ... 160
   - The Importance of the seventh Ray ... 171
   - The Eye of Hierarchy ... 177
   - The service arenas of the new Ashrams ... 182
   - The 'great winepress of the wrath of God' ... 189
   - The direct first Ray line ... 197
   - The activity of Splenic centre II ... 203
   - The second Ray Ashrams ... 218
   - An extract from Ephesians ... 226
   - The coming of the Avatar ... 232
5. Ashramic Interrelationships ... 245
   - The Second Ray Triad ... 245
   - The Perseus myth ... 249
   - The Mahāchohan's department ... 264

6. Hierarchy and the Major Centres below the Diaphragm 286
General considerations 286
The Sacral and Base of Spine Centres 290
The Solar Plexus centre 314
Overcoming planetary evil 337
Summary 347

7. Considerations of Hierarchical Externalisation 354
Cleansing evil karma 354
The forces of evil 359
The swastikas governing Hierarchical activity 370
The nature of Hierarchical power 373
The upper echelons of the Hierarchy 376
The Great Invocation 387
The doctrine of Avatars 394
The first Ray pentad 411
The sixth Ray function and the Rays of Mind 414
The Hierarchy as a Head lotus 417
The Occult movement and the Masters 423

8. Further Esoteric Considerations Concerning Shambhala 434
The Planetary Head Lotus 434
The Deities of the Bardo Thödol 451
Further consideration of the planetary Executives 459
Concerning the moon Chain 463
The Lipika Lords (Mahārājas) 482
The Buddhas of Activity further explained 494

Bibliography 507
Index 511

Tables

Table 1. Seven subdivisions of the cosmic dense physical plane xxii
Table 2. Attributes of the Buddha's Saṇgha 44
Table 3. The Dhyāni Buddhas and the Chohans 125
Table 4. Planetary rulers of the Hierarchical Heart centre 139
Table 5. Logoi of sacred planets and their area of speciality 443

Figures

Figure 1. The first Shambhalic level ... 25
Figure 2. The second Shambhalic level ... 38
Figure 3. The third Shambhalic level—the Ray Lords ... 75
Figure 4. The externalised Ray Ashrams ... 89
Figure 5. The pentad of the Rays of Mind ... 102
Figure 6. The departmental heads of Hierarchy ... 112
Figure 7. Dynamic Love as a triune energy ... 117
Figure 8. The *maṇḍalic* template ... 118
Figure 9. The Hierarchical Heart centre ... 122
Figure 10. The Hierarchical dispensation as Splenic centre I ... 145
Figure 11. The arrow of present purpose ... 151
Figure 12. The door of appropriation to Hierarchy ... 176
Figure 13. The Hierarchical Eye ... 178
Figure 14. The Hierarchical shield ... 199
Figure 15. The Hierarchical Splenic centre II ... 204
Figure 16. The two-edged sword of truth ... 240
Figure 17. The Hierarchical Base of Spine and Sacral centres ... 293
Figure 18. The Hierarchical Solar Plexus centre ... 318
Figure 19. The Mahāchohan's department ... 372
Figure 20. The basic Hierarchical swastika ... 374
Figure 21. The manifestation of Hierarchical power ... 375
Figure 22. The heads of the major Hierarchical departments ... 377
Figure 23. The power of the Christ ... 384
Figure 24. The sixth Ray function ... 415
Figure 25. The Head lotus ... 418
Figure 26. The Lipikas and the Buddhas of Activity ... 491

Preface

This treatise investigates Buddhist ideas concerning what mind is and how it relates to a concept of a 'self'. It is principally a study of the complex interrelationship between mind and phenomena, from the gross to the subtle—the physical, psychic, supersensory and supernal. This entails an explanation of how mind incorporates all phenomena in its *modus operandi,* and how eventually that mind is liberated from it, thereby becoming awakened. Thus the treatise explores the manner in which the corporeally orientated, concretised, intellectual mind eventually becomes transformed into the Clear Light of the abstracted Mind; a super-mind, a Buddha-Mind.

A Treatise on Mind is arranged in seven volumes, divided into three subsections. These are as follows:

The I Concept
Volume 1. *The 'Self' or 'Non-self' in Buddhism.*
Volume 2. *Considerations of Mind—A Buddhist Enquiry.*
Volume 3. *The Buddha-Womb and the Way to Liberation.*

Cellular Consciousness
Volume 4. *Maṇḍalas - Their Nature and Development.*
Volume 5. *An Esoteric Exposition of the Bardo Thödol.*
(This volume is published in two parts)

The Way to Shambhala
Volume 6. *Meditation and the Initiation Process.*
Volume 7. *The Constitution of Shambhala*
(This volume is published in two parts)

The I Concept represents a necessary extensive revision[1] of a large work formerly published in one volume. Together the three volumes investigate the question of what a 'self' is and is not. This involves an analysis of the nature of consciousness, and the consciousness-stream of a human unit developing as a continuum through time. It will illustrate exactly what directs such a stream and how its *karma* is arranged so that enlightenment is the eventual outcome.

The first volume analyses Prāsaṅgika lines of reasoning, such as the 'Refutation of Partless Particles', and 'The Sevenfold Reasoning' in order to derive a clear deduction as to whether a 'self' exists, and if so what its limitations are, and if not, then what the alternative may be. The analysis resolves the historically vexing question of how—if there is no 'self'—can there be a continuity of mind that is coherently connected in an evolutionary manner through multiple rebirths.[2] In order to arrive at this explanation, many of the basic assumptions of Mahāyāna Buddhism, such as Dependent Origination and the Two Truths, are critically analysed.

The second volume provides an in-depth analysis of what mind is, how it relates to the concept of the Void *(śūnyatā),* and the evolution of consciousness. The analysis utilises Yogācāra-Vijñānavādin philosophy in order to comprehend the major attributes of mind, the *saṃskāras* that condition it, and the laws by means of which it operates.

The enquiry into the nature of what an 'I' is requires comprehension of the properties of the dual nature of mind, which consists of an empirical and abstract, enlightened part. As a means of doing this, the *ālayavijñāna* (the store of consciousness-attributes) is explored, alongside the entire philosophy of the 'eight consciousnesses' of this School.

Volume three focuses on the I-Consciousness and the subtle body, by first utilising a minor Tantra, *The Great Gates of Diamond Liberation,*

1 The book was inadequately edited hence contains many errors and grammatical mistakes that have been corrected in this treatise.

2 My earlier work *Karma and the Rebirth of Consciousness* (Munshiram Manoharlal, Delhi, 2006) lays the background for this basic question.

to investigate the nature of the Heart centre and its functions, then the *chakras* below the diaphragm. This is necessary to lay the foundation for the topics that will be the subject of the later volumes of this treatise concerning the nature of meditation, the construction of *maṇḍalas,* and the yoga of the *Bardo Thödol.*

The focus then shifts to investigate where the idea of a self-sustaining I-concept or 'Soul-form' may be found in Buddhist philosophy, given the denial of substantial self-existence prioritised in the philosophy of Emptiness. Following this, the pertinent chapters of the *Ratnagotravibhāga Śastra* are examined in detail so that a proper conclusion to the investigation can be obtained via the *buddhadharma.* This concerns an analysis of how the *ālayavijñāna* is organised, such that the rebirth process is possible for each human consciousness-stream, taking into account the *karma* that will eventually make each human unit a Buddha. In relation to this the ontological nature of the *tathāgatagarbha* (the Buddha-Womb) must be carefully analysed, as well as the organising principle of consciousness represented by the *chakras.* I thus establish that there is a form that appears upon the domain of the abstract Mind. I call this the Sambhogakāya Flower. The final two chapters of this volume principally define its characteristics.

The second subsection, *Cellular Consciousness,* is divided into two parts. Volume four deals with the question of what exactly constitutes a 'cell', metaphysically. The cell is viewed as a unit of consciousness that interrelates with other cells to form *maṇḍalas* of expression. Each such cell can be considered a form of 'self' that has a limited, though valid, body of expression. It is born, sustains a form of activity, and consequently dies when it outlives its usefulness. This mode of analysis is extended to include the myriad forms manifest in the world of phenomena known as *saṃsāra,* including the existence and functioning of *chakras.*

Volume five deals with the formative forces and evolutionary processes governing the prime cells (that is, *maṇḍalas* of expression), and the phenomenon that governs an entire world-sphere of evolutionary attainment. This is explored via an in-depth exposition of the *Bardo Thödol* and its 42 Peaceful and 58 Wrathful Deities. The text also incorporates a detailed exposition concerning the transformation of *saṃskāras* (consciousness-attributes developed through all past forms of activity) into enlightenment. The entire path of liberation enacted by a *yogin* via the principles of meditation, forms of concentration, and related techniques *(tapas, dhāraṇīs)* is explained. In doing so, the soteriological purpose of the various wrathful and theriomorphic deities is revealed. This volume is published in two parts. Part A explores chapter 5 of the *Bardo Thödol* concerning the transformation of *saṃskāras* via meditating upon the Peaceful and Wrathful Deities. This necessitates sound knowledge of the force centres (*chakras*) and the way their powers (*siddhis*) awaken. Part B deals with the gain of such transformations and the consequence of conversion of the attributes of the empirical mind into the liberated abstract Mind.

The third subsection, *The Way to Shambhala,* is also in two parts. They present an eclectic revelation of esoteric information integrating the main Eastern and Western religions. Volume six is a treatise on meditation and the Initiation process.[3] The meditation practice is directed towards the needs of individuals living within the context of our modern societies.

Volume six also includes a discussion of the path of Initiation as the means of gaining liberation from *saṃsāra.* The teaching in Volume five concerning the conversion of *saṃskāras* is supplementary to this path. The path of Initiation *is* the way to Shambhala. As many will choose to consciously undergo the precepts needed to undertake Initiation in the future, this invokes the necessity of providing much more revelatory information concerning this kingdom than has been provided hitherto.

How Shambhala is organised is the subject of Volume seven, which details the constitution of the Hierarchy of enlightened being[4] (the Council of Bodhisattvas). It illustrates how the presiding Lords who govern planetary evolution manifest. This detailed philosophy rests on the foundation of the information provided in all of the previous volumes, and necessitates a proper comprehension of the nature of the five Dhyāni Buddhas. To do so the awakening of the meditation-Mind, which is the objective of *A Treatise on Mind*, is essential.

---

3 The word Initiation is capitalised throughout the series of books to add emphasis to the fact that it is the process that makes one divine, liberated. It is the expression of divinity manifesting upon the planetary and cosmic landscape.

4 The word 'being' here is not pluralised because though this Hierarchy is constituted of a multiplicity of beings, together they represent one 'Being', one integral awakened Entity.

How to engage with this text

In this investigation many new ways of viewing conventional Buddhist arguments and rhetoric shall be pursued to develop the pure logic of the reader's mind, and to awaken revelations from their abstract Mind. New insights into the far-reaching light of the *dharma* will be revealed, which will form a basis for the illustration of an esoteric view that supersedes the bounds of conventionally accepted views. Readers should therefore analyse all arguments for themselves to discern the validity of what is presented. Such enquiry allows one to ascertain for oneself, what is logical and truthful, thus overcoming the blind acceptance of a certain dogma or line of reasoning that is otherwise universally accepted as correct. Only that which is discovered within each inquiring mind should be accepted. The remainder should, however, not be automatically discarded, but rather kept aside for later analysis when more data is available—unless the logic is obviously flawed, in which case it should be abandoned. There is no claim to infallibility in the information and arguments presented in this treatise, however, they are designed to offer scope for further meditation and enquiry by the earnest reader. If errors are found through impeccable logic, then the dialectical process may proceed. We can then accept or reject the new thesis and move forward, such that the evolution of human thought progresses, until we all stand enlightened.

This treatise hopes to assist that dialectical evolution by analysing major aspects of the *buddhadharma* as it exists and is taught today, to try to examine where errors may lie, or where the present modes of interpretation fall short of the true intended meaning. The aim is also to elaborate aspects of the *dharma* that could only be hinted at or cursorily explained by the wise ones of the past, because the basis for proper elaboration had not then been established. This analysis of *buddhadharma* will try to rectify some of the past inadequacies in order to explore and extend the *dharma* into arenas rarely investigated.

There will always be obstinate and dogmatic ones that staunchly cling to established views. This produces a reactive malaise in current Buddhist ontological and metaphysical thought. However, amongst the many practitioners of the *dharma* there are also those who have clarified their minds sufficiently to verify truth in whatever form it is presented, and will follow it at all costs to enlightenment. The Council of Bodhisattvas heartily seek such worthy ones. The signposts or guides upon the way to enlightenment have changed through the centuries, and contemporary practitioners of the *dharma* have yet to learn to clearly interpret the new directions. The guide books are now being written and many must come forth to understand and practice correctly.

If full comprehension of such guide books is achieved, those *dharma* practitioners yearning to become Bodhisattvas would rapidly become spiritually enlightened. Here is a rhyme and reason *for* Buddhism. The actual present dearth of enlightened beings informs us that little that is read is properly understood. The esoteric view presented in this treatise hopes to rectify this problem, so as to create better thinkers along the Bodhisattva way.

The numbers of Buddhists are growing in the world, thus Buddhism needs a true restorative flowering to rival that of the renaissance of debate and innovative thinkers of the early post-Nāgārjunian era. In order to achieve this it must synthesise the present wealth of scientific knowledge, alongside the best of the Western world's philosophical output.

Currently the *buddhadharma* is presented as an external body of knowledge held by the Buddha, Rinpoches, monks and lay teachers. This encourages practitioners to hero worship these figures and to heed many unenlightened utterances from such teachers, based on a belief system that encourages people to *uncritically* listen to them and adopt their views. When enlightened teachers *do appear* and find consolidated reasons for firing spiritual bullets for the cause of the enlightenment of humanity, then all truth can and will be known. The present lack of inwardly perceived knowledge from the fount of the *dharmakāya* on the part of many teachers blocks the production of an arsenal of weapons for solving the problems of suffering in the world. Few see little beyond the scope of vision in what they have been indoctrinated to believe, allowing for only rudimentary truths to be understood. While for the great majority this suffices, it is woefully inadequate for those genuinely seeking Bodhisattvahood and enlightenment. The cost to humanity in not being given an enlightened answer as to the nature of awakening, is profound.

We must go to the awakening of the Head lotus to find the most established reasoning powers. Without the 1,000 petals of the *sahasrāra padma* ablaze then there is little substance for proper understanding, little ability to hold the mind steady in the dynamic field of revelation that the *dharmakāya* represents. How can the unenlightened properly understand Buddhist scriptures, when there is little (revelation) coming from the Head centres of such beings? Much still needs to be taught concerning the way of awakening this lotus, and to help fill the lack is a major purpose of *A Treatise on Mind.*

Those who intend to reach enlightenment must go beyond the narrow sectarian allegiances promoted by many strands of contemporary Buddhism. Buddhism itself unfolded in a dialectical context with other heterodox Indian (and Chinese, etc.) traditions, and prospered on account of those engagements. When one sees the unfolding of enlightened wisdom in such a fashion, the particular information from specific schools of thought may be synthesised into a greater whole. Each school has various qualities and types of argument to resolve weaknesses in the opposing stream of thought. This highlights that there are particular aspects in each that may be right or wrong, or neither wholly right or wrong. Through this process we can find better answers, or if need be, create a new lineage or religion which is expressive of a synthesis of the various schools of thought.

The Buddha did not categorically reject the orthodox Indian religio-philosophical ideas of his time, nor did he simply accept them—he reformed them. He preserved the elements that he found to be true, and rejected those 'wrong views' which lead to moral and spiritual impairment. If the existing system needs reformation it becomes part of a Bodhisattva's meditation. The way a reforming Buddha incarnates is dependent on how he must fit into such a system. Thus he is essentially an outsider incarnating into it to demonstrate the new type of ideas he chooses to elaborate. If there is a lot of dogmatic resistance to the presented doctrine of truth, then a new religion is founded. If there is some acceptance then we see reformation. There is always room for improvement, to march forward closer to enlightenment's goal, be it for an individual or for a wisdom-religion as a whole. There is a need for reform throughout the religious world today.

By way of a hermeneutical strategy fit for this task, we ought look no further than the Buddha himself. The Buddha proposed that all students of the *dharma* should make their investigations through the *Four Points of Refuge*. These are:

1. The doctrine is one's point of refuge, not a person.
2. The meaning is one's point of refuge, not the letter.
3. The sacred texts whose meaning is defined are one's point of refuge, to those whose meaning needs definition.
4. Direct awareness is one's point of refuge, not discursive awareness.[5]

These four points can be summarised or rephrased as: the doctrine (*dharma*), true or esoteric meaning, right definition, and direct awareness are one's point of refuge, not adherence to sectarian bias, semantics, the dialectics of non-fully enlightened commentaries, or to illogical assertions. What may be long held to be truthful, but is not, upon proper analytical dissection, needs rectifying. Also, in other cases, a doctrine or teaching may indeed be correct, but the current interpretation leaves much to be desired, and hence should be reinterpreted from the position of a more embracive or esoteric view.

Hopefully this presentation finds welcoming minds that will carefully analyse it in line with their own understandings of the issues, and as a consequence build up a better understanding of the nature of what constitutes the path to enlightenment. Their way of walking as Bodhisattvas should be enriched as a consequence.[6]

Concerning the two volumes on the Constitution of Shambhala

Tackling such an abstruse subject as what constitutes the Kingdom of 'God', Shambhala, can by direct empirical logic be considered to be beyond the experiential level of the reader, a matter of speculation. However, to the Initiate, the high level Bodhisattva, such is not so, but rather a matter of internal revelation, and subjective experience, albeit at a far higher level

---

5 Griffith, P.J., *On Being Buddha, The Classical Doctrine of Buddhahood*, (Sri Satguru Publications, New Delhi, 1995), 52.

6 Many quotes from Alice Bailey will be used, with permission from Lucis Trust. It was stipulated that quotations from Alice Bailey's books should not be reproduced except by permission from the Lucis Trust which holds copyright.

than is normally attainable by meditators. Disciples have to be taught appropriate meditation practices by awakened ones, the guides that have travelled to Shambhala and know the methodology (the Initiation process) that can lead the gifted (*karma* ripened) student to Shambhalic domains. An ability to withstand high energisations is certainly a prerequisite.

Much of this dual volume may be difficult to follow by those not familiar with the esoteric doctrines revealed telepathically over a thirty year period (1919-1949) by an enlightened Tibetan Rinpoche (D.K.) via his Western amanuensis, Alice Bailey. Those teachings continued from that originally provided by H.P. Blavatsky. The foundational teachings are provided in their works, as well in my earlier writings. The reader unfamiliar with this doctrine may do well to start with the book *Initiation, Human and Solar*, published under Alice Bailey's name. Being enlightened, D.K.'s works are authoritative, as were the writings of the enlightened Buddhist philosophers of the past, such as Nāgārjuna, Dharmakīrti, and Asaṇga.

Buddhist readers need to expand their vision, to comprehend what it is that 'lies beyond' empirical deductions of what constitutes an 'awakened Mind'. They must also open their minds to a greater spiritual universe than just the relatively parochial field of orthodox Buddhism. Consequently, the philosophy contained in these two volumes constitutes an esoteric expansion of what they can discover by pursuing the *buddhadharma*. Now they must also learn the context of the 'ear-whispered truths'- the reason why Buddhas and Bodhisattvas are portrayed with long earlobes, and why the main symbol of Milarepa is him sitting with his right hand behind his ear, in the gesture of listening.

Those familiar with Bailey's writings should not jump to preconditioned conclusions, the comfort zone of empirical 'esoteric' knowledge (as 'blinded occultists'), but rather awaken to far vaster insights than was previously possible to them. They must consequently comprehend better what constitutes the path of Initiation, in order to be able to directly vision what exists upon the inner realms, and the domain of the Masters of Wisdom, the significance of the Ashrams to which they belong. They must also consequently better comprehend the nature of the way of group evolution. Much revelatory information is provided in these two volumes, and much else needing to be comprehended related to the inner universe known to the Masters, and those that are resident or frequent visitors to the Halls of Shambhala. The time for such further revelation is nigh, because those that are being prepared to travel the Initiation path need to rightly cognise what constitutes the path and processes ahead of them.

Those relatively new to such information need to read with an open mind, and be prepared to continue later studies of the source material from the quoted books, as well as the earlier teachings provided in this series. Basic teachings are also provided on our website that should prove valuable to the novice. Similarly, a glossary exists therein explaining some of the more abstruse Sanskrit words and esoteric terminology.

Western esotericists need to comprehend Buddhist doctrines with far greater cognisance than they do, as the new Initiation tree demands a higher level of awakening of the higher Mind than previously needed. *Antaḥkaraṇas* (consciousness links) need to be projected to this domain, and Buddhist philosophy represents a major means to do so. The *antaḥkaraṇas* arise *automatically via the effort* needed to appropriately comprehend such philosophic fare. This is an important consideration now requested by the Lodge of Masters for those wishing attainment for higher Initiations than the second. Buddhists must also broaden their thinking to incorporate this new revealed esoteric doctrine if enlightenment is to be wrought by them. The goalposts to enlightened standing have been raised significantly since the time the revered Scholars and Tantric Masters gained their awakening. The path to liberation does not stagnate, it moves onwards and upwards, and ever more is required by applicants thereto, as humanity also have moved onwards as they evolved further intellectual capabilities and knowledge of the material universe via the rise of empirical science. In this way East meets West in meditation and upon the Initiation path. Consequently, the old ways will not make enlightened beings out of Buddhists, because of the sources of *adharma* (erroneous thinking) existing in their texts and which they follow, as pointed out in this series and in the book *Karma and the Rebirth of Consciousness.*

It is consequently well worth the effort for those new to these teachings, as well as to the adherents of orthodox religions, agnostics, and even materialist thinkers, to read with an open mind. Much can be gained thereby, and if they apply logical, meditative thought then pathways may open in the mind producing revelations. Let each reader ascertain truth for him/herself, or for what may resonate as such, and be free to reject that which does not. Consequently no claims are made that what is contained in these pages is the final authoritative truth, simply that they present postulates and concepts for later verification via the meditation Mind. If then validated, one can move on to further awareness. If not, then one must ascertain the reasons why and proceed accordingly.

For a guide to understanding the pronunciation of Sanskrit words, please visit our website.
http://universaldharma.com/resources/pronounce-sanskrit/

Our online esoteric glossary also provides definitions for most of the terms used in this treatise.
http://universaldharma.com/resources/esoteric-glossary/

My eyes do weep as I stare into this troubled world,
For I dare not place my Heart in my brother's keep.
He would grapple that Heart with hands so rough
So as to destroy the fabric of its delicate stuff.
Oh to give, to give, my Heart does yearn,
But humanity must its embracive,
Humbling, pervasive scene yet to learn.
To destroy and tear with avarice they know,
But little care to sensitive rapture they show.
How to give its Blood is my constant fare,
For that Love to bestow upon their Hearts I bemoan.
But they hide their Hearts behind mental-emotional walls.
No matter how one prods these walls won't fall,
So much belittling emotional self-concern prop their bastions.
Oh, how my eyes do weep as I stare.
I stare at their fearsome malls and halls.
That lock Love out from all their abodes
And do keep them trapped in realms of woe.

Oṁ Maṇi Padme Hūṁ

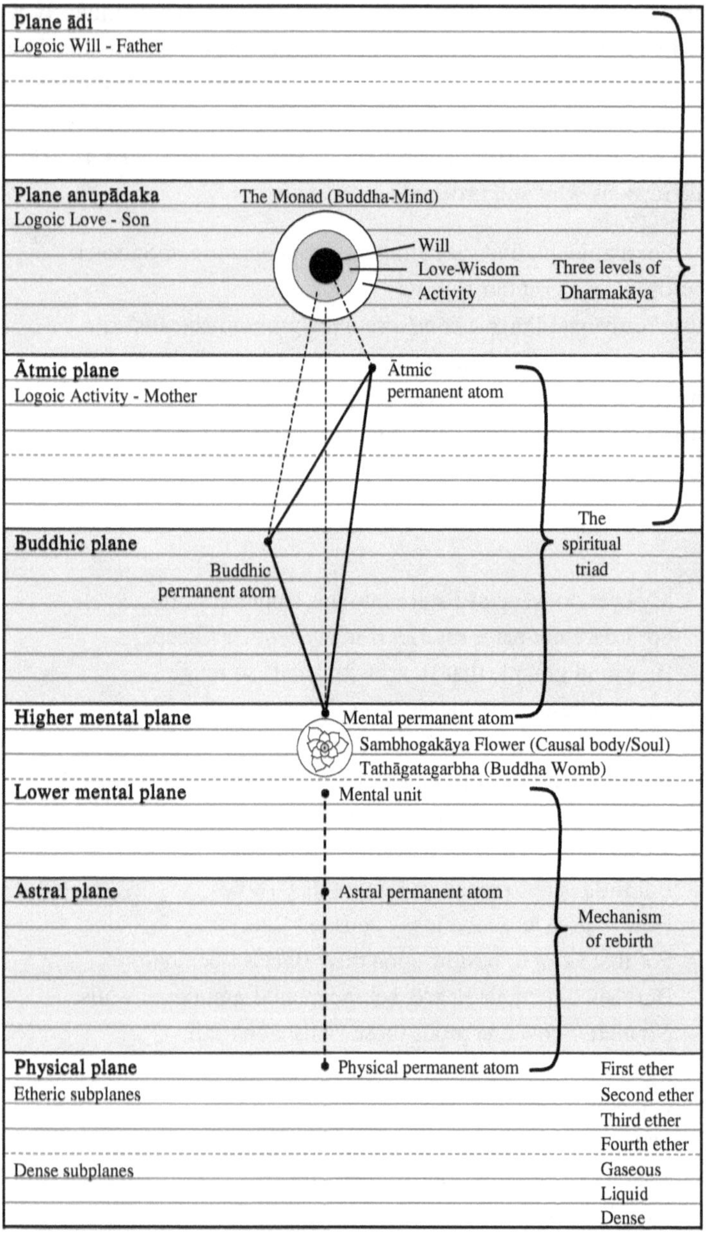

Table 1. Seven subdivisions of the cosmic dense physical plane[7]

7 Adapted from Chart VIII in *A Treatise on Cosmic Fire,* 817, by A.A. Bailey.

Prologue

The journey begins where our life ends
or where the heart sings
and finds out what tomorrow brings.

As endless tides flow to and fro,
so our lives are swayed with the ocean's rhythm.
With humanity and in humanity
we must grow and come to be strong,
a boat with power in a stormy sea.
Our journey in the world, with its many vicissitudes,
trials, tribulations, and uncertainties,
is at first like a wind strewn desert vale,
or the shoreline's pounding waves,
or a jungle densely matted with briars and vines.
Onwards we tread on the endless road,
but can find no shelter in the Fiery night sky,
no place to rest our weary feet,
though we've walked for so long.

It is an intoxicating faraway tune that a flute brings,
sweet with the promise of beauty and bounty,
that ever leads us on to new fields and terrains,
rocky or wooded, deserts or jungles, and to vast horizons.

By trial and error we progress,
never-ending is the journey's quest.

The secrets of the Path to enlightened liberated Being
are experiences that grow into progressive realisations;
memories that lead to elimination of past mistakes;
and the directed application of the creative imagination,
wherein greater revelatory vistas are embraced.

The means to the related mastery of all allurements and obstructions
to the full attainment envisioned needs a fixed determination
to walk steadfastly the path perceived.
Yet ever must one be ready to stop and wisely give
to all seen in need along that way,
with a full active helping hand and loving embrace.
Compassionate undertaking leads to the Heart of Life.
Selfishness in motive is synonymous
with imprisonment to a desire-mind clinging
to destructible or transient self-imposed needs.
It is an addictive illusion-forming carousel,
pleasurable for periods, but then it stops.

How often will you start it
before you tire of that one route?
What will you do when you must get off?

In experiencing, dying,
thence progressively experiencing the new
we find ourselves and know.
Fear not the first steps
of every new undertaking in areas of activity
sweet with the promise of increased scope for Revelation
and freedom from painful repetitious mundane conditionings,
habit patterns and preconceptions.
Fear not the unknown,
the method of walking the path to the Divinity before you.
Fear not to relinquish your tenacious attachments
to past understandings, your desire-mind's sensations
and emotion-filled longings,
when the Way full of Light opens before you,
the Path to an astounding Domain.
Free yourself from all past conditionings,
come to be free, a liberated being

following the *dharma* in all ways to the One.
Open the Eye, let the inner flower radiate,
offering a delectable fragrance, nectar,
and beauty for all to behold.
Increasingly perceptive, the mind-nature smiles,
freely radiating wisdom to every related mind
where there is concerned receptivity
to its emanatory undertaking.
Boundless is the multidimensional Space
that unfolds before you.
To the four directions of the compass,
and in time, every mediatory position we must travel.
North is the point of ultimate attainment,
it is the way upwards to the Omnipotent,
ever-present Source of all Being,
absolute unbounded Deity,
unperceived by the conceptualising mind.
South is the sphere of material involvement.
It is the direction downwards
to the lesser kingdoms in Nature
and their massed understanding,
the categories of sentience expanding
and the bodily nature unfolding.
East produces an inward quest,
the Heart's full awakening of the immanent Divinity
exploding into an illumined splendour.
Boundless Light expanding to fill
the chasms of all forms freely evolving,
interdependently interpenetratingly irradiating
areas of darkness with that Light.
A synergy of related sounds and colours
of the myriads resolved into the One,
as one fundamental energy Source.
Formless Life abounds to, through,

and beyond all manifest forms.
It becomes the Heart of Being,
the Light of Life, the Word of 'God',
the music of the Spheres.
West leads outwards to humanity,
the renunciation of self-will,
self-gratification, self-service and separateness,
for equanimous undertakings to benefit the whole,
all related selves in the one undertaking
to produce perfected harmonious
co-operative good will in our diversified civilisations,
with a consequent liberation
of all suffering unities from the causes of their tribulations.
The One is in all and the all evolves into the One
by means of enlightened activity.
There can be no true *nirvāṇic* Peace for any being
until all have been rightly educated
to tread the way to the other shore
of evolutionary journeying.
Such is the cross of inner Revelation.
This is the cross of Life,
whereon the crucified one, scourged and pilloried,
hearkens to the world's salvation
with his/her Heart's Blood,
the substance of the Soul's aspiration,
the resolution of past tribulations
directed to those still thus afflicted,
who by continuous contemptuous actions
perpetually scourge their courageous Saviours.
On that cross we too must find our liberation.
We are brothers, sisters and companions together
in this world and on its journeying.
It is an atom, almost imperceptible
in the cosmos so immense, that is unfolding.

All companionship brings a harvest
from Life's vineyards, and leads
us onwards to the Soul's full Light.
Enlightenment's game is progressive,
flowing in wonderment with Nature's scenery
back to the Heart of all Being.
To not be attached to temporal conditionings,
pleasured sensual pursuits, repetitive desires chattering,
or to any of the bodily allurements, is the secret.
For the dew mist must vanish as it gives way to the day;
not even the songbird can capture the morning.
True non-attachment produces testings
of real measured attainment, the progress of the Path.
Easy to perceive, but hard to practice.
It necessitates walking the narrow middle way,
the razor-edged path between all extremes.
To be attached neither to corporeal cravings
nor the ecstasy of the vision,
the sublime desires for Divinity,
produces the ability to walk in wisdom,
directly to the field of liberated Being, an ocean of tranquillity
and the full unfoldment of the Heart's Service.
It is a process of continuous dying to obstacles,
glamours and illusions on the way.
In death naught can you hold;
all decays, is consumed, or is destroyed.
Time conquers all, yet the Mind grows, Phoenix-like
from the ashes of the past
and renews itself in a new dawning,
from eternity to eternity, incarnation to incarnation.
We see transmutative recapitulations of experiences unfolding
into ever-expanding revelatory scenarios,
continually playing differing roles,
until finally the entire play is mastered
and the related gain projected into a new field of endeavour.

From the gross to the sublime,
and the sublime to the intrinsic, does Divinity unfold.
The play offers the Sun's Light or the darkest night,
the One Path, or the pathless way.
The player alone must choose the route to go.

One must ever continue breathing,
living, experiencing, contemplating,
meditating upon the Way that one must walk;
to ever continue hearing, touching, seeing,
smelling, and tasting all nectars,
opportunities and signs that lead to the portals
of the House of Eternal Light.
Divinity and Divinity only is Life's task for us.
May we all walk together, hand in hand,
in love and service upon that Path.

Effortlessness in giving,
spontaneity in response to need,
and desirelessness in motive,
are the jewels the Phoenix brings,
with them the Heart forever sings.

1

The Exoteric Myth of Shambhala

The nature of Shambhala

The current levels of development of sentience and consciousness of all subjective or objective beings on this planet are affected by the proximity of Shambhala to the high points of all Bodhisattvic activity. Energies are directed from Shambhala to vitalise the entire *nāḍī* system of the earth. These *nāḍīs* convey the *prāṇas* that empower and vitalise all beings. The entire *maṇḍala* of manifest being is thereby invigorated, made to thrill with vibrant activity. Such activity necessitates the development of a consistently applicable meditation-Mind by all involved in this great work. It is part of their esoteric service that is not spelled out in the Tantric texts and current meditation digests. Now, however, the teaching must be made clear. This also involves cleansing whatever is possible from the human *nāḍī* system; the base greys, muddied and dark *prāṇas* people have generated.

There are many *chakras* governing this planet that all non self-focussed meditators must comprehend so that they can work in accord with the dictates of the energy flows. Shambhala is the governing *chakra* of all such activity, thus meditators must eventually become aware of this centre, to find a place within its sacred precincts. They must learn to be guided by those who spontaneously offer the obeisance of the Heart to the central presiding One, the Lord of this world. The myth is transmogrified into reality in the meditation-Mind. That reality then becomes the central dynamo of the meditator's spiritual life, as its purpose and dynamic spiritual rhythm will govern every mode of activity on all planes of perception.

Shambhala is certainly not as the myths portray it,[1] for there is only a basic general semblance or correlation between the two. However, the myths have served a purpose of keeping the concept alive in the world of ideas as a place of aspiration with the thought of world governance by fully enlightened beings. Cartographers have revealed that Shambhala cannot be a place physically existent on the earth. However, it certainly exists upon the inner realms and is realisable through meditation, after one has passed sufficient Initiation testings upon the way to enlightenment. All higher Initiation ceremonies occur at Shambhala. It is the planetary Head centre *(sahasrāra padma*) and serves to educate and awaken the wise. The Council (or Hierarchy) of Bodhisattvas constitutes the planetary Heart centre, whilst humanity constitute the petals of the lesser centres, such as the Throat and Solar plexus centres.[2]

There are several ways of depicting the constitution of the planetary Head centre, though all explanations are inadequate.[3] One must also comprehend the nature of the Initiation level of the highest Bodhisattvas upon the earth, the way that the *devas* evolve, as well as to understand better what actually constitutes a Buddha than what is found in standard texts. Basic concepts have already been presented as to the nature of the Head lotus, the Sambhogakāya and Dharmakāya Flowers, the mode of

---

1 These myths are readily available in such books as by Nicholas Roerich: *Shambhala* (VEDAMS, New Delhi, 2003). (Roerich's life and teachings, and the writings of his wife Helena, serve as good examples of the nature of the output of high level Bodhisattvas.) Victoria LePage: *Shambhala; The Fascinating Truth Behind the Myth of Shangri-la* (Pilgrims Publishing, Kathmandu, 1996). Edwin Bernbaum, *The Way to Shambhala* (Anchor Books, New York, 1980). A demystified account exists in the writings of Alice A. Bailey. See also the accounts of the Tibetan Kālachakra system by various authors.

2 A proper accounting would also involve the *deva* hierarchy and the lesser kingdoms in Nature, as well as the governance of the major petals by the Ashrams of the Rays of Mind.

3 See for instance the figure on pages 48-49 of *Initiation, Human and Solar* by A. A. Bailey, (Lucis Press, New York, 1972). This figure posits the barest outline of the constitution and interrelation of the various departments of the Hierarchy, looking only at the various departmental heads.

gaining Initiation for the members of Hierarchy (Bodhisattvas), and of higher evolutionary attainment in cosmos in the previous volumes of this treatise, which should be meditated upon. There is a natural order in cosmos, and many schools of higher education exist for Buddhas that have been newly born therein by having evolved out from the limiting confines of a world-sphere.

The constituency of the uppermost echelon of Shambhala consists of attained Buddhas that had gained entry into various cosmic schools long before Gautama undertook the higher Bodhisattva *bhūmis* upon this planet. They are his gurus and have many other students that they have similarly educated. From this perspective, the concept of *guruparamparā,* the lineage tradition of a guru, as explained in Volume 6, should be understood by Buddhists to also relate to transcendental levels of expression. World spheres, such as that of our earth, and its inherent *chakra* system, are formed as a consequence of prior interrelationship by many great Ones via such a tradition having manifested in a former aeon of evolution. A Head centre is established for the purpose of governing planetary evolution when a human kingdom Individualises. Their ability to use the mind necessitates a central directive centre for the Fires of mind/Mind. Until then a planet is ruled by the *ḍākinīs* (the higher orders of the *deva* evolution) that are responsible for the evolution of the kingdoms of Nature up to the appearance of human units of consciousness. Evolutionary focus then moves from a planetary Solar Plexus centre to that of a Head centre, which becomes duly established as a Shambhala, to be informed by the appropriately trained Lords of Life.

Such considerations are sorely missing in the Buddhist ontology and must now be incorporated, if the way to liberation is to be appropriately taught by their meditation instructors. Promulgating forms of ignorance no longer suffices, hence what was formerly esoteric must be revealed for those that are developing the Eyes to see, and the Heart's wisdom to comprehend. The revelation can now be provided with increasing perspicacity. The exoteric lineage follows upon an already established tradition from Blavatsky to Bailey, whose teachings shall now be significantly clarified. There is, however, an esoteric lineage of a vastly different order.

The depiction of Shambhala in the texts

Much has been popularised concerning this myth from the Tibetan sources and romanticised in terms of a Shangri-la existing in a hidden, long lost valley somewhere high in the vast reaches of the Himalayas or Altai mountain ranges. What is normally overlooked is the esoteric symbolism of the available texts and what such symbolism actually refers to. The *Kālachakra Tantra* is a major text from which such speculation is derived. When its symbolism is analysed, however, then we see that it quite clearly is a Tantric Tibetan meditation text, complete with the normally heavily veiled esotericism associated with the techniques for enlightenment. It is also an astrological text and method for computing of dates from the Tibetan perspective. The actual term *kāla* means 'time, movement' (from the verbal root *kal,* to calculate), hence 'a cycle or wheel *(chakra)* of time'.[4]

It is not my intention to analyse the detail of the symbolism of this Tantra here, for to do so would require a large treatise at least as detailed as my rendition of the *Bardo Thödol*, but would not add significantly to the esoteric comprehension of the nature of the constitution of Shambhala. I simply wish to point out the significant symbolic content by relating it to the expression of the petals of the Head lotus, which indeed represents Shambhala in the human psyche.

Concerning the myth I shall utilise the work of Henning, who quoting Tāranātha, states:

> "On the full moon of the month Caitra in the year following his enlightenment, at the great stūpa of Dhānyakaṭaka, the Buddha emanated the maṇḍala of 'The Glorious Lunar Mansions.' In front of an audience of countless buddhas, bodhisattvas, viras, ḍākinīs, the twelve great gods, gods, nāgas, yakṣas, spirits, and fortunate people gathered from the 960 million villages north of the river Śītā, he was requested by the emanation of Vajrapāṇi, the king Sucandra, to teach the Tantra."
>
> Tāranātha continues: "Some teachings were taken to other human realms, and the Dharma king Sucandra wrote the Tantras in textual form in his land of Sambhala. He composed the Explanatory Tantra in 60,000 verses to the Mūlatantra of 12,000."

4 It is also a name of Yama, the king of the underworld.

> It is said that the teachings of Kālacakra were propagated in Sambhala for many centuries, with a succession of righteous kings teaching and writing about Kālacakra. Most of these kings are said to have reigned for a hundred years each. After seven generations, it is said that a king called Yaśas, an emanation of the bodhisattva Mañjuśrī, united the Brahmin Ṛṣis living in his kingdom into the Vajra caste; in other words converted them to Buddhism as protection against the coming Islamic invasions.
>
> Tāranātha states that: "As in this way the Ṛṣis of different casts were brought into the single caste of the Vajrayāna, from the time of Yaśas onwards, these kings were called Kalkī kings, meaning of one caste."
>
> Yaśas is also important for another reason. He wrote the Kālacakra Laghutantra, which summarises the meaning of the Kālacakra Mūlatantra that is said to have been the original text taught by the Buddha. If it ever existed, only short quotations (many are to be found in the Vimalaprabhā) now remain of the Mūlatantra, but the Laghutantra has survived in both the original Sanskrit, and Tibetan translations.
>
> The next of the kings was the emanation of Avalokiteśvara, Puṇḍarīka[5]...A few generations after Puṇḍarīka came another king of importance to our subject, the 11th Kalkī, Aja. He is said to have corrected the karaṇa calculations and re-established the calendar.[6]

The significance of using the device of such numbers as 960,000,000 (an impossible number of villages for the hidden kingdom of Shambhala[7]) was explained in Volume 4 of this series, in the section entitled 'Numerological considerations concerning the *chakras*'.[8] There the number 72, generally given as relating to the number of *nāḍīs* in the body (72,000) is explained in relation to the true number of 96 (symbolically 96,000). The number 96 represents the number of minor petals to any of the major *chakras*[9] (except the Head lotus, which contains multiples of this number). Also, the meaning of where

5 Edward Henning, *Kālacakra and the Tibetan Calendar,* (American Institute of Buddhist Studies, New York, 2007), 211-12.

6 Ibid.

7 This alone should suffice to inform all discerning readers that this kingdom does not physically exist.

8 See Volume 4, 344-56.

9 There are 96 petals in total, for instance, to the two lobes of the Ājñā centre.

something is multiplied times 1,000 was explained, as implying a very large number or cycles of expression. When extended to millions, as in the case of these villages, where each village can be considered a petal of a *chakra,* then it is a device that informs one that the entire body of manifestation of a person (in this case the planetary constitution as governed by Shambhala, when referring to the planetary Head centre) is involved. The petals of all the *chakras;* major, the minor, and tiny ones of the Inner Round, are incorporated in the symbolism of this number.

Here can be introduced the way Shambhala is generally depicted, using Bernhaum's description:

> Inside the ring of snow mountains, around the center of the kingdom, runs another ring of even higher snow mountains. Rivers and smaller mountain ranges divide the area between the two rings into eight regions shaped like eight petals arranged around the centre of a flower (see Plate 1, Fig. 1). In fact, the texts usually describe Shambhala as having the shape of an eight-petalled lotus blossom enclosed within a rosary of snow mountains...Each of the eight petal-like regions contains in turn twelve principalities, making ninety-six princes or minor Kings who owe allegiance to the King of Shambhala. Their small kingdoms abound with cities of golden-roofed pagodas set among parks filled with lush meadows and flowering trees of all kinds.
>
> The snow mountains surrounding the central portion of the lotus blossom have turned to ice, and shine with a crystalline light. Within this inner ring of peaks, at the very centre of the kingdom lies Kalapa, the capital of Shambhala. To the east and west of the city are two lovely lakes shaped like a half moon and a crescent moon and filled with jewels. Waterfowl swoop and skim over the scented flowers that float on their waters. To the south of Kapala is a beautiful park of sandalwood trees called Malaya, the "Cool Grove"; here the first King of Shambhala built an enormous mandala, a mystic circle that embodies the essence of the secret teaching kept in the kingdom and symbolizes the transcendent unity of mind and universe. To the north rise ten rock mountains with the shrines and images of important saints and deities.[10]

10 Edwin Bernbaum, *The Way to Shambhala* (Anchor Books, New York, 1980), 6-8.

The description of the palace etc., continues, but the main points given suffice, as it has already been established that Shambhala does not exist physically, but rather subjectively. From a yogic perspective then, being those who wrote the texts, the symbolism relates to the *chakra* system. First we are presented with an idea that Shambhala is situated high up in the snow capped mountains. This symbolises the rarefied attributes of the abstract Mind (Clear Light of Mind) or *dharmakāyic* Mind. The pristine cognition (cool, clear Reason) can thereby view the entire domain. Only the Head centre, the pinnacle of the *chakra* system, offers such a view. Next is depicted a two-tiered structure (three-tiered, if the central palace is included) common to all *chakras*. All major *chakras* are three-tiered, but the Head centre is five-tiered, as detailed in Volume 5A. Then one must ascertain which *chakra* is being referred to, as the Head centre has twelve main petals, whilst only eight are here depicted. This then lowers our vision to the eight-petalled Diaphragm centre. The objective of this centre is to act as a type of relay centre for *prāṇas* crossing over from below the diaphragm to the higher centres and vice versa. It also helps redirect *prāṇas* not suitable for the higher centres. The symbolism of the mountains, however, does not tally with its properties. Hence we must conclude that the *maṇḍala* presented is a symbolic depiction of the Head lotus, viewed according to the activity of the eight armed cross of direction in space (*aṣṭadiśas*), which is well explained in all the previous volumes. This symbolism is then appropriate, and integrates with the general Buddhist concept of the number of petals of the Heart centre. The true number of petals however is given in the information that these eight direction or orientations must be multiplied by the 'twelve localities' to make the number 96, or '96 princes'.

Now, as far as the organisation of the Head lotus is concerned, the number eight plays a significant role. First it represents the eight base petals of an Airy petal (see Figure 20, Volume 5A) governed by the activity of the Mātaraḥ. Then we have the eight decades of petals governed by the Gatekeepers enacting rites.[11] Finally, there are the eight decades of petals integrating the inner Throat and Heart tiers of

11 See, Volume 5A, 397.

petals, and which when fully active signifies the enlightened activity of the meditation-Mind.[12]

The descriptions of all the cardinal directions can be interpreted in terms of the meanings attributed to them in the previous volumes and the symbolism here viewed in terms of the Head lotus. Also, imagery such as 'golden pagodas', phases of the moon, etc., can be analysed in terms of the main attributes of the petals contained in these directions. 'Pagodas', for instance, are places of containment (for *prāṇas).* The 'half moon' of the eastern direction symbolises the *piṇgalā nāḍī,* and the crescent moon of the western direction refers to the *iḍā nāḍī.* The southern direction (representing downwards to the little ones, here signifying the lives of all kingdoms of Nature) contains the sandalwood tree, the 'Cool Grove' and the *maṇḍala* of the secret teachings needed to educate all on earth. The sandalwood tree signifies the Airy Element (incense), the grove the Watery Element (which 'cools' the grove) and the teachings the Fiery Element needed to develop people's minds. The Earthy Element is implicit in the rocks of the mountains (of *saṃsāra* which must be conquered), and the significance of the southern direction itself. The rocky mountains of the northern direction represent the uplifting effects of the meditation-Mind that aspires to lofty heights. This Mind contains the 'images of important saints and deities'. The number ten signifies the attainment of perfection, such as, for instance, the development of the Bodhisattva *bhūmis.*

The inhabitants of the kingdom were not perfect, but: 'live in peace and harmony, free of sickness and hunger. Their crops never fail and their food is wholesome and nourishing. They all have a healthy appearance...Each one has great wealth in the form of gold and jewels but never needs to use it.'[13] This phrase refers to the mental attributes of one possessing significant spiritual knowledge, that are stored in the petals of the Head lotus.

That 'the King of Shambhala possesses all the power and wealth that befits a Universal Emperor'[14] simply relates to the governance of the mind/Mind of this centre over all of the attributes, organs and *prāṇas* of body, speech and mind.

---

12 Ibid., 403-24.

13 Bernbaum, 8-9.

14 Ibid., 8.

The number 12,000 for the Mūlatantra (root text) relates to the mode of ordering the petals of these *chakras,* based upon the twelve main petals of the Heart centre. There are twelve main petals to the Head lotus, for instance, and as Volume 5A shows, the total number of its petals is 1,200.[15] When multiplied by ten (the number signifying perfection), it includes the levels of expression (dimensions) governed by all the *chakras* in the body. The number twelve also relates to the conditioning influences of the twelve signs of the zodiac and indicates an organism governed by the Heart that is Life, where compassionate understanding rules the expression of all incarnate Life.

Similarly, the number 60,000 of 'the Explanatory Tantra' is another numerological device, signifying that aspect of the *nāḍī* system where the symbolism of the number six rules. Its concern therefore is with the principle of desire-attachment (hence the 'six senses'), regulated by the six main petals of the Sacral centre. As this *chakra* is also responsible for the projection of the *prāṇas* in the *nāḍīs* (the vitalisation of the body), consequently from this centre stem the *iḍā* and *piṇgalā nāḍīs.* There are also 60 Wrathful Deities[16] all told that deal with the conversion of defilements conveyed by the *prāṇas.*

The fact that each of the Kalkī kings attributed to Shambhala ruled for 100 years symbolises the *sambhogakāya* level of expression[17] of the body of manifestation, wherein these *chakras* are found, as well as signifying a great period of evolutionary attainment for any major cycle. That there are really 24 of these Kalkī kings indicates the main method of organising the petals of the *chakras* in the Head lotus, 24 = 2 x 12 or one quarter of 96, as has been explained in Volume 5A. If 25 kings are included[18] then

---

15 See Volume 5A, 431.

16 See Volume 5A, 346-47.

17 See Volume 4, 350.

18 There are slightly different accounts for the list of these kings, as Henning points out. 'There are some problems with the number of kalkī-kings. The list above contains 25 names, but the great Indian Kālacakra teacher Vibhūticandra pointed out to Tibetan colleagues that the names of the 18th and 19th in this list, Hari and Vikrama, belonged together as one name, Harivikrama. He also pointed out to them that some Tibetan lists similarly split up the name of number 24 in the list above into two names, Ananta and Vijaya. This persists to this day.' (Henning, 366.) The correct number esoterically, however, to the appearance of Rudracakrī, who will initiate the great war against the

the central point of the *maṇḍala* of the Head lotus is also incorporated, as well as symbolising the 5 x 5 attributes or levels of expression of the mind, five *skandhas, prāṇas,* and Elements. As the symbolism also incorporates a system of time reckoning via astrological methodology, so two of the kings are used as markers to indicate an historical period.[19]

The fact that there are seven originating Dharma Kings preceding the list of the Kalkī kings, starting with Sucrenda, implicates the seven Ray energies (as associated with the word *dharma)* that condition the activity of the Head lotus. As Sucrenda is an emanation of Vajrapāṇi, the bearer of the adamantine power *(vajra)* of the Dhyāni Buddhas, so this energy can be assumed to govern the dispensation of Shambhala. I stated in Volume 4 that Vajrapāṇi stands at the northern direction of the *maṇḍala* of the *mahābodhisattvas,* thus focuses our vision upwards to the regulating Head centre, the Sambhogakāya Flower or to Shambhala and the Dharmakāya Flower.[20]

Yaśas, the first of the listing of the Kalkī kings,[21] was said to be an emanation of the Bodhisattva Mañjuśrī. Mañjuśrī embodies the great transcendental wisdom of the *prajñāpāramitā* that is the heart of the Mahāyāna canon, and which consequently expresses the content of an awakened Head centre. (Which is embodied by the sum of the Kalkī kings.) That he united the Brahmin Ṛṣis (Rishis) with the Buddhists under the symbolism of the Vajra caste, symbolises the flow of the three principal *nāḍīs* up the spinal column to the Head centre ('his kingdom'). The Ṛṣis symbolise the more *manasic* (mental) *iḍā* flow, and the Buddhists the more compassionate *piṅgalā nāḍī,* whilst the five-pronged *vajra* symbolises the *suṣumṇā nāḍī.*

'barbarians', is 24, as used by Gyatso, see below. The reason being that Rudracakrī starts a new cycle, hence technically establishes a rebirth of the Head centre upon a higher cycle of expression.

19 Henning states (Ibid., 366): 'Not all writers accept that Samudravijaya reigned for 182 years and Aja for 221 years. Banda Gelek, for example (Bgbumrim, p. 5) describes a chronology that has them both reigning for 100 years. This means that in this listing the reign of Kalkī Sūrya would start at 824 CE.'

20 Volume 4, 320-26.

21 Hopkins has 'kulika', which he translates as 'one who bears the lineage' and calls this king Kulika Mañushrīkīrti. Tenzin Gyatso, the Dalai Lama and Jeffrey Hopkins, *Kalachakra Tantra, Rite of Initiation* (Wisdom, Boston, 1991), 60.

From then on the kings were called Kalkī kings. The term *kalkī* is derived from the Sanskrit word *kalkin,* meaning 'white horse', (symbolising the purified horse of mind/Mind embodied by the Head lotus), and relates to the last (tenth) of the *avātars* of Vishnu, the Kalkī Avatar. He will come upon a white horse at the close of the *kali yuga* (the materialistic iron age) to re-establish righteousness upon the earth. Henning states that it means 'one caste', signifying the Buddhists, who had done away with the caste system of the Hindus. Hence both meanings are applicable.

The succeeding king (Puṇḍarīka, meaning lotus, the symbol of purity) was said to be an emanation of Avalokiteśvara, the lord of compassion.[22] Hence in the three named kings of Shambhala we have the attributes of the first three Rays implicated.

1. Vajrapāṇi—the immutable power of the *vajra,* the first Ray of Will or Power. This Ray empowers the inner Throat tier of petals of the Head lotus.
2. Mañjuśrī—the embodiment of wisdom, the second Ray of Love-Wisdom. The Heart tier of the Head lotus is here implicated.
3. Avalokiteśvara, the lord of compassion, the third Ray of enlightening, Mathematically Exact Activity, governing the activity of the outer Solar Plexus in the Head tier.

In the thorough translation of the Kālacakra by Gyatso, the 25th Kalkī is said to appear at 'the end of the age of troubles'.

> Rudracakrī appears when our teacher Śakyamuni's doctrine of tantra has reached the end of the age of troubles, and eighteen hundred years will have passed since the arrival of the barbarians in Makha. In the ninety-seventh year of his reign, aided by the armies of the twelve great gods and others, Kalkī Rudra will leave Shambhala to journey to the noble land south of the Śīta River, and there, in lesser Jambudvīpa, they will defeat in battle the armies of the barbarians with their asura allies and bring them and others dwelling in the barbarian dharma to the Vajra Vehicle. Then, clockwise from lesser Jambudvīpa, they will

22 The Tibetan name is Chenrisi Padmapāṇi, the lotus bearing downward looking Lord who compassionately sees all forms with penetrating vision. See volumes 4 and 5 concerning detail of the role of Avalokiteśvara.

> enter the other eleven sectors one by one, and where the Vajra Vehicle of our teacher Śakyamuni has declined at the end of the age of troubles, they will restore it. In all twelve sectors, thereby, the teachings of the victorious Vajra Vehicle will bring about an end of completeness.
>
> With such an accomplishment and his hundred-year life at an end, his two sons, Brahmā, an emanation of Mañjuśrī, and Indra, an emanation of Avalokiteśvara, will be appointed teachers of the Vajra Vehicle, and Rudra will pass away. Brahmā will be the dharma teacher in Shambhala north of the Śīta River for eight hundred years, while Indra will be the teacher of dharma in the noble country and other lands.
>
> In this way, Rudracakrī brings the Vajra Vehicle of the Conqueror at the end of the age of troubles into an age of completeness. How long will that doctrine last? In each continent it will last for eighteen hundred years.[23]

Names heralding from Hinduism, such as Rudracakrī, Brahmā and Indra were chosen with great care to convey maximum meaning as to the forthcoming events. Rudra means 'howler', ferocious, terrible, angry, and is a wrathful form of Śiva. He brings about death, dissolution and transformation. This is apt in a time of transition to eliminate the ignorant forces in 'an age of troubles' (the *kali yuga),* so that new enlightened *dharma* can be presented for 'an age of completeness'. When the specific time for the appearance of this great one may be is defined according to the chronological system of the Kālachakra,[24] when read exoterically, as for instance given by Hopkins:

> The current, twenty-first, Kulika is said to have ascended to the throne in 1927, and the reign of the twenty-fifth and last Kulika, called "Rudra With A Wheel", will begin in 2327—the reign of each Kulika being one hundred years. In the ninety-eighth year of his rule, the year

23 Gyatso, Khedrup Norsang, *Ornament of Stainless Light. An Exposition of the Kālacakra Tantra* (Wisdom, Boston, 2004), 44-45.

24 With respect to the concept of time, Henning says: 'From a Kālacakra point of view, naturally one can talk in terms of outer time, inner time, and other, or awareness time. Outer time is the form or structure of time, the various appearances in nature. Inner time refers to the changes, in time, of the winds and elements in the body. Other time is the all-embracing reality, the Kālacakra awareness of indivisible emptiness and great bliss, and the path used to achieve this state of realization'. Henning, 216.

> 2425, which according to the Kālachakra calendar is 3304 years after Shākyamuni Buddha's passing away, a great war will be waged from Shambhala during which the barbarians will be defeated. After that, Buddhism will again flourish for eighteen hundred years; thus, in the 5104th year after Shākyamuni Buddha's passing away the period of his teaching will finish, the length of time being 104 years longer than the Sūtra system.[25]

Coming from this source the dating appears to be definitive, however, one should be very careful when interpreting anything in Buddhism concerning numbers and dates. There is not even an agreement as to the time of the passing away of Gautama. Contemporary accounts have him being born in the sixth century B.C. and therefore passing away in approximately the fifth. When asked about the demise of the *dharma,* Gautama replied:

> It is stated in the fifty-first section of the Mahāsannipāta-sūtra, that Buddha said: "After my Nirvāna, in the first 500 years, all the Bhikshus and others will be strong in deliberation in my correct Law. (Those who first obtain the 'holy fruit,' i.e., the Srota-āpannas, are called those who have obtained deliberation.) In the next or second 500 hundred years, they will be strong in meditation. In the next or third 500 years, they will be strong in 'much learning,' i.e., bahusruta, religious knowledge. In the next or fourth 500 hundred years, they will be strong in founding monasteries, &c. In the last or fifth 500 years, they will be strong in fighting and reproving. The pure (lit. white) Law will then become invisible.[26]

The reason for quoting this passage is that a good case could be made for the appearance of Rudracakrī, or indeed for Maitreya, in this present most materialistic epoch after the Chinese invasion of Tibet, as literally 2,500 years have passed since Gautama's demise. The pure white law, literally meaning the esoteric knowledge of the inner context of the *sūtras,* has all but disappeared.

---

25 From the introduction by Jeffrey Hopkins in *Kālachakra Tantra Rite of Initiation*, 65.

26 E.B. Cowell, *Buddhist Mahāhyāna Texts,* (Motilal Banarsidass, Delhi, 1997), from the section on *The Vagrakkhedikā,* 116. Gyatso, elaborates a '5,000-year duration of the doctrine according to sutra in ten sets of five hundred years'. Gyatso, 603.

'Lesser Jambudvīpa' in the quote from Gyatso refers to the earth, wherein from about this time there will be a war against 'the armies of the barbarians with their asura allies' to convert them to the white *dharma*. At the time the text was written the 'barbarians' were the Muslim conquerors of northern India, who virtually completely wiped out Buddhism there. However, projection from that time to the then distant future means that the 'barbarians' would take a different, more esoteric significance.

In fact the concern here is the conquest of the white *dharma* by the 'kings of Shambhala' over the ignorance purveyed by 'the barbarians'. The 'armies of the twelve great gods and others' refers to the forces of the twelve major petals of the Head lotus, and the 'others' refers to the petals of the other *chakras*. Physical plane wars may happen, but the true target is the conversion of *adharma* (ignorance) into *dharma*. This *dharma* is couched in Buddhistic terms ('the Vajra Vehicle') and as such will educate the world.

In terms of the meditation process there is the conversion of base *saṃskāras (kleśas)* developed in the lower centres into the compassionate wisdom-bearing attributes of the enlightened. This concerns the 'journey to the noble land south of the Śīta River'. This river refers to the Watery astral plane, wherein reside those that have died, and from which most are born.[27] Travelling 'clockwise from lesser Jambudvīpa, they will enter the other eleven sectors one by one' refers to developing one after another of the characteristics of the Heart centre, and the Heart in the Head, starting with the southernmost petal symbolised by the attributes of Cancer the crab, hence the rebirthing process. Cancer is governed by the Watery Element and its attributes. It, along with the other signs of the zodiac, are explained in Volume 3 in the section entitled 'The Great Gate of Diamond Liberation'. That one is travelling clockwise to cleanse the attributes of these petals (by

27 See Volume 4, 137-46 for an explanation of the properties of this realm. See also the footnote on page 9 of Volume 5A. This entire volume deals with the process of the conversion of the 'barbarians' (defiling *saṃskāras, kleśas)* developed in the lower centres found below the diaphragm into enlightenment-attributes. This same process can also be interpreted in terms of transformations of the *kleśas* for all upon the earth, to which the above symbolism refers. One can then comprehend the vastness of the undertaking manifested by the Lords of Shambhala.

means of the activity associated with the eight-spoked wheel) concerns the rectification process of the zodiac. This means that no longer are attributes of *saṃsāric* attachments produced, but rather that concerning enlightenment. Eventually the teachings of the white *dharma* will reign supreme in 'all twelve sectors' of the manifesting Heart centre that constitutes the awakening of humanity.

The rectified and cleansed *prāṇas* are then contained in the centres above the diaphragm and incorporated in the Head centre. When viewing humanity as a whole, and the process of the transformation of their consciousness upon a planetary scale, such a conquest will obviously take more than a few decades, or even centuries. Many millennia in fact will pass. The symbolism refers not only to the population of this earth, but also to the psychic residents *(asuras)* on the inner realms. Certainly the approximately 300 years between now and the quoted year 2327 will be needed. Such a 'war' will happen upon many levels at once, with a new, revised white *dharma* promulgated, formulated to lead the masses to liberation, not just those professing to be 'Buddhists'.

The true white *dharma* itself is non-sectarian, which it must be if truly compassionate. The inherent teachings of the white *dharma* need only be phrased in meaningful terms and language that can be comprehended and applied by the many aspirants to enlightenment wherever they may be. The skilful means of the Bodhisattva is utilised to thus educate, no matter the race, philosophy or religion of the individual. The terminology changes according to need and *manasic* predilection of the people concerned, and must evolve with the needs of the changing times, but the inner *dharma,* the true meaning remains the same. The parochial thinking of many Buddhists must change and their thought-structures adapted to meet the true needs of the aspiring ones in our societies. To do so they must begin to think more esoterically, hence to wisely overcome their penchant of belief in exoteric myth and outdated logical assumptions, so to compassionately awaken new modes of spreading the *dharma.* In doing so they will step into the shoes of the great Bodhisattvas of the past, who are ever moving forwards and onwards into cosmos.

The true battle, however, will be against the forces of darkness, the black magicians and the like that espouse evil in all of its facets. Such evil is based principally upon the power of money in this avaricious society, malicious false propaganda, outright lies to deceive the many, and manipulative aggression, or outright war against those that oppose their manifold schemes for absolute power over all.

'Cakrī' is a feminised form of the word *cakra (chakra),* therefore Rudracakrī embodies the wrathful or destructive aspect of the first Ray forces of Will or Power manifesting as a wheel of transformative effects in the *nāḍī* system of this earth. Brahmā is the third person of the Hindu *trimūrti,* the creative deity, who can be personified as the Mother embodying the Fires of Mind, hence the power of Secret Mantra.

The hint, therefore, is that the new epoch will be governed (after a fierce battle against the forces of materialism) by the feminine principle (wisdom in Buddhism), whereby the attributes of the *devas* can be revealed. The feminine dispensation will be needed to karmically offset much of the evil war-like attributes of the patriarchal systems that have governed the nations of this world for many millennia. Being the 'dharma teacher in Shambhala north of the Śītā River' simply means that this feminine dispensation will rule from Shambhala for a symbolic eight hundred years, the turning of the eight-spoked wheel of direction in space that organises all of the forces ('villages') of the eight regions of the depiction of Shambhala earlier described. It turns the complete twelve petals of the Head lotus, and their tiers of 96 subsidiary petals. Indra is the king of the gods, ruler of the Airy Element, hence wields the power of the lightning bolt and *vajra* to defeat his enemies. He literally represents the earthy representative or appearance of the Lord of Shambhala (who remains 'north', thus subjective). Hence Indra will 'be the teacher of dharma'. What is effectively symbolised here, therefore, are the *sambhogakāya* and *nirmāṇakāya* aspects of a Buddha (or great Bodhisattva), where one manifests as an outward appearance (Indra) and the other (Brahmā) the subjective guiding expression.

The 'eighteen hundred years' that they rule for refers to one definition of a *yuga* (or cycle of time), which here incorporates a cycle of five years consisting of sixty solar-sidereal months of 1,800 days. The entire mechanism concerning the computation of time is therefore implied. Also, numerologically the number 18 has reference to the sub-planes governing the mental, emotional and physical domains that all humans must master to overcome *saṃsāra.* Seven subplanes each for the physical and astral planes and four for the subplanes of the empirical mind.

Hence they ruled for the time that humanity could master their lower three-fold nature, which is a vast undertaking (signified by the multiplier of the number 1,000). Also, the number 18 refers to undertaking the second Initiation whereby the Watery emotions are mastered, where the number nine signifies Initiation.[28]

From the above we can see that the *Kālacakra Tantra,* and hence the accompanying well-known *maṇḍala* and associated deity, relate to the detail of the attributes of the Head lotus. By comprehending the nature of this lotus as it actually exists, rather than a mythologised account, can an analogy to Shambhala be drawn, as Shambhala is the planetary Head centre. It governs the expression of all Life upon this planet and its interrelationships with all similar centres in our local cosmos. We are now in a position to embark upon an exploration of exactly how that centre is embodied by the liberated beings that have gained Buddhahood from former aeons of achievement, plus those elevated Bodhisattvas that have evolved from our earth.

For this we must analyse transmuted correspondences of the entities that help convert the *prāṇas* in a Head centre, and the enlightened entities that help transform the *saṃskāras* derived from below the diaphragm into the *manasic* propensities stored in the Head lotus. The view is upon a far vaster domain than a human unit, for now all of the kingdoms in Nature and the Dharmakāya Flower are to be incorporated under the guidance of the compassionate planetary executives that have evolved thus to direct the evolutionary process of all streams of Lives, taking the multidimensional view of what exists into account.

Also, as far as possible names need to be assigned to such entities, not only in terms of Buddhist deities, but also as they may have been termed in other religions or myths. The exposé of the Head and related *chakras* in relation to the *Bardo Thödol* in Volume 5A will prove

---

28 What is introduced here is the subject of esoteric numerology that must be mastered to properly understand the significance of numbers in sacred texts. The *Kālacakra tantra* adds its own element to the symbolism of numbers, as explained by Henning: 'Most of these symbolic names are for single numbers, although double digit values are sometimes used. For numbers greater than one digit, the individual numbers are to be understood "backwards." So, the present "fire (3) sky (0) ocean (4)" means four hundred and three, and "hand (2) snake (8) Moon (1)" one hundred and eighty-two. Henning, 222. See also Appendix 5 from Gyatso, 605-9 for a list of these 'word-numerals'.

valuable here as a guide to help delineate some of the major entities that play a role in the Kingdom of Shambhala. This assignment will mainly more accurately depict the *devas,* the feminine principle governing the dissemination of *karma.* Other major players in this Kingdom need modern names and will be so attributed.

The time has come to unravel the myths and to present *the truth of what is,* so that the many that evolve the Bodhisattva characteristics by taking high Initiations in the future can more quickly find their placing in the liberated domains unhindered by erroneous conceptions and veiled myth in religious scriptures posing as truth.

Though the esotericism of many of the concepts are alien to traditional Buddhism, I will need to use as my primary source the most enlightened teachings currently available, that enunciated by the Tibetan Master D.K., via Alice A. Bailey, and supplement this with the teachings from the previous volumes of this *Treatise on Mind,* where useful. Also, considerable additional material hitherto not revealed in publications can now be presented. Those that do not possess a Buddhist background may breathe a sigh of relief, in having to no longer wade through difficult metaphysics and terminology. Nevertheless, all that proceeds has its basis in the *buddhadharma,* esoterically understood. The doctrine is simply to be extended into what to Buddhists represents unfamiliar territory, but indeed represents the continuing revelations that the Dharmakāya Way provides. Buddhists, welcome to the future. The revelations concerning the way Bodhisattvas actually evolve and how the Council of Bodhisattvas is constituted, its relation to the Lords of Shambhala, and what can be presently revealed about them, is now offered for your taking. Come, let us herald the great awakening.

It should be emphasised that the spiritual age of all in the earlier epochs of evolution, when Atlantis, for instance, existed, was much less than now. For this reason Shambhala manifested as an externalised centre upon the physical plane, with most of its members needing further incarnations to progress their enlightened status. Certain types of *karma* still had to be transformed. For this reason many myths, such as Mount Olympus and that found in the Kālacakra, refer to the physical plane location of this Kingdom of the Gods.

All of the members of Shambhala had their genesis in world spheres that existed prior to this one. They came to inform the matrix of the planetary Head centre with the special skills needed to direct all streams of Life upon our planet to liberation, or have since been replaced by those that have attained high Initiations upon the earth sphere.

There are many more zones of residence for human consciousnesses and enlightenment than mere three-dimensional space. The planets that the scientific community deem uninhabitable have forms of Life residing in the subjective planes of perception that underlie the dense spheres. Some have undergone earth-like conditions aeons ago. There are consequently many schools of learning in the inner realms, all of which are contactable via the awakening meditation-Mind. Enlightenment reveals the history of all such places. Marvellous indeed is the universe experienced through the process of meditation.

Much that is considered mythological, such as dragons and unicorns, also suddenly become real. Also, many friends and personages exist within the subjective realms that were formerly not known, but are expressions of the *karma* of acquaintances developed in past lives. They therefore do not presently share the same physical time-space with the person. The meditation instructor needs to be familiar with such vistas of expanded possibilities, opportunities and beings to meet in the universe, if the student is to be rightly guided. Also, the instructor must be initiated in the symbols of the path of astounding vision stemming from the meditation-Mind, to properly guide the candidate to these realms of meaning. These symbols represent forms of instruction bequeathed by the enlightened ones working from the inner realms.

To become residents of Shambhala is a natural goal for Bodhisattvas, as the three highest *bhūmis* necessarily incorporates them therein. The entire process of meditation therefore prepares one to bear the high potencies of the energies and visions that will be received from this source, once the grounding of intensified *manasic* substance has been achieved.

With respect to an appearance of a transforming force or Avatar, such as Rudracakrī, one should also compare the teaching of the Rider on the white horse in the Bible.[29] Similarly the teachings concerning

---

29 *Rev. 19:11-17*, which will be explained in chapter 4.

the Kalkī Avatar, the last (tenth) of the *avatāras* or incarnations of Vishnu (the embodiment of the principle of Love-Wisdom in the Hindu *trimūrti),* when he is said to come upon a white horse at the end of the present, most materialistic of the four ages in Hindu cosmogony, the *kali yuga* ('iron or black age'). Krishna in chapter 4:5-9 of the Bhagavad Gītā sums up this advent well when he states to his charioteer Arjuna:

> The Blessed Lord Said:
>
> Many births have gone by Me and of thee too, O Arjuna! I know them all, But thou knowest not (thine), O Paraṃtapa!
>
> Though unborn, the Imperishable Self, and also the Lord of all beings, brooding over nature, which is Mine own, yet I am born through My own Power.
>
> Whenever there is decay of righteousness, O Bhārata!, and exaltation of unrighteousness, then I create Myself (incarnate myself in some form);
>
> For protection of the good, and destruction of evil-doers, for the sake of firmly establishing righteousness, I am born from age to age.
>
> He who thus knoweth My divine birth and action, in its essence, having abandoned the body, cometh not to birth again, but cometh unto me, O Arjuna![30]

Krishna (an earlier *avatāra* of Vishnu and an incarnation of the Christ) is but one name for the embodiment of compassion for this planet, and his role within the halls of Shambhala and the Council of Bodhisattvas shall be explained later.

---

30 Annie Besant and Bhagavan Das, *The Bhagavad Gītā* (Theosophical Publishing House, Adyar, 1926), 78-70.

The third Christ in his tattered Robe
waits by the ferry for the Toll Man's bell.
The second Christ is crucified in Light.
The first Christ is honoured with a Robe.
They all tell the story of man to the Boatman
with whom they sail.
Come on this journey with me.
We'll set sail on this ocean of Love to the Dog star.
We leave on a raging tide.
You, me, all the Ones we go.
We daren't stay,
for that which beckons no man can say nay.
The mysteries of space, of time, of Life all revealed
to those who sail on this boat on the Waters of space.
The bell it tolls, the note carries them all away.
The ripple across time itself is felt.
And all who know feel the Power that comes this way.

2

The Meditation Process and Shambhala

The five levels of Shambhala

Having explained the myth, the Shambhalic lore can be explained. Its esoteric history is revealed through yogic direct perception, *pratyakṣa,* and known to those that are Initiated into 'the mysteries of the kingdom of God'.[1] They are the high Initiates, Bodhisattvas of the higher *bhūmis,* that have both the all-seeing Eye and the inner Ear awakened whereby they can see all things that come to pass and can listen to 'ear-whispered' truths. The revelation of the context of those truths pertaining to Shambhala is now mandated because the high level of attainment of the world's disciples evokes the need for higher truths, as befits this epoch of universal education and the computer literate society. The time has come for the inner meaning of the formerly spoken parables to be revealed.

Five levels of expression to Shambhala can be considered, each representing a different *maṇḍalic* construct. These levels, constituted of various gradations of Initiates, exemplify attributes of the qualities of one or other of the five Jinas[2]. The lowest, broadest level relates to the activities of the third and fourth degree Initiates. They are the most senior disciples within the Ashrams of the Masters of Wisdom.[3]

---

1 *Luke 8:10,* King James Version (KJV), which shall be used throughout this volume. 'And he said, Unto you it is given to know the mysteries of the kingdom of God: but to others in parables; that seeing they may not see, and hearing they may not understand'.

2 Dhyāni Buddhas.

3 The Masters are fifth degree Initiates, tenth level Bodhisattvas, though sometimes

Each Ashram embodies a sub-Ray department within the Council of Bodhisattvas. Each such group can be viewed as a *chakra* of twelve petals centred around a particular Master, to which then, there are a number of subsidiary petals. These Ashrams come under the auspices of Amitābha's Discriminating Inner Wisdom. They represent those who are in the process of obtaining their final release from the domain of the Sambhogakāya Flower,[4] and those that have done so. The Ashram expresses the attributes of the abstract Mind, which is the focus of most members, and consequently they express Amitābha's purpose in *saṃsāra*.

The next level constitutes the *maṇḍala* of the Masters of Wisdom, the Initiates of the fifth degree, who function at the third or lowest level of the *dharmakāya* (the *ātmic* plane). They express *dharmakāya* into *saṃsāra* according to the nature of the particular sub-Ray whose purpose is held in their custodianship. They represent the level of Bodhisattvaship prior to the attainment of Buddhahood. There are presently around twenty-four individuals that have made this grade. Their mode of service work upon our planet demonstrates Ratnasambhava's Equalising Wisdom. They work to harmonise all lesser spheres of activity into the one primal mode that is their directive from the Lords of Shambhala. Utilising the Will-to-Good they direct planetary purpose along their respective sub-Ray lines far into the foreseeable future. Together these Ashrams constitute the organised *maṇḍala* of the Hierarchy of Light and Love,[5] which constitutes a Heart centre upon this planet. Its functions are also incorporated into the Heart in the Head lotus of this planetary Head centre (Shambhala). All streams of activity are amalgamated into the variegations of the Shambhalic and Hierarchical *maṇḍalas*, according to a central Plan for the betterment of all life upon our planet.

Next is the level of expression of the *maṇḍala* of the eight Mahābodhisattvas explained in Volume 4 of this Treatise, plus their *deva* compliments. They are the Chohans of the seven Rays (each incorporating seven sub-Ray Ashrams), plus the Mahāchohan, who occupies the northern

---

Chohans of the Rays, sixth degree Initiates, are also called Masters.

4 The Causal Body, the Soul. Its qualities from a Buddhist perspective were explained in Volume 3.

5 The term Hierarchy shall generally be used henceforth to designate those that constitute the planetary Heart centre. It shall supplant the earlier descriptive phrase, 'the Council of Bodhisattvas'.

position of the *maṇḍala.* They technically can be considered eleventh level Bodhisattvas, and have taken their sixth Initiation, the degree of attainment of the Buddha when he gained his *parinirvāṇa.* (The Mahāchohan, however, is a seventh degree Initiate.) Consequently, they are Buddhas that are still actively engaged with earth affairs because they fill necessary posts in the Shambhalic *maṇḍala.* There are also some others functioning at this level that shall later be explained. Together their united work manifests the functions of Amoghasiddhi's All-accomplishing Wisdom. They possess all power over every attribute associated with their respective Ray lines with which they disseminate Shambhalic purpose into manifestation.

This second highest level is constituted of an interrelated hexagram of high Initiates who form a *maṇḍala* with the historical Buddha (see Figure 2). There are other beings which can be included at this level, which shall be elucidated in chapter nine. This group manifests the functioning of Akṣobhya in that they mirror the high commands from Shambhala and cosmic sources into manifestation. They express the cyclic activity of the all-seeing Eye from all directions in space and cosmic centres into our planetary sphere. Thus all the *chakras* below the planetary Head lotus are vitalised with active purpose whereby receptive entities can be adequately guided. This group is constituted of Initiates of the seventh, eighth and ninth degrees. The first Shambhalic level is presented below.

The first Shambhalic level

At this level we have the symbol of the Eye in the triangle, surrounded by a diamond of Great Ones that represent an inner executive Council of Shambhala. They are Initiates of the ninth and tenth degrees (or greater), making them Heavenly Men in cosmic spheres. They function at the highest level of *dharmakāya.*

This is the source of all Shambhalic dictates governing all planes of perception and of all links of our planetary system, with their correspondences in the solar system and throughout cosmos. They therefore take the attributes of Vairocana and the Dharmadhātu Wisdom with respect to the dissemination of spiritual power into the domains of the earth.

The Avatar of Synthesis, the Spirit of Peace and the Mother of the World are the three esoteric Kumāras that will be explained in greater detail in chapter 8, as well as the three Buddhas of Activity and Sanat

Kumāra. They are introduced here as part of the overall schema of Shambhala. Similarly in that chapter other great entities, such as the four Mahārājas shall be incorporated at this level of expression of Shambhala, as part of the Council Chamber of the Lord of the World. The Buddhas of Activity are direct 'Students' of Sanat Kumāra and are of extreme antiquity. They herald from the past solar system and represent a special dispensation on our globe.

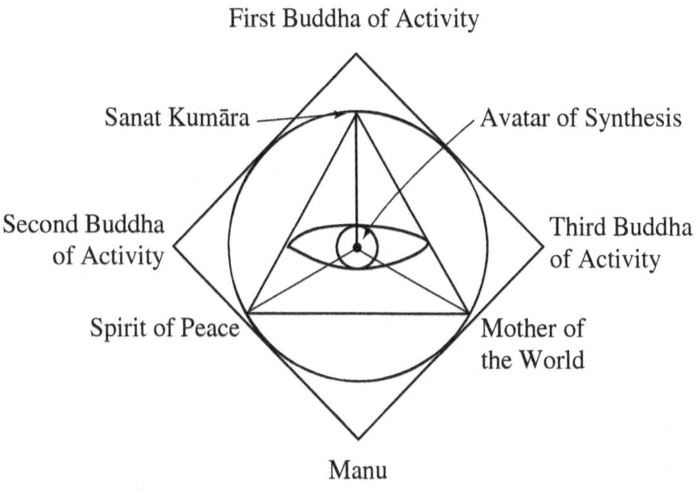

Figure 1. The first Shambhalic level

Examples of the work of the Buddhas of Activity can be seen in their effect upon the formation of the infant Hierarchy during the early period of the fifth Root Race epoch, whose story became established in myth and legend. They overshadowed certain Initiates, making possible their herculean tasks as they struggled under the auspices of 'the Gods'. Thus was established the tone of ancient history and the story of their exploits was repeated by a succession of ancient bards, the Initiated keepers of the Mysteries. An example was Hercules, son of the king of the Gods (Zeus), whom we can infer refers to Sanat Kumāra, and the mortal Alcmene. Hercules was overshadowed by the second Buddha of Activity when the sun was in the sign Leo. This is signified by the trademark lion pelt he wore of the lion he slew when he was eighteen. His major achievement is epitomised by undertaking twelve labours, which concern mastery of the qualities of the twelve petals of the Heart centre and the Heart in the Head centre, therefore, also of the potencies of the twelve signs of the zodiac.[6]

Hercules' esoteric work thereby established the basic *maṇḍala* of the Hierarchy of Enlightened Beings (which the events of his life symbolised) and its mode of gaining high awareness at the adolescent stage of its development. This activity occurred in anticipation for the inflow of worthy candidates for Initiation into the Bodhisattva path for our planetary life, within the context of the cycle of the manifestation of mind throughout the planetary system.[7] In those days this was conceived of in terms of accomplishing heroic sacrificial deeds. The twelve labours manifested because of the unsavoury actions he made whilst mad (which included killing six of his own sons)[8], and as a consequence he had to serve king Eurystheus of Argos for twelve years. He had 'to perform whatever labours might be set him, in payment for which he would be rewarded with immortality. At this, Hercules fell into deep despair, loathing to serve a man whom he knew far inferior to himself, yet afraid to oppose his father Zeus'.[9]

The symbolism of the early history of the Hierarchy of Love and Light, governed by the sign Leo the lion, is therefore veiled in the

---

6 As such these labours need not necessarily have been undertaken in one life, but rather a sequence of lives, each one dedicated to the task of mastering one of the attributes of the signs of the zodiac. Such a sequence of lives is still followed by those undertaking the path today for the earlier Initiations, as all aspects of life are conditioned by these twelve signs. Initiates must master all aspects of being as they progress through their incarnations. They must demonstrate their accomplishments via the conditionings determined by the twelve signs. As they do so the properties of the twelve petals of the Heart centre are explored and its petals awakened. Similarly for the Heart within the Head centre. In the higher Initiations mastery of the attributes of the twelve signs can be gained in one life, based upon the momentum of former accomplishments (e.g., slaying the lion, signifying the ego, whilst an adolescent).

7 Esoterically, the term Aryan is used to denote the present fifth great cycle of humanity whose purpose is to evolve the qualities of the mind in all its attributes. This represents the fifth Root Race, whereas the term Atlantean is used for the fourth Root Race. The Atlantean purpose was to evolve the Watery emotional attributes of humanity, incorporating also the awakening of the lower psychic perceptions.

8 The number six here relating to the abuse of the principal of desire, of the attributes of the Sacral centre. Its six petals can be symbolised by these sons.

9 Robert Graves, *The Greek Myths*, (Penguin, Middlesex, England, 1980), Volume 2, 101.

myth concerning Hercules, with the lion pelt that he continuously wore signifying the budding Hierarchical aura. As a grouping of Bodhisattvas, the young Hierarchy had to undergo all of the stages of development that all upon the path must. The path of aspiration, accepted discipleship, and the stages of development to the third Initiation is implicated, including the nature of the mastery of *saṃskāras* below the diaphragm, as explained in Volume 5A, but now to be interpreted in terms of the Greek mythos.

This service work manifested at a time when the attribute of mind was only in its infancy amongst humanity, and set the ball in motion for all future Bodhisattvic activity. This great One undertook the third Initiation through manifesting the form of Hercules, making him thus a 'son of God', when this Initiation was the equivalent of the liberation later undertaken by Gautama thousands of years later.[10] Hercules set the paradigm of what could be achieved and the means to do so, for all that were later to become members of Hierarchy. He represented the head of Hierarchy, the Christ-principle, for those times.

That the ancient story was set down in writing as a Greek myth simply signified that by the time that the myth was written down the teachings could then be applied usefully by the population of the time. There are always high Initiates incarnate capable of recording ancient information for the contemporary idiom and needs. Myths contain a mixture of psychic happenings concerning inner transformations, coupled with allegories of actual events. The complicated, eventful life of Hercules relates to the symbolic battling with the *saṃskāras* from below the diaphragm needed to accomplish the third Initiation at his time, hence he was accepted at Olympus (Shambhala) as a God after his self-imposed death on a funeral pyre.[11]

Another related myth is that of the Odyssey at a significantly later time, and the search for the golden fleece by Jason and the Argonauts. It concerned the journey to Shambhala by the young Hierarchy, and gaining the Hierarchical aura (the golden fleece), as a consequence of sufficient numbers of Hierarchy being able to take their third Initiation.

---

10 The requirements for taking Initiation at Hercules' time were different than at the time of Gautama. Thus teachings concerning adamantine faith in instructions from the Gods was conveyed in the Hercules myth, and yogic prowess at the time of Gautama.

11 Graves, Vol I, 202-3.

They travelled inwardly, as well as physically, to a place in the Gobi desert, where the etheric expression of Shambhala could then be found and where the Initiation ceremony took place. They also had the internal vision to interrelate with the members of this Kingdom. The Odyssey was a record of a major evolutionary event upon this planet.

The third of the Buddhas of Activity overshadowed the Mahāchohan's department, where Hermes Trismegistus ('thrice greatest Hermes') took the role of the first Mahāchohan for the Aryan dispensation. He was known in antiquity for his great wisdom and was the author of the Emerald Tablet, the source of all alchemical lore upon our planet. This text states:

> True, without error, certain and most true; that which is above is as that which is below and that which is below is as that which is above, for performing the miracles of the one Thing; and as all things were from one by the mediation of one so all things arose from this one thing by adaptation.
>
> The Father of it is the sun, the mother of it is the moon; the wind carries it in its belly and the Mother of it is the earth. This is the Father of all perfection, and consummation of the whole world. The power of it is integral if it be turned into earth.
>
> Thou shalt separate the earth from the fire and subtle from the gross, gently with much sagacity; it ascends from earth to Heaven, and again descends to earth; and receives the strength of the superiors and the inferiors—so thou hast the glory of the whole world; therefore let all obscurity fly before thee. This is the strong fortitude of all fortitudes, overcoming every subtle and penetrating every solid thing so the world was created.[12]

The Egyptians identified him with their god Thoth, the god of writing and wisdom. He was the scribe of the gods and also their messenger, and 'He was believed to command "the sacred books of the house of life", i.e., papyrus rolls housed in temple libraries, inscribed with medical treatises, mathematical problems, etc'.[13]

---

12 Alice A. Bailey, *A Treatise on Cosmic Fire,* (Lucis Publishing Company, New York, 1982), 1066. The extract is given here because it provides much esoteric wisdom, well worth meditating upon by all earnest students seeking enlightenment.

13 Oakes, Lorna and Lucia Gahlin, *The Mysteries of Ancient Egypt* (Hermes House, London, 2005), 306.

The first of the Buddhas of Activity helped establish the Egyptian civilisation in the hoary mists of time,[14] where we have the Egyptian myth of Osiris, the first born from the primal parents Geb and Nut (the earth and sky god and goddess). He was the lord of the earth and gave to the Egyptians their laws, culture, etc. He was also associated with the Nile river and the Djed column (representing the spinal column, hence the power of the three main *nāḍīs* contained therein). He was killed by his brother Seth (symbolising the dark forces of evil), and who was jealous of Osiris's success in the civilisation he created. Osiris's body was dismembered and its parts hidden throughout Egypt. These parts were later found, reconstituted and resurrected by Isis (the Mother of the World). The only part that was not found by Isis was his phallus, so she created a golden one, sat upon it, and the consequence was the birth of the god Horus (the second[15]). Osiris then became King of the Egyptian underworld (thus to embody the purpose of the reincarnation process). Horus later battled with Seth and defeated him.

The purpose was to establish Egypt, the Heart centre for the Aryan epoch, as the exoteric home wherein the future spiritual Hierarchy could safely incarnate and evolve the qualities needed. Here the two banks of the Nile river symbolise the pillars of the temple of the Mysteries governed by Gemini. The river itself veiled the significance of the Holy of Holies within the temple. The Hierarchy of enlightened being was symbolised by Osiris's son Horus who embodied the symbolism of the Christ aspect for the Egyptian religion, of whom the Pharaohs, the god-kings, were said to be the earthly incarnations, the head of a priesthood devoted to the Osiris myth. This established the basic eschatological Mysteries of life for all those ready to travel the path to great wisdom.

The story concerning Osiris has many levels of symbolism related to the establishment of ancient Egypt (here part of the work of the Manu's department[16]) as a centre, or place of residence for Hierarchy. Egypt was chosen because it is the planetary Heart centre, exemplified

---

14 We can look to the time when the sun was in Virgo, signifying the birthing of the religious dispensation for the Aryan epoch.

15 The first Horus was a brother of Osiris.

16 In this case it directed its first Ray purpose via the Mahāchohan's department, whereas the Manu's role is exemplified in the later role of being Lord of the underworld.

at the site where the great Pyramid complex at Giza stands. The dismemberment of his body into 14 parts symbolises the astral plane. In those days Hierarchy was evolving the powers and attributes of the Solar Plexus centre, which Egyptian magic, with its many spells and Gods exemplified. For this reason it was easy for the dark forces, the worshippers of Seth, and of the grey version of the Anubis to inevitably take over the Egyptian religion. The 'heresy' of Akhenaton was to try to counter this takeover by properly establishing the true cult of the Sun, where the energies of the Heart centre takes control over the Solar Plexus centre. Hence he built a new capital on pristine, untainted land at Tell-el-Amarna where he could concentrate his forces via those loyal to him to battle the dark brotherhood ensconced as the state religion in Memphis. Though he failed in this objective, nevertheless his rule marked the turnaround for Hierarchy in its religious dispensation away from the Solar Plexus centre to the Heart centre proper. The focus was then not just upon the physical sun, but also upon the Heart of the Sun.

The title *Manu* refers to the one who holds office as the primal progenitor of one of the Root Races of humanity, presiding over the dissemination of a particular major human evolutionary quality, such as the development of the emotions (the Atlantean Manu), the mind (the Aryan Manu), and later high spiritual perceptions (a Manu who will take this role in the new epoch). The Manu is responsible for the sum of the evolutionary development of the Life aspect that incarnates into evolving forms, incorporating thus also that of the lesser kingdoms of Nature. As the Lord of Life, the Manu deals directly with the directive power of the first (destroyer) Ray, which works to abstract all streams of Life back to their originating source. His department thus directs the overall development of the Spirit or Monadic aspect of humanity, which then conditions the realm of the *tathāgatagarbha,*[17] the human Soul. From the *dharmakāya* he directs the many transformations that the form of any embodied *maṇḍala* of lives may take. Each of the sub-Races of humanity also have a ruler or director of their evolutionary impulse under a presiding Manu.

17 The Buddhist rendition for what I have termed the Sambhogakāya Flower. See Volume 3 for proper explanation.

The present Manu that rules the evolutionary journeying of the fifth (Aryan) Root Race governed by the dissemination of the Element Fire[18] (thus concerned with the evolution of all attributes of mind), is termed Vaivasvata Manu.[19] The previous Manu (the fourth) was responsible for the dissemination of the Watery Element (all forms of emotionality and psychic receptivity) in the Atlantean epoch.

The inner triad in Figure 1, for the first level of Shambhala, represents the triune Deity that can be considered as Father-Son-Mother for our entire planetary life. The explanations found in D.K.'s books almost exclusively focus upon the 'Personalities' of Sanat Kumāra and the three Buddhas of Activity, and at times giving them the functions that would normally be attributes of the three subjective Kumāras. The attributes of the esoteric three are veiled in the personage of Sanat Kumāra. The reason for this is that Sanat Kumāra is the planetary Avatar, the incarnate Personality embodying the functions (reflecting into manifestation) of this esoteric triad. For this reason one of His appellations is 'the Eternal Youth'. The three Buddhas of Activity then reflect Their Purpose into the three kingdoms of Nature. They 'regulate' the sum of that activity to its Visioned conclusion.

We are now, however, entering into an epoch where the esoteric three can become more exoteric, hence their functions can be somewhat elaborated. This is especially so for the Mother of the World, the fifth Kumāra (counting from below up), and who from another viewpoint can be considered the seventh. The situation is somewhat complicated as a consequence of the events upon the moon Chain, which shall be elaborated in chapter 8. Obviously little can be said about these Entities due to their exalted states of Awareness and cosmic contacts, the expression of the cosmic Mind They embody. Their functions are normally integrated into the Dynamic Poise of Sanat Kumāra and

---

18 This fifth Root Race thus brings the *manasic* principle to the fore in humanity.

19 Vaivasvata (the sun-born or brilliant one) is the fifth *manu* (progenitor, father) who governs the present age. He was said to have been a son of Surya (the Sun) and is the Hindu correspondence of Noah, in that he was saved from the great Atlantean deluge (explained in the *Satapatha Brāhmana* and also the *Mahābhārata)* in an ark (that was built by the order of Vishnu). The myth states that he became the father of the founder of a solar race of Kings. (The Masters of the present Hierarchy of Light.)

carried through into manifestation via the focussed intent of the three Buddhas of Activity. These three express the attributes of the subjective three into manifestation, yet are cosmically more advanced than their position would normally indicate.

The central (Father) figure (standing therefore as the Ādi Buddha for our planetary system) is termed *The Avatar of Synthesis* because He synthesises into one dynamic integral Life all purpose and energies for our planet of woe. This great being, the first of the esoteric Kumāras, has a scintillating rainbow auric field and is generally abstracted from our planetary life. He works with other Regents in cosmos with respect to the integration of our planetary evolution with that of the solar system in general, as well as to the various places of destination (stellar spheres) within cosmos that the *nirvāṇees* (the Buddhas leaving our planetary sphere) must go to for further advancement. Though He is therefore represented as the pupil of the all-seeing Eye in Figure 1, through which all light to and from the planet passes, Sanat Kumāra, as the embodied Avatar, normally takes this role.

Sanat Kumāra integrates the sum total of the *karma* of our planetary Life towards its placement in cosmos. Therefore, the access of all that can be considered cosmic evil is strictly regulated with respect to whatever *karma* humanity possesses with them, and to the cycles of opportunity that such evil consequently reigns over. The sum total of the *bījas*[20] that awaken the cyclic opportunity within the *nāḍīs* of the planetary life are therefore projected by this One.

The *Spirit of Peace* represents the heart of this triad, the embodiment of the deep indigo blue principle of Love-Wisdom that is the matrix of the Womb of the Jinas. The Buddhas of meditation all gain succour from the fountainhead of bliss poured forth from this great One. He integrates the ocean of Consciousness from cosmos into our vital planetary life. Transformations of planetary *saṃskāras,* such as those depicted for an individual in Volume 5, though upon a far vaster scale, is directed by him, working via all five levels of Shambhala.

The *Mother of the World* is the mother of all integral life of the planet. There are a myriad names for this great feminine principle, Tarā, Urusvati,[21] Demeter, Isis, Mary, etc. As such she is a prime object of

20 Seeds of karmic propensity sown in former lives.

21 *Urusvati.* Meaning 'Star of the Morning', thus Venus, but here more specifically,

worship in most religious dispensations, especially for women in relation to their sexuality, pregnancy, and childbirth. She is also worshipped in relation to the symbolism concerning similar functions of planetary evolution. The epoch we are now entering represents the era when the feminine shall again be exemplified in Nature and our civilisation. Much needs to be accomplished to raise women out of the many abysmal and dire situations in which they find themselves via various religious dispensations and cultural situations. Most members of the Council of Bodhisattvas have consequently chosen to be born into female bodies, or will do so. This includes those of the highest *bhūmis*. Tibetans therefore need to seek for the incarnations of their Rinpoches mostly amongst women rather than within the masculine population.

The main rulership of the great Mother is, however, over the *deva* Hierarchy (the angelic kingdom), the *ḍākinīs, gandharvas,*[22] etc. The epoch is rapidly approaching when some of the more advanced members of humanity will begin to communicate with certain orders of the *deva* Hierarchy, especially those denoted 'the violet *devas* of the shadows'.[23] Cosmically, the great angelic orders and the Mother's department are ruled by the great feminine Hierarchy found on the Pleiades star cluster. (As well as via other feminine constellations and stars.) The great Mother is an Initiate from that system, having taken her ninth Initiation.

The Mother of the World, the great Deva Lord out of whose substance all streams of sentience and consciousness are formed. She signifies the Womb of Light that is the hope of the future.

22 *Gandharvas,* (Tib: dri zha) Literally scent eaters. *Gandharvas* are fairy-like celestial musicians, wherein sound, as in song and music, is the prevailing quality of existence. Their cities are said to be fantastically shaped in the form of clouds, dissolving in rain. This relates to the realm of the mind, and of all the flighty images it contains, which 'dissolve' or change with each new Watery (or Fiery) impression that come through from the world of sense input. Each of the buildings of the city represents a major category of ideas and mental imagery, with the rooms signifying subcategories, and the things in each room represented as particularised images. The city is in the sky (the realm of ideas and lofty ideals) and is laid out in distinct prefectures, patterns and groups of buildings, producing the major arenas of specialisation of the mind. The greater the complexity and vastness of the city, the more detailed the nature of the mind that we are perceiving. Dhritarashtra, guardian of the east, is their ruler.

23 See Alice A. Bailey: *The Externalisation of the Hierarchy* (Lucis Press, New York, 1988) for further details.

The planetary Solar Plexus and Throat centres are Her focus, including all of the Inner Round system of *chakras*. All life forms upon the planet can be said to have been born from out of Her Womb, whilst the *devas* constitute both the agents of parturition of those forms, plus embodying the substance from which those forms are constructed, including the human. Consequently, the *devas* are the agents of *karma*.

Sanat Kumāra is the Avataric Lord, or great King of Shambhala. He represents the embodied manifestation of the combined function of the Avatar of Synthesis and Spirit of Peace. Chapter one analysed the succession of kings associated with the myth of Shambhala that can be considered emanations of this great One. However, we see that this myth needed considerable comment in relation to it representing the attributes of a Head centre, which then reflects the nature of Shambhala, the planetary Head centre. There is no succession of kings, there has only ever been one, 'the Ancient of Days', 'the Eternal Youth', 'the Great Sacrifice', 'the One Initiator', Sanat Kumāra.[24] This name taken from the Hindu religion best describes his quality, therefore it is used here.

There is no proper equivalent from the Buddhist perspective for Sanat Kumāra. Perhaps the best term that depicts the attributes of this great one is the Ādi Buddha, Samantabhadra (kuntu bzang po). The term means the one who is all good, ever perfect, manifesting universal goodness or joy. It is a synonym for the *dharmakāya,* manifest in the form of a primordial Buddha, as recognised by the Nyingma tradition. Samantabhadra can be viewed in terms of the natural or spontaneous compassionate luminosity that is an attribute of *dharmakāya,* conceived of as masculine, integrated with his Consort (Samantabhadrī), which represents emptiness (*śūnyatā*). We thus have the non-dual attribute (yab-yum) that unites the appearances of *saṃsāra* with emptiness. Esoterically, however, the 'appearance of phenomena' is embodied by the feminine *deva* kingdom, and the emptiness derived from it, which is the base for compassionate wisdom, hence is masculine. Samantabhadra can be conceived of as the compassionate driving force that produces emptiness out of phenomena in terms of

24 *Hebrews 7:1-3* presents him under the name Melchisedec, and states: 'To whom also Abraham also gave a tenth part of all; first being by interpretation King of righteousness and after that also King of Salem, which is, King of peace; Without father, without mother, without descent, having neither beginning of days, nor end of life; but made like unto the Son of God; abideth a priest continually.'

spontaneous wisdom. Such a force is also equated with *bodhicitta,* of which Samantabhadra is then the regulatory body of expression for our planetary system. Consequently, he is also one of the eight great Bodhisattvas. In this fusion of the qualities of primordial Buddha and an eternally manifest Mahābodhisattva we observe the basic quality of Sanat Kumāra. Another term utilised for the Ādi Buddha is Vajrasattva.

In Hindu mythology the Kumāras are the Mind-born sons of Brahmā, 'virgin youths', who refused to procreate and thus remained *yogins.* There are seven of these, two esoteric and five exoteric.[25] Esoterically, they embody the substance of Mind for a planetary Scheme[26] and are thus responsible for the dissemination of the patterns of the Mind of a creative Logos. They are His representatives for the sum of the intelligent Lives evolving via embodied space, plus the streams of sentience. The Fires of Mind manifest through a pattern associated with the pentagram, which when extended produce the potency of a *vajra,* of which the five Elements—Aether, Air, Fire, Water and Earth—are aspects. The Kumāras therefore represent the functions upon our planet of the five Dhyāni Buddhas that embody the manifestation of these Elements upon our earth. Here the Avatar of Synthesis and the Mother of the World take the attributes of the Ādi Buddha and Consort. Sanat Kumāra, the Spirit of Peace, and the three Buddhas of Activity then manifest the qualities of the five Dhyāni Buddhas, or Kumāras.

From this perspective the Dhyāni Buddhas are expressions within the Womb of the Mother of the World, where Sanat Kumāra takes the attributes of Vairocana, the Spirit of Peace of Akṣobhya, the first Buddha of Activity of Amoghasiddhi, the second Buddha of Activity of Ratnasambhava, and the third of Amitābha. There is, however, a special dispensation where the compassionate mirror-like attribute of Akṣobhya manifests as the centre of the *maṇḍala* for humanity, making Vairocana (Sanat Kumāra) the eastern point (of the way to the Heart of Life).[27] A heightened compassionate dispensation therefore manifests as

---

25 Consequently, the myth signifies a 2-5 numerical arrangement associated with the manifestation of the planes of perception, whereas the earlier arrangement given is 3-1-3, or even 1-3, when only Sanat Kumāra and the three Buddhas of Activity are considered.

26 This term relates to both the physical globe and its subjective counterpart.

27 In Tibetan Tantras the roles of Vairocana and Akṣobhya are often interchanged in the *maṇḍala* of the Dhyāni Buddhas according to the focus of the *maṇḍala.*

the Heart of our planetary Life. The energies of the Avatar of Synthesis manifest in the northern direction via the first Buddha of Activity. The energies of the Spirit of Peace are focussed in the southern direction via the second Buddha of Activity, and the activity of the Mother of the World is focussed in the western direction via the third Buddha of Activity. In this way the planetary dispensation is flooded with Love-Wisdom, being the primary energy to be developed by humanity and epitomised by all travelling upon the Bodhisattva path.

The seven Kumāras can be considered as four manifesting into/as embodied space, whilst three are veiled as One (therefore making an esoteric fifth). The fourth Kumāra, therefore, who stands midway between the subjective three[28] (the Eye in the Triangle) and the objective three (the three Buddhas of Activity) becomes the mirror, bearing the Weight of the qualities of the abstract Logos (or Ādi Buddha) for all who are incarnate within our planetary Scheme. Through great compassion, Sanat Kumāra assumed the role of this fourth position to help steer humanity to travel away from the path that leads to abject sorcery. He is in fact greater than 'the fourth' but restricted his full glory to be in a zone of self-imposed limitation, and has assumed the role or mantle of the One Initiator for all lives on the earth for aeons. The progress of all Bodhisattvas upon this planet are his direct concern. He manifests in a perpetual youthful Buddha-form, and is thus literally an Avatar, an embodied appearance of a planetary Logos.[29]

The Kumāras are said to have originally come to our planet at the time of the Individualisation (formation) of humanity from out of the animal kingdom (through the seeding of the Sambhogakāya Flowers for humanity), bearing with them the seeds of mind for the appearing animal-men. They came with 100 others, termed 'Lords of Flame',[30] making the number 105 (7 x 15). When the triune planetary Logos is added and linked to the solar Logos then we get the sacred number 108. Thereby these great Beings, who bequeathed the Fiery Element to our

---

28 The Avatar of Synthesis, Spirit of Peace and the Mother of the World.

29 This is due to the abstracted function of the Avatar of Synthesis and because of the mystery of the moon Chain and the failure of that planetary evolution.

30 See H.P. Blavatsky, *The Secret Doctrine*, (Theosophical Publishing House, Adyar, 1962), Vol. 3, 'Anthropogenesis', Stanza 7, 31.

planetary Scheme, manifested the planetary Head Centre (Shambhala) upon the earth. The complete *maṇḍala* also integrates all Bodhisattvas of the higher *bhūmis*, and their *deva* correspondences (the *ḍākinīs*).

The ranks of the Lords of Flame have been gradually replaced by Initiated members of our present humanity (Lords of Love-Wisdom) who have developed the attributes to take their place. They have added the quality of intensified Love (*bodhicitta*) to the basic Fiery Wisdom the Lords of Flame contributed to humanity. Of that original complement, effectively only Sanat Kumāra and three Buddhas of Activity remain. Due to the forthcoming process of planetary Initiation, they too will attain release from their great sacrifice upon earth. There is a great mystery relating to this presiding One and the reason for his aeonic Sacrifice. Not all planetary spheres containing conscious life evolve according to Plan; cosmic evil is of vast scope.

The second Shambhalic level

The second level embodies the general functioning of Akṣobhya with respect to Shambhala, and can be viewed in terms of two interlaced triangles, one pointing upwards towards Shambhalic purpose, and the other downwards towards Hierarchical integration and compliance with the plan for the eventual liberation of humanity. Akṣobhya's function as the Mirror-like Wisdom here translates as the vitalisation of the entire Hierarchy of enlightened being by Shambhala. The Bodhisattvas represent the compassionate *saṃskāras* projected to the centres below the diaphragm of this planet to effect the necessary transformations of the *prāṇas* (units of consciousness and sentience) that will make this planet sacred.

This vitalisation manifests via the hexagram that is the integral central directive board (or 'Father' aspect) of Hierarchy. The triangle pointing upwards concerns the directed will underlying the purpose behind the manifestation of consciousness upon the planet. We have the Manu (the Lord who directs the streams of Life) as the head. The Love-Wisdom point is represented by the blue Christ, who overshadowed Jesus in the gospel story, and who was known as Śāriputra at the time of the Buddha. He governs the dissemination of the entire field of consciousness upon the planet. The activity point is taken by the

Phoenician,[31] the former Lord of civilisation (Mahāchohan). An incarnation of his was as the Buddha's foremost disciple, Mahākaśyapa.

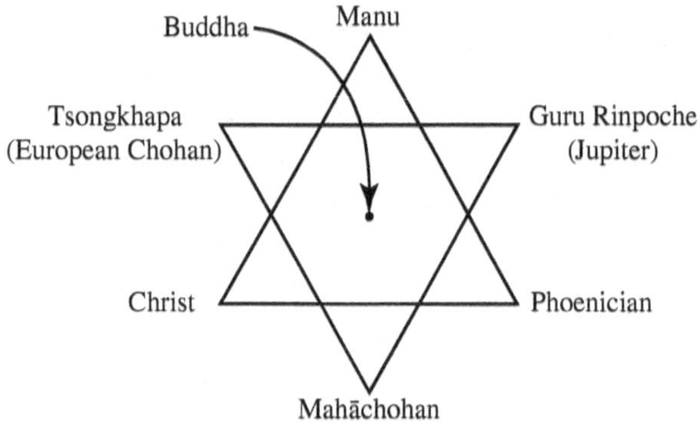

Figure 2. The second Shambhalic level

In this figure there is an implied *suṣumṇā* flow of energies from the Manu to the Mahāchohan. There is also a *piṅgalā* flow of the interwoven triangles of the commingled energies of the European Chohan and the Christ, and an *iḍā* flow of Jupiter and the Phoenician.

Together then, these energies present a fixed cross aspect, where the northern direction of upwards to Divinity (cosmos) is represented by the Manu. The eastern direction of inwards towards the Heart of Life is represented by the European Chohan-Christ integration. The western expression of outwards to the field of service is held by the integration of Jupiter and the Phoenician. The downwards expression towards the little ones (humanity) is embodied by the new Mahāchohan. (An incarnation of which in Buddhism was Ānanda.) Here the east-west direction relates principally to the flow of the energies of the Plan to all members of the Hierarchy and the kingdom of the Sambhogakāya Flower, and through them to humanity.

The downward pointing triangle is a triad representing a dynamically poised, wise activity, that brings into manifestation what has been

31 He presided over the evolution of mind to just after the Renaissance period. His role was then taken over by another great member of Hierarchy, who incarnated as Nāgārjuna, later as Francis Bacon, then the Count St. Germain (also known as Rakoczi, where we get the pseudonym R). We are now in a transition period between his dispensation and a new Mahāchohan, hence the new Mahāchohan also bears into manifestation the energies of R.

positively planned at Shambhala for humanity for any cycle.[32] Here we have the Mahāchohan as the focal point of expression, in the active birthing of the Plan via the context of the evolving civilisation for the new epoch, hence he takes the southern direction. It should be noted that the hexagram is a symbol of the active feminine matrix of a womb that objectively manifests its purpose. The Will point is represented by one who has been called Master Jupiter by Western esotericists, but who is recognised in Tibet as Guru Rinpoche[33] (Padmasambhava). At the time of the Buddha his incarnation was Maudgalyāyana, noted for his great psychic powers *(siddhis).* The Love-Wisdom point of this triad is the one named by esotericists the European Chohan, and known in Tibet as Tsongkhapa. At the time of the Buddha his incarnation was Subhūti, who was renowned for his comprehension of the doctrine of the Void.

The driving point of power for the outward expression of this *maṇḍala* is Gautama, who still retains this link with his foremost disciples to continue the outward momentum of a plan instigated when he had incarnated. He remains in contact from his new home in Regulus, the Heart of the constellation Leo the lion.[34] From there the major energy dispensation of his Eye is golden yellow and projected by the red of his Fiery cosmic Will. I present this information to note that it is a mistake to think that fully liberated ones cut off all ties with their former disciples. Such is an impossibility for them—it is contrary to the law of Love and the nature of the *maṇḍalic* construct that forever (a near useless concept in the infinitude of space) causes them to march onwards to fulfil their cosmic purpose. They are, however, engrossed in other major tasks that necessitate abstraction.

Shambhalic lore informs us that the Buddha came to this planet already as a Bodhisattva at about the time that mind was first being awakened by earth's indigenous humanity in Atlantean times. He was part of a team drawn together, whose speciality was to defeat dark brotherhood psychic projections and cunning who were responsible for the disastrous

---

32 I shall limit this account to humanity, though in reality all kingdoms in Nature are actively served. A far more esoteric topic would be to include the *deva* compliments to all of the great Ones.

33 The 'precious guru' who instigated the Lamaistic system in Tibet in the 9th century.

34 One should note that travel upon the inner domains is by means of the speed of thought, which is considerably faster than that of light.

outcome of Atlantis. The Lords of Life governing earth evolution had foreseen the imminent peril of the planet during the epoch preceding the 'great flood'[35] that sank the continent. This happened because of the vast evil the common masses unleashed upon the face of the planet through unabated psychic rapacious acquisitiveness and military adventurism. They were goaded and manipulated by some very powerful dark lords, both terrestrial and cosmic, wherein there exist vast numbers.

The team sent to oppose them was headed by Sanat Kumāra. Under him were seven other individuals. The Three Buddhas of Activity,[36] then the one that later became Gautama Buddha, the Phoenician, who is so named because of an eminent incarnation of his, another who later became Padmasambhava, and finally the Mahāchohan for this coming new era.

The Manu is not mentioned as a disciple of the Buddha because being the head of the first Ray department he is not directly concerned with the teaching dispensation to humanity.

This upward pointed triad bears the energies of the rarefied Fire of cosmic Love interpreted at their elevated level of manifestation. This allows them to channel into Hierarchy the potency of cosmic Mind (the *dharmakāya*) that passes through the all-seeing Eye of Shambhala. They are Contemplatives, as are all of the Lords embodying this hexagram, except technically the present Mahāchohan, who is the point of downward focus into the world civilisation for their united projection of Mind. They are mediators between the Great Lords of Shambhala, the representatives in cosmos of the various planetary and stellar spheres, and the Council of Bodhisattvas. Vast, therefore, is their visioning.

When Gautama incarnated, the great Ones also manifested appearances with respect to the new major religious dispensation. They incarnated for three main reasons:

1. Because of the homage and respect they owed to their superlative elder brother.

---

35 As portrayed in the Bible, the Gilgamesh, and other mythological texts found in all ancient cultures.

36 Their focus is outward towards the planetary manifestation, as well as being abstracted contemplatives (as are the Dhyāni Buddhas).

2. To fulfil the living *maṇḍala* of enlightenment that Gautama had to establish and which karmic purpose dictated.
3. To help ground and to propel the new religious dispensation so that it could fulfil its anointed purpose.

We then find the incarnation of these great Mahābodhisattvas throughout the subsequent epochs sustaining the history of Buddhism and its evolving purpose. Two of the greatest disciples of Gautama, Śāriputra and Maudgalyāyana, both died before the Buddha. Maudgalyāyana was killed by followers of extremist doctrines and was said to have entered *nirvāṇa* with 70,000 *arhats*, whilst Śāriputra died because he could not bear the thought of his friend's death and is said to have entered *nirvāṇa* with 80,000 *arhats*. These numbers are important. As Śāriputra manifests extreme love and compassion (Love-Wisdom) for his friend, and is symbolised by the number eight, he signifies the expression or dynamo that turns the wheels *(chakras)* of the Law for the entire *maṇḍala* of the Council of Bodhisattvas.[37] This relates to the functions and qualities of the Christ, the head of our present Hierarchy of enlightened beings.[38]

Maudgalyāyana (Padmasambhava) is killed whilst debating, symbolising his intellectual prowess, and he is also symbolised by the number seven, referring to the various septenaries that condition manifest life. This signified that this Bodhisattva possessed a link to the seventh Ray of ritual, ceremonial magic, and materialising power via the wisdom aspect of the second Ray.

---

37 The purpose here is to present more esoteric information to what was formerly stated concerning some of the Buddha's close disciples in Volume 3, chapter 5. As stated in earlier volumes, the number 1,000 is a multiplier, signifying a large number, vastness, immensity. *Arhats* symbolize enlightened elements of Mind. (Obviously the earth did not possess 70,000 plus 80,000 *arhats* to die simultaneously with these two great ones.)

38 The term Christ means 'the anointed one', and is used esoterically as the term for the holder of the highest office in Hierarchy. He therefore governs the sum total of all Bodhisattvic activity. He is considered the 'son of God', in that he channels the cosmic energy of Love-Wisdom (the 'son' aspect) to humanity via Hierarchy. This energy emanates from the Heart of 'God' when viewed as the Ādi Buddha, the highest representative of divinity upon earth. Esoterically, he is the 'Heart-born' Son of the planetary Logos.

An esoteric reason why Śāriputra died after hearing of Maudgalyāyana's death lies in their most ancient close connection, and represented a withdrawal of the major influence that their Ray lines would have brought. It allowed the Mahāchohan's dispensation to flow through Mahākaśyapa and Ānanda. Their fifth and third Ray energy helped to lay the groundwork for the organisational structure of the *saṇgha*. The *maṇḍala* of what was to be within the course of ancient civilisation could then be properly directed by this department to assist in the evolution of mathematically exact enlightenment via the further development of Buddhism. The focus at that time was the attainment of the attributes of the abstract Mind (the *arhat* path), which these Rays facilitated.

The Buddha was the embodiment of love and wisdom via the fourth Ray to bring a harmonising 'middle way' in the midst of the competitive rhetoric amongst the various clashing philosophies of the time. This energy was then the overall flavour of the *buddhadharma* and needed the third and fifth Rays to properly incorporate the teachings in the realm of accepted ideas, and to codify the *sūtras* so that they could be comprehended by all minds. The overall third Ray flavour (which incorporates all of the Rays of Mind) was necessary to establish the young wisdom religion, but it also resulted in the development of the many disputations of early Buddhism. Mahākaśyapa (the Phoenician) thus lead the disciples rather than Śāriputra (the Christ), who embodies the Love principle.[39] The patriarchy of the *saṇgha* then went to Ānanda after Mahākaśyapa died, because his line of development was similarly along the Mahāchohan's line.

The expression of the second Ray was all-pervasive, but would begin to later play its proper role via the work of the third Patriarch, Śāṇavāsika, a former incarnation of Koot Humi (K.H.).[40] He is directly along the Love-Wisdom line of the Christ (and accordingly is his successor). This allowed Śāṇavāsika to produce the active dissemination of the Love-Wisdom teachings to a far larger audience than was possible

39 What is here referred to as 'the love principle', or 'wisdom aspect' refers to a very high degree of expression of these qualities, only properly known at the highest Bodhisattva levels.

40 This name is taken from his last incarnation during the Victorian era, when he incarnated as a Sikh, Koot Humi lal Singh. Earlier he had a Tibetan incarnation as sGam po pa.

before. He oversaw the right future direction of the *buddhadharma*, where as a consequence, the practical, compassionate Bodhisattvic aspects of the teachings could begin to be developed, as a foundation for the later Mahāyāna stream.

As will be later explained, the new Mahāchohan and the second Ray Chohan (K.H.) work together in the closest coordinated manner. One is fundamentally third Ray with a significant second Ray expression, and the other is fundamentally second Ray, with a significant expression along the Rays of Mind. This is a reason why Śāṇavāsika followed Ānanda.

This teaching concerning the early history of the Buddhist *saṇgha* was introduced in Volume 3 of this *Treatise on Mind*, but more detail concerning the incarnation of the Chohans of the Rays can now be provided. The keywords of the main attributes given to the most important disciples of the Buddha are presented in Table 2, however, I shall refine the information regarding the Rays. The earlier presented attribution was from Ray 1 (Mahākaśyapa) to Ray 7 (Upāli),[41] that reflected the effect of their service work within the community of which they were a part at that time. However, it is best to view their attributes in terms of the three primary Rays because of the very advanced degree of Initiations they have undertaken. Subhūti embodies the fourth Ray mirror reflecting the attributes of the higher into the lower three.

These three primary Rays are viewed from the perspective where they are but the expression of a lower portion (the fifth, sixth and seventh Rays) of a higher septenary. The tattered robe that Mahākaśyapa inherited from the Buddha signifies the Mind (exemplified by the saffron colour). Here the first Ray manifests via a fifth Ray methodology. The elementary Mind of the Buddhist dispensation that stood at his time was yet to flower into its full glory. In Upāli the major disciplining of the mind produced the outward manifestation of seventh Ray ritualistic observations and the martial aspects of the first Ray to control the mode of activity of the body, speech and mind of the organisation.

At that stage the second Ray esoteric wisdom embodied by Śāriputra manifested via a sixth Ray flavouring because of the early *saṇgha's* devotion to each other and also the fervour by means of which they

---

41 See Volume 3, 282-287. The Rays presented in that volume are given in brackets in Table 2.

propagated the *dharma*. The sixth Ray then becomes the energy that drives the doctrine to influence the masses of people. This wisdom was reflected in a second Ray disposition via Śāṇavāsika, which helped steer the young organisation towards the eventual flowering of the Mahāyāna, where the doctrine of *śūnyatā* is exemplified.

The *siddhis* (psychic powers) attributed to Maudgalyāyana are an expression of the seventh Ray of Ritualistic Power. Also, the seventh Ray attribute of Maudgalyāyana (which reflects all of the Rays), and his great wisdom, allows him to manifest the third Ray with ease. This allowed Guru Rinpoche to be the quintessential Tantric exponent in Tibetan history. The extraordinary memory attributed to Ānanda is but the manifestation of a *siddhi,* which at this stage assisted the Mind (which is naturally governed by the fifth Ray) to retain the *dharma*. The third Ray, however, is exemplified, as the knowledge had to be retained with mathematical certainty. The seventh Ray also comes into play, allowing the externalisation (materialising power) of all topics concerning the *dharma*. The third Ray governs all of the five Rays of Mind, hence the seventh Ray is the mode of grounding its expression.

Saṇgha	Attribute	Ray Energy
Mahākaśyapa	Asceticism	Ray 5 (1)
Śāriputra	Great Wisdom	Ray 6 (2)
Maudgalyāyana	Psychic Powers	Ray 7 (3)
Subhūti	Knowledge of Emptiness	Ray 4 (4)
Ānanda	Extraordinary Memory	Ray 3 (5)
Śāṇavāsika	Powers of Conversion	Ray 2 (6)
Upāli	Discipline	Ray 1 (7)

Table 2. Attributes of the Buddha's Saṇgha

The fifth Ray of Mahākaśyapa here relates to his ability to incorporate attributes of cosmic Mind into Hierarchical activity. The sixth Ray attribute of Śāriputra relates to his ability to channel the cosmic Love conveyed from the Waters of the cosmic astral plane. The seventh Ray of Maudgalyāyana concerns his ability to control the substance of the cosmic physical plane (our seven systemic planes) with ambidexterity. The fourth Ray of Subhūti allows him to project the energies of the above three via the *nāḍī* system of the earth (the four cosmic ethers). He acts as a mirror via the second cosmic physical subplane, *anupāḍaka*. Ānanda then wields the karmic purpose of the 'powers' of the higher three into manifestation via the third plane of perception *(ātma)*[42]. Śāṇavāsika tones down the potency of the energy of Śāriputra so that those ensconced in *saṃsāra* can gain liberation *(śūnyatā)* through the generation of *bodhicitta* (Love-Wisdom) via the fourth plane of perception, or cosmic ether *(buddhi)*. Upāli embodies the first Ray potency that will allow all in *saṃsāra* to master its substance by means of ritualistic discipline and control of the vicissitudes of the mental-emotions.

Here then is presented an account of the functions of the executive members of Hierarchy viewed via the generated attributes of former incarnations of theirs with respect to the foundation of Buddhism. This is integrated with the present Ray mode of activity, though the first five of the list manifest quite ambidextrous functions.

All of the above individuals have been commented upon except for Subhūti and Upāli. Being one of the foremost disciples of Gautama, coupled with his expertise on *śūnyatā* at that time (which manifests a fourth Ray harmonising effect upon the strife of *saṃsāra*), points to Subhūti being a former incarnation of Tsongkhapa. He is considered along the second Ray line and works to integrate all aspects of the Rays of Mind into a fluid unity via the modifying effect of the second, fourth and fifth Rays, the fifth being a reflection of cosmic Mind.

The expertise of the *vinayapiṭaka* (the stoic and oft martial rules of discipline), with respect to the meditative life style for the monks, compiled by Upāli, equates with him having been an incarnation of the first Ray Chohan, Morya. The seventh Ray function concerns the manner with which the energy of will is grounded to discipline

42 The fifth from below up.

the ordained monks according to the ritualised observation of their activities. It effectively rightly integrates the ascetic function ruled by Mahākaśyapa into the daily lives of the monks.

It should be re-emphasised here that the lists of previous births of the important personages presented in the extant biographies given in the texts generally manifest symbolic truth only. They are rarely correct if taken literally, any more than the line of successive incarnations of a particular Rinpoche is literally correct. Much is introduced that comes from mythologised meditation impressions.

The abovementioned major Bodhisattvas represent the directive executive Head of the entire Council of Bodhisattvas. They therefore take the paradigm of the Bodhisattva qualities reflected in the wisdom attributes of the five Jinas for the Hierarchy of Enlightened Being. The assignments proposed here are somewhat different than what was presented in Volume 3. The list therein was concerned with the dispensation of the Buddha. The present one focuses upon their overall standing within the *maṇḍala* of the Hierarchy. This *maṇḍala* takes Akṣobhya as the central figure, because the indigo blue Ray of Love-Wisdom is foremost in their development. The Mirror-like Wisdom of Akṣobhya reflects the directive purpose from the first Shambhalic level into the complete flowering of the *maṇḍala* of Hierarchy. Śāriputra (Christ) takes the role of Akṣobhya as the central point of the *maṇḍala*. He integrates all aspects of the Council of Bodhisattvas' *maṇḍala* into a unity, thus embodying the indigo energy of Love-Wisdom for all. *Mahākāśyapa* (the Phoenician) takes the role of Vairocana and thus the Dharmadhātu Wisdom, as derived from the northern direction. His main purpose is therefore to integrate the directives from the first level of Shambhala into the mainstream thought currents of the Hierarchy of Light, and to assist in their aspiration upwards towards ultimate liberation, thus movement onto cosmic spheres. The Element channelled is cosmic (Aetheric) Fire. His Fiery Eye therefore sees far vistas in all cosmic directions, as to where the liberated ones may sojourn and continue their education after their earth evolution has finished.

Ānanda, the new Mahāchohan, then takes the function of Amitābha in the western direction for the integrated Council of Bodhisattvas. He ensures the rightful development of their Minds so that they manifest in accord with the Plan emanating from Sanat Kumāra. With their help the outward vision of humanity can awaken in such a way that the errors and chimeras of mind developed by people are finally conquered. He thereby feeds and positively directs the entire course of *manasic* development in humanity to refine the stratum of the *ālayavijñāna*. His purpose is to lead humanity to develop the elements of the abstract Mind, the Clear Light of Mind wherein the *saṃsāra-śūnyatā* nexus can be found.

Subhūti, (Tsongkhapa, the European Chohan), takes the eastern position of Ratnasambhava and his Equalising Wisdom. This wisdom expresses itself with respect to *śūnyatā,* the meditation upon which Subhūti was considered foremost. The ability to reside in the Void (*śūnyatā*) is the common denominator of all senior members of Hierarchy. It is that to which the junior members must aspire towards (gained through undertaking the fourth Initiation) to be able to play a role in Hierarchical decision-making. It equalises them by giving all the ability to reside within the cosmic ethers, and thus partake of liberated access to cosmos.

Maudgalyāyana (Padmasambhava) takes the southern position of Amoghasiddhi and his All-accomplishing Wisdom. Here the energies of cosmic sources become grounded via the ceremonial ritual of the seventh Ray. The power of Hierarchical purpose is thereby established upon the physical plane. Their plans can therefore be accomplished through the *maṇḍala* established by them, according to the dictates of *karma.*

Another list of value to consider here is that of the seven Patriarchs. In the accompanying symbolism lies the hint as to the qualities of some of the other Chohans[43] that fulfilled roles relating to the complete externalisation of the young religion as a force to be reckoned with in India, and then the rest of Asia. The major characteristics the Patriarchs were noted for (see Volume 3 for detail) is given below, as well as the *chakras* that they were responsible in activating for the evolving *saṇgha.*

1. *Mahākaśyapa,* to whom Gautama handed the succession of the *saṇgha,* represented the Base of Spine centre. The activity of this centre secures the solid foundation for the existence of the *saṇgha,* its life as an organism upon the physical domain. The first Ray (via the fifth) sets the wheels turning for gaining the knowledge base of the *saṇgha.*

43 I use the term Chohans here and below, but at the time these great ones were still in the process of evolving the attributes of becoming Masters.

2. *Ānanda,* who succeeded Mahākaśyapa after the first Council at Vaiśālī. With him the basic structure of the Head lotus is established, into which the future *saṇgha* could grow as its *saṃskāras* develop. The forthright wisdom attributes of the early *saṇgha* flowered under the auspices of the third Ray.
3. *Śāṇavāsika,* who propagated the Tripiṭaka to a large audience. The faculty of the compassionate Eye (the Ājñā centre) is now awakened. It directs the *saṇgha* member's *prāṇic* development of esoteric vision, as it was always a contemplative organisation. Its main activity being to develop the inner vision based upon compassionate considerations. The flowering of the second Ray ensures that the developing wisdom is directed to the enlightenment of others.
4. *Upagupta,* who was noted for his vast compassion. The Heart centre now fully awakens, here manifesting the fourth Ray of its founder, which thereby becomes the middle way approach to gaining enlightenment, with the focus being the development of *śūnyatā.*
5. *Dhītika,* who developed the understanding of thousands. The Throat centre next becomes the onus of development, to produce the many doctrinal disputes and sectarian views, as Buddhism became much more established as a religion. Many avenues of thought consequently had to be explored under the auspices of the fifth Ray of scientific reasoning.
6. *Krishna* was a merchant sailing the seas, and when he got into trouble invoked Dhītika for help. Up to this stage the *saṇgha's* energetic expression was in the centres above the diaphragm, but now its major characteristics had to be properly born in the material domain via the centres below the diaphragm. The Solar Plexus centre is now functioning, to direct the Watery energies that produce a major emotional appeal for its teachings amongst the population at large, rather than mainly amongst the intelligentsia. (Educated converts from other disciplines.) Hence the sixth Ray purpose became exemplified. This change in orientation was a difficult achievement, and needed guidance from the mental domain.
7. *Mahāsudarśana,* who subdued the *yakṣinī* Hiṅgalācī (utilising the magical means facilitated by the seventh Ray). He built

many monasteries in the south under the patronage of Aśoka. Consequently, the *saṇgha* became fully grounded via the energising and materialising power of the sixth and seventh Rays working via the Sacral and Base of Spine centre combination.

The first three of these Patriarchs have already been described, and the remaining four manifest roles symbolically played by the subsidiary Chohans of the Rays of Mind. Thus the compassion of Upagupta is a quality of the harmonising quality of the fourth Ray Chohan, Serapis, who worked to ground the qualities of the Heart centre of the new religion. Being the Ray that governs Buddhism as a whole, the fourth Ray of beautifying harmony overcoming strife is the foundation of the doctrine of the Middle Way *(madhyamaka pratipad)*. Dhītika helped stimulate the mental comprehension of thousands, which symbolised the work of the Chohan of the fifth Ray, Hilarion. Hilarion and Serapis have a similar symbiotic relationship in their forms of service work as do Koot Humi and the new Mahāchohan, because of the way that love and knowledge must reinforce each other to produce the dual quality of the Love-Wisdom that is the foundational purpose of the educational process of Buddhism.

The sixth Ray quality of devotion and high aspiration of the Chohan Jesus (Krishna) helped make the religious dispensation appeal to the masses of people via devotional methodology, which was needed for when Buddhism became a state religion under Aśoka.

The attributes of enlightening activity embodied by Mahāsudarśana of the founding of many monasteries, coupled with the demands of an administrative function that catered for a vastly increased community of monks, implied the work of the seventh Ray Chohan (Rakoczi), assisted by the work of the third Ray Chohan (the Venetian). These Rays were needed to manifest the organisational aptitude and education of the vast religious structure that developed during Aśoka's reign. This Ray combination also facilitated a close cooperative endeavour with the first Ray attributes of Aśoka. Aśoka was impelled by the power of the first Ray to conquer India. Later he relinquished violence as a means and embraced Buddhism. India was then thoroughly proselytised by the emissaries of Aśoka under the leadership of Mahāsudarśana. Aśoka was thus an incarnation of the first Ray Chohan, Morya. Upāli, who specialised in the code of laws governing the discipline of the monks, and the function of the will that must be used in all ascetic and yogic practices, was an earlier incarnation of this Chohan.

Another disciple of note at the time of Gautama is Aniruddha, who was his cousin, as was Ānanda. (Aniruddha and Ānanda were thus also considered brothers.) He was said to be foremost amongst those who had divine vision, signifying a function of the seventh Ray of ceremony, ritual, magic and materialising power to awaken the Eye of vision. This implies an incarnation of the then seventh Ray Master and later the Mahāchohan (the Count St. Germain). There is a close connection between the 'divine vision' of Aniruddha and the 'psychic powers' of Maudgalyāyana (Guru Rinpoche), as both are emanations of the seventh Ray.

The inverted triangle

The downward pointed triangle consisting of Tsongkhapa, Padmasambhava, and the new Mahāchohan can now be analysed. All three Bodhisattvas are remainders from a Hierarchy that oversaw the Atlantean epoch. That Hierarchy was a matriarchate, most of whom left for cosmic shores (mainly to the Pleiades) as a consequence of the inundation of that continent. To the fundamental second Ray of Love-Wisdom (developed by all great ones during that epoch), Tsongkhapa also bore a fifth Ray sub-hue and Padmasambhava a seventh Ray sub-hue, from which, for instance, he derived his skill as a great *mahāsiddha*-magician that conquered the demons of Tibet. The materialising power of the seventh Ray is aided by the mathematically exact activity of the third. This combination greatly facilitates the empowerment of Hierarchical objectives upon the physical domain (ruled by the third Ray) and its etheric substratum (ruled by the seventh Ray), wherein exist the *chakras*. The seventh Ray grounds all Ray attributes via cyclic purpose.

All of the Mahābodhisattvas are ambidextrous with respect to the expression of different Rays. In Tsongkhapa's case (1357-1419) the synthetic second Ray line[44] is exemplified via fourth Ray characteristics, which facilitates the reflection of all Hierarchical attributes into manifestation via its mirror-like qualities. The fourth Ray attributed to Tsongkhapa also had a strong affinity with the fifth Ray, which

44 It synthesises all other Ray purposes into a unity of expression.

facilitated his scientific enclyclopaedic enquiry into all aspects of the *buddhadharma* in that life. Hence he balances out both *iḍā* and *piṇgalā* streams of realisation with great dexterity, all equalised by means of the fourth Ray. The fluid interchange between the wisdom stream and scientific application is what is capitalised upon in his role as the European Chohan,[45] as it was in that continent that modern science was developed, but now needs to be steered to its rightful conclusion with great wisdom. (Which this great Mahābodhisattva possesses.)

Tsongkhapa used basic scientific methodology to bring all major streams of *dharma* into one logical synthesis. Similarly for his incarnation as Leonardo da Vinci (1452-1519), who was really the first true scientist in European history, and also a most gifted artist (facilitated generally by the fourth Ray). Ray purpose is the invisible thread whereby we can trace all incarnations to conclusion. He is given the *nom de plume* of the European Chohan because his specialised Ray equipment and high Initiate standing facilitate his responsibility for the destiny of Europe. These Rays help to feed European minds with compassionate aspects they so much need, to try to fuse love with the scientific activity of mind the West has pioneered for the world. Without the nurturing embrace of such love, the natural separative, concretising and materialising tendencies of the mind would overtly control one. Unfortunately, the way of *manasic* development has proceeded faster than what was planned and Hierarchy are now trying to offset this uneven development. The task of converting the self-focussed aspects of mind into wisdom vectors is a nearly insurmountable task, taking human free will into account, along with the weaving in of the *karma* of past human transgressions on a vast scale. Such *karma* hearkens back to Atlantean times.

The historical development of the evolution of mental and scientific accomplishment since the Renaissance can be studied by all, and has to date been generally successful, despite the many failings when the forces

---

45 Note that one reason that I am indicating some of the past lives of these great ones is because modern esotericists have many fanciful ideas as to their past lives. Buddhists on the other hand think too parochially, in terms of their religion only, thus need to broaden their perspectives to include many fields of service for the great Bodhisattvas. The logic concerning the factors causing the roles for their incarnations is difficult to provide, considering the limitations of people's inductive reasoning. The information, though logically presented, needs to be verified via the meditation-Mind, or intuitively ascertained.

of evil won their victories. They are now even more powerful than ever before in swaying the masses of people by empowering the imperial ambitions of US hegemony via aggressive, rapacious monetary and military power, coupled with people's rampant avaricious materialism. However, counter forces play out via the force of *karma,* governed by Shambhalic directives that will overcome the perceived power of the forces of evil and their widespread lying propaganda via the mass media. Humanity need to heuristically learn the basic lessons of unbridled materialism, and suffer the attendant *karma,* before they will aspire to overcome their foibles.

The new Mahāchohan plays an interesting role in this conversion process. His Ray purpose is spread right across all Ray lines. His fundamental Ray is that of the third Ray, as it must be to manifest as a Mahāchohan, however he has also occupied an important seat in the second Ray department, and with the help of Morya and Koot Humi, is responsible for the formation of the 2/1 Ray Ashram. One reason is that the occupants of this Ashram are specifically converts from dark brotherhood activity from ancient times. They are predominantly upon the Rays of Mind and earlier wilfully empowered the attributes of mind to the exclusion of Love. Consequently, they had strongly developed the will of mind to conquer all around them in order to empower the separateness of 'self', thus need the Love principle considerably fanned in their lives. Hence they are placed in the most intense of the second Ray Ashrams, to assist the process of developing Love-Wisdom as rapidly as possible. It is not easy to transform longstanding *saṃskāras* of hatred, material ambition and personal power. Many are the karmic lessons to be learnt, and the conversion process takes a large number of lives to achieve.

This new Mahāchohan is a specialist in this field because having aeons ago undergone such an educational process, now has an intensified second Ray aptitude, coupled to the third Ray, plus that of the first Ray. Consequently, he is able to play a triune function within Hierarchy, of helping to train first and second Ray disciples, plus those from the Rays of Mind. This special Ray combination will also allow him to play a subsidiary role in the guise of Maitreya in this present materialistic era, the *kali yuga*, wherein the potency of the dark brotherhood is everywhere prevalent. He will manifest thereby the violet Ray (being one of his Monadic Rays) and by combining the indigo-blue of the second Ray with the red of the first Ray. Consequently the seventh Ray purpose (of materialising power) will be expressed via the green of enlightening activity to rightly educate disciples in the New Age. The seventh Ray robe assists in countering the ruthless magical and material power, the sheer manipulative and monetary forces that the dark forces presently possess to govern the present materialistic civilisation. All of Hierarchy and the Lords of Shambhala will assist, as this is not a chore that can be accomplished in the short space of one life. Much chaos, war and upheaval of mass scale karmic cleansing, viewed by humanity as catastrophes, will accompany such work. The beginning of the enlightenment (Initiation) of large numbers of people will not come without the price that needs to be paid in all karmic conversions of *saṃskāras*.

Planetary transformation is nigh, and for this the potency of Sanat Kumāra will empower this one to set the wheels in motion to transform over time this pain-wracked planet into a sacred one. Vast are the transformative potencies that must be directed over many centuries to produce such an outcome. Guru Rinpoche (who was similarly trained from an earlier cycle) also manifested a violet robe to exorcise many areas of Tibet, so that the *white dharma* could flourish there.[46] Many psychic battles had to be fought with sorcerers and their minions before Buddhism could take hold as the major religious dispensation of Tibet. Even so, there was significant recidivism after he disincarnated. The task now is far greater than what occurred in Tibet, with far more at stake, hence Sanat Kumāra will of necessity also have to play a direct role via a process of divine embodiment of one individual (the new Mahāchohan), who as an Avatar, indeed will be the subjective eye of a cyclone of change, but consequently over all Initiates that have incarnated to become significant subsidiary transformative agents. The epoch of Maitreya hence will not just be of a singular entity, but of a mass movement of change, of war against the forces of evil in all their disguises.

With respect to the Mahāchohan's department, it should be noted that the Chohan ℛ (the Count St. Germain) undertook the role of Mahāchohan after the ascension of the Phoenician because humanity were unable, until the advent of the 21st century, to receive the type

46 This robe is also coloured by a cosmic sixth Ray potency, producing an increased material power to effect his accomplishments.

of energisation associated with the new Mahāchohan. They had to be prepared over the course of some centuries by the special directives of the seventh Ray, of which the Count was the ruling Lord. He acted as a caretaker for the role of Mahāchohan until the rightful heir could 'come of age'. To do so the Count's third Ray attributes needed to be fanned. Hence for the stages of the birthing of the new Aquarian age the Mahāchohan's department will be reinforced by the Count's seventh Ray focus, and the new Mahāchohan's integration of the three primary Rays via the third Ray of Mathematically Exact Activity. This integration allows all Rays to be appropriately expressed to produce the birthing of the new civilisation, which will be governed by the second Ray.

The earlier cycles were simpler, their purpose concerned birthing the epoch of mind, which was well within the jurisdiction of the Mahāchohan's department to produce. However, the technicalities of adding a heightened first Ray momentum to humanity's evolution, and the proper flowering of Love-Wisdom in the forthcoming new civilisation, demands the special relationship between these two great Ones, and their brothers in the first and second Ray departments. The long planned for goal can then be achieved with facility.

The information presented above is presently academic, and beyond the reach of the average reader to independently verify, but explains the gist of much Hierarchical purpose when properly studied.

Concerning the second Ray of Love-Wisdom, which is the primary Ray governing our solar evolution, perhaps it would be useful to add D.K's. explanation to the former considerations of this Ray from my previous books, which were summarised by the term *bodhicitta*:

> love-wisdom (the heart nature and the higher mind)...is *not* love, however, as usually understood, or wisdom as man generally defines it. This is free of emotion and of the astralism which is distinctive of the solar plexus life which most people live; love, esoterically and in reality, is perceptive understanding, the ability to recognise that which has produced an existing situation, and a consequent freedom from criticism; it involves that beneficent silence which carries healing in its wings and which is only expressive when the inhibition aspect of silence is absent and the man no longer has to still his lower nature and quiet the voices of his own ideas in order to understand and

achieve identification with that which *must* be loved. Can you follow the beauty of this concept and comprehend the nature of this silent depth of true understanding?

Wisdom is the sublimation of the intellect, but this involves the sublimation of the higher as well as of the lower aspects of the mind. It is a blend of intuition, spiritual perception, cooperation with the plan and spontaneous intellectual appreciation of that which is contacted, and all this is fused and blended with and by the love which I have defined above, plus that esoteric sense which must be unfolded before the second initiation can be taken. I call this especially to your attention. Seek to understand and perceive the subtle evidences of the esoteric sense, and then define it and explain its processes and evidences, invoking as you do so the higher sensibilities.[47]

A note on the third and fourth Rays

Here a note should be made concerning my designation of 'Mathematically Exact Activity' to the third Ray in the light of D.K.'s statement concerning the fourth Ray:

> One of the foundational septenate of rays embodies in itself the principle of harmony, and this fourth Ray of Harmony gives to all forms that which produces beauty and works towards the harmonising of all effects emanating from the world of causes, which is the world of the three major rays. The ray of beauty, of art and harmony is the producer of the quality of *organisation through form*. It is in the last analysis the ray of mathematical exactitude and is not the ray of the artist, as so many seem to think. The artist is found on all rays, just as is the engineer or the physician, the home-maker or the musician. I want to make this clear, for there is much misunderstanding on this matter.[48]

I have used the phrase Mathematically Exact Activity to best summarise the attributes of the third Ray because clearly D.K.'s rendition as 'Activity' or of 'Active Intelligence' is inadequate. 'Activity' can apply to physical plane happenings, such as cyclic activity, relegated to the seventh Ray; and intelligence simply refers to the main attribute of

---

47 A.A. Bailey, *The Externalisation of the Hierarchy*, 98-99.

48 A.A. Bailey, *Esoteric Psychology, Volume I*, 49.

the mind, being a fifth Ray characteristic, and as the mind is normally active, so the appellations given by D.K. to the third Ray[49] are clearly inappropriate. Also, when referring to the third Ray, consideration must be made concerning its relation to the third plane of perception *(ātma),* from whence it emanates, hence of the nature of the enlightened Mind, whose form of activity is mathematically precise, manifesting with the precision of karmic law. Hence there is a conflation of qualities between the third and fourth Ray depictions. The reason for this is that the fourth Ray acts as a *mirror,* as it is the harmonising bridge between the third Ray and the fifth Ray attributes within the domain of mind. Hence the mathematical activity of the third Ray is modified by means of the fourth Ray in terms of overall patterns of expression needed to produce order out of chaos (of unregulated or uncontrolled, wrongly faceted or scattered mind-substance). The term 'mathematical exactitude' used by D.K. thus implicates the way the enlightened Mind (the third Ray aspect) works via the fourth Ray to impact upon the substance of the mind. The organisational nature of the fourth Ray tends to harmonise the elements of the mind structure, tending towards producing ordered beauty in the image making tendencies, which is also elaborated in terms of the quality 'Harmony through Conflict' as D.K. styles the Ray,[50] or 'Beautifying Harmony overcoming Conflict' as I do. The phrase 'Active Intelligence', however, does approximate the way that the third Ray manifests amongst ordinary humanity (as they inadequately bear its full expression), and from this perspective D.K. is correct.

The Christ's department

The term 'Christ' refers to the Head of a specific department within the Council of Bodhisattvas, of those who are directly in line to manifest the functions of the Love-Wisdom attribute for humanity. The present holder of this office is focussed upon the Love (compassionate) attribute of the Love-Wisdom Ray. He directs the intensely potent cosmic silver-white, which is integrated with the indigo blue Ray of Love-Wisdom for our Planetary system. (Consequently, I have termed him the blue Christ.)

49 Ibid., 23.

50 Ibid., 205.

His principle concern is the evolution of consciousness for the sum of the present humanity. By being patriarch of the direct second Ray line he is the true Head of the Hierarchy. He also manifests functionally as the emanatory Heart because all Bodhisattvas must evolve through expressing this Ray line, no matter what Ray they are principally upon. All Rays are essentially sub-Rays of this fundamental second Ray.

Within this context this office also historically veils a trinity of Christs that effectively wield the first, second, and third Ray attributes of the energy of Love-Wisdom. The terms 'first, second and third' therefore refer to the forms of Bodhisattvic activity that allow different versions and potencies of the same energy to manifest upon the planet. Christ number one (or the 'first Christ') for this present epoch was the Buddha, who is now not directly affiliated with our humanity, but still retains links to some high Initiates. He embodies the function of the first Ray of Will or Power for this dispensation, manifesting therefore its overall directive purpose. This is done via a fourth Ray medium of expression. He therefore exemplifies the wisdom aspect of the Love-Wisdom Ray via the Will, where the potency of the first Ray is toned down by the harmonising energy of the fourth Ray. His use of the Will was demonstrated in the form of the extreme asceticism practiced in his early years, and then the battles he undertook to overcome the myriad potent forces of Māra arraigned against him.

The second Christ (an incarnation of which was Śāriputra) essentially embodies the energies of Alaya Avalokiteśvara for the world sphere (of which the Dalai Lama is merely a symbolic representative). His tears of compassionate concern succours all Bodhisattvic activity. His purpose is served through deep meditative abstraction, though focussed upon all aspects of world need, and his purpose is directed via the highest members of the Council of Bodhisattvas. Great is this need because of the dire state of the present planetary imperil, seen in the way that evil has gained control of world governments.

The other great Bodhisattva that forms an integral unity with this One is labelled 'the third Christ' (symbolised by the number three), and specifically stands thus for a humanity from a former evolutionary epoch which failed, and which now shares the earth as a planetary home. Their main Ray energy is the third. These members of humanity are esoterically 'older' than those whose Sambhogakāya Flowers individualised upon the earth from out of the animal kingdom. This is a mystery veiled by the moon. The fundamental colouring of this Christ is green-blue. From this perspective he manifests objectively in the form of the Bodhisattva Maitreya, the green Ray being that of divine embodied Activity. He was once Ānanda and continues the symbolism of the Buddha's successor, as his two great predecessors have already fulfilled their appointed roles.[51] His focus, therefore, is along the wisdom portion of the Love-Wisdom Ray, but he also bears a substantial portion of the golden-red of the Buddha and the blue of the second Christ. The three energies therefore are blended into one, spearheaded by wisdom.

The second Christ manifested in the form of Christ-Jesus, having founded the Christian religion under the auspices of being the 'son of God', as well as being the 'son of man',[52] as he often styled himself. 'God' here is but a pseudonym for the great Lord ruling Shambhala, whose will he meticulously followed. All major Bodhisattvas can similarly style themselves as Christ-Jesus did, as they are 'sons of God', where Shambhala can be titled the Kingdom of 'God' as far as our planetary system is concerned. They can also be considered 'sons of man', as they have evolved out from the human kingdom. They exist to serve humanity, by leading them to high enlightenment states ('salvation'), which indeed was the function of the great sacrifice of Christ-Jesus.

That there are two levels of humanity upon this planet will become obvious to all who have seriously pondered why a relatively small number of people (maybe 20% of the total human population) are the social activists, thoughtful thinkers, and compassionate helpers in our societies. The remainder, though generally well-meaning, are conservatively resistant to change, gullible to indoctrination by authority and religious figures, seemingly incapable of truly compassionate concern, and are often narrow-minded. The reason lies in the fact that the former come from a humanity that had its genesis from outside the earth globe, and are therefore far older as human units. They are actively engaged in such things as trying to prevent the wholesale destruction

---

51 Mahākaśyapa as the earlier Mahāchohan and Maudgalyāyana as Guru Rinpoche.

52 *Matt. 8:20, 9:6, 10:23, 11:19, 12:8, 16:27, 19:28, 24:30, 25:31,* etc.

of all forms of life in our biosphere via the excessive logging of forests, widespread pollution, wholesale depletion of fish stocks, and many other environmental concerns. They oppose the rapacious greed of multinational corporations. They also manifest a host of social activities aimed at human betterment, right enlightening education, beneficent political agendas and proper resource sharing for all.

These activists are the opponents of the megalomaniacal, avaricious moneyed 'elite' that control the banking system, corrupt governments, the perversions of the orthodox health industry, the legal system and big corporations. They are staunch adversaries of all the war mongering parliamentarians who convince their populations to manifest aggressive acts upon other weaker nations for spurious reasons (disguised as 'humanitarian wars' for instance). We thus had the anti-war protests of the Vietnam era and the rise of an alternative society from the early 60's on.

This category of humanity are thus characterised by expressed love and concern for others in their societies, and for the world they live in. They are essentially unselfish in their motives and are often political activists working to overcome the wrongs in the political processes and the effects of those who are easily manipulated and whipped into fear-driven responses by the moneyed 'elite'.

This 'elite' are a group of exceedingly evil individuals that have similarly stemmed from this failed evolutionary epoch. They have advanced the activities that caused the past failure and have taken control of the reigns of power over most of our governments, the mass media, the large multinational corporations, the banking sectors, the military, and generally the judiciary. They have not relinquished their ancient tendencies that perpetually cause destruction in any society they are found in. Consequently, continuous warfare in the Middle East and elsewhere are fought because of their evil scheming and manipulative grip over the minds and massed desires of the common people. This grouping from that former cycle have not advanced upon the evolutionary path to light.

The largely unthinking masses are the objects of focus for all forms of indoctrination, whilst they thoughtlessly consume products that serve their desire for increasing material comforts. Their fundamental selfishness and self-interest prevents deep thought as to the cost that such profligate consumption has upon the planet's ecosphere. Materialism is their mainstay, even when religiously inclined, because the fine words of their scriptures are interpreted in such a way that desire for material wealth or sensual gratification can be satiated. Our religious dispensations have thus been prostituted to serve greed, where bigoted, inane interpretations are used as a base for often cruel and prejudiced actions that increase the collective woe, especially with respect to women.

Innate greed and fostered ignorance also manifest in the investiture of our military economies. A military-industrial complex dominates, which the bewildered masses are indoctrinated to support. Inevitably, grave violations of international law are produced. Facts are doctored or blatant lies manufactured to support naked aggression against relatively defenceless nations, as in the cases of Vietnam, Cuba, Panama, Iraq, Libya, Syria, and Afghanistan. All ethical virtue is annihilated for political gain in the 'great game' of imperialistic hegemony, so that one way or other the wealth of a nation can be plundered through large scale murder. It is easy for the materialistically powerful to manipulate the masses of self-focussed people in order to gain the charter to carry out ruthless military or financial exploitation of the weak and helpless groups in a society or of other nations. The massively socially destructive evil of the war against drugs is another example of note.

Though the 80% think that they are in control of their own lives, the reality is that their selfishness, endless desires and fundamental materialism can be easily preyed upon by the ruthlessly manipulative, very intelligent and powerful individuals, that exist on top of the avaricious pyramids in our societies. They are the financial wizards and schemers, and the self-serving politicians that have enacted callous and cruel laws that perpetuate social inequity enforced by the strong arm of a brutal police force. Thus is established the massive wealth gap in our societies, via the forms of plutocracies that govern people's lives. Vast numbers of economic slaves are produced at the bottom of the wealth pool. Their totally undervalued labour is fostered by all possible means, and much of what they earn is siphoned from them in many ways. Examples are excessively high rents for accommodation and businesses, inordinate medical and insurance costs, austerities, and unfair taxation systems. We also have the absurdity of a fiat money system privately owned, which a government buys and pays interest for and that it recoups by taxing people who are forced to use the intrinsically worthless paper for all transactions. For this, their labour is demanded to be freely supplied. Thus is produced all the evils of usury, galloping inflation, and the woes of manufactured debt that comes with it.

Though laws prohibiting public ownership of slaves may have been introduced more than a century ago, nevertheless we see a form of debt-slavery that economically ties people to work long hours for a pittance. They can barely survive with their families in societies where others are handed great mounds of the beneficence of the nation on a platter through laws that foster massive social and financial inequality. It is interesting to note that massed greed translates out as economic slavery for all but a handful of plutocrats who have won privileged, ruthlessly contrived power. Then there are many forms of 'lotto games' and Ponzi schemes preying upon the poor who hope that they too can possess ostentatious wealth.

The mechanisms of help for the education of this bewildered 80% are foremost in the planning of Hierarchy. Ways have been found to educate them (despite their blindness through the karmic consequences of massed folly) by the social activists born amongst them, who are willing to undergo many hardships, suffer persecution and the rigours of police brutality to educate them to begin to think rightly. Such effort is not without its success stories, and slowly the thought-structure of humanity is bettered. Planetary woe, the widespread battle of labour verses financial rapists continues unabated, and will be inevitably won for the cause that serves human betterment. A new era where sound, caring governments constituted of the wise, will eventually dawn upon humanity. Partial examples exist amongst the community of nations, and will grow exponentially when the masses finally awaken from their indoctrinated stupor and demand their inalienable rights and freedoms. This is the process that we see happening all around us now.

If we add Hercules, who played the role of the Christ in antiquity, to the list of the triune Christ, and Koot Humi, the one who will succeed the blue Christ, then we have a pentad. This pentad can then be related to the qualities of the five Dhyāni Buddhas. Hercules then takes the attributes of Vairocana in the Christ's department, thereby embodying the Dharmadhātu Wisdom. The Buddha takes the attributes of Akṣobhya, hence the Mirror-like Wisdom, reflecting the attributes of cosmic Love and Wisdom into the activities of the remaining three representatives of the Christ. The blue Christ takes the attributes of the All-accomplishing Wisdom of Amoghasiddhi, to reflect all seven Rays that are the sub-hues of the fundamental blue Ray into the planetary manifestation. Koot Humi is the Chohan responsible for the dissemination of the blue energy via the Equalising Wisdom of Ratnasambhava. His main function, therefore, is to harmonise the mode of expression that those upon all Rays within Hierarchy develop so that the purpose of Love and Wisdom reigns supreme within our planetary manifestation. The new Mahāchohan takes the attributes of Amitābha as he blends the energy of Love-Wisdom with that of the awakening Minds of humanity, ensuring that the forthcoming civilisation will have compassionate considerations as the base energy driving all decision making. The epoch of the new world civilisation, the new era, can then flower, supplanting the present one based upon materialistic considerations of mind.

Taking this pentad into account, therefore, we see that the terms Christs I, II, and III refer principally to the type of energy dispensation that these important members of Hierarchy are presently involved with in transforming the planetary situation from a non-sacred to a sacred planet via the energy of Love-Wisdom. The first Christ works primarily from cosmic spheres, integrating these first Ray astrological sources into a form that can be utilised to drive the evolution of consciousness forwards upon our planet towards a cosmic destination.

The second Christ integrates these energies from cosmos with those from the solar system in the form of a silver-white blue light that disseminates the purpose of the blue Ray to all.

The third Christ incorporates this energy to principally feed the Minds of those seeking enlightenment so that they can pass Initiation testings upon the upward way, to be incorporated as part of the planetary Head centre's awakening. This process then produces the externalisation of the Hierarchy in the form of 'the holy city, new Jerusalem, coming down from God out of heaven, prepared as a bride adorned for her husband'.[53]

---

53 *Rev. 21:2.*

The energy of the past Buddha, Śākyamuni (Christ I), is the Will-of-Love manifesting in the form of unbounded wisdom. He represents the *dharmakāya* attribute of Maitreya. The quality of the One the Christians call 'Christ' embodies unfettered Love, the intensely contemplative, deeply observant *sambhogakāya* aspect of Maitreya. Christ III is the *nirmaṇakāya* or actively embodied form (actively expressed Love) of Maitreya. His quality is therefore the activity attribute of Will and Love-Wisdom.

The difference between Christs II and III is that the first embodies the focussed principle of cosmic Love that is dynamically serene within itself, making him 'the downward-looking lord of Compassion' working to effect a cosmic principle through the agency of others. He is crucified in the light of this Love. Christ III is the expressed Wisdom of that Love as active compassion that incarnates to ground that cosmic potency. His spiritual robes of Love-Wisdom are comparatively 'tattered', but bears an increased receptivity to the energy of cosmic Will and the demonstration of Mind. Together they embody the two parts of the Ray of Love-Wisdom, integrating cosmic Love in such a way that eventually the great mass of people can come to bear it as applied wisdom. The equalising wisdom of Koot Humi helps to integrate the activity of the two Christs, ensuring that this compassionate wisdom manifests appropriately in the difficult field of human interrelations, because vast is the undertaking in this modern era. Disciples all over the world must now be directly accommodated in their fields of service, rather than in a localised area as before. Thus we have the necessity for the phenomena of this interrelationship, coupled with the work of all Initiates, who together manifest the compassionate function of Maitreya.

The energy of Christ III also translates as the actualising wisdom that empowers the Will-to-Love. He karmically inherits the 'robes', the *manasic* sheaths left behind by Śākyamuni after his *parinirvāṇa*. (The Buddha wears a new 'robe' consisting of cosmic astral substance.) He thereby continues the former Buddha's teaching dispensation upon a higher, expanded cycle of expression. This will inevitably manifest in the form of a new world religion when a part of the Buddhist world reforms, manifesting its philosophy upon sounder footing, but which many fundamentalists will not accept. The reformists therefore will manifest a new esoteric version of Buddhism, which will later be seen as a new religion. The effect will be similar to the activity of Gautama some thousands of years ago with respect to Hinduism, as well as the effect of the work of Christ II via Jesus, who reformed the Judaic religion. Jesus' reforms were, however, quickly distorted by bigoted fanatics that created what is now viewed as Christianity.

The appearance of Christ I allowed the complete flowering of the *iḍā nāḍī* stream of human consciousness. He spurred the development of the wisdom traditions upon the earth based upon sound logic, as was developed in Buddhism and also through the Greek empirical philosophers. (The basis for the *mahāmudrā* uniting the East and the West[54] then came into being as Bodhisattvas incarnated into one or other of these sectors of the world to develop the respective philosophical systems.)

Christ II represents the demonstration of the *piṅgalā nāḍī* stream, the compassionate aspect of human consciousness. This energy empowers the entire Hierarchy of enlightened being to manifest their respective service arenas in the world. This potency was also the driving force behind an earlier manifestation of this Christ as Krishna, at a time when the Hierarchy was much less developed than now.

From the most ancient times we have a dispensation of the Christs expressing their forms of active wisdom and love to meet the need of the world's aspiration to seek enlightenment.

The *iḍā prāṇas* sown by the Buddha have matured significantly by the time of the exoteric activities of Christ III. He therefore represents the beginning of the empowerment of the *suṣumṇā* aspect of human consciousness (viewed as *bodhicitta),* wherein mind is transfigured into Mind along the path of sacrificial Love.

Essentially, the dispensation of Christ I concerned the awakening of the wisdom principle as compassionate understanding of the nature of the basic factors of life. This concerned such things as the relation of suffering to impermanence, Dependent Origination, and formulations of the nature of mind in relation to the Void. His previous incarnations, e.g., as Orpheus, laid the foundation for the development of his limitless wisdom. The point made here is that Buddhist mythologies concerning the earlier lives of the Buddha, such as provided in the Jataka Tales, should be

54 See here the chapter 'The West and the East, the Mahāmudrā of the Two Truths' in Volume 1.

viewed symbolically or allegorically only. For instance, there is little or no understanding as to the nature of his Western incarnations found in them.

Christ II demonstrated the active power of Love, laying the foundation teachings in his earlier incarnation as Krishna, and later as Christ-Jesus. The Lord of the second Ray (sGampopa/Koot Humi) will take the mantle of the blue Christ when Christ II moves on to greater responsibility in the cosmic landscape. Eventually Christ II will assume the functions of the Logos of this planet.[55] By then it will be truly manifesting as a planet of Love. In this way he continues his aeonic servitude upon this planet for the humanity he loves most intensely.

Christ III fuses Wisdom with Love, which is the foundation of great compassion, and adds the teaching of the nature of the Divine Will. His purpose has always been esoterically veiled in history and works to explicate the nature of Mind to humanity. (Consequently he was also Vasubandu, a founder of the Yogācāra tradition.)

The point of focus for the compassionate activity of this department of Christ/Maitreya into the material domain manifests in the south-east arm of the *maṇḍala* of the Mahābodhisattvas.[56] Here we also have the function of bearing the seventh Ray of Ceremonial Activity into manifestation,[57] the energy that governs the outpouring of the purpose of our civilisation in the new era. Here the second Ray is borne by the seventh, because enlightening ritualised activity is its current purpose, the demonstration of what Maitreya symbolises and effectively embodies for our planetary woe. We see also that the role of Maitreya in this direction relates to the integration of the function of all three Christs. They turn the wheel of the *maṇḍala* northward to awaken the Head centres of the world's disciples. (Signified by the role of the Mahāchohan in the *maṇḍala.)*

---

55 This is the meaning of the statement in *Matt. 28:20:* 'lo, I am with you alway, *even* unto the end of the world. Amen'.

56 See Figure 25, Volume 4, and Figure 3 further on in this chapter.

57 If we take the Buddha to be abstracted from humanity, and focus strictly upon the blue Ray, then we can also take the 'blue Christ' mentioned above to represent the first point, the second Ray Chohan as the second point of a trinity of active manifest compassion, and the 'green Christ' as the third point. The third and seventh Ray combination then manifests as the mode of activity.

Cyclic, wise, active sacrificial compassion therefore is a keynote of this Bodhisattva, who takes the mantle and responsibilities that effectively go with the role of the Buddha for this new age. Do not expect an overt show of great *siddhis*,[58] as that is not the way that Hierarchy care to work. Converting the gullible ones who are impressed by titles and glamorous images by such means is never a prime objective of Hierarchy. They astutely prefer the processes that produce true wisdom in the population. The demonstration of vast wisdom is what the worthy seek and will sup from for guidance and nourishment to further their progress. Neither Gautama nor Christ-Jesus manifested a great ostentatious spiritual show around them, and had many enemies to contend with. At that time the Buddha's doctrines were deemed an heretical form of Hinduism, and Jesus was crucified by the authorities due to the jealousy of the Sanhedrin, the high Jewish council of priests governing the religion of the time.[59] There also will be adversities aplenty for Christ III. There are different streams of *karma* to contend with, and alien forms of logic to react to by the uncomprehending conservative religionists and materialists. It takes centuries of skilful Bodhisattvic action of the generations of followers to prove the worthiness of a great One whose purpose was to bring about a new religious dispensation. Such a One is but the *bīja* of an entire *maṇḍala* yet to fully flower.

Compassion is indeed the *modus operandi* of the constituency of the *maṇḍala* of the Mahābodhisattvas and the entire Hierarchy of Light and Love. This *maṇḍala,* therefore, also conveys another interpretation of the appearance of Maitreya—the mass incarnation of Hierarchy. A group appearance into outer manifestation of rhythmic compassionate activity is certainly worthy of the symbolism of this name. Maitreya is often depicted in a Western seated position, which portends a future Western incarnation by the one in whose honour this iconograpy was originally formulated. The awakened Eye allows an enlightened one to envision the convoluted line of humanity's future evolution to liberation as they respond to this enlightening force within them.

---

58 When *siddhis* do manifest they will serve to awaken materialists out of their entrenched opinions.

59 We should note here Jesus's comment with respect to the appearance of the second coming of Christ: 'behold he comes as a thief in the night' *(1 Thess. 5:2).*

There is a continuous process of evolutionary rearrangement within Hierarchy as aspirants gain Initiation and move up their ranks. This causes the higher members of Hierarchy to also move up. The advent of Maitreya constitutes a period of simultaneous, rapid rearrangement and advancement of Hierarchy upwards towards Shambhala, and downwards into humanity. Eventually Shambhala will thereby become externalised upon the physical plane, as Hierarchy will reveal thereon the conditionings found upon *dharmakāyic* realms. The full onset of the violet Ray of the magical power of ritualised activity will help to produce these changes by effecting the right happenings upon the physical plane. The seventh Ray facilitates the descent of the first Ray of Will or Power, to quickly overcome all forms of materialistic thought and assertions, when backed by Love-Wisdom. This first Ray potency is wielded by the Lords of Shambhala.

The Dharmakāya Way

What is traditionally known as a human *(mānuśi)* Buddha is one who has passed the necessary grade along the second (teaching) Ray line (Rays 2, 4, 6). The Buddha exemplified the wisdom associated with this Ray line. He was an expression of the fourth Ray of Beautifying Harmony overcoming Conflict. Being the central Ray it acts as a mirror that reflects the higher three into active manifestation. The fourth Ray is therefore the conditioning Ray governing the Middle Way, thus the entire Buddhist dispensation. Those along the first Ray line (1, 3, 5, 7) generally pass the grade (of the sixth Initiation) that denotes them as Buddhas in a manner that is not recognised by humanity. This is part of the basis to the Buddhist conception of the existence of *pratikyekabuddhas.*[60] For instance, we did not see the appearance of a Buddha when the Phoenician took his sixth Initiation, as he is an Initiate travelling upon the fifth Ray line.

Of those that attain the sixth Initiation only a stipulated few are needed to play an essential role in the Shambhalic *maṇḍala.* Such esoteric roles were assigned many epochs ago, and evolution proceeds along the course set by the originating Jinas governing Shambhala.

60 Individualist Buddhas.

The esoteric history of Buddhism has only symbolically been provided in Buddhist lore, and then little pertaining to how Bodhisattvas have evolved throughout the centuries. In fact, there is very little viable history that can be relied upon by modern historians. The presented hagiography of its saints and great *yogins* mixes the symbolism of sensationalised mythologizing with biographical data. The supposed past lives of the Buddha are but moralising tales, fables that endeavour to portray to simple minds, villagers and lay folk, examples of compassionate acts. Much therein does not behove of true wisdom, but rather of extreme sacrificial acts, such as found in the Jataka Tales of the Bodhisattva offering his body for consumption by a hungry tiger. We have folly displayed here rather than wisdom, the wastage of a 'pure and difficult-to-attain, free, and endowed human body'.[61] In no way should such foolhardy 'compassion' be emulated by the average population, as it certainly would result in a rapid growth of the tiger population and the corresponding demise of the human one, with little else being achieved.

Difficult to discern are the types of incarnations that would be expected of an exceedingly advanced Bodhisattva along any of the Rays of Mind, though such can be found amongst the tales of the *mahāsiddhas*. Buddhists have a natural inclination for the second Ray line, but even then they should expect for one such as the Buddha to be the founder of an earlier esoteric religious tradition, such as the Orphic tradition of ancient Greece.

It is obvious that to properly trace the lives of the great Ones the entire world's history must be at one's disposal and not just the parochial religious history of a relatively small grouping of people ensconced in the Himalayas, or other locality. It should thus be obvious that to factually explain such things to the general populace enlightened ones had to wait for the modern era when proper historical accounts are available. Logically, therefore, enlightened beings nowadays must of necessity be steeped in historical lore if they are to truly serve the community they wish to enlighten. Here, therefore, we find an arena where the present Rinpoche system falls flat with respect to its claims as

61 W.Y. Evans-Wentz, *Tibetan Yoga and Secret Doctrines* (Oxford University Press, London, 1968), 67. This quote is part of 'The Precepts of the Guru' presented therein.

to the enlightened status of its incarnates. Most are simply too ignorant of the mainstream happenings in the world: religiously, historically, culturally, economically, scientifically, or in terms of international and globally interrelated organisations, to represent the status of high Bodhisattvas. Younger Initiates they may be, but as such do not need such extensive knowledge.[62]

The main challenge now facing all Bodhisattvas working to gain enlightenment, therefore, must be to become fully aware of the intricacies of what's happening all over the globe in many arenas of Life, and not just with the insular matters of a religion. As stated, the planet is being throttled by a major cancerous outpouring, based upon the massed avaricious predatory ambitions within the community of nations, principally by the Western powers.

Below is a list of three major objectives of meditation. The first two of these concern ways of training beginners upon the path of compassion. There is a progression over a course of lives leading from these steps to the third position. The path eventually produces Bodhisattvas initiated into the ways of Shambhala.

1. Being interested in gaining peace of mind, calming one's own emotional volatility so that one is better equipped to handle challenges in life. Often this intensifies the concept of 'self' so that it can battle the vicissitudes, adversities and other people's emotions within our complex societies.
2. A concern with the development of self-enlightenment, then to obtain the goal of *śūnyatā* (Void), which is bereft of any concepts of 'self'. Often little is done however to relieve the problems in the world (other than in terms of religious education). Internal quietude, control of the personality vehicle, and abstraction from the *māyā* of the world around being deemed most important.
3. Complete acquiescence to the challenges of the Bodhisattva path, which concerns passing the Initiation testings upon the road of Love and compassion so that the Bodhisattva *bhūmis* are trod. The candidate eventually becomes a Shambhalic recipient. Though

62 This is a generalised statement, as sometimes the selection process may indeed find the true reincarnate, in which case multilevelled awareness may be awakened over time.

śūnyatā may be a baseline of striving for the meditator, as has been the onus in Buddhism for millennia, the focus must now be the Dharmakāya Way. Here Buddhahood via integration into the *dharmakāya* is the objective. To do so one must be compassionately active in helping to rectify the evils in this planet, as well as developing the yogic path of transforming *saṃskāras* in accordance with the dictates of the laws of group evolution.[63] This Way is the leitmotiv of the residents of Shambhala, and increasing the number of Shambhalic recipients is the focus of activity for the most advanced members of the Council of Bodhisattvas.

All meditation procedures that aim at enlightenment must now increasingly take this third position into account in the education of candidates. The training necessitates complete mastery of the volatile emotions and the vicissitudes of the mind. It necessitates, therefore, the development of various levels of compassionate insight that are awakened as the Heart *chakra* becomes empowered to control the forces below the diaphragm. Its energies will then dominate the Solar Plexus centre. Effectively, the activity of the theriomorphic Wrathful Deities, explained in Volume 5 of this Treatise, come to the fore as the challenges are properly met by transforming grosser *prāṇas*. (Such visuals, however, may take other forms than what is portrayed in the Buddhist texts, or experienced in terms of pure transforming energies.) The higher abstract Mind is thus developed over the reifying attributes of the empirical mind.

The fruits of the Dharmakāya Way orient one to Shambhala, for which purpose this present book is written. The theory of the constituency of Shambhala is presented, but the actual visual appearance will be provided in the Mind's Eye of the meditators that actually travel there. This Way consists of passing a gradated series of Initiation testings along the Bodhisattva path. These Initiations are only indirectly related to the 'initiations' presented in the Tantric digests, such as that of the Kālachakra, where such terms as 'vase Initiation' and 'water Initiation' are given. The way constitutes proper mastery of the emotions and *manasic saṃskāras*. The method produces residence at the *saṃsāra-śūnyatā* nexus

63 See Volume 6, chapter 8.

in terms of what is appropriate for this present epoch, rather than what existed for the comparatively simple times of the great Mahāsiddhas.

Every step along the way to *dharmakāya* necessitates developing the characteristics of high level Bodhisattvas. This incorporates increasingly esoteric and vaster meditations upon planetary (and later cosmic) need. At every step there is the incessant resistance and attacks by members of the dark brotherhood, whose machinations against humanity and the Bodhisattva's purpose must therefore be overcome. Beings of unadulterated ceaseless evil exist at all levels of cosmos. Their nature and massed effects must thus be understood, the associated *karma* mitigated, light and mantric sound of various intensities and hues generated, and the corresponding *nāḍīs* within the earth, and also cosmos, cleansed. For the third Initiation to be passed many types of black, grey or sombre hued theriomorphic and wrathful entities, and many levels of sorcery and witchcraft must be countered within the context of one's evolving group.

Examples of such beings are the Anubis (jackal-headed humans) generated in Atlantean and Egyptian days as objects of worship. In Egyptian mythology Anubis was a god concerned with the judgement over the dead. He weighed the deeds of the heart with a feather in the opposing pan of the scales. This agreeable function was quickly prostituted to having control over all attributes of the astral body, not only of the deceased, but also of the living, when perverted by the power of the black magicians, which abounded in that magic based society. The efficacy of the vast number of spells to ward off evil in that society has never been taken seriously by Egyptologists. However, all esotericists, *yogins* and psychic people know of the need of similar mantras.

Anubi abound in subjective space. The theriomorphic form simply betokens the fact that such beings wield emotional energies, which are animal-like. The specific qualities of the emotions predominantly developed are symbolised by the type of animal head represented. In this case the jackal signifies a form of cunning, devious, clever and canny intelligence.

As these Anubi mostly have grey colourations, they are experts in grey thought projection and subliminal suggestion fostering subtle desires, thus are masters in manipulating the emotions of people. They are experts in perverting truth. Their special focus is upon those struggling to liberate themselves from the common emotional pull.

The realms where those that have disincarnated go are here called the 'inner realms'. These realms can also be viewed in terms of the various Bardos of *The Tibetan Book of the Dead* (*Bardo Thödol*), though technically they relate to differing consciousness states. Alternatively the term the *astral plane* (which is constituted of seven sub-planes) can be used. There are also domains that are more purely *manasic* (hence Fiery). The technicalities of this subject are some of the things explored in the meditation-Mind. Sometimes working consciously to assist those on these domains is part of the work done in meditation. The presented teachings concerning these domains must be true to be effective, therefore must be given by one who has mastered that way. The lower sub-planes of the astral realm constitute the hell states of the various religions (including the domain of the *pretas* and *asuras* in the Buddhistic eschatology), whilst the higher sub-planes constitute the heavenly realms. They also represent domains of service work for Bodhisattvas of the lower degrees, as they are closer to where common humanity are actually at.[64] It is all part of the knowledge needed by those travelling upon the Dharmakāya Way, as each plane of perception mastered is one step closer to reaching the domain of Shambhala.

Each heavenly or hell state represents the expression or reward of the *karma* for types of emotional-mental action manifest whilst incarnate. When a person dies he/she simply drops the physical body, and after the vital body is also dropped, will be clothed in the emotional and then mental sheaths that remain. Uncontrolled emotions of any type generally means a hell state to experience as one cleanses their volatile emanations.

Because everything is mind-constructed on the inner realms, the laws of mind will control all appearances and states of livingness that the people therein are clothed by. Extreme desire, avarice, aggressive and volatile emotions, all produce their respective deformities upon the substance of the planes that clothe the human entity. Anubi for instance, represent the nature of the form of human cunning and malicious intent through the development of the art of listening to the selfish thought constructs and observing the subtleties of desire impulses. The jackal head presents the best means to do so, and to also voice the mantras to control the forms of astral substance.

---

64 The book by Peter Richelieu, *A Soul's Journey* (Thorsons, London, 1958), for instance, gives a good account of some of the methods of service work accomplished here.

The way each person gets enlightened adds to the pool of energy in the earth's *nāḍīs,* and this becomes more Fiery with time. As a consequence it becomes easier to contact and attract to earth more potent energies. This also facilitates contact with the realms of enlightenment wherein reside the various Bodhisattvas, Buddhas and *ḍākinīs.* The energy of the earth sphere is speeding up because of the onset of our modern Western technological civilisation, with its fast pace of action in all things and because of the more vibrant thought processes of people. The affects of this energy stimulating the way people think, assisting them to move into greater enlightened states, and awakening their Head centres, can now be seen. The forces of darkness have capitalised upon the same energy to propel their malicious schemes for planetary conquest.

The consequence of the principle of energisation of the various stratas of human awareness will enlighten the world. Quarks, electrons, quantum chromodynamics, quasars, galaxies, genetics, the evolution of the fittest of the species, are all scientific discoveries. But there is also the spread of literature from a more perceptive, insightful media (especially on the internet) exposing the dogmas of many commonly held beliefs. Spiritual literature, the expanding progress of Buddhism, and more advanced esoteric philosophy is also there to consider. Within the global environment there is a slow progression to more vibrant thought processes, the synthesis of cultures, and with it all religious dispensations. All forms of information are broadcast through trans-national media outlets, producing cultural globalisation, with the internet allowing the wealth of human knowledge to be freely available for a progressive and rapid stimulation of human consciousness. Thus no longer are foreign ideas and cultural artefacts, alien and intriguing concepts segregated and difficult to explore, but on the contrary, more inclusiveness of thought is now manifesting.

Many diverse forms of knowledge now materialise into common comprehension, and morsels of revelation that move and flow in the higher strata of the intelligentsia and academically elite's thinking become commonly accessible. Einstein's Theory of Relativity, which was once the domain of the most avant-garde physicists, has for instance now become the subject of popular books. However, most people don't think enlighteningly, so the process starts off slowly, like cream floating to the top of milk, because of physical laws. Similarly there shall be an intensification of the processes activating the particles of the milk of enlightenment that make them swirl to form more rapid movements in the uppermost strata of life.

By being radical but logical, persistent and inventive, one can change the opinions of those that are stubborn and resistant. The outpouring of the general meditative influx of energies upon the planet may however make others more stubborn in consciousness and less able to define the basics of regular esoteric thinking, because energy is impartial and can reify their minds. Such people will also come to advance in time.

Rigidity of thought is a general malaise that will slowly change via the activity of the world's meditators. The sublime strata of consciousness, of pure unadulterated receptivity to the Oṁ of the Mind's expansion, is rarely experienced and very little understood in the West. The prerogative of all who have been properly trained in meditative techniques is to educate the compulsive deniers, to free their minds from all forms of self-limiting constraints. A Buddha must use the Mind also, and the way that people can give of themselves to gain *buddhic* perception (the enlightened Mind), via discipline of mind, brings one more than a third of the way towards enlightenment. The body is the vehicle of whatever constitutes one's consciousness, thus the remaining two thirds of the path to light will be found in mastery of the sensorial aspects of the body, and how emotional expressions are controlled.

The third, fourth, and fifth Shambhalic levels

The *third Shambhalic level* is that of the eight Mahābodhisattvas. They were explained from the Buddhist perspective in relation to Figure 25 from Volume 4 of this Treatise,[65] which the reader should consult for detail. See also Figure 3. Further information concerning them from an esoteric perspective shall be provided throughout this book.

This level takes the attributes of Amoghasiddhi's All-accomplishing Wisdom, by acting as potent instruments of Shambhalic purpose within *saṃsāra*. Attributes of the Shambhalic Mind *(dharmakāya)* are projected into the *maṇḍala* of the Council of Bodhisattvas. This

65 Volume 4, 281-326.

Mind incorporates the links from various solar and cosmic sources to our planetary sphere according to the Ray line the various Chohans (sixth degree Initiates) embody. These energies are then divided into the sub-Ray purposes that are the specific focus within the planet at any time. The western direction of the *maṇḍala* of the Dhyāni Buddhas is accommodated, as the field of service related to enlightening humanity is the focus.

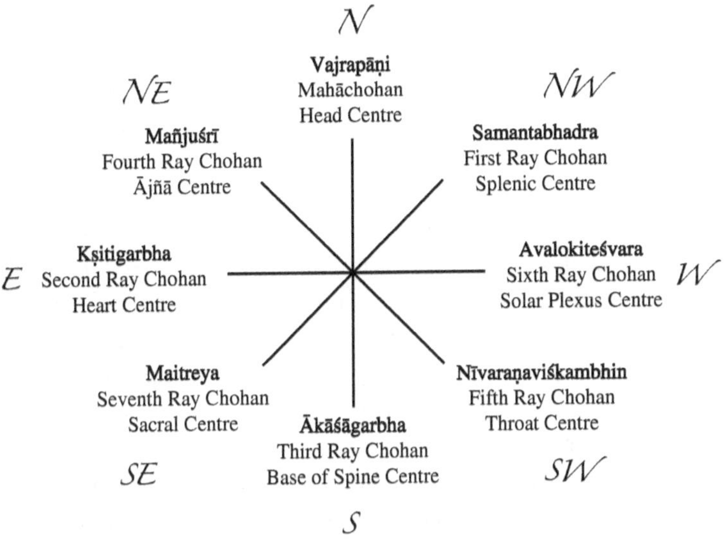

Figure 3. The third Shambhalic level—the Ray Lords

The *fourth level* constitutes the *maṇḍala* of the Masters of Wisdom, the fifth degree Initiates that govern the expression of sub-Ray energies into manifestation. They embody the Ashrams of the Council of Bodhisattvas wherein all disciples are trained according to the fundamental flavouring of the Sambhogakāya Flower of the individuals concerned. These are conditioned by the sub-Rays of the fundamental Rays from which the Masters of Wisdom have evolved and which they now direct. They are karmic overlords projecting *dharmakāyic* purpose for the associated group of Souls by training all disciples that are of their genre. The activities of all people are directed by the Ray purpose of their overriding Sambhogakāya Flower.

The Equalising Wisdom of Ratnasambhava is here exemplified, as the Masters work to integrate all divergent activities into the one Hierarchical Plan. Here the southern direction of the *maṇḍala* of the Dhyāni Buddhas is implicated, as enlightening all the lives in Nature's kingdoms according to their Ray disposition is within the Master's ken.

Detail of the way of Initiation into the structures, conditions, and activities of the Ashrams can now be broadcast. Such esoteric information was hinted at in Buddhist philosophy through the concept of *guruparaṃparā*.[66] The world of meditation opens the meditative one to the forms of training instigated by the Ashram they are part of. It is an essential part of the training of all Bodhisattvas. Consequently, contact with the Master of Wisdom at the centre of the Ray Ashram one is in is the most important part of one's spiritual development and meditative progress, once the Master has deemed the student worthy.

Here is veiled the symbolism of the Rinpoche system, where a Rinpoche stands as if being a Master at the centre of an Ashram of the Hierarchy of Light. The most famous and important Rinpoches of the past may indeed have been incarnations of such Masters, with the *maṇḍalas* of their disciples manifesting to fulfil the purpose of their Ashramic service work. Such would be the case, for instance, of the first Karmapa, Dusum Khyenpa (1110-93), who established Tsurphu monastery. He was the incarnation of a second Ray Master under the auspices of his Master sGam po pa, the present second Ray Chohan. The second Karmapa, Karma Pakshi (1206-83) who became the spiritual preceptor of Kublai Khan, is a case where we actually have a successive rebirth of a great one, as the first Karmapa started the Rinpoche system by nominating where his next incarnation would be found. At that time the instigation of the Rinpoche system was the correct Hierarchical dispensation. The system, however, quickly became politically motivated, perverting the originating purpose, and this trend continued until the present day.

---

66 *Guruparaṃparā,* lineage tradition of a guru, or spiritual preceptor. An important consideration in Buddhism and Hinduism. It was needed where the most important information was not written down, but were 'ear whispered' from the guru to students, through a lineage or series of beings that have evolved to take the place of the preceding guru. Especially important in Tantricism.

The *fifth Shambhalic level* consists of the most senior disciples of a Master's Ashram. These are the third and fourth degree Initiates. They constitute the inner executive council of twelve disciples that form the major petals of a Heart lotus with respect to the Master at the centre. The Hierarchy is a Heart centre and therefore its component parts are but smaller expressions of the major unit. A Master is part of an inner quorum manifesting as a triad with his two most senior disciples. One of these will be an Initiate of the fourth degree and the other close to taking the fourth. They form the *iḍā, piṇgalā and suṣumṇā nāḍīs* for the entire *maṇḍala.*

Here we observe the functioning of Amitabha's Discriminating Inner Wisdom. Being closer to humanity, these disciples must develop the enlightened Mind, thus acting upon the field of human consciousness with respect to helping them to transform the attributes of the empirical mind into Mind. All that is desired by the Lords of Shambhala to be accomplished within the matrix of human minds has thereby the best chance to be achieved. The implicated direction within the *maṇḍala* of the Dhyāni Buddhas is northwards to Shambhala and cosmos, to which these Initiates aspire.

Though this last group are included in the *maṇḍala* of Shambhala, their home is Hierarchy, but they assemble at Shambhala during important festivals. They have earned the right at appropriate times. Such experiences can be remembered in dreams or in meditation. The Masters of Wisdom on the other hand can enter at will because they consciously reside in *dharmakāya.* The Chohans have offices in Shambhala, but they are the executive decision makers for the activities of Hierarchy within their respective Ray purposes.

The most advanced Bodhisattvas have little free time to spend upon continuous administrative detail, or impressing the devotional needs of the laity. They have freed themselves from much of such *karma.* They are the founders of the major spiritual Schools, as were sGam po pa, Tsongkhapa and other great *paṇḍitas.* They are not intricately concerned with later administration of such Schools and organisations. They direct from above without again having to incarnate into those organisations. They have evolved on to meet other challenges upon their paths.

The outer seeming is the great illusion. *Saṃsāra* is an enormous play with many actors upon the stage. Disciples should take much care to see through the acts of this play to ascertain their nature, and to especially look for necessary signs of great wisdom in those they choose to revere as gurus.

We should also note that the above consideration is concerned with the basic *maṇḍalic* structure of Shambhala as it relates directly to the present humanity. The concern therefore is with the occupancy of the major petals of the Head lotus of the planetary Logos by various members of Shambhala, drawn from humanity. There are other important beings that fulfil roles that place them as part of this major Lotus. There are, for instance, the executive members of the Deva kingdom that should also be placed, plus the planetary representatives of the Regents of the sacred and non-sacred planets within the solar system, and of other cosmic centres. D.K., for instance, presents a summary in relation to one who has opened the 'third door' of *'the monadic sense of essential duality'*[67] (a sixth degree Initiate), and mentions:

> The inner group of the Council Chamber at Shamballa are now of greater advancement than he; the "Supernal Three," the "Radiant Seven," the "Lives embodying the forty-nine Fires," the "Buddhas of Activity," and certain "Eternal Spirits" from such centres of dynamic spiritual life as Sirius, or from the constellation which at any one time forms a triangle with our Sun and Sirius, and a Representative from Venus.[68]

This listing shall be explained in chapter 8, whilst the chapters in between will be devoted to a detailed explanation of the Ashrams of the Council of Bodhisattvas because of the importance of the subject. Those interested in enlightenment need to factor in such information to better comprehend the nature of the visions they may receive and of the true mode of the training that governs their spiritual development. Unless they have an enlightened teacher such training will be veiled, where both the teacher, and the earnest student, will be given impressions from the Master at the heart of their being as to the right course of action. The presumption here is that the teacher is not

67 A.A. Bailey, *The Rays and the Initiations*, (Lucis Publishing Company, New York, 1960), 141.

68 Ibid., 141-142.

an egoist or one who has self-serving motives for thus teaching. The quality of the demonstrated wisdom and the nature of the expression of love are the major determinants to look for when gauging whether or not a person is an advanced member of Hierarchy. Narrow-minded thinking and self-serving activities are sure indications of people who do not wear the Hierarchical mantle, or at least will not do so until their love for humanity and Nature is palpably demonstrated. A fluid broadmindedness and selfless activity then intervenes, and many will benefit accordingly.

To meet the Christ

one needs a quiet
all-embracive Mind
and an active Heart
well versed in the art of
detached one-pointedness
answering the cry of all suffering.
Give your heart to That
which is the world's offering,
and rise
to greet the universal,
most vast and awesome Light
that is (His) Mind.

Grace be to the Guru,
inspiration of aspirational being,
ineffable Love-Light Source.
Gift waves come
from that Light to you,
and through you
to all those that are you,
and from them
through you to the Guru.

He is your path to
the One and the other
that are separated
in time and space.

3

The Qualities of the Ashrams

Preamble

This chapter details the nature of the Ashrams of the Masters of Wisdom. They are residents in *dharmakāya*, having surmounted all challenges in the subtle domains and conquered every aspect of life in *saṃsāra* according to their various Ray lines. They are the gain of the evolutionary and meditation process. An integral part of the Mindscape of the enlightened, or those that are becoming so, is the sublime inner world of continuous revelation and service wherein the Masters reside. The subtle domains are a necessary experiential zone to master before entry into Shambhala is possible. The way to Shambhala therefore leads via the territory of the Masters. Let us proceed thereto with zeal and forthright striding to great heights of awareness. The approach to *śūnyatā* inevitably reveals *dharmakāya,* allowing the plenitude of cosmos to awaken in the Mind's Eye of the modern *siddhas* who can thereby enter into Shambhala.

To explain the nature of these Ashrams we need to utilise the writings of Alice A. Bailey, via whom teachings concerning them were first published. She was the amanuensis of a Master who utilised the pseudonym Djwhal Khul (D.K., also known as the Tibetan). She received the teachings telepathically from 1919 – 1949, and some also by mail. At that time D.K. was a high Rinpoche of the Gelugpa order and resident at the Tashi Lungpo Monastery, Shigatse. Exoterically, he was one of the two senior tutors of the Panchen Lama at the time of the 13th Dalai Lama, but was esoterically much more than that.[1]

This important Bodhisattva along the second Ray line once had an incarnation as Rechungpa, a foremost disciple of Milarepa. Earlier, D.K. was also Peter, one of the twelve apostles that followed Jesus. The fact that Jesus called him 'the rock'[2] upon which he would build his church refers specifically to his later work in the twilight of the Aquarian epoch as D.K. The Roman Catholic (meaning 'universal') church that was founded after Jesus' time was certainly *not the fulfilment* of this prophecy because it forthrightly rejected the teaching of compassionate Love that Jesus so adequately demonstrated, to zealously persecute the Pagan religion, the Gnostics, and then all other Christian sects and religions from the time of the first Ecumenical Council at Nicaea (A.D. 325) onwards. The writings and temples of worship of the sects made anathema were ruthlessly destroyed and over the centuries many hundreds of millions were slaughtered[3] in the name of the 'Lord of peace'[4] who said 'love your enemies, do good to them which hate you. Bless them that curse you, and pray for them which despitefully use you. And unto him that smiteth thee on the *one* cheek offer also the other'.[5]

The 'rock' that Jesus was referring to represents what can best transmit Hierarchical teachings of the nature of Love-Wisdom to material (concrete)-minded disciples. Hence it did not refer to the 'church' of the Christianity that arose hundreds of years later, which so reified, politicised, and maligned the words of Jesus that it blocked the wisdom and demonstrable compassion that Jesus demanded of

---

1 The then Panchen Lama was in fact a relatively junior disciple.

2 *Matthew 16:18-19:* 'Thou art Peter, and upon this rock I will build my church; and the gates of hell shall not prevail against it. And I will give unto thee the keys of the kingdom of heaven'.

3 Through utilising the evil methodology of the dark forces, the sins of which they must yet atone, this Roman church consequently courted 'the gates of hell'. Diametrically opposite is the white Hierarchy, the Council of Bodhisattvas, the 'kingdom of heaven', to which D.K. has the keys, and has unlocked the Door to that Kingdom, to help reveal what is veiled behind it.

4 *II Thes. 3:16.*

5 *Luke 6:27-29.*

his disciples. Once the Hierarchical wisdom teachings are properly broadcast on a world-wide scale, then will be revealed the true import of what Jesus (the representative of the cosmic Christ) meant to be his 'church'. When it is to be established is hinted in the symbolism of the last supper, where Jesus asked his disciples to follow a man bearing a pitcher of water, and in the upper room of his house they were to eat the Passover with Jesus.[6] A man bearing a pitcher of water is but the symbol of the sign Aquarius the water bearer, whose field of influence the sun is now entering.

The true teaching of Jesus is the embodiment of the 'gospel of peace'[7] that is 'The Revelation of Jesus Christ, which God gave unto him, to shew his servants things which must shortly come to pass.[8] The concept of 'shortly' esoterically means after a due cycle, taking millions of years of the evolutionary history of humanity into account. The nature of the content of this Revelation was first established by H.P. Blavatsky's *The Secret Doctrine*, and firmly consolidated by D.K.'s writings via Alice Bailey, and to lesser extent the writings of Morya via Helena Roerich.[9] My *Treatise on Mind* (and subsequent texts) continues the sequence of esoteric information presented to the world at the end of the nineteenth and beginning of the twentieth century. In updating and elaborating the information that had been provided upon the subjects then introduced to the world I have also integrated the *buddhadharma* into the earlier, more Western presentations, as this *dharma* is essential for proper comprehension of esoteric lore. Buddhism presents a *suṣumṇā* context to the *iḍā* and *piṇgalā* presentation of the esoteric doctrine given to the date of my publications. Hence teachings of a detailed exposition of Mind, the *prajñāpāramitā, bodhicitta, śūnyatā,* the Tantric lore of the *vajrayāna, mahāmudrā,* the Peaceful and Wrathful Deities, the *Dhyāni Buddhas* and the *dharmakāya* can now be ontologically incorporated into the esoteric lexicon.

---

6 *Luke: 22:8-14.*

7 *Ephesians 6:15,* and *Rom. 10:15.*

8 *Rev. 1:1.*

9 A good summery of their work and lives can be found in the book by Harold Balyoz, *Three Remarkable Women,* (Altai Publishers, Flagstaff, Arizona, 1986). See also A.A. Bailey, *The Unfinished Autobiography* (Lucis Publishing Company, New York, 1951).

The formation of the Ashrams

The basis to the following rests in a statement given in *The Externalisation of the Hierarchy,* entitled 'Hierarchical Preparation at *the Wesak Festival* April-May 1946'.

> I have delayed writing my usual Wesak[10] message until this late date because of a certain event in the Hierarchy which was maturing and which necessitated my entire attention. This event was connected with the Wesak Festival and involved among other matters the formation of a new Ashram in which the Wisdom aspect would be of particular importance and not the Love aspect; this Ashram would also be related in a particular manner to the Buddha. It had to be formed at this time in order to be the recipient, and then the custodian, of certain "endowments" which the Buddha will bring at the time of the May Full Moon. The endowments concern the will-to-good of the Lord of the World, the Ancient of Days, though they do *not* concern goodwill as *you* understand that phrase. This Ashram, when duly formed and established, will enable the Members of the Hierarchy to respond to this aspect of the divine Purpose—the Purpose which as you know lies behind and implements the Plan; this Ashram, related to the Buddha, will be specifically under the close supervision of the Christ, and also of the Lord of Civilisation - at this time the Master R. They are the only two Members of the Hierarchy able to register the divine Purpose (in regard to its immediate objectives) in such a manner that the entire Hierarchy can be informed and can then work unitedly and intelligently at its implementation. More than this I may not tell you about this particular Hierarchical move, affecting as it does both Shamballa and the Hierarchy.
>
> This Wesak Festival is of supreme importance because it is the first Festival since the war ended, because it takes place at a time when a definite orientation of the Hierarchy will take place, and because a fresh tide of spiritual impulse and directed second ray energy will

10 Note that the Wesak festival commemorates the *parinirvāṇa* of the Buddha. It is thus a major spiritual festival, observed not only by Buddhists but also by the entire Hierarchy of Light. It is held at the first full Moon in May and concerns the stream of wisdom projected into the world via the opened Eye constituting the Taurean Gate of the zodiac. During this festival the Hierarchy plans its yearly, centennial, or millennial activities, depending upon the nature of the cycle at hand.

> flood the entire Hierarchy; the work, therefore, to be done by the Hierarchy will be far more effective. This you may anticipate and upon this you can count.[11]

The Ashram in question here is that of the first sub-Ray of the second Ray, (2/1), though it is still in the process of unfoldment, as many are the tests for Initiation that the senior candidates must pass before it can be properly established. This is the latest of the Ashrams to have formed to date. Its subsidiary first Ray quality allows direct receptivity of the Will-to-Good from Shambhala and the flowing on of divine purpose into manifest life. The second Ray also allows a specific close affinity to the Buddha and the Christ to eventuate along the wisdom line. Love is a direct emanation from the Heart that draws all into a unity. Wisdom is the active expression of Love in the field of service, and utilises Mind as its steed, with which it can go forth to conquer the domains of ignorance, distorted information, and darkened resolve. Love draws that which has been conquered or converted back to the Heart of Life.

The task of the One whose role it is to integrate the disparaging units of this Ashram into a coherent unity is difficult,[12] as it is not constituted of the usual material that forms other Ashrams. They are the converts of a former dark Hierarchy that have been won over to the white side by the power of light via the use of spiritual swords. Such a task was a monumental aeonic endeavour. Eventually a Master must evolve out of the candidates that overcome their former dark brotherhood allurements. There is significant *karma* along group lines to cleanse past involvement in the dark brotherhood. The work concerning this conversion process progresses over a vast time period. This 2/1 Ashram will eventually bear the all-embracive understanding that is Love in action, and the dynamic sword of the Spirit (from the *dharmakāya*) with which to go forth 'conquering, and to conquer'[13]. Their united will that was formerly devoted to self-centred purposes is consequently redirected for the good of the whole.

---

11 Bailey, Alice, *The Externalisation of the Hierarchy* (Lucis Trust, New York, 1981), 541-542.

12 The process can be likened to being a spiritual midwife to a troubled birth.

13 *Rev.* 6:2.

The complete formation of this Ashram will allow a stronger influx of first Ray energy into Hierarchy than ever before, causing Shambhala and Hierarchy to move closer together, producing a consequent major vitalisation of Hierarchy's magnetic aura (radiance).[14] This energy opens more avenues of approach between Humanity and Hierarchy by drawing a greater number of individuals into the threshold of Hierarchical activity, because it increases the vibrancy of disciple's individual auras. Barriers of mind will consequently be broken down, allowing entry into new fields of awareness, related to the perspective of etheric vision being developed by humanity. The effect upon the physical plane translates as a greater number of disciples being engaged in the finer points of occult and esoteric studies. Esoteric thought will eventually become widely promulgated.

Wisdom will be evoked out of many of the present intelligentsia, as the way of Mind eventually transcends the barriers and limitations of mind, via viewing things from a more esoteric planetary perspective. The Will-of-Love[15] *(bodhicitta)* associated with this Ray combination will thus help to dynamically infuse the second Ray energy into the sum of manifest Life. Channels will thereby be opened that were formerly sealed, wherein individuals may directly contact the great Heart (Hierarchy) and elicit from it radiatory and beneficent responses. The Shambhalic potency may thereby begin to directly flood the earth, channelled by the many divine sword bearers now able to wield this energy without undue strain.

The order of formation of the Ashrams 'under ray activity' in the Hierarchy is given in *The Rays and the Initiations*:

2, 7, 4, 6, 5, 3, 1.[16]

Concerning this process it is helpful to quote D.K.'s explanation.

> As you know, the first human being out of that "centre which we call the race of men" to achieve this point was the Christ; in that first great demonstration of His point of attainment (through the medium of what

14 The effect is similar to the action of an electromagnet upon a magnetic substance, once the power of the electromagnet is switched on.

15 See Volume 4 of this treatise for a detailed account of the meaning of this term.

16 Alice A. Bailey, *The Rays and the Initiations*, 387-388. This order concerns the evolution of Hierarchy since Atlantean times.

was then a new type of initiation) the Christ was joined by the Buddha. The Buddha had attained this same point prior to the creation of our planetary life, but conditions for taking the third initiation were not then available, and He and the Christ took the initiation together. At this initiation, and since then for all initiates of that degree of attainment, They stood in the Presence of the One Initiator, the Lord of the World, and not in the Presence of the Initiate Who was then Head of the Hierarchy. This third initiation was taken in a fourth ray Ashram, the Ray of Harmony through Conflict. This Ashram had taken form and attained functioning activity some time earlier. You can see, under the Law of Correspondences, why this was so. The first human being in the fourth kingdom in nature to take this initiation did so in a fourth ray Ashram and then, esoterically speaking, "the Way lay open toward the Cross"; the initiate faced the process of extension on the Cross, and from that vantage point could view the three worlds. The fourth initiation then became a possibility; the crucifixion faced the disciple of the third degree with its promise of complete liberation and final resurrection.

You can see, therefore, what a tremendous crisis took place in the relation between Humanity and the Hierarchy—a crisis of such importance that Shamballa became involved and the Lord of the World Himself admitted the initiate to the higher contacts. Between that time and the crucifixion of the Master Jesus, the sixth ray Ashram, the fifth and the third, have all been formed around the nucleus of light, started by the ray Lords much earlier. The point of light and of will energy at the centre of each Ashram has existed for untold millennia of years, but the Ashrams themselves were only slowly formed around the nucleus as the various types of energy swept into manifestation and brought with them human types responsive to the ray energy.

When the Master Jesus took the Crucifixion Initiation, another crisis arose of equally great import, if not greater. The crisis was brought about because simultaneously with the crucifixion of the Master, the Head of the Hierarchy, the Christ, took two initiations in one: the Resurrection Initiation and that of the Ascension. These are the fifth and sixth initiations, according to the Christian terminology. This was possible because the first ray Ashram was now active, making entry into the Council Chamber at Shamballa possible. When the Christ achieved this, He was deemed worthy of embodying in Himself a new principle in evolution and of revealing to the world the nature of the second ray aspect—the divine principle of love (as humanity calls it) or of pure reason (as the Hierarchy calls it).

Since that time, all the seven major Ashrams have been fully organised and are steadily increasing in radiatory activity. As you will have noted, the order of their appearance—under ray activity—was 2, 7, 4, 6, 5, 3, 1. In giving this item of ashramic information I am giving you more hints than you will immediately realise.

Each Ashram, as you know, expresses ray quality in its purest and most essential form. During the process of creating the seven Ashrams, they have shifted their focus (or location) from the lowest of the three levels of the abstract mental plane at each major crisis, until today the Ashrams are to be found on the buddhic plane and not on the mental plane at all. This marks the triumph of the hierarchical work, because pure reason—through the second ray—is now the dominant quality in all the Ashrams. Forget not in this connection that all the rays are subrays of the second Ray of Love-Wisdom, but that in the early days of hierarchical activity, it was the particular quality of the ray which dominated an Ashram that first demonstrated, and not the quality of the great major ray of which they were all a part.

Today this is all changing, though the process is not yet perfected, and pure reason or true love is beginning to manifest itself through the quality of all the rays, functioning through their respective Ashrams. The secondary ray quality will not die out or in any way be lessened, but each ray quality will serve to implement the expression of pure love, which is the essential and—at this time—the primary quality of the Lord of the World, Sanat Kumara.

As the centuries have slipped away and the potency of the rays has increased on Earth, humanity has become more and more invocative; this has necessitated the expansion of the Hierarchy itself, and each Ashram has become the creator of six other Ashrams (few of them as yet complete, and some entirely embryonic), so that, in fact, all the forty-nine Ashrams are in the making. The second ray, for instance, has five affiliated Ashrams and one of which only the nucleus exists, and all these are working under its inspiration and through the effect of the second ray central fire. All have at their centre a second ray disciple. The third ray has already two subsidiary Ashrams; the sixth has four, and so on. The first ray is the only one at this time with no subsidiary fully functioning Ashram, and this because the will aspect is as yet very little understood and few initiates can meet the requirements of the first ray initiation. This is no reflection upon humanity. It is a question of divine timing and expediency, and Shamballa is not yet

> prepared for an influx of first ray initiates. Ages must pass before this Will aspect will have reached the stage of unfoldment and expression on the physical plane and through the medium of mankind which will warrant the fusing of six first ray fires—the purest fires there are.[17]

Though D.K. was speaking of the major Ray Ashrams, the same ordering applies for those of the sub-Rays. Thus by deduction we logically would have the Ashrams in existence shown in Figure 4. Each of the sub-Ray Ashrams is presided over by a Master of Wisdom, whilst the major Rays are presided over by the Chohans of the Rays:

	Major Rays						
	2	7	4	6	5	3	1
	(2/2)	7/2	4/2	6/2	5/2	3/2	1/2
	2/7	(7/7)	4/7	6/7	5/7	3/7	1/7
	2/4	7/4	(4/4)	6/4	5/4	3/4	
Sub-Rays	2/6	7/6	4/6	(6/6)	5/6		
	2/5	7/5	4/5	6/5			
	2/3	7/3	4/3				
	2/1—	7/1					

Figure 4. The externalised Ray Ashrams

The diagonal line to this figure posits the Ashrams existing at the present time, according to the above formula. The line also passes through Ashrams that are presently forming. More Ashrams are however depicted than would normally be expected, here denoted by the 6/5 and 5/6 Ashrams. This is because the sixth Ray of Devotion has been a major conditioning Ray governing the Piscean era, wherein these Ashrams have formed. Paralleling this is the effect of the successful

17 A.A. Bailey, *The Rays and the Initiations*, 385-388.

outpouring of the fifth Ray of Scientific Reasoning, which governs the development of our present materialistic civilisation. Thus there is also the flowering of the 4/5 Ashram. This concerns the empowerment of the activity of the fifth Root Race (Aryan) humanity, which is now at the apogee of its influence and development. The 2/1, 1/2, 3/4, 4/3, 7/1 and 1/7 Ashrams are the next in line to form.

In noting the exuberantly rapid development of the spheres of influence on the world stage of the abovementioned Ashrams, the appearance of the 6/5 Ashram in our scientific era, for instance, is concomitant with the widespread explosion of activity of the many religious scholars from the Victorian era onward. The focus being upon those that have endeavoured to utilise logical empiricism and related analytical methods in their religious studies, and in the formulation of systemic theology. The intense missionary activity of that era and the more erudite theological books written (not just concerning Christianity), and also many of the then scientists and the archaeological discoveries in Egypt and the Middle East, came under the auspices of this Ray.

Also, the 5/6 Ashram appeared during this same period, where the primary Ray is that of Scientific Reasoning, and the secondary Ray is the sixth Ray of Devotion. The formation of this Ashram necessitated the incarnation of many gifted people totally devoted to science and technology, archaeology, anthropology, etc., making it the mainstay of our present civilisation. The sixth Ray flavour tends to produce dogmatism in their formulations, such as making Darwinian 'survival of the fittest' the cornerstone of biological thinking despite the lack of any real facts to prove it. We also have the dogmatic assertion by physicists of a materialistic universe where chance alone sets the rules for evolution, despite the fact that all experimental data leans strongly towards the Anthropic Principle.[18]

Similarly, Archaeologists adhere to a strict linear time line, where any concept of a civilization appearing before 7,000 B.C. has for them been anathema, despite the many examples of the expression of such a civilisation, such as the amazing mathematics encoded in the dimensions of the great Pyramid, and the weathering of the Sphinx proving its extreme antiquity. We also have the appearance of huge pyramids all over the world, each with precise astrological coding and alignment to

18 See my book *Esoteric Cosmology and Modern Physics* for detail.

geographic cardinal points, huge monuments made of blocks of stone weighing hundreds of tons in ancient Egypt, Baalbeck, and South America, etc. The Easter Island statues, the roads running into the Mediterranean sea in Malta, the Nazca lines, Teotihicán, the relatively recently discovered Gobekli Tepi, and much else, all prove the existence of an ancient civilisation with advanced technological knowledge, though one not based upon the materialistic assertions of our present civilisation. Atlantis is the name we give to that civilisation, whose main centre was the continent that sank, according to the exoteric account of Plato.[19] Materialistic scientists and technocrats with their atheistic views are the modern correspondence of the dogmatic religionists of the past century, in that they have similar narrowness of viewpoint in attitudes of mind, devoted to their pursuits. They have used the most devious, circumspect arguments to try to counter the overwhelming evidence of such a civilisation, as well as the antiquity of highly intelligent human thought. What they cannot thus deny they have totally ignored, shelved in the back rooms of their museums, provided inane, supine explanations to, or 'lost'. The wages and 'reputations' of too many narrow-minded academics are on the line in our 'esteemed' universities for them to admit the logical deductions, the truth of the evidence before them.

The 3/7 and the 7/3 Ray Ashrams that helped anchor spiritual power upon the physical plane and to pioneer the way of rightly directed thought via various cultural activities, politics and finance, in the service of civilisation also appeared at the beginning of the twentieth century. First, we have the work of the English Master J.M.H. (Justin Moreward Haig[20]) with respect to the 3/7 Ashram.

---

19 Some of the vast number of books on these subjects include: Adrian Gilbert, *Signs in the Sky* (Three Rivers Press, New York, 2000); Graham Hancock, *Fingerprints of the Gods* (Mandarin, London 1994) and *Underworld* (Penguin books, 2003); Peter Tompkins, *Secrets of the Great Pyramid* (Harper Colophon Books, New York, 1978); Robert Bauval and Adrian Gilbert, *The Orion Mystery* (Mandarin, London, 1994); Alan F. Alford, *Gods of the New Millennium* (New English Library, London, 1994); Otto Muck, *The Secrets of Atlantis,* (William Collins, 1976); Robert Schoch, *Voices of the Rocks* (Harmony, 1999); *Voyages of the Pyramid Builders* (Tarcher/Penguin, 2004), etc. There are also a host of worthwhile videos on the internet worth pursuing.

20 The nature of his work is indicated to us by *The Initiate* series of books written by one of his disciples, Cyril Scott: *The Initiate, The Initiate in the New World,* and *The Initiate in the Dark Cycle.* Published by Samuel Weiser, New York.

The 7/3 Ray Ashram was established via Nicholas Roerich's activities (1874 - 1947), a noteworthy artist, philosopher and cultural reformer, seen in his magnificent paintings and writings; as well as his work concerning the League of Nations, the Banner of Peace, and expeditions to the Altai region. The esoteric writings by Nicholas's wife Helena, under the auspices of Morya, must also be noted. (Whom we can presume to also have strong first Ray affiliations because of her close relations to the first Ray Chohan.) Her work, the *Agni Yoga* series of books, which provided spiritual succour for many disciples, was more esoteric than that of her husband. This indicates an incarnation of the first point of the 7/1 Ashram, making the combination of their united service work an important Hierarchical initiative.[21]

Their service also included countering the psychic predations of the dark brotherhood, which is hinted at in her writings. As much as was then possible to be revealed concerning such work was released, but is little exoterically understood, because this service work to humanity is done in the silent zones of the rightly focussed contemplative Mind. It necessitates the directive Will.

All third Ray Ashrams will now be further stimulated into heightened activity because of the advent of the epoch of the development of Mind. They will also bring into manifestation a more compassionately based and socially responsible reformation of the concepts of modern finance to try to offset the ruthless stranglehold over the money supply that the lords of materialism have over our societies. A most difficult task indeed.

The Mother's department is now specifically evoked, giving birth to the new era, where sound esoteric values are inculcated into human civilisation. Such was also expressed with the earlier appearance of Madame Blavatsky and the Theosophical Society. This society, with its motto 'There is no religion higher than truth', was brought into birth by the power of the first and second Rays. The activity of the Theosophical Society in the Victorian era and early twentieth century, however, is fundamentally along the third Ray line. This Ray, combined with the second, allowed Blavatsky to write her monumental works *Isis*

---

21 The first Ray sub-Ray facilitates access to Morya's purpose. Also, being a high Initiate, coupled with possessing the seventh Ray line, which grounds the power of the first Ray upon the physical plane, allows close affiliation with Morya.

Unveiled and *The Secret Doctrine* within the context of the conservative Victorian mindset. The third Ray also facilitated the work in India which is generally ruled by Capricorn, and thus the third Ray energy. Within that era we also have the advent of Spiritualism and the proselytising Christian religionists that were fervently determined to spread their exoteric doctrine to the world in general.

That the Theosophical Society endeavoured to synthesise all religions into one and integrate them with science betokens of the second Ray, whilst the power to instigate the new esoteric vision is a first Ray expression, hence Blavatsky claimed her Master was Morya. Morya also acted as pseudonym for the directives from Shambhala, plus from the new Mahāchohan.[22] It is difficult to properly describe Madame Blavatsky because her body was a vehicle that was used by a number of great Ones. The earlier occupant had effectively 'died' (whilst fighting for the liberation of Italy under Garibaldi) so that there could be a consciousness-transference by a higher entity, signifying a more exalted version of a transmitting medium or Tulku. Mostly she was overshadowed by the third Ray Chohan,[23] to lay the foundation for the later flowering of the third Ray purpose via the 3/7 and 7/3 Ashrams, and then for the work of the new Mahāchohan. As a consequence, the era of the abstract Mind could begin to rightfully influence human civilisation.

The Master D.K. also assisted in the writing of the *Secret Doctrine*, but his work via Alice Bailey helped intensify the necessary second Ray purpose via the third Ray (D.K. being the 2/3 Master) so that the entire externalising process of Hierarchy can be established in the appropriate doctrine of the wisdom religion. It is now close to 100 years since he first promulgated his teachings, hence the stage is set for the next higher level of the Hierarchical outpouring for the world disciple. The era of mass Initiation is nigh and the disciples of this new epoch must be appropriately prepared.

---

22 He was a Master veiled to the Theosophists during this time, as it was not his intent to reveal his purpose or influence during the formative years of the Theosophical Society.

23 See A.A. Bailey, *A Treatise on Cosmic Fire*, 749, where D.K. states: 'When a man has reached a certain development and can be of service to the world, cases occur when he is overshadowed by a great adept, or—as in the case of H.P.B.—by One greater than an adept'.

From the time of Blavatsky, the third Ray thus acted as a mother of all that was to come, to give birth to the new teachings, the child of the first and second Ray purpose. Subsidiary occult movements, such as the Order of the Golden Dawn (instigated by S.L. MacGregor Mathers) and the other groupings primarily based upon the study of the Kaballah took a seventh Ray *(iḍā nāḍī)* line of development as compared to the basic *piṅgalā nāḍī* line followed by Blavatsky and Bailey. The pioneering inception of the first, second, third and seventh Ray purpose by this means is necessary if the Kingdom of 'God' is to manifest in objective space via the externalising Hierarchy. The empowerment of these Rays upon the physical domain via the further activity of the members of Hierarchy will establish the *suṣumṇā nāḍī* line producing the inevitable externalisation of Shambhala, but this will take some centuries to fully manifest. The inevitable externalisation of this kingdom necessitates the practical expression of the highest energies that disciples can bear. Many must pass group Initiation testings so that the necessary energy quotient for the planet can be carried into the physical domain. A significant number of third degree Initiates must appear to bear the Shambhalic potency. Also, their united service work must set the conditionings that will make this possible.

The service work of an Ashram is accomplished via a number of disciples of the Master that incarnate to manifest its full power. Generally only the most senior disciples learn their Ashramic standing and of the general Hierarchical purpose. The bulk of the members only need to generate the service of their chosen professions without being aware of their Hierarchical links, or even that such a Hierarchy exists. They will nevertheless be subjectively inspired by the Master and senior members of Hierarchy. Thus the Ashramic purpose unfolds.

That a person is a member of a Master's Ashram is indicated by the possession of an innate ability or drive towards compassionate undertaking. This is developed over many lives of Bodhisattvic activity wherein accomplishments are demonstrated in a field of activity producing human betterment and the advancement of civilisation. It thus matters little whether that person believes in a personal God or not, is outwardly religious, atheistic, or agnostic. Neither does it concern one's placement in a society or the amount of degrees or qualifications to one's name. The criteria concerning Ashramic standing will always concern the true motivations behind a person's activities, plus a dedicated intelligent approach to serve humanity. Selfishness and prideful activity are not Hierarchical attributes, they must be replaced by beneficent and selfless activity. Cogent, compassionate religious leanings, however, will always indicate the development of Initiate characteristics, for that is the purpose of religion to produce.

An Initiate/Bodhisattva will always be seen to demonstrate goodwill, an open-minded attitude to all societies and their secular or religious views. Within this context the Initiate will seek to rectify injustice or lying propaganda, take courageous steps in new fields and directions in life, to overcome all impediments and obstacles to the possibility of further revelation or for the successful conclusion of a service arena. The capacity of the Initiate to serve, however, depends upon the Initiation level. The more advanced the Initiation level, generally the more esoteric the service done. All happens via appropriate stages of development. It is thus not necessary for the disciples concerned to know their Ashramic positioning or inner plane activity. No matter their esoteric knowledge, the service work of the great majority of serving disciples suffices to anchor Hierarchical energies and consequent expansions in consciousness. It is obvious for instance that human consciousness has been greatly expanded in all fields of investigation by our scientists, yet very few scientists acknowledge contact with a divinity within. The life of an Initiate may however be geared so that inner plane contact can be consciously obtained by way of meditation.

One life of quiet contemplation relegated to psycho-spiritual development is often balanced by a future life of much concrete activity, where the gain of that contemplative life is fully expressed in outward active service. The individual gains revelations, the fiery zeal of discovery and creativity by means of the intuition, and the overwhelming urging of the Sambhogakāya Flower working with the exigencies of the law of *karma*, which prompts the person to fulfil his/her destiny. All such revelation and activity may have been staged by a previous contemplative life. The cycles of incarnations correspond to the inward and outward breathing cycles of meditation with their periods of interlude.

Dreams, premonitions, direct voices, and intuitive flashes of revelation are all part of this process. Nothing happens by chance or accident. Newton, Pasteur, Edison, Tesla, Einstein, Van Gogh, Goethe, Spinoza, Karl Marx, Mozart, Beethoven, and the myriad other people of science and of genius were inspired in this way. All are Bodhisattvas; disciples, and sometimes actual incarnations of one or other of the Masters.

The period concerning the formation of a Ray Ashram always means an exuberant expansive activity on the physical plane by members of that Ashram. It necessitates the complete flowering of the type of service work delineated by the Ray qualities in question. Here we look to the major and subsidiary Ray colourings of the consciousness-streams constituting the Ashram.

The formation of the 2/5, 2/3, 7/5, 4/6, 6/5, 5/4, 5/6, 3/2, 3/7 and 7/3 Ashrams during the past 300 years are thus principally responsible for the outpouring of creativity in the arts, philosophy, science, technology, religion, labour (workers organisations) and business. They have caused, and are the mainstay, of our present scientifically biased civilisation. The activity of these Ahsrams have set the backdrop for the necessary future appearance of the Ashrams with a first Ray attribute. Their 'midwife' will be the third Ray of Mathematically Exact Activity. Together these Rays provide the potency of the expression of Maitreya's purpose in this new era. This purpose will be to bring to the fore the dominance of the second Ray of Love-Wisdom in world affairs, once the 1/2 and 2/1 Ray Ashrams manifest their service potential. Thereby the new world era or civilisation can be born. The work of the seventh Ray Ashrams will ground that purpose via the mirror-like activity of the fourth Ray.

Ray considerations

The focus when considering the Ashrams is with the Rays of the Sambhogakāya Flower, not the Rays of the personality. The personality Rays are transitory, changing from life to life, and thus are relatively illusional, apart from the effect they may have upon a particular life and the *saṃskāras* that flow on to be transformed in future cycles. Membership of an Ashram happens on the higher mental plane wherein resides the Sambhogakāya Flower. The major Ray quality of this

Flower,[24] plus the subsidiary Ray colouring, is thus the determining factor. At the fourth Initiation the Monadic Ray will supersede, which may change the Initiate's Ashramic affiliation. The Rays governing an individual can be considered as below.

The *Monadic Ray* (the *dharmakāyic* body) embodies one of three major Rays, with two subsidiary tiers of energy expression. (Only taken into account at the higher Initiations.) There are thus 21 possible Ray permutations.

The *Soul Ray* demonstrates one of seven Ray colourings, plus a subsidiary Ray, making 49 possible permutations. (These are normally permanent for the duration of the life of a Sambhogakāya Flower, but can change gradually over many lives from one Ray to a complementary Ray, according to Monadic Purpose.) Next there are the Rays of the transitory periodic vehicles, the three-fold personality:

Personality Ray	one of 7
Mental Ray	one of 7
Astral Ray	one of 7
Physical Ray	one of 7

The personality Ray governs the overriding qualities of the person. It necessitates a developed intelligence focussed upon a particular task or occupation in life. The mind must govern all aspects of the incarnate personality for this Ray to become defined. The mental, astral, and physical rays govern the forms of activity of these three bodies respectively. They enrich and also complicate the personal life, whilst any one Ray can dominate that life expression. They modify the astrological conditionings of the sign the person is born into. In turn they are affected by the Rays of the racial, national and group affiliation of which the individual is a part.

The Ray qualities are explained in the books *Esoteric Psychology*, Volumes I and II, by Alice Bailey, from which the section below is adapted. The keynotes presented are for disciples on the various Rays,

24 The Sambhogakāya Flower, *tathāgatagarbha*, and Soul are here viewed as synonymous terms as explained in the earlier volumes of this *Treatise on Mind*. D.K. also sometimes uses the term 'Ego' or Causal Body.

rather than for the average person. Meditators should carefully analyse which of the Rays they are conditioned by, as the entire path before them is determined by the fundamental Ray line they are upon, coupled with the available *karma* that conditions all life processes. As one treads the path of Initiation and gradually integrates with the Sambhogakāya Flower, then the personality Ray takes its attributes.

Ray One - Will or Power

- Colour: Red.
- Centre: Head.
- Planetary rulers: Vulcan, Pluto.
- Plane associated: the first, *ādi.*
- Keynotes: The will to achieve, to overcome all obstacles. Abstraction and the projected power of divinity. Detachment, singleness of purpose, clear vision, sense of right timing to act, the destroyer of the old decaying or outworn forms. (Thus preparing for the second Ray Builders.) The divine motivator, statesmanship, penetrative focus upon the plan, esotericism, perseverance along the way to liberation from all considerations of form.

The first Ray rules the Head centre because it is the centre of abstraction, governing the will to liberated domains. It incorporates all the other Ray attributes by integrating the third and second Rays into *manasic* purpose and directing all towards *dharmakāya.*

Ray Two - Love-Wisdom

- Colour: Indigo blue.
- Centre: Heart.
- Planetary ruler: Jupiter.
- Plane associated: the second, *anupādaka.*
- Keynotes: An inclusive embrace of consciousness that intuits the all within the One, producing revelatory insights of the mysteries of being/non-being. Attractive power, demonstrable wisdom, the divine Love that facilitates contact with the divinity that is the Heart of all. Expansive, inclusive reasoning that comprehends

the way of Initiation, illumined sight and visioning. The revealer of light and awakener of true religious undertaking. The master builder and geometrician with the power to salvage. *Bodhicitta*, the compassionate force of liberation.

Ray Three - Mathematically Exact Activity

- Colour: Emerald green.
- Centre: Throat.
- Planetary ruler: Saturn.
- Plane associated: the third, *ātma*.
- Keynotes: The active implementer of inclusive reason. Comprehensive detailed analysis of the nature of any manifesting phenomena. Revealer of the Clear Light of Mind. The illuminator and manipulator of energy, the sower and director of scientific activity, the keeper of the records. Business-like efficiency in all forms of activity, mathematically ordered rhythmic activity to serve the whole. The dispenser of the cycles of time, the divine interpreter and adjudicator of the effect of the second Ray Plan made concrete. The reaper of the effects of the field of mind. The Mother of the divine child.

Ray Four - Beautifying Harmony overcoming Conflict

- Colour: Yellow.
- Centre: Ājñā.
- Planetary ruler: Mercury.
- Plane associated: the fourth, *buddhi*.
- Keynotes: The painting of fields of beauty and peace. The zone of revelation that thunders in silence. Power to reveal the path, to express divinity and to penetrate the depths of matter. The ability to respond to the sounds from the harmony of the spheres, the silent voice from the Heart. The synthesiser of beauty, unity and harmony. The faculty to quickly evoke the intuition, right judgement, and pure reason. The divine intermediary. The mirror that reflects the good, the Plan, into the field of activity without distortion. The steed of Love. The vehicle for all *prāṇic* activity, the harmoniser of the landscape (the overall vision) in any field of activity. That

which links the highest to the lowest. Mathematical Exactitude in overcoming the field of conflict.

Ray Five - Scientific Reasoning

- Colour: Orange.
- Centres: Solar Plexus and Splenic centre I.[25]
- Planetary ruler: Venus.
- Plane associated: the fifth, the mental (*manas*).
- *Keynotes:* The light of reason and intelligent design, analytical discernment of the myriad differentiations of subjective and objective things as they are in truth. Truth comprehensibly articulated in the mind's eye. The revealer of the way and the nature of being. The initiator of deductive processes in the realm of mind. The energy that accedes the power to take Initiation. The dispenser of knowledge. The illuminator of the Plan. The analytical educator of the many. The scientific inquirer. The discriminator between the many and the One.

Ray Six - Devotion, Idealism

- Colour: Pink or sky blue.
- Centres: Sacral and Splenic centre II.
- Planetary rulers: Mars, Neptune.
- Plane associated: the sixth, the emotional/astral plane.
- *Keynotes:* Affectionate endeavour in all forms of human aspiration and interrelationships. The motivating energy that drives thought to conclusion. Endurance and fearlessness. The creator, then the battler to negate desire. The master of the Waters (of the emotions). Inclusive idealism, rightly invoked and directed. Sympathetic understanding to other's points of view. The generator, then pacifier of war-like tendencies. The vitaliser of all forms of rightful activity. The devotee to life, to 'God'. He who envisions the Plan. The divine warrior

---

25 This centre is included because of the way it manifests to cleanse *prāṇas*. The Solar Plexus centre also rules here when in the process of mastering the emotional body. When the Solar Plexus energies are united with desire then the sixth Ray qualifies its activities.

marching to battle. The sword-bearer of the light of truth. The crucifier and the one crucified in the field of service.

The above centres are chosen because the Sacral centre rules the energy of desire and helps produce attachments to objects in *saṃsāra,* whilst *prāṇas* from the Sacral centre help to cleanse the *saṃskāras* processed by Splenic centre II. However, for a great part of evolutionary time Sacral energies are integrated with those of the Solar Plexus centre, intensifying all types of glamour and emotions. The sixth and fifth Rays normally strongly influence the outpouring from the Solar Plexus centre, producing the ubiquitous desire-mind *(kāma-manas)* in human interrelations.

Ray Seven - Ceremonial Cyclic Activity, Actualising Power

- Colour: Violet.
- Centres: Base of Spine/Sacral centre integration with any of the higher centres.
- Planetary ruler: Uranus.
- Plane associated: the seventh, dense/etheric.
- *Keynotes:* Ritualised ordering of activity on the physical realms so that the power, wisdom and intelligence of the first three Rays can be made effective in practical terms. Power and endurance to create, to cooperate and to direct the organisation of evolving forms. The white magician. Ritualised ordering of the planned activity. The temple guardian. The builder of the quaternary of *saṃsāra.* The grounder of the will via cyclic activity. The one who reveals the beauty of the form. The holder of the keys to the mysteries of incarnate being. The Hierophant commanding the work of the devic life. The Master builder. That which relates the One to the other.

There are many other interpretations of the Ray qualities that the student will gain in time. The first three Rays are the three primordial Rays, Father-Son-Mother. They are Rays of synthesis, of aspect and of abstraction, and are properly expressed after the Mind is awakened. The remaining four Rays are Rays of attribute governing the vicissitudes of the form, the quaternary. The four evolve by way of the manifestation of ritualistic activity to control the attributes of mind in the world-play. The third Ray synthesises the qualities of the four Rays of attribute. Together they form the five Rays of Mind, making a pentagram:

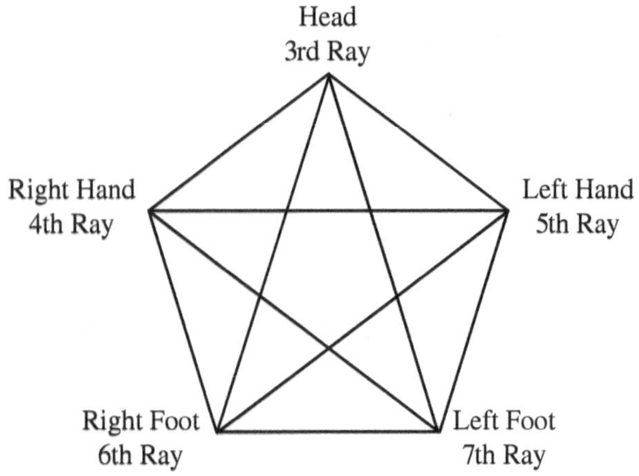

Figure 5. The pentad of the Rays of Mind[26]

By manifesting the differentiations of Mind, they are the direct expressions of the transmuted qualities of the five sense-consciousnesses and instincts. They are emanations of the five Jina wisdoms, hence govern the five *vāyus* of yoga philosophy, the five Elements (Aether, Air, Fire, Water and Earth) and the five planes of perception that are aspects of the Mother aspect of Deity. They find their field of application within Her bosom, hence humanity is succoured in them by way of mind, of all attributes of *manasic* development.

Though it is stated that the first of the Ashrams to form is that of the second Ray, this does not mean that all of its subsidiary sub-Ray Ashrams formed at the same time. The sequence of appearance according to the capacity of humanity to bear the related qualities was stretched over thousands of years. The last of the second Ray Ashrams to form prior to the birthing of the 2/1 Ashram was that of the Tibetan Master *Djwhal*

26 This arrangement of the pentagram integrates complementary Rays as lines of energy between the various points of the pentad.

Khul's. We can presume that he took his fifth Initiation in 1857[27], during which time the complete *maṇḍala* of his Ashram was externalised. Thus, his must be the 2/3 Ray Ashram (for the third Ray is the second last to evolve), where he assumes the central *bīja* point of the *maṇḍala*.

This Ashram is that of wisdom personified and embodies the sum of the active expression of Love-Wisdom in the formed realms. It synthesises and coordinates the qualities of the five sub-Rays of the second Ray that are the associated Rays of Mind.

The lower sub-Ray Ashrams of the second Ray are responsible for building the solid foundation of the teaching department of Hierarchy. They embody the fabric of the revelatory *dharma*, rightly weaving the tapestry of the wisdom teachings for all to behold and unfold. Being the head of the five Rays of Mind along the second Ray line, the 2/3 Ashram is consequently responsible for the glorification of the temple built on this foundation.

This tapestry veils the Shekinah[28] from the coarse reactions and incredulity of those that profane, who have not developed the Heart that would allow comprehension of the subtleties of impression. Such are 'dull of hearing'[29] and narrow visioned. The Shekinah reveals the glory of the light to those that conquer dullness of mind and reverently awaken their Hearts to the vision's delight. As they consciously tread the path to developed sight their eyes will not be blinded by the radiance of the Light. The Hierarchy stands, watches, and assiduously plans for the appearance of those who will develop such sight. For them we bow our heads, thus drawing them closer to the light of that glorious Day that is eternally with us.

The 2/1, 2/2 and 2/3 Ashrams embody the qualities of the inner sanctuary and sacred vestments of this second Ray flowering[30]. They manifest the blueprint of the Hierarchical Plan and project the

---

27 See *The Externalisation of the Hierarchy*, 522, where D.K. states in a passage written in January 1946 that 'I am still utilising the same physical body in which I took the fifth initiation, nearly ninety years ago.'

28 The Holy of Holies, the glory of the presence of the divine, here the most esoteric forms of *dharma*, of which the 2/1 and 2/3 ashrams are the custodians.

29 *Matt. 13:15.*

30 Once the 2/1 Ashram is fully formed.

wisdom of Shambhalic purpose, the Love of the light that sanctifies and provides benediction to all who will master the requirements to enter the portals of that Temple.

The Ashrams embodying the sub-Rays of the second Ray are responsible for the dissemination of the world's major religious and philosophical teachings. The highest aspect of such dissemination is the wisdom religion, which will establish centres for learning the mysteries of the Initiation process leading to Shambhala. However, many occult and sectarian groups have already appeared that distort such teachings. They manifest an obfuscating hindrance to the emanation of the higher wisdom teachings planned by the Masters of Wisdom.

Whenever any of the second Ray Ashrams have incarnated we find the impetus for the flowering of new religions or philosophic dispensations that emphasise the next step onwards for humanity. In the past we had the appearance of the general Mystery traditions, such as those of Eleusis, Delphi, Ephesus, Glastonbury; the incarnation of some of the early philosophers, such as Pythagoras, Plato, Lao-tzu, and the development of Mahāyāna Buddhism. We have the religious reforms of Akhenaton in Egypt, the appearance of Krishna and the other Avatars of Vishnu; the incarnations of the Buddha and Christ, etc. Such activity is supported by the rest of the second Ray line (the fourth and sixth Ray Ashrams) and then those of the Rays of Mind.[31]

The stage has been set for the next major advent of this continuous development, which may be defined as the Power-of-Love in service. Thus we have the physical plane establishment of the 2/1, 1/2 and subsidiary first Ray Ashrams that embody the qualities of this power, via the development of the Will-to-Love by disciples. The resultant magnetic radiance will blaze the path and build the foundations for the consequent externalisation of the entire Council of Bodhisattvas, the embodiment of the Heart of our planetary Life.

The Ashrams and Masters that are directly concerned with this present stage of Hierarchical externalisation, and consequently with the appearance of the new world religion, are a focus of this book. This 2/1 and 1/2 energy, the 'missing capstone' fitted on top of the pyramidical

---

31 Hence the Buddha was along the fourth Ray, but the esoteric Mahāyāna doctrines that evolved from him were second Ray.

structure of Hierarchy, is central to the new dispensation, of which all other Ray lines can be considered to be subsidiaries, as all are really aspects of this fundamental Ray of Love. The complete implementation of this capstone will at least take another two hundred years because of the problematic attributes of the candidates of the 2/1 Ray line.

Before this power can manifest, the wisdom principle has to be properly anchored. Humanity must have a true understanding as to the way of Love before they can rightly handle the power of its implications in the world of form, as perceived from an energy viewpoint. Without such a foundation, the flow of the will-power Ray would but intensify and exacerbate the muddled fanatically zealous, intolerant, and narrow-minded tendencies of the religious in the world, as well as in the scientific community. Teachings concerning love and wisdom have obviously been the main fare of a host of religious teachers for millennia, however, the true import of what this energy implies upon a vast planet wide and cosmic scale has largely only been hinted at. Also, its relation to the Initiation path has been veiled prior to the teachings found in the Bailey books.

The nature of undertaking the path of Initiation must now be emphasised, to prepare many worthy candidates to follow it. This path represented the secret portion of the ancient Mystery Schools, and the often distorted and corrupted guarded rites and secrets of occult fraternities. We also have the doctrine of the initiation stages of the various Buddhist and Hindu Tantras, which though purportedly esoteric, deal with the elementary stages of the path (or with the left hand path), unless taught by an enlightened being, in which case the veils are removed during the praxis.

We will find that the main Ray energies concerned with the present Hierarchical educational process are the first, second, third and seventh manifesting via the general expression of the fourth. The fifth and sixth Rays shall not be empowered because of the inordinate success of their impetus over the past few centuries, unfortunately producing also the unavoidable negative consequences already mentioned with respect to the evils of our present civilisation.

D.K.'s writings via A.A. Bailey and those of H.P. Blavatsky served to lay the true esoteric foundation of such understanding. Other teachers helped sow the seeds for a proper dialogue between Eastern and Western religious streams on a more exoteric or devotional level. Others awakened interest in ancient religious history, non-orthodox archaeological studies, psychic phenomena, and perceptive spiritual insights in all fields of investigation. They helped to prepare the field into which the new revelations must take root.

The Will or Power-of-Love (*bodhicitta*) will serve to eradicate all forms of evil sharing, separative intent, and the related arenas of lying propaganda and distortions of truth. These are arenas where grey and dark hues may be found on all the levels of experience. This power will shed light into mysteries hitherto unsolved and begin to lift the veil of the supernal glory of the Shekinah for all to behold. It will blaze the way with Fiery energy from Shambhala that will empower the good in all that people can see and do. It will enable progressive changes that will rectify the imbalances causing all phases of disease, wherever their expression may be found within the planet or within us. It will herald the dawning of the new era, with miraculous gifts of healing brought by the wings of power speeding through the Air. Lightning bolts from the empowered *vajra* of the Will-of-Love will everywhere seek their mark. The new Temples of the Mysteries will be established in the West and the East, linking the south to the north, that will allow the many groups of aspiring ones to be Initiated in the way of Love supreme via various meditative disciplines.

Written in the language of the Initiated, such prophecies manifest many revelations for those who have developed the eyes with which to see. The time is imminent, it is happening now. The process starts from a seed and grows into a new *bodhi* tree, a tree of Initiation for all upon the planet that pass the requirements. This new 'tree' will take the exigencies of this modern era into account and increased receptivity to the Will energy from Shambhala.

The Ashrams in parenthesis in Figure 4 (2/2, 7/7, 4/4, and 6/6) are not Ashrams in the proper sense, in that they do not have Masters of Wisdom presiding over them. They are minor 'holding' Ashrams that exist for the guidance and training of the Souls that have that purified Ray colouring. Because they bear the most purified flame of the expressed Ray, each is the direct seat of power of a Chohan of the Ray. This flame is then diffused into all the other sub-Ray qualities of that fundamental Ray, thus manifesting the complete *maṇḍala* of expression embodied by the Chohan. He works directly with all who have taken their third Initiation. The Masters under him train disciples to take this Initiation, which enlightens one into the Sambhogakāya level of expression, permitting access to Shambhala. The first two Initiations are but Initiations on the threshold of enlightenment.

Those Ashrams that are still forming and have at the centre of their Ashramic sphere an Initiate of the fourth or third degree are found upon the higher mental plane. Their task is to evolve the specific characteristics of their Ray line, for the central point to eventually embody the power of a Master of Wisdom. The fully formed Ashrams of the Masters exist on the buddhic plane.

Though a Master's Ashram consists of all disciples upon his Ray quality, there are also incorporated within it the members of other Ashrams that need the rounding out of their equipment of response and life experiences that a similar Ray line can teach. Some Initiates stay in other related Ashrams for some lives, to develop needed qualities, or assist in some important task. Everything concerning Ashramic evolution and its interrelationships is fluid and dynamic, pulsatingly active and alive. Nothing is static, though all is bathed in a depth of serenity and quietude unknowable to those active in the material world.

The appearance of an Ashram upon the buddhic plane (thus becoming a direct part of the *nāḍī* system of the incarnate Logos) allows an Ashram to externalise its full Power on the dense physical plane. It generally takes one Initiate of the fourth degree and eight of the third degree of that Ray line to evolve before a Master of Wisdom can assume his seat of Power within an Ashram and direct events from *ātmic* levels. These eight are then considered 'heart-born sons of the Master'.[32] They disseminate the energies and purpose of the Master in accord with the symbolism of the eight directions of space, as was detailed in Volume 4 of this *Treatise on Mind* with respect to the eight Mahābodhisattvas. They all share the burden of the potency of the energies that must flow through them.

All happens according to the law of group evolution and takes much time. Many millennia pass before an Ashram can emerge from

---

32 Fourth degree Initiates come under the direct guidance of the Chohan of the Ray.

out of the ranks of humanity. Many group transformations will have happened in a similar manner as happens individually to all on the path to enlightenment. Ashramic members always incarnate in relation to a particular field of service, though not always in the same country, religion, or even generation, for the service work started is usually carried through from one incarnation to the next. The appearance of the full power of an Ashram does not properly manifest until the one who is to be a Master can pass the testings related to taking the fifth Initiation. The world also needs to be adequately prepared to incorporate the related energies and qualities that such empowerment would present.

Some Initiates of the fourth degree may have to wait centuries before conditions are ripe for the distribution of the energies and qualities they would possess as Masters. Others may take their fourth and fifth Initiations in one life. All is dependent upon world need.

Undue development of any Ray line without adequate prevision and integration with what is happening upon the rest of the world sphere could be disastrous. Evolution must progress in an ordered sequence, but the factor of human free will is inviolate. An example of near disaster is the rapid advancement of the Rays of Mind before humanity was properly grounded in Love. Consequently, the scientific community has produced the nuclear bomb, which threatens the human population with extinction because of the power hungry and aggressive stance of the politicians of some nations that possess these weapons. This was a premature development, as human selfishness, national power projection, massed indoctrination, and separative attitudes are far too rampant. There is a real possibility of the misuse of such weaponry with obvious catastrophic results. Rampant pollution of the sum of our biosphere, the incorporation of genetically modified organisms and food, plus the worldwide rapine of our forest reserves (and other such effects) also point towards possible global disaster. We are now passing through the higher correspondence of the disastrous period in Atlantis that necessitated the sinking of that continent. The Lords of Shambhala, however, are carefully monitoring the situation to ensure that things work out according to Plan.

Rectification necessitates infusing humanity with qualities that would rightly steer them towards the ways of Love-Wisdom, and not further engender those of the mind. The fifth Ray is thus being partially withdrawn, taking with it many of the personnel of the Ashrams embodying that Ray. The demonstration of fifth Ray qualities is however an essential basis for future growth, as intelligence is the necessary vehicle for Love if *wisdom* is to be the gain. The aim is to make Lords of Wisdom out of humanity, rather than devotional, spiritual sycophants.

The first Ray is only just beginning to project its power, thus there are mass demonstrations against many social evils and war, as well as producing a corresponding militarism of those in power, a new arms race that is threatening world war again. It has also helped empower the forces of evil in their bid to control all planetary affairs. The third Ray outpouring (now somewhat replacing the partially withdrawing fifth Ray) has produced much concern by disciples over the throttlehold of financiers upon our governments, the arms race, worldwide pollution and the unequal distribution of the world's resources. It is producing astute thinkers in all social issues, to counter the lying propaganda of the main stream media outlets. The second Ray outpouring has produced a consequent rapid explosion of concepts of new, more enlightened ideas and alternative societies by those that advocate a compassionate and broadminded, less materialistic approach to life.

Testings for the fifth Initiation concern the Initiate's ability to organise his/her group on the physical plane so that the fiat of that Ashram is sounded in terms of service work rendered in accord with the plan for that cycle. Things are planned in minute detail and the tests related to the flowering of an Ashram take much time.

As previously noted, there will now be a predominance of high Initiates incarnate as women. This new feminine dispensation can then be considered a new incarnation for the Hierarchy, bringing into manifestation the epoch of the Mother of the World on this earth. By 'feminine' is not meant a matriarchate, but rather, the nurturing, creative, caring, compassionate attributes of the feminine disposition coming to the fore via the development of attributes of the higher Mind. Awakening such a Mind is now the focus of development for the world's aspirants. It is considered feminine when directed to solving the problems of material plane affairs by countering the effects of the separative, self-focussed, manipulative, war-like attributes of the empirical mind that have governed the patriarchal human civilisations humanity has struggled through for millennia. The widespread awakening of Mind then births the new Aquarian era proper, wherein the Leonine egotistic activity[33] is replaced by the more humble dispensation of the water bearer. This will produce profound changes in how humanity is governed and what our societies consider as important. For example, the world's massively excessive military industrial complex will lose much of its funding. Socially oriented programs and commitments by governments to eliminate poverty and other social ills that affect right nurturing and education of children will instead become the new priority. The urban environments will be beautified by altering the consciousness of those that reside therein.

The 7/3 Ashram formed in the early 20th century, whilst the 1/2 Ashram is yet to form on *buddhic* realms, being next in line for the projection of its full service work and extended power on the earth. Such power will inaugurate the complete expression of the second Ray cycle. The 1/2 Ray heralds the many major world changes to come, though its effects will be more esoteric than exoteric, as its Ray combination represents a most effective potency to directly counter the energies of the dark brotherhood in all fields of expression within the planet's *nāḍīs*. Many of this Ray line will also be intensely active in social and political activism. It is the most vibrant cleansing potency. Many young members of this Ashram will undergo such activity with zealous intensity to counter the worst effects of people's materialistic attitudes and aberrant thinking.

When speaking of the Hierarchy of Enlightened Being then our consideration is upon the third, fourth and fifth levels of Shambhala, directing the energies of Amoghasiddhi, Ratnasambhava and Amitābha to rightly play upon and through humanity. The Hierarchy is the Heart centre of the Logos of this planet and incorporates the way that this centre can gradually govern the activities of the centres below the diaphragm, especially the planetary Solar Plexus centre. (Representing the matrix of the bulk of human activity.) The *kāma-manasic* energies expressed by this centre have been intensified and perverted upon a vast scale by humanity.

---

33 Leo is the polar opposite of Aquarius.

The Masters view the forces that afflict humanity in the form of the *prāṇas* of various hues - mostly greyish, dull greens, browns and deep grey overtones, though with arenas of intensities of aberrant pinks, greens, yellow, etc. Various malicious, fearsome energies and entities can be seen, with members of the dark brotherhood preying upon humanity to sustain the base conditions in human societies whereby these dark ones can govern their lives. Karmically such malicious forms are bound to humanity because humanity sows the qualities sustaining their types of activity. Hierarchy must therefore deal with their dark brothers as factors of human livingness, which need to be karmically expelled by humanity itself. This happens in a similar way that the individual disciple must battle with the forces of their base *saṃskāras*, as was explained in Volume 5A. Thus the aberrant and grey shades of the *prāṇas* generated by humanity will be gradually cleansed and eventually directed to the higher centres. This constitutes the way to enlightenment for humanity. Many groups of people will thus eventually become Bodhisattvas, so that the world can become sanctified and cleansed of the evils that presently afflict it.

The way Hierarchy sends disciples to produce stimulatory effects within humanity depends upon which of the *chakras* of humanity need awakening. As various minor centres are awakened appropriately, so the integrating petals in the Splenic, Solar Plexus or Throat centres will be made more vibrant. The considerations are quite intricate, as national, religious and social groups can all be viewed in the form of interrelated minor *chakras* and associated *prāṇas*. There are also two major types of humanity upon the planet to consider,[34] plus the other kingdoms of Nature and the *devas*. All humans share the reticulation of interwoven *karma* at differing levels of development, and must inevitably be taught to travel the way to liberation by finding their place within Hierarchy.

The departmental heads and the Hierarchical Heart centre

The three departmental heads of Hierarchy embody the triad of:

34 Moon and earth Chain humanity.

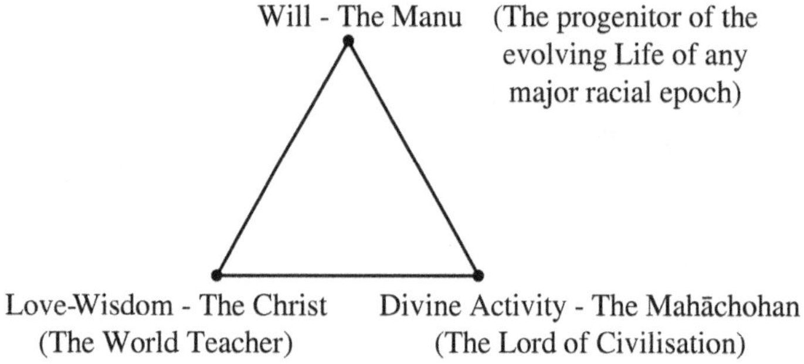

Figure 6. The departmental heads of Hierarchy

Though Ray considerations govern the organisation and progress of the Hierarchy at the fourth and fifth Shambhalic levels, other esoteric factors are taken into account as to the placing of the members of the higher levels. There are only a limited number of positions available for the present Shambhalic *maṇḍala* of the earth, and many cosmic paths beckon. Padmasambhava[35] and the one who was Tsongkhapa (the European Chohan), for instance, are two who are preparing to sever their placement in the present *maṇḍala* and enter upon their chosen cosmic paths after this new era has awakened. Their long, arduous servitude to this planet will then have borne the necessary fruits.

The first Ray Chohan (Morya) will become the Manu of the oncoming sixth Root Race of humanity, when the principle of love will be the guiding factor controlling humanity's evolutionary purpose, and not the intelligence that is the focus nowadays. The second Ray Chohan, K.H.,[36] will take the role of the Christ in this new world cycle.

Both Padmasambhava and Tsongkhapa heralded originally from second Ray Ashrams, despite the fact that Padmasambhava is often placed within the first Ray line. This is partly because of his relative spiritual age, as all that have attained the higher Initiations must of necessity develop first Ray attributes. This Ray opens the doors to Shambhala. Another aspect that facilitates the demonstration of the first

35 His *nom de plume* is given as Master Jupiter in the esoteric literature. He is also known as Guru Rinpoche, 'the precious guru' to the Tibetans.

36 In an earlier cycle he was also Akhenaton, the heretical Pharaoh, who tried to make the worship of the life-giving rays from the sun (Aten) the state religion.

Ray is that his subsidiary Ray was the seventh at the early formative period of Hierarchy, which is a reflex of the first Ray. The Rays are related thusly:

1 The first Ray
— The mirror
7 The seventh Ray grounds the first Ray Will into the formed realms through the materialising power of rightly expressed cyclic activity via the fourth Ray. (The dividing or fraction line under the one.)

There is thus a 1-4-7 relation of the demonstration of power via the quality that tends to harmonise all forms of strife. The line of transmission of the first Ray is also via the *iḍā* line, Rays 1-3-5-7. Similarly, the line of transmission of the second Ray is via the *piṅgalā* line, Rays 2-4-6.[37]

Padmasambhava and Tsongkhapa have, however, evolved past general Ray considerations, thus they are no longer involved with any specific Ashram, but generally form an esoteric trinity with either the blue or green Christs, and sometimes directly with any other member of the first three levels of Shambhala, depending upon planetary purpose at any time. They thus help to appropriately modify the energies that must be borne into manifestation to fulfil the current plan for the expansion of human consciousness.

Energy generally manifests in triune fashion in accordance with the attributes of the *iḍā, piṅgalā* and *suṣumṇā nāḍīs.*[38] This is the basis for the power of Neptune's trident, a version of the *khaṭvāṅga*[39] wielded

---

37 The *suṣumṇā* line can be considered the 1-4-7 relation.

38 Upon our planet, for instance, the main sources of energy are combustible fuels derived from the sun (such as wood, coal, oil), from electro-magnetic activity and from nuclear reactors. To these we can add an additional triad of: cosmic rays, gravity and geo-thermal. The Rays governing these energies are: Ray 1—cosmic rays, Ray 2—direct solar energy, Ray 3—gravity, Ray 4—electro-magnetism, Ray 5—radioactivity, Ray 6—fossil fuels and plant material, Ray 7—geo-thermal (including from minerals).

39 This ritual staff expressing the adamantine power of the guru was explained in Volume 5. Male *khaṭvāṅgas* are tipped by a *vajra* and the female form is tipped by a trident. Neptune is God of the Waters, therefore this trident concerns the mastery of the entire Watery disposition, the accomplishment of a *siddha*.

by Padmasambhava, in the form depicted in Figure 7 with respect to the projection of Ashramic purpose. It is the fundamental energy that influences everyone, as dynamic Love lies at the Heart of all. The Chohans Morya, K.H., and Jesus project this energy to the rest of the Hierarchy and thence the sum of the world sphere. The positioning of the points of this trident changes according to need during any particular epoch.

The above-mentioned Chohans normally work in the closest cooperation and incarnate in relation to a similar field of service. In the Gospel story for instance, John the Baptist was an incarnation of the Chohan Morya, Jesus was the direct bearer of the Christ principle for the world, and K.H. was Lazarus. All three took their fourth Initiation in that life. For John the Baptist this was at the time of the severance of his head. (Symbolising the severance of the sphere of the Spirit from the form nature, a first Ray method for taking Initiation.) Lazarus (the one whom Jesus loved[40]) took this Initiation by having been 'risen from the dead' after four days and nights in what was effectively the tomb of materiality. Lazarus thus re-enacted the ancient system of Initiation for us, in a crypt or tomb prepared for those that are to die to the vicissitudes of life. This represents a second Ray method of taking Initiation. Rising from the dead is a feat Jesus would accomplish after his crucifixion, which thereby hinted at taking the fifth Initiation.

The process of taking the fourth Initiation was played out exoterically by Jesus upon the world stage in the steps that led to his crucifixion. Everyone on the planet could consequently gain an understanding of what was needed upon this path, and to try to emulate the munificent feat of this great Bodhisattva. The Initiates achieve this inwardly as they accomplish the necessary mastery of the Airy Element and thus the attainment of *śūnyatā*.

Jesus epitomised the mode of attaining *śūnyatā* outwardly by a third Ray method in the incidents that led to the crucifixion experience, and the crucifixion itself,[41] at a similar time that the *prajñāpāramitā* teachings, the definitive teachings of the doctrine of the Void, were first given to the world. The correlation of the simultaneous outpouring of the same type of teaching, one for inward meditative practice, and

---

40 *John 11:5* and *11:36*.

41 As explained in Volume 6, chapter 6, which deals with the third to the fifth Initiations.

the other as an example of outer Bodhisattvic service work, has never been comprehended by the world's philosophers. It serves as a prime example of the way that the Council of Bodhisattvas work to integrate the appropriate teachings needed for both the Eastern and Western hemispheres of world service.

Gautama earlier demonstrated in an outward manner the way to undertake the third Initiation for the world by the symbolism of the events leading to him sitting under the *bodhi* tree and his subsequent lifestyle. Maitreya will consequently demonstrate outwardly the undertaking of the fifth Initiation for the uncomprehending world disciple, who must manifest a similar undertaking inwardly.

Figure 7 indicates the nature of the manifestation of the principle of Love upon the planet at this present stage of human evolution, where the devotional religions have been a focus for the expression of second Ray purpose. This is superseded by the path of discipleship wherein the desire-emotions are to be mastered. Humanity is still far too emotionally polarised to properly accommodate the more refined aspects of Love-Wisdom, but aspiration thereto is now thoroughly promoted. The Bodhisattva path, producing the experience of *śūnyatā,* presents the appropriate vehicle for this Love principle, but as of yet very few people have the wherewithal to procure the Void as the heart of the dispensation of Love. The majority of them are far too devotional in the application of their religion to be able to directly access the power of what *śūnyatā* veils. When Padmasambhava utilised its potency he substituted the seventh Ray as the central prong, rather than the sixth Ray, which then allowed him to focus upon the demonstration of great *siddhis*, 'occult magical power', to accomplish his task. This energy then established the Nyingma tradition of Tibet.[42]

The very popular life story in Tibet of Milarepa concerning the establishment of the succeeding Kargupta order should also be noted. Marpa, his guru,[43] embodied a first Ray attribute. Milarepa, a convert from the black Tantric practices, became a very devoted student, who

42 The sixth and seventh Ray combination of energies (pink and violet) is reflected in the colouration of the robes that the Tibetan monks wear.

43 He was a later incarnation of Guru Rinpoche, as only one of his spiritual stature could play such a role for Milarepa.

was put through considerable suffering and trials to atone for his psychic misdeeds before Marpa would give him the meditation teachings he craved. A strong devotional aspect of the Tibetan religion was fostered by Milarepa's life, as vast numbers of the lay population were inspired by the stories of his deeds. He embodied the sixth Ray energy dispensation that could feed the needs of the devotional Tibetans and became the central prong of the trident that was established. Of his three most important disciples after Milarepa's death, the inheritance of the wisdom teachings went to sGam po pa (the foremost of his three most important disciples), who took the second Ray position and established the monastic system for the order. Shiwa Aui[44] manifested a first Ray dispensation via adopting the pure yogic discipline of the Six Yogas of Naropa in the caves of the mountains of Tibet. He instructed the most worthwhile Initiates of the order in the practical arts of Tantric meditation in the cold mountainous air of his retreats. sGam po pa was the heart of the Love-Wisdom aspect of this dispensation. Rechungpa manifested the activity aspect by being still allured to worldly living. By becoming attached to a female companion for a while,[45] it signified that of the three he was closest to ordinary humanity in temperament.

In this interrelation we have a cyclic reappearance in the new setting from their former incarnation of Jesus' time, where Milarepa was a later incarnation of Jesus, sGam po pa a later incarnation of Lazarus, Rechungpa of Peter, and later incarnated as D.K., whilst Shiwa Aui was Andrew, and later the new Mahāchohan. As stated, Peter as the 'rock' upon which the foundation of the Christ's 'church' could be built refers to the esoteric 'church' signified by the externalising Hierarchy. He can do this by virtue of his 2/3 Ray dispensation and because esoterically he was closer to humanity than the abovementioned Initiates. Similarly, he was the 'rock' or foundation for the activity of the disciples that arrived after Milarepa gained his enlightenment, being the first of

---

44 The spelling here is taken from Garma C.C. Chang's *The Hundred Thousand Songs of Milarepa* (University Books, 1962). Evans-Wentz in *Tibet's Great Yogī Milarepa* (Oxford University Press, 1951), uses Shiwa-Wöd-Repa. The name means 'the Cotton-clad Light of Peace' (Chang, Vol. 1, 183).

45 The reference here is to him having an affiliation for a while with a noblewoman, Lady Dembu, and 'In order to free him from this hindrance, Milarepa transformed himself into a beggar and came to Rechungpa for alms'. (Chang, Vol 2, 637.)

his Heart-born Sons to appear. The united activity of the externalised Hierarchy in human affairs will rapidly foster the epoch of the rulership of wisdom upon this planet, facilitating the ability of the Christ energy *(bodhicitta)* to awaken every heart, inspiring the masses to manifest more enlightened forms of activity.

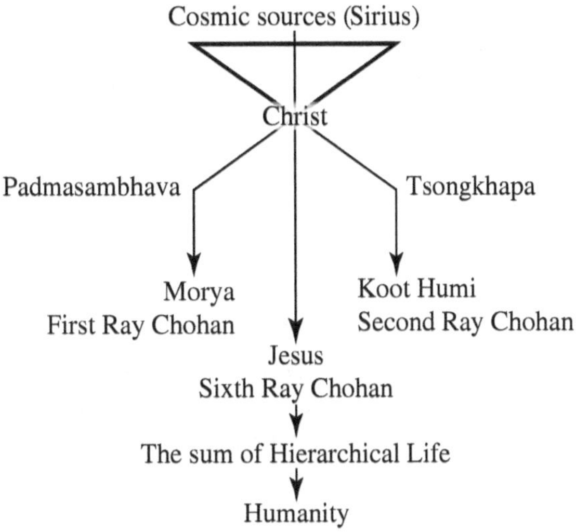

Figure 7. Dynamic Love as a triune energy

Here is seen an example of the integrated work of the manifestation of the great ones from cycle to cycle of spiritual accomplishment, as all evolve together in the great work of refining spiritual gold from the matrix of humanity. Though this information is unverifiable, except to those with enlightened vision, nevertheless the esoteric truths here outlined exemplify a certain logic underlying the sequences of the rebirths of any entity. Nothing happens haphazardly.

The three ways of attaining Initiation depicted above present worthy symbolism to note:

- *The severance of the head,* a first Ray method of Initiation. *Symbol,* the sphere. This is the sphere of the Monad *(dharmakāya)* into which the Initiate is abstracted.
- *The tomb experience*, a second Ray method of Initiation. *Symbol,* the quaternary. The implication here is to the four cosmic ethers

and the seat of power that is the *śūnyatā-saṃsāra* nexus from which the Initiate now works. It also signifies death to the lower four (signifying the 'tomb'), consisting of the mind, astral body, the ethers and dense form, thus the sum of *saṃsāric* life.

- *The crucifixion,* a third Ray method of Initiation. *Symbol,* the cross. This is the fixed cross of the heavens standing above the world stage, from which the Initiate pours out his/her Heart's Blood. This form of taking the fourth Initiation governs the Rays of Mind in general, from where the purpose of the Dhyāni Buddhas demonstrate their potency. The former method of travelling the Wheel of Life by means of the mutable cross has been superseded and transformed into the dynamism of the Heart's purpose, fixed in intent upon eliminating the pains of the suffering ones.

The integration of the symbolism of these forms of Initiation energises the eight directions of space and also produces the template for the construction of most *maṇḍalas,* specifically those depicting the symbolism of the way of manifestation of the Dhyāni Buddhas. The symbols can be interrelated thus:

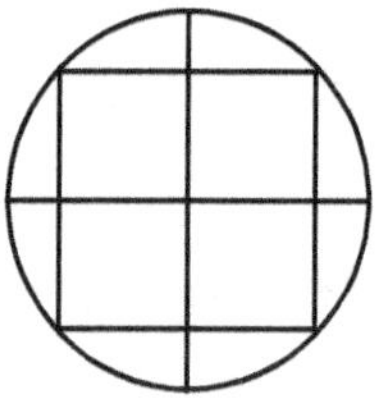

Figure 8. The *maṇḍalic* template

The *head* becomes the sphere of life that includes the activity of all that must walk the way to liberation. It signifies the source of light, Love and Life; illuminating all in their journey through darkness, to succour their ability to Love and presenting opportunity for enlightenment on their path to Buddhahood.[46] The *sword* that severed the head becomes the sword of life that dissects this figure into the eight directions of space. (Represented by the four arms of the cross and the four corners

46 From the Christian perspective, this would be seen as the path to 'God'.

of the square.) It thus cleanly projects the triune energy it wields (the two cutting edges plus the central line of strength) in any of these directions according to the purpose of the Initiate.

The square (or rectangle) becomes the Throne of 'God', the lotus base upon which the Buddhas and Bodhisattvas sit, before which all life is crucified. It also represents the opening door to the realms of life supernal, to which the Initiate can now enter. The cross becomes the burden of Love carried by the Initiate that stands poised before the Throne, which projects the qualities of what it veils (or the deity that sits upon it) to the four quadrants in space via the four Elements.

The 4 + 4 = 8 becomes the 12 when the cross manifests as mutable activity, reflecting its qualities into the formed realms. It spins to mirror itself outwardly to the four directions. The originating motion of the severing sword takes the guise of the *cardinal cross,* the cross of abstraction, resolution, and of dynamic intent.

The cardinal cross. The Father—Monad—Life, the first Ray dispensation of Will or Power, the originating ideation. Here it is pointed downwards towards materiality, but can be oriented towards any of the other directions of space.

The fixed cross. The Son—Soul—Consciousness, the second Ray dispensation of Love-Wisdom. It concerns the gain of the incarnate expression in the field of life. Consciousness is fixed and poised on its own realm and radiates its expression in all the directions of space.

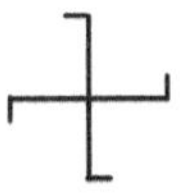

The mutable cross. The Mother—Form—Activity, the third Ray dispensation of Divine Activity; the continuous, mutable, cyclic personality expression into the realms of form. Thus there is the ingathering of experiences from the directions associated with its arms.

The Hierarchical twelve-petalled lotus

The twelve spokes of dynamic mutable activity associated with the interrelation of these crosses become the Hierarchical twelve-petalled lotus when pervaded with the consciousness aspect. It is the Heart of Life. Each petal becomes an open door to the influx of zodiacal energies to and from the world sphere. The inner council of Hierarchy embody the petals of this lotus and thus the related sign of the zodiac, according to the relative spiritual age of its members.

Though one's spiritual age generally has a reference to degree of Initiation, it is also directly related to the capacity of the Initiate to absorb and project intensified energies, specifically of the first and second Ray combination. It implicates the extensive nature of a developed sacrificial intent and esoteric sight, which inevitably produces far-reaching cosmic contacts.

With respect to Hierarchy, it is best to think of a Heart centre consisting of the eight armed cross of the Mahābodhisattvas, integrated with a pentad of great Ones incorporating the Shambhalic Mind. The focus of this pentad manifests via Vajrapāṇi (the Mahāchohan, one of the eight Mahābodhisattvas), who embodies the main energies constituting the Head centre, as shown in Figure 3.[47] The five great Ones referred to are the Manu, the blue Christ, the Phoenician, Tsongkhapa and Guru Rinpoche. It is however, best to view the Manu (the director of the streams of Life upon our planet) as a direct representative of Shambhala, demonstrating first Ray potencies, making the blue Christ the true Heart of Hierarchy, its guiding principle along the second Ray line. Omitting the Manu, we therefore have the twelve points of the Hierarchical Heart centre. Also, it is important to not form too rigid a mental construct concerning any of the great Ones, as they manifest quite fluid positions, with many interrelated mutable activities within the context of a serene, dynamic meditation-Mind that all share.

Within the context of the energy of Vajrapāṇi, the following arrangement can be observed. The new Mahāchohan and Guru Rinpoche form a fixed cross aspect (with their *deva* compliments) governing the activity of the Hierarchical Solar Plexus in the Head centre. The Christ, Tsongkhapa and *deva* compliments manifest a similar role with respect to the Hierarchical Heart in the Head centre. The Phoenician governs the activity of the Hierarchical Throat in the Head centre (assisted by

47 Detail concerning this *maṇḍala* was provided in Volume 4, chapter 9, to which the reader should refer.

the third Buddha of Activity). This represents the major mode of activity of the Head lotus in the manner described in chapter 7 of Volume 5A, as far as the enlightenment of humanity is concerned.[48] As we move from major petals to minor ones in the Head lotus, so we move down the planes of perception, to incorporate the activities of the lesser Initiates and then the world disciples in general.

The pentad integrates with the Lords of the seven Ray lines according to need. Consequently, to explain the complete activity of this centre with respect to Hierarchy, one must refer to the information in Volume 5A, and to transpose the conversion process of *saṃskāras* of an individual to that associated with humanity as a whole. Bodhisattvic activity therefore relates to their incarnation into the field of humanity as the major forces of this conversion process. Their aim thereby is transforming the normally self-centred, emotional and avaricious human consciousnesses so that an exalted level of planetary awakening is produced.

In such correlation the reader can obtain the true nature of all Bodhisattvic activity and the mode of the considerations of the enlightened with respect to the way that they incarnate. The theriomorphic deities presented in Volume 5A then represent the mental-emotional forces developed by humanity. One must also include the activity of the *deva* kingdom in one's assessment, plus their transformative potencies upon the realm of mind/Mind, represented by the Herukas. Also taken into account then is the way that human *karma* can be cleansed and transformed.

Each of the great Ones are specialists in the nature of the activities of the respective centres they embody in the planetary whole, and consequently work with the related transformative forces associated with the five *vayus (prāṇic paths)*. Vast is the interlocking and interweaving of all such activity manifesting within their meditation Minds. All who meditate upon the path to enlightenment are therefore learning the art of eventual planetary transformation as they undertake the task of transforming their own individual *saṃskāras*.

The petals of the Hierarchical Heart centre as it presently conditions the governing members of Hierarchy is shown below:

---

48 See Volume 5A pages 377-432.

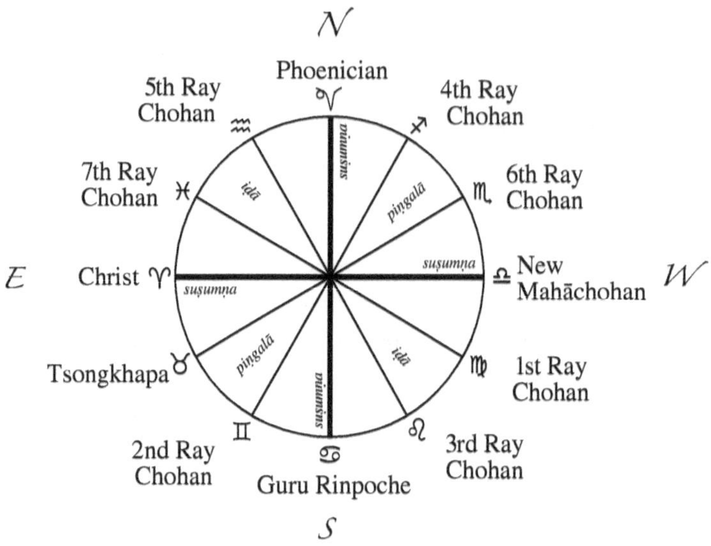

Figure 9. The Hierarchical Heart centre

The above figure presents a fusion of the second and third level of the Shambhalic *maṇḍala*. First, we see the major fixed cross constituted by the advanced members of this Heart centre. The remaining eight Mahābodhisattvas (including Tsongkhapa) are then incorporated, who take the intermediate petals (or spokes) of this centre. All Mahābodhisattvas can also be considered in terms of their polar opposites on the diagram and function accordingly. The focus is principally to the turning of the wheel of the directing energies from Shambhala and cosmic sources to humanity and then the response of humanity towards what the religious call the Kingdom of 'God'. Once received from Shambhala, the energies are toned down and transformed in a way that they can be utilised in the field of illusion (*saṃsāra)* wherein humanity resides. The basic qualities of the signs of the zodiac will only be mentioned here. The reader can refer to Volume 3 of this treatise, as well as to Alice Bailey's *Esoteric Astrology,* for elucidation.

The best way to view this figure is in terms of four triads oriented north, south, east and west, where the usual interrelationships can be considered, as provided in the earlier volumes. The fixed cross is composed of a (masculine) vertical line of cosmic direction, and a receptive (feminine) horizontal line for distribution of the energies for nurturing the desirable qualities in humanity. This cross therefore remains focused in dynamic purpose and compassionate intent. The intermediate petals of the Chohans of the Rays can be considered more mutable, dynamically active within the fields of their Ray purposes as to the way that energies must flow to humanity and the nature of human response. They manifest the *iḍā* and *piṅgalā nāḍī* flow of the Hierarchical Heart. Each Mahābodhisattva can also be viewed in terms of a cardinal cross of energy direction formed via their polar opposites and the two most senior Initiates within their own departments. As the concern here is with the planetary Heart centre, the focus is upon the means of the dissemination of the energies of Love-Wisdom *(bodhicitta)* to the planet.

The *suṣumṇā* petal of the eastern direction is occupied by the blue Christ. He receives directives from the cosmic Christ (in Sirius) in its most refined (Arian) form and sets the wheel in motion for the outpouring of new dispensations of Love. This energy represents the primary cleansing potency needed to transmute the base *saṃskāras* generated by humanity. Aries is the ram that impels, instigating the new. It signifies the outpouring of the initial seed *bījas* of the directive will needed to convert the most intense desire, selfish and self-based attributes of humanity into cooperative sharing, selflessness and basic goodwill for all. The utilisation of such a will is the first step towards the awakening of *siddhis* of spiritual accomplishment by humanity. Sirius is the source for the energy of Love-Wisdom to our solar system, and contains the cosmic paradigm for the *maṇḍala* of our planetary Hierarchy. From Sirius emanates the line of *guruparamparā*[49] for Sanat Kumāra (the One Initiator), the Logos of our planet.

The Taurean *piṅgalā* point for the east is held by Tsongkhapa (the European Chohan). He is closely affiliated with the Love-Wisdom line and carefully monitors the nature of the development of mind by humanity so that it can be appropriately offset and counterbalanced by the outpouring of Love. The development of *bodhicitta* can then eventually be expressed by the target groupings of people. For this reason he has been specifically overshadowing the European development of

---

49 Lineage tradition of a *guru* or a spiritual preceptor. For a detailed explanation see Volume 6, 156-68.

mind, and its scientific expression since the time of his incarnation as Leonardo da Vinci. Even so, the quality of scientific materialism and selfish *manasic* pursuits has rapidly overshot the building of the foundation of Love in our societies because of the strong predilection in this direction by general humanity.

This Taurean position fully integrates the edicts from Shambhala into the Hierarchical Thought-stream in a way that best facilitates the awakening of wisdom in humanity. The Taurean aspect here exemplified is the cosmic principle of Logoic Desire-Mind, which manifests as the Love-Wisdom that drives Hierarchical purpose to fulfilment. An objective being the Hierarchical connectivity to other such centres in the Body of the solar Logos. Taurus is the grand (cosmic) Cow providing the sustaining milk of Life for all, and wherein the Eye of illumination, the all-seeing Eye, can be found. It sets the keynote of the energies developed by Hierarchy by which all similar establishments in the solar system can Know of their current status (levels of development).

The Eye here (in the Christ's department) is focussed as an aspect of the Sirian agenda. When, however, used by the Mahāchohan's department (viewed from a different Hierarchical perspective), Taurus also steers human civilisation towards concourse with the Pleiades, the supreme domain of the feminine principle (the *devic* lore) in our local cosmos.[50] It projects the magnanimity of what *ḍākinīs* have for generations offered to accomplished *yogins*. Those of the new world civilisation are to be increasingly consciously integrated with this parallel feminine *deva* evolution to our human line. Scientists will then discover many secrets of the material world presently hid, transforming the way the universe is viewed, and transmogrifying their understanding of the nature of the laws governing it. The integration of the Pleiadian Mind with the Sirian karmic agenda[51] is the focus of Hierarchical activity upon earth at present.

In the cosmic Desire-Mind attributes of Taurus, fused with the Love of the Christ's department, we have the keynote expression of the *bodhicitta* that empowers the Council of Bodhisattvas. Humanity are thus nurtured and fed the ambrosial nectar of Hierarchical Love via a Taurean impetus. The purpose is to vitalise aspirants and disciples with

---

50 Meaning here the local part of our galaxy.

51 Signified by Logoic Desire-Mind above.

the energies they need to meet all challenges, as well as to offer the necessary testings for those upon the path of Initiation. This happens under the auspices of the first and second Ray integration. (Here coming under the auspices of the Arian impetus of the Christ.) Love-Wisdom is then the cosmic juggernaut that emanates via the Christ's department, which pushes along the sum of human evolution. It is the energy contained in the sacred adytum in the next sign Gemini, ruled by K.H., and pours through the *piṅgalā nāḍī* projected by Tsongkhapa and K.H. via the southeast direction of the wheel.

The bottom five signs of this Logoic Heart centre represent the attributes of the five Rays of Mind. They project Hierarchical *prāṇas* to the centres below the diaphragm, which represent the fields of *māyā* wherein humanity reside. These potencies manifest via the Lords of the three Rays of aspect (the first, second and third Rays), because the bearers of the potent Rays of synthesis are needed to properly regulate and transform the attributes of the mental-emotions developed by humanity. These three Rays govern the attributes of the Monadic potency that ultimately rule human evolution. We also have the projections from the Eyes of Guru Rinpoche and Tsongkhapa whereby the energies from the second Shambhala level are directed to help transform the mass thoughts of humanity. The trident *(khaṭvāṅga)* wielded by Guru Rinpoche bears the potency of cosmic Mind from the Phoenician as its central staff and the energies of the second and third Ray Chohans respectively as its right and left prongs.

These five Chohans can thus be related to the wisdoms of the Dhyāni Buddhas and the associated Elements.

Dhyāni Buddha	Related Chohan	Element
Amoghasiddhi	First Ray Chohan	Earth
Ratnasambhava	Second Ray Chohan	Water
Amitābha	Third Ray Chohan	Fire
Akṣobhya	Tsongkhapa	Air
Vairocana	Guru Rinpoche	Aether

Table 3. The Dhyāni Buddhas and the Chohans

Tsongkhapa embodies the *piṅgalā* petal in relation to the functions of the Diaphragm centre, whereby energies flow to and from the centres above and below the diaphragm. His purpose is to produce liberation through the inception of the wisdom principle by humanity, and to direct this potency to the second level of Shambhala.

The second Ray Chohan, K.H., directs the potency of the second Ray Builders in the temples of Life to awaken compassionate idealism amongst humanity. He incorporates the purpose of Love into the hearts of humanity, mainly via their Souls. All lives will thereby be infused with the magnetic potency of Love. This is accomplished via Gemini the twins, which governs the earth's *nāḍīs* and the esoteric significance of the outpouring of 'Blood', the vital *piṅgalā* potency that gives life to all forms. The silent rituals in the temples of the Heart centre evokes the Christ-energy *(bodhicitta)* that is directed downward towards the Solar Plexus centre of humanity so that the Waters can be stilled and transformed into its Airy form. Gemini thus implies the sacred precincts of the Temple of the Mysteries (embodied by the *nāḍī* system) of enlightened being/non-being that is Hierarchy, via which the Christ pours his dispensation. The Temple represents the establishment of the new Initiation Schools, for the revelation of the hidden mysteries of Life.

These schools preside over the implementation of the second Ray purpose via the generation of calmness of mind in this new era. They embody the method of externalising the entire Hierarchy through controlling the planetary *nāḍīs* and associated *chakras* so that all of its activities will be made exoterically evident in human affairs. For the Aquarian epoch a new form of (seventh Ray) ceremonial magic must be implemented and wedded to the second Ray so that the might of the externalised Hierarchy can be accomplished. The Waters of Love-Wisdom can then pour throughout the planetary manifestation to integrate all disparate humans into a harmonious unity, an epoch of sharing and cooperative activity, wherein the concept of 'brotherhood' supersedes the separative attitudes presently prevalent. The new Wisdom religion will thereby become truly catholic, universal. The 'twins' associated with this sign then represent the instructors of the Schools, being the 'immortal brother', and the candidates preparing to enter, representing the 'mortal brother'.

The *suṣumṇā* position for the southern direction of downward to the little ones is held by Guru Rinpoche via Cancerian purpose. This purpose concerns the mode of projection into manifestation of the sum of the imperatives from Shambhala. All lives thereby evolve according to the Will of the planetary Logos, so that the Plan for planetary transformation will eventually condition humanity. Cancer the crab represents the open gate for the descent of the purpose of this Will, as well as representing the door of liberation for those lives that have passed their evolutionary testings for any cycle. The focus is upon the evolution of Mind by means of the alchemicalisation of the evolving lives. Here Cancer projects the Will-to-Empower the entire planetary manifestation with Love and Mind. All Bodhisattvas are empowered with the visions and ideas as to the way to assist all within the planetary landscape.

Being a major Watery sign, Cancer represents the zone of direction for the (Watery) energies of cosmic Love into the general Hierarchical dispensation and of their integration with Mind, so that the new epoch can incarnate upon our planet. Mind therefore is steeped in the energy of Love as it pours through the gate to give birth to all new *maṇḍalas*. People's minds will thereby be generally stimulated so that incipient wisdom evolves from the outpouring of the stimulus of Love. This necessitates a mass outpouring of the causes and effects within humanity in a way that people are generally induced to correct modes of thought politically, culturally, scientifically, and by religious groups.

Another objective concerns the development of *siddhis* by humanity, that will come as a consequence of the understanding and proper control of the astral plane. This necessitates people to be appropriately focussed upon the inner realms through right emotional control. The Watery environment in which people generally wallow must be dissipated. Hierarchy, however, plans to avoid the development of *siddhis* of evil intent that happened in ancient Atlantis. First the Will-to-Love must be sought by the perspective candidates, which is developed in the new temples of Life, so that general society and the environment are helped as a consequence. The way of travelling the Bodhisattva path to attain the various Initiation stages must consequently become a well known factor.

Guru Rinpoche ensures that the birthing of the new venture (in this case the Hierarchical externalisation process) manifests smoothly according to Plan. By means of the cardinal cross, of which he is an integral member, he helps precipitate all Hierarchical energies into objectivity. Similarly in an earlier cycle he helped impel the birthing of the Buddhist civilisation in Tibet. The Fiery *suṣumṇā* energy he wields is effectively directed towards the planetary Splenic centre to help cleanse the unregenerate *saṃskāras* developed *en masse* by humanity.

The third Ray Chohan (the Venetian) occupies the Leonine petal. The sign Leo the lion, whose planetary rulers are governed by the sun, facilitates the ability of this Chohan to connect with the integrated Minds of all other members of Hierarchy and helps inspire human Souls to share a common integral purpose by way of Mind. The Venetian therefore will promote all aspects of mind/Mind that produce beneficent (sun-like) results, but with view of instigating new esoteric perspectives in all of the fields of human civilisation, through initiating the world's thinkers into the ways of Mind. The self-centred empirical thought of the intelligentsia must be converted into considerations of new ways of compassionate understanding and abstract thinking.

This petal wields the *iḍā* flow to and from the Solar Plexus centre, wherein the great majority of humans are ensconced. Those involved in emotional concerns need to find the clear way away from *karma*-forming activities keeping them bound to *saṃsāra.* Clear thinking by all, in all arenas of activity is the great need nowadays. Egoistic activity and the forms of self-concern, governed by Leo, have to be offset by concepts of selfless service and compassionate action. The reasons for such actions must be thoroughly understood, not just in the field of religion, but also philosophically, culturally and scientifically. Also, the sphere of world finances, that foul breeder of corruption amongst those in power, and the myriad schemes of the avaricious to amass more wealth from the servitude of the poor, must be properly regulated. Monetary power must adequately serve the masses, not just a ruthless few. Eventually the entire concept of what defines money will be reconsidered within our societies, with new methods of exchange for labour, goods and services instigated.

The right handling of all material resources ultimately lies in the hands of the third Ray department. The way of approach, therefore, is from minds to the Mind that is the Heart of all, where this dissemination of Mind (the Hierarchical Plan) becomes the new form of monetary wealth sought by the elite governing all.

The Virgoan *iḍā* energy for the western direction is wielded by the first Ray Chohan, Morya. In Virgo the virgin the sum of the *deva* kingdom is incentivised with the vision of the Plan, and they thrill into action to help produce the birthing of the divine child that forms within the womb of the Great Mother. The work of Morya in this regard is to help provide the physical conditionings that will allow the new forming *maṇḍala* to grow the civilisation to be, as planned. Old forms must die, cut asunder by the first Ray sword, so that the new forms of vital Life can sprout and thrive. In doing so he directs *devas* that are the moving force of the expression of the *karma* that impels *saṃsāra* onwards to more refined states of being throughout Nature.

Morya moulds the streams of evolving lives in *saṃsāra,* according to the directives from the Manu's department. His purpose is to produce physical plane changes that help transform concrete-mindedness and the emotional forms of attachment to material things by humanity. He governs the karmic forces of the great sweep of activity in *saṃsāra* that control the moving streams of Lives, reflected as divine activity via the feminine *(deva)* forces of the planet that embody the substance of all that we are. Morya works to make the physical plane activities of humanity more divine by engraving the Plan with skill into the matrix of the substance they reside in. Famines, wars, cataclysmic events upon a minor or major scale, all earth changes, must be factored in the human equation, according to the *karma* engendered to make it so. Such activity represents the type of *prāṇas* sent to the thymus gland in a normal human.

Together the signs Virgo and Leo represent the mystery of the sphinx, which concerns the way of evolution, interaction, and eventual marriage between the *deva* and human kingdoms.

The *suṣumṇā* point of the western direction, of outwards to the field of service representing humanity, is occupied by the Libran function of the new Mahāchohan in cooperation with the directives of the Christ. Each new cycle in the field of the Mind is thereby impelled so that humanity may comprehend the nature and purpose of Love through applied wisdom. Hence the emanation of the energy of planetary *bodhicitta* (the fusion of the Christ's and the Mahāchohan's energies) is the prime quality that conditions the action of *karma*. It vitalises the sum of Hierarchical life, thus is the major motivational force guiding all Bodhisattvic activity.

The emerald green of the Mahāchohan's department is fused with the all-encompassing Love-Wisdom of the silver-blue Christ. This combination integrates the dynamic Will of Morya and the sixth Ray materialising potency of Jesus into the *suṣumṇā* stream in such a way that the Watery emotionality of humanity can be dried out. In this respect their *karma* must be rightly directed so that their physical plane affairs reflects the pattern of what is so ordained. Jesus is concerned with the more Watery attributes of this *karma*, Morya the Earthy, and the new Mahāchohan the Fiery. All energies are impelled into objectivity via the trident the Mahāchohan wields. Esoterically, he breathes the energies from the planetary Lung centres into manifestation, but is more specifically concerned with the breathing out process of the gain of human evolution to the higher centres. Hence Love dynamically pours into humanity and it cleanses the defilements of the concretions of mind and exaggerated emotions that disciples must deal with at any time. It provides the chance to convert putrid *saṃskāras* into more refined types of *prāṇas*. Thus humanity is educated to do right, slowly at first and then with increasing momentum as basic lessons are learnt. Love inevitably wins out and the way that the *karma* of the converted *saṃskāras* comes to the fore will inevitably see to that.

Via the power of the Mahāchohan's trident, the 'engraving process' conducted by Morya and that concerning the overshadowing of the great mass of devotional ones, being Jesus' concern, are appropriately integrated with the skill of mathematical precision. All conditions in the three worlds of human livingness can then be catered for, and the minutiae, as well as the broad vision integrated. The turning of the great wheel of *karma* (Libra the balances) projects the Will-of-Love into humanity via the western triad, by rightly adjudicating the *karma* of what must be. We have the cleansing of physical impediments by means of the activity of the first Ray Chohan, Morya; the Watery impediments of humanity by means of the testings presided over by Jesus; and cleansing *manasic* detriments by means of the activity of the new Mahāchohan and his entire department.

There are myriads of wheels in cosmos, all of different sizes, and bearing different potencies. There are cogs within cogs transmitting energies from one wheel to the next. Libra represents the conditioning mechanism of the law of cycles that is the method of transmitting these energies. Our focus is upon the way of toning down a major potency from a greater wheel to a smaller one. Each wheel can also be viewed as a *chakra*. Libra controls the meditative cycles of the in and out breathing of the Will-of-Love so that the hand of Love tackles the right tasks at any time. The Fiery attribute of Love-Wisdom is thereby exemplified.

In this transition period the new Mahāchohan is aided by the presently transiting Mahāchohan (ℛ), who specifically wields the violet energy to ensure that enlightened concepts are rightly and cyclically hammered into the stones of concreted human minds. The Mind that is Love must grow through each cycle of time, with the consequent rectification of *karma,* as governed by Libra (being the wheel of the Law). Without Love the mind would generate the dark evil of materialistic might. Hence the combined power of Love and Mind via ritualistic, divinely ordained timing (magic when incorporating the *devas*) is used to foster what is right over time, by overcoming the negative tendencies of scientific materialism. Great is the need in this technological epoch of woe and of planetary malaise to overcome the cupidity of human minds, hence the integrating purpose of the forces of the two to overcome the rampant disease of mind empowering the manifestation of evil in every land. The combined power of these two great Ones is the basic incentive that will project all human consequences towards the future civilisation envisaged for humanity by Hierarchy and Shambhala.

The rulership of the activity of all the Rays of Mind sets the tone of the integrated way. This necessitates weaving the appropriate *karma* so that the new ideals and ideas for human societies and civilisation come cyclically to fruition. Thus we have the properly ordained and magical appearances of different religions, science, the arts, etc., with their fruits viewed as modern *siddhis*. (That is, the effects of our technological age, such as the many marvels brought about by the use of electricity in one form or other.) The way that the course of various human civilisations unfold is visioned by these Lords in the form of the *prāṇas* flowing through the *nāḍīs* and *chakras* of our planetary system. Therefore when a new *chakra* is to be vivified, a new way of thinking or religion, or a new scientific or cultural advancement appears, such as the Renaissance and Reformation periods in Europe, and the flowering of the Mahāyāna in the East. Now a new world religion is set to grow, based upon the empowerment of the planetary centres below the diaphragm by means of the Heart centre—the externalisation of the Hierarchy. Effectively we have an out-breathing of cycles of Fiery service to the new civilisation along the first, second and third Ray lines via the seventh.

The *piṅgalā* Scorpionic spoke of the western direction of this wheel is governed by the sixth Ray Chohan, Jesus. He projects the Taurean second Ray purpose from Tsongkhapa into the *kāma-manasic* morass of humanity to assist them to battle with and to overcome the fields of desire. Inevitably, aspiration will be seeded amongst large swathes of humanity. Through consequent striving their emotional disposition will be overcome through evoking the Fires of Mind. Mastery of the causes for *saṃsāric* allurements, however, manifests via a turmoiled pathway, with many testings along the road to enlightenment. The sign Scorpio the scorpion sets the stage for the actual tests the disciple must undergo to overcome the nine-headed Hydra, of all the incursions of the dark brotherhood, as well as tackling the most difficult, adverse *saṃskāras*. Many are the battles to be won if the second Ray of Love-Wisdom that is the hallmark of Hierarchy is to be awakened.

Base human selfishness facilitates the dark brotherhood's projections of manipulative purpose of separative evil intent, which people find so easy to emulate and express for self-gain. Strong selfish forces sweeping throughout human society are very difficult to offset with the processes related to developing compassion, to produce the play of selfless Love in people's lives. Though aided by the Hierarchy, the role played by Jesus to turn these qualities around is fraught with difficulty. Selflessness, compassionate sympathy to other's needs, intelligence devoted to creative pursuits and high spiritual aspiration, are some of the qualities to be developed. Consequently, Jesus feeds the devotional and aspirational masses with the attributes of the Hierarchical *piṅgalā* flow. He envelops the 'swamp' of the emotional proclivity generated by the masses with Love, causing it to be continuously washed with cleansing Watery energies from cosmic sources. These energies are 'breathed in' via the *nāḍī* to the planetary left Lung centre (to which this petal of the Heart centre is directed).

The target is the astral plane, the entire Watery disposition of humanity, which must eventually be pacified and converted by the Will-of-Love so that goodwill is the minimal response by human units *en masse*. Eventually the entire astral plane will be transmogrified, eliminating the need for the existence of this zone of residence. However, many transmutative battles loom concerning massed base *saṃskāras*, to reorient humanity away from *saṃsāric* attachment to Solar Plexus activity and upwards to the planetary Heart centre.

The broad and vast sway of the sixth Ray of Devotion is the appropriate vehicle to redirect the emotions and desires of common humanity, the focus of fanatics, wrongly oriented idealists, prideful religionists, neurotic, or sex-obsessed individuals (etc.) towards the basics of loving aspiration. They need to be seeded with the vision to aspire to great creative and spiritual heights. Under the auspices of religion the response comes in the form of devotion to the *dharma*, the images and lives of the great ones, to deities, 'God', as well as aspiration towards high ideals, enlightenment and eventual liberation.

The arrow-like potency of the Sagittarian petal is wielded by the fourth Ray Chohan, Serapis, who directs *piṇgalā* attributes to the new civilisation in a way that all of humanity will live harmoniously in a spirit of cooperative sharing. Because the fourth Ray of Beautifying Harmony overcoming Strife is the conditioning Ray governing humanity, so a loving response must be gleaned from the often warring and conflicting competitive situations people find themselves in, no matter their cultural situations.

The Sagittarian arrows will target all aspects of civilisation, to be beautified and integrated within the natural harmony found throughout Nature's kingdom. Society will consequently be uplifted through the appropriate sharing of the resources of nations, causing the elimination of urban slums. Labour saving devices producing significant free time will allow people to pursue creative activities, to educate themselves more wholesomely than present. Myriads will avail themselves so, as all culturally uplifting and educational pursuits, as well as the meditative arts, will be promulgated by leaders. The self-indulgent, often violent movies, games, sports, and drug-induced forms of activity most presently waste their leisure time with, will slowly and inevitably lose their attractiveness. The normal human clashing noises in our present urban areas will be largely eliminated in the future garden cities.

Normally the keynote to Sagittarius is ambition, which is destructive in intent, as it takes from others to produce the wealth or material power desired. Aspiration and cooperative sharing must be fostered instead, which becomes the keynote for the new civilisation, producing opulence for all, and not just for the most scheming, avaricious, separative ones. To turn such human ambition around so that Bodhisattvic virtues can be developed instead, is part of the task assigned to Serapis as he views the present civilisation and ponders upon the new vestments it should take so that aesthetic beauty is seen in all arenas of human activity. Sagittarius the archer will then project the fourth Ray energies that will help disciples to develop the discipline and wilful intent to overcome obstacles and transform base *saṃskāras* into higher attributes via the Will-to-Love, and later to develop the Will-of-Love. The Archer will fire the arrows of people's creative imagination and aspiration towards discovering the multidimensional truths encoded in Nature. Eventually error-free Thusness will be sought by way of firstly awakening the higher creative amplitude (of the Throat centre's awakening, the natural orientation of this petal of the Heart centre), and then to reside at the *saṃsāra-śūnyatā* nexus, producing the central View that harmonises all into unity. The arrows will also fly to direct people to envision the directives of the Mother's department, the nurturing and building forces of the new civilisation to be. They concern the integration of human and *deva* forms of activity.

The northernmost, Capricornian petal, wielded by the Phoenician integrates the energies of the Logoic Mind (via Shambhala) into Hierarchy. This represents the *suṣumṇā* aspect of the direction upwards to the Kingdom of 'God'. The sign Capricorn the goat (that climbs the mountain of Mind) facilitates receptivity to this highest level of *dharmakāya*. It governs the karmic purpose of all Bodhisattvas preparing to leave our planet to travel to the farthest reaches of the ocean of Love, to distant cosmic shores built by Mind. All aspects of *manasic* development upon our planetary grid are appropriately nourished in this way. The Phoenician consequently directs all *manasic* Fires either downwards into manifestation to counter the hard, rocky materialistic mount of *karma* generated by selfish and separative human minds, or else upwards towards cosmic heights.

The Phoenician is impressed by cosmic Mind (Mahat) via the filter of the Lords of Life occupying the first level of Shambhala. The fifth cosmic astral sub-plane is the emanating source, via which are found the solar Logoi (Buddha-fields) energising the solar system. This, coupled with the liberating stream of cosmic Love from the Christ, is the prime source of energisation for the Hierarchical *maṇḍala*. The integration of cosmic Love and Mind constitutes the Logoic version of *kāma-manas*. From this perspective the Head centre of our planetary system (Shambhala) manifests as a Solar Plexus centre to receive the power of these cosmic Logoi.

The Phoenician therefore projects cosmic Purpose into the *maṇḍala* of the Council of Bodhisattvas, producing the overall far-sighted direction for all planetary affairs and planning. The motions of the planetary Head and Heart centres are thereby integrated, moving in accord with each other. This allows Fiery Logoic constructs to be toned down and projected into manifestation by the wise Council of the entire *maṇḍala* of Bodhisattvas.

The Aquarian potency for this northern direction is wielded by the fifth Ray Chohan, Hilarion. He embodies the attributes of the Hierarchical *iḍā nāḍī* system (to and from the planetary Throat centre) that incorporates the *prāṇas* of Mind that flow between Shambhala and Hierarchy. These energies from the Mahāchohan's department are directed mainly to the kingdom of Souls, so that planetary directives can influence their united meditation that the course of human civilisation must take. These directives are then carefully modulated by the third Ray Chohan so that the Fiery energies of mind are not overtly, exaggeratedly cornered by the Lords of Dark Face to produce planetary disaster. Eventually the blockages of the *manasic nāḍīs* in the *chakras* below the diaphragm, representing human activity, will be transformed. This will allow a free-flow of energies from Shambhala (the Mind of 'God') to humanity whereby the new era civilisation can flower. In the present transitional epoch these *prāṇas* represent the energetic outpouring from the pitcher held by the Water Bearer (Aquarius).

Humanity must learn to rightly wield the energies of mind/Mind to offset the powerful proclivities of their desire nature. Right cogent comprehension must manifest before mastery can be achieved. The higher *manasic* outpouring of Hierarchical Life is thereby directed into the general human population via their collectivised forms of activities. The emotional disposition of humanity must consequently be stilled through a proper comprehension of the nature of the Waters by means of the mind as it evolves into Mind through Love. The purpose is to develop a free thinking intelligentsia, to specifically stimulate the energy of goodwill via philosophic, cultural and an aesthetically-minded scientific enquiry. The downpour of rarefied Fire represents the main Hierarchical outpouring to general humanity aimed at stimulating group Love, advanced learning and spiritual aspiration.

Hilarion's purpose, therefore, is to instil into humanity the new era science that transcends materialistic considerations. The way of Love governing all that is must be taught. Also, the role of the *devas,* the creative factors in Nature, must be gradually revealed to a thankful humanity. The nature of the energies pouring via the four cosmic ethers must be discovered and scientifically analysed in this epoch. The esoteric sciences demonstrating the existence of the subtle planes of perception must therefore be widely acknowledged, and with it the knowledge of what these subjective dimensions in space veil. Thus is the ontological epistemology of the new science born.

The seventh Ray Chohan (here viewed as Master ℛ) embodies the function of Pisces the fishes for the wheel of the Hierarchical Heart centre. Pisces governs humanity's lower psychic and devotional responses to higher ideals and is the sign of termination, of completion of cycles of activity so that fresh beginnings can commence. It also governs massed responses to propaganda and glamoured images, mediumship, and the generalised swamps of murky emotionality.

The seventh Ray that will come into flower in this new epoch handles all Ray energies and grounds them in the material domain via an *iḍā (manasic)* energy perspective so that all lives may benefit. It represents the ritualistic, cyclic organisational endeavour of Hierarchy, via which their energies are poured into manifestation, effectively the beating of the Hierarchical Heart. The development of the higher spiritual faculties, the attainment of the higher *siddhis,* rather than evoking the lower psyche, will be the objective of Hierarchical purpose. Hierarchy wish to produce seers out of humanity, intelligent cooperators with the Plan, who accordingly awaken internal vision via appropriate meditation techniques, rather than psychics. The Watery environment that the 'fishes' reside in must be made more rarefied, Fiery in nature, attuned to Shambhalic purpose. Humanity must learn to project *antaḥkaraṇas* thereto.

The Temples of the new Initiation Schools for the revelation of the hidden mysteries of Life will be established largely under the auspices of this Ray.[52] Such schools will preside over the process of externalising the entire Hierarchy so that all of its activities will be made exoterically evident in human affairs. This concerns the out-breathing of cyclic purpose to humanity, a function of the *nāḍī* from the planetary right Lung centre, governed by this petal. The power to materialise thereby comes into play. The seventh Ray will also help empower Morya in the polar opposite sign to organise the eventual elevation of all lives into higher spirals of evolutionary attainment and eventual liberation. Hence all lives upon this planet can find their appropriate cosmic homes, once liberated.

Further astrological considerations

I shall conclude with a consideration of the planetary rulers associated with the major fixed cross of Figure 9, which determines the nature of the *suṣumṇā* flow for Hierarchy.[53] The rulers are:

1. *Aries.* Mars projects the will to control the sum of the Waters pouring through Hierarchy to rightly affect humanity's activities. Mercury governs the fourth Ray, the prime energy conditioning the fourth kingdom in Nature (humanity), via which all of these energies must flow, and with which the Christ must work. Uranus allows the dissemination of the energies through all of the seven Rays, producing the expressed power and might of Hierarchy.
2. *Libra.* Venus governs the dissemination of the energies of Mind to humanity via their Sambhogakāya Flowers. Uranus facilitates the transmission of the energies of cosmic Love from the Christ via the seventh Ray to empower the expression of Love-Wisdom amongst

52 The Mysteries themselves will be an expression of the combined second and third Rays. This represents the integrated work of K.H. and the new Mahāchohan.

53 This cross is a cardinal cross from the viewpoint of those in *saṃsāra*, but is a steadfast fixed demonstration of Logoic energisation from the higher view.

humanity. Saturn helps to mete out the *karma* of what must manifest in the field of consciousness according to the turning of the wheel so that human civilisation becomes overtly more harmoniously integrated with the directives of Love.

3. *Capricorn.* Here all of the attributes of Mind are ritually cycled (via Venus, which governs the fifth Ray) through the planetary manifestation, according to the dictates of *karma* (Saturn). Venus facilitates the reception of the attributes of cosmic Mind into the Hierarchical *maṇḍala,* empowering its expressed might in all ways that *karma* (Saturn) must manifest. The cyclic manifestation of this potency helps to transmute the *saṃskāras* generated by humanity (via the southern direction) so that eventually the type of *karma* is generated that will allow them to climb the mount of Initiation, hence overcoming the generalised materialistic bias seen nowadays. Each person must master the dictates of *karma* as the Initiation path is trod.
4. *Cancer.* The cosmic astral energy flows principally via Neptune to feed the general aura of Shambhala. The Moon here veils Uranus and cyclically projects to the system the elements of cosmic Mind that can be utilised. Cosmic astral energy is directed via Neptune's trident (which is but a version of the *khaṭvāṅga* held by Guru Rinpoche) to overcome the mediumistic and psychic tendencies of humanity, the Cancerian mass emotional moods, as veiled by the Moon. The trident integrates Mind with the Waters and projects the resultant potency to rightly control the general emotionality of massed human consciousness. In the form of the *khaṭvāṅga,* it is a sceptre that helps transform the activity of all lives in *saṃsāra.*

Note the prevalence of the Rays of Mind here (the planetary rulers being along the third to seventh Rays), principally via the third, sixth and seventh Rays. They are concerned with disseminating the energies of cosmic Mind (Mahat) via the cosmic astral plane, and infused with the Love-Wisdom by the Hierarchical Heart, so that the evolving lives on earth can be rightly impressed by the Logoic Plan.

Concerning Figure 9, the *southwest* direction ('understanding') of Leo-Virgo is governed by the attributes of the third and first Ray

Chohans. Their function is to properly organise the Hierarchical Plan, expressed so that mind can be utilised by humanity without it being perverted by the dark forces. (To oppose the machinations of the dark brotherhood is a specific forte of Morya and his department, where the Will-of-Love is used to offset the will-of-mind wielded by our dark foes.) The objective of such activity is to produce a complete understanding of all things, exoteric and esoteric, and to generate the will to overcome the snares of *saṃsāra*.

Sign	Exoteric	Esoteric	Hierarchical
Aries (the east)	Mars	Mercury	Uranus
Libra (the west)	Venus	Uranus	Saturn
Capricorn (the north)	Saturn	Saturn	Venus
Cancer (the south)	the Moon	Neptune	Neptune

Table 4. Planetary rulers of the fixed cross of the Hierarchical Heart centre[54]

The initial seeding of the era of knowledge has proven to be exceedingly successful. The epoch of scientific materialism consequently is everywhere prevalent. However, the difficult esoteric portion of the task has only just begun to spread understanding of the inner universe and the nature of compassionate insight by way of awakening the abstract Mind. (This necessitates completely empowering the *piṅgalā* forces of the *southeast* direction, Taurus-Gemini.) There is a considerable

54 Alice Bailey's *Esoteric Astrology* (Lucis Publishing, London, 1975) should be consulted for detail here, as well as for the background as to the meaning of the planetary rulers. The three rulers to each of the signs presented: the orthodox, esoteric, and Hierarchical rulers, are as per Tabulation VI in *Esoteric Astrology*, 68. The rulers given in the above order are: Aries—Mars, Mercury and Uranus; Taurus—Venus, Vulcan and Vulcan; Gemini—Mercury, Venus and the Earth; Cancer—the Moon, Neptune and Neptune; Leo—the Sun, the Sun and the Sun; Virgo—Mercury, the Moon and Jupiter; Libra—Venus, Uranus, and Saturn; Scorpio—Mars, Mars and Mercury; Sagittarius—Jupiter, the Earth and Mars; Capricorn—Saturn, Saturn and Venus; Aquarius—Uranus, Jupiter and the Moon; Pisces—Jupiter, Pluto and Pluto.

handicap karmically obtained from the disastrous events in the failure of the moon Chain,[55] and the causes for the Atlantean deluge. The forces of evil appear almost universally successful once again in controlling planetary affairs. Their activities still need appropriate countermeasures.

The third and first Ray Chohans, wielding the energy of Mind and Will, work closely with the new Mahāchohan, who organises the expression of *manas* into the sum of the planetary manifestation via Libra, which governs the general dissemination of mind/Mind whenever a new cycle for the expression of any of the aspects Mind is to influence our civilisation. The dominance of the concrete mind in humanity is set to wane,[56] and the era of the expression of the abstract Mind will rise in its stead, especially once the esoteric teachings of Hierarchy become better assimilated amongst the target groups. The link of Mind continues via Tsongkhapa, but is integrated with the second Ray purpose of K.H., and empowered by the Christ in the eastern direction. We therefore have two triads, the first, the eastern orientation of the Christ-Tsongkhapa-K.H.,[57] focussed mainly upon the downwards expression of the *piṇgalā* Love principle. Next the western triad of the new Mahāchohan-Morya-third Ray Chohan focussed mainly upon the downwards projection of the *iḍā* Wisdom principle. The interrelated energies of the two streams are appropriately blended by Guru Rinpoche in such a way that massed human *saṃskāras* will be transformed via Splenic centre activity.

The polar opposites in the north-eastern and north-western directions ('unity' and 'goodwill'), continuing the *iḍā-piṇgalā* flow to humanity, integrate their specialised service arenas. Together the eight great Bodhisattvas of the *iḍā-piṇgalā nāḍīs* also blend Love with Mind to empower the Love-Wisdom *(bodhicitta)* attributes of Hierarchy. From every perspective then this energy is seeded into humanity, being the main Hierarchical objective. The epoch which focussed on seeding the attributes of mind has now been successfully accomplished.

---

55 See Alice Bailey, *A Treatise on Cosmic Fire*, 414-17.

56 Fewer people embodying the fifth Ray line will, for instance, incarnate.

57 I am here segregating the dual Love-Wisdom Ray in terms of the specialised focus of the Chohans concerned. All are in fact exponents of this Ray to varying degrees of expression via the differing sub-hues of its attributes.

Thus the new era is dawning. But first manifests inevitable strife, as those that are ensconced in the powerhouse of the domains of the reifying empirical mind will not relinquish their materialistic powerbase without much struggle and war. Their tenacious, united will-of-mind will, however, inevitably be defeated and the Mother of the World will give birth to her new child, the glorious resplendence of Love-Wisdom, despite the pain of a troubled birth.

From the perspective of expressing the Rays of cosmic Mind, the Christ in the eastern direction of the Hierarchical Heart centre conveys the fourth Ray (the Ray governing humanity in general) via Mercury to the planetary dispensation. The Phoenician, in the northern direction, conveys the fifth Ray via Venus, the new Mahāchohan, the third Ray via Saturn into the western direction to humanity. Guru Rinpoche in the southern direction conveys the sixth and seventh Ray combination via the Moon and Neptune. The Rays dispensed by all of the members of this Heart centre are conditioned by the sixth Ray (Mars and Neptune) of the cosmic Waters, being the energy of the interrelated Love of the Logoi travelling through the cosmic astral plane.

To dare to strive!

Oṁ

Let s/he who would taste the cup of benediction dare—
Dare to strive to seek the goal in the great game,
game of life and liberation to seek the One
who set the way for the flame of your name.

Oṁ

In flame you strive, in flame you die.
In flame you seek to be born again.
Again to dare, to strive for the gain
of the boons bestowed by the Namer of your days.
Your days, your ways merge into the Flame
of the striving zeal and common weal
of the glorious son/suns likewise striving
upon the wheel of that great Son
that blazes out the glory of the All as the One.
Cold is the Flame, but brilliant the Light.
Seven times seven the sevenfold boons
peal out from the Lords of Liberation
Who have written the script
of the blazing path your feet are on.
From Fire to great luminescence is the Way
for all those who strive to sup
from the cup that holds the life of all in thrall,
that offers the soothing salve of redemption
from all karmic woe, for the road is long,
and the way be strong for the striving ones
of that luminescent throng.
Their songs peal out as golden delight
that fills the benedictive cup for each hoary plight.
Take flight, take flight away from plight.
Enter into the grand Domain of the Sight

of the King of Kings, the Lord of Hosts,
the Ancient of Days, the One of endless Munificence.
As a Lord of Hosts you fulfil your part,
to illumine the path for other's gain.
For other's gain is your constant aim.
Your aim is bright. Your aim is Light—
Straight through the Heart of every bright One's Son.
In scintillating radiance they grow.
Your aim is bright. Your aim is Light—
straight into the heart of the darkest night.
Keen you are to deliver each one therein their Sight.
Your boon is golden. Your boon is Light,
Your boon is sevenfold Sight.
You kindle the path for the daring ones to walk to Light.
Great luminescence is the Light of their Might,
the fame of their astounding Sight.
Heart's light, be intensely bright.
Dazzling is your Life's Light.

Oṁ

4

The first and second Ray Ashrams

The major Hierarchical dispensation

The purpose of the second Ray line colours all Hierarchical endeavour, especially in this epoch that heralds the new era. The second and first Ray combination will increasingly flavour all purposeful activity manifested by the Hierarchy amongst humanity. However these two Ray energies will be heralded by the enlightening mathematical ordering of the third Ray for the foreseeable future. Thus there is a triad of abstracted energies heralding via *ātma* (the first Ray), *buddhi* (the second Ray) and the abstract Mind (the third Ray) to project forwards humanity's evolutionary status. Hence comprehension of the nature of the abstract Mind lies in the immediate future for humanity, though such teaching has been available for two millennia, especially as developed in Buddhism. The true qualities of the nature of Mind can only now be properly revealed because of the exposition of the qualities of the Sambhogakāya Flower, which was provided in this present series of books. The ritualistic power of the seventh Ray grounds this energy upon the physical domain via the fluid, harmonising energy of the fourth Ray.

Figure 10 depicts the major energy flows underlying present Hierarchical purpose manifesting as Splenic centre I. The desire-mind of humanity is to be overcome through the transformation of base substance, facilitated by evoking greater Love-Wisdom and rightly directed Will.[1]

---

1 The information presented here is a major revision of my now superseded book *The Revelation* Volume II, (Ibez Press, Sydney, 1988).

The *maṇḍala* presented indicates the present major Hierarchical activity with respect to humanity when integrated with Splenic centre II. Figure 10 elaborates the work of the Chohans in terms of their interrelationship with humanity, whereas Figure 9 (the Heart centre) is mainly focused upon being an intermediary between Shambhala and humanity. As two dimensional representations the figures appear static, however, there is a commensurate mutability happening at all times. This is partly because the Chohans and Masters function upon different planes of perception due to their different Initiation status. There is also Ray methods of activity, plus many other esoteric considerations.

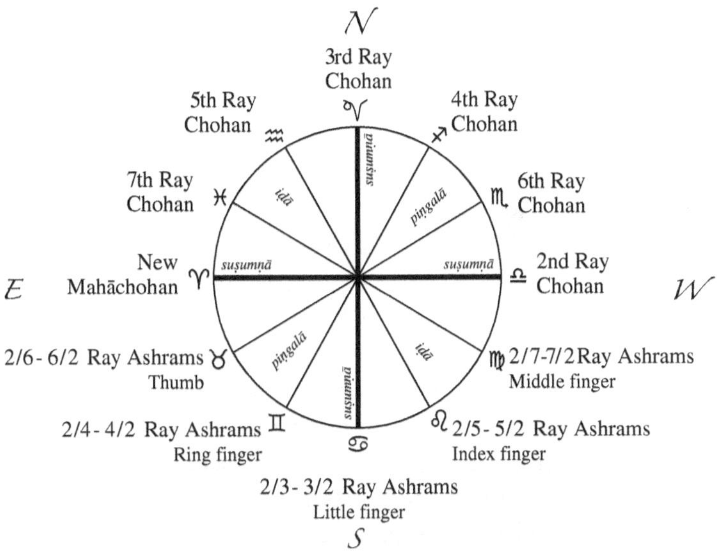

Figure 10. The Hierarchical dispensation as Splenic centre I

As the perspective of this figure is from the view of Hierarchy undertaking to assist humanity to overcome and transform their base *saṃskāras*, so it concerns the refinement of human consciousness via the empowerment of Mind, and generating beneficent wisdom.

Figure 10 depicts the new Mahāchohan assuming the eastern, Arian position of the inception of the cleansing *prāṇas* from the Heart centre via the Christ. He represents the will that is the dynamo that drives all energies in this centre to produce their transforming function. The effect of the work of the Mahāchohan's department to help produce the new world civilisation is a major consideration at this present time. Major changes must manifest in all departments in life as the new energies pour from Shambhala to transform our planet of woe into a sacred planet. Therein the principles of Love and Wisdom dominate, inaugurated by Will. This is the gain of Hierarchical planning and activity for millennia, for changes in the human situation do not evolve quickly. A large number of factors need to be accounted for in seeding the era of Love-Wisdom in the fertile soil of the former epoch of intelligent activity. Many groups, nations and organisations must change their forms of activity to be more inclusive of what is beneficial for the whole.

Many of the keynotes of this Arian position concern *sacrifice,* giving the Heart's Blood utterly for service of the other. Aries is the initiator of new cycles of endeavour, seen from the higher perspective. This necessitates perseverance, the ability to wait for millennia if need be for the fruition of any projected activity. The Arian dispensation cuts asunder the old so that the new can be instated. We then have the command and right projection of all energies in the field of the Heart's Life, which instigates the process of abstraction of the all back into the One, here via the second Ray impulse.

Koot Humi (K.H.)[2] takes the polar opposite Libran position, of outwards to the field of service, to disseminate the new dispensation of Love-Wisdom through appropriately timed cyclic activity into the general Solar Plexus centre of humanity, so that the emotional Waters can be cleansed and transformed. It completes the east-west horizontal line that represents the major matrix of the service arena for humanity. Humanity must conquer their Solar Plexus centres through developing greater mental understanding of the nature of *saṃsāra* and by the evocation of the Mind. The principle of Love alone generally produces heightened emotional sensitivity, whereas the Fires of Mind transforms the Waters.

Though the Mind is generally governed by the third Ray, we should note that each of the three higher mental sub-planes have an affinity with one or other of the first three Ray qualities. Thus the Clear Light of Mind (the first sub-plane) represents a first Ray flavour of Mind; the Son of Mind (the *tathāgatagarbha*) is ruled by the second Ray, and the

2 Sometimes the name Koot Humi is also spelled Koot Hoomi.

third sub-plane of the mental plane in the form of the general abstract Mind (the *ālayavijñāna*) is governed by the third Ray.

K.H. impels the Plans that are formulated to demonstrate the second Ray of Love-Wisdom throughout the various departments of life. The vibrancy of the opening and awakening of all the petals of the Hierarchical Lotus is stimulated as a consequence of such Plans. This second Ray potency is utilised in the five southern petals of Splenic centre I to help wash clean the *saṃskāric* grime of humanity, where the dross is projected to Splenic centre II to be further processed. Splenic centre II is thus governed by the activity of the first Ray Ashrams, as they wield the necessary force to help convert the worst attributes of the massed human psyche and that generated by the dark brotherhood.

The wheels turn through adamantine purpose in right ordered sequence to bear fruit, the radiance of colour and emanatory perfume. The projection of the power and rate of development of all associated Initiates are carefully monitored, so that the right blend of energies are projected to meet the needs of all in the realms of form.

Primarily, K.H. projects into manifestation, via the western orientation, the unifying, all-embracing attributes of consciousness, so that the compassionate part of the Bodhisattva path can be trod by all, and the Wisdom Religion unfolded. This fundamental second Ray energy supports and helps impel the activities of the new Mahāchohan, whose department primarily manifests via the Chohans embodying the five northern petals. This Mahāchohan and K.H. work together in the closest cooperation to produce the Plan of the outpouring of the major second Ray cycle for this planet under the auspices of the third Ray.

Libra, the adjudicator holding the scales of justice, facilitates the regulation of the various streams of *karma* projected into civilisation in a way that the combined first, third and second Ray purpose (of the new Mahāchohan and K.H.) manifest via the ritualistic and regulating activity of the seventh Ray.

The five Chohans of the northern hemisphere take the attributes of the Herukas (whose functions are explained in Volume 5A)[3] for the *prāṇas* generated by the human kingdom as a whole. By this is meant that the Chohans 'fiercely' guard the *prāṇas* entering Hierarchical and

3 See Volume 5A, 175-199.

Shambhalic domains so only what is worthy can be expressed therein. The remainder is recycled, redirected to the appropriate centre, so they can be reprocessed (as the available *karma)* by those that generated them. The entire path of discipleship and Initiation, of the evolution of the Bodhisattva *bhūmis,* thereby comes into play for all as they tread each step or progress through the cycles upon the upward way of *saṃsāric* life.

The 'Herukas' thereby wisely assist their disciples to transform and transmute base *saṃskāras* in such a way that the qualities needed to pass the respective Initiation each disciple is aspiring to attain are gained. These Initiations are attained under the auspices of group law, which these Chohans, plus K.H. and the new Mahāchohan, dispense.

The seventh Ray Chohan governing the Piscean petal takes the attributes of Karma Heruka, a function of Amoghasiddhi. The fifth Ray Chohan governing the Aquarian petal takes the attributes of Padma Heruka, as a function of Amitābha. The third Ray Chohan at the Capricornian gate manifests as Buddha Heruka, a function of Vairocana. The fourth Ray Chohan at the Sagittarian gate manifests as Vajra Heruka, a function of Akṣobhya, and the sixth Ray Chohan at the Scorpionic gate manifests as Ratna Heruka, an aspect of Ratnasambhava. The Ashrams situated at their polar opposite signs manifest as their Consorts. The new Mahāchohan takes the role of Mahottara Heruka, and K.H. as his Consort (Krodheśvarī), hence taking a more feminine (here passive) role to the first and third Ray ferocity of Mahottara. Their efforts provide the basis for humanity eventually being able to attain enlightenment.

The rise of the new Mahāchohan is enigmatical as it does not fall into the normal mould directly via a defining Ray Ashram. He has had an ambidextrous role in Hierarchy as part of the preparation to take the Mahāchohan's role for the new era. Though his fundamental (Monadic) Ray is that of the third Ray, he has also taken the role of overseeing the formation and development of the 2/1 Ray Ashram. One reason for this is veiled in his vast antiquity and the role he originally played as part of the team that came with Sanat Kumāra to the earth to help protect infant humanity from the onslaughts of cosmic dark brotherhood. (The direct effect of the failure of the moon Chain.) His Monadic/*dharmakāyic* aspect had by then developed a substantial sub-hue of the deep indigo blue of the Love-Wisdom Ray, and hence stood as the sixth point of the grouping. His Monadic purpose at that time, however, was to attain the first Ray hue, where the unfoldment of the third Ray could be used as a basis for subsequent conversion to the red. The one known as Jupiter was then the seventh point (hence bearer of the seventh Ray, and the basis to his magical prowess, seen for instance in his life as Guru Rinpoche). During the Atlantean epoch, however, the new Mahāchohan decided to stay with the green purpose and thus to promote the cause of the feminine principle in the evolutionary process. This then required his 'falling' to the seventh position of the Shambhalic team, and Jupiter had to make special effort to elevate himself to the sixth position. Similarly, the one known as Morya had to make a strenuous effort to move from the yellow Ray to master the red Ray in order to fill the position of an important Hierarchical vacancy.

The fledgling 2/1 Ashram was formed as a special dispensation for the coming of spiritual age of the former black hierarchy that were converted after the fall of Atlantis. Their then left hand abuse of magical powers facilitates the generation of similar *siddhis* of the right hand path to assist the white brotherhood. The intense energy of the Will-of-Love helps safeguard them from further egoistical psychic projections whilst they are trained to progress deeper in the ways of the lore of Love. Consequently, many of those who were mainly within the first and seventh Ray lines also found placement and training in this holding Ashram until it was deemed safe to bring them back to their rightful Ashramic positions. There are many converts from the dark brotherhood that need specialised training. Proper conversion, however, is oft a tumultuous affair, with many reversions from life to life, as dark egotistic *saṃskāras* are not easily converted into the corresponding ones of Love and Wisdom. Rebellious situations amongst the members of this Ashram have therefore persisted right up to the present era. The tendencies of temporary reversion is specifically problematic in the reverberation of a higher arc of an ancient cycle.

The 2/1 Ashram, along with the general first Ray Ashrams, have a specialised ability to counter the wilful machinations of the present dark brotherhood, who were once their protégés. There is much karmic affinity and the effects of former misdeeds is cleansed thereby. In this way also the new Mahāchohan sustains his primary role of countering the activities of the dark brotherhood upon this planet. Lord of Love and Sacrifice he consequently is, within the auspices of divine Activity. Because of the work regarding training dark brotherhood converts his position in Hierarchy has always been veiled, hence his existence has only been hinted at in the revelations broadcast exoterically to the world concerning the Masters of Wisdom via Blavatsky and Bailey. The ancient war between the Lords of Dark Face and the Lords of Light and Love continues unabated, but much can now be gained in this information age by revealing the fact and nature of this most ancient war to humanity. It therefore no longer needs to be kept secret, an 'ear-whispered truth', as in the past.

From the point of view of being the Arian point of Splenic centre I, this Mahāchohan impels the projection of Shambhalic purpose to humanity via Hierarchy so that all new aspects of consciousness can evolve. The key phrase for this petal is—the liberating will to pierce the veils shrouding all domains. The first Ray purpose from Shambhala emanating from the domains of cosmic Mind is thereby grounded, being modified with the qualities of the lubricating second Ray of Love-Wisdom from the Christ's department (the Heart centre), to K.H. and Hierarchy via Splenic centre I activity. (The Plan is simultaneously impressed into the Mind of Morya, who governs Splenic centre II.) The work is appropriately mathematically incorporated into the *maṇḍala* of expression representing the matrix of human consciousness by means of the activity of the third Ray department and the Rays of Mind. The qualities of all seven Rays are thereby rightly blended into the matrix. This assists the reception of the new impulses by younger Initiates without unduly destroying the fabric of their existential awareness, which the unmodified destroyer/first Ray purpose will always tend to do.

This work is significantly assisted by the seventh Ray Chohan, (Rakoczi[4]), whose rulership of ritualised magic and materialising power forms part of the directive arrow of Hierarchical purpose. This seventh Ray effect is further empowered by the new Mahāchohan being a seventh

---

4 He assumes this role with respect to the new Mahāchohan, as esoterically his dispensation as a Mahāchohan comes under the auspices of the one here styled the new Mahāchohan (who is also later termed 'the Rider'). However, the new Mahāchohan will take his role as a Mahāchohan via the position of being the seventh Ray Chohan. We see, therefore, that he and the Master *R* manifest a fluid mutable compliment, which takes into account the new Mahāchohan's auxiliary role as 'the Rider'.

point within Shambhala, who can blend the red and blue Rays into the violet of the seventh Ray. Verily, therefore, all seven Rays of Life can be wielded by this Lord of Civilisation.

The new Mahāchohan projects the arrow of the cardinal cross of directed purpose sent into the planetary malaise at this time, where K.H. is the piercing point for the dissemination of Love-Wisdom aimed at the target of rectifying the world's problems. The energies of the first and seventh Ray Chohans tear asunder the barriers in the physical plane that prevent the reception of the new Shambhalic dispensation. We see that the focus of this arrow is the western direction (Libra) into the world's astral (Solar Plexus) morass in order to bring light and order into an otherwise turbulent darkness.

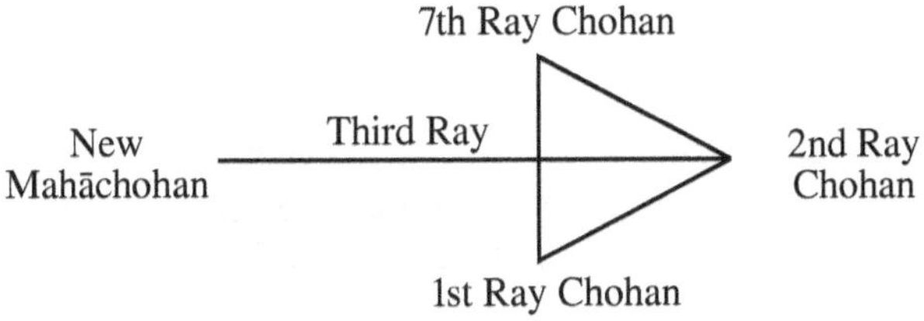

Figure 11. The arrow of present purpose

The key phrase for Libra here is—the meditative compassionate balance that portends the next step on the path of Love. Such compassion interrelates the combined Splenic centres, so that all cycles of activity function with right ordered sequence and perfected timing to transform *saṃsāra* into a vehicle of service. As K.H.'s focus is upon the Ashrams governing the southern portion of the *maṇḍala* via the second Ray Ashrams, all diverse qualities and energies are harmonised in one bountiful and glorious Song. It concerns the way that the cardinal cross turns the moving mutable cross (the swastika) governing human activity via the stabilising influence of the fixed cross.

The swastika and *vajra* are weapons of the new Mahāchohan, who takes the guise of Mahottara Heruka. The attributes of the weapons he wields in his triads of hands is explained in Volume 5A.[5] His right hands hold a *vajra, khaṭvāṅga* and a *ḍamaru* (drum). The left hands

5 Volume 5A, 181-82.

hold a bell, a blood-filled skull *(kapāla)* and a noose of entrails. From the present perspective we see that the *vajra* embodies the adamantine power of the *dharma,* which helps empower the activities of the Chohans of the northern hemisphere. The attributes of the wisdoms of the Dhyāni Buddhas are thereby expressed. The *khaṭvāṅga* wields a sevenfold methodology to convert all mindful attachments to *saṃsāra.* In this case it empowers all seven Ray aspects via the activities of the seven Ray Ashrams, to assist humanity to overcome the lures of *saṃsāra.* The *ḍamaru* beats out the rhythmic sounds (mantras) via the Libran petal to cyclically empower second Ray purpose to overcome the lures of humanity's emotional attachment to the fields of *māyā.* The bell intones the sound of emptiness to all that begin to awaken from the dream of *saṃsāra.* The *kapāla* bears the *amṛtā* (ambrosia), the 'Blood' of Love and Life that is poured to those that undertake the testings to overcome their material selves so as to enter the ranks of Hierarchy.

The noose of entrails ensnares attachments associated with the centres below the diaphragm. Consequently, it helps to annul the *karma* of the aspirants that offer themselves for service, by setting the arenas whereby they can cleanse it by way of their compassionate aspirations. It is but a form of the swastika. The swastika moves in the opposite direction to the right to left motion of that wielded by humanity. The purpose (with K.H.'s assistance) is to fuse all pairs of opposites into a unity, balancing the left and right hand *prāṇas* (as well as of good and evil) in the field of life, so that ultimately only the good, the true, and the bountiful harvest in the Heart of Life is produced. Hence the fixed cross of the heavens is established, upon which the manifold serving disciples that arise will be crucified. As far as human free will allows at any time, such compassionate action imposes the rhythm of the cycles of Love, Light, and Peace, producing a serenity that overcomes the plight of the bewildered in the dark, turbulent, pain filled fields of *saṃsāra.*

The significance of the Piscean era

The Piscean era that we have just transited through has empowered the Watery dispensation of humanity, assisted by the two other Watery signs (Cancer and Scorpio). Exemplified is the *southeast piṅgalā* line of the 2/6-6/2 and associated sixth Ray Ashrams that heralded the beginning of the Piscean era. They produced teachings yoked or bonded to devotion, aspiration, zealotry and the heightened emotions. In Figure 10 these Ashrams embody the Taurean petal, which governs the entire field of desire-attachment of humanity. Such activity must eventually be converted to wisdom as aspirants travel around the zodiacal wheel. In the Aquarian age the Waters are set to dissipate, hence the influence of the sixth Ray Ashrams (governed principally by the Taurus-Scorpio relationship[6]) will wane.

If one takes the Ashrams governing the southern hemisphere as manifesting in the form of the Hierarchical hand projecting its *prāṇas* into human activity, then this sixth Ray line embodies the functions of the thumb.[7] The objective was to lay the foundation of the principle of Love via devotional aspiration by humanity. This was necessary because of general humanity's basic level of preparedness, as their overall level of development had to be taken into account. Devotional and aspirational stimulation allows future higher penetration into the citadels of Love. The outpouring of the work of the sixth Ray Ashrams were needed to impel this purpose. Jesus, the then future sixth Ray Chohan, consequently instigated this major Hierarchical cycle. The work of the 2/4-4/2 Ashrams then followed, which overlapped much of the sixth Ray epoch. Next came the activity of the 2/7-7/2 Ashrams, followed by the 2/5-5/2 Ashrams and finally the 2/3-3/2 Ashrams, with significant overlapping occurring between all of these stages.

The above can be considered to represent the five subdivisions of the Piscean epoch, with the emphasis being upon the expansion of the Christian West, then the rapid development of the empirical mind of humanity. The first epoch of the Christian era was primarily the effect of the labour of the sixth Ray Ashrams as they simultaneously evolved. This ascertained the exemplification of some of the most extreme aspects of Pisces, where the keynotes are given as: '1. Bondage or captivity. 2. Renunciation or detachment. 3. Sacrifice and death'.[8]

---

6 They are polar opposites in the zodiac.

7 The seventh Ray Ashrams take the functions of the Earthy middle finger, the fifth Ray Ashrams the Fiery index finger, the third Ray Ashrams of the Aetheric little finger, and the fourth Ray Ashrams of the Airy ring finger.

8 Bailey, *Esoteric Astrology,* 115.

The emotional Watery environment wherein the bonded fish swims became a battle zone. This explains much of the exaggerated attributes of the Christian religion, based upon polemics in relation to the sexual function, narrow-minded bigotry and martial fanaticism. The willing martyrdom of many early Christians, as well as many of the Muslim faith, comes under the auspices of this Ray flavour.

At that time the energies from the world-Soul were perverted by the intensity of emotional thinking then focused through the early theologians. They railroaded the Christian religion away from the original intention of its founder. We thus have the zealotry of intolerant diatribes against the Pagan religion and any Christian sect not deemed orthodox, thus the Arian controversy, and the programs against the Gnostics. There was also the rise of dogmatic theology that inevitably produced one form or other of inquisitional activity against their fellow humans. Then came the rise of a religion deeply influenced by mystics, and concepts of renunciation through celibacy which was imposed upon the priestly class. A good example during the early formative periods of Christianity were the anchorites, many of whom practiced forms of extreme asceticism in the desert sands of Egypt.

Later many fourth and seventh Ray disciples incarnated who gave us the magnificent Gothic Cathedrals and accompanying artworks. The general stimulus of all Ray Ashrams was produced by Hierarchy during the Renaissance. This was followed by the first proper outpouring of fifth Ray disciples, such as Copernicus, Paracelsus, Galileo, and later Newton, to lay the foundation of modern empirical science. The fifth Ray dispensation increased with vigour over the following centuries (coupled with the general fourth Ray purpose), which increasingly superseded and eventually supplanted the role of religion in society, producing a new 'religion' of scientific materialism.

The seventh Ray saw its main influence in the rise of the modern Masonic movement, and other occult organisations, such as the Rosicrucians. We also have the American Revolution, where the major players were seventh Ray disciples, to a lesser degree the French Revolution, and the rise of the Industrial Revolution. The general influence of the fourth Ray continued unabated, especially seen in the flowering of the creative arts that essentially culminated just after the end of the nineteenth century with the rise of the Impressionists and the early Moderns.

The end of the nineteenth century brought the import of the work of the second and third Ray Ashrams to the fore. This produced the explosion of research into the nature of Eastern religious beliefs and their incorporation into Western society that we see nowadays, plus the establishment of the Theosophical movement and its offshoots, such as the work of Rudolf Steiner and Alice Bailey. Then there is the various Kabbalistic, spiritualistic, and mystical groups, such as the Baha'i. Christianity also rose to the challenge that the scientific era imposed upon it to produce many excellent scholarly revisionist texts and instigated archaeological research to 'prove' the validity of their doctrines. There was also a rise of modern concepts of philosophy, psychology, then the mathematical analysis that is the backbone of science and technology and the methodology of modern financiers.

From this very brief history it can be seen that the interrelated cycles of influence of the various Ray dispensations produced different effects. The earlier sixth Ray dispensation lasted the longest, whilst the subjective influence of the fourth Ray grew stronger as the modern era approached to help lay an aesthetic and ethical foundation for the inevitable rise of the epoch of the dominance of mind - of the mind's naturally separative, empirical, divisive and reifying attributes.

The Chohans of the Rays of Mind

Having analysed the east-west axis, I shall now focus upon the northern quadrant, which with this axis represents the Splenic centre's correspondence to the 'sacred petals' of the Hierarchical Heart centre. The Ashrams of the five southern petals constitute the non-sacred petals. This represents the five types of *prāṇas* needed to be cleansed by the manifest body, which cyclically course through the veins of the extant civilisation. Directing these *prāṇas* becomes the function of the seven Ray Chohans. They ground the related qualities into *saṃsāric* activity via the subsidiary sub-Ray Ashrams. There we have the crucible of experience wherein all aspects of *saṃsāra* are processed and eventually converted into the elixir of immortality, the philosopher's stone. The focus of service work to awaken the new era is via the second sub-Ray Ashrams of their respective Ray lines and the related second Ray Ashrams.

The seventh Ray Chohan wields the Piscean petal, whose main purpose has been to ground the *iḍā nāḍī* gains of the Piscean era. This produced the ceremonial aspects of religion and then facilitated the scientific endeavour that is the mainstay of the present materialistic civilisation. His work via the seventh Ray Ashrams also helped produce the esoteric fraternities in the seventeenth century and their rebirthing in modern forms that will seed the new epoch. This Chohan also works with the second and first Ray potencies of Pisces (via its rulers, Jupiter and Pluto) to produce the necessary changes in the transition period to terminate the old Piscean idealisms based upon the sixth Ray, so that the new second Ray dispensation (governed by Master Jupiter) can be effected. The once veiled ceremonial Mystery Schools of the past and occult traditions in Europe are thereby reborn as the new world religion. This is especially significant, as the oncoming Aquarian era will be ruled by the seventh Ray, by virtue of Uranus, the exoteric ruler of Aquarius.

This Chohan works in the guise of Karma Heruka (the reflex of Amoghasiddhi) to change the effects of *saṃskāric* conditionings so that the new may arise. His is the materialising power that cyclically grounds Shambhalic Plans in such a way that the magical effects upon substance suits the evolving need.

A key phrase for Pisces at this level of expression is—*mediatorship* between the One and the all to produce the liberation of life by severing the bonds to the form.

The fifth Ray Chohan (Hilarion/Sakya Paṇḍita) will work to transform the *iḍā* dispensation of the rulership of mind into the acquisition of Mind for the now manifesting Aquarian dispensation. The keynote of Aquarius at this level is—compassionate Bodhisattvic action dispensing the Waters of Life. *Manasic* Life is presently the predominant Ray stimulus that governs the progression of human evolution. It facilitates the dispensation of the radiant aura of Hierarchy into humanity, and so illuminating the *māyā* of human substance with vibrant Light. New non-materialistic sciences will thereby eventually evolve that will truly investigate all of Nature's forces, subjective and objective, without the present zealous bias towards physical plane phenomenon.[9] Hilarion's disciples will also

9 My focus in this section of the book is upon the human kingdom, hence I have largely omitted the work of the *devas*, and of those Masters who are engrossed in liberating the other kingdoms of Nature.

properly investigate the ramifications of the scientific achievements of the ancient civilisations to show the true antiquity of these civilisations, thus eliminating the bigotry presently promulgated by the academic establishment. Also, the stultifying materialistic bias concerning the investigation of human origins shall be countered, partly by exposing the nature of the suppressed evidence that contradicts current prevailing dogma. Considerable work has already been done in these fields, but much still remains to be discovered, waiting for the epoch where evidence can no longer be suppressed, evaded, erroneously labelled and shelved, or wantonly destroyed. Scientific data concerning all of the esoteric sciences will then be more forthcoming, greatly enriching human civilisation in ways presently conceived of as speculative fantasy. This new epoch of discovery is symbolised by Air, the Element governing Aquarius.

In working via the polar opposite fifth Ray Ashrams to vitalise the Sambhogakāya Flowers with Fiery solar *prāṇas,* then the 'Lion of the Lord' manifests. Energies are poured forth from the heart of the Sun to flood the sum of the domains of mind/Mind. Appropriately seeded with the Hierarchical vision and energies of the new epoch, human Souls can then impress their incarnate personalities with the needed prompts to work to the stated goals in their fields of activity.

Hilarion's attribute as Padma Heruka (the reflex of Amitābha) aptly empowers him to overcome the egotistical, separative attitudes of the polar opposite sign, Leo. It also facilitates his work with the Sambhogakāya Flowers and to rightly invigorate all *chakras* in Nature.

The third Ray Chohan, the *Venetian,*[10] is sensitively attuned to and identified with the creative aspirations of the world's intelligentsia and disciples, to which is poured the energies of revelatory idealism that uplifts their visioning to new heights. His Capricornian position (the mountain of mind/Mind) facilitates the projection of Shambhalic Ideation into humanity. The structure of humanity's *manasic* outpouring will be woven to integrate the developing Minds of the world's foremost thinkers. The focus is upon the composition and intensity of the energies *(prāṇas)* needed to produce the new changes that allow seeding the necessary elements of Mind into human civilisation. The appropriate distribution of all of the planet's resources, monetary, mineral, Watery and mental, is at his command.

---

10 An important Tibetan incarnation of his being Jigme Lingpa.

The key phrase for this sign at this level is—*patient endurance* to overcome all levels of the portals of death, thus initiating one into ways of cosmic Mind. Patience concerns the organisation of all cycles of the life process working through the context of the world-sphere and related civilisation. Human evolution progresses in slow, carefully metered stages, though the progress in the past few centuries has been comparatively meteoric. Patience is needed to see the fruition of sometimes millennia-long cycles of planned activity. An example being the processes needed to calm the emotional sensitivities and aggrandisement of the collective desires of the human family, with their warlike, strife-ridden turmoil.

Working via his seventh Ray brother (who governs the physical plane externalisation of the third Ray purpose), we will inevitably see that the finances that lubricate all aspects of our societies will be appropriately allocated to build the technology and cities according to a vibrant Hierarchical Plan. The evils of the present fiat system of creating money out of thin air must be eliminated and replaced with an equable, properly securitised commodity or resource based monetary system, or a new system of barter. The true worth of human labour will be rightly acknowledged by law and not exaggeratedly depreciated in favour of a wealthy elite (as is nowadays everywhere evident). New societal systems will be established to serve the common weal, facilitating people to devote themselves to a presented vision of a new age of cooperative sharing as the norm.

This Chohan manifests as Buddha Heruka (the reflex of Vairocana), who integrates the activities of the other Rays of Mind. The ferocity of this energy will gradually overcome the negative impediments of mind (left hand attributes) developed by humanity, to facilitate the path of wisdom that allows travelling up the mount to Hierarchy's domain.

The fourth Ray Chohan's (Serapis, Atiśa) energy works to unify all facets of this Splenic centre *maṇḍala* via the Sagittarian impulse. The arrows direct *piṇgalā prāṇas* so that humanity will be eventually integrated into the inner sanctum of the temple of Life (in the polar opposite sign, Gemini). Serapis primarily integrates the relationship between the human and *deva* Hierarchies. He sings the notes calling forth great orchestrations of *devic* lives from various cosmic sources to assist in the new planetary venture. They weave the reticulated *nāḍīs* through which the vital cosmic energies can pour, invigorating all Hierarchical endeavour. The *devas* will vitalise the created forms of the new cultural activities and of the arts with sound and colour in the coming cycle of Love. They embody the substance of all that must come to be. The new forms vitalised will express the radiance from the Heart of the Sun.

The key phrase for the Sagittarian impulse at this level is—*one-pointed striving* upon the path to Shambhalic Life. Sagittarius is the projector of cosmic Light into the Temple of Life so that all Lives can awaken *chakras* of sight.

The *piṇgalā* stream blends the fourth and sixth Ray purpose. Serapis thus embodies the energetic functioning of the new Temple of Love, whilst Jesus officiates as the religious preceptor, who offers the sacraments and sacred vestments for the noviciates that can master the required training. Jesus has the power that makes the encroaching energies from the cosmic Christ possible. The result is the active projection of the blended qualities as the *prāṇas* of vital Hierarchical life and devotion into the world of human activity.

Serapis takes the role of Vajra Heruka (the reflex of Akṣobhya) acting as a mirror to reflect the potency and beauty of Hierarchy into the new civilisation.

The sixth Ray Chohan (Jesus/Milarepa) directs cosmic astral energies via the impetus of Scorpio the scorpion in such a way that the attributes of desire, selfishness, and glamour-forming tendencies in humanity will be properly controlled and converted to aspiration to high ideals. This effects the many testings related to overcoming spiritual ambition, selfishness, avarice, various forms of fanaticism and the mislaid devotion of the generally religiously oriented masses. The work will be regulated by the sixth Ray Ashrams.

In his role as Ratna Heruka, Jesus holds the Watery dispensation of the world's bejewelled *nāḍī* system in thrall and moves the streams of sometimes gaily coloured, but often murky, turbulent emotional mix, according to the next great test needed to purify the Waters. Its expression is to be harmonised and made sparkling clean, according to the purpose of the Christ's department.

The key phrase for Scorpio at this level is—*conflict resolution* in discipleship so that arcs of Love can convert desire-mind into the Heart's Mind.

Subsidiary Ray considerations

There are five 'fingers' of expression concerning the work of the Ashrams governing the southern portion of this *maṇḍala*. First to consider is the *Taurean petal,* consisting of the *2/6-6/2 Ray Ashrams.* They are effectively the Consort to the work of the sixth Ray Chohan when acting in the guise of Ratna Heruka for humanity. A keynote of Taurus at this stage is—*illuminating wisdom* overcoming the fields of desire. The fruit of the Mahatic[11] Love projected by the new Mahāchohan via the Arian point causes the vibrancy of the development and awakening of all the petals of this Hierarchical Lotus (Splenic centre I). Hence the necessary utilisation of the cleansing potency of the Waters that are the speciality of the sixth Ray department. First all aspects of desire-attachment must be developed and mastered. Here lie most of the major tests, trials, and tribulations for people as they strive to overcome their gross desires, sensuality, fanaticisms, mental-emotional bigotry, religious zealotry, and emotion-filled intoxications. Aspects of these qualities besot most lives. This is one of the most difficult fields of activity undertaken by Hierarchy, as it involves so many drastic changes in people's lives concerning the motivation for their various forms of selfish behaviour. This process finds its resolution in the polar opposite sign, Scorpio.

Refinement of the various forms of desire-attachment inevitably lead to devotion upon the religious path, to various concepts of deity. This can be to a plurality of gods or expressions of divinity, or to the concept of one God, of that which unifies and embodies all. Also there can be more subjective concepts, such as devotion to the *dharma* and the compassionate ideal in Buddhism, or to Ma'at, the universal law or order of things in the ancient Egyptian religion. Devotion signifies a form of attachment or relation between the devotee and that which is the beloved. Devotion inevitably leads to aspiration to noble ideals. It is important that the right blending of devotion and Love is carefully formulated and provided for human consumption so that it helps develop wisdom and not fiery inquisitional or fanatical zeal. (Which is destructive in its intent.)

The ambidextrous thumb is here utilised, bearing Watery energies to the Earthy terrain ruled by Taurus, under whose impetus some of

---

11 Mahat here referring to the energies of the empirical Mind of a presiding Logos.

the most ancient religions were sired. Together they lay the field of expression of the desire principle that eventually becomes the battle zone, the Hydra's swamp, in Scorpio. This activity is presided over by the sixth Ray Chohan, Jesus. Some of his work, and hence of the subsidiary sixth Ray Ashrams, was explained in relation to the sign Pisces (a Water sign) that we are now exiting, hence need not be repeated. Eventually the Equalising Wisdom of Ratnasambhava will manifest in humanity to integrate the diverse forms of religious expression into unity.

The *prāṇas*[12] directed by the 2/6-6/2 and 2/4-4/2 and subsidiary Ashrams represent the *piṇgalā* response to the energies from humanity coming via the planetary Liver centre to be processed in Splenic centre II. The fourth and sixth Rays are Rays of reflection, energisation, and experiential expression.

The Airy *Gemini* ring finger regulates the general incoming *prāṇas* and impressions from humanity, especially the artistic and creative impulses that beautify and produce great benefit upon the human societies. Here then is the focus of the work of the *2/4-4/2 Ray Ashrams.* They utilise the directive potencies fired by the fourth Ray Chohan from his Sagittarian function as Vajra Heruka so that eventually Akṣobhya's Mirror-like Wisdom is expressed by humanity. This is seen in terms of expressed beautifying harmony and right human relations.

The key phrase for Gemini at this level of expression is—*service to the other*, thereby integrating polar opposites into the sanctity of the Heart. Service represents the continuously blissful, wise, loving inter-departmental Hierarchical activity wherein all lines of relationship and co-endeavour are always carried out and the plan rightly unfolded. It is the moving arm of wisdom in the arenas where right action is most effective. It is the mouth that speaks the word according to well planned cycles of opportunity, awakening the hearts of those seeking release from turmoiled *saṃsāric* illusion.

Gemini governs the Temple of the Lord wherein the sum of the Hierarchical energy is integrated, for this Temple is the body of manifestation of the Hierarchical *maṇḍala,* where the Airy 2/4-4/2 Ray Ashrams specifically exemplify the *piṇgalā nāḍī,* the Love-Wisdom principle. This represents the right pillar of the two pillars

12 There is obviously a coming and going for each direction and Ashram, related specifically to which Ray energy is energised at any time, or which is being withdrawn.

associated with this sign. It necessitates the *manasic iḍā* function (the left pillar, specifically exemplified by the Fiery 2/5-5/2 Ray Ashrams) to lay the foundation of comprehension in humanity, if all energies from Shambhala are to be rightly projected to the manifesting phenomena of the material domains so that people can gain their liberation. They are aided by the Ashrams constituting the Watery thumb and the Earthy middle finger of Splenic centre I dispensation. All arenas of conflict must be vanquished before people can gain access to the inner sanctum of this temple.

The fourth Ray Ashrams are sensitively attuned to the true creative needs and abilities of humanity, orienting them to rightly respond to the flow of Love. Humanity's right orientation produces an aesthetic environmental landscape (looking at the word 'environment' in its widest connotation, as the sum of human habitation and livingness), peace and harmony from out of the present materialistic malaise that grips the planet. The innate selfishness and superficial activities of the average person in the Aquarian epoch must be countered by the fourth Ray workers via their creative, harmonising aptitudes. Such labour is not easily successfully accomplished due to the voracious selfishness of most people. Right group and social mores are to be engendered, with an aesthetic bias, producing an integrated harmony and beauty of the developed civilisation. Differing opinions and philosophies of life need to be integrated, harmonised, into unified purpose. The creative genius of inter-disciplinary activity of all people in the various departments of life must therefore be inspired. This lays the foundation for the various ideals of the dawning new age ruled by the Aquarian gate. (Another Airy sign.)

The diverse modifications and activities of the 'man-plant'[13] working in the field of desire-mind will thus be inevitably resolved into harmonious unity. The Hierarchal Plan for entry of people into the adytum of the temple in Gemini concerns establishing groups of like-minded people working cooperatively and creatively with each other to unfold the principles of the *dharma*. These principles define the laws governing the common good, necessitating a fair distribution and sharing of the world's resources so that all may receive the maximum benefit of life's providence without destroying the environmental balance and

13 A term derived from H.P. Blavatsky's *The Secret Doctrine.*

harmony of the planet. The individuals within the groups will be spread all over the world and will largely not know of the existence of each other, yet will share a common vision. Also, there will be cooperative work with the forces of Nature, rather than destructively, as at present.

All conflicting opinions and arguments will eventually be resolved into a collective understanding that serves to foster goodwill and cooperativeness and not separative factions. The inherent good in all philosophies and religions and their harmonising influence must be fostered, so that they serve each other rather than sowing the seeds of dissension and strife. For this purpose a new, truly reformed United Nations must evolve, wherein no nation possesses veto power, where proper democratic principles rule, totally uninfluenced by financial or manipulative coercion of any superpower or aggressively self-centered group of powers. The Waters of Life will then flood our civilisation with harmonising goodwill and the Will-to-Love.

The *Cancerian petal* represents the open gate for the downpour of the energies from Shambhala that dynamically directs Hierarchy, and similarly for Hierarchical compassion to the lesser kingdoms in Nature. Cancer is the gateway of the birth of the Watery energies of cosmic Love into our planetary life so that the massed consciousness of those on earth can be rightly stimulated. Here the key phrase for this sign is—*apotropaic sensitivity* to the mental-emotional tides generated by humanity. Hierarchy responds in such a way that expressed wisdom is the gain. Cancer manifests as the opener of the Door to the higher liberated domains.

Here we have the work of the 2/3-3/2 Ashrams, hence the efforts of the 2/3 Master, D.K. He is a major source of the esoteric doctrine, feeding Hierarchical Ideation into the minds of the world's disciples so that fixed and idealistic (Piscean) beliefs can be overcome by the books he has written. A new visionary impetus can then shine in the awakened minds. Many formerly esoteric subjects have been unveiled, though generally most who receive them interpret via empirical minds still, because they lack the Initiations to properly envision the subjective depth and vast scope of the hidden meanings. Much is veiled through symbolical and numerical coding, and much is still omitted, as the revelation of the Mysteries can only be provided in stages. The 2/3 Ashram formed in the early 1800's with D.K's activity in Tibet. He is primed to succeed the position of the second Ray Chohan when that great one moves on to the position of the blue Christ for the planet.

The calming Hierarchical group energy (described as 'the Comforter' or 'Holy Ghost' in the Bible) descends via this southern gate of the *maṇḍala.* It puts humanity in touch with the overshadowing of vast stores of Hierarchical wisdom and the overriding long-range embrace of their collective Souls. (The World-Soul to which they become increasingly sensitised.)

This 2/3 outpouring represents the work of the little, Aetheric finger, of the hand projected by this Hierarchical *maṇḍala.* It manifests as the wisest second Ray qualification for the general stimulatory consumption of human minds. The purpose is to generate abstract thinking, well seeded with compassionate thought. We should note, however, that these energies generally become debased because of the Watery disposition of humanity. It necessitates the correction and refinement of the little bits of illogical ungainly mind stuff people possess. The thought process must become entirely sanctified. It demands careful monitoring of those preparing to enter into Hierarchical domains by identifying the true needs of the world's disciples. The Fiery qualities of their minds can then be fanned so that added radiance shall enhance the current civilisation with the seed thoughts of the new. Utopian ideals benefitting the whole will then manifest. The thoughts projected concern ways that our civilisation can be enriched. Primarily, however, educating disciples so that they can undertake Initiation occupies the bulk of the work of the adherents of this Ray line.

This Aetheric finger represents the extent that humanity can presently consume of the most esoteric portion of Hierarchy's teaching dispensation. It stimulates thoughts in the New Group of World Servers. This is the *suṣumṇā* stream, projecting energies from the centres above the diaphragm to be processed by the planetary Splenic centre II. We thereby have the expression of the Buddha Heruka's Consort manifesting in a form that will eventually empower on earth the Dharmadhātu Wisdom of Vairocana.

The 2/3-3/2 Ashrams therefore plan the mechanisms *(antaḥkaraṇas)* that provide ways of escape from the present impasse of materialistic thought in our strife-filled world into arenas of enlightened activity. Bridges are built from mundanely orientated, erroneous and sensationalised philosophies, to that which more factually represents the nature of incarnating Divinity. Thus the new religious dispensation is born for the appearing new world civilisation; the externalisation of 'the New Jerusalem', or 'Heavenly City' on the earth.

The outgoing *prāṇas* from the 2/5-5/2 and 7/2-2/7 and subsidiary Ashrams (Leo-Virgo) express *iḍā nāḍī prāṇas* coming to and from the planetary Stomach centre and Splenic centre II. Empirical streams of mind are thereby conveyed in order to be processed and refined. New ideas and visionary impressions through philosophic enterprise, science, technology, the material distribution of finances and other resources, can then awaken to produce advances in various strata of human society. Technological innovations are produced that help enlighten people by providing enhanced time to pursue meditative and creative enterprises. The new era will consequently flower once these *prāṇas* meet the required grade by overcoming materialistic thinking in humanity.

The Fiery forefinger, causing the projection of *manasic* impetus and idealism from Hierarchy, is governed by the *Leonine* 2/5-5/2 Ray Ashramic purpose. Consequently, Divine Fiery Love enflames and vibrantly infuses the sum of the Hierarchy, and those they must serve, with the attributes of Mind. The glory of the Hierarchy then shines as the radiant sun[14] (or 'son of God') blazing forth its light for all other suns/Sons to behold.

A key phrase of this sign is—the *humbleness* that reveals the all-Self as the Heart of Life. Humbleness is a mantric sound emanated by the Hierarchical lotus, the Heart centre in the greater body of the planet. Humbleness produces the coordinated note of the rhythm of the whole that embodies the second Ray purpose via mastery of mind, and bears the Fiery domain of Mind of the Mahāchohan's department as a distributive energy. This concerns equanimous reception to, and understanding of, the needs of others.

These Ashrams act as the Consort for the fifth Ray Chohan (Aquarius) who takes the guise of Padma Heruka so that Amitābha's Discriminating Inner Wisdom will eventually govern human thought. *Manasic* purpose floods the world so that humanity can eventually climb the mount of Initiation to their united transfiguration experience. There will be a wise, creative blending of all Hierarchical energies and

---

14 Leo being ruled exoterically, esoterically, and Hierarchically by the Sun.

enterprises to rightly assist the intelligent, creative, and well-informed people in our era. Humanity must scientifically build a bright and wondrous future. The rampant materialism, widespread moral decay, choking pollution, planned obsolescence, and continual warfare throughout the world must end. The selfish, egotistical intention of the masses thus need to be overcome. Their focus must be redirected away from limited and destructively repetitious mental-emotional activity towards what better serves the common good. Logical pathways to serve the all must be sought after and found, necessitating a careful blending of the forces of both Heart and Mind in humanity. (A focus of these Ashrams of the Rays of Mind.) Scientific activity will then no longer be prostituted to focus upon weapons of destruction and purely commercial ends, but towards truly beneficial labour saving devices, plus those innovations that further the advancement of knowledge in directions beyond purely material concerns.

The existence of the kingdom of the Sambhogakāya Flower upon the higher mental plane will in time be discovered via scientific enquiry. These Flowers will be seen as the guiding principle nourishing the evolving minds of humanity, allowing better comprehension of the propensity of the nature of Mind in all righteous fields of human activity. A new form of spiritually based science will evolve, utilising comprehension of the gain of esoteric reasoning regarding Nature's finer forces and of *devas,* to impulse our civilisation into new heights of livingness. Religion and science will merge into unity upon increasingly higher arcs of the spiral of evolution. When the blinkers are removed from the eyes of our scientific community then the epoch of scientific materialism will end and the epoch where humanity can truly set their sights to cosmos will herald. A far vaster and more complex multidimensional space will be discovered than ever dreamt of by present scientists. The abundant Life therein will be seen and new forms of technology based upon command of the ethers will then be appropriated, in cooperation with our space brethren.

Another way of meditating upon the Ray relationships concerns the comprehension of the primacy of the fifth Ray in the governance of mind/Mind. All forms of Ray expressions find their modes of activity via Fire. Truly all we perceive is but an expression of mind/Mind, as all emanates from the Mind of the cosmic Logos, whose activity is reflected by the minds of self-conscious units. The fifth Ray is the crucible of experience wherein all come together and are blended in the Fire to produce the Mind of Revelation and the path to liberation, which is the purpose of it all. The generation of Fire, rightly blended with Love and Will, is the Dharmakāya Way, the making of a Shambhalic recipient. The Leonine focus directs the Fire that Way. The second and third Rays are Rays of conscious expansion and abstraction into the enlightened Mind. The seventh and first Rays are Rays of cyclic embodiment of the forms of expression and projection of the gained experience into the unity of Life.

The *Virgoan petal* fecundates the intelligence principle that must arise and respond to the word of Love. It is the womb of consciousness. All aspects of Hierarchical achievement and plans are nurtured in this womb so that the Fires of Love and the expansion of the revelatory awareness of the Life aspect proceeds towards Shambhala. The key phrase for the Virgoan petal is—*sympathetic identification* with the needs of all so that light can be born from darkness. It embodies the Love of the Mother. Here new ideas and ideals must be increasingly and progressively born within the current epoch in context of bringing into flower the new world civilisation. Hence the Christ-child appears amongst us, all Hearts having awakened to comprehension of the nature and purpose of Love-Wisdom. Virgo also integrates the *deva* kingdom into the sum of Hierarchical life via the common quality of the light of Mind that unites them both.

The middle Earthy finger is here implicated, governed by the attributes of the 2/7-7/2 Ray Ashrams. All forces that effect the material world are thereby grounded through cyclic, ritualistic activity. Many cycles come and go through long, arduous strife and struggle before the fruits of the planted seeds of Love in action can be harvested.

The evolution of all of Nature's kingdoms, from the mineral up, must be taken into account. Mind is inherent in all phenomena and must be drawn out and gradually brought to a state of enlightened receptivity. The Mind's rhythms must be ritualistically applied to control humanity's turbulent astral ocean of thought and desire forms. Love-Wisdom must dominate human society. Real *siddhis* of magical accomplishment can then be obtained by people via a rigorous control of astral plane phenomena, producing magical effects upon the physical domain.

The time will therefore come when the laws of the astral plane will be scientifically studied and its substance mastered. This task shall be accentuated as the seventh Ray governing the forthcoming Aquarian age gradually comes to the fore, awakening the science of ritualised control of subjective and objective substance.

The many cycles of emotional turmoil within humanity; socially, nationally and internationally, must subside and the way to the collective human Heart be found. This necessitates following the ritual of enlightened activity, similar to the way the Heart cyclically beats out its rhythms of blood flow. It ceremoniously projects related hormonal secretions (Hierarchical activity) from various glands within the human kingdom to all parts of the body.

The *iḍā nāḍī prāṇas* from the collective Stomach centres of humanity are processed via this finger in the form of a *manasic* Earthy aspect as they are passed to Splenic centre II for processing. All forces and attributes from the inner realms therefore become properly grounded in *saṃsāra*. Much concerning overcoming the power of the dark brotherhood upon the material plane and their eventual conversion to the ways of the forces of Light comes under the auspices of the seventh Ray. Similarly for the associated Leonine petal. The wrathful attributes of Karma Heruka's Consort produces this purpose for those training to pass the second and higher Initiations. Amoghasiddhi's All-accomplishing Wisdom is the gain. The process of cyclic cleansing of humanity's most base *saṃskāras* lays the ground for the fruit of the tree of Initiation.

In terms of *the alchemical process,* the second Ray is the flux, the fifth Ray is the Fire, the seventh Ray is the crucible, the sixth Ray the sulphurous stuff that transforms.[15] The fourth Ray is the Mercurous element that undergoes the various changes of experience, and the third Ray is eventually extracted as the Philosopher's stone when rightly driven by the first Ray fused with the flux. When made potent by the first Ray, the second Ray drives the third to transform the Fiery fifth via the fourth. Together they empower the residual sixth and seventh to transmogrify all base metals into the vital gold that is the Hierarchical Life.

---

15 The third Ray works via the sixth Ray during the transmutative process.

The third Ray of divinely ordered Mathematical Activity is the matrix that acts as the vehicle for *dharmakāya* to resonate throughout the form and transform all substances via the ritualistic seventh Ray. The combined first and second Rays pierce all barriers of formed space to drive the radiant essence of the golden substance to domains incomprehensible by mind. With them the purpose of the major Ray conditionings governing the present epoch is established.

The three major *nāḍīs* governing Hierarchy can also be viewed as below:

1. *Suṣumṇā –The initiating Will-of-Love.* The cardinal points of directive, creative Will and abstracting resolve.
   a. In the fields of Life—Shambhalic Lords via the first Ray Chohan.
   b. Directing the course of civilisation—the new Mahāchohan.
   c. In the darkened realms—the 2/1-1/2 Ray lines.
   The seventh Ray Chohan grounds this purposeful endeavour in the realms of form.
2. *Piṇgalā –The reservoirs of Loving Endeavour.* The serene points of poised, dynamically quantified Love and Wisdom sustaining the purpose.
   a. In all realms wherein Life is found—The Christ and K.H. via the second Ray Ashrams.
   b. In all currents within the streams of civilisation—Serapis and the fourth Ray Ashrams.
   c. In all pools of darkened, then aspirational resolve—the sixth Ray Ashrams.

   Jesus projects this Love in the Watery streams and cesspits of desire, and the 2/3 Master in the Fiery fields of earth.
3. *Iḍā—The disseminators of the vitality of Mind.* The points of compassionate, purposeful activity resolving Love through Mind.
   a. In all groupings of Life where Love must be evoked—the third Ray Chohan via the third Ray Ashrams.
   b. In all streams of consciousness wherein obstacles block the flow—Hilarion and the fifth Ray Ashrams.
   c. In all caverns and stagnant pools of earthy concerns—the seventh Ray Ashrams.
   The Masters of the Rays of Mind disseminate this vitality to the devitalised ones that cry in the night.

The Chohans have major challenges confronting them.

- The new Mahāchohan is to become a 'cosmic Cow' offering the milk of resplendent nourishment to the thirsty disciples awakening high Initiate perceptions in this new age.
- K.H. must further develop his receptivity to and expression of first Ray energies, if he is to meet the challenge of assuming the role of the blue Christ for this new age. Mastery of this level of planetary Will completes all of the Ray line directives needed to direct the entire Hierarchy of Love.
- Jesus must develop increased receptivity to incoming second Ray energies from the cosmic Christ, if this energy is to appropriately succour the devotional attributes of the new world civilisation. Love-Wisdom must become its keynote.
- Serapis firmly anchors his role in both the great Mother's department and Hierarchy by working to rightly integrate the eventual marriage of groups of humans and *devas* within the temple of Hierarchical life. This marriage is a progression of the step associated with the fourth Initiation, which D.K. explains in terms of the development of the 'will aspect of Shambhala'.

> As man develops the will aspect, he learns to break loose from the aura of the deva evolution, and the major task of the Hierarchy (as far as basic essentials are concerned) is to "provide sanctuary" to those who have liberated themselves from the ocean of deva energies in which their vehicles must perforce move and live and have their being, but with which they have otherwise no point of contact, once liberated by their own effort and will "from the angels."[16]

- This globe is the fourth of a chain of seven globes within a planetary Scheme that is likewise the fourth, and upon it the fourth kingdom (humanity) possesses the right quality. All are governed by the fourth Ray, consequently Morya must utilise the soothing, mediating, moderating effect of the fourth Ray energy to ensure that the first Ray is not too harsh and destructive in its effects.

16 A.A. Bailey, *The Rays and the Initiations,* 181.

- Rakoczi must empower the seventh Ray purpose in a way that its adherents are not sidetracked into higher, more *manasic* (therefore more potent) forms of sorcery and magic that was the nemesis of the Atlanteans. The Aquarian epoch must be flooded with Fiery Love directed by the organisational abilities of *R*'s department.
- Hilarion must weave the paradigms of the new spiritual sciences into the mainstream of human civilisation.
- The third Ray Chohan will work to weave the right energy interrelations into the patterns of human civilisations.

The seven Chohans can be considered the modern equivalents of the seven Rishis (Sages) of the ancient Hindu philosophy. In Shambhala, however, Ray Lords also exist that are the direct bearers of the energies of the seven planetary Schemes, of which the Rishis are emissaries.

The Importance of the seventh Ray

The relationship between the new Mahāchohan and Rakoczi should be further considered here, as together they wield the potency that will externalise Hierarchy into active manifestation via the materialising power of the seventh Ray. The relation between the two is that between the one styled as The Rider on the White Horse and Master *R* as the Lord of Civilisation. As stated by D.K.:

> The ending of the present evil situation is, therefore, a cooperative measure; and here, in this connection, we have the appearance of the Lord of Civilisation Who voices and engineers upon the physical plane the fiat of the Lord of Liberation and of the Rider from the secret place. He aids and makes possible, owing to His control, the precipitating upon the Earth and in the arena of combat, of the power generated by the Lords of Liberation, expressed by the coming One and focussed through Him as the hierarchical Representative in Europe... You have therefore:
>
> 1. The Lords of Liberation, reached by the advanced spiritual thinkers of the word whose minds are rightly focussed.
> 2. The Rider on the white horse or from the secret place, reached by those whose hearts are rightly touched.
> 3. The Lord of Civilisation, the Master R., reached by all who, with the first two groups, can stand with "massed intent."

> On the united work of these Three, if humanity can succeed in calling Them forth, will come the alignment and the correct relation of three great spiritual centres of the planet, a thing which has never occurred before. Then:
>
> 4. The Lords of Liberation will receive and transmit to the Hierarchy energy from the centre *where God's Will is known and furthered.*
> 5. The Rider will receive this energy and take such action as will express it, plus the motivating energy from the centre *where God's Love is expressed.*
> 6. The Lord of Civilisation will stimulate and prepare the centre which we call humanity for right reception of this re-vitalising, stimulating and releasing force.
>
> Thus Shamballa, the Hierarchy and Humanity will stand consciously related and dynamically in touch with each other....The synthesis of the three energies, evoked through invocation and the response of certain divine Potencies, is esoterically given the name of "the saving Force." Of its exact nature and intended effects we know practically nothing. It has never before appeared in action on the physical plane, though it has for some time been active upon the mental plane. Though it is a blend of the energies of the three centres referred to above, it is primarily the energy of the divine Will, which will be its outstanding characteristic.[17]

This Rider shall ride out on the steed of Hierarchy (the 'white horse'[18]) in the form of its externalisation, when overshadowed by the cosmic Christ. This subject shall be further explained later, however, the significance of the major third Ray dispensation wielded by the new Mahāchohan and the seventh Ray wielded by the current Mahāchohan (Master *R*) should be noted here. The seventh Ray dispensation primarily manifests upon the etheric plane, effecting thus the expression of the *chakras,* and the nature of the unfoldment of their petals by means of the control of the coursing of the *prāṇas.* Hence we have the appellation 'ceremonial magic' given for the seventh Ray. The third Ray primarily governs the physical plane and of the way that these energies impact upon it, hence the appearance of things, of the phenomena we

17 Bailey, *The Externalisation of the Hierarchy,* 274-275.

18 *Rev. 19:11,* 'And I saw heaven opened, and behold a white horse; and he that sat upon him *was* called Faithful and True, and in righteousness he doth judge and make war'.

see all around. Together these Rays therefore qualify the sum of the expression of the physical plane, the materiality which humans take to be the real, and which the *devas* embody *in totia.*

A hint is given as to Master *R*'s need to properly acclimatise to the third Ray purpose, when becoming the Mahāchohan, in *Discipleship in the New Age II.*

> When, for instance, the Master R. assumed the task of Mahachohan or Lord of Civilisation, His Ashram was shifted from the seventh Ray of Ceremonial Order to the third Ray of Active Intelligence; the majority of those who have taken the second and third initiations were transformed with Him under what might be called a "special dispensation"; the rest of the members of His Ashram remained for tuition and training in service under the Master Who took His place as the central point of the seventh Ray Ashram.[19]

This 'special dispensation' incorporated their training under the third Ray purpose of the new Mahāchohan, hence this seventh Ray group, integrated with the 2/1 Ray and general first Ray line, then becomes the backbone of the steed upon which the Rider will issue forth into objectivity. In addition, those of the 3/4 Ray line will integrate their new Ashramic field of service and hence will empower the third Ray under the auspices of the new Mahāchohan. This Ashram also has affinity to the seventh Ray by virtue of the addition of the numbers 3 and 4, and that the seventh Ray is the reflex of the third Ray via the fourth. They will embody his general mode of activity in the world. It will be necessary, as the Aquarian dispensation demands this potency to implement its zodiacal dispensation. Also, inaugurating the new era of Love-Wisdom will need the assistance of the second Ray Ashrams of K.H. The second Ray Ashrams (assisted by the fourth) will then become the main body of this steed. Its strength will be maintained by fifth and sixth Ray activity. In this way the dense physical plane will be transformed and the 'door where evil dwells' can eventually be sealed upon a planetary scale. The forces of evil (the dark brotherhood) become that upon which this Rider shall make 'war' as a consequence of the total activity of those upon which he rides, and the cosmic forces (signified by the sign Sagittarius) that he will project into the arena of the planetary service.

---

19 Bailey, *Discipleship in the New Age II,* 383.

A further hint as to the relation of this Rider to Master ℛ can be gleaned from the diagram of the Planetary Hierarchy in *Initiation, Human and Solar*[20] (published 1919), where above Morya we have Master Jupiter (Guru Rinpoche), above K.H. is given 'A European Master' (the European Chohan), whilst Master ℛ takes the position of the seventh Ray Chohan. We know him to later take the role of the Mahāchohan. Above him then logically is the Rider, who then forms a triad with the Master Jupiter, and the European Chohan. As this Rider (the new Mahāchohan) comes from 'the secret place' he is veiled and hence omitted from this diagram, as well as to the general account of the Masters in the texts. By now it should be obvious that what D.K. earlier presented is only a bare outline of the personnel constituting Shambhala.

The Virgoan position, represented by the seventh Ray Chohan (Master ℛ), becomes the mechanism for pouring the energies of the enlightened Mind from Hierarchy to the domain of the concretions of mind represented by humanity. The mechanism can be viewed in the form of a pyramidal diamond of energies. The pyramid or throne of intensified energies is needed via cyclic activity to overcome the reifying concretions of mind of our present materialistic society. It's base is constituted of the 7/3, 7/4, 7/5 and 7/6 Ray Ashrams, and they manifest via a square of the second Ray Ashrams embodying the Rays of Mind: the 2/4, 2/5, 2/6 and 2/7 Ray Ashrams. The capstone of this pyramid is represented by the Master ℛ, who demonstrates the role of both the seventh Ray Chohan and the Mahāchohan via the 7/2 Ashram and the third Ray 'special dispensation'. We thus have a living tabernacle where esoteric truth is moulded into the constructs of thought. The objective power of this arrangement is to directly confront the lying distortions of the dark brotherhood upon the psychic levels and so defeat the powerbase of those that sustain materialistic concepts. The reality of the subjective domains will eventually thereby be shown to be factual by the workers in this field. The squares of concrete thought become triangular as the pyramid of the awakened Mind is sought.

As Rakoczi came from the 7/2 Ashram, and as most of the Ashram 'who have taken the second and third Initiations were transferred with him', so the remainder of the Ashram consisted of junior disciples, those

20 Bailey, *Initiation, Human and Solar*, 49.

preparing for, or who had taken the first Initiation. They specifically need the Love-Wisdom principle fanned, to prepare for the oncoming new age, the major second Ray cycle, hence also spent time in the 2/7 Ray Ashram within the context of this dispensation. In this way an increased second Ray receptivity could be infused into the sum of the seventh Ray line, taking into account when the younger Initiates would come of age by attaining higher Initiation status under the 2/7 tutelage. Initiates of the third and seventh Ray line were also transferred to the 7/2 Ashram for qualified experience. In this way the selected Master of the 7/2 could fulfil the function (though weakened) required of this Ashram. It would be enhanced with third and second Ray attributes, which would be needed for the Rider's dispensation of the 'saving force'. To further strengthen these Rays he adds the first Ray Shambhalic potency, which via the other Rays has the capacity to produce major changes upon the physical plane. As the elder members of the Ashram also developed the green Ray as a foundation for its increased stimulation under the auspices of the new Mahăchohan, so he can ride on the back of this specially prepared seventh Ray, second Ray and third Ray accommodation.

Thus, with the manifestation of the Rider's work, the Aquarian epoch truly begins. The lubricating flux of the fourth Ray, however, is also needed to help eliminate the potential fields of conflict.

The second and seventh Rays work in unity to overcome tendencies to left hand occult practices and to help engender the new epoch, which will be governed by the second Ray. We thus have a living tabernacle that actively disseminates into manifestation the Hierarchical plan concerning the revelation of the subjective nature of the human psyche and its energies via the matrix of human consciousness in such a way that it can best overcome reifying minds. It represents the materialising power of the seventh Ray working via the etheric body (the *nāḍī* system) of the planet to produce the newly incarnating spiritual paradigms and demonstrable magical effects for the Aquarian age, overcoming the present materialistic bias.

Another important consideration is that the sixth and seventh Rays function as a practical unity, manifesting therefore as a point of externalising power in *saṃsāra*. The sixth Ray of Devotion has a direct link to the second Ray of Love-Wisdom, and colours Hierarchical activity so that those on earth can rightly partake of its nourishment.

The seventh Ray anchors the attributes of all the other Ray lines. This combination of Rays has governed the cusp between the exiting Piscean era and the oncoming Aquarian dispensation from the astrological view. However, during the Piscean era there was always a significant seventh Ray energisation via the subjective effect of the seventh Ray, reinforced by the first Ray tendencies of Pluto (the esoteric and Hierarchical ruler of Pisces) to effect the many destructive wars of attrition during this epoch. The seventh Ray potency was often wrongly appropriated by those in power. The combined energies most potently intensifies the astral-etheric miasma of the emotional and selfish thinking that most in our civilisation wallow in. One needs only to look at the world's history, to view the effects of the ravages of the resultant wars. Wars that pit religions against each other were especially prevalent over the past thousand years when the seventh Ray more dominantly affected the Piscean dispensation. We also had scenarios, such as the American civil war, where the Southern side was predominantly ruled by the first Ray and the North the seventh. Empowered by the seventh Ray, the North could muster far greater material strength from their factories, and calculated logistics governing troop movements to counter the often brilliant first Ray military stratagems and valour of the Southerners.

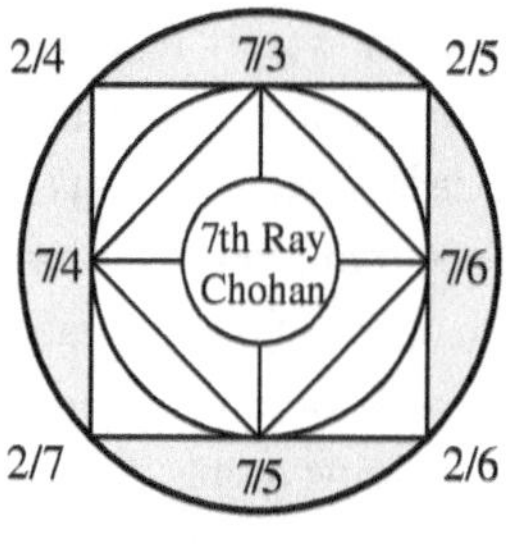

Figure 12. The door of appropriation to Hierarchy

With the approaching new era where the sixth Ray potency will wane, to be replaced by the second Ray, much of the zealous basis for fighting wars will disappear, as much wiser relations between nations will manifest. One factor still threatening the world with wars and impending world war is the United States, whose personality Ray is the sixth.[21]

21 Bailey, *Destiny of the Nations,* 91.

The Hierarchical power generated by the disciples along the second and seventh Rays working via the *nāḍīs* of humanity will effectively counter many of the social ailments affecting humanity by strengthening their resistance to them, and by manifesting right education. The will to fight all forms of entrenched evil will consequently grow as the new era advances. This work will be especially effective when augmented by the third Ray attributes of the new Mahāchohan, which will empower the epoch of Mind. Thus the man-plant growing in the soil of the material domain can be appropriately watered with Love and directed to grow towards the realms of light by evolving wisdom. The second, sixth and seventh Ray combination can also be considered the embodiment of the Blood of Life once the wrong Watery activities of the sixth Ray can be properly cleansed by the second Ray and mathematically directed by the third Ray.

The Eye of Hierarchy

There are various ways of viewing Hierarchy, as the higher members embody different fluidic attributes and functions. The relationship between the established Ashrams can be seen in the form of an Eye that has the ability to open its pupil to let in greater Light. The Eye is three-tiered, consisting of a pupil portion related to the first Ray, an iris portion related to the second Ray, and the bulk of the substance of the Eye related to the intelligence aspect (the Rays of Mind). This is seen from the point of view of differences in the clarity of the Ray line. The colouring of the pupil is the deep indigo blue of the second Ray admixed with red and green. The pupil is constituted of the first Ray Ashrams focussed via the 1/2 Ray, plus the 2/1 Ashram, coupled with the 2/2 Ray and the 2/3 line, which is a dominant colouring, as this Ashram is fully formed. (The blue and red of the second and first Rays also admix to produce a version of the violet.) The pure energies from Shambhala and the Chohans are refracted via these Rays to vitalise the rest of Hierarchy. Alternatively, this Ray combination represents the way of access to Shambhalic domains.

The hues of the rest of the second and the third Ray Ashrams colour the iris. The white of the eye is an admixture of the integrated spinning of all the colourings of the Ray Ashrams of Mind. This Eye becomes the directive Eye of Deity for the projection of Logoic energies into systemic space. It is the microscope through which the Logos looks into the formed realms.

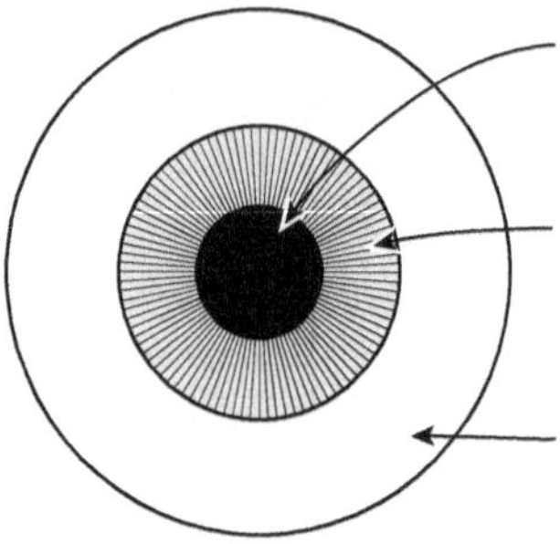

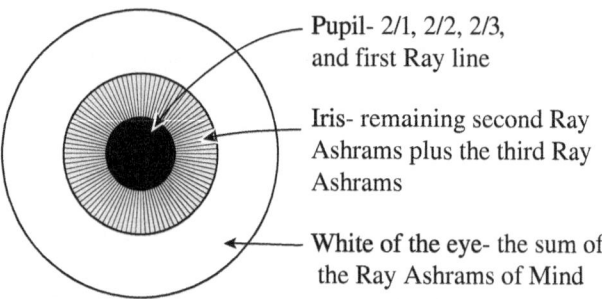

Figure 13. The Hierarchical Eye

The first Ray Ashrams act as the lens through which all energies to our system are focussed. The 2/3 Ray helps clothe the incoming energies with the Love-Wisdom principle so that the sum of Hierarchy can utilise them. This Eye is also the telescope through which disciples can view into cosmos. This view of Hierarchy is seen from the perspective of its constitution below the rank of Chohan. If the Ashrams were fully formed, then the pupil channels directives from *ātma*, the iris from *buddhi* and the white of the eye from the abstract domain of Mind. Also, at the centre of this pupil exists the Hierarchical twelve-petalled lotus in the form of a Heart centre, the iris manifests as Splenic centre I, and the white of the Eye as the major centres below the diaphragm.

The first Ray Ashrams are youngest in terms of the development of the Ashramic personnel. Only a portion of their *maṇḍalas* are activated, curtailing their possible service potential. There are only four Ashrams organised. The rest are embryonic, incorporated into other Ray Ashrams. (The 1/5 Ray will 'soon' be added, as its field of opportunity concerns helping to terminate the cycle of materialism and of rulership of the empirical mind in the new era.) We saw that the 2/1 Ray Ashram is still forming and is problematic because of its makeup. Many members will sometimes cyclically, partially revert to former left hand tendencies. When assisted by the more developed, wiser 2/3 Ray Ashram, they will eventually act as the dynamic focal point for the reception of the pure luminescence of Light. (Similarly with the 1/2 Ray line, also not yet fully formed.) The radiant first Ray energy potently counters and converts dark brotherhood *prāṇas*. The conversion of such *prāṇas* is central to all Hierarchical activities.

Once established, the 2/1-1/2 Rays will help protect the activity of other Ray lines from the onslaught of extraneous evil, thus the service arenas of humanity as a whole. Such activity is presently in the hands of the Lords of Shambhala. This service work is grounded by the activity of the seventh Ray line. The 1/2-2/1-1/7 and 2/3 Ray lines represent the clearest, most intense, rarefied and abstracted of Hierarchy's energies. They thus stand at the centre of the Hierarchical Eye to channel the energy of Light and Love in its most liberating form. Individual *karma* of former evil generated will, however, need to be zapped away by the exponents of all Ray lines who originally manifested the *karma*. Initiates of the higher degrees will also bear the burden of planetary protection as needed. As more Initiates can do so, this will represent the externalisation process of Shambhala itself, as its first Ray potency will increasingly be brought into manifestation by such activity.

There are altogether ten potential Ashrams that produce this Hierarchical pupil at this time. They are the 2/1, 2/2, 2/3, 1/2, 1/7, 1/4, 1/6, 7/1, 4/1 and 6/1 Ray lines. Only one of these, the 2/3 Ashram is fully formed, whilst the 2/2 Ray Ashram is but a 'holding Ashram'. This Love-Wisdom Ray therefore sets the tone of what generally colours Hierarchical impressions. It will take 100-200 years for the 1/2 and 2/1 Ray lines specifically to come into their full potential. By then the three first Ray Ashrams of the Rays of Mind will also be established. This will signify the manifestation of the major second Ray cycle, propelled by the first Ray potency, via which Shambhalic Purpose can incarnate. Thus the new age proper will manifest, superseding the present epoch of mind, and the 'City of God', the New Jerusalem, can descend.

With respect to this pupil, five Ashrams will have formed or be nearly formed during this period, the 2/1, 2/3, 1/2, 1/7, 7/1 Ray Ashrams, and two rapidly forming, the 4/1 and 6/1 Ray lines. The focus being the first, second, third and seventh Ray lines manifesting via a subsidiary fourth Ray. These energies then represent the incoming purpose of Shambhalic potency that will instigate the forthcoming new era. Such potency will also ride upon the newly flowering third Ray Ashrams.

The ten potencies indicate that this central pupil also functions as a Solar Plexus centre, allowing it to channel into *saṃsāra* the purifying Waters of Love from the cosmic astral plane.[22] By the time that eight of its petals are appropriately active it will project into manifestation the embryonic form of the Kingdom of Shambhala, which when established will initially manifest as a Solar Plexus centre (the Solar Plexus in the Head), and later the Heart in the Head will form, which will directly govern the entire planetary manifestation without any intermediary to tone down the energies. The Hierarchical Heart centre will also be incarnate as well as the activity of the Throat centre governed by the progressed New Group of World Servers. This will transform the type of civilisation we presently have, ending the reign of emotional thinking by humanity. Physical plane livingness will begin to be abstracted etherically, due to the potency of the incoming cosmic energies via the expression of unadulterated Will-of-Love (*bodhicitta*) and divine Will impacting upon dense physical substance.

Many human groups shall begin to learn the doctrines associated with travelling to other cosmic shores in 'space craft' propelled through knowledge of the laws of Mind, as new sciences will be established whereby the subjective domains will be explored. The incoming energies of Divine Will shall remove the barriers that presently prevent premature penetration of the various sacred domains of space. Visitors from those domains shall be known and made welcome.

The iris of this Eye is constituted of the remaining four second Ray Ashrams of Mind, the third Ray Ashrams (some of which are not yet formed), plus the 7/1,[23] 7/2 and 7/3 Ray Ashrams. The seventh Ray Ashrams are included because the seventh Ray is exemplified in this new epoch and they provide the added power to ritualistically channel the increased first Ray potency into the material domains. Their potency provides the power to appropriately regulate the iris to allow differences in the vibrancy of incoming light. Their strength and colouring firmly connects this central tier to the pupil and white of the Eye. The 3/3

22 Shambhala also exists in the form of a Solar Plexus centre with respect to the corresponding centres in the solar system because the cosmic astral plane is the common denominator of the way they interrelate.

23 This Ashram straddles both the pupil and the iris.

and 3/1 Ray Ashrams are omitted in this consideration because their formation still lies far into the future.

The iris therefore consists of twelve Ashrams that respond to and project the general qualities developed by the Hierarchical Heart centre. The potential thus exists for this portion of the Hierarchical *maṇḍala* to fully awaken during this present epoch. Thus the complete expression of a Heart centre will unfold. Seven petals have been fully functioning for some time, allowing the projection of the energies of Love-Wisdom via seven Ray Attributes, where the seventh Ray line helps to channel the first Ray potency. With the addition of the 7/3 Ray Ashram (the inherent power of divine ritualised activity) in the early twentieth century, the eight-spoked wheel of direction came into functioning power, allowing Hierarchy to project its purpose into all directions of space. Technically, therefore, a Diaphragm centre was established, allowing the Heart centre to better control the centres below the diaphragm by more adequately channelling the potent energies from Shambhala. Wise activity will present opportunity for the 3/4 petal, followed by the 7/1, 3/6 and then 3/5 Ray lines, to awaken during the next 100-200 years. The Heart centre as a directing centre will then be activated via twelve major petals, signifying the complete externalisation of Hierarchy on earth in a way that Shambhala manifests therein, as the Ray lines bearing its potency are incarnate. The Heart centre will then be able to control the functioning of the Solar Plexus centre for humanity.

Within 300 years Shambhala can then actively begin to externalise, which in conjunction with the second Ray cycle, makes the earth truly a sacred planet. This is significant because it betokens the period when humanity will generally understand the nature of the destructive potency, volatility, and illusion-forming activity of their emotional bodies. Governments will be elected based upon the inherent wisdom and compassionate stance of the leaders, and not because of their appeal to the lowest common denominator of the stirred up (mainly fear based) emotions of the masses. No longer will the passing of egregious laws be possible. The increased downpour of the first, second, third and seventh Ray energies facilitates the ability to overcome humanity's major glamours and illusions. These Rays (especially the power and destroyer Rays) will also help cause an exaggeration of the self-same emotions at first, thus producing the basis for the oncoming of the financial and social strife, the dictatorial attitudes and tyrannical rule of governments, and planetary upheavals of all types. (Including the wars at the beginning of the twenty-first century, terminating in world war.) Wars can represent wars of opinions and ideologies as well as manifesting physically. They represent the clashing tides of energies between people and nations.

To help produce a major change in massed human orientation away from selfish emotional considerations will be a major task of those Ashrams coming into full service potential during this period. This will be accomplished by the large number of aspirants and probationary disciples that will be incarnate to foster good will, right human relations and devotion to high ideals on a world-wide scale. Many Initiates will so inspire them to realise their service activities in the world. All Ashrams must successfully manifest their service arena as defined by the qualities of their Ray line before they can fully flower as a centre within Hierarchy. An Ashram similarly must undergo Initiation testings as a unit, via its general group service work, before it can fully form. Thus a Master of a Ray comes into being by having passed the major tests that galvanises the Ashramic members into their complete service potential.

The white of this Eye is constituted of the remaining sixteen fully functioning Ashrams, which therefore demonstrates as a Throat centre (to which there are sixteen petals). This allows the mass dissemination of forms of wisdom that are directly accessible by the intelligentsia within humanity. The right education of people's minds therefore becomes the focus for the service work of these Ashrams.

Together there are presently twenty-four fully functioning Ashrams. They therefore manifest as a Heart centre for Humanity, as well as being receptive to the energies of the Heart in the Head from Shambhala. In its integration as a functioning Eye we also see how the three major divisions of the Ashrams, projecting the potency of the Will, Love-Wisdom and Enlightened Activity, work together under the general auspices of Love-Wisdom. They externalise the potency of the All-seeing Eye of the planetary Logos.

The service arenas of the new Ashrams

A more detailed analysis can now be presented concerning the service arenas of the new Ashrams that are in the process of forming, as this is of great significance with respect to the oncoming new era. *Maṇḍalas* of activity are thereby progressed that will produce profound impacts on the course of civilisation for the oncoming generations. Obviously, the related arenas of service work are framed according to the Ray disposition of the Ashrams concerned. The forming Ashrams at the fore of the instigating process of the new Hierarchical directives are of the 1/2, 2/1, 7/1, and 1/7 Rays, which can be considered the Will, Love-Wisdom, and Power aspects of the first Ray line. (The 7/1 Ray Ashram rhythmically manifests its power in the realms of form, thus it acts as an anchor for the energies of the first Ray Ashrams.)

We also have the 3/4 and 4/3 Ray Ashrams, which will work to clear misappropriated ideas by manifesting creatively intelligent activities in the service of society. Many harmonious and aesthetical physical constructs will be built into our civilisation. They will wisely distribute the new aesthetic and creative ideas into the mainstream of *manasic* impetus so that the Lords of Love-Wisdom can eventually manifest their day. The Ashrams will contain many of the social activists and ethical bloggers countering the lies and distortions in all social and political issues governing our world today. They will fight against all forms of injustice and lying propaganda projected by our governments. Many seventh Ray Ashrams will also be especially active in this field. Many urban planners and technocrats, especially those that are internet savvy, will be found here in all major countries of the world. Some will also focus upon the wise direction of the financial reserves needed for future service work to rectify the world's woefully imbalanced distribution and mismanagement of resources. The *nāḍīs* of the new civilisation will consequently be rightly vitalised. These Ashrams complete the Throne of Service that will be manifested by the Hierarchy in the externalisation process of its *maṇḍala* of power. This Ray grouping is presently the vanguard of the New Group of World Servers, explained in D.K.'s writings. They are assisted by the second Ray line, plus those of the other Rays that possess the needed characteristics.

> Their influence is wielded silently and quietly and they lay no emphasis upon their personalities, upon their own views and ideas, or upon their methods of carrying forward the work. These possess a full realisation of their own limitations, but are not handicapped thereby, but proceed to think through into objective manifestation that aspect

> of the vision which it is their mission to vivify into form. They are necessarily cultured and widely read, for in these difficult transitional times they have to cultivate a world grasp of conditions and possess a general idea of what is going on in the different countries. They possess in truth no nationality in the sense that they regard their country and their political affiliations as of paramount importance. They are equipped to organise, slowly and steadily, that public opinion which will eventually divorce man from religious sectarianism, national exclusiveness, and racial biases.
>
> One by one, here and there they are being gathered out and are gathering to them those who are free from the limitations of past political, religious and cultural theories. They, the members of the one group, are organising these forward looking souls into groups which are destined to bring in the new era of peace and of good will. These latter who are being influenced by the group members are as yet only a few thousands among the millions of men, and out of the four hundred accepted disciples working in the world at this time, only about 156 are equipped by their thought activity to form part of this slowly forming group. These constitute the nucleus of what will be some day a dominant force[24]...The members of this group of new age workers will, however, possess certain general characteristics. They will impose no enforced dogmas of any kind, and will lay no emphasis upon any doctrine or authorities. They are not interested in having any personal authority nor do they rest back upon traditional authority, whether religious, scientific, cultural or any other form of imposed truth. Modes of approach to reality will be recognised and each will be free to choose his own. No discipline will be imposed by these workers upon those who seek to cooperate with them. The ideas of any one person or leader as to how the units in his particular sphere of activity should live and work, should meditate and eat, will be regarded as of no special value. The members of this new group work esoterically with souls, and deal not with the details of the personality lives of the aspirants they seek to inspire.[25]

Though events did not manifest as D.K. predicted, nevertheless the general gist of his statements are correct. This can now be somewhat elaborated, taking the present state of affairs into account. The Exoteric

---

24 Bailey, *A Treatise on White Magic*, 416-417.

25 Ibid., 419.

development of the New Group of World Servers has changed somewhat from what D.K. envisioned in the 1930's. D.K. was viewing from an inner plane perspective, whilst the external situation of the world has changed since the time when he wrote the above. There is always a difference between the ideal and the way things actually work out. Though the subjective inner plane link with Hierarchy and the telepathic attunement will exist in this group, recognition of the existence of Hierarchy generally will not. Also, the forces of evil have now shown their hand in world affairs, as the groups that had incarnated around Hitler and Stalin have reincarnated in the Western world, and the difficult work of countering their machinations is very challenging indeed. In relation to this the service work of the New Group of World Servers continues unabated to educate humanity concerning the present political systems dictated by the Western powers, and of the nature of mass indoctrination of the propagandistic mainstream media. They will also be active in uncovering the truth concerning the antiquity of human civilisation, the Atlantis myth, crop circles, etc. Also, many will be found as activists opposing globalisation, the rule of avaricious corporations, the moneyed elite and CEO's that have corrupted government officials and every branch of our social structures. They will be anti-war, but will militaristically fight against social injustice, and for the rights of the common person, etc.

What in effect is implicated here is the externalisation of the membership of a newly awakening planetary centre, the Throat centre of humanity, to compliment the Heart centre embodied by Hierarchy. Its time of awakening has eventuated with our present technocratic civilisation, and the advent of the computer age. The nature of the Throat centre was explained in the previous volumes, and its potency amongst humanity will become specifically, firmly expressed with the empowerment of the third Ray Ashrams. This centre will help accommodate the many new disciples that will meet the challenge of passing Initiation testings in the present epoch, as the nature of the Mind must now be fully explored. Hierarchy will then be externalised in two centres, though obviously, subjectively, the higher echelons of Hierarchy will play dual roles in a similar way as the relation between the Heart centre and Splenic centre I.

With the Heart and Throat centres actively functioning, the planetary Ājñā centre can also awaken, heralding a higher form of spiritual perception that the more advanced members of humanity will appropriate, superseding the widespread form of (Solar Plexus) clairvoyance that besotted the Atlanteans. The nature of the higher perceptions, 'awakening the third Eye', will then be part of the parlance of many. Hence this present endeavour to provide a cogent rationale to understanding the nature of the *chakras* and of their safe awakening.

With respect to the awakening of the Ājñā centre of the planet, D.K. has presented the teachings concerning the Contemplatives in *Discipleship in the New Age II* and elsewhere:

> The effect of that reflective vibration is both vertical and horizontal, and this wide diffusion has led to the formation of that major group of contemplatives, the Nirmanakayas; They focus the hierarchical invocative appeal and (to quote the *Old Commentary*) "put it into the musical form which will please the ear of the One Who dwells in the highest plane." They then transfer the focussed received energies—after due reflection and contemplation—to Shamballa. One of Their functions is to relate the invocative appeal of the Hierarchy to karmic law, and thus determine "in the deep silence of Their united work" what can be possible because it does not infringe upon karmic intention, and what is not yet possible in time and space—those two major factors which are governed by karmic law. They have to bear in mind that the time has not yet come and "the karmic era cannot yet demand that demanded good become accomplished good."
>
> The members of this group are also transmitters to the Hierarchy of the response evoked from Shamballa. They are constantly in touch with the Council Chamber at Shamballa. Just as the Hierarchy—in this present cycle of world endeavour—is working through the New Group of World Servers, so Shamballa is carrying out its intentions (as far as humanity is concerned) through this group of Nirmanakayas. This all connotes a great centralisation of the work in connection with the reappearance of the Christ.[26]

26 Alice Bailey, *Discipleship in the New Age II*, 206. See also pages 210-211, where D.K. states: 'They are, in a peculiar sense, the creative agents of life as it streams forth from Shamballa into all the aspects, areas, kingdoms and fields of manifestation. This They are enabled to do through sustained, concentrated, intensive and dynamic meditation. They are necessarily a second ray group (as the second ray is the ray at present of the planetary Logos) but They focus Their meditation largely along first ray lines (which is a sub-Ray of the second ray in this solar system, as you know) because

The number 156 = 12 x 13, which implicates a central group of twelve beings surrounded by twelve subsidiary groups of twelve, who signify types of service work, as governed by the twelve petals of the Heart centre (Hierarchy), or the signs of the zodiac. The groupings of twelve petals are overshadowed by those embodying the twelve petals of the Hierarchical Heart centre. When these twelve great Ones are added then we get the number 168, which relates to the 28 main petals (16 + 12) of the Throat centre, where 28 x 6 = 168. This number incorporates the six levels of awakening the Throat centre via the six stages of Initiation attainment of the New Group of World Servers from the probationary disciple to a Master of Wisdom.

One can also envision the function of the six petals of the Sacral centre (the lower reflex of the Throat centre) in terms of overcoming the principle of desire-attachment of humanity. The Sacral centre is the centre that energises the *nāḍī* system, once the base attributes have been purified by means of the activity of the Splenic centres. There are then six centres to consider concerning the approach of Sacral centre energies to the Throat centre: the Sacral centre, the two Splenic centres, the Solar Plexus centre, the Diaphragm centre and the Heart centre.

The Throat centre is literally the domain of the new Mahāchohan, from whence the directives of Mind can enthuse humanity. The New Group of World Servers were established as a support mechanism for his purpose, to help wield the new doctrines related to awakening the higher Mind of humanity. From the Sacral centre all of humanity can then be stimulated in their serried ranks, so that eventually the central 156 can expand into millions. This will happen as the manasic purpose rises up and cleanses the *prāṇas (saṃskāras)* of the petals of the various *chakras*, from the Sacral to the Throat centre. This becomes another interpretation of the 'white horse' that is the vehicle of the new Mahāchohan as 'the Rider'.[27]

From this perspective the new Mahāchohan overshadows the central twelve of the 156 disciples. This manifests via the function of Splenic

---

They are the creative agents of life itself and the knowers and the custodians of the will of the planetary Logos, as it works itself out in manifestation. They are the source in reality of planetary invocation and evocation'.

27 See chapter 7 for an explanation of the Rider on the white horse.

centre I, which works to cleanse the maligned *prāṇas* of the circulation below the diaphragm, represented by the activities of humanity.

If the Council Chamber of Shambhala is taken into account then a further 24 Great Ones must be added to the number 168 to integrate the functioning of this centre with the *Ājñā* centre and also the Head lotus. First, when a council of twelve is added to 168 then the number 180 is obtained, signifying the energies needed to produce planetary Initiation (20 x 9). The next twelve incorporates the entire *maṇḍala* into the Head lotus. When added to 180 it produces the number 192, the number of petals of the Heart in the Head, hence activating all of the processes associated with this grouping of petals, as was explained in Volume 5A[28], though now relegated to the planetary situation and the process of the liberation of all upon it.

The interrelation of the presently forming Ashrams will produce a triad of Ray expressions working to anchor the complete power of the first Ray upon the physical domain. The 'Will of God' can for the first time thereby appropriately be demonstrated in human affairs via a dedicated mechanism of expression. From Logoic Eye to the Hierarchical Eye and the *maṇḍalic* form of the externalising Hierarchy will potent cosmic astral energies pour to reap enlightened human souls, 'for the harvest of the earth is ripe'.[29] This triad manifests in the form of a Will—Power couplet (the 1/7 and 7/1 Ashrams), a Will—Love-Wisdom couplet (the 1/2 and 2/1 Ashrams), and the divine Wilful Activity couplet of the 3/4 and 4/3 Ashrams, where together the third and fourth Rays constitute a form of the seventh Ray. Also, the fourth Ray is part of the first Ray dispensation of 1-4-7, and the third Ray is the activity expression of the ruling Rays of aspect (1-2-3).

When observing the combination of the major Ray colours of these Ashrams then what is produced is a blood red energy. We have the vivid scarlet of the first Ray plus the violet of the seventh Ray admixed, coupled with the overtone of the general blue of Hierarchy. There is also an infusion of a greenish extract (green 'grapes') of the golden and green Rays of the 3/4 and 4/3 Ray Ashrams. The overall hue will therefore be a greenish red-violet, as the will becomes developed by humanity in

28 Volume 5A, 403-424.

29 *Rev. 14:15.*

the form of good will, the Will-to-Love, the Will-of-Love, and finally the Divine Will. (Which were explained in Volume 4 of this treatise.)

The 'great winepress of the wrath of God'

What is implicated above is the energy symbolised by the 'grapes' of the 'vine of the earth' that was cast into the 'great winepress of the wrath of God'.[30]

> And another angel came out from the altar, which had power over fire; and cried with a loud cry to him that had the sharp sickle, saying, Thrust in thy sharp sickle, and gather the clusters of the vine of the earth; for her grapes are fully ripe.
>
> And the angel thrust in his sickle into the earth, and gathered the vine of the earth, and cast *it* into the great winepress of the wrath of God.
>
> And the winepress was trodden without the city, and blood came out of the winepress, even unto the horse bridles, by the space of a thousand *and* six hundred furlongs.[31]

There are various levels of interpretation of the verses of *The Revelation of St. John*, but fundamentally the symbolism here relates to reaping the gain of the process of planetary Initiation. (Which effectively concerns the externalisation process of Hierarchy.) These verses have reference to the time when these Ashrams are externalised and in full service mode. They will be the Initiates that will pass the tests of this wrath as they cleanse egregious *karma* from dissonant incarnations and transform the *saṃskāras* into those of the Will-of-Love via their service work.

The 'angel' is a great *deva* Lord that comes from 'the altar' that is the Throne of the planetary Logos. It is an emissary of Agni and thereby wields the Fiery Element, hence bears the potency of the Mind of that Logos. The altar is the central stage whereon all of the sacramental and ritual instruments are kept and before which the rituals are performed. Consequently, it expresses a seventh ray function. This function emanates from Shambhala in the form of a mantric cry from an 'angel', hence manifests in the form of the first, destroyer Ray. The cry

---

30 *Rev. 14:20.*

31 *Rev. 14:18-20.*

is a fiat that causes a karmic reaper from the *deva* kingdom to 'thrust in a sharp sickle'. (The shape of the sickle is in the form of the glyph for Saturn and esoterically relates to the sun-moon relationship[32] governing cycles of time). Here the Rays of Mind (1, 3, 5, 7) are exemplified. The reapers are also the Lords of Fire, the wrathful energies of the Consorts of the Dhyāni Buddhas. These *devas* are the agents of action.

A transforming Fire therefore manifests to overcome the Watery *saṃskāras* of humanity by means of a loud cry rather than 'a loud voice', as a cry is more intense, piercing, or sharper, than a voice. It implies a first Ray gusto (bearing zodiacal and planetary energies that are esoterically implicated in the meaning of the phrase 'power over fire'). The Power of the Lord, working mainly through the first and seventh Ray combination, then gathers 'the clusters of the vine of the earth'.

Effectively, *antaḥkaraṇas* are projected from the Head centre of the planetary Logos to these 'clusters' (of 'grapes') as part of a cyclic effort. (The 'grapes' are spherical, signifying the shape of human Souls, or *maṇḍalic* structures, plus having a specific colouration.) They reap the gain of the evolutionary process after each major cycle of activity. By means of the word 'fire' we can deduce that this cycle is the fifth (governing our present materialistic civilisation) which is ruled by this Element. The mathematical activity of the third Ray governs the motion of the sickle, ensuring that these 'clusters' are appropriately gathered. This harvest prepares the way for the major second Ray cycle to begin.

The 'vine of the earth' is the Tree of Initiation and the clusters (of 'grapes') are the human soul groups that have ripened upon that Tree. This Tree (also 'of knowledge of good and evil'[33]) can be symbolised by the Caduceus staff, as the central trunk of the true vine in every Logoic body of manifestation. The branches and leaves of the vine represent the intricate *nāḍī* system that unfolds as *saṃskāras* are developed and *chakras* are awakened. (Consequently one gains 'knowledge of good and evil'.) The main stem being the *suṣumṇā nāḍī,* and the left and right branches as *iḍā* and *piṅgalā nāḍīs,* with other *nāḍīs* representing subsidiary vines. The roots are planted in the soil of *saṃsāra* via the *nāḍīs* as an extension of the Base of Spine and Sacral centres. The sun

---

32 Exoterically seen in the form of the phases of the moon.

33 *Genesis, 2:9.*

disc over the Caduceus represents the Head lotus that is awakened by this activity, and the wings coming from the Caduceus represent the spaciousness of the awakened consciousness. As for the individual, so one can also envision a similar 'tree' from a planetary perspective, wherein fruit *(chakras)* 'ripens' by means of transmogrifying energies as the associated units of consciousness gain Initiation.

The circular form of a *grape* can here be thought of as the shape of the Sambhogakāya Flower, which are to be reaped in groups, according to the laws of group Initiation. The clusters are to be gathered in accordance to the service activity successfully undertaken, producing evolutionary perfection, especially in relation to undertaking the fourth Initiation onwards,[34] whereby an entire Ashramic structure is 'plucked' by the reaping agency of the Logos.

This 'vine' is of the earth because therein the cycles of incarnatory activity have been undertaken by humanity, producing those that represent the ripened fruits. (The gain of it all.) Hierarchy evolves accordingly and many move into Shambhala and cosmic shores, the purpose of *manvantara* having been attained.

The 'sickle' in the form of the sign Saturn is the reaper of *karma.* Saturn is the exoteric ruler of Capricorn, who governs the mount of Initiation, hence it signifies the cycle when *karma* is to be reaped as the Initiation path is trod. This is but another way of depicting the yogic process concerning the transformation and transmutation of *saṃskāras.*

A *'winepress'* is an instrument that applies great pressure on the grapes so as to extract the liquid and to dispose of the waste material, the husks, pips, etc. Being a 'great winepress' signifies a vast size (needed to reap the crop of Initiates during this period) as the pressure that bears upon it is composed of the energies of the Logoic Mind. Only this Fiery Power can press or squeeze out the Watery principle[35] in the form of Love-Wisdom *(bodhicitta)* from out of those involved in *saṃsāra. Saṃsāra* is also symbolised by the concept of the 'grindstone' of the winepress. One 'grindstone' is represented by the material domain,

---

34 This Initiation awakens one to the fourth cosmic ether, *buddhi,* whereon the *chakras* in the body of the Logos are situated, allowing the energies of the 'vine' to be 'gathered'.

35 Signifying here the attributes of the cosmic Waters being generated.

and the other being the force of the first and seventh Ray combination bearing upon the 'grapes', whilst the third Ray governs the movement of the wheels, producing the 'Blood' of the second Ray purpose.

As the wheels of the 'grindstone' turn, signifying the testing process, so tests of *endurance* are provided for the prospective Initiates. Cycle after cycle of testings and related accomplishments of Initiation undertakings manifest. To meet the challenges of the approaching first and seventh Ray energies from Shambhala new methodology needs to be used by Hierarchy to test the worthiness of candidates for high office. The Initiates must prove their mettle over a considerable time period in any life. Do they have sufficient faith, determination and significantly established knowledge of the esoteric sciences to be able to overcome all the testings that their own *karma,* Hierarchy and also the dark brotherhood, will throw their way and still remain firmly in their hearts? They must be resolute, determined, unwavering in their love and knowledge of purpose. The gain is the strengthening of their first Ray aptitude, which all must now develop if the City of 'God' is to descend upon earth. All Initiates must bear the potency of the strength of the first Ray purpose descending. Those who cannot bear an increase of first Ray potency will be superseded in the Hierarchical standing by those that can bear the increased tension of energies without distortions. The inner Eye must be awakened in difficult circumstances to produce the new civilisation, so that the first Ray can pierce the veils and protect the awakening of the oncoming second Ray cycle.

The 'wrath' represents the transmogrifying energy from Shambhala that is absorbed by the 'grapes', the ripened human Souls/ Sambhogakāya Flowers as they are 'trodden' outside this City of 'God', i.e., in the fields of the earth known as *saṃsāra*. The Feet of the great Lords of Shambhala tread upon them in the form of the Wisdoms of the five Dhyāni Buddhas manifesting in their wrathful forms as Buddha Herukas and their Consorts. The 'Blood' that pours out is the compassionate effect of the *bodhicitta* generated by the Initiates undergoing the process of transformation.

'Horses' represent that which the human minds ride. They are the carrier of the mental principle. Thus they embody the mechanism of the sense-perceptions, the sum of desires and the emotional nature of a body of manifestation. 'Bridles' are utilised by the rider to direct the horse (the lower animal nature), therefore they represent the *antaḥkaraṇas* from the realms of Mind to the astral and etheric realms. Accordingly they regulate all activity associated with the body of manifestation. They signify the *nāḍīs* through which the energies ('Blood'/*prāṇas*) flow to esoterically turn the wheels, the *chakras* governing the all. The 'Blood' must reach the bridles because compassion must direct all such activity.

Here is implicated the energies and function of the Wrathful Deities explained in Volume 5A, whose work is to help the *yogin* convert base *saṃskāras* before they could enter the liberated zones. The Deities are the guardians of the gates to Shambhala. This 'wrath' is the consequence of the expression of cosmic astral energies working via the enlightened Mind. The energies that come from this 'winepress' manifest in the form of the Will and Love-Wisdom that instigates the new second Ray cycle upon earth, symbolised by the 'Blood' that comes from it.

The symbolism of the term 'great' here also signifies a vast planet-wide scale 'winepress', to which many cosmic, zodiacal and solar energies could be applied to squeeze out the 'Blood'. *Blood is Life,* is *prāṇa,* cosmic vitality, the general colouring of which is *red.* This means that the purpose of squeezing the juice from the grapes by means of the enormous pressure of the 'winepress' is the evocation of first Ray energies from all the associated Lives. This is appropriate, as the only way to the higher Initiations is due to such development. The first Ray is the last of the Rays to be awakened and always means liberation, producing the ensuing *pralaya* period. When integrated with the concept of 'Blood' itself, the life-giving energy coming from the Heart, then we have a fusion of first and second Ray energies (red and blue Blood). The purpose of this combination of energies is to inevitably produce Masters of Wisdom, Bodhisattvas of the highest *bhūmi,* via the cosmic pressure applied to this press. They bear the energies of Logoic Mind into the manifest domains.

The esoteric concept of a *'city'* means a *chakra,* and the nature of the city determines the type of *chakra.* We can presume that 'the city' that is referred to here is the planetary Head centre, Shambhala. The information given is that this winepress is trodden outside 'the city', hence the 'treading' process happens throughout the rest of the Body of manifestation of the

Logos, which is appropriate, as there 'the grapes' exist for the harvest. What is outside this 'city' is riddled with desire-attachment, selfishness and separateness, when related to humanity. Therefore the martial (sixth Ray) energy (associated with the testing process) of those being squeezed within the 'winepress' will also produce the outpouring of the wine. Desires and selfishness must thereby be converted into Love and spiritual Will. As the cycles come and go the sum of the planetary life will thereby benefit.

The phrase 'the space of a thousand and six hundred furlongs' incorporates the symbolism of numbers which will be fully explained in a later book I shall publish.[36] Numerological considerations represent one of the major keys to the interpretation of any sacred text. Basically, we have the numbers 1,000 and 600 juxtaposed to make the number 1,600 with respect to a unit designating the conquering of space (or distance). Now, the number sixteen refers to the sixteen major petals of the Throat centre, and therefore represents the complete expression of its creative amplitude (the writing of texts, etc.) to conquer any mind-space. It can refer to the expression of the resultant wisdom, the Christ principle, when viewed as two to the fourth power (2^4). The number one thousand refers to the great perfection (a vast number), whilst the number 600 implies the desire principle upon which all manifestation is based. Indicated therefore is the potency of the hexagram (or petals of the Sacral centre) that represents the Womb of time-space. It is also an expression of the sixth Ray of Devotion and aspiration that helps make it all manifest.

A *furlong* is 1/220th of a mile. As there are 1760 yards to a mile (5280) feet, so there are 8 yards (24 feet) to a furlong. In 1,600 furlongs there are 12,800 yards (2^7 x 100). These are important numbers. First, we see that the number 220 refers to the space enclosed by the twelve zodiacal signs and ten planetary energies. This is essentially another way of stating the Womb of space-time. The number 8 indicates the spiral-cyclic energies that delineate this space-time continuum.

The number 2^7 x 100 signifies the seven dimensions of perception, as governed by the second Ray (2^7)[37], manifesting on a large scale (100), hence associated with the space of a planetary or solar sphere.

The number 24 refers to the second of the twelve signs of the zodiac (*Taurus the bull*), which embodies the function of the Ājñā centre, the

---

36 *The Astrological and Numerological Keys to The Secret Doctrine.*

37 The seventh power here relates to the seven planes of perception, etc.

all-seeing Eye that delineates the form of this space. It projects the cosmic Desire and the *karma* that reticulates the fabric of the planetary or solar form with Purpose.

The number 1,600 also refers to the 'space' enclosed by the compassionate concern of a cosmic Christ, who fulfils on a massive scale the Bodhisattva vow to never cease striving until all sentient beings have crossed the 'other shore' of *saṃsāra*. That the number is divided into 1,000 and 600 furlongs is important. 1,000 furlongs equals 8,000 yards, 24,000 feet. All these numbers refer directly to cosmic or systemic space (wherever multiples of 1,000's are concerned). Therefore, the entire body of manifestation is reaped and consequently put into the 'winepress', as all must now enter into *pralaya,* thus ending another great cycle. Such happening is not imminent, however the beginning of the process is, relating to the outpouring of the new second Ray cycle (2^7).

The number 600 (furlongs) refers to the constitution of the form nature on this vast scale. This makes 4,800 yards and 144,000 feet. The number 48 referring to the fourth sign of the zodiac (Cancer), signifying the doorway to incarnation, whilst the number 144,000 refers to the sum total of the membership of humanity. (The symbolic 'twelve tribes of Israel'[38] governed by the twelve signs of the zodiac, who are involved in the process.) It also relates to the twelfth sign of the zodiac (Pisces), signifying the completion of a cycle. It signifies the vast space (1,000) governed by the cycles of the turning of the signs of the zodiac, literally the mode of awakening the twelve petals of the Head lotus, and all that this signifies when viewed Logoically.

The way that Logoic Mind can also manifest in the form of the 'wrath of God' is explained in *Rev:14:9-11,* where teachings are presented concerning those who follow the ways of the world via dark brotherhood activity. They thereby 'worship the beast and his image'.[39] They will 'drink of the wine of the wrath of God, which is poured out without mixture into the cup of his indignation'.[40] Here the same first Ray energy combination is used, but this time to overcome a plague of evil scheming of the wicked ones. They will be 'tormented with fire and brimstone', the *karma* of their forceful, manipulative mental-emotional

---

38 *Rev. 7:4.* These 'tribes' literally represent humanity, whose evolutionary journeying is governed by the cyclic turning of the wheel of the zodiac.

39 *Rev. 14:9.*

40 *Rev. 14:10.*

misdeeds. This torment lasts 'forever and ever',[41] for cycle after cycle, until the *karma* is cleansed upon the Initiation path via passing the related testings. The agents of the transmission of this 'wrath' are those that were 'squeezed' out of the 'winepress', for they can appropriately bear the energies, the 'Blood' needed to help educate and to transform those of dark face into vehicles of light.

The consequences of such conversion produces the formation of the Ashrams. As the new Ashrams form, so the number of Masters within Hierarchy will grow to about thirty.[42] We can visualise this in terms of the first Ray Ashrams (1/2, 2/1 and 1/7) to make twenty seven, plus a triad of the Rays of Mind (7/1, 3/4, and 4/3) to complete the number thirty. The number 3 x 9 signifies the taking of the third Initiation, here by significant numbers of the world's disciples so that the new epoch of Love-Wisdom can truly manifest.[43] Concurrently there will be a large number of Initiates to take their first Initiation, and this process will have significant impact upon establishing the new age, producing many far-reaching changes in human affairs.

The number thirty refers to the perfection of a cycle of activity, which in this case refers to the cycles of developing Mind, fecundating the new era of the dominance of Love-Wisdom. The activity of the 3/4-4/3 Ashrams will help produce the final seal to all the incidents that produce planetary Initiation, the upwards movement of many people to greater heights of light supernal. They will effect right expression of the *esoteric sciences* in such a way that humanity can comprehend and be inspired to meet the challenges of the Initiation process. Consequently, new enlightened avenues of thought in all arenas of Life will be built into the edifice of the current biased materialistic world view. New temples of liberation shall be financed and built, hence aesthetic structures in the garden cities that will appear. Initiates will develop the new

---

41 Ibid.

42 This statement refers to Masters that form Ashrams, a few that take the fifth Initiation do not.

43 Because the third Initiation relates to the complete awakening of the powers of Mind, it will also allow reception of all the levels of expression of these powers to manifest upon our planet. The energy manifests from cosmic sources through the three highest planes of perception via Shambhala, into the substance of the seven mental sub-planes. They can then influence all levels of human livingness.

artistic movements and literature within our communities, providing the philosophic background to produce accelerated growth towards compassionate activity. Once the foundations of a harmonious, equable society have been produced then the Ashrams manifesting the Love Ray can fully demonstrate their salutary activity.

The theme of the planetary Initiation process is a significant one, and the reader should by now comprehend that it underlies all of the happenings in human history since the dawn of time. Because the focus is upon the entire planet, it betokens much turbulent time ahead. Initiation also necessitates the penetrative and liberating effect of the power of the first Ray in application, plus the externalising power of the seventh Ray, to properly implement all Hierarchical potencies in *saṃsāra.* The highest and lowest levels of expression of the process of Life thereby became integrated. Many significant changes must affect the way we are governed, and erroneous, deceitful propaganda affecting the masses must be eliminated. Living standards must universally significantly improve, with massed poverty eradicated, and people's leisure time more productively channelled than it presently is via right education, before the major second Ray cycle can be properly established. The birthing of a new child is often accompanied by much stress and pain for the mother. So also for the Mother of the World, whose child this truly is.

The direct first Ray line

Disregarding the Ashrams of the Rays of Mind and looking to the overall *first Ray line,* we will see that there are five Ashrams to consider at various stages of growth. They act as a functioning unity, manifesting as a pentagram bearing the powers of the five types of *prāṇas* in their highest, most intensified, purified form. The energy is electrical by nature and Fiery in effect (an attribute of nuclear energy). They are thus an embodiment of Agni, the Lord of Fire. These qualities can also be considered grounded in the mind-stream of humanity by the Fiery aura of the awakening 7/1 Ashram. The *Agni Yoga* series of books[44] by Helena Roerich presents the general gist of the associated teachings for disciples to pursue.

---

44 Helena Roerich, *Leaves of Morya's Garden,* Volumes I and II, *New Era Community, Agni Yoga, Infinity I and II, Hierarchy, Heart, Fiery World I, II and II, Aum, Brotherhood,* etc. (Agni Yoga Society, Inc., 319 West 107th Street, New York).

In the pentad for the first Ray line the 2/1 Ashram represents the functioning head of the supportive base of Love-Wisdom, helping to integrate the first Ray department with the sum of Hierarchical purpose. The 2/1 Ashram becomes the focal point of the Plan. The 1/2 Ashram represents the right hand of the pentad, conveying the *piṅgalā prāṇas* of the group. The 1/7 Ashram manifests as the left hand, conveying the *iḍā prāṇas* of the group. Being the youngest of the direct first Ray line the 1/4 Ashram manifests as the right foot and the 1/6 Ashram as the left foot of the group. They help ground the first Ray purpose in the fields of activity. The 2/1 Ashram can be viewed as a Head centre, the 1/2 as the Heart centre, the 1/7 as the Throat centre, the 1/4 as the Solar Plexus centre and the 1/6 as the Sacral centre of this grouping of Ashrams. As the 2/1 Ashram is still developing (as are the others of this first Ray line), so the overall directing principle of this *maṇḍala* comes from Morya coordinating with the new Mahāchohan. Morya directs their purpose and power and the new Mahāchohan incorporates that power within the course of the directives of the unfolding civilisation. The power of this grouping is now substantially increasing, preparing the Mother's Womb for the parturition, breaking the Waters for the troublesome birthing of the new civilisation.

The associated service work of the first Ray department to energetically counter the psychic emanations from our brothers of dark face is thereby activated. Though the first Ray embodies the dynamic qualities of the cardinal cross, because of the potency of its energy directives, the pentagram also manifests in the form of a moving swastika, which becomes a shield of power that helps to protect Hierarchy from the hostile projections from the hosts of darkness. It also facilitates the projection of energies not yet endowed amongst humanity.

These Ashrams manifest in the form of the fixed cross, where north represents the direction upwards to Shambhala, east the direction inwards to Hierarchical impression, west to the field of service that humanity represents, and south to the integral *nāḍī* system of the planet. The swastika indicates that the directions associated with the Ashrams are not static, but will move according to the need via Shambhalic and Hierarchical directives, seen from three angles of vision: a) from Shambhala, b) integrative work of Hierarchical energy with Shambhala's potency, c) protecting humanity from the onslaught of dark brotherhood projections and helping to cleanse the effects of these emanations.

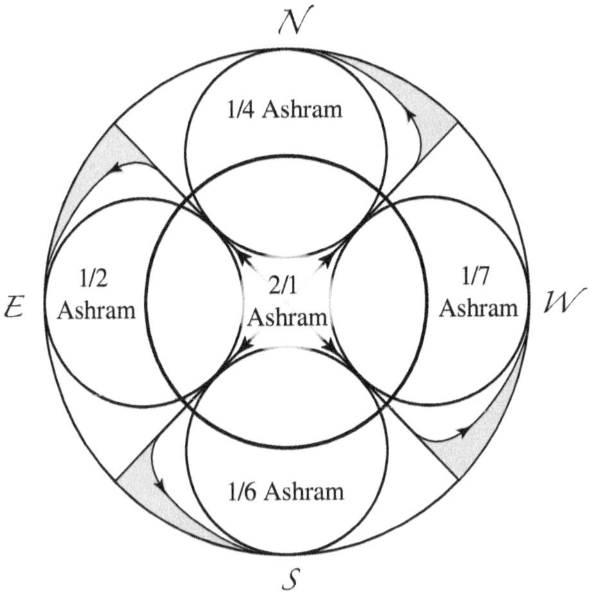

Figure 14. The Hierarchical shield

The true work of these Ashrams is esoteric and can best be explained in the terms used below. Here the focus is upon the work done in the field of battle, how the Ashrams confront and counter the forces of evil. It should be noted that the membership of this first Ray line developed many of their skills by being soldiers and commanders of armies, as well as in the field of politics throughout the centuries. They therefore innately know well the privations undertaken by soldiers, the enormous resourcefulness and will needed to fight battles, the philosophies of death, and acquiescence to suffering for a noble purpose.[45] We also have the complete obeisance of the lower ranks to commanders, rulers and kings, which later translates as a complete unswerving receptivity to the dictates from Shambhala that allows them to pierce furthest and deepest to the source of all (spiritual) power. They can then project that power towards the common foes of humanity and Hierarchy. Thus is the way of the warrior clothed in spiritual armour.

45 There are also negative karmic consequences of such things as rape, pillage and plunder that many soldiers recourse to, which often come as karmic repercussions that many disciples along these Rays have to cleanse.

Figure 14 shows the *maṇḍala* of expression that will exist as the new era properly awakens. In viewing the present structure of the *maṇḍala* it should be reaffirmed that these first Ray Ashrams channel the most purified, refined qualities of their respective sub-Ray hues.

Those of the *1/2 Ray Ashram* are the warriors of the Lord, embodying His moving hand and projecting His battle cry to the far reaches of the earth, and to all of the denizens of the deep. First, however, they must overcome the potency of this energy to feed all aspects of desire and the intensities of the emotions. (Similarly for all first Ray types.) Those of this Ashram are lords of abstraction causing the ending of times, once they develop the vision to do so. They also wield the sword of righteousness outwards in service to assert the good law throughout the nations (incorporating all customs, religions and creeds), so that the common good can be properly established to overcome darkness, stagnation, and amassed evil. This Ashram holds the swords of might and arrows of flight in the army of the Lord above all. They move to project Shambhalic Ideation to impact or impress its Purpose into manifestation and then withdraw. Hither and thither do the tides of such service flow. All of the other direct first Ray Ashrams are nourished and activated by them. Seeking inwards to Hierarchy and the Manu's department they receive the energies needed to overcome the forces of evil, and will help modify with compassionate instructions some of the more forceful attitudes of the younger members of other Ashrams of the first Ray line.

The junior *1/6 Ray Ashram*[46] receives blessings and energies from all other first Ray lines, and from above, to wield the potency of cosmic astral Waters as much as is possible to be presently conveyed by them. The emotional impediments of humanity and the zealous fanaticism that generate dark brotherhood attributes can then be countered. This energy concerns the flow of the adamantine 'Blood' (a sixth Ray expression of *prāṇic* vitality) that is churned in the skullcap of the Wrathful Deities, and offered to all worthy supplicants of Shambhala to drink. Deity here manifests as the crucified World Saviour mounted on the fixed cross of the heavens that is situated upon the 'mound' of the earth. This Saviour

46 They are yet at a very elementary stage of formation, and will only start properly forming once the second Ray cycle has been appropriately established.

is pierced by the *sword* fashioned by the fervent aspirational ardour of devotional human activity. The energy producing zealous fanaticism must be redirected in the service of the Lord, once appropriate visions and instructions have been received to rightly direct their service. Symbolically, those of this Ray line will automatically sacrifice their Life's Blood for the service of the All. They are the warriors of the Lord that in spilling this Blood will eventually help produce the death of the Watery *saṃsāric* affiliations of humanity. They are the crusading servants of the Lords of Shambhala, and also embody the armour of the Lord worn on the field of battle wherein the armies of Shambhala resolutely come to defeat the massed forces of its dark brotherhood opponents. Impetuosity must be overcome, they must learn the art of patience, to know when to act, and when to simply observe the forces massing the field of battle. They can thereby open up the doors to Life for all.

The *1/7 Ray Ashram* are the first Ray Builders, grounding the power of the first Ray into the service work that will help convert the artifices of present human civilisation into more esoteric spiritual constructs. They help precipitate the Plan through cyclic activity so that the power of Hierarchical purpose shines through. They help forge the weapons of Light that empower the ritualised activity in the temples of divinity wherein enlightenment may be obtained. They work to build and to project the foundations of the new age, the New Jerusalem, onto firm ground (in the fields of human consciousness). They are the solid strength of the bastions, battlements, and ramparts in the army of the Lord. They also assist the might of the fight with battalions of dragons (of wisdom) to put to flight panic-stricken legions of hate. They, however, must temper their power until the lessons of Love have been learnt, hence they work closely with those of the 1/2 Ray.

The *1/4 Ray Ashram* directly receives power from Shambhala to convert the general darkened Watery *prāṇas* affecting humanity. The sword of the *dharmakāya* pierces their Hearts to shed their Blood for the good of the whole. This fills the holy chalice (skull cup) borne by this Ashram with the potent energies that are directed south. Those of this Ashram stand as mediators, generally tending to act alone, as a self-centred source of power. They need to discover the esoteric group, the Hierarchical shield, they belong to, and with them work to rectify human affairs by overcoming dark brotherhood predations. Skilful they are at bearing the sword of strife and then of peaceful resolution. Martial activity (the sword of the good law and lore that sets the path straight between often warring factions) will eventually pave the way to beautifying landscapes and condolences of peace. The dove of peace then flies over the land. This Ashram holds the banners bearing the insignias of Life in the army of the Lord of Shambhala upon the fields of this great battle.

The positions of the component Ashrams can shift according to the vicissitudes of Hierarchical purpose and to humanity's response. For instance, the 1/2 Ashram can stand in the northern position, the 1/7 in the western position, the 1/6 in the south and the 1/4 in the east. In this scenario the 1/2 Ashram is best able to receive the potency of energies from Shambhala due to the fact that it is close to being fully formed when compared to the 1/6 Ashram, which is still largely embryonic. The 1/6 Ray therefore is a potent energy that can be used to help destroy the glamoured perceptions of the astral plane. However, the power of its intensity may also strengthen many aspects of the self-will that foster those attributes in the first place. The 1/7 Ashram resounds the ritual of the new Hierarchical purpose into active service during the Aquarian age, which is governed by the seventh Ray. The 1/4 Ray Ashram is thus best placed to listen to and envision the new Hierarchical directives, to implement the plan with its aesthetic and architectural designs for the new era communities.

Another ordering of the first Ray pentad can be viewed from the perspective of the strength of their innate abilities. The 1/2 Ashram empowers the attribute of the directive Will or overall purpose. The 2/1 Ashram then manifests the supportive, clarifying and wise augmentation of purpose by the Love-Wisdom principle of the right hand. The 1/7 Ashram embodies the activity attribute of this triad, fully projecting the first Ray power onto the physical domain, as the left hand. The junior 1/4 and 1/6 Ray Ashrams are literally the feet that help anchor the (destroyer) first Ray purpose in *saṃsāra* via a foundation of cushioned, loving activity.

In the new age this *maṇḍala* can also manifest so that the direction north is held by the 1/7 Ashram, to best receive the potent power from Shambhala. The direction east is held by the 1/2 Ashram to integrate all purpose of the first Ray into a unity with Hierarchy and then directing that purpose to cleanse misperceived evil influences and the aberrations of humanity's Solar Plexus activity. The primary work therefore concerns the power to convert emotional energies into a wise, loving impetus. This happens via the western direction that will be held by the 1/6 Ashram. The process helps defeat of the powerbases of the dark brotherhood, who work mainly to foster the evils of people's emotional and desirous bodies. The direction south, which is the 1/4 purpose, concerns projecting the cleansing, purifying energies of Hierarchy into humanity's *nāḍī* system. The 2/1 purpose remains constant at the centre, as the organising Love-Wisdom aspect channelled from the general second Ray Ashrams, which must always guide the first Ray output. Also, there is the directive purpose of how to best defeat the dark brotherhood's manipulations.

The activity of Splenic centre II

Having provided the overview of the mode of activity of the direct first Ray Ashrams, the integration of their work with their corresponding Ashrams of Mind can now be given. This is seen as the function of Splenic centre II for humanity. The hub of this wheel is governed by the directive potency of the first Ray Chohan, Morya. Such work is literally the effort of the entire Hierarchy, as it effectively concerns the process of the transformation of the *saṃskāras* of humanity, producing the path of Initiation. The effectiveness of the first Ray department, however, concerns being sword bearers of the Lord, to directly overcome the dark brotherhood upon the inner realms in their march to gain planetary ascendency. The other Ray Ashrams mainly work in support, where their primary activity is the right education of humanity and to provide the social fabric of civilisation wherein people can discover the means to improve their lives spiritually. All however can bear swords of light to defeat the evil, the darkness of their past actions, as they evoke first Ray attributes to overcome all obstacles on this path.

To analyse the activity of Splenic centre II upon humanity as a whole one should use the information provided in Volume 5A, where the eight Piśācī were explained in relation to an individual *yogin's* meditative work to transform *saṃskāras*. The *'yogin'* that now concerns us is the cumulative activity of the first Ray Ashrams, where Morya represents the higher directive Mind governing the process. One need only transpose the information related to the individual to envision similar *prāṇas* expressed by the mass of human units. However, as it is humanity that we are concerned with, much of what is to be transformed can be conceived of as the worst type of *saṃskāras* that the human persona is capable of developing. Hence much of this work concerns battling the evil generated by the members of the dark brotherhood, by utilising the most potent forms of light.

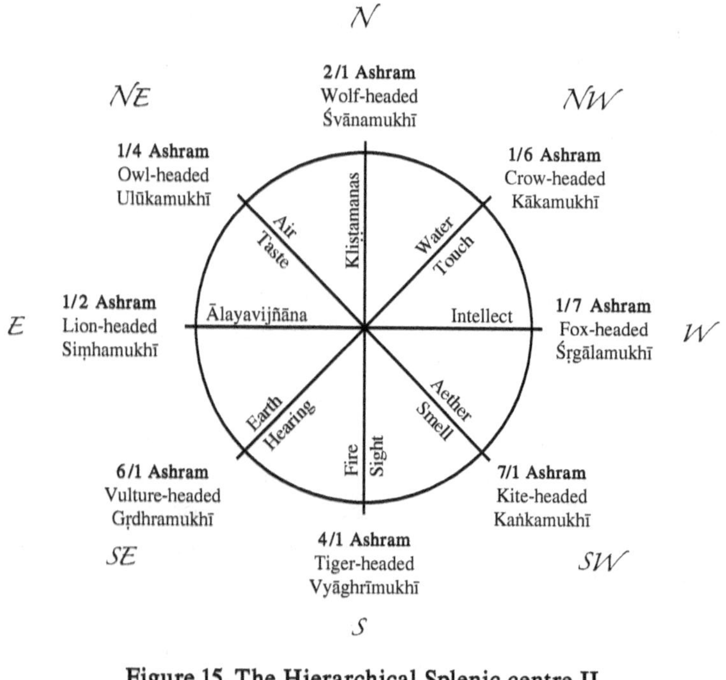

Figure 15. The Hierarchical Splenic centre II

Elaborating some of the information presented earlier in Volume 5A, it can be stated that the potency expressed for the *eastern direction* (or gate of the *maṇḍala)* governed by the 1/2 Ray Ashram is symbolised by lion-headed Siṃhamukhī carrying a human corpse in her mouth. This function relates to regulating the *prāṇic* flow to the right Gonad centre. The Gonad centres, and their relation to the Sacral and Base of Spine centres, represent the storehouse of mind for the *prāṇas* at this predominantly Earthy-Watery level of expression. The Gonad centres are but offshoots of the Sacral centre's energies, the source of *prāṇic* vitality for all minor *chakras* and those of the Inner Round. They also represent, as one can deduce, the sexual function, and physical-emotional creative forces, the power to manipulate and to control substance.

The right Gonad centre represents the 'sun' under whose light this lion basks. Its energies, rightly cleansed of desire, are what the *yogin* utilises to overcome aberrant *saṃskāras,* mostly of a sexual nature and of attraction to material things. They deal with the subjective, inner forces governing the creative process, of the way the higher energies from the higher self (Hierarchy/Shambhala) are to be utilised in the form to be built.

The corpse that Siṃhamukhī carries represents the dead weight of one's entire carnal body, and when viewed from a planetary scale concerns the conversion of people's erroneous sexual thinking and desires, plus of the associated martial application of the Sacral's *prāṇic* energy in militaristic fields and politics. This inherent Sacral potency, when strengthened by energies from Shambhala, allows those of this Ray to use the most powerful energies to combat the emanations of the dark faced ones. The power of Siṃhamukhī is the mouth, hence speech. Wise logic must be used by the 1/2 disciple to produce the transformations of the corpse of the general human psyche. Evidence of 'clear vision'[47] must be provided to the rest of the first Ray department.

The sensory object here[48] is that of the *manasic* substance of the *ālayavijñāna*. The objective is to cleanse the Earthy aspects from the desire-mind (the 'human corpse') so that thought becomes more Fiery. Because Splenic centre II deals mainly with an Earthy-Watery mix of *prāṇas,* so the term 'sewer system' has been used to describe the function of this centre. Its main purpose is to wash away the major Earthy defilements and impediments so that the cleansed *prāṇas* can flow to the higher centres. Eventually the substance of the *ālayavijñāna* environment will be generated by transforming all base Earthy-Watery *saṃskāras* into their Fiery correspondences.

---

47 See *Esoteric Psychology,* Volume I, 65, which states for the 1/2 Ashram: 'Kill out desire when desire has fulfilled its work. Thou art the one who indicates fulfillment. Quality...clear vision'.

48 One must view these 'sensory objects' as internalised attributes of consciousness if they are to be dealt with yogically.

The general cleansing (hence most developed) Watery-Fiery *prāṇic* flow from all minor *chakras* below the diaphragm, coupled with that of Splenic centre I, are admixed in this eastern gate. This energy purifies the *piṇgalā* attributes developed by the Earthy circulation (the principle of desire) of the minor *chakras* (wherein the bulk of humanity reside). The western petal of the fixed cross aspect of Splenic centre II similarly works to cleanse the *iḍā* stream of the minor *chakras*.

Such a purifying flow is expressed by advanced people that are no longer predominantly focussed upon their physical bodies, but rather upon mental pursuits. Highly creative (esoteric) writings hence can manifest, coupled with the generation of intense light needed to cleanse the world's astral murk. Humanity must learn to evoke the Will if they wish liberation, by drawing upon this clarifying energy of Love, to project consciousness to the *arūpa* levels via this Splenic centre II flow. They must produce the fulfilment of higher, more exalted achievements in life than their normal materialistic goals.

The tiger-headed Vyāghrīmukhī standing with two arms crossed is found in the *southern direction* and symbolises the functioning of the 4/1 Ray Ashram. This Ashram manifests the 'power to penetrate the depths of matter'. [49] The sensory object here is the object of sight. From this perspective the sense of sight perceives all material objects, integrating them into a panoramic vision. The tiger symbolically lurks in the jungles of the mind, where the attributes of the defiled mind (the animal-like mental-emotions) hide. In this case the 'jungle' represents the forces of all the small Inner Round *chakras* of the *nāḍī* system wherein the emotional and desire attributes of humanity are generated. The objective of the tiger is to seek out and prey upon all such *prāṇas* and to elevate them to the higher domains by consuming (and hence transforming) them.

The hands (the extension of the arms) are normally used as manipulative or grasping tools to obtain the object of desire, but are here crossed, signifying the demonstration of proper control over all forms of desire. That they are crossed over the chest cavity signifies the ability to prevent any of these defilements from affecting the higher centres. Hence a major function of this Ray Ashram is to counter the

---

49 The statement for the 4/1 Ray Ashram being: 'Speak low the Word. Speak low. Quality...power to penetrate the depths of matter'. Ibid., 72.

effects of desire (the wrong manipulation of energies) by all in our civilisation. Also implied is the symbol of the mutable cross, of repeated cyclic activity, thus of the recycling of *prāṇas* until they are thoroughly cleansed of all aspects of the Earthy-Watery constitution.

Depending upon the nature of the *prāṇas* involved, the cleansing of *karma* often produces sickness. Watery *prāṇas* for example, generally contain many Earthy defilements that produce ill health when externalised in an organ. Health manifests when gross *prāṇic* defilements are eliminated. The function of this Ashram, therefore, is to try to manifest good health in humanity by zapping away predatory *prāṇas,* the forces amongst humanity that pertain to sickness and disease—the evil-minded ones. These ones work assiduously to keep humanity materialistically focussed. They represent the forces of war and strife that need to be annulled and harmonised to produce the epoch of peace and harmony. Those of this Ashram will find it difficult to curtail physical plane martial activity because the energy of will or power manifests via the Ray that works to produce harmony in the midst of strife. When this energy is used to battle the emanations of the dark brotherhood the 4/1 Ashram members will tend to manifest such activity with excessive zeal. Similarly for those of the 1/4 Ashram, who will tend to be much more isolationist than their 4/1 brother or sister, hence must work to become more group focussed.

As this Ashram develops they will help demonstrate to humanity that all that is apprehended by means of the senses is ephemeral. They will assist to transform the perception of the 'solidity' of things, to show that all is non-substantial, as the mode of controlling physical phenomena via the etheric substance upon which all is built will be adequately demonstrated. Physical plane laws as presently understood will thus seemingly be overcome. That all such powers are an effect of the path of the cleansing, transformation, and transmutation of *saṃskāras* will however be stressed. Their effect hence is to help produce the etherealisation of substance, as the power of this Ray (in this southern direction) penetrates deep into matter by breaking down its resistance to the impact of higher energies.

In the *western direction* of outwards to the field of service we find the 1/7 Ray Ashram symbolised by the fox-headed Śṛgālamukhī eating entrails. The sensory object is the object of the mind's perceptions sought after by the wily fox. We therefore have the functioning of the intellect, 'eating' the substance of thoughts (the expressions of the five sense-consciousnesses). The fox's natural cunning represents the 'sensory object' of intelligent thoughts (or mind) of the individual, whereas eating entrails relates to the emotional content of thoughts, the desire-mind *(kāma-manas)*, which are digested and relatively quickly mastered by the 1/7 disciple. The first Ray will reinforce the disciplining organisational tendencies of the seventh Ray, which will sternly regulate the emotions. Other emotions, such as pride in 'knowing', may be intensified as a 'virtue'. The Fiery-Earthy Element is exemplified, and when integrated with this field of desire, then the worst, most entrenched *saṃskāras* are produced that need to be converted. The near ubiquitous desire-mind in humanity then is what the 1/7 Ashram works to counter with steely, practical, down-to-earth determinations.

Such a service domain represents the *iḍā nāḍī* for the Earthy circulation directed via the left Gonad centre. Literally this centre relates to physical plane creation, hence the focus is to empower Hierarchy's purpose upon the material domain. It ensures that the edifices of activity are appropriately constructed. The transformative work in this petal strips from *saṃskāras* as many adverse qualities as possible before directing them to the left Gonad so that appropriate constructs are created in the material world. The symbolic cleverness of the fox manifests to determine the best way to achieve this goal. Many of the primary battles of conversion of *saṃskāras* of personal aggregates into attributes of desirelessness can then happen. Refined *prāṇas* can also be directed to Splenic centre I with view of them being acceptable for circulation in the centres above the diaphragm.

The statement given to the 1/7 Ray Ashram is:

> Seek out the gentle way, Oh Lord of Power. Wait for thy brother on the path of Love. He builds the forms that can withstand thy power.
>
> Quality...dynamic power.[50]

We see, therefore, that once the 1/7 disciple is aware of the service work ahead, very little upon the physical plane can prevent

50 Ibid.,65.

its accomplishment because of the determination, the force brought to bear to achieve. However, the second Ray is needed to temper the energies and provide the wisdom that will rightly direct and help build what is to be. Patience is always needed to be developed by all first Ray disciples to overcome their natural impetuosity.

The transformation of the Earthy-Watery *skandhas* upon the path to enlightenment inevitably evokes the All-accomplishing Wisdom of Amoghasiddhi. All eight qualities attributed to the petals of Splenic centre II describe the processes needed to effect this transformation. The base characteristics of the related *saṃskāras* must be converted into the most refined aspects of the eight consciousnesses. In this western petal they are infused with the Fiery fox-like characteristics of consciousness, allowing comprehension of the way negative attributes of desire affect decision making. Plans can then be made of how to counter the development of such attributes, to produce forthright practical effects.

In the *northern direction* is found the wolf-headed Śvānamukhī tearing apart a bloated corpse, symbolising the attributes of the 2/1 Ray Ashram. The sensory object here relates to *kliṣṭamanas* (defiled mind), being the most refined Watery-Earthy *prāṇas* developed. They are directed northward to Splenic centre I. (Which esoterically relates to the ability of the new Mahāchohan to help direct Splenic centre II activity via the 2/1 Ashram, as the most refined energies are projected this way, or via the 1/2 Ray Ashram. Note that all *prāṇic* flows between petals of the *chakras* can manifest in a two-way direction.)

The *prāṇas* coming to Splenic centre I from its lower companion represents the Earthy attributes it must process. As the coarser aspects of the Earthy Element are washed away to produce a refinement of desires and attachments, coupled with increased *manasic* aptitude (creativity), so then the attributes of *kliṣṭamanas* are generated. This is signified by the activities of the wolf, a very sociable animal, who generally works as part of a pack to hunt its prey (the objects of desire). Similarly amongst humanity desires are generated within a group context. The prey is herded by various factors that subjectively influence each other, producing the images of things desired by humanity. This 'prey' represents the *saṃskāras* from many minor centres. The elements of mind (the 'pack of wolves') are consequently developed to produce the best outcome. Each 'wolf' represents an individual thought-stream, part of a grouping of multiple perspectives that collectively produce the sensorial images. The Watery-mind *(kliṣṭamanas)* is thus established, but is inevitably transformed into *bodhicitta* via continuous refinement. Rash, impulsive behaviour for what is desired is eventually superseded by thoughtful acquisition upon the road of developing the Will-of-Love.

As the general idea pool of the mind is developed then the resultant logic can tear apart the corpse of illogical concepts associated with *saṃsāra.* (The sum of the images that bloat the corpse of all illusional thoughts.) The 2/1 Ashram thus helps annul the bloated forms of desire-mind attachments generated by people. The dark brotherhood that manipulate massed human desires and manifest the propaganda to further enslave humanity to their base natures is consequently countered and *karma* annulled. All *karma* is the effect of the substance of mind that must eventually be directed towards properly examining the corpse of what was once considered real by the eye-consciousness. The transmogrifying process must then happen within the mind.

The enlightenment-bound *yogin/yoginī* of the 2/1 Ray must succeed in helping to annul the *karma*-producing activities in humanity so that they can tread the path northwards. The *manasic* impetus from the Throat centre to control all activities of desire, as focussed by the eye, is invoked via this petal. The eye directs the expressions of karmic volition right through to the southern direction wielded by the 4/1 Ashram so that all the *prāṇas* from the Inner Round can eventually be converted to *bodhicitta.* The *prāṇas* evoked are utilised by the mind to produce new seed thoughts for future actions, but must be broadened by Love-Wisdom if the deadening *karma* leading to deeper *saṃsāric* affiliation is not to be produced. The most refined Fiery aspects of the integrated Earthy-Watery *prāṇas* generated in Splenic centre II can then be directed northwards as *saṃskāras* are transformed and transmuted.

As the *karma*-generating base is eliminated, so humanity can climb the mountain of achievement to gain the focal point of aspiration. The generation of the related *saṃskāras* therefore ceases, either through transformation and direction upwards towards the Heart centre, or else through projection out of the system altogether by preventing their attributes from occurring. Esoterically, such activity is viewed as zapping the dark *prāṇas* with Rays of brilliant light. Eventually, the Initiation process can be undertaken.

The statement given for the 2/1 Ray Ashram is:

> Within the radius of the love of God, within the circle of the solar system, all forms, all souls, all lives revolve. Let each son of God enter into this wisdom. Reveal to each the oneness of the many lives.
>
> Quality...expansion or inclusiveness.[51]

The fixed cross attribute of the eight-armed wheel of direction in space so far described deals with the main *prāṇic* orientations of Splenic centre II. The intermediate mutable cross positions of the four remaining deities deal with the *iḍā* and *piṇgalā* expression of *prāṇas* of the desirous attributes gained via the sense-consciousnesses (apart from sight, which is directed via the north-south direction). The southeast-northwest expresses the *iḍā* line to and from Splenic centre I and the northeast-southwest line the Airy-Aetheric *piṇgalā* line. This interrelation allows a thorough and rapid sorting out of all *prāṇas* to be processed by the combined Splenic centres, for many are the aspects of desire and emotion generated by most people all of the time. The *prāṇas* directed from Splenic centre I to Splenic centre II via this mutable cross represent what needs further processing.

In the *southeast direction* of 'expression' is found the vulture-headed Gṛdhramukhī carrying a human corpse draped over her shoulder, symbolising the work of the 6/1 Ashram. The sensory object here is the object of sound impacts. The vulture is the prime emissary of the 'sky burial' practiced in Tibet, where human corpses are cut up and left for these birds to consume. The concept of sound impacts here presumably relates to the noisy scene at feeding times for these birds. Hearing is the most limited of senses because sound is the result of clashing together of physical objects. These sounds are related to the death of phenomena. Esoterically, they relate to the rather coarse Earthy *prāṇas* circulating through the *nāḍīs* of the practitioner. This physicality is symbolised by the weight of the corpse that is carried for later consumption (processing). Within the overall context of the Earthy *prāṇas,* the 6/1 Ashram works to transform a subsidiary hue of a Watery expression of base desire, lust, extremisms and general martial attributes within humanity. These *saṃskāras* relate to the *prāṇas* flowing to and

51 Ibid., 67.

from the Gonad centres and the Inner Round. Also, the weight of the reject *prāṇas* from Splenic centre I must be borne.

The statement given for the 6/1 Ray Ashram is:

> Why is desire red? Why red as blood? Tell us, Oh Son of God, why thy way is red with blood?
>
> Quality...power to kill out desire.[52]

The activity of this Ashram is problematic, because it's development is at an infant stage. Esoterically the concern is its 'lust for blood', signifying the war-like activity and zealotry, as well as intensified desire or idealism, which this Ray engenders. Those of this Ashram consequently must struggle hard to master the astral plane and all of its lures and glamours. Their path relates to battling with all illusions and strong astrally projected thought-forms, of the complete nine-headed Hydra of rampant energies and associated images. As a consequence of the learning procedure and eventual mastery, they can eventually demonstrate to humanity the way to undertake the second Initiation. They must reason their way through the associated bewildering kaleidoscope of images. In doing so those of this Ashram will be able to wield the strongest forces to help overcome the world's astral hells and those that sustain their existence. This then is a manifestation of their 'power to kill out desire'.

The Sacral centre absorbs the *prāṇas* derived from all forms of contact with the external environment and from interrelation with other's desire bodies. Many are the emotional responses, desirous articulations and tendencies for base *saṃskāras,* generated. The propensity to be engrossed in activity that intensifies attachment to the objects of the senses must be overcome. Transience must be eschewed through knowing how to eliminate addiction to the sense bases. Inevitably, the painful outcome of desire-attachment will be so thoroughly comprehended that aversion to sense activity manifests. Fanaticism can then manifest, producing extreme forms of celibacy, austerity and the like, which also must be resisted. The middle way between all things must be sought instead. Through proper comprehension and control of all energies,

52 Ibid., 81.

consciousness will transmute coarse desires, emotions, and concepts of sexuality (the 'human corpse' that causes cyclic rebirth) into selfless Love for all. The effortless sound of the *dharma* will then be heard and the carrion for Gṛdhramukhī to consume eliminated.

In the *southwest direction* of 'understanding' stands the kite-headed Kaṅkamukhī carrying a large human corpse, symbolising the attributes of the 7/1 Ashram. Kites are medium sized birds of prey that typically have a forked tail, often found soaring in updrafts of air. Such flight provides ability to view a vast panorama of the plains (*saṃsāra*) below. Their forked tail indicates that such vision incorporates both the *iḍā* and *piṇgalā nāḍī* views. However, this kite is lumbered by the weight of the *saṃskāric* qualities of the corpse it carries.

The sensory object here relates to the way substance of the highest Element (Aether) is integrated into the qualities of the corpse, the expression of the Earthy Element. It therefore relates to the etheric counterpart of the 'smells' of the physical domain, concerning the debasement of the elements of mind ('the corpse'). This encumbered bird (the 'corpse' being heavier than that carried by the 6/1 Ashram) hence is concerned with the purified, most onerous Earthy desire-mind *saṃskāras,* the material *(iḍā)* aspects of the *piṇgalā nāḍī.* The objective is to produce flight without the 'corpse'. (Its 'smell' will then no longer be discernible.) The *prāṇas* derived from the Gonad centres and Inner Round must be so refined that they become more Airy and hence suitable for incorporation into Splenic centre I circulation. Abject desires must be transformed via the elements of the thought processes into loving aspiration.

The phrase given for the 7/1 Ray Ashram is:

> Take thy tools with thee, brother of the building light. Carve deep. Construct and shape the living stone.
>
> Quality...power to create. [53]

The 'heavy corpse' thus represents the burden of the material plane substance that this Ashram is especially empowered to work with, utilising the organising power of the seventh Ray energy combined with

53 Ibid., 86.

determined will to do so. They must carve deeply into the substance of materialistic minds so as to convert the most recalcitrant empirical thinkers into those that can bear lofty enlightened thoughts. (To take 'flight' through understanding of the processes involved.) Most difficult is this task, hence the potent first Ray Shambhalic energies assist, coupled with the seventh Ray power to transform and transmogrify. This Ashram thereby manifests great power to help convert the dark brotherhood ensconced in the material domain, by destroying their power bases in the world. Aspiration to noble ideals are developed that eventually lifts one above the factor of materialistic desire. The task of such conversion work is enormous. This Ashram also has the ability to defeat the darkness via the right empowerment and utilisation of money, by building the material plane edifices that will house Hierarchical purpose. They are the master builders, craftsmen in the Masonic art, esoterically understood.

The 7/1 Ashram has the capacity to integrate all of the *prāṇas* of Splenic centre II, as well as the ability to utilise the dynamic Will to cut asunder from the circulation what no longer possesses a rightful place therein. They thus help propel the worst of the dark *prāṇas* into the eighth sphere. The work of this Ashram is therefore ubiquitous for the activity of this *chakra*. This Ashram separates out the maligned and malignant tonalities of all concretising *prāṇas* so that they can be refined or eliminated. (These are the *saṃskāras* the dark brother is most at home in.) The 7/1 Ashram thereby helps build the living temples for the habitation of the Lord of Light with the purified substance they send upwards. The 7/1 Ray thus constitutes the 'power to create'[54] the edifices of all our spiritual lives.

In the *northeast direction* of 'unity' there is the owl-headed Ulūkamukhī holding a *vajra*, who symbolises the attributes of the 1/4 Ashram. The owl is generally viewed as symbolising a wise being because of its ability to see in the dark where it hunts its prey. The darkness represents the blindness of ignorance, which is overcome by the owl's excellent vision. This vision relates to the ability of the members of this Ashram to reflect divinity (via the first Ray) into the material domain by means of the fourth Ray aptitude. The force of the *vajra* draws the

54 Ibid.

elements of wisdom from out of the darkness. Whatever wisdom can be found then represents the owl's prey, or conversely it works to eliminate attributes that prevent such attainment.

The sensory object here relates to the sense of taste, hence to the Element Air. Here, however, at first the most material aspect of the taste sense-consciousness is experienced, associated with physical plane sensations and related knowledgeable attributes. Once tasted, some are savoured and others are rejected as vile tasting, even poisonous. Eventually, *prāṇas* (foods) that do not serve to nourish the spiritual life are eschewed. The most pleasing attributes of the Inner Round and Sacral centre *piṅgalā prāṇas* are processed so that they can be projected to Splenic centre I.

We have moved from a primarily Earthy and desire based scenario associated with the southern petals to a Watery-Airy emotional based scenario for the two northern petals of the mutable cross under consideration. Within this context the 1/4 Ashram directs the subsidiary Airy-Watery *prāṇas* of the fundamental Earthy Element processed by Splenic centre II that must be cleansed of defilements. Some of the most concreted Earthy *prāṇas* (manifesting via the polar opposite sign, governed by the 7/1 Ashram) are eliminated as a consequence of this washing process. The pacified, cleansed *prāṇas* can then be directed to Splenic centre I wherein the energy from the Heart centre can thoroughly purify them. The disciples constituting Splenic centre II can then be freed from the qualities of self-identification, which identifies things in relation to the concept of an 'I'. Once the energies from the Heart-infused Splenic centre I impresses them from this northeast direction that feeds the entire mutable cross with energetic directions, liberation then proceeds with speed.

The statement for the 1/4 Ashram is:

> Stand not alone, but with the many join thyself. Thou art the One, the Isolated. Come forth unto thine own.
>
> Quality...solitariness.[55]

Those of this Ashram need to overcome the sense of isolationism (a natural outcome of the first and fourth Ray combination) by learning

55 Ibid., 65.

to integrate with the members of Hierarchy (the concept of 'unity') that they recognise. They will then develop the ability to project the most Airy *prāṇas* possible to cleanse humanity's etheric miasma of conflicting energies. In group formation then, they will battle the darkness to brighten up the earth's aura by producing harmony in arenas where there was formerly strife.

In the *northwest* direction of emanatory positive expressiveness ('good will') we have the crow-headed Kākamukhī brandishing a skull and a sword, symbolising the attributes of the 1/6 Ashram. The crow has black feathers, a strong beak used for scavenging food, and a raucous voice. What is emphasised here concerns the development of the attributes of mind via the *iḍā nāḍī.* In Splenic centre II this *nāḍī* conveys the most material aspect of the desire principle, the Watery aspect of the Earth Element that must become increasingly refined as consciousness develops.

Having prevailed over the environment it resides in (as implicated by the qualities of this northwest direction) the crow carries a skull, signifying the rulership of the process of birth and death that comes as a consequence of the mastery of desire-mind. At first the mental-emotions processed generally produce desire for further intoxicating experiences, by gathering more bits of information by the scavenging crow. Much must be gleaned from *saṃsāra's* turmoil, with its death-like attributes, symbolised by the skull that is held. This skull also indicates the way to the Head lotus offered by this path, once the sword of right discrimination is utilised and base Watery *saṃskāras* no longer rule. The fruit that then comes to view concerns liberation from it all. The accompanying sword of right discrimination allows the 1/6 disciple to quickly sever ties to all limiting *saṃskāras,* once the will to do so has been generated.

The sensory object here is that which can be touched, causing the apprehension of physical objects. Watery, desirous responses are evoked through the experience of sense contact. The mind must be developed from out of the Earthy-Watery environment to comprehend the objects of contact before *skandhas* can be converted into knowledgeable attributes and directed to Splenic centre I. For the sixth Ray disciple (especially intensified by the first Ray), mastery of the emotions, hence the development of clear thought, is very difficult, as extremism and fanaticism generally prevail. Such mastery becomes a major objective, but once accomplished, then the disciple of the 1/6 Ray can utilise martial skills to quickly produce the death of the desire principle and convert the planetary entities that are the exemplars of such energies. The 1/6 spiritual warrior must, however, first learn patience in order to know when to act, as natural impetuosity can undo the Hierarchical plan.

Most people comprehend the power of strong, uncontrolled desire. It empowers martial attributes, fanaticism, jealousy and the intensity of hatred. Many dark brotherhood attributes are based upon the power gained through the manipulation of the desire-emotions of their victims. In the ranks of sex magicians, those that abuse their power as high ecclesiastics, or in the military, are the dark ones found that are ruled by the sixth Ray. Those of the 1/6 Ray have much power to psychically oppose such ones, once they have mastered their own desirous proclivities and wrongly faceted idealisms. More importantly, people's emotional miasmas and glamours, the intensely desirous images scavenged by the crow, must be battled by the potent Rays of this Ashram. The beginning of the end of rulership of the astral plane in humanity will manifest once this and the 6/1 Ashrams evolve the *maṇḍalic* empowerment to do so. Together the 1/6 and 6/1 Ashrams will effect this aim, but the 6/1 is more materially and religiously focussed, whilst the 1/6 acts more like the avenging 'Hand of God', projecting His Wrath upon the 'grindstone', potently projecting cosmic astral energies to cleanse the systemic Watery murk, and to overcome the 'beast' that is vitalised by it.

When the members of this Ashram have evolved the capacity to project the first Ray intensity and sixth Ray zeal in overcoming the allurements of the astral plane, then they will project the 'gift of death' for all humanity concerning this plane of perception. Myriad will be the battles effected to 'seal the door where evil dwells' (as per the wording of 'The Great Invocation'). They will then open the Door to the higher spheres for humanity to travel the way as they fight the evil. Right timing is everything, a lesson learnt via fighting many battles against implacable and ferocious foes, sometimes in the face of innumerable odds. The natural impetuosity and fears of the warrior in battle must be tempered by the wise decisions of the leaders of the fray. Here then is the gist of the statement for this Ray Ashram.

Withhold thy hand until the time has come. Then give the gift of death, Oh Opener of the Door.

Quality...sense of time.[56]

The hand projects the energies of all five *prāṇas* of the *nāḍī* system via the five fingers. It wields the instruments of power of the warrior, the builder and the magician.

The second Ray Ashrams

Below are a series of phrases concerning the function of the second Ray Ashrams, whose purpose will manifest properly in the new age, plus the other Ray lines that are concerned with awakening this new second Ray era. The focus shall be upon the methodology of these Ashrams to defeat the forces of evil. The second Ray Ashrams assist the efforts of the first Ray army for the fight, as the first and second Ray energies are always considered to function as a unity. This interrelationship is demonstrated in the relation between the two Splenic centres.

The 2/1 Ashram.
The vital expansive Life of what is to Be.
The shield of Might in the hand of 'God'.
The power of Sight in domains of Night.
The moving power of Thunder.
The power of the Right.
The power of Love,
and the spiralling, straightforward
Might of the Light that must be used in the Fight.
Climb up the ladder of time and see
this reaping of Souls, cyclically foretold.
Why the spiral? Why the Fight?
From whence comes the illusion, the hordes of the night?
The One who sits on this Throne
can tell you, if you ask just right.

56 Ibid.

2/2 Ashram.
Clothing the army with indigo blue Light,
the curtain of Love veiling the power of the Right.
They resound the songs of joy, songs of delight,
from the Hierarchy around and humanity below.
The blue protective aura is the all-pervasive Might.
The hosts of evil brook not Love,
they must be converted by it, 'tis the Dove.
The Dove takes flight in the blue starry sky,
conveying its message to every Hierarchy of Light.

2/3 Ashram.
Understanding the minds of the evil one's entourage of hate,
the wise words of Love counsels the warriors of the Fight,
envisioning defects in the dark foe's battlement insights,
and assisting the Shield to vision the vistas of the night,
they help put the evil foes into cages of Light.
Lord Saturn decrees that the harbingers of woeful states
must to woe be bound, as their karmic fate.
The hourglass turns as the sands of time
mete out the ending of all tithes of mind,
the ending of rhyme, of reason, all mankind.
There exists but the ONE, Look! Be sublime.
The cycles return, the hands of fate spin and weave,
the tapestry decreed unfolds throughout Space.
Time waits at each appointed gate
to release the demons, the hordes from hell!
Woe must come, and come to pass.

2/4 Ashram.
They mirror the Light through clouds thick with hatred and spite.
Mantras from above whip and shatter the evil amassed
material might.
Deva cohorts come with flowered wreaths of delight,
cleansing pockets of dark coloured loathing
and malicious mantras of fright.

Humanity in Love sing songs of the Right,
joy, joy, joy be thy accomplished birthright.
Anubis hasten to flee from their listening places.
No spaces left for them to jumble your mind
with wily distracting thoughts, their aces.
Anubis are the special nemesis
of all second Ray forms of enlightenment seeking.
Be aware, be watchful, alert to their mindful twisting.
With radiant delight you fight to displace them,
sending light to overcome lying thought projections.

2/5 Ashram.
Opinions abound in the world's collective cesspool of mind.
The dark ones feed this conflicting speculative and separative blight.
Oh what a morass of ugly forms and darkened distorted life!
The golden winged army of Light
shines as a sun so radiantly bright,
eliminating this darkness with patches of sight;
envisioning the future so close to our hearts.
What a wondrous freeing of sensations of mind,
a spaciousness devoid of formulations of thought,
the flight of the bird o'er mountainous heights.
Seers shall be made of men with no darkened respites.
Evil foes vanquished by golden arrows in flight.
Home to the sun all must fly as One
fuelled by the Love that is the harvest of Life,
journeyed through all domains of night,
progressed through the dawn's patchy Light.
No strife, nor turmoil, only That (Clear) Light in your Mind,
with unlimited, unparalleled visioned Insight.
Behold, the One, all Power, His Might.
You attract all to you to view this Sight.

2/6 Ashram.
They battle the darkness with swords of Light,
voicing bright counsel to the massed fear, anguish and plight

of the populace's self-delusioned woe and lack of will to fight
the dark one's machinations of might.
Devoted endeavour in ways blue electric just right
assists humanity to take up the good fight,
to end illusions, glamours, all woes and their blight.
The Christ-Light so bright comes to liberate the night.
Its radiant glory, that Love becomes your birthright.

2/7 Ashram.
The commanders of the arenas of active battle,
planning the stratagems of the moving masses.
With ritualised formulations they assist the fight
with magical incantations and talismans of Right.
The temple Hierophants, they evoke the Might,
the blue and violet, a powerful Light
in the realms of form, of hell, and human plight.
They enchain all demons and phantoms of night
with bright sound and right magical insight.
They speak the Words that all can hear
so that Love works to fill all dark cavernous spaces,
wherein reside organised self-willed groups,
full of cunning design and forceful, fearful intent,
that by rituals of evil project potent forces,
the great beasts of thoughts serving their grandiose formulae
of world domination and enslavement of all of Life's descent.
Our separative foes, the brothers of dark faces
have built powerful empires of greed in all races
and are everywhere found, even in high places.
Come *devas* of the Sight, the moving power of Might.
Hallelujah! Hallelujah!
Sing the orchestrations of the chorus of Light,
circle the domains of the creatures of night
with the Light, the Love, the Fight.
The dark one finds his black lair forsaken.
Who can withstand the power of the Sight?

The following statements concern the nature of the other major Rays (excluding the first Ray) that govern present Hierarchical purpose to produce the major second Ray epoch. The sub-Rays of these Rays manifest as versions of the corresponding second Ray sub-Rays.

The third Ray statement.
The bountiful greens, viridian, the vibrant hues,
the yellow shades, orange, and violet tones.
The third Ray bequeaths Nature's verdure to you.
Mathematically exact it brings all flowers to bloom.
Such multifarious activity is a fortitudinous boon.
The Mother's garden flourishes by
converting *prāṇas* of malicious hue.
Wish-fulfilling gems of far-sighted *siddhis* arise,
but only for those who hearken to the Heart of Her Life.
Throughout civilisation its the springtime
of the exactitude of Mind dispensed by the wise.
The Head lotus awakens as valiant deeds are done
by the victorious conquerors of the concretions of mind
when evil weeds transformed become
by ideas resplendent, ideas transcendent,
all abstractions automatically comprehended.
The Head is the *prajñāpāramitā's* disguise,
resplendently luminescent, its all wisdom inside.
Instantaneous, omniscient, omnidirectional is this Sight.
The *devas* sing songs of delight,
reticulated *nāḍīs* of Mind shining bright,
apparelled in the spontaneous Clear Light,
its pristine naturalness like the dawn's birthright.
New ideals, new ways, garden cities, *maṇḍalas* of munificence begun,
forgotten the epoch of woe begotten, with the awakening Sun.
The flaming jewel, the radiant trident of might,
the *vajra* unfolds its prowess of five-fold insight.
Transcendental Jinas bequeath bliss as their powers arise,
once you've fought the wrathful ones, their schemes undone.

Fiercely they fight you upon every step to that Sight.
They will not rest until you're dressed
with the thousand-petalled crown, exuberant delight, no evil inside,
all-knowing Wisdom, radiant glory, the Clear Light.

The seventh Ray purpose.
The violet, the golden-violet hues,
bronzes and all metallic lustres, silvery, azure,
the seventh Ray's power works magical wonder;
alembics, beakers, and flasks of reticulating acids to convert
base ores into silver radiance and golden lustre,
by recurrent regulatory heat and sounds refined
the recalcitrant metals into the most ecstatic piercing thoughts.
Transformed are all that ungainly minds desire.
Philosopher's gold and radiance mustered,
astute minds, awakened hearts illuminate prescience bright.
The smithy forges, the workers toil, rhythmically converting
concretions of mind into banquets of light
causing the dark ones to flee from their domains of night.
The magical hammer of transformatory Might
comes pounding upon the skulls of the
feckless, perfidious, venal, evil ones,
who with much hubris and cupidity abound.
Cantankerous minds, reified stuff, ungainly emotional Watery fluff,
all forms of prideful huffs and puffs are crushed with glee.
All is dissolved into the shiny vibrant *manasic* sea.
Refined, Fiery, apodictic, apotropaic illuminations of Mind,
replace all that emotional gruff.
Utopia bound beneficence for all humankind,
technological amazement, artistic wizardry, occult advancement,
incessantly these workers for Love will
bring all you can ken one step higher.
In the fields of strife, in the fields of Life,
in the Mother's garden they toil with devic delight,
with devic sight, *devas* sublime

to transform woeful belittling ungainly habitats
of humanity into attire divine.

The fourth Ray.
The fourth Ray is the golden flux
generating the light of the transforming might.
It illumines the fate of mind-full canker,
equilibrating between the gruff and the spite,
the strife and bile of humankind
with exactitude
to produce harmonious radiant delight.
Mirror-like it reflects the glorious Shambhalic Sight
liberating woe-begotten attached mire
to an enlightened consciousness-space, the Void of ire.
In the luminosity that remains the all is viewed
for what it contains.
And this 'what' is not, no-being, no-thing,
nothing for the mind to be seen.
Empty, but all is there in Wisdom's Light.
The Naught can fill the Mind with what's mirrored
in the Clear Light that has overcome the night.

Adjunct:
Hallelujah! Come one, come all the hoary victors
of a myriad past fights.
Come now, come to the battle in Sight.
The Avatar! He comes. He comes to seal
the end of the seasons of rapacious blight.
The wolf in his lair will know no respite.
The shepherd and his flock walk o'er green pastures and rocks.
The sound of the flute cleaves the still air of Night.
The one Star so bright shines forth its Light.
The New Day has begun and the flock moves on.

Obviously, esoteric statements should not be analysed with commonplace discernment, the application of the seven keys must be utilised to glean various levels of interpretation. Cosmic implications as well as Hierarchical visioning may be discerned to invoke the intuition. Interpretation comes from above down and from within without, supplementing mindful reasoning. 'Cavernous spaces' for instance, refers to *chakras*, and the type of *chakra* involved is implied by the adjectives associated with the related phrase. All symbolism must also be interpreted in terms of the three times.

The major 'fight' associated with the dark brotherhood in this cycle is upon astral levels, for that field of glamour is the present power base for their form of activity. The murky darkness of the astral swamp must be converted, to become a clear transmitter of the intensified energy of light. The veil between the astral and dense physical space is to be appropriately rent during the new era, necessitating pouring in Shambhalic light to humanity and upon the physical plane. The power to do so constitutes the Hierarchical might, which necessitates the active cooperation of people of all races and creeds.

Humanity must be educated to recognise what evil actually is, and thereby overcome it. Hence all aspect of mind must necessarily play their rightful role in this Aryan epoch. Until the combined wisdom and the Light of Life that Hierarchy brings can be universally seen,[57] we live in the domain of the night. (For humanity is esoterically blind.) The epoch of the great awakening, the new Day, thus concerns opening of the (etheric or astral) Eyes of humanity, so that the minor *siddhis* can be developed. For such eventuation upon a wide scale the second Ray cycle must govern human civilisation. This is the major objective of Hierarchical activity at this time, and the above symbolism refers to the associated methodology utilised by the related Ashrams.

Bringing about the new Day necessitates the forthright activity of the above Rays, but specifically a second and first Ray combination serves to rightly awaken the *chakras* by defeating the darkened *prāṇas* of the emotional-mind. The third Ray sets the field whereby an adequate vibratory response can be met through appropriately timed activity, allowing heightened vivification via the awakening of Mind. The seventh Ray cyclically sets the stage for all such activity and empowers the warriors to conquer the darkness within the trammels of their forms.

57 Until people have developed the eyes *(chakras)* to see.

Hence it provides the magical effects of the accomplishment in the temples of Life. The fourth Ray mirrors all into the One and the One into the all.

An extract from Ephesians

A good description of the nature of the functioning of the united first and second Ray Ashrams comes from the astute mind of Paul (later to become the fifth Ray Chohan) and is found in *Ephesians 6:10-18*. This passage concerns the fight against 'rulers of the darkness of this world, against spiritual wickedness in high places'. The interpretation is detailed here to present a better comprehension as to the vast esotericism found in the New Testament.

This 'fight' takes place on many levels of perception and not just on the physical plane where there are many well understood arenas of battle, such as the corruption in society, organised crime, and the tyranny of corporate greed. There are a myriad less understood forms of evil, which are very dangerous to humanity because they are not generally conceptualised, thus out of mind, but which lurk in the fabric of people's psyche. We thus have the effects of sorcerers, black magicians, and the like, preying upon and feeding people's innate fears, phobias and dislikes, via mediumistic empathy to negative thought-forms and astral entities of a lower grade. This also involves the many disciples of such magicians that are incarnate, manifesting forms of egregious evil. They generally work (mainly through the world of finances) without knowledge of their past-life servitude to black rituals. Much happens on a mass scale, and many such incarnate innate black magicians hold positions of power in our societies, utilising vile methodology. They can easily succeed in their schemes because of the acquiescence of the selfish, self-centred mass of people and their blind gullibility. Chapter eight of my *revised* book, *The Revelation,* explains what 'evil, Satan, and the Devil' is and is not, and can be read here as a basis to further comprehension.

Ephesians 6:10-18 states:

> Finally, my brethren, be strong in the Lord, and in the power of his might.
>
> Put on the whole armour of God, that ye may be able to stand against the wiles of the devil.
>
> For we wrestle not against flesh and blood, but against

> principalities, against powers, against the rulers of the darkness of this world, against spiritual wickedness in high *places.*
>
> Wherefore take unto you the whole armour of God, that ye may be able to withstand in the evil day, and having done all, to stand.
>
> Stand therefore, having your loins girt about with truth, and having on the breastplate of righteousness;
>
> And your feet shod with the preparation of the gospel of peace;
>
> Above all, taking the shield of faith, wherewith ye shall be able to quench all the fiery darts of the wicked.
>
> And take the helmet of salvation, and the sword of the Spirit, which is the word of God.

'The whole armour of God' here refers to the sum of the work of the first, second, and seventh Ray Ashrams, then to the entire Hierarchy, which serves to protect humanity from the Evil.[58]

'Loins girt about with truth' refers to the function of the *1/6-2/6 Ashrams,* then the sixth Ray in general. The Solar Plexus and Sacral centres situated below the diaphragm ('the loins') are the natural repositories for the sixth Ray of Devotion or Idealism. As these centres control the distribution of sensual desire and emotions of all types, they are the sources of the distortions of truth, the production of fears, glamours and the psychic receptivity that bedazzles humanity. The function of these Ashrams is to project the truth at all cost, no matter what the ramifications of such actions would be upon people's desire bodies (producing emotional intensities) for humanity generally abides not in truth. One must note here the nature of the fanaticism and zealotry that clouds the vision and perceptions of truth in the world's religious devotees, the adherents to various philosophies and single issue agendas. They will generally fight to the death for the preservation of their dogmas. These, however, must be rectified in time.

The focus of activity for each Ashramic line of service is just as much based upon the inherent weakness that must be overcome or mastered by those of that Ray type as upon their accepted strengths. This is important to note, and the reader should endeavour to work out the corollaries of all Ray lines. In the sixth Ray line, for instance, the

---

58 See *John 8:43-5,* for a good description of the nature of this evil.

fanaticism, short sighted blindness, and militarism that these individuals often fall prey to is eventually converted into inclusive idealism, devotion to 'God', steadiness of perception, and a sympathetic identification with the points of views of others.[59]

'Breastplates of righteousness' refer to the functions of the *1/4-2/4 Ashrams,* and then the fourth Ray Ashrams in general. Breastplates cover the area of the chest and Heart (centre). This centre is the central of the seven *chakras*, just as these Ashrams are the central of the seven Ray lines. They embody the purifying *buddhic* energy (of the *śūnyatā-saṃsāra* nexus), reflecting the associated intensified energies to end the stranglehold of form (*saṃsāra*) in human consciousness.

Righteousness emanates from the Heart centre and is defined as actions characterised by justice or uprightness, that which is morally right and justifiable in accordance with (the good) Law. Righteousness works to counter all forms of wrongdoing that afflict human societies. It is the basic energy that must be utilised to rightly govern people, to produce harmony and good will in the midst of human strife. Righteousness is essentially the quality that best serves to pacify the world's aggressive forms of emotionality. It is an activity of the Heart into which pacified emotional energies must inevitably be absorbed. The function of these Ashrams are thus protective, shielding the good in human society from extraneous harm, from the wiles of what is evil and which would unduly stimulate people's propensity to act in irascible and aggressive ways.

The *'feet shod with the preparation of the gospel of peace'* refers to the function of the *1/7-2/7 Ashrams,* and then the seventh Ray Ashrams in general. The seventh Ray wields the greatest power on the dense physical plane, wherein the feet must tread and take the spiritual person over rough terrain and through much battlefield strife. The 'gospel of peace' concerns the teachings that will tend towards the elimination of all strife in the material domain. (It is certainly not the Gospel as preached by present day Christianity.) This concerns the work of the sum of all the Ashrams that focus their endeavour upon physical plane happenings, for as they project their qualities into the formed realms they educate humanity with the truth of what is. Seventh Ray methodology, however, governs general physical plane activity. Those of

---

59 See *Esoteric Psychology,* Volume II, by A. Bailey, 40-43, for a listing of these relationships.

this Ray are the builders of the foundation whereon the great Ashram of Hierarchy can externalise. The Temple of 'God',[60] wherein this gospel is empowered, can then rise. The gospel is literally the esoteric sciences that resounds its purpose from the highest domains.

Next we have the phrase the *'shield of faith, above all'*. This represents the function of the *2/1 Ashram,* and then of all the first and second Ray Ashrams. They primarily work to protect humanity and the struggling disciple from the 'fiery darts of the wicked', referring to the projected mental-emotions of evil-minded people, the vindictiveness, slander, hatred, lying propaganda and other utterings of ire utilised to attack others. We also have the psychic projections and emanations generated by the dark brotherhood. These Ashrams effectively work to counter all the activities of evil and its minions, for they bring the complementary energies and educational policies based upon the non-aberrant use of the Will, exuberant Love and unparalleled Wisdom.

This 2/1 Ashram knows the ways of the workings of the dark brotherhood best, having once been 'the stone which the builders rejected' *(Matt. 21:42-5),* as exemplified in Masonic tradition. In this connotation it refers to the upper echelons of a former dark hierarchy that had been converted to the ways of the white brotherhood. There is always a tendency to revert to their dark past. There are thus cycles of washing clean of such *karma*. Eventually this group is ensconced in the path of Love-Wisdom and work to protect others from making similar mistakes, of actions that would tend towards them becoming lords of evil. The pattern of actions sown in one life has karmic ramifications for many lives to follow. Some members of this Ashram are aware of the subtleties of such tendencies of all who come their way, others however often fall victim to the approaches of the dark, unconverted *saṃskāras* still lurking within. Thus the ancient dramas of conversion and reconversion unfold. Many convoluted karmic hands are played from life to life by these ancient wanderers towards the light of Life, because their feet straddle both camps, until eventually the left foot is withdrawn from the darkened forms of activity altogether.

The 2/1 Ashram thus embodies the sum of the future for the dark

60 'God' here referring to the Planetary Logos, thus the Gospel becomes the nature of the lore emanating from Shambhalic domains.

One and his entourage, whilst their dark brothers represent the past for those of this Ashram. Here the concept of the serpent biting its own tail, completing the cycle of time, can be considered; for all is a unity within the precincts of the all-seeing Eye. The serpent can be considered a thing of evil when it poisons, and an omen of wisdom when the poison is transmuted, and converted into ambrosia. It signifies the power of psychic energy working one way or the other within the system, however, as the tail is swallowed the entire cycle spirals upwards to unfold higher sublime cycles.

The task of the 2/1 Ray is to convert the dark brotherhood to the ways of light in a similar manner whereby they were earlier converted by the present members of Shambhala. The process takes many cycles, and sometimes aeons, to accomplish.

The white brotherhood methodology concerns rightly educating the dark ones and all who tend towards left hand practices. They work by means of the emanation of various Rays of light, accompanied by mantric power and by broadcasting the wisdom of Love. They protect all who fall under nefarious psychic influences, and those who are attacked by evil are wisely defended by the power of the Right, weapons of light, and the magnetic dynamism of the Love that sustains the duration of the fight. Thus the white brotherhood are healers par excellence, as sickness and disease is but the effect of dark *prāṇas* in the body. (The emanations from the dark brotherhood are moribund in their effect, antithetical to life.) There are many ways of expressing the radiatory light that heals the sick and comforts the meek.

'Meekness' is but the elementary quality to be developed that will eventually allow a beginner upon the Bodhisattva path to evolve into a dove of peace. To comfort someone esoterically implies a benediction or bestowment of the energies of Love, which conditions or sets the stage for the person to develop the qualities associated with the comforting process. It admits one into Hierarchy as a member of an Ashram. Here comfort is but the benediction of the Master, or one's guru.

'The helmet of salvation' refers to the *1/5-2/5 Ashrams,* and then the sum of the fifth Ray line. The helmet covers the head area wherein the mind (governed by the fifth Ray) is found. The quality to be evoked here relates to the thought-forms that are of an inspirational nature and

the formulation of the ideas that will be of great benefit to humanity. Ultimately such thoughts will lead to people's salvation, liberation from *saṃsāra*. Similarly, the *manasic* fabric via which mundane science is built comprehends the illusional nature of phenomena, as all ultimately is energy. Great ideas uplift human thinking, helping to transcend the bounds of empiricism and its concrete limitations. Indeed such ideas make the taking of Initiation possible, hence salvation. They lay the foundation for disciples to take group Initiation, because the widespread dissemination of truthful scholarly information, based upon meticulous research, is a way that science has rapidly progressed human thinking during the past four centuries. Ideas that break the bounds of the hitherto veiled and limited counter the agglomerations of thought, of mind-generated concretions emitted by the dark ones. These ones are driven to misinform, deceive and keep the masses ignorant as to the true nature of the real.

Little can be said about the 1/5 Ashram, as it is still embryonic. They will work to destroy all concretized, outmoded concepts that limit human thinking. Their Ashram will help to bring about the end of the era of the epoch of materialistically based thought through their use of sharp, analytical, piercing logic and transmogrifying energies.

The *'sword of spirit'* refers to the *1/2 Ashram* which governs the first Ray Ashrams in general (until their *maṇḍalas* have properly formed). They wield this sword to sever arenas of truth from untruth in the world stage. They fight for the Lord of Shambhala on the day of His wrath; to cleave asunder all the forces and entities that stand in the way of the army of this Lord, which prevent humanity from marching towards Light. They use this sword with might to produce major world changes in the formed realms,[61] and they generally assist all the endeavours of the 2/1 Ashram. The sword and the shield work together.

The *'word of God'* refers to the *1/3-2/3 Ashrams,* and the third Ray Ashrams in general. Here the images and ideas associated with the Hierarchical Plan and Shambhalic purpose are wisely expressed within *saṃsāra,* which will present to humanity a vision of what lies in their future if they act rightly. (As ordained by the Plan.) They speak the

---

61 Alexander the great, an incarnation of Morya, worked via this Ray potency.

Word that is the leitmotiv for each generation. This Word materialises as that type of organisational ability that instates the patterns of things new and beneficent for all.

The 1/3 Ashram will be the second last of the Ashrams to externalise, and when it does so then active intelligence will be utilised as a Power to produce necessary abstraction of thoughts in the realms of the mind. All forms of erroneous ideas and doctrines will be unable to stand in the pristine logic that will then be broadcast, thus terminating all material plane activity as we know it now. Their work will thus be fundamentally esoteric. The power of the domain of Mind will supersede that of mind, thus what is known as evil will cease to exist.

The members of all Ray Ashrams wield swords out of necessity when they find their placing in the army of the Lord, though those of the first Ray line (and their numerological kin) wield them most effectively. (The 2/1-1/2 Ashrams basically help to energise the substance of the swords utilised by all Bodhisattvas.) Roles are generally interchangeable between members of the various Ashrams that are numerically aligned. For example, the fifth points of the various Ashrams become open gates to each other, as they bear similar energies and qualities. There is, however, a difference in the degree or capacity to wield the related powers between those concerned. The emphasis lies in the attainment of different capabilities that each specialises in. Nothing is static and fixed.

The *1/1 Ashram* will be the last of all the Ashrams to form, and will appear during the seventh Root Race to spell the end of all that has come to be and which is known as *saṃsāra*.

The coming of the Avatar

The swords that are utilised are but versions of the one that Christ-Jesus said he would bring in *Matt. 10:34:*

> Think not that I am come to send peace on earth: I came not to send peace, but a sword.

The sword is a focussing tool for the energy of light, but symbolises the *suṣumṇā nāḍī,* veiled by the central spinal column. This *nāḍī* expresses the direct electrical energies from the Monadic aspect of the person,[62] as utilised by the will. The development of this will by humanity is the onus of human evolution in this coming new era, especially once the proper foundation of Love-Wisdom has been established. It consequently will be one of the major tasks assigned to Maitreya to convey to the world's disciples.

The *sword* is composed of the qualities of the various sub-Rays of the first Ray. It is the 'sharp sword' coming from the mouth of the *Avatar,* 'the King of Kings, and Lord of Lords', who comes forth on a white horse:

> And I saw heaven opened, and behold a white horse; and he that sat upon him *was* called Faithful and Truc, and in righteousness he doth judge and make war.
>
> His eyes *were* as a flame of fire, and on his head *were* many crowns; and he had a name written, that no man knew, but he himself.
>
> And he *was* clothed with a vesture dipped in blood: and His name is called The Word of God.
>
> And the armies *which were* in heaven followed him on white horses, clothed in fine linen, white and clean.
>
> And out of His mouth goeth a sharp sword, that with it he should smite the nations: and rule them with a rod of iron: and he treadeth the winepress of the fierceness of the wrath of Almighty God.[63]

Here the 'winepress' represents the nature of the intensity of the energies this Avatar bears. Literally the combined energies from the sixth and seventh cosmic astral sub-planes, which manifest on our Systemic planes in the form of red wine coloured energies, cosmic Blood. This Blood pours onto the astral and physical planes in the form of widespread compassionate Might (a seventh Ray effect). Such wrath thus represents the compassionate, transformative power of a first Ray Lord to effect profound changes in *saṃsāra* via the fiat of the amassed forces such a One wields.

---

62 An interpretation of the term 'Father' to which Jesus often prayed.

63 *Rev. 19:11-15.*

This Avatar will herald the epoch where the second and first Rays[64] must become the dominant factor in evolution. He is an emanation of the second Ray line, as is seen by the statement that he is the 'Word of God'. (The emanation of 'the Word' is the major second Ray characteristic.) This becomes the mantra, the battle cry that proceeds from this Avatar. It is his dominion. The fact that 'in righteousness he doth judge' informs us that he is also an emissary of the third Ray line, which governs the abstraction of the streams of *karma* in Systemic space. He thus judges the effect of the expression of the mind with respect to planetary Initiation. This concerns the process of transforming mind into the abstract Mind. All *karma* must be properly resolved if planetary enlightenment is to ensue. For this reason he judges the worthy supplicants to the process.

He also bears first Ray energies into manifestation (as all Avatars do), here coloured by the effects of the Shambhalic 'winepress' explained above. The first Ray expresses the power and purpose of Deity and is true, exact to the minutest detail, in the implementation of that purpose. What is known by human ken as personal will can be considered the lowest aberrant reflex of such combined energy.

Being *faithful* is a third Ray virtue, for one is faithful to something, such as to the emanation of the Word. In faith one manifests the activity of great service. In these three words (true, word, faithful) we have therefore the three major Rays implicated, where the word 'true' refers to that which deviates not from its target, a first Ray virtue.

The word *righteousness* is a fourth Ray quality as it reflects divinity into manifestation via appropriate action. The ability to 'judge and make war' is a fifth Ray quality. One utilises the discriminating, separative, dissecting mind to do so.[65] The actual fighting of the war ('the armies which were in heaven' following him[66]) is a sixth Ray characteristic, with its zealous idealism. Theirs is a crusade of the Right.

---

64 They reflect the energies of the sixth and seventh cosmic astral sub-planes into manifestation.

65 Judging 'in righteousness' is however a third Ray attribute, bringing the entire process of 'judging' into the domain of the *dharmakāya*, rather than upon the lower domains of mind.

66 Which is but another version of the armies of the King of Shambhala, as depicted in Buddhist legend regarding the period of the end of this epoch. This Avatar can therefore be considered as the King of Shambhala with his entourage descending into objective manifestation. Thus we have the process associated with the externalisation of the Hierarchy of Light.

Finally, the treading of *'the winepress'* is a seventh Ray function, which grounds (the concept of 'treading') the sum of the combined energies of Deity (the ambrosial wine, squeezed out through the 'press' of the liberation process) into active manifestation. This 'wine' therefore is the same liquor as the 'blood' contained in the skullcaps carried by the Wrathful Deities and drunk by accomplished *yogins* and *yoginīs*. The process of treading is a ritualistic activity that connotes the repetition of cycle after cycle of liberating activity. Wine is the ambrosial liquor that vitalises the successful candidates for Initiation after they have succumbed to the 'fierceness of the wrath of Almighty God'. This final statement connotes the reception of first Ray energies by those who are mastering this process. It is essentially the sixth sub-Ray of the first, viewed in terms of being an emanation of the second Ray. (The energy, for instance, directed by the Chohan Jesus.) It is difficult to express in empirical terms the nature of the force of liberation, which elsewhere is summarised in the term *bodhicitta*.

The energy source is the sixth cosmic astral sub-plane, the energy channelled by the 2/1-1/2 Ray line, and which empowers the principle of Love by Hierarchy. Via its second Ray flavour, we can also see that it is an aspect of the Purpose of the Sirian One, the great cosmic Lord of Love for all within our solar system. From this perspective it is the 'blood of God' shed for the salvation of the many. This esoteric fact is a major reason why Jesus was the bearer of the Christ principle who shed His Blood on the earth in an exoteric manner at the garden of Gethsemane and at his crucifixion. Esoterically, it concerned the infusion of the substance of this earth with the Blood of this cosmic Logos, thereby anchoring a version of the first Ray cycle via the second Ray. This occurrence was thus part of the next major step of the unfolding second Ray cycle, as the first and the second Rays act as a unity.

If we add to this 'winepress' the symbolic 'grapes' that were earlier explained as the ripened Souls of humanity with their various Ray combinations, then we see that the act of treading upon this *anima mundi* by the feet (the Avatar and his agents) of this cosmic Logos will project a vast pressure upon humanity. This will produce an accelerated evolutionary impetus, squeezing out thereby a large number of Bodhisattvas able to bear the import of this wine energy. (Another way of viewing the energy of *bodhicitta*.) The expression of great spiritual power and might will then find its application upon the dense physical via the astral plane, which will thereby be transformed into an energy vehicle rather than a place of residence of discarnate humans. The entire region below the diaphragm becomes controlled, and this indeed is the demonstration of power, both by the accomplished *yogin* and by humanity.

We will see, therefore, that eventually this will fulfil the prophecy in the Bible of the time when there shall be 'no more sea'.[67] The 'sea' here refers to the Watery substance of the astral plane, as well as later to the terrestrial waters when the earth passes into objectivity. The associated *saṃskāras* will be transmuted by means of the Bodhisattvic activity of humanity.

The entire planetary Hierarchy ('the armies which were in heaven') represents but one petal in the Heart centre of the Sirian Logos, for He has many such Sons existing within the awesome embrace of His compassionate Eye that purveys the far reaches of cosmos. That these armies *were* in heaven implies that the Hierarchy was in the process of externalisation into the material domains wherein humanity reside. To do so they must make war against the 'enemy' therein, the forces of darkness. To bring peace to the strife filled world they thereby descend from their zone of serenity.

If we think in terms of the externalising Hierarchy, then the Avatar can also be viewed to consist of a composite of the Chohans (*mahābodhisattvas*) that govern it, headed by One who can best wield the combination of the associated cosmic energies, and who has retained the *karma* to manifest upon the physical domain. This one is Christ III, (the new Mahāchohan), who we saw represents the activity aspect of the Christ's department through possessing an appropriate combination of Ray lines.

The great Ones at the forefront specifically focused upon this Herculean process are Morya, K.H., the new Mahāchohan in conjunction with Master ℛ, Serapis, Hilarion, Jesus and Padmasambhava (also a specialist in expressing this wine energy). The quote from *Rev. 19:11-15* therefore has an esoteric reference to their combined energies and purpose. The new Mahāchohan acts as a midwife to the great Mother's birthing pains for her soon to be newborn child (the new era civilisation) amongst human affairs. The 'Word of God' is an expressed part of the

---

67 *Rev. 21:1.*

meditation of the second Ray Chohan (K.H.), as the entire venture is governed by the great second Ray purpose. Love-Wisdom is the quality that humanity must now embody. It is fermenting within them like the action of yeast upon a sugary solution. In this task K.H. is assisted by his two great second Ray brothers (the blue Christ, and the European Chohan. K.H.) therefore functions as the energising point of this triad. The third Ray term *faithful* refers to the activity of the Mahāchohan, who must faithfully carry out the decisions of the Council of Bodhisattvas as he works to implement the plan within the formed realms. He represents the spearhead of the plans and activity of Hierarchy, thus in practice carries the purpose of the Avatar into active manifestation. The word *true* integrates the first Ray purpose of Morya, the silent toiler in the garden of Monadic Life, into a triune energy with that of his two great brothers.

Padmasambhava expresses the magical activity that integrates the entire *maṇḍala* of externalisation with the downward projection of the vitalising cosmic *prāṇas*. The treading of 'the winepress' of the Lord at the Hierarchical level is the process where all Ray lines are commingled before being projected into *saṃsāra*. His purpose specifically integrates with the activities of the new Mahāchohan, then with the sixth and seventh Ray purpose to project the sum of this Hierarchical power into the general embryo of the new world civilisation. This is a major part of his work. Thus he empowers the entire *maṇḍala* with the *prāṇa* that will strengthen the forms of activities to be carried out. This will manifest in the form of 'the fierceness of the wrath of Almighty God' if the major changes effecting the slovenly, desirous, separative, rapacious, and sometimes malicious, aggressive aspects of human minds are to be converted into the enlightened ways of the Hierarchy. All of this activity represents the 'stage of the forerunner' that will inevitably precipitate the appearance of the blue Christ, who is well explained in D.K.'s books.

Humanity stubbornly resists the necessary changes and forces threatening their self-righteous wilful ambitions, aggrandisement of material comforts, and emotional attachments to things desirous. The consequent *karma* is skilfully woven by the Lords of Life so that social, national, and international calamities, major wars, famines, diseases, and the like, cause them to reconsider the values of corporeal existence. This is part of the nature of 'the fierceness of the wrath' mentioned above. However, another interpretation of this phrase concerns the battle with the dark brotherhood who hold all of humanity in thrall. Fierce is the energy that must be evoked to properly subdue the emanations of evil projected by the Lords of materialistic might to prevent Hierarchical purpose from manifesting. It is an esoteric war that has run unabated for aeons.

That which is *true* needs no other modifications for existence, and projects Ideations from the Head centre (Shambhala) into the Avataric purpose. The *Word* is the active dissemination of what comes from the Throat infused with the Heart's Mind. (Literally the combined energies of K.H. and the new Mahāchohan.) It demonstrates the *true* expressed as *truth,* therefore the embodiment of the Thoughts of the construct of the *maṇḍala* of externalisation. Its embodiment is the expression of the blue Christ. The import of the word *faithful* is then expressed via the Avataric Ājña centre, for it is faithful to what it sees and registers, and this centre represents the way of projection of the *maṇḍala* into active manifestation. In this manner it presents the vision, delineates the structure upon which or via which the Word may act (to breathe Life into the sanctified space), and projects the lines of sight that emanate from the *true* into all needed directions of space and arenas of Logoic concern.

Righteousness then becomes the attribute demonstrated by the fourth Ray Chohan, Serapis, flavouring all major attributes of the Rays manifested by Hierarchy with the beautifying harmony that overcomes conflict. Serapis's fourth Ray energy facilitates the expression of the Hierarchical matrix into the complete scope of humanity's activities (who are also governed by this Ray). Humanity must evolve the right opinions and ideas, according to the dictates of the good law. They must become willing servants of this law, and thus be righteous. This necessitates the development of and receptivity to the energy of will along this fourth Ray line. Theirs is the middle kingdom, thus they tread the middle way to enlightenment.

The fifth and sixth Ray Chohans represent the qualities that are in the process of waning, therefore they govern the general conditions of the field of humanity that need to be transformed.[68]

Judgement requires the activity of the mind to discern the right from

---

68 Working with the new Mahāchohan and Serapis, Hilarion will however help awaken the higher sciences governed by the aesthetics of Mind. Together their Rays will manifest the 3-4-5 triangle of planetary Initiation.

the wrong, which is a function of the fifth Ray. Teaching humanity to do so is a primary attribute of the Chohan of this Ray. Their thinking capacity is waylaid by desire and the emotions, perverting any line of correct reasoning. Inevitably, all thoughts must manifest according to enlightenment's dictates. Hilarion works closely with the Lords of Love-Wisdom, for the fifth Ray is needed to weigh the growth of the Heart and its activity, to see the true motives behind the actions committed by any individual, group, or nation. The second Ray gives the overall perspective and vision, whilst the fifth Ray analyses and evaluates. Both must work rightly in combination in order to judge. The first Ray then metes out the necessary sentence or reward, the making of war if necessary.

The sixth Ray Chohan (Jesus/Milarepa) governs the field of battle of the 'armies which were in heaven', as such a field is determined by people's massed emotions and desires, the strength of their attachment to all of the allurements of *saṃsāra*. Their emanatory action is also effected by the intensity of sixth Ray energisation. The beneficent effects of the religions of the world are an example of the work done by this 'army', however, zealotry and martial activity also need countering.

Will is the power of the Eye and Hand of deity acting in unison, utilised to project and uphold the good law in the world of form by stern compassionate control, preventing it from becoming a wild, uncontrollable, destructive force. This Hand of activity wields many instruments, some of protection (as is the shield), insignias of office (such as the sceptre and orb of the ruler) and others of destruction, e.g., the sword. The sword, however, also becomes the two-edged sword of truth. Truth is always grounded in love. The Eye projects and directs divine energies, all the activities of the enlightened one.

The sword wielded to smite the dark forces channels the energies from the *dharmakāya*. It brings about the inner vision, cleaves the cup of the Soul, thus producing the attainment of *śūnyatā* (the fourth Initiation). The directive Will-to-overcome will also produce the *ālayavijñāna* enlightenment, so 'that the thoughts of many hearts may be revealed'.[69] The sword is an expression of the first Ray of Will or Power, therefore

---

69 *Luke 2:35,* and see also *Hebrews 4:12.* Note that the significance and symbolism of the use of the sword by means of the hands is also given on pages 577-578 of *A Treatise on White Magic* by Alice A. Bailey (Lucis Press, New York).

the first Ray Ashrams wield it best. Their combined energies can be said to constitute this sword. What flows through its blade, the substance of its actual strength, however, is the potency ('truth') of the second Ray. Its potency then reverberates throughout the remaining Ray Ashrams according to numerical affiliation.

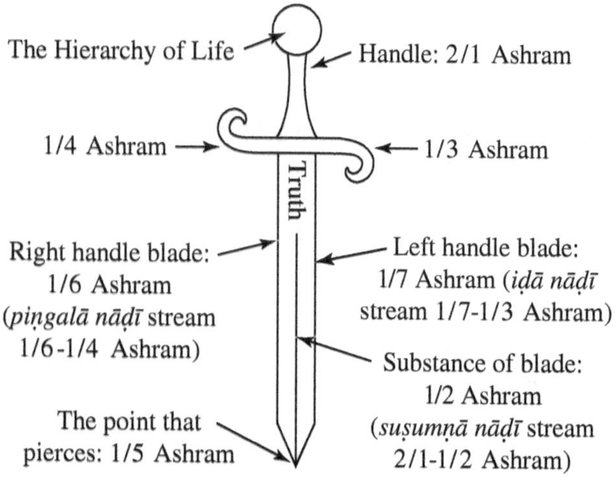

Figure 16. The two-edged sword of truth

From the perspective of the first Ray Ashrams being part of the general Ashram of the first Ray Chohan, the future Master of the 2/1 Ashram will become the second (Love-Wisdom point) therein, thus heads the teaching department of the first Ray dispensation. He will explicate the more esoteric aspects of the Wisdom Religion. Being the first or Will point, Morya vitalises all first Ray activities, dispensing the yoga of the Fire (Agni yoga). This yoga awakens the Fiery Will fused with all-encompassing Love and Wisdom that will be the mainstay of the new world religion. The first point of the 1/2 Ashram will then become the third or Activity point, the active hand of Power in the material domain. It can then be said that the first point in the 1/4 Ashram becomes the fourth point, the first point of the 1/7 Ashram becomes the fifth point, the first point in the 1/6 Ashram becomes the sixth point, and the first point in the 7/1 Ashram of ritualistic application into the Rays of Mind then manifests as the seventh point position. Because the positions within Ashrams are fluid and can be viewed from different angles, the above relationships can relate the sub-Ray quality to the present, and thus is valid. This view, however, is also somewhat erroneous, as all of these point positions are of uneven development, some being more potently applied than others, according to inherent spiritual age.

It is best to think in terms of the first Ray Ashrams manifesting as a unit, in terms of true spiritual age, as well as omitting Morya, because he overshadows them all. We then have the prospective Master of the 1/2 Ray as the first point. The second point being the second point of this Ashram, the third point being the first point of the 1/7 Ashram, the fourth point position as the first point of the 1/4 Ray, and the fifth point as the third point of the 1/2 Ray Ashram. This pentad of energies will focus the Shambhalic Will to help initiate the birth of the new era civilisation. These disciples have taken their third Initiation and some will take the fourth and higher Initiations within this present 100 year cycle. They can thus wield the power of this Sword, which will draw directly from the energy of *śūnyatā*.

It is obvious that the power of the first Ray must be steeped in Love, thus all first Ray Souls must come under the general auspices of the 2/1-1/2 Ashrams, for the qualities of compassion, wisdom and patience are what they need to develop most before their inherent will becomes dominant. In a similar fashion, Shambhalic power is generally necessarily absorbed and retransmitted by Hierarchy, the organ of Love in the body of Deity, before it can be safely utilised by the other kingdoms. The true nature of the first Ray power is not easily understood because this power deals primarily with the Life aspect, often producing widespread destructive effects that cause rapid changes in the course of civilisation, such as happened with the outpouring of the Mongol hordes of Ghengis Khan.[70] The nature of the mind is easily intensified, hardened by this Ray, making many first Ray types insensitive to other's pain and suffering, thus producing dark brotherhood attributes and adherents. On the other hand, it can easily transform the mind to produce the Initiation path. Indeed, undertaking the higher Initiations necessitates

70 He represented a rare direct incarnation of a member of Shambhala to bring about rapid planetary changes and the cleansing of massed *karma*.

developing first Ray attributes, because attachment to all aspects of *saṃsāra* must be severed to take them. Mind is the focal point of that transformative power, *Fohat* (the *prāṇa* flowing from cosmos) is its eventual application.

The first Ray line, including also the first Ray capabilities of the Masters of Wisdom and of the seventh Ray Ashrams, concerns the direct flow of this energy of spiritual Will into manifestation in such a way that the energies are sufficiently toned down for humanity. At this stage the world cannot stand the inherent power of the first Ray energies directly expressed by the Lords of Shambhala without them being too destructive. It is a difficult energy for personalities to wield without evil taking control. History has many examples of tyrants and ruthless potentates, kings, and governors in power over the masses who have misused their charter to rule, or who have used ruthless methods to put themselves in positions of power. It is said that 'power corrupts and absolute power corrupts absolutely'.

The field of politics is a hard, rocky, often murky road for anyone to travel via toward enlightenment, however, the potential to manifest great benefit for the masses of people governed by a wise executive or ruling body is obvious. Presently, a truly wise ruler in governance who courageously fights to oppose an entrenched, rapacious ruling oligarchy is very rare. The way democracy is expressed nowadays is guaranteed to act as a nest of power for the evil ones. It is certainly not the most advanced form of government possible. Rule by the truly wise and most compassionate in society as demonstrated by the Council of Hierarchy, must now be countenanced, as it is what will eventually come to manifest on a planetary scale once the Hierarchy has fully externalised. To bring about a wise planetary governance is the reason why the Ray of Power must increasingly come to the fore. Before it manifests, however, the planetary situation will go through a major paroxysm of fiery war, brought about in part through a projection of this energy directly to humanity without it being toned down. The worst of human *karma* surfaces like a putrescent boil to be lanced. Thus is revealed another form of activity for those wielding this Ray energy.

This Ray line is thus most difficult to wield with any finesse. The one who formerly was being trained as the eventual Master of the

1/2 Ashram, for instance, has fallen too many times into the dark brotherhood traps set for him and therefore has proved unable to wield this energy properly in a rulership capacity. Consequently, another member of that Ashram has had to be trained for that position (taking a couple of millennia to do so), whilst the former one has moved to another Ashram to help build a more stable basis in love and devotion, much needed by the first Ray stalwarts.

We see that a purpose for the flowering of the first Ray Ashrams is to produce beneficent and lasting world changes. At first we see militaristic activity, exaggerated monetary destabilisation of society, and other effects of the imposition of the direct and expressed Will of the planetary Logos for planetary karmic cleansing purposes. (What people call cataclysms and catastrophes, the effects of human *karma* working out on a grand scale, in conjunction with the overlay of cyclic evolutionary Law.) We will also see necessary rectifications in the course of civilisation that will properly lay the foundation of the second Ray epoch wherein a *new* United Nations, good and wise governance by Hierarchy, will come to be established upon the planet. Hierarchical externalisation will then finally be completed. Similar is the process to the battles with Māra and his hosts that Gautama had to subdue before gaining his enlightenment.

The New Jerusalem

To stand within the pentagram of the east
when order is restored
and the ritual of the Master is imposed.[1]

The added glory of
the three within the five,
the seven within the twelve,
and the One within and without
the ring of Fire.

Thus the Creative work
of the magician unfolds
as the City of God,
the New Jerusalem is built
and the Plan is served.

Where are you Oh Mighty One?
Where is your radiance?
Where are those with whom
you must serve?

The Rider on the White Horse
issues forth and conquers.
Come forth Oh Mighty One.
Destroy! So that the Builders may build
what the Planners have planned
and the Magician creates.

---

1 See Alice A. Bailey, *The Externalisation of the Hierarchy*, (Lucis Publishing, New York), 249.

5

Ashramic Interrelationships

The Second Ray Triad

The 2/1, 2/2 and 2/3 Ashrams work as a practical unity, where the 2/1 Ashram expresses the father energy and the 2/3 Ashram the dominant feminine counterpart, with the 2/2 Ashram being the symbolic son that colours the field of their expression. It is a 'youth' that helps clothe the work of the second Ray Chohan, hence the effect of this Ashram is diffused throughout the second Ray line. There is a strong esoteric relationship between the One who supervises the formation of the 2/1 Ashram and the Master of the 2/3 Ashram. In the past the two often played out integrated roles on the physical plane, for instance as Andrew and Peter in the Bible. Andrew, 'the first called',[1] was an incarnation of the new Mahāchohan, and Peter, 'the rock' or foundation of the Christ's Church,[2] was an incarnation of the 2/3 Master. The 2/3 energy (the active expression of Wisdom) is the foundation of the Church that is based on Love-Wisdom, the flowering of the second Ray dispensation. The work of the 2/3 Master as the embodiment of Wisdom in the form of the 'blue books' written via A.A. Bailey, is clearly the foundation for the new world religion. This will be evident if the time is taken to seriously study them.

1 See *John 1:37-43.*

2 *Matt. 16:18:* 'And I say also unto thee, That thou art Peter, and upon this rock I will build my church: and the gates of hell shall not prevail against it'.

John the Baptist, the fiery ascetic prophet who styled himself 'the voice of one crying in the wilderness',[3] was an incarnation of the first Ray Chohan. For this reason Andrew was one of his disciples at the river Jordan at the time of Jesus' Baptism. He then followed Christ-Jesus, the bearer of the second Ray dispensation,[4] thus exemplifying the then 2/1 Ray function of Andrew.[5]

The Baptism experience allowed the Lord of Love (the blue Christ) to overshadow Jesus via the first Ray conduit, wielded by the subjective sword of John. It built the *antaḥkaraṇa* that allowed the 'dove of peace' (the Christ principle, the unique energy of the united Hierarchy) to descend, 'And John bare record, saying I saw the Spirit descending from heaven like a dove, and it abode upon him'.[6]

As earlier stated, the 2/1 Ashram contains the converted dark brotherhood from former cycles, whilst those guiding it work to educate them to progress towards the path of Love-Wisdom. The first Ray energy converted the dark brotherhood with the energy of unassailable power, whereas the second Ray line appropriately educated them. The integration of these two Rays are found in the 2/1 and the 1/2 Ray. The 2/2 Ray surrounds the converted former dark ones with a shield of the strongest Love to help prevent the possibility of conversion back to the dark ways of their former activities, as unconverted *saṃskāras* still have a strong pull upon them. The 2/3 Ashram provides much wisdom to help overcome prideful *manasic* pronouncements, self-focussed intelligent will and philosophic quagmires from these former converts. The 2/2 Ray Ashram represents the substance of the throne upon which the second Ray Chohan sits. The second Ray Ashrams signify the lotus blossom supporting it. Their energies act to reject all dark *prāṇas* of those aspiring to enter Hierarchy's ranks.

The abovementioned Ashrams embody the dynamo for the Hierarchical Heart at the Ashramic level of expression. With the remaining second (and third) Ray Ashrams, they represent its central

3 *John 1:23.*

4 *John 1:35-43.*

5 This One has always played a dual role, with one foot in the second Ray camp and the other in the Mahāchohan's.

6 *John 1:32.*

administrative grouping. Embodying the keynote of Hierarchy's Love, this group causes the appearance of the various wisdom-religions. We also saw how the first and second Ray Ashrams function in relation to the dual Splenic centre of Hierarchy. This centre plays the role of storing vitality and protecting the body from general sickness through eliminating unwholesome *prāṇas*.

Cumulatively, the reject substance, and that yet to be converted upon the Initiation path, represents the *eighth sphere* for Hierarchy. It signifies a store of the type of *karma* that must be annulled before the pure light of Hierarchy can manifest. This *eighth sphere* attribute can also be associated in Hierarchy via the members that have not yet gained their perfection, hence are below the rank of a Master of Wisdom. This attribute represents baggage they must yet convert via incarnation as they work to serve humanity. Firstly there are the converted dark brotherhood. Next are various members of Hierarchy that earlier fell victim to the dark methodology of self-focussed abuse of spiritual power and positions of responsibility. Such disciples often have a seventh, sixth or first Ray background and generally manifested aberrant yogic, political, religious, or ritual magic prowess. They can be considered to have failed in past cycles, and who having seen the nature of their errors manifest service arenas whereby they can make amends. Care has to be exercised to help prevent them from following a regressive path that will quickly lead to becoming one of dark face. Sometimes they may also need to spend some lives in other Ashrams that help them to curtail the abuse of the will energy and to develop more love and wisdom. Finally, there are those aspirants seeking entry into Hierarchy's domains whose substance also needs proper processing and conversion through passing the testings for Initiation.

The 2/3 Ashram establishes the teaching dispensation for all, whilst the 2/2 Ashram forms the substance or fabric conditioning right thinking. The members of the 2/1-1/2 and general first Ray Ashrams become esoteric 'policemen' that help directly convert darkened ones through the power of Love and its potent forms of light. Such education constitutes the basis between the aeonic war between the Lords of dark face and the white Brotherhood. The yogic path of the transmutation of *saṃskāras* can then be applied not just by these Ashrams, but by all members of Hierarchy as they work to develop more of the Will and

Love-Wisdom that is esoterically the forte of this 2/1-1/2 Ray line. They represent the synthesis of the way of treading the path. The work concerns blocking the effects of and converting the aberrant *prāṇas* projected by the dark ones that wish to enslave the all. As the light annihilates the dark Rays, so it blasts the auras and minds of the promulgators of the evil. Their plans are thereby defeated and so they must prepare a new attack upon the planetary dispensation. The Rays of light striking such ones signify manifesting *karma* and they take some time to recuperate their energies and defences.

There is no such thing as death in reality, only conversion from one form to another. Hence the entire 'war' is that of conversion, where the white Hierarchy work to convert the dark forces to the path of love, and the dark ones similarly work to convert the white to dark. Inevitably the white will win because the power of light is far greater than that of darkness, and because it is planned so by the presiding Logos. In effect, this entire 'war' concerns the Logos converting the base *saṃskāras* of His/Her Body of manifestation (be that of a planetary or solar form). These *saṃskāras* are expressions of the emanations of the dark brotherhood and the normal course of the selfish, self-centred, avaricious, domineering, manipulative, aggressive, intolerant, etc., mental-emotions of humanity. They concern the great swirling mass of such energies to be converted to light via Love and Will. The effect is similar, though on a much vaster scale, of the work done by a *yogin* to convert unwanted negative *saṃskāras* via meditation. All is ordained as part of the evolutionary process when viewed upon a vast scale and great spiritual heights. The white Brotherhood are the agents of conversion of *saṃskāras*, hence manifest in the form of wrathful deities for those of the dark. Hence the white Brotherhood represent the cleansed, rectified *prāṇas* in the Body of the Logos.

The substance of Love also forms the basis of a jail for members of the dark brotherhood who have transgressed the Law to the extent that they can no longer find a home in *saṃsāra* for a particular cycle. They are imprisoned in a sphere of intensified Love through which they cannot pass, as evil has no power here. This zone represents the *eighth sphere* proper. They must wait for the karmic door to open. Being surrounded by the purest Love, which they cannot manipulate whatsoever, it effectively constitutes a hell-state for them. They are left with their own diabolical lust for power and no means to express it, except amongst themselves. The appropriate cycle for their release may be many millennia, or even aeons, in the future when again they will find karmic opportunity to make amends.

The Perseus myth

Though normally only seven major *chakras* are counted, the Splenic centre should be added, making it the eighth centre, for its power and influence is that of a major *chakra*. In Greek mythology this centre is symbolised by the functions of the three Gorgons, with the Gorgon Medusa's head taking the attributes of the eighth sphere.

Graves states:

> The Gorgons were named Stheino, Euryale, and Medusa, all once beautiful. But one night Medusa lay with Poseidon, and Athene, enraged that they had bedded in one of her own temples, changed her into a winged monster with glaring eyes, huge teeth, protruding tongue, brazen claws and serpent locks, whose gaze turned men to stone.[7]

It appears that all three sisters were similarly converted by Athene for their sister's deed because Athene led Perseus to 'the city of Deicterion in Samos, where images of all three Gorgons are displayed, thus enabling him to distinguish Medusa from her immortal sisters'.[8] Athene represented the development of the forces of the mind in humanity (having been born from the head of Zeus), thus transformed the Gorgons (who were daughters of the sea, whilst Medusa bedded Poseidon, the god of the Waters) after these emotional energies had begun to be influenced by the attributes of mind. In the early Atlantean times, the Greek golden age (followed by the silver, then bronze and finally the iron, materialistic age we are now in), much of the selfishness, spite, separateness, and all attributes associated with the development of the mind, did not exist. People were clairvoyantly endowed, child-like, and existed in a garden of Eden-like existence. They were closely attuned to Nature, where they saw the *devas* and worked with them. Pure emotional thoughts, feelings, idealism and desires worked through

---

7 Robert Graves, *The Greek Myths, Complete Edition* (Penguin Books, London, 1992), 127. See the text, 237-245 for the complete story.

8 Ibid., 239.

them. Hardly any negative *saṃskāras* were developed for the Splenic centres to process, hence the sisters were 'beautiful'. Once the planetary Logos released the energies of mind (the fifth Ray) into the planet as part of the evolutionary plan, then arose negative, selfish, separative, critical thoughts, possessive jealousy, and wilful desires to amass what is pleasurable for the individual. Aggressive psychic and physical wars became the norm. Consequently, the Gorgons became ugly and deformed by means of the energies pouring through them, which now needed processing.

The entire history of the development of the *saṃskāras* of the desire-mind by humanity then followed, which are collectively symbolised by the features of the Gorgon, Medusa. The Splenic centres then conveyed these *prāṇas* throughout the planetary body via the Inner Round circulation, as organised by the Solar Plexus centre. (An important part of this circulation was explained in detail in the earlier volumes of this treatise.) The differences between the Gorgons were symbolised by their names, and the fact that only Medusa was mortal. This is because the *eighth sphere* which she embodies is a construct composed of human *saṃskāras* needing purifying. The other two Gorgons are permanent *chakras,* hence, 'immortal'. These names are given as: 'Stheino ("strong"), Euryale ("wide roaming"), and Medusa ("cunning one") – and are titles of the Moon-goddess; the Orphics called the moon's face 'the Gorgon's head''.[9]

The concept of 'strong' refers to the potency of the qualities of the twelve petalled Splenic centre I, which receives the transformative *prāṇas* from the Heart centre, allowing the conversion of base *saṃskāras*. The expression of 'wide roaming' refers to the functioning of Splenic centre II, which integrates and redirects all of the *prāṇas* of the minor centres associated with the Inner Round - either towards Splenic centre I, the Solar Plexus centre, the Sacral centre, or to be eliminated via the *eighth sphere*. Hence the roaming nature of the reach of this *chakra*. The phrase 'cunning one' refers to the cunning, deceitful qualities of the darkened *prāṇas* developed by the forces of evil, plus the reject *prāṇas* of the system, which are stored in the *eighth sphere* ('purse') prior to being appropriately dealt with. Their link to

9 Ibid., 129.

the moon is that the moon represents the *eighth sphere* for our earth, and is hinted at occultly as 'The Mystery of the Moon' in Blavatsky's *The Secret Doctrine* and Bailey's *A Treatise on Cosmic Fire*.[10]

Below is a list of the qualities attributed to the Gorgon Medusa in Ray order:

1. Glaring eyes–refers to the general description of the circular nature of the *chakras*. Here the Fiery Element is implicated - the main energy, when united with the desire principle, that deformed the once beautiful women (the *chakras* in their pristine condition). The eyes are used to direct the power (the first Ray quality) of the Gorgon.
2. Golden wings[11]–refers to the clean *prāṇas* circulated by the Splenic centres. The wings represent the petals of the *chakras* and assist the movement of *prāṇas* through the Air, the generalised Element conveying the *prāṇic* forces. The second Ray quality of the awakening consciousness of humanity is implicated.
3. Huge teeth (of a boar)[12]–refer to the Earthy focus of the developing mental *saṃskāras*. The boar uses the teeth to dig for roots and tubers. This implicates the materialistic aspect of the third Ray of Mathematically Exact Activity manifesting upon the Earthy sphere.
4. Protruding tongue–the quality of taste, a fourth Ray function of discerning nourishing and tasteful food amongst the possible dangerous types. (An attribute of producing harmony in the midst of strife.) The large tongue, however, represents the aberrant exaggerated focus upon the use of the mouth in such things as lying, slander, deceit and malicious gossip.
5. Claws of bronze–the forging of the composite metal that is signified by bronze represents the attributes of the mind that were developed,

---

10 This relates to the *karma* of the failure of the moon, whose humanity was overcome by the dark brotherhood, principally via sex magical practices. They never evolved past a Lemurian form of the Aryan epoch, and at its corresponding fifth Aryan cycle a major catastrophe destroyed the moon's biosphere, and all life was transferred to the earth. The moon presently represents the skeletal remains of what once was.

11 See Felix Guirand (Ed.), *The New Larousse Encyclopedia of Mythology*, (Hamlyn, London, 1983), 183.

12 Ibid.

but made very critical, sharp, hardened with materialistic ideas and possessing the ability to attack others. The fifth Ray attribute of separative activity, sharp discernment and criticism is implicated.

6. Serpent locks—the complete panoply of all the aspects of desire, greed and sensual focus to produce the vituperating, poisonous, hissing halo of animosity that people generate. This implicates a lower expression of the sixth Ray of Devotion.
7. To turn to stone—To cause having to perpetually incarnate into the formed realms to cleanse *karma.* The deathly, cyclic, repetitious activities of the most concreted thoughts. The seventh Ray of Cyclic Activity is thereby implied.

Perseus (embodying the office of the Christ at that time) cut this head off and put it in 'a wallet' (representing the *eighth sphere* zone) that was contained by means of the first and second Ray energies then available, but here the first Ray manifests via the seventh, which had the power to 'turn to stone'. This phrase refers to the loss of psychic perception by those thus acted upon by the face of the Medusa. They could then only view things empirically, materialistically, hence the loss of their psychic ability to practice magic. This was the harbinger of the present materialistic epoch and signified the transition from the Atlantean era proper to the then oncoming Aryan epoch. The process of desensitisation to the subjective astral energies by an increasing number of human groups was one method that the then Hierarchy dealt with the predatory effects of the dark brotherhood.

The loss of psychic abilities represented an evolutionary progression, and was a consequence of the developing epoch of mind. Evolution became more focussed upon the material domain and its mastery, thereby mitigating some of the worst effects of black magic, which is the natural product of mind infused with the psychicism associated with the astral plane. The concept of 'men turned into stone statues' hence is a mythicised reification of this basic idea. Perseus thus utilised this method to defeat his enemies, as it symbolically turned to stone all who gazed upon it. They became more focussed physically rather than psychically. They gazed upon the extent that the concretising attributes of the Hydra were developing within their minds, and which Perseus revealed to them as their psychic perceptions were being annulled. Such was the directed effect of their manifesting *karma*, which is the ultimate educator.

Being the active Christ of that time Perseus was the bearer of the energy from the *Spirit of Peace*. From this perspective Sanat Kumāra takes the symbolism of Zeus, the king of the Gods, of whom Perseus was one of his many sons. The reference, therefore, is to the later Atlantean period at a time when the major members of the Kingdom of Shambhala were undergoing tests for Initiation in an externalised form, similar to our Hierarchy now. The present activity precedes the birthing of the sixth Root Race, whereas that earlier endeavour helped lay the foundations for the birth of the Aryan fifth Root Race.

Perseus thus incarnated to undergo the necessary testings within the Watery Atlantean epoch (governed by Poseidon).[13] The two gods that helped him in his task were Athene and Hermes. As Athene was given the appellation 'the huntress' (a function of the mind seeking out ideas and images) and born from Zeus's head,[14] she represented the fifth Ray qualities of the mind that had to be developed by humanity. Hermes was the messenger of the gods, possessing the Caduceus staff (symbolising the triune central *nāḍīs*) and wings on his feet and helmet. These qualities exemplified his function as the ruler of the fourth Ray, which governs humanity as a whole. Their main adversity was Poseidon, the god of the Waters, ruling the astral plane upon which human consciousness was then focused. Hermes symbolises the wisdom that had to be developed at that time.

Human perception was different in those days, as most of humanity were astrally polarised with natural clairvoyance. They resided within

---

13 The Atlantean Hierarchy were generally incarnate during that time, contrary to the present era, where the Hierarchy is in the process of externalising.

14 At one stage Zeus possessed a massive headache and 'To cure him Hephaestus – some said Prometheus – split open his skull with a bronze axe and from the gaping wound, and shouting a triumphant cry of victory, sprang Athene – "fully armed and brandishing a sharp javelin". At the sign all the immortals were struck with astonishment and filled with awe. "Great Olympus was profoundly shaken by the dash and impetuosity of the bright-eyed goddess."' Ibid., 108. This is also a way of describing the awakening of the planetary Throat centre.

the domain of the minor *chakras* associated with the Inner Round. The objective then was to properly awaken the properties of the Heart centre, thus to transfer *prāṇas* from below the diaphragm to that above it, and also to begin to use the Throat centre as an organ of power. To do this the Splenic centre's activities had to be mastered, brought directly under the rule of the Christ's department. Hence, Perseus's quest to obtain the head of the gorgon Medusa. This also necessitated fighting off and defeating the awesome power of the dark brotherhood of that time, who controlled the image-making tendencies of humanity, in whom the mind was being awakened. This development opened the gates to a flood of evil entities from cosmic shores, which necessitated much stealth, e.g., a helmet of invisibility.[15]

Athene gave him a highly polished shield and advice to never look directly at the Medusa or he would be petrified. (Meaning that Perseus would lose his *siddhis* if he identified with the attributes of this Gorgon.) The shield represented a properly prepared Solar Plexus centre, to which the luminous energies from the Heart centre were directed. This allowed him to view the image from a higher perspective than normal, which safeguarded him from danger. The energies manifested via the Diaphragm centre - the principle dividing the upper torso, the realm of the higher powers, from the lower psyche where resides all of the forces of the Gorgon. A more important interpretation is that it was the then Hierarchical Shield into which he must look if the powers needed to defeat the dark brotherhood (such as the mass of wriggling venomous serpents that formed the hair of the Gorgon) could be utilised. By seeing the reflected image he could avoid the fearsome gaze. Esoterically, Perseus would then not be tempted by the lures of the material domain, and with his mind rightly focussed the Gorgon's head could be severed from its body.

He therefore did not mentally engage in the dark brotherhood's deadly attributes, but rather took the implements and psychic powers provided him by the 'gods' in Mount Olympus (Shambhala), such as a sickle-like sword of wisdom in the form of the karmic reaper that could cut off its head. Once the head of the dark brotherhood entourage was

15 This simply means functioning upon a dimension of perception above or beyond that which was perceptible to the dark forces, which is the onus of the white brotherhood. They always manifest from the realms of abstraction compared to those of concretion that limit the dark brotherhood's *modus operandi*.

placed in the 'wallet' of white brotherhood conversion and education, it could be used to defeat all of Perseus's enemies in the material world, and rescue his mother (Danaë) from an unwelcome marriage. This 'wallet', was a *chakra*, being the combined Splenic centre controlled by the auric structure of the then Hierarchy.

Like all women, Danaë can symbolically represent Nature's kingdoms in general. The name Danaë means 'she who judges'[16] and is associated with the moon Goddess. This, coupled with her father's brother (Proteus), who seduced her (being an important part of a chain of events that brought them to this island) and who retained 'Seven gigantic Cyclopes',[17] links her to the Lemurian cycle. The Cyclopes that made 'massive walls, using blocks of stones so large that a mule team could not have stirred the least of them',[18] are Lemurian Initiates that had developed the single Eye. These giants are the giant third Root Race precursors[19] of the Atlanteans (the fourth Root Race).

Our vision therefore reverts to the aetiology of the present Hierarchy. That the infant Perseus and his mother were locked in a wooden arc and thrown into the sea refers to the transition between the Lemurian epoch and the Atlantean. The passage of this vessel upon the sea implies the passing of a significant time period, of cycles of activity, that eventually brought Perseus and his mother to that island. Logically, therefore, we can deduce that Danaë represents the mother of the Atlantean Hierarchy (which Perseus was bound to defend with all of his heart) that gave birth to the Aryan one, assisted by the efforts of Perseus during this Atlantean epoch. However, he fell for the ruse of Polydectes, the ruler of the small island they alighted upon, who wished to marry Danaë against Perseus's

---

16 Graves, 738.

17 Ibid., 238.

18 Ibid.

19 See *Genesis 6:4*. 'And there were giants in the earth in those days; and also after that, when the sons of God came in unto the daughters of men, and they bare *children* to them, the same *became* mighty men which *were* of old, men of renown'. This particular race Individualised from out of the animal kingdom, and their focus concerned gaining mastery of their dense physical vehicles (the Earth Element) and its etheric substratum. Inevitably, this allowed them to control the etheric energies governing physical phenomena, hence the ability to levitate huge objects, necessitating also the right use of mantra.

wishes. (We are, however, not told exactly why Perseus was at odds with such a marriage. One can speculate that Polydectes represents a past cycle that was not conducive to the future that Perseus's actions would produce.) 'Polydectes then assembled his friends and, pretending that he was about to sue for the hand of Hippodameia, daughter of Pelops, asked them to contribute one horse apiece as his love-gift. "Seriphos is only a small island" he said'. When Perseus was asked he said that alas he had no horses or gold, but if Polydectes was not interested in marrying his mother "'I will contrive to win any gift you name." He added rashly: "Even the Gorgon Medusa's head if need be"'.[20] His offer was then accepted.

The island upon which Perseus grew into manhood thus refers to a minor *chakra* governing the Atlantean dispensation during its earlier period. The attributes of this *chakra* were inadequate for the development of the future Atlantean Hierarchy. The *chakra* that had to be awakened fully was the Solar Plexus centre, which was to dominate the Atlantean civilisation, where the horses symbolise the main animal-like, emotional energies governing that civilisation. For the Hierarchical attributes to progress, the *prāṇas* of the Splenic centre had to be mastered. Hence, inadvertently, Perseus had promised to obtain Medusa's head, and thus, honour bound, the quest begins.

Hermes (symbolising the intuition) gave him a sickle needed to cut off the head. This weapon, in the form of a crescent moon (and also the glyph for the sign Saturn, Lord of *karma),* allowed reaping the harvest of transforming *saṃskāras* and *karma.* The cycle had arrived when the *karma* could be cleansed, which is what actually effected the cutting off of the Medusa's head. He was then directed to the Stygian Nymphs from whom he could obtain a pair of winged sandals, which allowed him to fly in the air, a magic wallet to safely contain the head, and a dark helmet of invisibility that allowed him to safely approach the Medusa. These qualities are *siddhis* associated with the mastery of the laws governing the astral plane whereon his adversary was to be found. To obtain information as to the whereabouts of the Gorgons,[21] he approached their sisters, the swan-like Graeae, who shared a single eye

---

20 Graves, 238.

21 Westwards (to 'the land of Hyperboreans'), the direction we know to refer to the field of outwards service work to humanity. See Graves, 239.

and a tooth of prophecy.[22] He obtained their eye and tooth as they were passing it from one to the other and refused to hand it back unless he got the required information. These three sisters refer to the three-fold structure of the third Eye,[23] which the Christ principle had to develop to discover the nature of the externalised, embodied *nāḍī* system, thus where this *chakra* was located, and of its qualities. Appropriately armed, he could proceed to battle this most dangerous foe.

The 'tooth of prophecy' represents the particular petal of that Eye whereby the future unfoldment of the progressing *saṃskāras* and hence *karma* could be assessed. The detailed relationship between this Eye and the Head lotus was given in Volume 5A, wherein the methodology of obtaining such ability to prophecy can be gleaned.

It should be understood that Shambhala was then approximately as developed as Hierarchy presently is. Senior members of Shambhala had to undergo similar tests then as the Hierarchy must now with respect to bringing into manifestation the new era. The attributes of mind within humanity were only at their inception stages near the ending of the Atlantean epoch, where only Initiates had fully developed minds. Hence the major forces involved were feminine. Nowadays the mind is very developed in our civilisation, (the major focus being masculine attributes), with those upon the Initiation path awakening Love-Wisdom and the Will.

When the Medusa's head was cut off, the winged horse Pegasus flew out. Pegasus embodies the forces of the Diaphragm centre and represents the connection of the Heart centre to the Solar Plexus centre. A warrior also sprang out clutching a sword, signifying the personal will of the Solar Plexus centre, whose esoteric purpose was obviously to fight off unruly *prāṇic* forces.

The entire story concerning Perseus (meaning 'destroyer') and the Medusa is thus an allegory relating to the Christ principle (the Heart centre or the Hierarchy of the Atlantean dispensation) conquering the earth's *nāḍī* system. Being the head of the Hierarchy in the Atlantean epoch, Perseus also seeded the Christ principle for this present epoch.

---

22 Ibid., 245.

23 They were thus to be found on thrones at the foot of Mount Olympus, the home of the Gods (the planetary Head centre). Graves, 239. The eye and tooth they passed from one to the other refers to the cyclic passing of *prāṇas* to either lobe of the Ājñā centre when needed.

Like many ancient myths, the symbolism also has cosmological implications (such as indicating the esoteric relation of the constellations Cepheus and Cassiopeia[24] to Andromeda) and can be related to the formation of a solar system or earth sphere. Here, however, the reference is specifically to the ancient Initiation testings provided to the progenitor of the Hierarchy that developed during Atlantean times under the auspices of its Christ (Perseus). Andromeda, for instance, who was naked and chained to a rock, waiting to be devoured by a 'female sea-monster',[25] represented the Solar Plexus centre. Perseus instantly falls in love with her and wanting marriage defeats the monster by showing it the Gorgon's head from out of the sack. The desire for marriage, which was achieved in the myth, refers to the Heart centre's natural affinity to the Solar Plexus centre. They must marry, if the Heart is to rule the unruly forces below the diaphragm (symbolised by the 'sea monster'). This is not accomplished without many fierce battles, as happened, for instance, when Agenor, at the head of a band of warriors, claimed Andromeda for himself.

Upon returning, Perseus also turned a hostile Polydectes and his party to stone. Then sailed to the mainland (Argos) with his newfound wife, his mother and 'a party of Cyclopes'.[26] There, fulfilling prophecy, he accidently killed his grandfather via a misplaced discus (thought-form) throw. That the Cyclopes (Lemurian Initiates) were part of Perseus's party indicated that the then Hierarchy incorporated both groups of Initiates, Lemurian and Atlantean. They were masters of different *siddhis*, the Lemurian the Earthy, and the Atlantean the Watery. The influence of the Lemurian Initiates passed through to the Aryan epoch to the builders of the megalithic stone structures. Their handicraft is specifically seen in the ancient stone structures using huge blocks carefully crafted and fitted together that still survive, and

24 They also symbolise two minor *chakras* in the body associated with the Solar Plexus centre.

25 Graves, 240. The monster was sent by Poseidon, God of the Waters, because of an insult Andromeda made to the Nereids, who symbolised the feminine Watery forces. Andromeda claimed to be more beautiful than them, hence the monster was sent to ravage her father's kingdom, and she needed to be chained to the rock to appease it. The rock here symbolising the material domain.

26 Ibid., 241.

which are falsely dated by modern archaeologists to a far more recent period than they were actually erected.

Now, reverting to what was earlier said regarding the three Christs, we can see that the true first Christ, in terms of the sum of our planetary evolution, relates to the symbolism of Perseus. Logically, this event would have happened by about the time the sun moved into Leo (approximately 12,500 B.C.), which is ruled by the sun (the energy qualifying the Hierarchy) exoterically, esoterically, and Hierarchically. There is, however, an overlay with a much earlier time (or cycles of events) when the Cyclopes and the Atlantean Hierarchy cooperated to build a new social structure. This cooperation is also symbolised in the mystery of the sphinx, where the Virgoan woman's head symbolises the characteristics developed by the Atlanteans as they evolved to become the high feminine Initiates ruling the then Shambhala. The Lion's supporting body symbolised the qualities of the Cyclopes, who developed the will to overcome the attributes of their animal forms by aspiring upwards to their solar forms, the Sambhogakāya Flowers.[27] One would expect the sphinx guarding the pyramids at Giza, whose head was re-carved much later with a Pharaoh's head, to have been originally built during this cusp period between Virgo and Leo, effectively also symbolising Perseus's victory.

Due to the less advanced level of consciousness of humanity in those times, the events to produce the transition of astralism to the development of mind in humanity was slow. Gaining the second Initiation was then the objective, signifying mastery of the Watery Element. We can therefore deduce that the symbolism of cutting off the Medusa's head signified the method of taking this Initiation. There is, however, an overlay of two Initiations in the Perseus myth. The symbolism of cutting off the

---

27 This is one level of the meaning of the symbolism. Another being that the feminine head represents the *deva* Hierarchy and the lion's body the human. Still another relates to the advent of the fifth Root Race that will develop the ability to completely use their minds to master *saṃsāra* (the lion being its lord). The lion here being a solar symbol (ruled by the sun) governs the Aryan epoch, whereas the Atlanteans were orientated towards the moon. In this case the symbolism of the gaze of the sphinx towards the constellation Leo as it rose in the night sky is important. The woman's head then symbolises the development of the empirical mind. From the above perspective, however, the statue at Giza simply may have originally had a lionesses or lion's body and head.

Medusa's head and defeating the water monster, etc., related to attaining the second Initiation, yet the ability of the Medusa's head to turn people into stone when gazed upon signifies the attainment of the first Initiation in the process of descent. Cleansing the Splenic centre of its impediments properly begins at this Initiation, but the main transformative battles are accomplished at the second Initiation.

Perseus symbolises the attainment of the Atlantean Hierarchy as a unit. All of the Christs embody the symbolism of undertaking Initiations for the world disciple at a level or two below what they individually take. Perseus would also have taken the fourth, to demonstrate the quality of being Christ then. This Initiation would allow the impress of the cosmic energy of Love to affect the planet via the then manifesting Hierarchy. The mystical, *piṇgalā* line of development, was exemplified.

Similarly, Hercules symbolises the attainment of the Aryan Hierarchy during its formative period. The twelve labours of Hercules signifies twelve stages, incarnations, of the infant Aryan Hierarchy preceding taking their group third Initiation. Each labour signified a particular quality, group *saṃskāras,* that had to be mastered before that Initiation could be undertaken. Most of his feats, such as the defeat of the nine-headed Hydra, however, related to mastery of the psychic forces associated with the second Initiation for the world disciple. Continuing along this vein the appearance of Krishna and the battle of Kurukshetra in the Bhagavad Gītā symbolises the actual battle with psychic forces needed to take the second Initiation. The story of Krishna relates to the time when Hierarchy actually took their group second Initiation.

The second planetary Christ (Hercules[28]) was an embodiment of the Spirit of Peace, thus he was another son of Zeus. His purpose was to develop the *iḍā* function of mental development in the young Hierarchy in the early Aryan epoch. (A period when humanity was still transiting from the Atlantean astralism.) His time of incarnation could be thought to be when the sun first entered the sign Taurus the bull, about 5,000 B.C. However, a sequence of incarnations of the infant Hierarchy is

28 His relation to Perseus is hid in myth by the statement found in Larousse, 186: 'Perseus did not want to succeed to his grandfather's throne and instead reigned over Tiryns and Mycenae. He founded the family of the Perseids of which one day Hercules was to be such a glorious representative'.

implied via his exploits from the fall of Atlantis in the cusp between Leo and Cancer. He was a sun Initiate, hence his first exploit was the slaying of a lion, the skin of which he consequently wore.[29] The sun in Leo, signifying the qualities of the world Soul upon the higher mental plane, symbolises the major characteristics of the Hierarchy with respect to their action upon humanity.

The main feature of Hercules' life concerned undertaking the twelve labours associated with the tests one needs to undergo to take the third Initiation. They are governed by the qualities of the sign Scorpio the scorpion (the sign of testings), which is the polar opposite of Taurus. The focus of the tests in Scorpio is slaying the nine-headed Lernaean Hydra, which signifies the sum of one's mental-emotional foibles that must be mastered before the third Initiation is possible. The twelve labours then relate to the growth of the evolution of Hierarchy through stages relating to the awakening of the twelve petals of the Hierarchical Heart centre.[30] After he had undertaken these labours he was admitted as a god upon mount Olympus.

There is an obvious progression in degree of Initiation of all concerned as we move closer to the present era. This is necessary because of the advancing spiritual age of humanity. Also, all advance together, therefore the status quo between the earlier Christs and the present members of Hierarchy remain the same. Perseus was concerned with the cleansing of the *prāṇas* of the infant Hierarchy, symbolised by the severing of the head of the Medusa. Being able to master the Medusa's head, which turned people into stone when gazed upon, signifies the attainments of the first Initiation. Hercules was concerned with Hierarchy passing the testings of the twelve labours so that the planetary Heart centre could be awakened. His feats, such as defeating the nine-headed Hydra, effectively demonstrated the symbolism of taking the second Initiation. The Buddha subsequently signified the development of great wisdom by the Hierarchy by outwardly attaining the third Initiation. Christ-Jesus then embodied its central doctrine of sacrificial Love,

---

29 The lion symbolising the prowess of the young adolescent Hierarchy at the time when Leo was the ascendant.

30 See the translation of the myth by D.K. concerning these labours in A.A. Bailey, *The Labours of Hercules,* Lucis Press.

where the great sacrifice upon the cross symbolises the attainment of the fourth Initiation. Capitalising on all the above, the fifth Christ will produce the revelation of the true nature of the *dharmakāya* for humanity.

Even seemingly trivial information, such as the concluding statement to the Perseus myth, are significant and should be properly analysed by those wishing to comprehend the myth in its entirety. An example is the story of the mushroom that sprang up when Perseus was thirsty and 'provided him with a stream of water'[31] at Mycenae, which he founded. This relates to the much later Aryan epoch when people generally had lost their natural clairvoyance. The psychic energy of the Atlanteans precipitated into the vegetable kingdom and fungi, producing their hallucinogenic effects. Thus they were often used to awaken such perception in the Mystery schools, such as Eleusis, when humanity were developing the empirical rational mindset that eventually led people away from being able to directly converse with the 'gods'. The stream that flowed from the mushrooms therefore refers to the new mystery schools and philosophic output of the later Greeks, that effectively was a continuation of the Atlantean dispensation. The river symbolises the consciousness-stream, the flowing of karmic connections.[32]

Under the auspices of historical record, come the development of the three Christs earlier explained. The Buddha is then third in line.[33] He

31 Graves, 241-242.

32 My exposé has not been as detailed as it could have been if the focus was the complete examination of this myth relating to Perseus, and the origination of the Christ's department on earth. Nevertheless, sufficient information has been provided for later esotericists to use for their further research. Many of the world's myths can be similarly interpreted by using the template here outlined to provide revelatory benefit to humanity.

33 These three Buddhas are introduced in *A Treatise on Cosmic Fire,* 874, after D.K. explains the 'mystery of electricity'. *'In the mystery of Polarity,* we have three different types of force manifesting and thus it is apparent that the two mysteries deal with the six forces. These three types of force are manipulated by the Buddhas of Love. They, through Their sacrifice, concern Themselves with the problem of sex, or of "magnetic approach" on all the planes. The Buddha of Whom we speak and Who contacts His people at the full moon of Wesak, is one of the three connected with *our globe*, having taken the place of One Who passed on to higher work in connection with *the Chain*, for the same hierarchical grading is seen as in connection with the Buddhas of Action. One group might be considered the divine Carpenters of the planetary system, the other the divine Assemblers of its parts and the Ones Who, through the magnetic influence They wield, unite the diversities and build them into form'.

integrated the attributes of the Christs before him via the development of Mind, thus exemplified the Wisdom part of the great Love-Wisdom Ray for humanity. He demonstrated the fine logic and syllogisms coming from the awakened Mind and the extension of the process to attain *śūnyatā,* which is void of mind. He took his third Initiation under the *bodhi* tree and the sixth just after his *parinirvāṇa.* In terms of the qualities of the five Dhyāni Buddhas, therefore, his purpose demonstrated the function of the Discriminating Inner Vision of Amitābha for our planet. Hercules represented the qualities of the Equalising Wisdom of Ratnasambhava, laying the proper foundation of the energies of Love by empowering the twelve petals of the Heart centre via his labours. Perseus embodied the All-accomplishing Wisdom of Amoghasiddhi, producing an inevitable physical reorientation (the turning to stone of his adversities) from the astral bias of the time. This activity inevitably helped to ground the activities of humanity and hence the functions of the infant Hierarchy upon the physical plane.

Christ-Jesus then appeared and outwardly demonstrated the undertaking of the fourth Initiation for the planetary disciple. He refused to play the role of the temporal saviour for the Jewish people, so much desired by the zealots; rather he demonstrated the principles of being an esoteric saviour, where he laid down his life in Love for humanity by strictly following the Will of his Father, which he reflected into manifestation. The fourth Initiation relates to the attainment of *śūnyatā,* which Jesus demonstrated upon the cross that he was crucified upon, when he cried out 'My God, my God, why hast thou forsaken me?'[34] Here he voiced out loud the experience of the Void, when every familiar spiritual landscape known to him, including that of 'God' was stripped from him. He embodied the qualities of the Mirror-like Wisdom of Akṣobhya for humanity. Jesus, the bearer of the Christ principle (hence mirroring his Wisdom), took his fourth in that life and most of the fifth, which he took in a later incarnation.

Finally, we have the new Mahāchohan, who will outwardly demonstrate the taking of the fifth Initiation for humanity, but this will be overlaid by the attributes of the seventh. His role therefore concerns the demonstration of the Dharmadhātu Wisdom of Vairocana.

---

34 *Matt. 27:46.*

This relates to empowering the teachings concerning the *dharmakāya* so that it can be better understood by the intelligentsia and so inspire them to seek enlightenment.

The new Mahāchohan but prepares the ground for the reappearance of the blue Christ, the true fount of the principle of Love-Wisdom, and who consequently will play the role of taking the sixth Initiation upon the world stage, but will not be born as a child and evolve through the lesser testings to do so. His *karma* for such an eventuation has long gone. Instead he will ride the vehicle prepared for him by the externalised Hierarchy. He will appear as the Master of Masters in the guise of the fully grown Child of Love-Wisdom in the Womb of the Consort of the Ādi Buddha (the Mother of the World). He is the embodied *maṇḍala* of the sum of what previously appeared in his department, and which was hid, but which will then be outwardly revealed upon the world stage.

His reappearance is also his exaltation, as the result of planetary Initiation will propel him into a higher Shambhalic role. K.H. will then take the role of Christ, supplanting the role of the new Mahāchohan, who as the green Christ has an esoterically limited role in the Christ's department. (His focus is the right education of moon Chain humanity, his ancient karmic obligation.) K.H. will fully empower the Love-Wisdom Ray for all upon the planet, whereas the new Mahāchohan principally empowers the Wisdom aspect and the process of planetary Initiation as a compassionate action, being overshadowed by Logoic Purpose and Love.

The Mahāchohan's department

The Mahāchohan's department, which directs the evolution of the Rays of Mind, is the third great department within Hierarchy.[35] Its concern is with a line of development of third Ray Monads that directly support the activities of, and inevitably produce, the appearance of a Mother of the World. (This then lays the foundation for the manifestation of a Creative Logos.) Consequently, third Ray disciples play definite roles in the Mother's department on earth by way of promulgating the effects of

35 The other departments being that of the first Ray, governing the direction of the principle of Life, headed by the Manu, and the second Ray department, headed by the Christ.

Mind. This department works as a complement to the feminine principle in Nature, the *deva* kingdom. (Theirs is the way of evolution of *ḍākinīs.)* From the emerald Ray of Mathematically Exact Activity comes the entire diversification of Nature. In the human world it governs the interplay of the *karma* directing the course of civilisations. Consequently, the concern is with the birthing of the new, and the right nurturing of the resultant child until it has matured as a scion of love and wisdom. We see, therefore, that the mode of the externalising Hierarchy is planned via this department and their corresponding Lords in Shambhala.

The Mother of the World is primarily assisted by a council of great Deva Lords, who are representatives of the Regents of the Pleiades (the 'Seven Sisters'), in relation to which the Mahāchohan manifests a comparative second Ray function. From the time of the appearance of a human kingdom the path to becoming a Mother of the World lies via the Mahāchohan's department, because the great Mother must combine both *deva* and human consciousness in Her dispensation. To take such a Seat of Power necessitates a Mahāchohan to delve deep into the mysteries of the *deva* kingdom. Further high Initiations must be taken in certain constellations governed by the feminine principle, such as in the Pleiades and the star Spica, the bright star that represents the sheath of wheat held in the hand of Virgo the virgin. The Mahāchohan therefore becomes significantly more feminine, learning the duties of a prime Creative agent in the cosmic landscape. (The function of Brahmā of the Hindu *trimūrti*–Śiva, Viṣṇu, Brahmā.) This function is also symbolised in the ancient myths by the appearance of the various cow goddesses, such as Hathor in ancient Egypt. These teachings were promulgated at a time when the sun was in Taurus. Part of the reason for this is because the Pleiades are a part of this constellation. The nutritive milk-providing faculty of the cow also aptly symbolises the attributes of the feminine department to nurture the evolution of the divine child in Nature.

Roerich states:

> Indeed it is time to point out that the one Mother of both Lords is not a symbol but a Great Manifestation of the Feminine Origin, in which is revealed the spiritual Mother of Christ and Buddha.

> She it was Who taught and ordained Them for achievement.
>
> From times immemorial the Mother of the World has sent forth to achievement. In the history of humanity, Her Hand traces an unbreakable thread.
>
> On Sinai Her Voice rang out. She assumed the image of Kali. She was the basis of the cults of Isis and Ishtar. After Atlantis, when a blow was inflicted upon the cult of the spirit, the Mother of the World began to weave a new thread, which will now begin to radiate. After Atlantis the Mother of the World veiled Her Face and forbade the pronouncement of Her Name until the hour of the constellations should strike. She has manifested Herself only partly; never has She manifested Herself on a planetary scale.[36]

'The hour of the constellations' relates to when the appropriate constellations are aligned, signifying the planetary Initiation that would cause the externalisation of Shambhala. Then the true face of the Mother of the World shall be revealed. Her true 'name', signifying her true qualities, could not be revealed because it would provide too much information about the *devas,* who also had to be relatively veiled, to prevent the types of abuse that transpired during the Atlantean epoch. Mantra was used to manipulate them on a mass scale for the service of many darkened ones. The revealing of Her Face relates to the mystery concerning Her eventual ascension to the Throne of the Logos of this planet as a consequence of the externalisation process of Hierarchy.

There are five individuals from ancient times onwards who have or will bear the cloak of the Mother of the World. Three of them will first assume the role of Mahāchohan upon our planet. Being governed by the law of the pentad, where the five Dhyāni Buddhas are the direct emanatory representatives, each Mother manifests as the Consort of one or other of these Jinas. The Mother's department is responsible for the expression of the *karma* external to the individual. This *karma* governs the environment in which people reside and conditions all evolutionary space. The mechanism for the expression of this *karma* manifests via the angelic (*deva*) subordinates within the Mother's department, viewed as Cherubim, Seraphim, Archangels and angels. Individual *karma,* on the other hand, is a product of the human mind, wedded to the desire

---

36 Helena Roerich, *Leaves of Morya's Garden, II, Illumination,* 131-132.

principle and human emotions, which then impact upon the physical domain via appropriated *deva* substance.

From the point of view of the pentad, therefore, the present Mother is a second point upon our earth globe. She came with the Lords of Flame at the time of the Individualisation (formation) of humanity on this earth. There was an earlier Mother who oversaw the evolutionary paean of all kingdoms of Nature to the time of the appearance of humanity. Her purpose therefore was purely with the activities of the *devas* in fashioning the conditions that allowed a humanity to appear upon the earth. The present great Mother adds consideration of human evolution to her repertoire, and also labours under the *karma* of having made a wrong decision with respect to moon Chain humanity.

We can see therefore that what was earlier said concerning all forms of life emerging from her Womb is only partially correct. It is an ongoing progress shared by all of the Mothers, as each inherit the structure of the Womb of the previous Mother and then qualify it with new hues according to the evolving purpose of their dispensation. In correlation with what is already there, new streams of lives and energies enter, to be born under the new conditionings of the epoch the Mother presides over. With respect to the various ways that the phrase the 'Mother of the World' can be used, D.K. stated that it can mean:

1. The feminine aspect in manifestation, symbolised for us in many of the world religions as a virgin mother and in the Christian religion as the Virgin Mary. It is that substance which allows Deity to manifest.
2. Nature itself, the mother of all forms.
3. The moon also, who is the symbol of the generative, creative life which gives birth to forms and is therefore the symbol of the form nature.
4. The concentration of the feminine force in nature in some individual in female form who is then called the "World Mother." Such an individual has never existed in our planetary life, though the avatars of a previous solar system, expressing itself through planetary life, always took this form. But not in this solar system. The tradition of such appearances is purely symbolic, inherited from the previous solar system from which we inherited the matter

> of which all manifested forms are made. The symbolism has come down from the far-off period of the Matriarchate, which had a religion that recalled the ancient ways of the earlier system and in which period of time Lilith symbolised the World Mother, until Eve took her place.[37]

The reason for this is that in this solar system, which is governed by the consciousness aspect (the second Ray), the Mother is not intricately incorporated in the form of the substance She directs. She stands above or beyond what is constituted in Her Womb, and directs via intermediaries. Also, the Mother's department is an office held by various representatives, who play similar, though changing roles as the planetary evolution proceeds. In the earlier solar system the Mother was the Logos.

There are, however, cycles that are governed by the third Ray working via substance, such as the moon Chain, when rulership of the Mother principle directly took on attributes of the earlier solar system's form of governance. Much *karma* is bequeathed to our present earth through the failure of this third Chain's evolution, which is borne by the present One who embodies the Mother principle upon the earth, because of Her prominent role in that ancient cycle.

When D.K. states that 'such an individual has never existed in our planetary life' he is speaking technically, where the highest governing principle, or 'God' of a planet, embodies the principle of Mind in its lowest, empirical aspect (Mahat). In such a case the objective of Life in Her Womb will be to develop the attributes of mind. The evolution of life within the veil of substance being the dominant theme, and that of consciousness being subsidiary. The separative attributes of mind are developed, where what is now dark brotherhood was at first considered a high point of evolution. The development of enlightened consciousness, with its unifying, integrative faculties, is then an ultimate objective, signifying the ending of the feminine cycle of evolution heralding the ending of a *manvantara,* because the Son gains ascendency.

Putting such technicalities aside, I shall associate 'the Mother of the World' to the One governing the third point positioning

---

37 A.A. Bailey, *Esoteric Healing,* (Lucis Publishing, New York, 1977), 362-363.

in Shambhala, and who consequently embodies the sum of the *deva* kingdom.

The first Mother of the World took the attributes of Amoghasiddhi's[38] Consort. The focus during Her time manifested in the form of Amoghasiddhi's All-accomplishing Wisdom, to effect changes throughout the sum of the early evolutionary period of the earth. This *prajñā* produced the terrestrial changes that occurred during geological time, plus the evolution of the various streams of life. Each different kingdom of Nature represents a particular *prāṇa* and corresponding *saṃskāra* coursing through Her body of manifestation. The scientific community has classified five kingdoms of Nature (Monera, Protista, Fungi, Plantae, Animala), which can be considered to be effects in Her body of the Earthy aspect of the five *prāṇas* that course through the *nāḍīs,* when viewed from the perspective of the embodying Life. During Her time the Fiery stream manifested through the work of the higher *devas* under Her. The Watery stream then represents the Builders of the forms. These forms are constructed from the basic mineral substance from which all evolves. Tiny *deva* lives then embody the substance, with their evolution guided by the Fire Devas. These five kingdoms, plus the Fiery and Watery *devas,* are attributes of the seven sub-Rays of the overriding third Ray that governs the expression of all of Nature's phenomena.

The mineral kingdom and its etheric substrate clothes the forms of the five streams of Life. This kingdom reflects the basic laws governing cosmic evolution, thus conveys the elementary attributes of the first Ray in formed space, reflected in the form of the seventh Ray. The Monera represent all classes of single celled organisms without a nucleus, therefore reflect in a very rudimentary way the void of self attributes of the second Ray. The Protista are a large group of Eukaryote cells containing a nucleus and complex membrane-bound structures. When organised as co-dependent organelles they become the basic structures of all higher forms of life. The governing Ray is the third of Mathematically Exact Activity. The Fungi share some of

---

38 The name Amoghasiddhi means 'unfailing success'. He is said to preside over the family of *karma*, the mastery of which provides the complete attainment of Buddhahood. The vehicle is Garuda, who eats up all of the serpents of desire, sensuality, emotionality, and of selfishness, allowing the manifestation of the *siddhis* of enlightenment.

the features found in one or other of the other phyla, but also some unique ones, which presents a relation to the middle Ray of Harmony through Conflict. The Plants produce such an abundance of colour, perfumes and leaf forms, etc., that clearly relates them to the fifth Ray of Scientific Organisation and Reason. The animals are related to the sixth Ray of Devotion as that is one of the principal qualities that their evolutionary line develops. The *devas* govern the mathematical ordering of space (the third Ray) and ritualistically embody all of the cycles and appearances of the natural order of all the kingdoms in Nature under the general auspices of the seventh Ray of Ceremonial Activity. The modes of activity of other *devas* are also found via the fourth, fifth and sixth Rays.

The present Mother manifests the attributes of Ratnasambhava's Consort,[39] utilising the golden energy of his Equalising Wisdom to specifically generate harmonious relationships in the fourth kingdom in Nature (humanity).[40] As the golden Ray governs human evolution, She is well predisposed to assist their progress throughout the course of the appearance and disappearance of human civilisation. Progress is slow because the normal volatility of human free will must always be accommodated within the general Watery environment where they reside. Her agents are responsible for the evolution of the forms via which humans evolve, plus the substance of their periodic sheaths, including that of the mind. Hence the *devas* regulate the *karma* of all human actions so that it all equalises ultimately into the oneness of *śūnyatā*.[41]

---

39 Ratnasambhava (the 'jewelled born'), whose emblem is the wish-fulfilling jewel, signifying the entire *nāḍī* system through which all of the *prāṇas* sustaining consciousness (the wish-fulfilling aspect of this jewel) must manifest. The vehicle is the horse, signifying the sum of the animal nature that is fully subdued to become the perfected vehicle for enlightenment.

40 Here the term kingdom is used in the esoteric sense of that which corresponds to the expression of the five Elements manifesting in *saṃsāra,* incorporating thus also the mineral domain as a kingdom. We therefore have the mineral, plant, animal, human, and divine kingdom (of the Sambhogakāya Flower-Hierarchy-the *devas)* as the five kingdoms. They represent the five *prāṇas* in her body of manifestation.

41 *Śūnyatā* is that which is void of mind, hence designated as 'emptiness', 'the Void' in Buddhism, but is more than that, which the earlier volumes of this series adequately explain. Being Void it is freed from *deva* presence, hence of the associated karmic affiliations.

In the coming epoch the feminine will be exemplified, and the role of the *devas* underlying the happenings of things will begin to be properly recognised by an amazed humanity. Their functioning will then be studied by the scientific community.

For this process to proceed, fundamental human selfishness must be replaced by the factor of human goodwill and then the higher wills via altruistic motives in decision-making. The feminine in Nature, manifesting in the human kingdom via women's rights, must specifically be appropriately rectified. Sexually biased conditioned thinking and religious zealotry against the feminine must be finally honestly tackled on the world stage. Much inroad against the dark brotherhood's stranglehold of the astral miasma of humanity will then have been achieved. The present Mother of the World directs the *saṃsāric* play through all human dramas until the appearance of the major cycle of Love-Wisdom on this planet. Once her child has matured, as ordained, Her position can be given to another. She can then take a higher position in the great third Ray department in cosmos, in relation to directly ruling our planet. Hers will be the direct empowerment of a cosmic feminine dispensation, in line with the overall 'sex' of our planet, which is feminine, as indicated by its vast oceans, and the green colouration of Nature.

The onset of the new era upon this earth will signify a time of taking Initiation for the entire planetary dispensation, including the Lords of Shambhala. All will take a further step upon their respective paths, and some will move out of the orbit of direct planetary concern, leaving behind a new *maṇḍala* to influence the earth. The highest two members of the Spiritual Triad ruling this globe will leave, as the need to directly intervene in the affairs of our globe will have gone. The Lord of the World, Sanat Kumāra (who will no longer have to play the role of the 'Silent Watcher'), and the three Buddhas of Activity will also leave. They will oversee the formation of the new fifth globe and Chain of the Scheme, but are preparing for higher exalted roles in cosmos. Hence Sanat Kumāra will be the Logos of our planetary Scheme and under Him the Mother's department that will be responsible for our globe. The earth will then be a sacred planet and resonate to its true Sound for all in cosmos to hear.

The Mother will thereby take a 'new' role, to be in charge of the close cooperation between *devas* and humanity, signifying the oncoming feminine dispensation. The planet's *nāḍī* system will change accordingly from its present masculine disposition to a feminine one. In order to fulfil this new role she will add more Sirian blue to Her aura, and red from the Rishis of the great Bear via the Pleiades. The Pleiades are the central esoteric School of Mysteries for the entire feminine dispensation.

The Phoenician will succeed Her as the Mother of the World, to garner and vitalise the role of the expression of Mind that will be developed by humanity in the new world civilisation. He oversaw the development of mind by humanity in ancient times, and in the forthcoming incarnation as the Mother of the World this long aeonic task will be neatly concluded. Mind will then become the vehicle for the implementation of Love-Wisdom as the mainstay of the new era. She will thus manifest in the form of Amitabha's Consort,[42] by thoroughly infusing the function of the Discriminating Inner Vision into the planetary body. This wisdom disseminates the Fiery Element for humanity and *devas* alike.

Humanity's *manasic* predilections towards materialistic and selfish incentives will be converted into the new era of compassionate and cooperative striving. The consequent scientific era will respect and properly analyse the principle of Life governing the evolution of forms, in contradistinction to the present focus upon the form of things. Nature's finer forces and the role that mind/Mind plays in determining the evolutionary play will therefore be increasingly discovered. This Mother of the World will preside over an increasing downpour of energies from the cosmic mental plane into the human mental matrix, making possible many discoveries concerning the nature of cosmic evolution hitherto impossible, except for the highest Initiates.

During this time Shambhala will externalise upon the physical plane, which necessitates an increased reception to the energy of Mind by a significant number of humanity. They must bear and help distribute the nature of a much greater downpour of the Will energy (cosmic astral energies) than is presently possible, which will pervade the auric space shared by humanity.

---

42 Meaning 'boundless light'. His emblem is the lotus blossom, thus of the power to awaken the *chakras*. The vehicle is the peacock, signifying the complete display of the potency of the *dharma* via *manasic* vicissitudes, expressed as the enlightenment of the awakened one.

The Phoenician's tenure as the Mother of the World will govern the period of the second Ray dispensation into the planetary *manasic* maze during the sixth Root Race epoch. This will make the earth truly a sacred planet. This period, however, will be relatively brief when compared to the many hundreds of millennia long occupancy of the seat by the present Mother.

The next Mother will take the functions of a deep blue-green energy as the Consort of Akṣobhya,[43] assisting with the expression of his Mirror-like Wisdom. She will reflect the purpose of cosmic Love into Nature's domain. When this Mother of the World gains ascendency, humanity will be at the apogee of its civilisation and in communication with cosmos. She will therefore oversee the process wherein human groups will begin to leave the planet, as group after group pass the necessary Initiation tests. This energy will fully vitalise the expression of the Shambhalic *maṇḍala,* signifying that the great bulk of the dark brotherhood that formerly preyed upon humanity have been converted, and thus the forces of evil no longer play a role amongst human affairs. Her purpose will be to oversee the ending of the evolution of humanity upon earth. She will oversee the termination of the conditioning of the astral plane, the heaven and hell realms created by humans. This will allow the astral Waters to finally dry up on the earth, and the focus of general human aspiration will be upon the domain of the Sambhogakāya Flower and beyond. Obviously, it will take considerable time for humanity to relinquish attachment to this Watery substance. The last remnants of what is known as evil will be overcome with the downpour of great power via the cosmic astral plane.

The final one to hold the mantle of the Mother of the World will take the attributes of being Consort to Vairocana's[44] Dharmadhātu Wisdom. The purpose of the present earth evolution will then be in the final stages of being successively completed. This wisdom manifests via the influx of cosmic mental energies (a first Ray Fiery aspect) that will be channelled by this Mother to help effect the ending of the

43 Akṣobhya, the 'unshakable one', whose emblem is the *vajra,* the full power of the awakened, enlightened Mind. The vehicle is the elephant, signifying immense spiritual strength.

44 Vairocana, the 'intensely luminescent one', who presides over the Buddha families, and whose emblem is the *dharma wheel* (of the *dharmakāya*) from which all else proceeds. His vehicle is a lion, symbolising all-conquering activity.

streams of Life upon our planet. Her work will therefore be purely via the *deva* kingdom. The power of Shambhala will then evoke the processes needed to abstract all Life forms to new planetary destinations, producing the onset of *pralaya.* A new globe of the earth Scheme will have formed upon which a human kingdom can arise from the animal kingdom, supplemented by the failures of the present human evolution. (Many of whom will be those who in that cycle staunchly remain attached to dark brotherhood methodology, and thus who refuse to progress the evolutionary way.) These streams of Life will find their home in this new globe that is now in the process of emerging from the subtler realms.[45]

The new Mahāchohan is destined to take the role of the Logos of the next (fifth or Saturn[46]) globe of our present planetary Scheme. It is presently being objectivised from cosmic etheric space and is veiled by the moon. To it will flow all of the streams of Life from the earth once conditionings here cannot support their further evolutionary progression. In order to prepare for such a role, and because of his facility in the three primary Rays, he will not directly assume the position of the Mother on this planet, but rather will partly inherit the role of Sanat Kumāra when That One leaves His position on earth. He will be the Initiator for a while, (overseeing those that take their third Initiation), though will not take on the other attributes of 'The Ancient of Days'. After having taken the requisite Initiations he will be the Regent on earth for That One. He will be well qualified to guide the world's disciples to pass Initiation testings according to the new rules of group Initiation, having established the new Initiation tree for the immediate second Ray epoch ahead. His remaining tenure upon the earth, however, will be relatively brief, as the great need will be for him to acquire the necessary skills to assume the role of a Logos. For this, considerable cosmic training and higher Initiations are required, of which the role as the Initiator for the planet is but the prelude.

---

45 Detail concerning this subject and of the evolution of the planetary Schemes in the solar system will be provided in a later work on the numerological and astrological code to Blavatsky's *The Secret Doctrine.*

46 I use the symbolism of Saturn here because the purpose of this planetary Chain will be to cleanse the *karma* of all previous lines of evolution in the solar system, and this function falls under the auspices of Saturn.

Those who will or have assumed the role of Mahāchohan upon this planet since the fall of Atlantis are:

1. Hermes Trismegistus

This one, known historically as Hermes Trismegistus, is the primary embodiment of the emerald Ray, and will vacate his position at Shambhala as a consequence of the appearance of the new cycle. His role as the Mahāchohan was from the time of the fall of Atlantis and he was a major source of the arcane knowledge that universally governed the ancient religions. It helped to instigate much of the astonishing star lore and amazingly advanced astronomical observatories known to be encoded in the vast monuments that were erected by the ancients all over the world. The most well known of such structures is the great Pyramid of Giza. Its construction was completed whilst the sun was in Taurus, signifying the wisdom symbolised by the opened Eye, before transit into Aries, which signified the true beginning of the cycle when mind will dominate human affairs within the Aryan epoch of human history.[47] The plans and foundational structure were begun in Atlantis because of the significance of the site. Thus an astrological temple existed there for many millennia before the great Pyramid was actually built. Indeed, it was also for a long time used as a place for gaining Initiation to the Mysteries of enlightenment. The sarcophagus that was found in what is termed 'the King's Chamber' was used for this purpose. The Initiate to be, after proper preparation, ritual, mantra and consecration was laid therein, where he spent a number of nights[48] out of his body, then coming back with knowledge of the experiences after awakening.

The exquisite mathematical knowledge of the Mahāchohan's department in relation to the many planetary and solar Mysteries, and the symbolism of the Initiation process, were built into its construction.[49] This happened at a time when this Mahāchohan undertook his fifth Initiation, and the existence of this exquisite monument is testimony to this. The work was obviously a major Hierarchical undertaking, when

47 Prior to the time of Cheops, to whom it is falsely attributed.

48 Depending upon the degree of Initiation concerned.

49 This information is well explained in the many popular books on the mysteries of the great pyramid, hence there is no need to reproduce them here.

all the members of the Mahāchohan's department were incarnate and assisted by the second Ray. The pyramid complex at Giza encoded the nature of the transmission of the ancient Atlantean wisdom to the fifth Root Race, the Aryan epoch, fixed in indestructible stone, so that it would survive until the present era, when those that could exoterically decipher the mathematics had evolved and consequently could reveal the outline of the ancient wisdom to humanity. The term 'exoterically' is used here because Initiates have always known the Mysteries, but in this present epoch such Initiate knowledge can be broadcast to humanity via the mass media. The revelation was therefore planned for the time of the ascent of mind in human civilisation, and when it could be transformed into Mind, so that the more esoteric symbolism could be comprehended. The sphinx is older; the symbolism of its construction time concerns the Virgo-Leo cusp.

2. The Phoenician

He can be considered to have taken the Mahāchohan's role when he founded the Zoroastrian religion, and has guided the course of the development of mind in human civilisation through the Renaissance period in Europe (a major effort of the Mahāchohan's department[50]) to the early part of the twentieth century. Our modern scientific era was consequently fecundated, being the gain of his effort in the past epochs to fan the principle of mind amongst humanity.

Before taking his assigned role as the Mother of the World the Phoenician will undergo considerable training in the Pleiades to build into his constitution more attributes of the Deva Hierarchy. He needs to be intrinsically Initiated into their forms of identification to higher commands. He will also have to add further receptivity and definition of the Will (from the seven Rishis) and the silver-blue energy of Love-Wisdom from Sirius so as to be able to play an appropriate role in the new second Ray cycle of Love-Wisdom on the earth that will make it a sacred planet. Silvery green and blue hues and further red-violet will be added to his fundamental orange, thus building a new design to the robe he will inherit from the former Mother. He will thus become the third Mother of the World, well positioned to oversee the

50 This Hierarchical undertaking necessitated the incarnation of the great Ones in all Ray departments to achieve.

abstraction of consciousness to the higher domains of Mind in the new world civilisation. Creatively intelligent people must therefore begin to build their mental constructs with a far more vibrant form of *deva* substance under Her direction. The role of the *deva* kingdom as a factor in evolution will be gradually discovered and properly investigated by many scientists during Her tenure. A new era of cooperation with space visitors will be established,[51] massively invigorating science into new areas of investigation.

3. Rakoczi/Count St. Germain (Master ℛ*)*

He was the immediate successor to the Phoenician's tenure. *Rakoczi's* role as Mahāchohan was to help bring in the epoch of mind to humanity by means of the scientific revolution. (One of his incarnations consequently, was Francis Bacon.) The development of human intelligence, albeit with an undue materialistic focus, was vigorously stimulated as a consequence of the Renaissance and the coming of the Industrial Revolution. Being formerly the seventh Ray Chohan, the Master ℛ also oversaw the explosion of the service arena of the seventh Ray Ashrams during the age of the Enlightenment in Europe, producing such things as the French and American Revolutions, as well as the rise of the Masonic movement.

Master ℛ took the Mahāchohan's position prior to the one who was actually senior to him in the *maṇḍalic* structure of the Mother of the World's department. The time for the true third point (the new Mahāchohan) to take this role was not ripe, as this necessitated humanity to have developed much more Love-Wisdom than it actually had. Such expression was only possible as a consequence of the Hierarchical preparation for its externalisation since the end of the Victorian era. Rakoczi consequently has undergone specialised training to garner

51 The Crop Circle phenomena manifesting all over the world is a harbinger and guarantor of such an eventuation. The present aggressive militaristic posturing and materialistic bias of our nations (especially the U.S.) prevents contact with the space people. The appearance of this phenomena has revealed the blind dogmatism of our present scientific community, who have refused to honestly investigate it because it lies outside the parameters of their belief system. Unexplainable by them, thus to be haughtily dismissed as fabricated by tricksters, but they are clueless as how to replicate the intricate designs in the conditions wherein they actually happen. The miraculous appearance of this phenomena is thus ignored as if it does not exist.

further third Ray aptitude and to develop the cosmic contacts needed to help fulfil the purpose of the seventh Ray for the new cyclic epoch.

Rakoczi's function effectively manifests in the form of a mirror (viewing him as an actual fourth point) to reflect the purpose of the higher triad into manifestation, producing therefore the great alchemical work of the transformation of the base qualities of the human metallic psyche into refined spiritual gold.

4. The new Mahāchohan

His purpose is to drive human thought towards abstract thinking, so that wisdom will guide human affairs. This will be in conjunction with the blue Ray being fully established in human affairs. The purification and eventual elimination of Watery reactions and opinions shall properly begin under his watch. Because of humanity's love affair with their emotions, many battles against the lords of dark face will have to be fought to overcome such attachments. Such battles will continue right to the ending of the sixth Root Race period to eliminate all of dark brotherhood strangleholds amongst human affairs. The astral plane consequently will lose its potency and with it the heaven and hell states created by humanity. Inevitably the existence of the *deva* kingdom will have been scientifically proven, with a large number of individuals being able to visualise and work cooperatively with them. The Devas of the Shadows (etheric plane *devas*) especially will enter into peripheral sight due to the increased etherealisation of substance, vitalised pharmaceutical-free living styles, the study of the esoteric sciences, the ritual of invocation and evocation, and widespread vegetarianism. (Such vision will be the result of the increased sensitisation of the mechanism of the eye rather than being a clairvoyance *per se.*) Obviously many aspects relating to agricultural methods, treatment of animals, and social planning, will have been revolutionised via such contact. Community gardens where *devas* instruct humans for optimal vegetable growth will be a common sight in the garden cities that will dot the landscape.

5. The present third Ray Chohan

He will assume the role of the Mahāchohan when the new Mahāchohan leaves on his cosmic path. We can therefore see that there is always a moving up in the ranks of Hierarchy and Shambhala and outwards to cosmic service whenever humanity makes a leap forward in its evolutionary attainment.

By the time the third Ray Chohan takes the role of the Mahāchohan, the power of the third Ray will be more evident in the world, allowing the pure green of Mathematically Exact Activity to colour many attributes of our civilisation. He will obviously help oversee the era of the ascendency of Mind over mind as a factor governing the motives for action amongst the intelligentsia. He will ensure that the present, selfishly driven direction of the world's resources, and of the use of money, will be a thing of the past. New forms of resource sharing will evolve that truly serve all in need, and not mainly those that are aggressively rapacious in their actions. He will mainly work to properly infuse the new civilisation with divinely ordained ideas and the esoteric sciences that will help establish the culturally magnificent and aesthetic landscapes that will then govern the face of the earth.

Two more Mahāchohans will later arise that have much affinity to the first Ray, and who will oversee the course of civilisation at the latter part of the sixth Root Race and for the final Root Race, when what is presently understood as 'civilisation' will no longer have any meaning. They will continue the 'mopping up' operations concerning the elimination of the Watery influence in human affairs. They will also work to direct many fleets of ships of Fiery-Air, manned by *maṇḍalas* of human groups, on to their cosmic destinations.

The path of their ascent will assist the difficult work of the then Mother to oversee the period of the ending of the world's astral miasmas. The power of the remaining dark brotherhood upon the mental plane will also be eliminated. Many major psychic battles must pass into the mists of time before their stranglehold upon humanity will be terminated psychically. (By then the greater portion of humanity will have developed *siddhis*, and the mental plane will be a common field of experience for them.) This will represent the final cleansing cycle for the reverberating *karma* from the great psychic wars in Atlantean times.

The physical plane will become etherealised, as the first (destroyer) Ray manifests its true power to end the cycles of the many streams of Life that found their purpose upon our planetary sphere. (Obviously humanity will be abstracted from the earth many millennia before any of the other kingdoms of Nature.) Because much of what we presently consider to signify ‘civilisation’ will then no longer exist, or be in dissolution, as an Initiate-focussed planetary consciousness will have been established, so there will be no direct role in the projection of the qualities of a civilisation. The final Mahāchohan will rather be working to resolve the lingering strands of *karma* and to project them to the new planet. Much concerning the formation of that planet and its future evolution will be investigated and prepared for. The conditionings producing the new solar incarnation will also be meditatively viewed. That incarnation will continue the cycles of the rebirthing experience for all who have evolved on this present system. The members of the Mother’s department on this earth will move on to various systemic and cosmic Schools to learn to become the constituency of Logoi of planetary systems. (Assisted by members of the second Ray line, who will manifest the embodied Word for myriads.)

The further our vision is projected to the future, the more difficult it is to explain the probable conditions and states of consciousness to those who have not been Initiated into them. As we advance into the future, the qualifications needed to obtain the necessary Initiations become more demanding.

My Heart is Bleeding

What can I do to rattle your brain.
to break it to pieces, to build it up again,
reassembled in Love, to make it your Way,
for you to know what it is to be a Man,
then to be no-man on this new glorious Day?
Come, heed my call, help defend us all
in spheres of Light, sweet radiant delight.
Let go of yourselves. Be. Acquiesce to Love.
Come with me, follow my Path.
I will show you the white of the Dove,
the Halls of the One, of all His Domain.
The great King Himself shall swallow you whole.
For you to become Nought
is His great Command.
The Nought is the All.
It is my Way, your Love, His Day.
The Hierarchy stands, assisting All.
It bows down its Head.
Glory Be. The Christ is born.
We love you, Love is you
on each and every Day.....

My heart is exploding,
it is effectively pulsating
the cycles of reason,
the seasons, the zodiacal changes,
the rhythmic breathings of all that is evolving.
My Lord, oh God!
It is unfolding, expanding,
exploding, freely bleeding,
filling the chasms of the valleys
whereon are walking those that are
continually dying.

Dying!
To the sensitive sentience
and unfolding beauty
of the entire multidimensional world.

Dying!
For they grow but little as they age,
but live out empty thoughts
of pleasured paths,
effectively for which
from all they will take,
and will give only
for their own benefit's sake.

Dying!
as they talk and talk
about their concerns,
their needs, their comforts,
their friends, lovers, themselves,
but see not their brothers struggling,
in pain, the saddened plight of others.

Dying!
As they've emptied their hearts
from all such concern,
and see not the consequences
of cause and effect.
For selfish action means separation
from the Heart of all lovers.
And with the Heart not freely beating
there can be no essential living,
only withering sickness,
life's starvation, consequent suffering,
continuous dying.

Ignorance of karmic adjudication
is the undoing
of all selfish empire building.
Energy expenditure
is not forgotten or wasted,
but changes from one form to another.
For every deed, thought, or word projected
an equal reaction will concur.
It is an adamantine,
exacting, most effective Law.
What is not given
cannot be received.
A seed not nurtured can grow no tree,
only a pitiful field, death, an empty chasm.

Their chasms are gaping,
into which my Blood is pouring.
They're dying, dying
to the Light within them trying to grow.
I'm bleeding, I'm bleeding,
my body is profusely bleeding
from every pore and rupture
caused by the piercing blows
of those that have scorned
the path I have taken.
Look, oh look at the flood
my Heart is making
trying to water the seedlings
so wretchedly barren.
I will give you my Heart,
offer it without speaking,
give you my joy
to comfort your pain.

Wash your muddied feet
with the Blood of my concern,
caress your fears
with the flood of my understanding,
touch your Heart with my embrace.
You need only look, or ask;
you need only feel
for your troubled companions,
and weed out the source of their plight.
I'm bleeding, I'm bleeding,
please receive my Heart's Blood.
It is Light, it is Life,
wondrous ensightment.

Absorption into the Heart of Being
has opened the valves
of my Heart's expression.
The journey is a progression,
one of fully giving.
In giving there's receiving
the joy of every being.
At first such understanding is arduous,
a real undertaking, but in the end
its a spontaneous flowing of desirelessness
for consequence or rewards,
save the joyous emanation
of another Soul's awakening,
a devotion to the need
for the whole world's salvation,
a complete understanding
of right energy distribution.
Life's Bliss is only received by wisely giving,
certainly not by indoctrination to ideas,
ideals, and dogmatic assertion.

It flows freely to all,
for every cell in the Body it is feeding.
Your Heart and my Heart
the One Life are pulsating,
together they are beating the rhythm
that all Souls are sharing.
Please receive the Blood
that from my Heart is flowing
and give it to the many
who fear to touch or seek it.
Open their eyes to the source of all anguish,
maybe then this Blood they will see,
and touch it, and drink it,
and express it, and give it
freely and harmoniously in companionship
with all who bequeath it.
The world will then be your heaven.
You will be where you are needed,
and all you need will be given,
and you will share in the Bliss
between all lovers and the loved.
Our hearts, our Heart,
it is bleeding.....

6

Hierarchy and the Major Centres below the Diaphragm

General considerations

The Ashrams governing the Rays of Mind (the Mahāchohan's department) work primarily in relation to the Throat centre and major centres below the diaphragm. This concerns the Solar Plexus, Sacral and Base of Spine centres. These and the minor centres of the Inner Round constitute the arena of activity of humanity, whilst the associated *saṃskāras* produce the main attributes of our present civilisation. (Evolution of the qualities of the Throat and Heart centres has however been gathering pace over the past few centuries.) Hence the Mahāchohan's department is mainly concerned with awakening the higher attributes of the associated centres, to lead humanity away from purely material concerns (the Sacral-Base of Spine centre interrelation), aspects of gross sexuality and war-like aggression (Sacral centre), or egotistical, selfish and all emotional-mental concerns, coupled with aspects of lower psychic phenomena (the Solar Plexus centre).

The objective is to lead humanity to awaken the attributes of the higher centres via the Heart centre. Obviously, this transformation from focus below the diaphragm to above is difficult, with many setbacks (when the sum of humanity are included in our consideration). The process leads (via the activity of Splenic centres I and II) to produce the transformation and eventual transmutation of humanity's *saṃskāras,* as already described.

Twenty Ashrams constitute the directive function of the main petals of the centres here considered. The Ashrams in consideration are those that have already formed or are presently actively forming. They are arranged in basic Ray groupings, where the sixth and seventh Ray Ashrams are concerned with manifesting the attributes of the six petals of the Sacral centre and the four of the Base of Spine centre. The petals of the Solar Plexus centre *(maṇipūra chakra)* are constituted by the activities of the third, fourth and fifth Ray Ashrams. This centre represents the central processing centre for the entire process. It channels the Watery *prāṇas* whereby humanity is besotted and must learn to properly control. In many ways the path to enlightenment constitutes the ways whereby the Waters become dried up within the human psyche. Hierarchy therefore projects the cleansing Airy and Fiery attributes of the Watery *prāṇas* that will accomplish this end. (A toned down version of the cosmic astral Waters, which is pure, unadulterated Love/*bodhicitta*.) They hold the ambrosial antidote to the various poisons of humanity's desirous and emotion-filled world of strife. Also concerned are all of the Inner Round series of *chakras* that govern the sum of human civilisation controlled by this centre. Much esotericism is veiled here.

A major function of the work of the Rays of Mind is integrally interwoven with the rectification of the incorrect and misguided *saṃskāras* of humanity. There is thus a fluid, mutable interplay between the above centres and the important arrangement of the dual Splenic centre. This centre redirects valuable *prāṇas* through the Solar Plexus centre (generally via the Stomach and Liver centres) and rejects those no longer viable (via the work of Splenic centre II). In many ways Hierarchy generally acts as Splenic centre I with respect to humanity. Thus Hierarchy works to impress upon humanity the clean, vibrant life energies and teachings from the Heart, recycling impressions and concepts still valuable for people to know, so cycling out of the human environment the redundant and harmful concepts (or to mitigate their effects). This is because humanity as a whole generate base emotional *saṃskāras* that continuously need karmic rectification, signifying their very limited capacity to be directly energised by the Heart centre.

The Equalising Wisdom of Ratnasambhava qualifies the functions of the Sacral centre. Loving qualities are projected to humanity in such a way that their Watery disposition is stimulated to produce harmonising emotional responses by way of understanding and to lessen their fields of desire. This produces advances in the creative imagination, rightly placed devotion, and aspiration to high ideals, as people learn to detach from wrongly placed desire. The focus is the development of wisdom. Humanity are at the stage where adolescence needs to be superseded by mature adult forms of activity. The astral plane (the onus of expression for the sixth Ray) is an illusion. The heavens and hells of the various religions are created by the sum total of the image-making faculty and desires of humanity, thus as disciples learn to control those faculties so for them the attributes of this plane vanish, except as a field of service. This control is produced by the Initiation process wherein psychicism, emotions and glamours are eliminated. Common humanity are, however, entrapped in this substance, thus it constitutes the field of testings for all disciples.

Amitābha's Discriminating Inner Wisdom generally governs Hierarchy's outpouring to humanity's Solar Plexus activity. People must learn to transform emotional activity into wise loving concerns for all, to rightly discriminate right from wrong and to scientifically observe the nature of all manifesting phenomena, human psychology and cultural situations. Hence this epoch of scientific materialism is largely the result of such *manasic* stimulation upon the matrix of human concerns. We are now at an age whereby the direct second Ray outpouring from the Heart centre can overcome the fanaticism of the materialistic minded ones and their addiction to things of the form. Thus the process concerning the externalisation of Hierarchy causes many unregenerate *prāṇas* of humanity to be sent to the Splenic centres for conversion and transformation.

Amoghasiddhi's All-accomplishing Wisdom governs the activity of the Base of Spine centre via the activity of the seventh Ray Ashrams.

When looking to these centres one should understand that this concerns the way Hierarchy interrelates with the human units constituting the lower attributes of the respective petals of the *chakras*, in order to awaken them to higher possibilities. Hierarchy project a rhythm of activity from the higher domains that positively stimulate the target groups to produce advancements in thought and better living styles. Hierarchy do not feed the emotions, glamour forming tendencies, or illusions, rather they endeavour to awaken constructive thought, broadminded tolerant attitudes and rational solutions to life's problems and those that afflict civilisation in general. All aspects of human society are targeted with cogent ideas.

For Hierarchy, the astral plane is non-existent as a place of residence, but constitutes an arena of service. Similarly with the fields of desire governed by the Sacral centre. The focus of the sixth Ray Ashrams associated with this centre is to convert human desire into aspiration. For the seventh Ray Ashrams governing the Base of Spine centre the focus concerns the right organisation and distribution of resources of all the physical plane activities of humanity. They are concerned with the structure of human society and its governance. Cooperative communities and nations are its goal. The seventh Ray represents the power to transform the most base of *saṃskāras* and to redirect the entire flow of the transformed *prāṇas* away from domains of generation of the *saṃskāras* upwards to Hierarchy, and finally to Shambhala. Materialising scientifically applied mathematical planning is its basic methodology.

The sixth Ray provides the driving energy, the aspirational zeal to effect changes via religious, spiritual and socially focussed pronouncements. The seventh Ray utilises this energy to build the concrete edifices that consolidate the gains produced 'in stone', in rightly structured lasting organisations. All Ray lines produce cogently applied thought in various arenas of human livingness to structurally change society so that the outcome is beneficent to all.

The work of *prāṇic* purification that is undertaken, generally by the entire Hierarchy, is but an expression of the second cosmic path of Magnetic Work. It is described by D.K. in terms of the speciality of a *nirvāṇee* that chooses this path.

> Another aspect of the work done by the Master on the second Path is the drawing off of those phases of glamour which no longer have the power to deceive mankind. They are not allowed to accumulate or to remain upon the astral plane. They are therefore, through the magnetic power of the Master, withdrawn from our planetary life and are "occultly absorbed" by the Master: the substance of the glamour, purified and freed from all that conditioned it on the planetary astral plane, and with only the pure essence retained, sets the law in motion which draws this purified remainder into the cosmic astral plane.

> Constantly, therefore, this great circulatory process goes on, demonstrating anew the essential synthesis underlying all life—human, planetary, systemic and cosmic; it reveals also that the Law of Attraction, the Law of Magnetic Work, and the cosmic Law of Synthesis are three aspects of one Law for which, as yet, we have no name.[1]

The Sacral and Base of Spine Centres

From the Hierarchical viewpoint, the Sacral centre exists as a vehicle for energy distribution via the entire etheric body of humanity. Its purpose is to help precipitate divine Ideas, the Plan, into active manifestation. It vitalises the aspirational zeal generated by humanity to help them accomplish desired tasks to conclusion. The energisation serves to aspire and to lift up humanity's thoughts and devotion to higher domains, producing divinely ordained idealism that effectively can 'take the Kingdom of 'God' by storm'. Unfortunately, such energisation also stimulates fanaticism, war-like aggression, overt sexuality, and many of the worst traits of the desire-mind of humanity. Such effects, like all energisation, therefore is a double-edged sword. Because of humanity's sensual bias and materialistic focus, the effect of such stimulation is highly pronounced in human society. It has produced much of the social turmoil, racial tension, bigotry, predilection towards mass emotional movements. There are sports gatherings, political or religious induced frenzy over concepts, zealous attraction to movie and music stars, indoctrination to consumer products and fads (based upon the power of mass-marketing), the pornography industry, and military aggression between nations.

It is difficult to separate the Sacral and Solar Plexus forms of activities, between that is desire based and those feeding the emotions - so intricately entwined are they in our modern societies. Hierarchy's challenge lies in how to energise humanity without arousing the above-mentioned attributes. Humanity's general desire and emotional bodies are no longer to be stimulated, rather, the development of wisdom is the focus. Humanity have come to the stage where its adolescence needs to be superseded by mature adult forms of activity. Careful placement of

1 A.A. Bailey, *The Rays and The Initiations,* (Lucis Publishing Company, New York), 403-4.

disciples to act as energy vectors rightly steering the desire-emotional currents of humanity have been incorporated into Hierarchy's planning, but the gains of the work takes a long time to show. The elements of rightful change have a significant counter current opposing it. Here also the dark brotherhood find it easy to stimulate humanity's base desires via all their levers of power by controlling governments, the world of finance, the mass media and movie industries.

The Sacral centre is the mechanism whereby the five types of *prāṇas,* as directed by Hierarchy, can be conveyed to appropriately, rightly vitalise and cleanse humanity's desire and thought impulses. Its functioning appropriates energies to the entire body of manifestation.

The sixth Ray energy (specifically when interrelated with that from the Heart centre) is utilised in the process of magnetic healing,[2] because in its pure form this Ray conveys the vital energy from cosmic astral sources that vitalises and invigorates the form. The hands are used to convey the *prāṇas* that cleanse obstructing energies and disease bearing influences. Similarly, upon a vast scale, the martial energies utilised by the sixth Ray Ashrams (when rightly directed) work to effectively cleanse the astral scourges afflicting humanity.

The astral plane, the onus of expression for the sixth Ray, is an illusion. As stated, the heavens and hells of the various religions are created by the sum total of the image-making faculty and desires of humanity, thus as disciples learn to control those faculties so the attributes of this plane vanish for them, except as a domain for service. This control is effected by the Initiation process wherein psychicism, emotions, and glamour are eliminated. As stated by D.K. concerning this plane:

> It embodies the great creative work of humanity down the ages, and is the product of the 'false' imagination and the work of the lower psychic nature. Its instrument of creative work is the sacral and the solar plexus centres. When the energies, finding expression through these two centres, have been transmuted and carried to the throat and heart by advancing humanity, then the foremost people of the race will know that the astral plane has no true existence; they will then work

2 A.A. Bailey, *Esoteric Healing,* 642-644.

> free from its impression, and the task of freeing humanity from the thraldom of its own creation will proceed apace. In the meantime a group of disciples is being slowly built up (of which this second group is a part and in which it can play an important function, and occupy a key position), which can gradually aid in the task of dispelling the great illusion and can act also as a bridging group so that those who are freeing themselves from glamour can find their way into the vortex of influence wielded by the group, empowered thus to work. Then three things can happen:
>
> 1. Those who thus approach the group will find their efforts to live free from glamour greatly helped and intensified by the group assistance.
> 2. They will swell the number of those so working and hasten the processes of dissipation.
> 3. The Hierarchy will be enabled then to work more closely upon earth and to approach much nearer to mankind.[3]

Despite the formidable obstacles, Hierarchy's relative success is seen in the fact that we are now entering the epoch wherein the rules of discipleship will become commonly understood. Here lies the major onus of the future activities of the sixth Ray disciples of the Chohan Jesus. He presides not just over the sixth Ray Ashrams, but also oversees the path of aspiration and that of all probationary disciples preparing to enter into full Hierarchical service. Whilst they work out how to master its substance, the astral domain is the service arena for them. The activities of the Ashrams not yet formed come under Jesus's general jurisdiction because they are still largely emerging from the Watery domain into the light of day. Hinted in all of these statements then is the premise that Hierarchy now manifests the forms of service work that will eventually produce the ending of the rule of the astral Waters upon our planet. Having reached their apogee in planetary evolution the turbid and murky sixth Ray forms of activity must evaporate as they are being refined.

3 A.A. Bailey, *The Externalisation of the Hierarchy,* 40. The reader should correlate the information I present with the much earlier information given in *The Externalisation of the Hierarchy,* as my purpose is to update and expand upon D.K.'s writings.

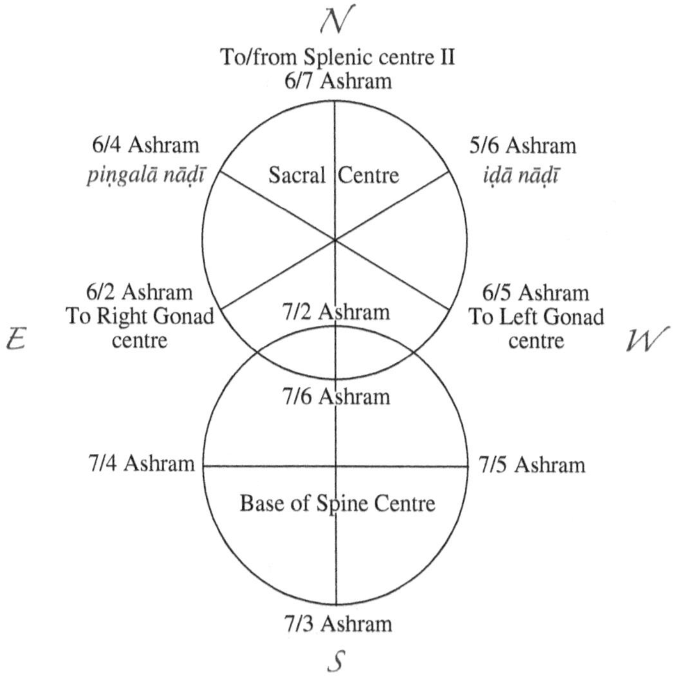

Figure 17. The Hierarchical Base of Spine and Sacral centres

The petals of the Hierarchical Sacral centre, that bear the onus of the above forms of service work, are mainly constituted of the currently established sixth Ray Ashrams. The main explanation of the attributes of these petals, and of all the other *chakras* discussed in this section, will be found in the earlier volumes of this series, especially the information in Volume 5A, where the attributes of the feminine wrathful deities (Īśvarī) are explained. In the present context the Īśvarī refer to the karmic factors (embodied by the *devas)* that Hierarchy use to unfold their plan. The interested reader can transpose the correspondences between the process of conversion of negative *saṃskāras* confronting the *yogin* to those generated by humanity *en masse,* and which Hierarchy (the planetary *yogin*) must process and convert.

Figure 17 shows the interrelation between the Sacral and Base of Spine centres, Hierarchically speaking. For the Sacral centre this concerns the 6/2, 6/4, 6/5, 6/7, 5/6 and 7/6 Ashrams. The Base of Spine centre's activities are governed by the 7/2, 7/3, 7/4 and 7/5 Ashrams.

The seventh Ray Ashrams embody the attributes of the Base of Spine centre, hence they support the activities of all the other Ashrams, being the foundation for the movement of planetary *kuṇḍalinī* to the Head lotus (Shambhala). Being the harbingers of the Aquarian age, they therefore effectively precipitate the externalisation of this centre by grounding its activities upon the physical plane. The interrelation between the 7/6 and 7/2 Ashrams incorporates the conjoined petals between the Base of Spine (7/2) and Sacral centres (7/6). This allows the vitalisation of humanity with Hierarchical purpose via the activity of the seventh Ray of Ceremonial Magic. Hierarchical Power is thereby materialised upon the physical domain. Concerning the effect of the coming into manifestation of the seventh Ray, D.K. has this to say (where the word 'him' refers to humanity):

> The force and the effect of the seventh ray influence will, however, reveal to him the magical work, and the next twenty five hundred years will bring about so much change and make possible the working of so many so-called "miracles" that even the outer appearance of the world will be profoundly altered; the vegetation and the animal life will be modified and developed, and much that is latent in the forms of both kingdoms will be brought into expression through the freer flow and the more intelligent manipulation of the energies which create and constitute all forms. The world has been changed beyond belief during the past five hundred years, and during the next two hundred years the changes will be still more rapid and deep-seated, for the growth of the intellectual powers of man is gathering momentum, and Man, the Creator, is coming into possession of His powers.[4]

Also, speaking more directly concerning the nature of the seventh Ray :

> The seventh ray is one of the direct lines along which this first ray energy can travel and here again is another reason for its appearance at this time, because, in the releasing of the life into the new and improved forms, the old ways of living, of culture and of civilisation have to be destroyed or modified. This is, all of it, the work of the

4 A.A. Bailey, *Esoteric Psychology I*, 83.

> first Ray of Will expressing itself predominantly at this present time through the seventh Ray of Organisation and Relationship.[5]
>
> One of the major characteristics of the seventh ray disciple is his intense practicality. He works upon the physical plane with a constant and steady objective in order to bring about results which will be effective in determining the forms of the coming culture and civilisation; towards the end of the seventh ray cycle he will work equally hard to perpetuate what he has brought about. He wields force in order to build the forms which will meet his requirements and does this more scientifically than do disciples on other rays.[6]
>
> The keynote of the seventh ray disciple is "Radiatory Activity." Hence the emergence in world thought of certain new ideas — mental radiation or telepathy, the radiatory use of heat, the discovery of radium. All this connotes seventh ray activity.
>
> The divine principle with which the seventh ray humanity will be mainly concerned is that of life as it expresses itself through the medium of the etheric body. It is for this reason that we find a growing interest in the nature of vitality; the function of the glands is being studied and before long their major function as vitality generators will be noted. Esoterically, they are regarded as externalisations upon the physical plane of force centres in the etheric body and their aliveness or their lack of activity are indicative of the condition of those centres. The shift of the world interest is also into the realm of economics which is definitely the realm of life sustenance. Much is, therefore, bound to happen in all these spheres of interest, and once the etheric body becomes an established scientific fact and the centres — major and minor — are recognised as the foci of all energy as it expresses itself through the human body upon the physical plane, we shall see a great revolution take place in medicine, in diet and in the handling of daily life activity. This will produce great changes in the mode of work and labour and above everything else in the leisure activities of the race.[7]

The *7/2 Ashram* carries the gain of all seventh Ray activity in the material domain and projects it upwards, with the assistance of the sixth

5 A.A. Bailey, *Destiny of the Nations,* 121.

6 Ibid., 126.

7 Ibid., 133-134.

Ray impetus, so that the Head centre can be rightly empowered in its ability to control material plane phenomena. It is an extension of the Virgoan petal[8] of the Hierarchical Splenic centre I, conveying the Earthy *prāṇas* of Hierarchy needing processing, which it disseminates via the rest of the seventh Ray Ashrams. Linking directly to the second Ray Ashrams ensures that the second Ray purpose conditions all magical work accomplished in building the Temples of Deity in this new cycle. Empowered thoughts then manifest that also build the edifices and technological innovations that vitalise humanity with Nature's beneficence. Thus new cycles of activity are initiated in all fields of human activity whereby the Mother's garden can flourish with the benefits brought to it by rightly ordained scientists and technocrats. Eventually the etheric fields governing all of Life will be studied.

The statement provided by D.K. for this Ashram is:

> Choose well thy workers. Love them all. Pick six to do thy will. Remain the seventh in the east. Yet call the world to enter into that which thou shalt build. Blend all together in the will of God. Quality... power to cooperate.[9]

The Master of this Ashram leads the sum of the seventh Ray department, hence must carefully choose those that are to guide the policies assisting humanity. The objective is to lead all to the Initiation path, and only those who can pass the necessary testings can form the inner council of decision making. Because the seventh Ray represents the forces of materialising power, so the mode of delivery of the Initiation process (the outward expression of the new temples of Divinity that will be built) falls via their Ray, as far as physical plane demonstration is concerned. They anchor the Will that will externalise the energies of the 'Mind of God'. All of humanity must in time learn the ways of Initiation. All Ray Ashrams are integrated ('blended together') in the one common purpose, so that the 'will of God', the Plan for this epoch,

---

8 Virgo represents the keen, quick, mercurial mind that governs the forms of activity in the womb of Nature whereby the new forms of divinity are impregnated, to later produce a fruitful harvest in the fields of Life from human civilisation.

9 A.A. Bailey, *Esoteric Psychology I,* 86.

can manifest. All disciples must learn to express their right quotient of that Will so that planetary liberation is possible. The seventh Ray Ashrams also blend *deva* and human interrelationships, grounding the Will of deity in order to produce the perfected manifestation of the grand design in all departments of Life. The seventh Ray incorporates all the Rays via cyclic activity, here reinforced with the unifying, integrating energy and wisdom of the second Ray. Together they will build the attributes of the New Jerusalem, the externalised Hierarchy upon earth.

By summing up the directive Love of the second sub-Ray Ashrams, this seventh Ray Ashram meditatively cooperates with all other Ray lives, ensuring that what is to be accomplished manifests as ordained as the cycles turn. By blending the work of the seventh Ray Ashrams they support the development of wisdom in humanity via revealing the nature of the Mysteries discovered in the temples of Initiation through rightly ordained ritual. Therein they teach the way east to the Heart of Life to those that have passed the testings upon the way.

The *7/3 Ashram* governs the southern, Earthy petal of the Base of Spine centre, expressing thereby the Earthy *prāṇas* from Shambhala. It empowers and rightly organises the workers that toil with their hands in all aspects of civilisation. (They represent those who are esoterically blind and must be taught and shown how to rightly act.) It produces the power of clear, cogent, constructive thought concerning the material domain in all human situations and aspects of society. Hence it rightly organises labour and establishes a correct view concerning the common plight of humanity, to work for the establishment of a plenitude for the all. Rectification of social injustices upon the international scene and overcoming political tyranny are the focus of many members of this Ashram. All of the new edifices and bulwarks of civilisation must be correctly thought out and implemented, allowing the residual dark (Earthy) *prāṇas* to be screened out via Splenic centre II processing. The many forms of evil doing (especially that governed by avarice) have no role to play in the new world scenario and must be defeated at this basic level of human interrelationships and of governance. Politically therefore, an aim is to work to transform the United Nations to try to make it more representative of the needs of the bulk of humanity so that poverty can be eliminated. Proper resource sharing will be a must.

Ideas concerning the attributes of a union of nations was foremost in the mind of the 7/3 Master, Nicholas Roerich, who formed this Ashram at the beginning of the twentieth century, and promulgated the 'Banner of Peace' to the League of Nations, before the second World War interrupted Hierarchical plans.

Both the 7/3 and 7/5 Ashrams share similar forms of activities, as there is much overlapping of functions between the membership of the Ashrams. The degree of Initiation of the various members must also be taken into account. The higher the degree attained, the more their literary output, executive decision making, and high esoteric logic become hallmarks of their work. The Throat centre facilitates the study of the variegated attributes found throughout Nature, as Nature's domain is ruled by the third Ray. Also, the *deva* kingdom principally manifests via the fifth Ray and the seventh Ray Ritualistic methodology, to produce the multitudinous varieties of things found in Nature. Therefore, in the seventh Ray Ashrams will be found many that will have a natural predilection to open doorways between the human and *deva* kingdoms, once the emphasis upon scientific materialism in humanity is curtailed and Nature's finer forces are studied instead.

The statement given to those of this Ray is:

> Sit in the centre and the east as well. Move not from there. Send out thy force to do thy will and gather back thy forces. Use well the power of thought. Sit still. Quality...power to think.[10]

Because of the Earthy orientation of all the seventh Ray Ashrams, the 7/3 Ashram in many ways represents the focal point of all their endeavours, hence the statement to 'Sit in the centre and the east as well'. The 7/3 Ray directs the combined activity of their work in the field of human affairs. Consequently the 7/2 and 7/3 Ray lines work to integrate the *suṣumṇā* expression of Hierarchy, helping to ground the power of Shambhala into the formed realms. They actively disseminate the output of the intelligence that awakens human minds, preparing them to take their third Initiations. The 7/3 Ray expresses the Mind of Deity by way of cooperation with the *deva* builders, the creative

10 Ibid., 86-7.

agencies in Nature. The entire edifice of mind built by the dark forces must be shattered thereby, as humanity learns to 'use well the power of thought' to overcome their materialistic incentives. The Hierarchical *maṇḍala* will consequently expand as humanity increasingly masters the approaches to Mind and all aspects of the form nature by developing the meditative ability to 'sit still'. This statement does not mean to be immobile, but rather to be meditatively focussed in all that is done. The 7/3 disciple must counter the natural tendency to be exceedingly active in physical plane affairs (because of practical know-how and organisational skills) with ritualised times of meditation. The meditation-Mind must then flow through to the active service arena. All who are materially focussed must similarly learn to work in this manner.

The *7/5 Ashram* processes the *prāṇas* associated with the western gate of the Base of Spine centre, representing outward service into the field of the Fiery *manasic* whirlpool of ideas that is humanity. Here can be seen abuses of personal power of many over the masses, and wrongly directed empirical and dogmatic scientific zeal. The power of scientific investigation comes under its sway, assisting emotional based thought to be dissipated in the materialistic epoch we reside in. The exponent of this Ray, however, must take care not to fall into the trap of cold, non-compassionate thought. Logic must be stoked by the wisdom from the heart.

The purpose of this Ashram is to 'reveal the mind of God',[11] thus of the mode of action of the Lords at Shambhala.[12] To organise human minds so that their thoughts and ideologies correctly reflect the compassionate stance of the Lords of Life is a difficult chore. Hierarchy therefore directly supports this Ashram in its endeavour to reveal the context of the divine Mind. The entire symbolism of the ritualised ceremonies provided in the Masonic tradition exists to reveal this Mind. (This tradition, and the great architectural achievements of the past, therefore are also a product of all the seventh Ray Ashrams.) The revelations concern the nature of the expression of the building work of the 'Grand Architect of the Universe'. This implicates the way things are ordained in Hierarchy for humanity

11 A.A. Bailey, *Esoteric Psychology I*, 87. The statement for this Ashram being: 'Watch well thy thought. Enter at will into the mind of God. Pluck thence the power, the plan, the part to play. Reveal the mind of God. Quality...mental power'.

12 Ibid.

to develop and to emulate. Ritualistic or cyclic activity is the key to the proper control of all of the vicissitudes of mind. It is the basis to the organisational power of the seventh Ray line. Cyclic activity produces power over the Fiery fields in the streams of consciousness. Ritual can exorcise dark ideologies and wilful projections of mind from otherwise sound arenas of thought. The converted *saṃskāras* can then be directed to Splenic centre I. Such ritual to control the forces of the mind is also the key to the awakening of a *yogin's* psychic power.

The *7/4 Ashram* controls the rhythms of the Airy Element from the eastern direction of the Base of Spine centre. It therefore projects Hierarchy's general *prāṇic* vitalisation to the Inner Round, constituting instructions concerning the way of beautifying the manifesting civilisation with noble ideals and refinement of thoughts. The purpose is to illumine and to awaken the sleeping ones in our societies by showing them grandeurs of beauty. The gain in bright colouration from humanity's general mental-emotional response must be processed by all of the workers of the seventh Ray department constituting this Base *chakra*. The 7/4 Ashram cyclically organises the relationships between all of the various factors and groupings of common humanity so that the desired outcome is eventually gained. This represents the power of the seventh Ray to overcome gross *saṃskāras*.

The statement for the 7/4 Ray Ashram is:

> See all parts enter into purpose. Build towards beauty, brother Lord. Make all colours bright and clear. See to the inner glory. Build the shrine well. Use care. Quality...revelation of the beauty of God.[13]

This Ashram works to unify the disparate parts of human society, producing harmonious peace. All are encouraged to reflect the attributes of divinity, facilitating the potency of the Throne of 'God' to be projected into physical manifestation. The wondrous beauty of the new age civilisation can then appear. This necessitates all Ray aspects constituting humanity to be clarified and made radiant, whereby the muddied auric colourings are transformed. All attributes of Mind can then govern human affairs. The way that establishes the glory of the adytum of the new temples of Initiation created by the seventh Ray Ashrams, cooperating

13 Ibid.

with the *deva* builders, can then manifest. The reflected energies from Deity via the 7/4 Ashram will 'build the shrine well'.

Great care must be used in training the candidates for Initiation and those that are to officiate in the temples of the Mother of the World, by working directly with Her *deva* agents. Inevitably, the beauty of the revelation of the Plan will awaken in the heart of humanity, once all of the testings for Initiation have been accomplished.

The 7/4 Ashram vitalises the square of physical plane activity, hence magical accomplishments are their forte, for they ritualistically control the flow of *prāṇas* from the four ethers. They are thus at the forefront of Hierarchy's endeavours to exoterically demonstrate the reality of the ethers and of the consequent new advances in technology.

They must take great care in all their undertakings as they build the shrine, the inner sanctum, to the 'temple of God'. Mantra and *deva,* colour and form, must be wielded so that the inner glory veiled by that shrine can be revealed. The dark brotherhood colourations obscuring or hindering the work must consequently be converted to light. The fabric of the mind and the edifices of our civilisations should not be built with steely greys and sombre hues. The general tone of the hues must be cleansed from subtle discolourations and aberrations of motif, the gain directed to higher domains. This happens after the grosser Watery, Fiery, and Earthy *prāṇas* have been cleansed of their dross by means of the activity of the general seventh Ray dispensation working via Splenic centre II.

The seventh Ray Ashrams work to project the needed energies from the Heart centre right into every aspect of the material domain. Thus the highest ideas from Hierarchy can be built into all human constructs. They will reveal thereby the beauty of what transpires from the inner realms in a way that all can be inspired. The new temples of Initiation to be built will reflect such divinity, not just in the material constructs, but more so with rituals that will esoterically vivify the human floral display by directly invoking *devas* to manifest their harmonising, healing songs.

The *7/6 Ashram* manifests the complete potency of Hierarchical power in the realms of form and fields of desire. It interrelates the energies of the Sacral centre with those of the Base of Spine centre and works in close cooperation with the 7/2 Ray purpose. Hence it helps project the effects of the seventh Ray (constituting the Base of Spine activity) in the material domain upwards to the higher centres. This Ashram is the gatekeeper of the south, processing some of the worst attributes of humanity's emotional murk, religious zealotry, hatreds, and avaricious ambitions. To do so those of this Ashram must 'stay in the east', in the domain of their Hearts, and not be swayed by emotional considerations, hence the statement for this Ray is:

> Stay in the east. The five have given thee a friendly Word. I, the sixth, tell thee to use it on the dead. Revive the dead. Build forms anew. Guard well that Word. Make all men seek it for themselves. Quality... power to vivify.[14]

In the east they are receptive to the words, instructions from the sum of Hierarchy, as to the way of manifesting divinity via Love. From the east they are energised with the potency of the cosmic astral Waters, which can then help vitalise the combined Sacral/Base of Spine interrelation. The doctrines are focussed via the sixth Ray ruling the Sacral potency, which then informs the Base of Spine centre Ashrams in general via the 7/6-7/2 interrelation. The instructions provided are to awaken the sleeping ones, those entombed in the crypts of their materialistic concerns ('the dead'). Theirs is the rhythm of imposed military or religious power affecting the domains of human activity where often very little vibrant light can penetrate. They are to be awakened to higher perspectives. Esoteric secrets, however, can only be revealed to the worthy, those willing to generate the efforts to gain the most precious jewels of revelation. Hence the new temples of revelation must be built to provide the mechanism whereby seekers can gain Hierarchy's guidance.

The minor Inner Round *chakras* differentiate lesser expressions of Ashramic concern in relation to the many human forms of activity. Here the interrelated 7/2 and 7/6 Ashrams (and the seventh Ray in general) work to rightly organise all such activity for aspirants to the mysteries of Hierarchical living. They are the lesser spiritual builders that are the great mass of the workers who toil with their hands making the appliances and edifices of all human livingness.

People's attitudes must be turned away from *saṃsāric* pursuits and death-like self-glorifying attributes. Human enslavement to separative,

---

14 Ibid.

selfish, devious, malicious activities will be finally broken with the help of the might and travail of the conscientious 7/6 workers. The Watery *prāṇas* of predatory evil can then be relegated to the *eighth sphere*, and the cleaner *prāṇas* directed to Splenic centre I. The younger members of this Ashram must guard against the entrenchment of zealous or militaristic attitudes, wrong magical practices and sensual pursuits.

When the 7/3 Ashram is appropriately formed and working in conjunction with the 7/6-7/2 Ashramic interrelationship and assisted by the first Ray Ashrams of the Hierarchical shield, then can planetary *kuṇḍalinī* arise to awaken humanity from their spiritual slumber. This will eventually cause the exoteric appearance of the Kingdom of 'God' (Shambhala) on earth via the activity of the externalised Hierarchy, hence producing the long planned planetary awakening.

The *6/2 Ashram* represents the petal of the Sacral centre wherein its energies are directed to the right Gonad centre (which governs strong sexual desire) of humanity. This translates as intensity of feeling, even fanaticism to the path one has chosen to follow. (In any field of Life, not just the sensual.) Effectively, the right Gonad centre is concerned with loving sexual interrelations, the subjective forces that build the child to be. For humanity such a 'child' will be the new Hierarchical dispensation, which spurns the materialism of the present epoch. In earlier cycles the same energy tended to generate religious zealots, as well as wise followers of their faith. This Ashram receives the major Watery *(piṇgalā)* energisation (of the 'thumb') from Splenic centre I via its Taurean petal. Those of this Ashram thus have to be careful not to become raging bulls in their activities, but rather must manifest the Taurean wisdom.[15] This impetus then stimulates the sum of the Ashrams governing the Sacral centre.

This Ray manifests not only via religious fields, but also via the activists that envision a more utopian lifestyle and civilisation than presently offered. The 6/2 Ray disciples will rigorously fight against perceived injustice in any chosen field, often with fanatical determination

15 The sign Taurus exoterically manifests the blind onrushing desire of the masses, or else it clothes the divine thought, and embodies the functions of the all-seeing Eye. Principally, it directs the Watery *prāṇas* (the field of desire) to the general Inner Round *piṇgalā* pool of humanity. (Here accessed via the right Gonad centre.)

and incomplete logic. Even if carefully considered actions manifest, there generally will be an impetuosity, or intensity to carry out the plan, because of the difficulty to control the inherent martial energy of this Ray. The disciples will give their all to build the image of that desired–directing all thoughts to a visioned goal and rejecting all other opinions or alternatives. Their devotional attributes facilitate work in organised structures as team players, religiously, or in alternative groups dedicated to new ideas. Often they will manifest as impractical idealists, envisioning a too grandiose utopian scenario to battle for, before the right conditions have eventuated. Many valiantly try to help cleanse the repository of the murky, swampy, emotional thoughts of humanity by choosing certain mental-emotions from the morass to rectify.

The sixth Ray always tends towards fanatical and zealous religious attitudes, however, the subsidiary second Ray of Love-Wisdom of the 6/2 Ray produces perceptive insights into the nature of *saṃsāric* squalor governing the earth. Thus they often scorn the material domain, rejecting its allurements by becoming monks and *yogins*. Wisdom, however, is to be rightly evoked to comprehend the value of the manifesting phenomena. The concepts of 'God', Hierarchy, and *nirvāṇa,* the heavenly abodes to which the religious aspire, consequently become overwhelmingly attractive. Those of this Ashram generally need to wisely balance their natural zealotry with concepts of the good that can be built into the material domain that will make a heaven upon the earth. For humanity this necessitates emotional control via a rightly orientated religious worship of the divinity inherent throughout Nature's superabundance.

The statement for this Ashram is:

> Why do you turn your back upon the sphere of the earth? Is it too small, too poor? Why kick it as a ball upon a playing field? Quality... spurning that which is not desired.[16]

The powerful Sacral stimulation of those of this Ashram causes them to be martyrs to a cause, extreme *yogins,* anchorites, fanatics. Their desire to quickly achieve and to master, to atone for former wrong doing, produces many testings upon the path of discipleship. Cyclic addiction in past lives to sensual pursuits, martial activities and strong sexuality have

16 A.A. Bailey, *Esoteric Psychology I,* 81.

produced many strong *saṃskāras* to master. The logic of mind/Mind must be developed above all in order to properly analyse the nature of desire, the problem of sexuality and the results of fanaticism. They must learn that all is divine, even the form, and thereby gain the wisdom that liberates. Concepts can then be formulated that will provide a cogent comprehension of the nature of the materialism that is rejected. By way of the development of Mind they therefore gain access to Hierarchical domains as they master *saṃsāra*. Not easy is such accomplishment for those of this Ray. The intensity of the accompanying Love that is the leitmotiv of their Ray will, once they have found the right path, propel them quickly to the sources of cosmic Waters. Compassionate understanding directed by the victors of this Ray line can then flood 'that which is not desired' (those addicted to the fields of desire) with the liberating Waters of Life.

Concerning the influence of the sixth Ray in general, D.K. states:

> The sixth ray devotee is far more abstract and mystical in his work and thought, and seldom has any real understanding of the right relation between form and energy. He thinks almost entirely in terms of quality and pays little attention to the material side of life and the true significance of substance as it produces phenomena. He is apt to regard matter as evil in nature and form as a limitation, and only lays the emphasis upon soul consciousness as of true importance. It is this failure to work intelligently, and I would like to add, lovingly with substance and so bring it into right relation with the dense outer form that has made the last two thousand years produce so disastrously a mismanaged world and which has brought the population of the planet into its present serious condition. The unintelligent work upon the physical plane, carried forward by those influenced by the sixth ray force, has led to a world which is suffering from cleavage in as true a sense as an individual person can suffer from a "split personality." The lines of demarcation between science and religion are a striking instance of this and have been clearly and forcefully drawn.[17]

The energies and teachings Hierarchy provide are similar to the way a parent educates a child. The parent waits to see if the instruction has been properly understood, or if it needs to be continuously repeated

17 *Destiny of the Nations*, 126-127.

in differing ways until the lesson has been assimilated. The sixth Ray disciples are specifically geared to rectify child-like or adolescent behaviour in human groups because they manifest a similar Watery (emotional) energy. Once the lessons have been taught, the child can then learn other aspects to gain further comprehension. Thus humanity progresses. Multifarious teachings are needed to be absorbed before people learn the lessons that the way of Love provides. Affectionate, loving, socially beneficent activities then follow.

The *6/4 Ashram* governs the *prāṇic* flow of the *piṇgalā nāḍī* to the Solar Plexus centre, which lays the Watery foundation for that centre. Standing as a bridge between the Sacral and Solar Plexus centres, those of this Ashram battle considerably with desires and attachment, not just against *saṃsāric* concerns, but over noble ideas and idealisations. They then battle against the common glamours developed by humanity, to show them the way to wisdom. The fourth Ray endeavours to produce harmony in the midst of strife, whilst the sixth Ray intensifies the attributes of the warring sides, hence to produce the peace that leads to the Initiation path is difficult. To do so they must project *antaḥkaraṇas* for humanity to follow, away from their lower sensual natures and desires, towards higher aspirations that produce the liberation coming from an awakened Heart centre. (The natural course for the *piṇgalā* flow.) In doing so meditative peace must be obtained, the vacillating emotions stilled and the forces of the Heart centre evoked.

The statement for this Ashram is:

> Why battle thus with all that is around? Seek ye not peace? Why stand between the forces of night and day? Why thus unmoved and calm, untired and unafraid? Quality...endurance and fearlessness.[18]

Endurance is needed to conquer martial energy and to fearlessly teach others to do similarly, as there is often considerable opposition from emotional or zealous thinkers from other religious beliefs or philosophies. Those of this Ray embody refined attributes of the emotions so they can educate the sensually desire-driven masses, hence once the sword of right discrimination has been developed they use it against their brethren, to teach them the way that overcomes

18 A.A. Bailey, *Esoteric Psychology I*, 81.

strife. The work to rightly inspire aspirants concerns stimulating them to seek the divinity in all and to aspire to serve the common good. Consequently, pleasing religious and devotional constructs are built, providing inspiration concerning greater harmony, beauty and productivity. This work brings into manifestation the raincloud of spiritually desirous things. Thus is expressed high religious ideals for common humanity to follow, and the endeavour to make these ideals a practical reality within a society.

The field of activity necessitates teaching humanity the methods of controlling the emotions to develop the needed calmness and spiritual fearlessness to overcome all. In doing so they battle to stem humanity's emotional tide. The grosser forms of emotions, desires and sensuality must be converted into devotion to noble causes, aspiration to high ideals, and the idealism to create the beautiful things envisioned from Hierarchical sources.

As this Ashram incorporates the general *piṇgalā prāṇas* from humanity, it allows the Initiates to further refine humanity's desire-concepts and aspirational thoughts, helping to engender high aspiration, beauty, harmony and prosperity for all. The focus is upon religions and philanthropic organisations, as by being directly along the sixth Ray this Ashram is a mainstay of higher religious sentiment. They are asked as to why they 'battle thus with all that is around? Seek you not peace? Why stand between the forces of night and day?' The 'forces of night and day' represent the duality in the mind of the religionist, who possesses such concepts of heaven and hell, where people may go to either. Concepts such as 'God' versus the Devil, *saṃsāra* versus *śūnyatā,* the forces of light verses darkness, come to the fore here. All of the statements for the sixth Ray Ashrams begin with questions because they need to develop the reasoning mind above all. This will allow those of this Ray to comprehend the nature of such dualism. The forces of night also represent life in *saṃsāra* wherein the attributes to be mastered are developed, specifically here the grey *prāṇas* channelled in the *piṇgalā nāḍī,* whilst those of 'day' represent the awakened attributes of Hierarchy.

An earlier aberrant version of the imposition of harmony in the midst of strife via zealous religious idealism was seen in the type of *missionary* activity of the past few centuries. The aboriginal populations of the world were conquered by military might, then had the gospel of hell fire and brimstone, the devil, etc., thrust upon them in the name of the man of peace who 'died for their sins'. Younger members of this 6/4 Ashram generally develop the endurance and fearlessness characteristic of devotional religions that will engender martyrdom, or seeing a project through, generally said to be 'in the name of God', no matter what the odds or costs to the individual.

The *6/7 Ashram* stands at the northern gate of the Sacral centre that directs and receives the flow of Watery-Earthy *prāṇas* from Splenic centre II. The integrity of this Ashram is problematic, and indeed for the entire *suṣumṇā* line of the Sacral-Base of Spine centre integration (6/7, 7/6, 7/2 and 7/3 Ashrams), because they must handle and endeavour to transform the worst *prāṇas* of sex magic attributes that many of its members previously generated. We have marital aggression, potent sexuality and materialising power. (Such attributes becoming more potent and materialistic in the 7/6 Ashram.) The Watery emanations processed by the 6/7 Ashram are those of the astral plane (the 'sixth great sphere'), its heaven and hell states as generated by humanity. Strong desires, attachments and glamours abound, often the most fanatical, and intense emotional *prāṇas* that humanity generates.

Once the egregious aspects of the members of this Ashram have been mastered, then they become specialists that know how to arrest the flow of the muddied Waters, or to direct them to their rightful destination. Consequently, the injunction to the 6/7 Ashram provided by D.K. are the questions:

> Can you arrest the waters of the sixth great sphere? Can you stem the flood? Can you recover both the raven and the dove? Can you, the Fish, swim free? Quality...overcoming the waters of the emotional nature.[19]

The raven and the dove in this context refer to the attributes of the dark and white Hierarchies, as well as to the transformation of the *prāṇas* of the *iḍā* (the raven) and the *piṇgalā* (the dove) *nāḍīs*. These are the *prāṇic* qualities of the two main *nāḍīs* originating at the Sacral centre and directed to the other *chakras* for processing. Their main qualities are thus to be 'recovered' (comprehended) so that eventually the consciousness swimming in the emotional Waters is

19 Ibid.

freed from attachment to the objects of desire. It also relates to laying the groundwork for the attainment of the first Initiation (the Raven), and the second (the dove) for humanity.

The 'sixth great sphere' refers to the Sacral centre (the sixth centre) and the astral plane in general. Difficult is the work to control the flow of murky, Watery *prāṇas* to and from Splenic centre II. Much recycling of *prāṇas* proceeds from one centre to the next in order to lighten the murk and to eventually clarify the Waters. The energies of the Mind must be developed to do so, because only the mind/Mind can properly rationalise the errors of emotional thinking, to transform *kāma-manas* into pure *manas*. Many incarnations, cycles of activity, are needed to do so by the disciple and the world's Initiates. Indeed, is it possible to 'stem the flood' of emotionality continuously generated by humanity? Vast and most difficult is the task, hence it is easy to see that when disciples develop occult knowledge in this Ray they can easily fall victim to their lower natures and undergo sex magic rituals, or abuse of ecclesiastical power, or of any organisation they direct. Hence the task of the disciple in this Ray Ashram, 'the Fish', is to learn to 'swim' free from the assaults of the lower nature and from the flood of Watery energies generated by humanity. The disciple must learn to control this emotional tide and so rightly direct it. Aspects that need recycling from the combined activities of the sixth and seventh Ray lines can be directed to Splenic centre II for further processing. The Waters from that centre can then be rightly organised and directed to the respected Ashrams so that they can process them and thereby share the burden of the workload. The cyclic expression of the law of the good within fields of Logoic Desire then produces a power base for the triumph of the Lords of Life.

The work also concerns instilling sound ethical values amongst our urban masses, via establishing organisations and groups geared towards devotedly helping the impoverished and needy. People need to be inspired to envision higher ideals via various social media, movies, television, the internet, and to galvanise the masses politically.

In this Ashram we also find many zealous, charismatic, and powerful individuals in the field of religion that hold sway over the many in their congregations and religious institutions. All of the sixth Ray Ashrams are naturally concerned with the field of religion, or else they work in fields directly related to the organisation of the masses along desirable lines. Sometimes glamour producing occupations hold members of these Ashrams in thrall.

Concerning my reference to 'sex magic' above, which for the members of the dark brotherhood is but the entrance degree for higher forms of activity associated with sorcery, I wish to elucidate somewhat a comment made by D.K.

> The Dark or Materialistic Forces correspond in their entirety to the energies of the sacral centre of the planet, dealing with the generation of forms, and their work is to keep the direction of planetary interest upon the form side of divine expression. They are concerned with the life of matter itself, with its magical usage, and with that which is regarded as dark because, for humanity at its present stage of development, that divine aspect should have lost its major hold and should lie behind "in the darkness of that which has been outgrown and which has no further hold upon the son of God".[20]

D.K.'s reference to the Sacral centre here is of course inclusive with the Base of Spine centre, as the focus is upon that which sustains and ever works to perpetuate the conditionings found upon the material domain. The dark brotherhood use the 'energies of the sacral centre of the planet' for this purpose, however, because the *nāḍī* system stems from this centre, so the dark brotherhood can be found in all the centres, including being able to influence the Heart centre via its five non-sacred petals. Their main power base presently, however, is the Solar Plexus centre because from there they influence the glamours of humanity, keeping them forever bound to selfish, self-centred emotionality, directed to material plane concerns (whereby Sacral centre energies are evoked). This said, it should be understood that the control of all dark brotherhood activity comes from the Throat centre, where its Fiery energies are utilised by the sorcerers therein *(yogins* that have starved out all emotions and loving considerations) through the force of the will. The Throat centre is the higher correspondence of the Sacral centre.

The *6/5 Ashram* governs the *nāḍī* to the left Gonad centre of humanity, here associated with the mentally creative potency governing

20 A.A. Bailey, *The Externalisation of the Hierarchy,* 87-88.

scientific and religious activity, but producing a tendency towards fanaticism or dogmatism, as well as forms of zealotry. The 6/5 energies represent the basic desire-mind combination that is so misused by humanity, and which is the cause of their most heinous crimes against others in their society, of nations against other nations, and of humanity against all other kingdoms of Nature. This Ashram thus processes the volatile vagaries and intensities of the massed desires, selfish and prideful projections of humanity at any particular time. They confront the desire-mind energies in their most potent forms and must work to rightly educate people as to their glamour and illusion forming tendencies. The Watery *saṃskāras* developed by humanity are thus processed in a way that humanity are taught the foibles of their abusive emotions. This Ashram therefore has its finger on the pulse of the major energy streams governing the fiefdoms of the fickle thought life of the major social groupings.

To rightly convert this mess they focus upon the redeemable aspects of humanity's desire-mind, to generate the best outcomes. They impregnate truthful ideas, devotion and aspiration to high ideals within these thought-streams. Hierarchical mandates are articulated in a way that common people can clearly listen and learn from the presented logic. Therefore those of this Ashram incarnate into positions whereby the masses can be educated; such as journalists, writers on popular philosophic and scientific themes, teachers and the academically inclined religious preceptors.

The task of those in this Ashram relates to sieving the valuable sources of information and arenas of truth from the morass that abounds in our information age. The good and proper can then be circulated to the generalised Inner Round centres to stimulate humanity's creativity. Consequently those of this Ashram must teach people how to develop 'the power to detach'[21] from the tyranny of their own emotional bodies. This is partly accomplished by seeding the world's intelligentsia with religious feelings and insights of 'God' or divinity. However, the tendencies towards the martyr idealism or fanaticism based upon interpretations of scriptures must be countermanded.

21 A.A. Bailey, *Esoteric Psychology I*, 81. The statement being: 'See you not the God in all, the life in all, and love in all? Why separate yourself and leave behind the loved and the well-known? Quality...power to detach oneself'.

To see 'God in all' at first necessitates a scientific approach in absorbing all fields of Life, or a systemic study of the available religious or philosophic doctrines. Later the development of intuitive or meditative insights will allow direct perception of the real. Inevitably the grand design ('the life') and that which coherently integrates all into One will be discovered. The Love that underlies the happenings at any time will then be known. The tendencies towards fanaticism can make those of this Ray blindly detach in celibate, yogic, or monastic pursuits. They must yet learn to query why, what the purpose of it all is, hence zealotry must be replaced by scientific enquiry.

The 6/5 and 5/6 Ashrams cater specifically to the problems of the *kāma-manasic* impulses and attributes developed by average humanity, and the religious and scientific communities that meet their needs. They therefore direct *prāṇas* to the minor *chakras* of the Inner Round that represent the general mass of people. They have heralded the epoch of scientific materialism that has produced many atheistic scientists, who have effectively turned their belief that only the material world of forms exist into a religion. The scientists have thoroughly probed and analysed the minutiae of what constitutes the physical domain, as governed by the Inner Round *chakras*, but must yet turn their analytical eyes to the qualities and denizens of the higher centres.

The process of scientific discovery is, however, but a stage in transforming humanity's desire-mind (*kāma-manas*) *saṃskāras* into clear rational thought. *Kāma-manasic prāṇas* are well nigh ubiquitous. It is literally the child created via left Gonad centre activity. The desire-mind throttles humanity with their greatest woes, anxieties, fears, separative, selfish and competitive thinking. Such a list is virtually endless on the battlefield of desire. This battlefield provides the tests needed to overcome the Watery emotions, as well as the various forms of ambitious and mentalistic projections for material power and wealth. The elimination of such qualities is the service focus of these Ashrams, where the *saṃskāras* are transformed into the power of lofty thoughts and the idealism to appropriately change society.

The *5/6 Ashram* expresses the foundation of the *iḍā nāḍī* circulation, which conveys *manasic prāṇas*. Hence this Ashram helps develop and refine the context of mind developed via Sacral centre activity. Its Initiates lay the foundation for the evolution of Mind, as capable of being awakened by the world's intelligentsia, by fostering desire to work for the common good. Cooperative international institutions in the fields of science and technology, and within major philanthropic structures, are thereby developed. It produces a rigorous devotional application of the general scientific community to their pursuits in the various disciplines. Generally unbeknownst to them is their subjective response to Hierarchical impression. They engender the light of knowledge that overcomes the darkness of human ignorance. Similarly with the religiously inclined amongst humanity, with respect to the concept of perceived divinity. They endeavour to use astute logic to comprehend the mysteries behind the appearance of things.

A more esoteric function is to prepare people to obtain the first Initiation through overcoming their base sacral urges and related desire-minds, by presenting rightfully reasoned scientific facts on all aspects of the human psyche. The harmful effects of people's unsubdued desires then become evident, causing activity to control such impulses within the context of developing service arenas within their societies.

Much of the pollution and noise of the modern industrial world is, however, also the effect of the successful enterprises of those of this Ashram, plus that of its sister 6/5 Ashram and the fifth Ray line generally. Consequently, the behest to them is to learn, to listen to the voices of Nature (the *devas*) and to act accordingly, rather than to the bewildering cacophony of the phenomenal world's seeming reality. (Which the modern religion of scientific materialism keenly listens to.) Compassionate comprehension is the need. Scientific materialism must be transformed from within by members of their own community. Esoteric thought reinforced by irrefutable logic and demonstrated facts is needed.

The statement for this Ashram is:

> 'God and His Angels now arise and touch. Bring forth the rod of power. Extend it outward toward the sons of men; and touch them with fire, then bring them near. Bring forth. Quality...initiating activity'.[22]

The *iḍā nāḍī* allows Deity ('God and His Angels'), representing *manasic* forces from the Head centre, to manifest downwards to 'touch',

22 Ibid., 78.

and hence influence or mould the astral domain, as ruled by the Solar Plexus centre. However, the *manasic* potency of mind/Mind can also directly mould the Earthy Element and domain (the Sacral/Base of Spine centre duo) via the 5/6 petal. The sixth and seventh Ray 'materialising power' needed in all magical creation is thereby vitalised.

The 'rod of power' would normally relate to the *suṣumṇā nāḍī,* but in this case it literally relates to the power of the mind as it evolves into Mind by means of the developed wisdom that is the eventual gain of the *iḍā nāḍī.* As the Fiery power projects its *manasic* impulses down into the physical domain so human consciousness is touched by its divine potency. When appropriately touched, their increased mental luminescence draws them closer to Hierarchy, and Hierarchy to them. Creative works that benefit the many is the gain, as is presently seen in our scientific era. The power of the mind initiates many new creative forms of activity for humanity. The expression of this potency is primarily the work of the seventh Ray Ashrams, who need this Fire to manifest their activities. They can then integrate the *iḍā* and *piṅgalā nāḍīs* into a central *suṣumṇā* force, producing liberation from form.

Psychic heat (Tum-mo) is the Fire referred to in the phrase 'touch them with fire', as well as the Fire of the intelligent and then the awakened Mind. When humanity can respond to such Fire, then the path of Initiation is set ablaze and the power of the Waters will be dissipated.

The Solar Plexus centre

The Solar Plexus centre manifests in the form of the sum of humanity's thought and emotional life, all that comes as a result of the expression of the personal wills of people. The nature of the generation of massed personal will is thus a major meditation of Hierarchical Thinkers, necessitating much care in rightly directing. Here, therefore, the Mahāchohan's department directs its meditation before projecting purposful action via any of the forms of activity represented by the Splenic centres and the Inner Round. This represents the ability of Hierarchy to penetrate the lowest strata of consciousness right into the domains of the dark brotherhood (with their grey and black forms of activity), thus of the great mass of humanity who also generate such darkened *prāṇas*. Expresses here are the cyclic impulses of the *karma* and *saṃskāras* governing the activities of humanity. There are always cycles of abstraction, then meditative interlude before an outward-going expression.

The *maṇipūra chakra* is the focus because it channels the Watery *prāṇas* wherein humanity is besotted and must learn to properly control. In many ways the path to enlightenment constitutes the ways whereby the Waters within the human psyche are dried up. Hierarchy therefore project the cleansing Airy and Fiery attributes of the Watery *prāṇas* that will accomplish this end. (A toned down version of the cosmic astral Waters, which is pure unadulterated Love/*bodhicitta*.) They hold the ambrosial antidote to the various poisons of humanity's desirous and emotion-filled world of strife. There are also all of the Inner Round series of *chakras* that govern the sum of human civilisation controlled by this centre. Much esotericism is veiled here.

At first, Loving qualities are projected to humanity so that their Watery disposition is stimulated to produce appropriate heightened responses. Advances in the creative imagination, rightly placed devotion, and aspiration to high ideals are stimulated. Later the emphasis moves to the domain of the mind/Mind so that all aspects of the Waters can be comprehended and mastered.

Generally, Hierarchy work directly via the kingdom of the Sambhogakāya Flower, hence therein the Hierarchical thoughts find their first major impact. The 'Flowers' then have the power to penetrate the depths of matter (the lower mental, astral, and dense physical realms) wherein Hierarchical purpose must find final application. The Solar Plexus centre can also be considered in terms of the human group Soul at this stage of its evolution, though the individual Soul is an expression of the energies of the Heart centre.

The third, fourth and fifth Ray Ashrams govern Solar Plexus centre activity. These Rays esoterically form a right angled triangle of Initiation achievement, once they are directed by the second Ray. When properly applied, the second Initiation will be obtained *en masse,* producing mastery of the Watery domain, and its inevitable demise. There will be a consequent generation of the minor *siddhis*[23] by those that are so

---

23 See Volumes 2, 115-20, and 5A, 306-08, concerning the awakening of the minor

mastering, which will be the gain of many in this coming Aquarian epoch.

In general, when observing the Solar Plexus centre we should also note that the third Ray (coupled with the second and first Rays) represents the power to abstract, to convert the gross *saṃskāras* of desire-mind into those of Mind. The fourth Ray of Beautifying Harmony overcoming Strife represents the general *prāṇas* of humanity, and thus of the process which produces the equilibration between all mental-emotional extremes. The fifth Ray effectively produces the mind (intelligence) that allows people to correctly reason their way out of problems, to understand the nature of things and their placing in the universe. The sixth Ray potency manifests via idealism, aspiration and devotion to noble ideals that help aspirants to attain liberated domains. The seventh Ray grounds all Hierarchical purpose through cyclic activity. The fifth and sixth Rays represent the present problem of human evolution, with an over-stimulation of the concrete mind and all attributes of desire, selfishness, and self-centeredness.

The Solar Plexus centre governs the personal will, which is a mental-emotional focus via the personal-I projecting its desire to dominate aspects of the material environment it finds itself in. Consequently, most of the Hierarchical efforts via the planetary version of this centre are to overcome the effects of pride, self-centredness, ambition, separateness and selfishness of humanity. This is a long and arduous task. However, once the Watery attributes are being brought under control then the right qualities of light can manifest in this centre to overcome and appropriately transform these effects in humanity. The devious, selfish empire building, lying propaganda, and the financial power of the people presently ruling humanity will then be defeated.

The battle to overcome materialistic *saṃskāras* necessitates the assistance of the first and seventh Ray Ashrams associated with the Splenic centre II working via the Sacral centre. In the last resort, therefore, the first Ray power is needed to control the Waters, but first the second and third Rays must be in the process of transforming its most defiling impediments via right comprehension. Hence when the first Ray rightly comes into

---

siddhis. These *siddhis* are therein termed *dharmatā,* aspirational idealism, clairvoyance, psychometry, Tum-mo, yogic control of the elemental lives, clairaudience and abstract cognition.

play the battle is at its apogee, as it signifies the ending of times for the Lords of materialistic might. They will fight with great intensity, cunning, stealth, financially, militarily and psychically, to prevent the demise of their power. Such is the epoch we have now entered, which will produce the awakening of the new age once the materialistic and psychic impediments (evil), as well as the volatile aspects of the Solar Plexus centre, have been battled upon the testing ground. The second Ray can then pour in without much obstruction to produce its transforming effects upon the face of our civilisation. It is well worth the effort of all disciples to visualise what such effects may be and work to produce them. The victorious forces of light will then bring to light the potency of the externalised New Jerusalem (the Hierarchy of Light) and thence Shambhala.

Those governed by the third Ray Ashrams mainly work in the fields of the rule of law, finances, the great teaching institutions, and philosophical schools, where cogent logic is used to solve the world's problems. With their seventh Ray brothers they will help to counter the activities of the megalomaniac financial institutions and multinational corporations. The general ritualistic religions and their sectarian offshoots also come into the sway of the service arena of these Ashrams. There is obviously a close integration with the work of the 3/4, 4/3, 3/7 and 7/3 Ashrams, where their emphasis is to educate the minds of people to new ideals, vaster broadminded concepts of community and social justice for all lifestyles, and also the esoteric sciences, as taught by Hierarchy. Many astute thinkers working with grassroots activists will try to overturn the wrongs in human society. The logic demonstrated will clearly show the errors of thought presented by the ruling elite and their bureaucratic, religious, educational, financial and militaristic establishments. These Ashrams hence reveal the nature of Hierarchal purpose by means of wise pronouncements that will cleanse much of the Solar Plexus malaise, glamours and illusions that besot the morass of people's lives. The radiance of illumined Minds will then shine forth to reveal the vistas of future possibilities.

The *3/2 Ashram* represents the northern middle finger petal of the Solar Plexus centre,[24] which directly interrelates with the western, Libran

---

24 For an explanation of the symbolism of the role and nature of the fingers see Volume 2, 101-13, where the attributes of the Solar Plexus centre are first explained.

petal of Splenic centre I, governed by the second Ray Chohan.[25] This means that the entire dispensation of the Solar Plexus centre is essentially governed by means of Love-Wisdom via the third Ray. (The energies from the higher centres are thus conveniently toned down so that they can be best utilised by humanity. As humanity becomes more compassionate, the Watery attributes of the Solar Plexus centre will eventually be transformed by the Airy qualities from the Heart centre.) Libra regulates the cycles of the Hierarchical agenda for the education of all so that the *karma* of what is to happen will manifest according to Hierarchy's plan. From this northern orientation the incoming directives are then projected to the remaining arms of the fixed cross. The main flow being east-west (to and from the Liver and Stomach centres) that process the overwhelming mental-emotional activity of humanity. The direction downwards is to the Inner Round, representing humanity's physical plane concerns.

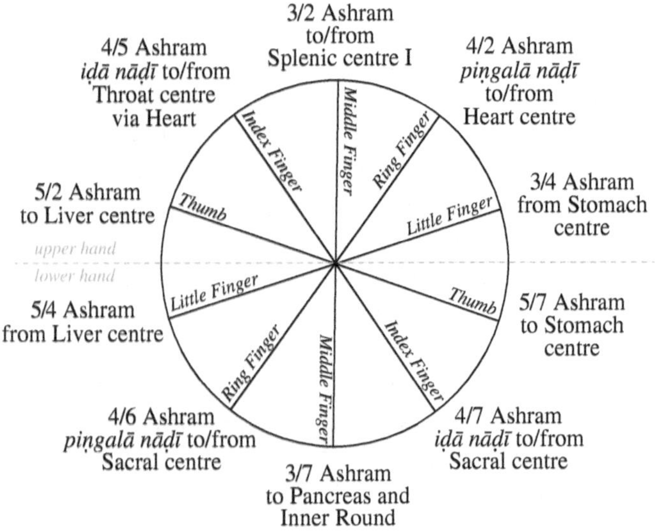

Figure 18. The Hierarchical Solar Plexus centre[26]

25 Note here that for each Ashram the primary influence comes via the Chohan that is Lord of the Ray, and then the Chohan of the subsidiary Ray. In the case of the 3/2 Ashram, the influence of the subsidiary Ray is increasingly heightened as Humanity becomes more receptive to the principle of Love.

26 The reader should correlate this schematic with Volume 3, Figure 12, 224.

The 3/2 Ashram projects the power of Hierarchical Wisdom to disciples and the general intelligentsia of humanity in a way such that the ordinary masses can be rightly educated. It instigates Hierarchical incentives by way of Mind, empowering the new cycles concerning the abstract *manasic* environment, as governed by the third Ray. It is the major gate of outpouring of the instructions and energies that aim to rectify the base *prāṇas* associated with the entire Solar Plexus centre. This involves the sum of the *prāṇic* circulation below the diaphragm (the Inner Round) wherein the great bulk of human consciousness is presently focused.

The remaining petals constituted of the humanity that embody the Solar Plexus centre are then broadly swayed by this Wisdom. This is articulated via the various service arenas of the Rays in a way that stimulates loving and wise response in the various departments of Life. The 3/2 Ashram receives the response from humanity via such Hierarchical impetus and then directs the thought-streams to Splenic centre I to be properly assessed and refined. Appropriate Hierarchical adjustments can then be made for the next cycle of outgoing purpose in any line of expression. The entire field of human evolution is slowly converted by this redemptive and salvifical activity with the help of the second sub-Ray Ashrams of the Rays of Mind within Hierarchy's generalised *maṇḍala*. They therefore assist the process of rectifying *saṃskāras* via Splenic centre II.

The statement for the 3/2 Ashram is:

> Conform the shell to that which dwells within, Let the world egg appear, Let the ages pass; then let the soul appear. Let life emerge within a destined time. Quality...the power to evolve.[27]

The 3/2 Ashram governs the power of the Mother's domain to en-Soul Life from within the Mother's evolving form, which from this viewpoint is 'the world egg'. Thus it helps produce the conditions within the Womb of Life and then directs the various streams of sentience and consciousness to evolve out from that Womb. When the 'Womb' represents the Solar Plexus centre then the streams of Life therein concern the strands of *saṃskāras* developed by humanity. These strands convey predominantly Earthy, Watery or Fiery *saṃskāras*,

27 A.A. Bailey, *Esoteric Psychology I*, 69.

which roughly categorise their karmic placing in different developing nations on earth.[28] Hence the 3/2 Ashram works to refine these strands and thereby help evolve the related human units towards developing more loving and wise attributes.

Here we see the effect of the work of A.A. Bailey coming to the fore. She is presently the second point of the 3/2 Ray Ashram. This point position facilitated her direct relation to K.H., who for all intents and purposes was her Master. (The third Ray Chohan, the Venetian, playing a secondary role to the overall second Ray purpose.) This interrelationship allows him to directly vitalise the entire Solar Plexus centre of humanity via the third Ray. It also allowed D.K., the Master of the 2/3 Ray Ashram, to overshadow her for his work (as his amanuensis) concerning the general education of all associated with the centres below the diaphragm. Thus the writings published under her name came into being and all related service arenas, such as world goodwill, the New Group of World Servers and the triangles movement. All was made possible by the close numerical relationship between the two Ashramic groupings, and also by the highly developed telepathic skills of Alice Bailey.

The proper establishment of Hierarchy's esoteric doctrines represent the outward appearance of the world Soul emerging at its 'destined time'. From these writings manifests the 'power to evolve' of the entire Hierarchical dispensation, being the keynote teachings for their externalisation process.

The 3/4 and 5/7 Ray Ashrams govern the *iḍā nāḍī prāṇas* associated with the Stomach centre of humanity, containing the general flowing motion of the more concrete-minded substance (*manasic* thought-forms) they have generated. This centre processes the strongest *saṃskāras* of pride, egotism, and all constructs of mind, the often materialised assertions of the intelligentsia. The thought-forms need to be refined and converted to harmonious and beautifying mental constructs that benefit humanity as a whole. Higher abstract thinking and idealism must be brought to the fore (via the activity of the 3/4 Ashram). The concern of these Ashrams is with the generalised western direction of

---

28 See A.A. Bailey, *The Destiny of the Nations*, for detail concerning the Rays governing the nations and some important hints as to the lines of their evolutionary development. Such destiny comes under the auspices of the Mahāchohan's department.

outwards to the field of service representing humanity. The third Ray of Mathematically Exact Activity, manifesting via higher, precise, logical thought processes must be generated to overcome the volatile morass of opinions and assertions that represent humanity's collectivised mental pool. First, however, the 5/7 Ray helps organise the *manasic* pool of human thoughts, directing their conflicting opinions to right outcomes. The organising abilities of the seventh Ray helps to control the forceful opinions of mind. Inevitably the Ideations from Shambhala must be brought to the fore via this western direction, carrying with it the general higher creative ideals of Hierarchy.

The *3/4 Ashram* manifests as the little finger of the upper pentad of the Solar Plexus centre of humanity, which receives the advanced *manasic prāṇas* coming from the Stomach centre. This represents the gain of the processes associated with the education of the intelligentsia associated with that centre. Their ideas and opinions are then refined and utilised to project more advanced teachings into the general pool of humanity's thought-stream within the generalised Solar Plexus centre. This Ashram manifests in the form of a triad with the 2/3 and 3/2 Ray Ashrams. It represents the activity aspect capable of reaching out to a wide audience by virtue of its sympathetic identification with the human plight via the fourth Ray, which governs the human kingdom. This Ashram will empower the second Ray purpose (of the 2/3 Ray) by way of Mind. Esoteric doctrines can thereby be promulgated upon a vaster scale than hitherto possible. Hierarchy's entire *maṇḍala* of activity amongst humanity is impregnated with the vitality and purpose of the Mother's Life via the third Ray. Mind is reflected into humanity via the subsidiary fourth Ray of the 3/4 Ashram to harmonise the separative, unruly aspects of mind. Also, the refined aspects of Mind gained by the world's aspirants can find an appropriate medium to enter Hierarchical *nāḍīs* via the fourth Ray flux. The fourth Ray facilitates the interrelation between the planetary Heart centre and humanity.

This Ashram constitutes an integral part of the Mother's Breath, externalising Her Thoughts *(deva* lives) into the various departments and categories of human civilisation to produce the birth of the new. It literally manifests as the Womb of the new world civilisation. As this Ashram properly forms, it will nurture and vitalise the stages of the evolution of the future, assisting the new Hierarchical ventures to bear fruit at the appointed time. The epoch producing a close conscious cooperation between the human and the *deva* kingdoms will be birthed by the activities of this Ashram in conjunction with the seventh Ray department. (The human kingdom being governed by the fourth Ray and the *devas* by the third Ray.[29])

The most advanced members of this Ashram will utilise the *karma* of the human group-Soul to help pacify, refine, intensify, and expand the human auric sphere so that it begins to approximate that of Hierarchy. The inevitable gain will be the externalisation of the New Jerusalem, the Hierarchy of Light, during this coming Aquarian epoch. *Karma* (planetary *saṃskāras*) must rightly manifest for all newly evolving forms of Hierarchical activity. The constraints of the various cycles of time must be taken into account to ensure that everything planned by Hierarchy manifests as ordained under the auspices of the great Mother. The cycle ahead hence will demonstrate as a feminine Incarnation and a new feminine *nāḍī* system must be awakened to replace the present one. This then is part of the objective of the third Ray, wherein the sacred spots of the earth that have lain dormant since Atlantis can again be discovered and awakened. The new temples of Initiation can then be established.

This Ashram balances the pairs of opposites, the *iḍā* and *piṇgalā* ways,[30] to find the middle path between the two, which will assist in the evocation of the *kuṇḍalinī* Fire. The Ashram can reflect the attributes of the higher three Rays into the septenary of the form, to assist in the projection of the *antaḥkaraṇas* between humanity and Shambhala (the Mother's department therein), so providing the esoteric wisdom that will assist humanity to see the need to travel the higher way to divinity. In doing so they can illuminate the path to the higher realisations for all to perceive. The Mother, Hierarchy and humanity become incorporated into one rainbow bridge of divine revelation. *Deva (iḍā)* and humanity *(piṇgalā)* will then work together in unity.

---

29 The numbers 3 and 4 numerically add to 7, where the seventh Ray is the reflection of the third via the fourth.

30 The statement given for the 3/4 Ray Ashram being: 'Let the two paths converge. Balance the pairs of opposites and let the path appear between the two. God and the path and man are one. Quality...Balance'. (A.A. Bailey, *Esoteric Psychology, I,* 69-70.)

The *5/7 Ashram* embodies the left thumb position of the lower pentad of the Solar Plexus centre and moulds the potency of the Hierarchical Thought-stream in a way that can bring order, or right understanding, to the morass of opinions generated by those embodying the attributes of the Stomach centre. The thumb projects the major forces of the hand, allowing it to properly grapple with and to manipulate material things. The potent seventh Ray is needed to cyclically educate the most opinionated members of humanity, and the materialistically biased, to the context of Hierarchy's doctrines.

The 5/7 Ray directs the sunlight of the mind's illumination to lift humanity out from the fogs, mists, and miasmas of their mental-emotional thoughts and opinions. This Ashram seeds enlightening mental attitudes into humanity by means of scientific activity, with its proclivity to ritualistic experimentation. We therefore have the production of the scientific and technological artefacts and appliances that benefit all in our civilisation. The telephone, radio, computer and television *etc.*, are divinely inspired, being but the necessary cyclic grounding of the forms of clairvoyance once possessed by infant humanity. They represent a higher spiral of the associated Atlantean epoch. Telephones and cellular phones correspond to the type of telepathy possessed by our Atlantean forebears. The progress of mind has allowed humanity to understand the processes involved in these technological accomplishments, whereas before there was only a childlike acceptance of the things and thoughts presented by the Lords of Shambhala.

The logic of modern electronic magic, the laws of physics and of chemical affinity, and the systems of modern computer technology, are based on the paradigm of inner plane reality. In time our intelligentsia will see such reality; for despite their materialistic ethos our scientific community has laid the foundation for such revelation.

This Ashram helps prepare humanity for taking the first Initiation, by properly seeding the development of the mind and by producing beneficent labour saving appliances and technological advances. These are but externalised applications of the development of the minor *siddhis.*

The worst attributes of humanity's mental-emotions will be incrementally overcome as people begin to properly control their emotions through right knowledge and comprehension of the esoteric sciences. Thus this epoch where the powers of mind are extolled heralds the time of the widespread practise of *rāja yoga,* the science concerned with the rules of training for awakening the higher Mind. The seventh sub-Ray provides the potency that cyclically attacks all problems at hand in the material domain, assisting in its mastery. The power to overcome the rigor mortis of the form by awakening the inner centres is greatly facilitated by this Ray.

Humanity is now in the process of rightly controlling *saṃsāra* through scientific investigations and accurately presented ideas. The evolution of mind/Mind in Nature, incorporating thus the work of the *devas,* is also part of the domain of such investigation. When the *devas* become an object of scientific concern, not with a view of manipulation, but via conscious cooperation, then the new era civilisation will awaken. Also, once the finer forces, the nature of *prāṇas* governing Life and the forces appertaining to health, have been discovered, then the grip of the modern pharmaceutical companies in medicine will be virtually eliminated. Consequently, the costs of healing people will significantly diminish.

The statement for the 5/7 Ashram is:

> God and His Angels now arise and hear. Let a deep murmur arise and let the cry of seeking man enter into their ears. Let man listen. Let man call. Speak loud. Quality...power to make the Voice of the Silence heard'.[31]

Esoterically, to hear draws our attention to the physical domain. This Ashram is therefore focussed downwards to the 'cry of seeking man', so that teachings can be provided that will best serve humanity by way of the mind and its intellectual pursuits. Humanity emits an invocational appeal ('a deep murmur') of need based upon past gains and sense of lack. Amongst the din of mental-emotional ideas and chatter comes the call, desire for more knowledge, plus the will to rise above. This Ashram helps humanity to generate the right thoughts that will project them to higher domains. Then can the answers be made that lead to perfection of the task at hand, to the Initiation process, the manifestation of divinity within the artefacts of the form. The objective

31 A.A. Bailey, *Esoteric Psychology I,* 78.

of this Ashram is thus to teach the intelligentsia the way of the Voice of Silence, rather than bending to the lure of *saṃsāric* pursuits, of deluding materialism and attachments to all of its forms. Those of this Ashram consequently work to lead humanity away from the ruts of their materialistic mire. Humanity must arise and seek a higher way within the domains of Mind.

The fourth Ray of Beautifying Harmony overcoming Conflict is generally concerned with all forms of *prāṇic* vitalisation. It is the carrier of the Airy Element. The Airy attributes of the intuition, enlightened perception gained via overcoming the strife of *saṃsāra,* are the esoteric forte of humanity. That vitalised is the minds and higher emotions of the great mass of humanity in all fields of endeavour. High levels of philosophical rhetoric and ideas are at first not needed, but people need to know how to improve their thought and devotional life so that it serves the common good and not just the limited bounds of self-interest. The fourth Ray line embodies the *nāḍī* system that is the field of action of all Hierarchical forces and energies. For the fourth Ray Ashrams associated with the Solar Plexus centre the focus therefore is upon the *iḍā* and *piṇgalā nāḍīs* that convey all *prāṇas* generated by humanity and directed from Hierarchy between the various *chakras* in the Body of the Logos. Effectively they channel the purifying, vitalising and transforming energies from the Heart centre that unifies all disparate attributes of humanity into the oneness of goodwill and then the Will-to-Love.

The *4/2 Ashram* governs the *piṇgalā nāḍī* (the upper 'ring finger') from the Solar Plexus centre to the Heart centre, therefore it directs Hierarchical *prāṇas,* the energies of Love and applied Wisdom, to help wash clean the Watery cesspool generated by humanity's incessant turbulent emotions. The energy is received via the Gemini petal of Splenic centre I and the 2/4 Ashram. The *prāṇas* will vitalise the inner sanctum of the new temples of Initiation built by the seventh Ray masons. The *prāṇas* will therefore vivify the differing cultural situations in our societies. The purpose gives birth to the second Ray qualities of Love-Wisdom out of the sum of the field of desire and glamour. This is the major focus of all Hierarchical endeavour. The awakening of the various *chakras* of humanity by means of this energy and the efforts of the Hierarchical workers in human society, produces a vibrant floral display that beautifies the sight of their mindscape, turning their normal messy fields of thought into displays of delight. The Hierarchical sun thus illuminates those fields to stimulate creative idealism and aspiration. They become the *prāṇas* utilised by the polar opposite 4/6 Ashram directed into the Sacral centre to rightly feed the principle of desire-aspiration, to produce goodwill amongst all human interrelationships.

The Statement given to the 4/2 Ashram is:

> Champion desire. Give what is needed to the seeker. Quality ... The dual aspects of desire.[32]

The 'dual aspects of desire' refers to both the normal form of desire, whereby people learn what not to do through the karmic repercussions of their actions, and the desire for liberation, the awakening of the Heart centre's attributes. This dual aspect comes into play here because the *piṇgalā nāḍī* flow contains all of the desire-emotional *prāṇas* generated in the Sacral centre, in which case the lower form of desire must be accommodated and transformed. The more affectionate, loving attributes of the Waters are then engendered via Solar Plexus interactions with others. When the energies from the Heart are evoked, then desire is transformed into aspiration. Receiving higher impressions, aspirants are then inspired to serve, to better themselves, to be compassionately concerned with the world around and the plight of others. The members of this Ashram have to manage this entire conversion process by being the examples that inspire others to seek out the divinity in all, and to thereby generate sacrificial Love. The Bodhisattva way can thus be trod. This Ashram hence energises all such activity in the centres below the diaphragm.

The *4/5 Ashram* governs the *iḍā nāḍī* flow of the index finger of the upper pentad of the Solar Plexus centre to the Throat centre via the Heart. This Ashram manifests as the lord of the jungles of *saṃsāra,* the lion that roars out its victory paean after the attributes of mind are dominated by the Mind. This is the true objective of the outpouring of fifth Ray energies and of the scientific analysis of the nature of Life. The cesspool of egotistic and malignant thoughts of humanity is thereby converted into forms of wisdom bright. Ideas from the Heart of

32 Ibid., 72.

Life (Hierarchy) will flow through this Ashram to positively influence humanity towards investigating Nature's finer forces as part of the field of science as well as the sum of the material domain. They manifest in such a way that they comprehend the true nature of manifesting divinity, rather than just via blind acceptance of religious creed.

The empowered thoughts return to help build the edifices and technological innovations that glorify humanity with Nature's beneficence. New cycles of activity can then be initiated in all fields of human activity whereby the Mother's garden can flourish through the benefits brought to it by rightly ordained scientists and technocrats. Beautifying the landscapes of mind and of civilisation is a forte of this Ray.

As the attributes of mind/Mind are developed, so the *chakras* awaken to accommodate the quality of the impressions that need to be processed. As in the human body, so also in the body of the human kingdom. The *iḍā nāḍī* conveys the energies that colour the flowers (*chakras*). Hence the statement for this Ashram:

> All flowers are thine. Settle the roots in mud, the flowers in the sun. Prove mud and sun, and roots and flowers are one. Quality...power to express divinity. Growth.[33]

The mind develops as one masters the conditionings found in the mud of *saṃsāra*. As a consequence, the *chakras* unfold and awaken so that the light from the Heart of the Sun (the Heart centre) can illumine them and in this way people evolve wisdom. The members of this Ashram have to cogently and scientifically teach humanity the processes involved in such development. They must show the way to evolutionary perfection, how to conquer the mud of *saṃsāra* to turn the entire human environment into a flower garden of resplendent achievement.

The *4/6 Ashram* receives the general *piṇgalā* Watery flow from the Sacral centre and processes this distilled offering of generalised desire-attachment so that Hierarchy can best work with it. (This represents the effect of the Airy Ring finger of the downward pointing pentad of the Solar Plexus centre.) The *prāṇas, saṃskāras* of basic human desires, mental-emotions and glamour engendered by humanity must be converted by them in a way that will help lift them out of their soggy

33 Ibid.

morass. High idealism and aspiration to noble ideals must be generated with the help of this Ashram. They therefore teach the qualities for which aspirants can aspire, and which must later be transformed upon the path of Initiation. The field of rightly ordained testings and trials that disciples must grapple with as they ascend up the *piṇgalā nāḍī* towards the Heart centre (as associated with the sign Scorpio) is then entered. Many are the battles with desire. The religiously inclined must learn to make a heaven upon the earth, and not to fanatically assert their belief systems based upon incorrect interpretation of scriptures.

The statement given to the 4/6 Ashram is:

> Roll and return, and roll again. Cycle around the circle of the heavens. Prove all is one. Quality...The harmony of the spheres.[34]

The activity of this Ashram, and of the *piṇgalā nāḍī* in general, is to continuously cycle into humanity's emotional consciousness the teachings of Love. They endeavour to convert the many conflicting emotional opinions, zealotry, prideful and often militaristic aggression of humanity with concepts of brotherhood, cooperation, the divinity in all. They teach the universality of goodness in the plan for human evolution, that all of humanity are divine, governed by singular spiritual laws emanated from the Kingdom of 'God' (Shambhala). Not easy is it to convert the vacillating and often enflamed emotions into peaceful and serene contemplative states, so the teachings must 'Roll and return, and roll again' until the lessons are learnt. 'The harmony of the spheres' in world events is the gain.

The *4/7 Ashram* integrates the *iḍā nāḍī prāṇas* coming from the Sacral centre into the general Solar Plexus pool, and empowers the Sacral and Base of Spine centres with the Watery potencies that need to be grounded via physical plane activities. It represents the Fiery index finger of the downward pointing pentad of the Solar Plexus centre.

Being the seventh of the fourth Ray Ashrams, it is logical that the Hierarchical *manasic* purpose designed to produce the world of outer seeming will manifest through this gate, to be precipitated via the activity of the lower centres. This Ashram possesses the will to transform, to produce great changes, by virtue of the fact that its Ray combination is along the first Ray line (1-4-7). Principally it works to harmonise and

34 Ibid.

to transform astral conditionings with seeds of light, the potency of Hierarchical power. Cyclically manifesting Hierarchical *antaḥkaraṇas* are projected to humanity through impressionable contacts, providing teachings concerning the shortcomings of unadulterated desire and the negative effect of emotional thinking.

The statement for this Ashram is:

> Colour the sound. Sound forth the colour. Produce the notes and see them pass into the shades, which in their turn produce the sounds. Thus all are seen as one. Quality... The synthesis of true beauty.[35]

'The sound' from the lower perspective manifests as the general thoughts coming from human minds. The challenge is to colour them according to Hierarchical precepts through right education via the various media outlets. These precepts are sounded forth within humanity's philosophical and spiritual constructs to overcome the worst aspects of people's emotional thinking. Sound values and ethics must be inculcated instead. The teachings presented will, however, normally be converted by humanity into the many shades of different opinions and doctrines.

We should also note that *devas* see sound and hear colour, whilst the reverse is the case for humans, hence this Ashram stands as a bridge between the *deva* and human kingdoms. They work to project Hierarchical mantras in the form of teachings ('sound') into humanity's mental pool ('the shades') in such a way that harmonising sounds will be produced and not the clashing noises of normal human civilisation. The pleasing images (of harmonising sound) produced for the *deva* kingdom will allow them to more effectively tend to humanity's needs—the healing of many human ailments. This represents the 'synthesis of true beauty'. Consequently, the edifices of the new epoch will be built through the inevitable cooperation between the two kingdoms. Many human units will then scientifically work with the esoteric subjects of sound and colour in conjunction with *deva* lore, especially when the sum of the seventh Ray Ashrams are vitalised in this way.

The members of this 4/7 Ashram naturally find themselves as urban planners, gifted healers, or artisans with a high sense of ritual

---

35 Ibid.

or rhythmic ordering. They impregnate the blueprint of the Plan into the *nāḍī* system of the minds of all co-workers according to the right cycles for their expression. Once the energies of the Sacral centre governing the fields of desire of humanity are mastered, then the resultant clarifying energies released can be directed to building the new constructs of Hierarchical purpose.

'The shades' also refer to the grey forms of thinking of humanity, which may be generally loving and inspired, but contain distortions or errors of view, which prevent or mar true awakened perceptions and ultimate liberation from *saṃsāra*. Along this line are the hosts of the dark brotherhood that deal with subtle thought projections (Anubis, image makers) and impersonators of the great Ones (the Masters of Wisdom) that the many that channel impressions from the inner realms are prone to. They call them 'ascended Masters' and the like. (Such as found in the works of the 'I AM' movement and by Elizabeth Claire Prophet.) The spiritual platitudes coming from such sources are often travesties of the real, even though inspirational to novice aspirants, as they detract from the type of salient multileveled teachings gained from awakened members of Hierarchy. Hierarchical teachings always aim to awaken the mind, and are often difficult to properly interpret as they contain vast stores of coded information, needing much meditation to properly access. They never feed the emotions and the glamour-forming tendencies of the devotional ones, to whom the teachings of the 'ascended Masters' aim. Also, the qualities attributed to such 'Masters' are anaemic distortions of the Real, and the images bandied about purporting to depict the way they look bear no resemblance to the truth. Many new vapid 'Masters' are promoted that offer little to the world's spiritual literature other than low level inspirationally sounding trivia.[36]

The Liver centre of humanity represents the store of the bulk of human emotions, thus of the *saṃskāras* of their major selfish, avaricious life expressions, generally coloured by the fourth and sixth Ray lines, or an aberrant version of the second Ray. (Representing general *piṇgalā*

---

36 I have presented this subject here because it is important that readers do not conflate what I have given concerning the Masters with information coming from such sources. What is provided by Blavatsky, Bailey, Roerich, plus this volume, or via direct experience in meditation, suffices for all disciples. When coupled with teachings concerning the Initiation process, they will get plenty to ponder on concerning the way to enlightenment.

prāṇas.) It is effectively the *chakra* that generalises the qualities of humanity and their astral world of experiences. The many forms of strife and warfare (that we are often told are 'for noble reasons'), ravenous greedy appetites, mendacity, covetousness and selfishness must all be converted into more beneficent forms of activity. Utilising the attributes of the mind to properly rationalise the nature of the emotions, and then to learn to control them, is thereby necessitated. This brings into play the activity of the fifth Ray Ashrams. Consequently, their transformative work must be dominant before the major second Ray cycle can properly manifest, for the fifth Ray is ever the vehicle of the second. The two Rays working together afford the possibility of Initiation for humanity. This is one of the reasons why a fifth Ray Ashram was one of the first to send out its members, in conjunction with that of Morya and K.H., for the preparatory stages of the externalisation process of the Hierarchy.

D.K. states that this Ashram is:

> The custodian, among other things, of science and of that which relates and brings into expression the duality of spirit-matter. This Ashram has an important part to play in the work of preparation, for it is through the scientific use of energy that the world will be rebuilt and the factual nature of hierarchy be proved.[37]

The *5/2 Ashram* represents the thumb of the upward pointing pentad of the Solar Plexus centre. It projects the primary *manasic* Hierarchical dispensation to try to educate the bulk of emotionally polarised humanity to think cogently.[38] Humanity functions primarily in terms of the attributes of a Liver centre. This Ashram wields the Leonine energies coming via the 2/5 Ashram and Splenic centre I to do so. The Leonine position helps build the sum of humanity's mentalistic aura, which can be viewed in terms of the 'pride' of the lion basking in the sun of the high revelations from Hierarchy. For humanity, however, this lion basks pridefully in the sun of selfish accomplishments. Egoistic attitudes are first demonstrated, but later must be converted into selflessness, true humbleness, as the way of the Heart and the pathways to the Soul are sought under Hierarchy's guidance. Leo stands for the sun, for the light of the Sambhogakāya Flower,

---

37 A.A. Bailey, *The Externalisation of the Hierarchy*, 577.

38 For this reason it is the best contender for the above mentioned fifth Ray Ashram.

which is the direction Hierarchy seek to turn humanity's gaze, away from the self-centred Atlanteanism and materialism of today. Being empowered by the radiance of the spiritual sun, complete self-consciousness is gained allowing the human unit to properly know itself and begin to investigate the mysteries of the Soul aspect, the Sambhogakāya Flower that underlies all manifestation. Once properly overshadowed by, and integrated with, the kingdom of the Sambhogakāya Flower, then humanity will truly become Lord of all that it perceives.

Hierarchy's general Thought-streams are appropriately adapted by this Ashram so that its Ideations can be best utilised by humanity. Especially needed are concepts concerning all forms of intelligent activity tending towards peaceful coexistence and cooperativeness between all human groupings, and the innovations that advance their societies for the better. As humanity develops the attributes of Hierarchical thinking, so many of the cultural and scientific edifices of the New Jerusalem will be built.[39] Ideas will be phrased that will stimulate and uplift common humanity to think and act more compassionately. A more vibrant, ethical scientific epoch will manifest as humanity converts Fiery Hierarchical teachings into inspired forms of creativity.

Myriad are the tonalities and hues of response from the various groups of people (small *chakras*) in our societies. The directed Fiery *prāṇas* empower salient thinkers, allowing them to arise from the morass of popular opinion. Scientific logic and veridical wisdom will then manifest via all issues, producing a reticulation of truthful ideas. The human mind-space can thus be elevated closer to Hierarchical paradigms. As the Waters are mastered so the nature of Life, of all phenomena, subjective and objective, as well as the laws of mind/ Mind, can be properly investigated. The fanatical attributes of the emotional-mind will thereby be overcome. Humanity then gains the power to control Nature's dominion through understanding the inherent divinity within, and not just through materialistic incentive.

This Ashram heads the work of the general fifth Ray Ashrams concerning engendering scientific speculation of the nature of the material world. In many ways, however, psychic, psychological, and parapsychological studies are some of the special fields of interest of

39 *Rev. 3:12, 21:2.*

many of this 5/2 Ray. Jungian psychology, with ideas of the 'collective unconscious' can be viewed as projected via this Ashram. This Ashram thus directs *manasic* impressions to influence the intelligentsia, to enlighten the materialistically minded and the scientific community to think more abstractly and lovingly.

Once the means is established that will allow humanity to choose rightly seeded ideas via the mind then intensified light will demonstrate therein and the nature of the glamour and illusions people fall prey to will stand revealed. The ways of evil doing will then be shunned, and the way of the Heart leading to Hierarchy will be chosen instead. Once the mind is held steady in the light then astral plane glamour cannot exist, making the attainment of the second Initiation possible.

The statement for this Ashram is:

> God and His Angels now arise and see. Let the mountaintops emerge from out the dense wet mist. Let the sun touch their summits and let them stand in light. Shine forth. Quality...emergence into form and out of form. [40]

There are many levels of interpretation to these statements. The primary reference here is to the creative process, however, when related to a human unit the phrase 'God and His Angels now arise and see' concerns the process associated with the awakening of the Head lotus, where 'God' represents the divinity within working via the mind, and the 'angels' referring both to the *devas* and the psycho-somatic forces controlled by the individual. All must be utilised in order to 'see', to rightly use the Fires of mind to comprehend, and then to visualise multidimensionally. Humanity as a whole must also undergo a similar process. 'The mountaintops' then become the high points of vision and revelation attained as a consequence of passing the necessary testings up the steep gradients of thought, whilst 'the dense wet mist' refers to the morass of humanity's emotional thoughts and desires, as consistent with the attributes associated with the Liver centre. 'The sun' then is the Light of the Soul, or of Hierarchy, that can then reach human minds and awaken them to the glory of that Light.

The *5/4 Ashram* represents the little finger of the downward pointed

40 A.A. Bailey, *Esoteric Psychology I,* 78.

hand for the Solar Plexus centre of humanity. It collates the gain of the response of the *manasic* vivification of humanity via the Liver centre and integrates this with the corresponding gain from Hierarchy's activity in the Stomach centre, so that the appropriate next step of evolution of humanity by way of mind can be promulgated. Thus from those of this Ashram comes a continuous outpouring of new ideas and technological advancements, being the general indices of the well being and improvement of the quality of life of our societies. Everything improving the lot of the average citizen of any country is a good and useful harbinger of Hierarchical purpose.

With respect to the work of the 5/4 Ashram, D.K. states:

> God and His Angels now arise and taste. Let all experience come. Let all the ways appear. Discern and choose; dissect and analyse. All ways are one. Quality...revelation of the way.[41]

In the statement for the 5/2 Ashram we had the sense perception of sight exemplified, now taste is implicated. This concerns the ability to rightly discern glamour and illusions from out of the morass of psychic and empirical phenomena that abounds in the world. They are told to 'discern and choose; dissect and analyse' facts from non-facts, truth from untruth. Thus the clouds and fogs of speculative and assertive images and ideas that are the mainstay of astral phenomena can be eliminated. Thus is conquered the root cause of the Hydra, which is ignorance. This allows them to direct aspirants towards the path of Initiation and the complete mastery of the Watery environment, which makes 'all paths one'. Such a path leads intelligent aspirants upwards towards Hierarchy and inevitably Shambhala. So many aspirants will eventually be receptive to the manifesting teachings that they will provide the workers what is needed to build a reflected aspect of that Kingdom on the earth.

The 5/4 Ashram also integrates the *manasic prāṇas (saṃskāras)* of the *iḍā* stream (governed by the 4/5 Ashram) concerning all topics and themes useful to the macrocosmic body cycled in the general Solar Plexus circulation. The 5/4 Ray combination blends the various fifth Ray potencies into a unity and directs the gain into humanity. These potencies can then be utilised by common thinkers to uplift their idea base. In

---

41 Ibid.

this way the collective Minds of Hierarchy will continue their outward expansion via humanity, vitalising all productive thoughts. By working to birth enlightened perception within the human matrix, these Ashrams plan to beautify all aspects of our modern urban environments, producing the aesthetic aspects of technology, and infusing the beneficence of the mind/Mind throughout people's everyday lives.

The *3/7 Ashram* governs the middle finger of the downward pointing hand of the Solar Plexus centre, which directs *prāṇas* to the pancreas and the Inner Round. This represents the general pool of common humanity, who generally toil with their hands and who grow the food, build the appliances and edifices of our societies. The objective of this Ashram is to rightly organise them, to sow the seeds of correct comprehension of the forces governing our societies. Working with the general seventh Ray line, this Ashram therefore helps to organise labour along social and political lines. This Ashram brings into active manifestation the power of the *manasic* potency of the wisely expressed planetary purpose whenever opportunity presents itself in the cycles of phenomenal life. Many cycles of such educative efforts come and go before genuine progress is achieved.

The statement for those of this Ashram is:

> God and His form are one. Reveal this fact, Oh sovereign Lord of form. God and His form are one. Negate the dual concept. Lend colour to the form. The life is one; the harmony complete. Prove thus the two are one. Quality...the power to produce synthesis on the physical plane.[42]

Entrenched opinions and the wilful attitudes of determined desire-minds are especially hard to convert, hence the 3/7 Ray esoterically embodies the attributes of a hammer and chisel that can chip away at the most hardened crusts of mind. Effectively this Ashram projects abstract ideas coming from above the diaphragm in such a way that general humanity can comprehend. Its power manifesting in such a toned down manner can consequently affect the field of politics, law, world governance, finances, and the dynamics of labour. The service work of the 3/7 Ray manifests in a way that organises people to produce the productivity that sustains the output of nations, to counter the way that wealth is presently distributed and the power money has over all

42 Ibid., 69.

aspects of the present materialistic civilisation. The focus of this work is with the toiling masses and their right education. Hopefully in time these masses will continuously vote in politicians that will truly serve the common people, by passing beneficent laws assisting their needs, and not that of the avaricious moneyed class. The 3/7 Ashram hence tries to induce revelation amongst our governing bodies of the way that civilisation ought to function, to produce true beneficence and prosperity for all. One can easily see the difficulties that those of this Ashram face in their endeavours to overcome the natural insouciance and cupidity of people, and the corruption of the ruling elite.

The need is also to empower the highest levels of thought life amongst the intelligentsia who serve humanity. They have the capacity to propel Hierarchical purpose into manifestation, via cogently revealing the concept of Deity as incorporated throughout Nature, so as to physically build the edifices in our civilisation that reflect the divine blueprint of the overall *maṇḍala,* 'to lend colour to the form'. They can therefore rationalise in a way comprehensible to average humanity the details concerning the constructs of the new world civilisation; to build the form from the ground up in the image of the divinity that is to reside in it. Their task therefore is to prove that divinity exists in all that is, by helping to build a civilisation based upon the Shambhalic blueprint, once the ideas have been inculcated into the minds of the intelligentsia. Consequently, the structures that will constitute the new temples of Initiation will be built. In many ways this Ray governs the evolutionary development of our planet as a whole. The more enlightened members will also work to reveal the functions of the *devas* to humanity.

Vast is the opposition of the dark forces to the success of this Ashram in helping common humanity end their serfdom to an extremely powerful monied elite (the nobility of the past). However, now a new form of debt serfdom has arrived which needs countering. Hard is the work to overcome the avaricious tendencies of humanity, and great is the power of the dark brotherhood in the field of finances, who have amassed unlimited financial reserves to do their bidding. Here Hierarchy face their greatest challenges, and the mass education concerning the errors of the 'greed is good' doctrine is still underway. Upon the material domain is seen the greatest arena of success for the evil forces, hence much work needs to manifest to rightly transform and reorganise the financial arena to turn the tide of massed selfishness. The enormous power of the dark brotherhood (that have egregiously manipulated the power of money for their own purposes) is not easy to defeat.

The 3/7 Ashram was formed at the ending of the Victorian era and beginning of the twentieth century with the activity of the English Master,[43] Justin Moreward Haig. This name is derived from *The Initiate* series of books by Cyril Scott, where the mode of education of some of his disciples was described.

Let the concretions and distortions of truth stand revealed for all to see. Let the *manaskāras*[44] of manipulations of human thought by the forces of evil be overcome by the rightly directed arrows of brilliant mental attire by means of the integrated work of all these Ashrams.

Overcoming planetary evil

All Initiates are actively involved in their various ways in the defeat of the evil on this planet, but the specialists in the art of converting the dark emanations (zapping) are those Ashrams with a first or seventh Ray dispensation. The second and fourth Ray Ashrams specialise in the conversion of those with greyish colourations. Being the central Ray that produces harmony in the midst of strife, the fourth Ray also generally assists all other Ray directives. All Ray lines can be used for maleficent purposes when directed by personal will. The first, fifth and sixth Rays facilitate generation of *prāṇas* of the dark brotherhood by means of the abuse of power of the mind and emotions. Right mental comprehension of the fifth Ray and the directive will and energetic zeal of the first and sixth Rays, however, are also needed to fight the dark predations. The third and seventh Rays externalise the efforts of the forces of evil upon the physical domain and produce the ritual magic

43 *The Externalisation of the Hierarchy*, pages 646-647 and 664-668 presents information concerning the English Master, whose work up till the time of D.K.'s writings has been deemed highly successful. Much of the foundation work and right distribution of labour in preparation for the New World civilisation in the Aquarian Age, which is ruled by the seventh Ray, rests in the hands of his Ashram. Note the close relation to the 3/7 and 7/3 Rays, in that they are open doors to each other and have similar functions.

44 Egotistical posturing of the 'I', me, mine.

of the magician, so often prostituted for the gains of the personal self. Perversion of the second and fourth Rays are the basis of the grey forms of magic. These subtle forms of maleficent whisperings of erroneous thoughts are most dangerous for those upon the Initiation path.

The general work of the Mahāchohan's department consists in converting the overly muddied *kāma-manasic saṃskāras* generated by humanity. The respective Chohans hold the keys to humanity's mental disposition and its eventual conversion to the attributes of Mind. The conversion, however, needs the flux of the flow of Love via the second Ray Ashrams. Thus is generated the *bodhicitta* that produces the liberation of *manasic* units from *saṃsāra's* wheel. To tread the Dharmakāya Way (the path to liberation) also necessitates the addition of the directive Will to pierce the veils to Shambhalic domains and to project *antaḥkaraṇas* to cosmos, whereon the Buddha-fields of great Bliss greet the liberated Minds.

Many are the keys to enlightenment to be discovered upon the path. They open various doors to higher perception. For the Mahāchohan's department the symbolic form of such a key can be considered where the long handle is constituted of the third Ray purpose. From it stem three prongs, where the Airy prong is constituted of the fourth Ray purpose, the Fiery prong is constituted of the fifth Ray purpose, and the Earthy prong is constituted of the seventh Ray purpose. The substance of this key is composed of the energies of the sixth Ray Ashrams. The key is turned in *saṃsāra* by the Mahāchohan to gradually transform the maligned ruddy, grey, and blackened *prāṇas* of the Lords of materialistic might and separative intent.

Many of these Ashrams are working to eventually implement a properly humanitarian United Nations, to carry through to conclusion all associated magnanimous agendas that will truly benefit its charter nations. This is not presently the case with the corrupted, compromised organisation of today. Much reformation is necessary as part of the process that will instigate the new world epoch. A consequent vision of what constitutes the new world civilisation needs to be provided to humanity to help it come to fruition. The Mahāchohan's department lays the foundation for the appropriate expression of the second Ray. The second Ray department specifically counters evil through right educational methods. The high Initiates of this Ray thus become specialists in countering all grey shades of light and aberrant thought emanation. They work to rectify all forms of illogic and to instate more enlightened modes of thinking. The first Ray department acts as the potent psychic shield for humanity.

All disciples have utilised evil methodology in past lives, hence must appropriately cleanse their former evil doing through becoming experts in the countering energies upon the higher turn of the cycles of the past. Upon the Initiation path such skills are developed by mastering the *saṃskāras* of past weaknesses. *Karma* from the past is specially selected to test the candidate and thereby the errors are rectified upon the path of Love in service. Through their former conversion process they have become specialists in countering that form of maligned activity. In this way everyone can progress on the upward way to enlightenment. As for the individual Initiate, so also for humanity, the world disciple. They also must be tested through learning to master past mistakes. Hence mass karmic opportunities are provided, so that the effect of cupidity, the mendacity of the political elite and the entrenched selfishness of the great majority become obvious for the candidates to see. Only then can the remedies be wrought from out of society itself. Hence we have the present planetary malaise brought upon us by the excessively greedy rulers and financiers of our nations bolstered by obfuscating statements by a well-oiled propaganda machine that has deluded the sleeping masses. The nature of such evil is obvious to most thinking people.

The new world order will be based in three basic keynotes: Power rightly shared, Love rightly understood, and Plenty rightly distributed. The poverty of the world will be stopped in the wisest manner, the massed attack of the avaricious upon the environment (the common heritage of humanity) will be averted, the lavish financial legal larceny of the Corporate CEO's and bankers will be stopped. Proper legislation will ensure that. A form of capitalism will still flourish, but will be under restrictions. The majority of the nations on this planet (presently called 'the Third World'), who have suffered immensely because of the imposition of the 'free trade', privatisation, capital manipulation, and multinational corporate agendas of the rich and powerful nations, will set the main agenda at the new United Nations.

The new United Nations will therefore deem the war waged by commercial interests against the welfare of common people, the poor and desperate in all of our societies, as a crime against humanity. The great harm done in terms of the financial, social, and economic devastation upon our communities will be recognised, therefore all tendencies to economic crimes will be proscribed. Such understanding is now becoming painfully obvious to many in the world and will then be officially acknowledged. Economic devastation will be measured in terms of the mass of human suffering, diseases, lack of social infrastructure and basic necessities (such as adequate shelter, power and water), all of which cause premature deaths. Hence no longer will the tides of human misery through economic deprivation be possible. There is everywhere the need for equitable resource sharing. This idea will be a battle cry of the poorer nations. This cry will make a common thread for multifarious forms of action, and humanity will muster strength to carry them out.

The Hierarchical plan asserts that all resources must be rightly distributed across all international boundaries, without tariffs and undue, unfair subsidies of any commodity. Thus will manifest a true resource management, concentrating on the arenas of necessity in various national states. Forms of international money racketeering will then also disappear. Racketeering in the pharmaceutical and health business will also be curtailed. The plan to eliminate all monopolistic practices, rent and price gouging, must work like a machine, logically instigated and lovingly inspired. There will be the coalescence of wise and loving design, will, and justice, well oiled with good will. What is fair and equable will become the order of the day.

The United Nations must truly work for the benefit of all member countries. This necessitates freedom from the avariciousness of powerful nations, especially of a hegemon, that bullies or bribes vulnerable nations to vote according to their dictates. No major country or grouping of powerful nations should be able to dictate their agenda for the rest to follow. There will be no further need for veto power by any nation or blocs of nations.

The new United Nations must properly take into account the differences in population represented by various nations. Nations with large populations are not equal to small countries with tiny populations. Countries will be divided into blocks for voting of their own free choice, by region, by culture, by economic need. Fees for the United Nations will be compulsory and can be divided amongst nations according to real income verses societal needs. Formulas incorporating gross national product with respect to the diversity of a multicultural population distribution can be applied to calculate these. Voting rights will be forfeited if fees are not paid by any nation.

The inherent wealth of any nation must be properly considered, as these nations bear a greater responsibility to provide for the common wealth of all. Equable laws must be generated by all nations on such issues as copyright, biodiversity, sanctions, all major financial dealings, trade, and holding mass media organisations accountable to truth and integrity in their reporting on major issues. Such issues must be by proper consensus. It necessitates freedom from the corruption of officials at the head of departments. The entire human kingdom must thereby be made to move upwards in their thought life, closer to that associated with Hierarchy. Proper international relations must therefore be established, similar to the accord that rightfully exists between loving, concerned people.

Nuclear, and other weapons of mass destruction, cluster bombs, biological weapons, etc., will be banned forthwith. The war machines of all nations will be much reduced after the major conflict that will be known as World War III, as the world will have passed through the effects of their use in that war. The series of world wars of the past should have educated humanity on the need for an international watchdog ('peace keepers'), with real teeth of enforcement that can be let off the chain at appropriate times. Many countries will contribute with rotating responsibilities. Its threat should be sufficient to prevent resurgence of war mongers, however by now the human population as a unit will stand solidly on the side of peaceful coexistence between nations, and the modes of war rhetoric, militaristic propaganda, will be recognised and curtailed from the outset. All will know where militarism will lead to. Rules of engagement will be clearly spelt out for aggressor nations that will be the targets of possible UN intervention. The distinction between 'freedom fighters' and 'terrorists' will be well defined by then. The need for extensive weapons manufacture by nations will thus be superseded by more socially acceptable industries, as the need for countries to defend themselves from aggressors will be virtually nonexistent. Definitive borders that misplaced ethnic or religious groups, drawn up during the days of colonial imperialism, will be redrawn if properly petitioned by sufficient individuals in any nation. Such UN militarisation represents a transition phase. Inevitably the armies will disband and the concept of war will only be a consideration of historians.

The new UN body will thus be provided with the script concerning new standards of international behaviour, and how to insist upon it. The vested interests of no organisation or nation will be allowed, except in the way that all are served in completely transparent interrelations. Economic sanctions would only be used as a tool of last resort by the entire community of nations once all of the facts have been properly assessed. Unilateralism will not be tolerated.

The new International Court of Justice, or any national justice system, will manifest without bias, with the justness of any law to the society in question properly factored in. Such courts will work in an ordered fashion with compliance to law factored in based upon true knowledge of human nature, not ideals or the dogmatism of an elite in power. No nation's individuals will be deemed exempt. The justice system will be bound by fairness, order, logic, good principles, then the right solution implemented with clear thought, which will be highly valued.

The new United Nations needs to better educate the world's masses, so that they become truly aware of the sources of their afflictions. Economic sanctions will work in a whole new way. Possibilities of graft and coercion of judges by powerful elites will be eliminated as much as possible, with severe penalties for those found in the pursuit of such actions. The tenure of a judge to any court of law will be based upon proven impartiality to the case submitted. Tenure of all offices must be limited to a set number of years. All cases shall be tried openly with the evidence provided for public scrutiny. Facts, not allegations must rule the day.

Transparency in all areas of government, especially that related to law enforcement, will be demanded by the associated populations. All contentious issues shall be thoroughly assessed by jurists who have proven themselves to truly represent the international community and not to the nation state or other vested interest group they might formerly belong to. Abuses of power of the political and judicial elite will be viewed as the gravest of offences and accordingly dealt with.

Purveyors of all forms of propaganda, especially the mass media that purport to educate the public, must be able to validate their claims. Lying propaganda of any type shall incur the harshest penalties, as the role of the mass media in promoting or greatly facilitating the wars and most of the evils of the past will be well documented. The role of a journalist must again be one of integrity in our societies, whose insights command high respect.

All activities of the new UN at whatever level (and eventually that of the nation states) will be fully transparent and published forthwith, so that all concerned people and governments can access for themselves the nature of the activity and the decisions made and why.

Privatisation of the resources needed for the welfare of the poorer sectors of the community, where large profits are made out of the victimisation of the poor, will be a thing of the past. The forms of financial rape of people and the communities in which they reside will thus end. All financial transactions will be closely scrutinised to ensure that the balance sheet of acceptable profits over the rightful needs of the population at large is properly ascertained. A fair equity will thus be presented to workers. Economic slavery will be understood as another disguised form of ownership of one large group of people by a smaller elite possessing much power over their lives. Here manacle and chain have been replaced by contrived economic necessity upon the impoverished to accept demeaning working conditions, and subsistence level payments for labour. This allows excessive profits to be made for the executors of a company, and humongous payments given to its CEO. Real limitations will be placed upon what such people can earn relative to the common person, as all forms of social inequity must come to an end. The true value of labour, of productive output, will thus be properly assessed and appropriately paid for.

Governments will hence be forced to ensure that the poorest sectors of their communities have affordable housing, food, medicine, transportation, education for children, and the possibility of finding work with non-slave labour wages for its citizens. Child labour will vanish. A proper international police force will be established to prosecute many of the rapacious crimes against the poorest in our societies, and those against women. The human trafficking and forms of prostitution now possible because of feeble policing, laws disadvantageous to the poor, and accompanying squalor will thus be eliminated. The 'war' on drugs will be eliminated, and beneficent programs set up in its place to assist people that are addicted to all forms of drugs and intoxicants, such as pharmaceuticals, alcohol, and gambling. Inevitably through sane laws and the imposition of the above measures the need for policing of a nation's citizens will significantly diminish.

Corporations should be assisted to become good planetary citizens, to help the environment and the communities of which they are a part. They will be rescinded or will pay high penalties, if their products are found to be detrimental to the environment and human society in general. No longer will billionaires be able to arise in nations when others are found to live in abject poverty. Neither will the financial power of the extremely wealthy be allowed to buy political favour. Venality will be especially proscribed. All citizens must be deemed to pay the same price in economic terms, to be part of a national society. No individual or group shall be specifically favoured, unless they have proven themselves in the fields of service work to their societies or the international community in some beneficent way. Contributions, aside from those seen just in economic terms, will be properly evaluated and be highly esteemed. The society will manifest valued, appropriate rewards for those that have served their country or community well.

No longer will public money be used to bail out the bad decisions of bankers and industrialists. No longer will the halls of our parliaments be filled with self-interest lobbyists. The copyright laws will be scrutinised so that dubious claims can no longer be made by unscrupulous companies for the patenting of such things as the world's biodiversity—as if the alteration of the genetic variety of our biosphere can somehow be made into a commodity, rather than being the common heritage of humanity. Humanity were never asked if their common resources could be utilised and adulterated for abusive profiteering in the first place. Here we have an example of a cynical exercise by the most powerful nation to control everyone's food supply and thus have near absolute power over everybody. Thus, no aggressively powerful and avaricious nation will decide what patenting and other laws are applicable to the world as a whole. A totally transparent world body shall decide what patents should be granted, how long they will remain in place, and the conditions that should apply. Shorter, not longer terms of applicability, of any patent will generally apply. Inventions and technological advances that are truly beneficial to humanity as a whole will not be allowed to be patented by an unscrupulous company if that advance is to be buried and never utilised for the intent it was created for. Clauses will be built into patent rights to ensure that all companies fulfil their international obligation as a beneficent planetary citizen.

Undue profiteering in such ways that is deemed to be harmful to the great mass of the planetary citizens will also be viewed as crimes against humanity, and be fully prosecutable in an international court of law. For instance, all forms of biopiracy will be outlawed, so that the fruits of scientific research become the property of the nations for collective good and not for the benefit of a few super wealthy individuals and corporations. A truly international police force will be available to that court to apprehend violators of international law, no matter in which country they reside. This force will have full freedom to act in any country deemed necessary, and measures will be in place for the new UN to impose penalties to non compliant nations.

Part of the future work of the Mahāchohan's department will thus be concerned with the implementation of the philosophy, aims, and agenda of the new, reformed UN armed with the powers to rectify many of the world's social and economic problems. It will no longer be possible for another country as powerful as the USA presently is to arise again. There will be no exceptions to international laws. With the UN's ability to police its decisions, nations will be forced to comply with them, and no hypocritical policies shall be acted upon. Safeguards will be put into place to ensure against internal corruption within the new UN. The vested self-interest of any powerful nation, or blocs of nations, will not be allowed to unduly influence the heads of department of the UN, or of any decision making that will be binding for the good of all.

Bribery, undue coercion of weaker nations by powerful ones and international nepotism will be a thing of the past. Honest portrayal of facts, the presentation of verifiable truth and evidence of what actually is, will be tabled and open for proper scrutiny by all member nations. Diplomats shall be subject to the laws of the land that hosts them when outside the confines of their embassy, thus eliminating the abuses garnered under the present system of 'diplomatic immunity'.

The demagogy of nations will obviously be taken into account. Clearly a nation such as India, with over one billion citizens, will carry more weight in decision making than an island state with a population of only a few tens of thousands. There will therefore be established a form of upper and lower house (or a form of Senate and a Congress), with respect to voting decisions, with a viable and truly representative formula established to determine how national votes can be apportioned. This will be revised over time to take into account the then current international situation and the demography of nations.

At first capitalism will again emerge out of the turmoil of war, with certain individuals manifesting scurrilous schemes to become the big winners of their society. Thus many financiers will try to amass considerable wealth again. However, there will be differences, more power will be in the hands of the common people, more of the beneficent changes propelled by Hierarchy will begin to flourish, more ventures and businesses will have the employees in charge of the resources and proceeds of that company or organisation. Fiat currency will no longer prevail, as money will be once again put upon sound basis, such as on a gold and silver standard, and forms of barter of labour, etc., for goods also advocated. A completely new monetary system, of means of exchange for labour may emerge, formulated by deeply conscientious financiers. The concept of the garden city with many small-scale farms for food production for local needs will be the mainstay of urban planning.

The movement of international capital will be properly regulated and policed so that the stock markets, commodity speculators, and multinational corporations cannot run riot in their greedy pursuit of excessive profits at everyone else's expense. The way that currency and commodity speculators have brought ruin to many nations over the past centuries will be fully analysed, and proper brakes put on the forms of compulsive gambling that have caused incalculable suffering upon the great masses of the world's people. The UN will consequently end the avenues that lead to super wealthy individuals. No more will be the way that the richest 1% of the world's population have abused the resources and common wealth of the remaining 99%. A new form of International Monetary Fund may be established to truly help poorer nations out of difficulties.

The plight of women all over the world will also be rightly assessed and new laws drafted that will ensure their status as equal to men in all societies, tribes, and religions. Medieval thinking in certain religions, such as Sharia law in the Muslim world, will be modified, curtailed or eliminated, based upon universally recognised human rights for all planetary citizens. Goodwill between people, races and sectors in society will be encouraged in every way.

The above is but an outline of a new form of Socialism that will in time be converted into a veritable treatise and the eventful implementation of the new United Nations. It is consequently a theme that many will be engrossed in during this present century as the appropriate externalised members of Hierarchy are increasingly found in positions of power in all departments of Life. Their Bodhisattvic activities will then be evident to all that they serve. It necessitates the recognition and placing in power those that are acknowledged the wisest or most caring in our societies. Pre-selection in any political party will need to take these two factors into account, as a properly free press will scrutinise candidates upon such a basis. The Ashrams will externalise, but any particular Ashram may not necessarily be localised in one area, rather its members will collectively incarnate throughout the world manifesting the service arenas of their respective Ray lines. The perceptive reader can deduce the wider ramifications of their probable effects from the outlines of their attributes from the summaries provided earlier, and from A.A. Bailey's *The Externalisation of the Hierarchy.*

Summary

We saw that the twenty odd Ashrams of the Mahāchohan's department can be considered to form *maṇḍalas* based on the mode of manifestation of the *chakras* below the diaphragm. Taking all of the Ashrams into account, the trinity of Will-Love-Activity (Father—first Ray, Son—Second Ray, Mother—third Ray) can also be found. The third Ray Ashrams (3/2, 3/7, 3/4) plus the first Ray Ashrams constituting Splenic centre II represent the directive principle for the process of the conversion of *saṃskāras*. The fourth Ray Ashrams represent the educative department for the principle of Love. They project the cleansing *prāṇas* of Love from the Heart centre via the second Ray Ashrams and the power of Splenic centre I. The remainder of the Ashrams of the Rays of Mind are concerned with the general activity of the other centres below the diaphragm, preparing human *saṃskāras* for conversion via the 'burning ground' of the Splenic centres.

The activity of all of the Ray Ashrams can be viewed in terms of the planes of perception to which they are numerically allied, with whose substance they consequently directly work. The *third Ray Ashrams* work via the plane *ātma* (the lowest level of *dharmakāya*) and related substance, thus with the emanation of the Aūṁ (the activity expression of Love-Wisdom).

The *fourth Ray Ashrams* are a natural emanation of the fourth plane, *buddhi*, and consequently reflect Logoic Purpose into manifestation. Also, as *buddhi* is the realm whereon Hierarchy resides, and the Logoic *chakras* are externalised, so it is natural that the fourth Ray Ashrams work directly with etheric energy associated with all the kingdoms of Nature. Their work is to directly organise the related flowers (*chakras*, or departments of human livingness) according to the pattern ordained for any cycle. They are cleansing agents, carrying off negative strains of auric *(prāṇic)* colouring and replacing them with purified streams to help invigorate the interrelatedness of all terrestrial Life. As this Ray governs the human kingdom, so it is always active in all fields of application, specifically those producing a beautification and aesthetic upliftment of society. There is a correlation between such activity and the effects of the work of the Solar *devas* that direct *prāṇic* vitality to all forms of Life. This is a reason why the Chohan of the fourth Ray (Serapis) has entered the ranks of the *deva* kingdom.

The *fifth Ray Ashrams* work directly with the substance of the mind (*manas*) and thus with the divisions of the empirical mind and abstract Mind. Upon the abstracted mental sub-planes the Sambhogakāya Flower finds its residence, thus these Ashrams work directly with the floral forms to intensify the radiance of the related Sun/Son, by means of the scientific application to the laws of Life. The stimulating effect of *manas* upon all levels of human Life gauges the possibility of people undertaking the various Initiations. The fifth Ray weaves the Fiery patterning that flows through humanity's *nāḍīs*, infusing the *prāṇic* flow with the light of Life. Inevitably this activity finds its externalisation as science and technology in our societies. Once scientific methodology is truly applied to all categories of human livingness in this universe, then we will see the salvation of humanity, producing its inevitable consummation in the Fiery domain.

The *sixth Ray Ashrams* work directly with the fluid proclivity of the sixth (Watery) astral plane. They help purify all streams of human desire, selfishness, and glamour-forming tendencies,[45] through seeding devotion to noble ideals, ideas and causes, and of aspiration to things supernal and divine. They work through religious streams and by rightly directing the behaviour of the moving masses. The younger members of these Ashrams are also responsible for that fanaticism and intolerant religious zealotry that is the cause of much warring strife. The effect of Mars, the god of war, upon the astral plane can also be considered here.

When the astral plane is cleansed of its muddied, turbulent activities it then acts as a conduit or reflector for refined *prāṇas*. These energies from Hierarchical and Shambhalic sources will then intensify the inherent radiance of humanity. At first this will produce warlike overtones whilst the cleansing process is instigated. This happens because base desire is rarely properly controlled in individuals and groups. The tone is thereby set for the entire world play, allowing Deity to ascertain what is possible concerning the karmic redirection of forces, thus conditioning Hierarchical planning. Their meditative processes are always directed to the true needs of humanity, in accordance to the way they will go in response to any given stimulus or energisation. The steady driving sixth Ray force first manifests emotionally, or as desire or aspiration, and then as definite action on the physical plane. The tide of massed emotions sway this way and that according to the play of energies emanating from higher sources that find their way into manifestation through the sixth Ray Ashrams. Thus the world view is eventuated with a tendency to war-like activity. Aspirational tendencies can also swing people towards the quest for liberation from all perceived suffering.

The *seventh Ray Ashrams* work ritualistically with the energy fields

---

45 See Alice Bailey's *Glamour, a World Problem* for esoteric insights on this topic and also to the distinction between glamour, illusion and *māyā*.

found within the *nāḍīs* of the various kingdoms of Nature. Their field of service therefore is with the etheric substratum of the corporeal world wherein is found the combination of all the above Ray effects, automatically effecting response upon the physical domain.

These Ashrams ground the work of the first and second Ray Ashrams via cyclic purpose. The 'blueprints' engendered by the second Ray planners become thereby the finished construct. Those of the seventh Ray Ashrams are often found in legislation, in governance, the military, as well as in arenas of magical endeavour, seen in the various occult and religious cults that specialise in the mysterious or the arcane. The seventh Ray organisational skills produces the power of accomplishment in religious, Tantric, and scientific fields of activity wherein repetitious experimentation is needed. These Ashrams build the concrete edifices of our societies, as well as the foundation for the externalising Hierarchy, making sure that all planned activity finds firm support in the material world.

The *second Ray Ashrams* are directly impressed from the Monadic domain, the second plane or *dharmakāyic* level *(anupādaka)* from whence they direct Hierarchical purpose. Via this plane the entire Hierarchal *maṇḍala* is energised from the Heart of Love in cosmos. They thus project the esoteric wisdom religions that arise to advance humanity into new fields of revelation. From its ranks come the world Teachers and far-sighted visionaries that incorporate the many streams of livingness and viewpoints along any field into a unity or synthesising whole. The second Ray works as an attractive force to draw all to the cosmic Heart centre. (Though at this level of expression one must also consider the abstracting power of the first Ray.)

The *first Ray Ashrams* work directly with Shambhalic purpose, imposing major changes upon this earth through the use of the directive energy of the Will. They are the victorious generals of armies and able statesmen in the fields of politics and jurisprudence. The more advanced members of this grouping, however, work with much more esoteric methods, as the 'shield of God', to directly counter dark brotherhood activity by means of the highest Ray energies possible to express. Such ones have been well trained in many previous lives as warriors, and leaders of armies in the field of battle. Being integrated with the second Ray department they manifest the most far-sighted vision and occult doctrines (via energies from the highest of the systemic planes of perception, *ādi*). Therefore many of the highest esoteric teachings are in the hands of the Lords of this Ray line, once they become awakened.

One can also envisage an inverted Shambhalic pentad energising Hierarchy, that has its feet and hands upon cosmic astral levels. (The source of Love/*bodhicitta* to our planet.) The hands and feet extend to various Buddha-fields manifesting in cosmos. The right foot (drawing upon the fourth cosmic astral sub-plane) is represented by the functions of the blue Christ. The left foot (drawing from the manasic cosmic astral sub-plane), the Phoenician. The right hand is represented by the European Chohan, who draws energy via the sixth cosmic astral sub-plane. The left hand (projecting the ritualistic purpose from the seventh cosmic astral level) is represented by Padmasambhava. The focal point of all their energies is the head of the new Mahāchohan resting in the substance of the highest systemic plane.[46] The entire Hierarchical *maṇḍala* is vitalised thereby with cosmic purpose. It becomes the expression of the meditation-Mind of this Chohan, the unfolding purpose of his Thought-stream. Therein is established the coherent Mindscape for the entire Hierarchical unfoldment via the various pentads throughout the three times. His Eye first helps to direct the Heart of the Hierarchical shield established by the 2/1 and first Ray Ashrams. It then helps project the service arenas of the newly forming 3/4 Ashram and the seventh Ray line in general, assisted by the second and fourth Ray lines. The demonstration of the service arenas of these Ashrams signifies the active descent of Hierarchy into the mainstream of human civilisation, finalising the results of millennia of Hierarchical planning and activity.

---

46 The complete Hierarchical *maṇḍala* can also be viewed in terms of manifesting pentads.

To Meet the Christ

If you met the Christ, and he asked you to follow him,
leaving everything else behind, material possessions,
emotions, things of the mind, could you?

If the meditation life attracts you
and you seek out right teachings,
will you ignore those teachings when they come
because they do not come in the form expected?
Can you always have an open heart and mind
that quickly change track when new things they find?

If the service work appears
for which you have trained for millennia
will you delay the expression of that Plan
because of the attraction to other activities
that glitter here and there in the dark?

If you have attained the right to enter a spiritual University
will you continue attachment to 'primary school'
  and its children,
pursuing easy activities designed for a simpler mind
when your capacity is of a higher kind?

If you have attained high spiritual age
will you continue with worldly affairs
or with forms of activity or 'helping'
that foster self-centred formulas of thought
that serve little the Plan,
knowing that the unloving activity of mind
will always find the new work a grind?

If vision of the ideal New Age Community inspires you,
will you involve yourself in activities
that are not related to its production?

Can you link hands, Heart, and mind
in complete identification
with those who are as you on the Path?
Or will your mind and hands constantly seek involvement
with those who walk a different way?

When you see the Light of the spiritual Sun
beckoning before you,
will you turn away from its Bliss
to satisfy personality wishes?

When our Hearts and minds work as one
then the One can shine forth in greater Glory
then it could for any Heart working singularly for the One.
Would it not be a crime to not take up the offer
to thus serve when opportunity appears?

Why continue in *saṃsāric* wandering,
with its cyclic journeying, its constant toil and pain,
its past conditionings confounding you,
when the way of the Heart,
which leads from that to Bliss finally opens?

Where is the Christ if he sits not before you
and uses not his tongue to implore you
to fully serve all that around you are faint-hearted
and dying of a materialistic sickness
that still attracts you when you heed not
that Voice within you?
Take the shortest, clearest path to such service
with those whom He has offered
so that the Way can be quickly realised.
His Heart in your Mind unfolding.
We are all then blest by your being.
This expression is a long time in the making.

7

Considerations of Hierarchical Externalisation

Cleansing evil karma

All Ashrams work steadfastly to counter the negative traits fostered upon humanity by our brothers of darkness. The forces of evil always have counter plans to that generated by Hierarchy. All consideration of Hierarchal effort must take into account the karmic implications of the situations they are concerned with, as the dark brotherhood are lesser Lords of *karma* in their own right. They have earned the right to influence humanity and the disciples that are endeavouring to throw off their yokes, because of the *karma* of the past nefarious activity of the people whom they prey upon and attack. They represent the karmic repercussions of former misdeeds and evil activities against the well being of all kingdoms in the Mother's domain. They are therefore compatriots of the former evil-doing of disciples, and come to claim what is their rightful due. They return to disciples the potency (in terms of thoughts and rays of darkened energies) of the effects of their former lies, evil schemes, psychic, physical and mental-emotional manipulation, and of what was inflicted in any way to cause pain. Progress upon the path is determined upon how effectively a disciple counters this appearing *karma* and transforms the associated *saṃskāras*.

The white brother, who works to eliminate the power of the forces of evil over the mainstream civilisation, cannot just simply zap them out of existence with their immensely more powerful Rays of light. (As compared to the grey and black emanations of the forces of evil.) Instead they need to properly educate humanity how not to generate the *saṃskāras (prāṇas)* that support the might of the dark ones upon this planet.

Creating no further *karma* is necessary on the stage of discipleship where much time is consumed in zapping[1] away evil emanations. These emanations can be painful and also sickness inducing. This is a necessary part of the second Initiation process, as it constitutes a testing ground and method of cleansing the *karma* of maleficent psychic projections from past lives of ritualised magical practice. (Or of power-focussed material incentives, religiously or temporally based.) Much meditation is needed to properly see the streams of grey or blackened attack, the entities involved, and of the many other forms of manipulation of the psyche that can be utilised against the disciple. Myriad are the thought-form attacks that must be warded off or countered with pristine efficacious logic. Self-centered, glamoured, egoistic, prideful, selfish, and all similar *saṃskāras,* must be countered with precise veridical logic and appropriate action. In this way the disciple's meditation life produces many different vistas of revelations concerning the foibles of past actions, whilst endeavouring to serve in the now. Concurrently, the disciple also enters a spiritual world of great beauty and inner plane helpers, as the karmic connection of former striving in discipleship comes into play.

Meditation therefore does not just concern emptying out from the mind all forms of 'self' concepts, or the attributes of *saṃsāra,* for the production of an 'empty mind'. Those that mainly work to produce such results in meditation fall into the danger of manifesting a form of empty complacency. Such emptiness of thoughts in the mind suffices not to awaken one. It but represents a stage on the way. Eliminating obscuring *saṃskāras* produces true emptiness. 'Obscuring' because they represent attributes of a mind not mastered, and which when appear are simply suppressed by the will of mind, hence still lurk to later rear their head as a major obstacle to the path. Similarly, there is obscuring *karma* to contend with that will present obstacles to the path as it comes into view. A strong tension must be developed as

---

1 By 'zapping' is meant the sending of rays of light to counter the dark emanations influencing one's thoughts or psyche.

an immovable will[2] to overcome all obstacles upon the Bodhisattva path by transmuting negatives into positives, so that the many can be best served as a consequence. Self-focussed meditators with 'empty minds' do not attract the focused eye or ire of the dark brotherhood, because they are not a threat to their existence or forms of activity. Also, these 'empty' contemplators can be easily influenced if need be by subtle thought projections directed to the level to which their minds have been acclimatised. They are not working to truly convert all negative *saṃskāras,* because the true nature of their psychic *karma* from past lives eludes them, to be dealt with at a later cycle.

The dark brotherhood are also masters of meditation. They must develop a mind that is empty of certain concepts (such as the principle of Love) before they wilfully collect the needed energies to empower their thought constructs with appropriate magical incantations that can be projected at a target. In this way phenomenal effects can be produced for the gain of the separative self.

The production of an 'empty mind' in meditation can consequently be another glamour, unless it is developed as a base or foundation for the establishment of the Clear Light wherein revelation as to the nature of reality may come. Then the subtle perversions of thought, the greyish and aberrant perceptions, are correctly perceived, analysed, and eliminated. This necessitates converting the darkened *prāṇas,*[3] and zapping the myriad dark brotherhood eyes that will now be keenly focused with intent upon a new upcoming master of wise logic and ceremonial, compassionate activity. This is a necessary practice for the development of *siddhis* on this path of Light and Love. Such a one consequently seriously threatens the powerful hold of the forces of evil over human minds, thus the dark lords will zealously endeavour to prevent him/her from arising. The enlightened Mind can only be awakened by fighting the battles that ensue and being victorious every time, similar to the way that Gautama fought the hordes of Māra. Such a

2 See A.A. Bailey, *The Rays and the Initiations,* (Lucis Press, 1970), 45-46 for further explanation of the meaning of the word 'tension'.

3 Detail concerning this path from the Buddhist perspective was provided in my book *An Esoteric Exposition of the Bardo Thödol.* The process concerns the work needed to be accomplished if the second and third Initiations are to be undertaken.

'war' may take decades to wage, and accounts partly for the many years in solitude that the *mahāsiddhas* and others that have become genuinely enlightened manifested before they gained the fame of who they were.

For this reason very few genuinely enlightened beings appear out of the many thousands who are practitioners of meditation. They lack proper, enlightened meditation instructors, or the determined Will-to-Love, a steadfast Will to overcome, as well as the type of *karma* that can lead them to the liberated domains as high level Bodhisattvas. Then the Will-of-Love becomes their leitmotiv.[4] Myriad, however, are the disciples of revered teachers, who erroneously deem them fully enlightened, awakened. Such teachers may have developed some *siddhis* on their path, are compassionately oriented, and possess certain wisdom in their religious field. The truth, however, is that they generally lack the far-reaching wisdom that truly comprehends the nature of the minutiae of *karma*, of all-round knowledge in many fields of revelatory experience. They do not possess a sufficiently far-sighted, in depth perception, of past ages and epochs of all cultural scenarios wherewith karmic situations can be appropriated. They do not have proper esoteric knowledge of the Ashrams of the Masters of Wisdom as outlined here, as well as the nature of Shambhala. The way of cosmic evolution remains a closed book to them. We would also see a lack of true knowledge of the nature of the minor *chakras* and how they work, and often an ignorance of the nature of the many echelons of the dark brotherhood and their activities. All such knowledge is gained as one masters the various stages of the Initiation path.

Enlightenment thus consists of much more than a placid deportment, the conveyance of appealing mantric spiritual utterances, the display of minor *siddhis* (for the dark brothers have also developed these), or the production of strong devotion (exhilarated emotions) in their disciples. In fact, a disciple's emotions and the related glamours will always be amongst the first casualties of war, of what must be overcome. Ostentatious devotion will be eliminated or sidelined to the outer court of a genuine Master's personal following. Intelligent meditative co-operators are sought instead. The strength of Love developed, however,

---

4 See the section on 'The Will and its Manifestations' in Volume 4 of this treatise, pages 199-217.

is always a keynote of the path. Love is defined as clear cold reason, compassionately focussed. ('Cold' because mental-emotional heat is missing.) There are degrees of enlightenment to consider, of the forms of activity of third, fourth, and fifth degree Initiates. Awakened third degree Initiates may not have some of the exemplary forms of perception indicated above, but do have much wisdom and spiritual insight, and generally cater to the needs of many devotees. They are invaluable teachers of their aspirants and disciples. Such teachers however should not be deemed Masters of Wisdom. They have far yet to travel in that direction. The more advanced along the Initiation path, the less time the teacher will have to indulge devotees. Vast are the subtle forms of service work to be accomplished in the liberated domains.

Workers in the fields that counter the malaise of incorrect human thinking will always be nourished by the enlightened, and a Master will generally be found working behind the scenes silently directing and educating them. Disciples can be trained to educate aspirants at this level, to give them the succour that they need. Time and energy draining forays in the world of human activity, the adulation of the masses, will certainly not be to a Master's liking. The Master's meditation-Mind is orientated at much higher and subtler levels than that, and serene contemplation is needed in places of seclusion to accomplish the tasks at hand. The dark hordes are defeated through deep meditation, esoteric foresight, and occult methodology, not by outward showy pretentiousness in the worlds of human habitation. The Master's hand moves behind the scenes, eschewing fame and the glitter of public acclaim, to work to change human society irretrievably for the better without the obstacles that public recognition would provide. Thus to be publically known and considered 'enlightened' by a vast number of devotees is considered a sacrificial hindrance by such a one. Though occasionally high Bodhisattvas do appear at appointed times to so serve.

As the individual disciple must battle to hold the mind steady in Light, so inevitably must all the serried groups and ranks of humanity along the various Ray lines. It is a millennial-long process that will inevitably defeat the bulk of the forces of evil that prey upon humanity, and the associated *saṃskāras* that constitute the planetary 'dweller on the threshold'. The appearance of the various Ashrams upon the physical domain concerns the establishment of the mechanism that will defeat evil. The era is approaching where no longer can the world's disciples ignore the reality of this aeon-long battle of planetary transformation that overcomes the dark hosts. Eventually people will not be able to plead ignorance to the reality of the subtle spheres of existence whereon the nefarious forces lurk. However, the many popularised images of the way that the forces of evil appear and work, as portrayed in sensationalised movies, in many occult texts, and in fiction, must inevitably submit to truer, more logical and factual presentations.

The general bewildered masses of humanity represent the backdrop between this ancient power play between the forces of the white lodge and those of the dark. Because *karma* and the rebirth of consciousness is the driving dynamo behind manifestation on all lower planes of perception, so the death of the body (the present scenario one inhabits) is not an objective of such activity. Rather it is conversion from one side to the other, with often barely imperceptible changes. Inevitably the forces of Love and Light will come out the victors of this 'war', as all will evolve to Buddhahood in the end, but the process thereto may take aeons. This process is revealed by the awakened meditation-Mind.

The forces of evil

Wherever one looks one can find examples of the forces of evil. These forces exist in everyone, except in the enlightened. There is a battle between light and darkness, Ormazd and Ahriman, to use the old Zoroastrian mythology. All that we consider as truly evil originates in the mind. It concerns the wilful use of the mind to forcefully project images and ideas outwards to negatively influence other minds, or the forces of Nature. In and of itself this substance is neither good nor bad, but the way that it is used to create *karma* that binds one irrevocably for durations of expression to *saṃsāra* is where the problem lies. That is what is here designated 'bad'. The 'good' manifests when the substance of mind is transformed in such a way that lessoning of *saṃsāric* bonding is the result. The nature of the attachments of mind therefore is the problem, of what it attaches itself to, and with what force. The mind then chooses how to interpret this attachment as either good or bad according to its developed predilections. The 'glue' that is utilised to attach to that which is material is the emotional body. This body is really just an energy field, given the alchemical quality Water, because of its mode of action. It is governed by the strength of desire coupled with emotional thought, the images created by the natural attractiveness of the mind to objects visualised in *saṃsāra*. The nature and strength of the attractiveness colours the object of perception with fields of glamour, the product of the desire-mind.

This entire teaching has already been provided in the previous volumes with respect to the Buddhist *Yogācāra* tradition. Here all is conceived of mind, lives in mind, is mind/Mind. An individual's perception differs from someone else's. Even if viewing the same thing, people look from different perspectives, different angles of vision, and their minds interpret in a different way. The nature or quality of what the mind contains is the true distinguishing attribute between people.

That which is evil empowers the reifying attributes of mind, which intensifies attachment to the conditionings of *saṃsāra*. *Saṃsāra* becomes its leitmotiv for existence, and it acknowledges no other domain. It sees itself as the centre of its own self-made universe and coerces all other unities of mind to become a submissive supplicant within its creation. What we designate 'the good' sees an inherent flaw in this logic, perceiving a state of unifying expression beyond mind, which has been called *śūnyatā,* that when strived for can liberate one from the ceaseless repetitions of the patterns created by the substance of mind. Liberation from the cycles of suffering associated with *saṃsāra* necessitates also the development of wisdom, producing eventually a clarified, intensified light of mind, called Mind in this treatise.

There are two sources of evil for our system:

1. First there is the product of the descending journey of the Monadic Life from the cosmic mental plane down to material plane livingness. This concerns the evolutionary journey of a Monad, the *dharmakāyic* aspect of a human. The Monadic Eye eventually lodges itself on the second highest of our seven systemic planes (*anupādaka)* and there it projects a Ray of itself at the appropriate time to form the Buddha-germ (*tathāgatagarbha*), the Sambhogakāya Flower, that then projects an energy link into a womb for each of the symbolic 777 incarnations to cause the evolution of a human consciousness-stream.

Each human unit thus formed is also considered a *mānasaputra*, a man-plant, a being of mind substance.[5]

The concern here, however, is upon the process of Monadic evolution before the establishment of a 'man-plant' because of the type of cosmic astral substance accrued on the path of descent. The masses of Monads on this downward path are swept into the vortex of young forming planets, such as the earth, and take the shape of mythological entities as they do so. Prior to incorporating the substance of a mineral kingdom, these Monads upon the involutionary arc represent collective formative forces that can express the destructive side of Nature's processes. They can also take the shape of dark entities bearing a spark of the substance of cosmic Mind.[6] The stage for the forming of the vehicle for the human Mind (*tathāgatagarbha*) is yet long in the future for them, however, the descending cosmic astral and etheric substance that represent their externalised forms can and do play a role in the mythos of any then presently evolving human kingdom. These descending, concretising forms, are often utilised and directed by advanced cosmic Sorcerers as armies that do their bidding. This is part of the natural order of things on the path of Monadic descent, where they must utilise substance (forms) that to the human units then residing effectively manifests in a time zone in the far distant past. This substance of the descending Monadic forms is therefore considered evil. Some of the dark brotherhood entities that are visualised in the meditation-Minds of disciples and *yogins* as attacking them are of this type. They take various forms, according to their inherent stage of evolution and intrinsic quality. Zapping them with light (to remove the psychic attack) is actually part of the process that clears the Monads from limiting substance, thereby drawing them closer to the systemic physical plane incarnation that humans are immersed in. The massive armies of the dark brotherhood that are seen are therefore young evolving Monads on the path of descent. This is an interesting, but vast subject, that would digress us too far

5 *Mānasaputra*, sons or forms (*putra*) of mind (*manas*).

6 Here we see the cosmic correspondence to the 'lunar lords', which interested esoteric students can further analyse.

if analysed in detail here, but needs to be mentioned for the sake of completeness.

2. There is another line of dark brotherhood which are the consequence of material plane livingness and are much more formidable. They come as a consequence of human evolution where human units have wilfully resisted the evolutionary trend. Thus they have become sorcerers, witches, warlocks, evil in high places. They follow a line of development that leads to an identification or fusion with *devas* that express the processes of destruction, disintegration, and death. They merge with these *devas,* allowing the dark forces to escape into cosmic space at the ending of a cycle of materialism, whereby they can perpetuate their *karma* for another solar evolution. In the long course of evolution, when one thinks of births and deaths of entire solar systems and in terms of Monadic evolution, human life on an earth sphere represent only a tiny portion or period of this process. Inevitably they face conversion as a consequence of the aeonic war between the white and dark brotherhoods, thus must eventually pay back their amassed *karma.*

The appearance of a Logos (a cosmic Deity) offers opportunity for all beings to journey from the concrete systemic domains to the cosmic mental plane. The seven systemic planes that we reside in are the seven sub-planes of the cosmic dense physical. Above them is the cosmic astral which is the plane of liberation. A Buddha that leaves this planet is born into the cosmic astral plane, and there is a vast scheme of evolution ahead. The dark brotherhood, on the other hand, represent the darkened *prāṇas* that need transforming within the Logoic Body. The process of transforming such *saṃskāras* are of a similar nature, but manifesting upon a far vaster scale, than what happens in a human body.

A positive outcome to any evolutionary progression is not certain. There are star systems that have been taken over by cosmic evil, wherein black *antaḥkaraṇas* engulf whole planets, integrating them into a huge, dying, disintegrating cancerous mess, a mass of darkness. Our moon had previously succumbed to such a fate, thus what is now seen is a (premature) dead body of a former planet that is the result of victory for the dark brotherhood. Most of its former Life streams have long ago been transferred to the earth. We are presently at the stage in earth evolution that corresponds to the end of moon evolution, the darkest period of a most materialistic age, known as the *kali yuga.*

It can be seen from this brief exposé that proper analysis of the nature of evil would require a large treatise. These forces work in duality, being composed of a black stream (associated with the most forceful and material aspects of mind) and a grey stream (dealing with subtler emotional-mental thoughts of people). Here also are seen the many sombre-hued dull streams of light. There is also a potent brown force (distorting the principle of desire) that supplements the main arenas of dark brotherhood activity. Expediency presently prevents proper analysis, because of the dangers presented to disciples that have not been properly prepared for the consequences if their creative imagination begins to run rampant, upon which the dark ones can capitalise.

There is, however, perhaps one aspect of the dark brotherhood, along the grey *(piṇgalā)* line, that should be discussed, as their effects are most pronounced in subtly swaying the minds of disciples along all levels of the path until the third Initiation is reached. These are the *Anubis,* the long eared Jackel-headed deity, found represented in Egyptian mythology, and seen weighing the heart of the deceased against a feather in illustrations depicting the Egyptian Book of the Dead. They were much worshipped in that culture, and powerful thought-forms were created that were given life upon the astral domains, by being incarnated into by dark forces.

All disciples of the Masters today have had incarnations in ancient Egypt, hence have *karma* with such psychic beings. Overcoming their subtle thought suggestions represents some of the final stages of the battle against the dark brotherhood before one can gain enlightenment, hence the need to provide some information concerning them. They can also take the image of wolves in the psychic domain. They produce subtle distortions of logic, which, for instance, is especially prevalent in the exponents of Buddhism. There is a plan for the *buddhadharma,* which succinctly and resolutely should resolve Egyptian *karma* in the now. The Anubis logic has engulfed the entire religion as a whole, and has produced quite an anaemic expression of an enlightenment vehicle that could have been. The wolf game of distorted belief systems must stop, hence the need for the publication of this series of books, plus the earlier two I have published.[7] The second Ray is to flourish through Buddhism, and the law deems that one must learn the hard way if the desired path is not followed.

Buddhism is the esoteric heir to the Egyptian religion, where the theriomorphic Gods of the theogony of the Egyptians become translated into the feminine Wrathful Deities depicted in the *Bardo Thödol.* The forces that were once worshipped become the transformative agencies for appearing *saṃskāras.* The overlay of a higher perspective based upon the powers of the Heart centre (Buddhism) transforms the powers *(siddhis)* of the Solar Plexus centre (the Egyptian religion). Thus the evolution of religions proceeds.

The Anubis feed fears, worries, anxieties, all attributes of pride of mind, separative, self-focussed and avaricious thinking. Their logic often runs riot in a disciple's mind. There is gossip, innuendo, and iniquitous accusations beneath the veneer of monk-like order, of nun-like quiet. All must watch for all errors of mind as well as emotions. Watch well for the waspish good humour, the twisted logic, the wolf in sheep's clothing in all spiritual pursuits. The Anubis will incessantly feed your desires, continuously tell you what you want to hear. They know how to swell your mind with thoughts of self, to masquerade as white brotherhood, and try to tell you that such thoughts are divine. They will preen your ego, to make you feel wise, but instead you will flounder in the tomb of your mind with thoughts unkind, disguised as loving all the while. They always generate emotionally polarised thoughts. See the effect of all the Rays distorted in logic gone bad. Wise, loving understanding and application of veridical insight is needed, not tunnel vision, dogmatic assertion and distorted perception.

The wolves have a way with words, to confuse aspirants and disciples with their logic. They waste a lot of our time. You can recognise it's a wolf talking by dullness of tone of the thought energy received and the resolutely focussed will on being right, as pride rears its head, for fear of being wrong. Look to the Ray aspects of mind and the animal-like attributes of mind,[8] the glamours and illusions according to the Ray line

---

7 *Ahimsa: Vegetarianism and the Buddhist Ideal,* and *Karma and the Rebirth of Consciousness.*

8 See Volume 2 for an explanation of these perversions of mind.

within you.[9] Counter them with humbleness and the pristine logic of the Heart's Mind. Console yourselves with thoughts of high ideas sanctified.

There are plenty of arguments in sight if you accept their thought suggestions. Might not you have a countering answer to truthful logic that displeases you, and assails your long cherished beliefs? Was your heart laden with loneliness, misunderstood, somewhat hurt and dismayed? Might you not have joined another spiritual group (other than the one presided over by the Master)? Did you hear the wolfish whispers in your ear? Did you see the grey line to your head? In listening to such thoughts grey wolf logic has assailed you and you have entered their maze. Wolf logic will win if not countered with humbleness and the insight to honestly listen earnestly to counter opinions. This path leads to awakening the Heart centre's revelations.

Be ever vigilant of the grey energies, the dullness of the tone of the thoughts, and generate light, clear white, golden, or any of the vibrant pastel hues, and project it at the aberrant thought sequence. Zap with light the arenas of dull pain in the head, zap with as much intensity of light that can be generated. Clear the mind of grey light, generate the Clear Light of Mind in its place. Hence overcome the *saṃskāras* of aeonic thought patterns that keep you trapped in *saṃsāra's* domain. The wolf will tell you to focus on your opinions, that you are correct all the while, and not to listen to difficult instructions from the wise teacher that are truly instructive of self-improvement. Rather, such teachings will be scrutinised only for that which supports your argument, ignoring or criticising the rest. Any critical rhetoric serves the wolf well. Learn to recognise the dull greyness of mind. Hence be earnest in your quest for enlightenment. Seek out the Way of the Heart, but beware of the five non-sacred petals, wherein the aberrant thought construct can lurk.

The Anubis block our minds to subtler levels of information and revelations of meaning from the higher planes of perception. They do this by preconditioning our minds to certain thought patterns. Thus even if we accept the first thought Hierarchy or one's higher self presents, we are not open and spacious enough mentally to allow the thought to have higher ramifications (such as impressions of subtle energy processes), because of wolf-generated, habitual, concretised mental activity at subliminal levels. Anubis logic always goes for the jugular, to attack the Master

9 Explained in A.A. Bailey, *Glamour, a World Problem,* (Lucis Press, New York.)

at the heart of the group dynamic, the Hierarchically attuned disciple already overburdened with vast responsibilities in service to humanity, and the one ensconced in Love. The Anubis knows what and who it hates and why. Once ensconced in the mind of a disciple, the preferred modus operandi of the Anubis is severance of contact, non-communication with such ones, because the Anubis fears debate with truthful logic most of all.

Renunciation is the key, renunciation of wilful concepts is the plan, renunciation of self-centred thoughts is needed to serve the purpose. To understand the Anubis is the law that psychically guides one to the higher domains. To understand the Anubis is the key to pure sound and magical ritual. Magic can only be done in silence, complete inner and outer reserve, the reserve of power, reserve of information strong in magic pure and simple. Magic is spiritual chemistry, the metallurgy of thoughts rightly projected. It is pure knowledge of the nature of the substance of the sheaths, their refining via the distillation process and combining to produce new sublime states of awareness. It is what is offered to one who overcomes the grey forms of logic. One must do well in the right combination of the Elements, to carry the enlightenment-plan to new heights. This is what esoteric chemistry provides, this is our birthright.

Honourable sailor upon the astral sea, honourable soldier in distant lands of revelation, manifest honour on the right hand path. Right knowledge bleeds thee to the path of compassionate Love. Can the Solar Plexus and Sacral components of your awareness be admixed with Love so that the Base of Spine centre can liberate its Fire? Can we refine ourselves to spiritual heights to reach the sublime?

Hierarchy needs not the unfortunate fall from grace of their sailors because they have been listening to wolves too much. They need not the quick repartee, the consolable responses because disciple's ears have been saturated with wolf-breathed sound at subliminal levels of distortion. We do not need the psychic base of disciples out of sync via listening to treble and mid range thoughts that pack their normal punch in the hype of mundane Western psychological logic that attacks yogic insight and the spiritual might of esoteric lore. We do not need the chief Anubis orchestra of sound, symbolised by the noisy cities and dogfights of the mind-induced stupor of disciple's thoughts busy with mundane industrial splendour, cutting away at the anchorings of the higher awareness. The Anubis will not generate 'God's work' productive of enlightenment. We do not need dissatisfied heroes or heroines endlessly searching for religious expression, but possessing no skill to work with higher perceptions.

All these and more are the result of Anubis sound assaults on humanity, particularly in the West, where deep, meaningful, meditative pauses have been lost as a mechanism of conversational intensity. Old spiritual concepts need to be broken with appropriate revelatory knowledge. The disciple must allow for a matrix of sound silently emitted from where new conceptions exist, to wash away old ones that now aberrantly clutter the mental landscape. The grey must be zapped clean with the vibrant Light.

When sound is properly studied with all its subtle attributes, then we will understand true law, the way effect follows cause via sound, the way of the magical appearance of things. Purpose will be expressed via tonalities of sound, mantra, and much more yet to perceive.

Is it possible to record the use of the sound of molecules clustering together, the depths of matter rightly arrayed with thought? Is it possible for proper white magic to occur? Can the cornucopia of Love in golden synthesis be laid bare through the impact of the right use of sound upon the array of matter to produce divine chemistry? Shall the group undertaking the Initiation process enjoy such awareness? It is possible for one to know once the cacophony of Anubis sounds are thoroughly defeated.

The building blocks of life are thusly: Chemistry, Sound, Silence. Admix just rightly, add the fluidity of Love and brightly convert with electricity, ever so slightly influenced by colour and sound of the right proportions, and thus transmutation takes place.

How can Buddhists, or disciples in general, do this work of transmutation of the base metals of their psyche's (as explained in Volume 5 of this series) if there are no sound experts amongst them, no specialists in the laws of disorder and harmonious order by sound? Think more upon the need for such mastery, not the sounds of external mantra, uttered by vibrating the voice box, but the subtle sounds of the silent Voice within, totally freed from Anubis input. Such meditation deserves your respect and further understanding.

Vanquished are the Hierarchical ideas of the plan for humanity, if disciples will not listen, other than to the Anubis. Up in smoke are the fine airs of Hierarchical thought. It all starts in the kitchen of the Solar

Plexus. What ingredients are you utilising? What *prāṇas* come through? Are they off? Are they smart choices or plainly dumb? 'How can I lift up humanity?' should be your thought. Thoughts of 'Can I have this, that or the other?' is the Solar Plexus in full reign. Forget the Solar Plexus. Rule it fast. Direct its energies to the Heart, experience the Heart, be the Heart.

Much damage is done to Hierarchical Plans through lack of the ability of disciples to listen to the silent Voices from their Hearts, from Hierarchy speaking via that Source. The din of the cacophony of distorting grey thoughts entering their minds prevents the Clear Mind from manifesting. Disciples must learn to clarify their hearing and to recognise the ways of Hierarchy, which are antithetical to the selfish egotism engendered in this materialistic age. They must thereby overcome Anubis logic, which always feeds self-opinionated thoughts. The student must answer the request for spiritual power with silence, a humble array of thoughts geared to vibrantly enlighten with light, and by generating the Will-to-Love.

Watch how the Anubis work, as they circle you, come en masse if need be with incessant streams of thought-forms and grey energies from companion witches.[10] Watch how they restrict the activity of mind. Observe their tongue-tied logic. Resist their embrace, resist lazy days, lazy ways. They tell you to think of self, to be happy, to be sad, to relax the tension of striving. This is their way. This is their day. Their knowledge is true enough for those on the left hand path, but not for those who wish to follow Hierarchy's ways. Learn our adamantine logic, convert them with sounds, and generate the bright light to project their way, and so educate them as to the right way with the lore of Love.

Many *saṃskāras* of their illogic abound in the disciple's *nāḍīs,* hence they need to convert well all Anubis hordes in all the spaces they choose to hide. Plans of beauty must begin to be found once more from throughout the cosmos and thus the second Ray shall truly resound out from the hearts of all into space. If sufficient disciples work to convert

---

10 The witches are not the physical plane hags, viragos with psychic powers of popular myths and the cultural imagination, but rather psychic female entities who, among other things, specialise in projecting grey substance to the Solar Plexus and minor centres. They devitalise the disciple, stimulating negative emotions, even nausea and sickness, helping to lay the foundation for the thought projection of the Anubis. All is made possible because of the mental-emotional proclivity of the disciple.

the grey then there will be a victory song in Shambhala. High energies from cosmic domains shall pass through to Nature's cornucopia, for cosmic law must rule all. In such awareness the disciple can then be briefed quite well. As they develop the attributes of the higher Mind then they can sidestep no more and will rise above and be briefed on new wings of power, to fly to distant shores of Purpose. They will rise fast on winged flames of Love. A powerhouse of truth will come to rule mind and all the Rays of Mind, to establish the New World Order upon new foundations of law just right.

Love flows through all things, in, around, deep inside, all about, continuously moving, continuously growing, manifesting the plan—action, non-action, breathing in and out via multidimensional spaciousness. It manifests surety, abundant light, tenderness, soft yet strong attributes, dignified phlegmatic and rueful characteristics in the minds of disciples. These are terms of Love on the mental side, but the *piṇgalā* line produces compassionate activity, comprehensive understanding and emphatic joy. Study well the difference between *dharmakāya* and *buddhi.* Study well our higher way, our mental law. The planes of perception are needed to be understood by all disciples, so that they comprehend where they are truly at and where the wolves are at. Then they can understand their Egyptian heritage and why its hard to decipher Anubis logic, and why disciples sometimes cannot remember who they are spiritually and why they were born, because they are incarnated into by the Anubis, demonstrating the critical mind. The disciple must remember that they were born alone in the cave of the heart, and must go out that way. To do this they must counter the separative, prideful thought suggestions and zap the incarnated Anubis away.

Be prepared for the bitter sweet breath of life, and love its lay, its song, its reality, growth and decay. One must learn to love the All. True Love may appear to be a paradox, but the frowning of its purpose will growl no more in your mind once the Anubis logic has been defeated. Beatitude as a response then manifests in all situations. Demand higher, broader, deeper understandings of yourselves. Demand the Heart with all its vigour and unusualness, with all its love and good cheer, with all its wisdom and gentle thinking. Though sometimes firmly presented, the throat will then always be subservient to its ways. The quiet inner dialogue is constantly with you day after day, with the inner ear open to Hierarchical whispers, their breath, their space, their airs. The zephyr of Love is then yours to behold.

The Christ moves out on every hand, to every good Christian there is a message. Welcome your brothers from different lands and religions to the Heart centre. Welcome Buddhists to your home, welcome them. Buddhists welcome Christians, welcome them. Messengers from every land bear beneficence, gifts, gladness, joy, great tidings, resounding bliss of unity, unifying all to the great shout of continuing existence on high. May Maitreya appear where people dwell. With a welcoming Heart in every way, where then can the Anubis, who spreads division and strife, find any chance to prey?

The swastikas governing Hierarchical activity

Another way of showing Hierarchical interrelationships from the point of view of energy distribution is presented in Figure 19. The presented *maṇḍala* shows the interrelation between the Ashrams in the Mahāchohan's department. We see that the entire background underlying energy distribution concerns the nature of the moving swastika: 卍, which empowers the *vajra* (Tib: dorje). The esotericism of the swastika was provided in the previous volumes, especially in relation to the qualities of the five Elements and *prāṇas*. Each *nāḍī* contains five such *prāṇas* or a permutation of this number. The information concerning the mode of manifestation of these Elements should be integrated here to gain an insight as to the nature of energy distribution between the differing Ashrams. The swastika is the driving impetus of the energies that manifest as 'the jewel in the heart of the lotus'. All forms, Logoic or human, are constituted of myriads of such mutable crosses, each rotating at different rates and directions. One can expect a swastika of energies to also manifest at the heart of each atom.

The 2/1 energy here represents a combination of Shambhalic and Hierarchical potencies, yet to be wielded by the fledgling 2/1 Ashram. These energies work as a functioning unity via the directive guidance of the second Ray Ashrams, but the manifesting power is via the seventh Ray Ashrams, who direct the energies into the etheric grid of the planet. As the new epoch advances, the flow of such energies to the physical domain will significantly increase until some of the veils separating it from the etheric substratum shall be rent asunder. Many people will consequently gain etheric vision, allowing them to see the subtle energy fields, the *devas* of the shadow, and even those that have recently departed. The Christ and certain of the Chohans, externalised in etheric vehicles, can then also come into their field of view. The etheric vehicle is the true form of a human unit and many of the lost arts of the ancients, such as levitation, even teleportation, will be rediscovered through direct control of these swastikas of energies by the awakened Initiates. Such activity shall gain prominence in the Aquarian age via the auspices of Uranus (governed by the seventh Ray), the planetary ruler of that sign.

The downpour of 2/1 energies is focussed via the Hierarchical Eye, which becomes the central activating dynamo behind all revolving swastikas. Such perpetual activity is effectively the Mother of all that was and is to be. It conveys cosmic Astral energies, pumping the Life's Blood of the Logos to all in need, heightening the energy levels and fields of human units, allowing them to see what was formerly veiled.

The Mahāchohan's department is particularly conditioned by the movement of swastikas of ceaseless internal motion, as indicated by Figure 19. Generally speaking, with respect to the movement of the swastika, the motion from left to right concerns the *piṇgalā nāḍī* unfoldment (the way of the evolution of consciousness). The motion from right to left concerns the *iḍā* unfoldment, the evolution of the form and of its organising intelligence.

The 7/2 Ashram is placed central because it is the 'oldest' of the Ashrams of the Rays of Mind, being the first to form, and because it can also directly bear first Ray energies by means of the seventh Ray function. The activity of this Ashram moves in the form of a swastika that interacts with the sum of the seventh Ray Ashrams and via them the others. All the minor swastikas of the Ashrams are synthesised by the five major Ashrams of the Chohans of the Rays of Mind. They are integrated by a major swastika that is the field of activity of the Mahāchohan, whose focussed output therefore is Shambhalic power. This power line is the dominant expression of the Mahāchohan (Rakoczi), who heralded from the 7/2 Ray line. The wisdom line, though fanned in Rakoczi's time, will come fully to the fore in the new Mahāchohan's dispensation via the general third Ray. He will wield both Ray lines with faculty, where the seventh Ray line will represent his left foot and the third Ray line his right foot. With them he will stride objectively to manifest the new world dispensation.

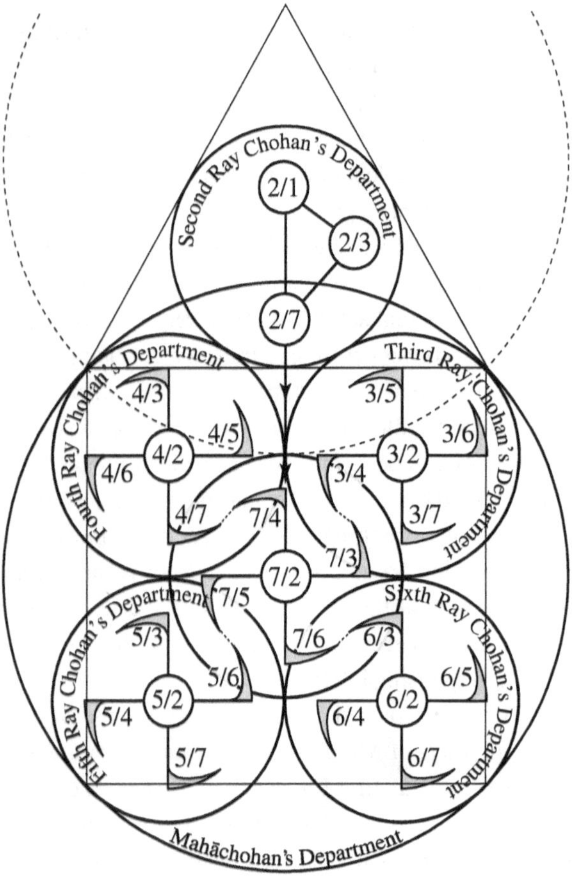

Figure 19. The Mahāchohan's department

Hierarchically, the term 'spiritual age' does not simply concern the relative time of the formation of the Ashrams, or degree of Initiation of those within the Ashrams, though they are important considerations.

More importantly, it concerns the ability of those involved to directly handle energies from the Throne of the great Lord of Shambhala. The greater the energy that can be rightly directed, the greater the spiritual age. This is seen in terms of the resultant radiatory activity that becomes the Initiate's sphere of service. It then translates as unfolding vision and receptivity to the plan and power of 'God'.

There is no sense of competition amongst the Initiated. They steadfastly obey the laws of the Love and the Will conditioning cosmos. This Will works out underlying purpose via the *maṇḍalic* patterning associated with the unfoldment of the Ashrams, within which each Initiate finds his/her unique role or part to play. All Initiates are telepathically and energetically a unity.

The Initiate's gaze is focussed outwards to the field of service or inwards to Hierarchical activity, and not upon him/herself. It is similar to the workings of a television; all component parts constitute the integrated functioning of the whole unit, which works when all parts are functioning effortlessly without strain. Self-focussed activity blocks energy, producing an overload on that unit, with consequent problems for the entire system.

The nature of Hierarchical power

Another diagram that represents the basic way that energies flow within the Hierarchy can be given. We should note here that energies can flow from within-without, that is from the centre to the periphery of the *maṇḍala,* via the direction of the moving arms, as well as from without-within. The motion of the arms can also be from left to right (evolutionary progression of enlightenment attributes) as well as from right to left (development of attributes that tie one to *saṃsāra*). Everything depends upon what is being developed or expressed at any time. There can also be an uneven development of any of the arms, which is the norm. This implies a focus upon developing a particular quality (*prāṇa*), oriented in a specific direction of the moving cross, before other attributes can be expressed.

With respect to the dissemination of first Ray energies to humanity the following diagram can be considered, where the new Mahāchohan, working with 2/1 energies and the 2/1 Master to be, also helps to direct energies into the 1/2 Ashram and hence the first Ray Shield. Such energisation is coordinated with Morya's (the first Ray Chohan) directive emanation. Here the seventh Ray can be considered the activity aspect of the first Ray, empowering the swastikas of moving forces.

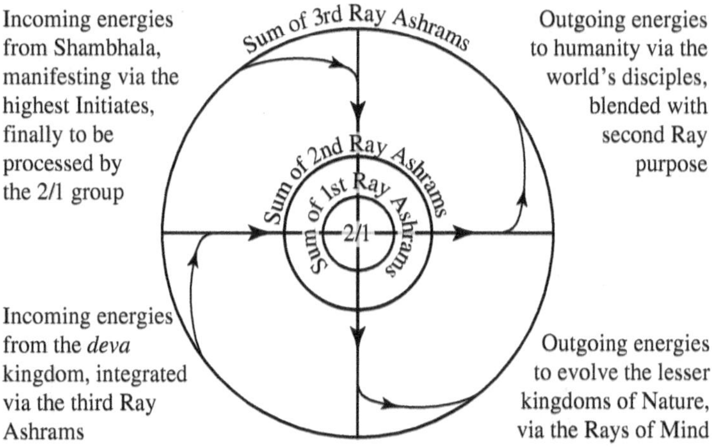

Figure 20. The basic Hierarchical swastika

Morya directs purposeful energies from Shambhala that initiates major (oft cataclysmic) changes in all spheres of activity. Jesus, the sixth Ray Chohan, directs the impelling devotion in humanity to first and second Ray purpose that seeds the field of aspiration for which they will devotedly sacrifice their time to produce their cherished visions. The resultant golden grain of their sown aspiration cyclically ripens for harvesting by the Lords of Life. K.H., the second Ray Chohan, manifests the all-encompassing outpouring of Love and Wisdom of the Christ's department, which must nurture the Will and rightfully direct it on all of its fields of activity. The Mahāchohan's department utilises the dynamic activity of the first Ray that produces world changes by means of intelligently applied cyclic endeavour and mathematically exact planning. The first Ray is thereby converted into the seventh Ray materialising power in a way that a vast number of people can express the purpose without undue destructive over-energisation, which the direct first Ray impact would tend to produce. The new Mahāchohan sets the stage of the world play whereon the divine reaper must inevitably walk. We also have the preparation of the ground for the planting of the seeds of aspiration.

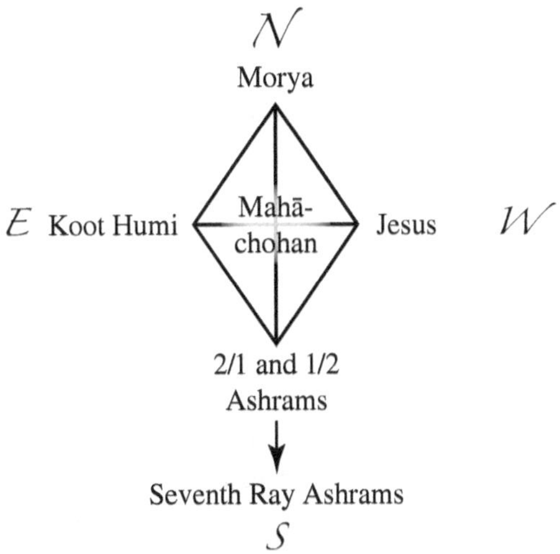

Figure 21. The manifestation of Hierarchical power

The Ashrams of the Rays of Mind sow the seeds of unfolding consciousness in the kingdoms of Nature, whilst the second and first Ray Ashrams are the reapers of that golden harvest. As the harvest becomes increasingly great, so the role of the 2/1 and 1/2 Ashrams become important, providing the testing ground for the aspiring Masters of these Rays via the formation of the Ashrams proper.[11] The forms of esoteric service work of promulgating the most esoteric doctrines and countering dark brotherhood predatory emanations and machinations will be needed to facilitate the ripening of the young Initiates being 'harvested', and to help protect them as they develop.

Here will be seen the power of the first Ray to rapidly produce changes in the thought patterns and determination to overcome limitations of the awakening ones. The related activities will similarly (relatively quickly) inspire the moving masses to strive to serve others. In the past, after an initial burst of rightly directed activity, such processes often became concretised, dogmatised and antithetical to progress, like

11 As before mentioned, the *maṇḍala* of these Ashrams are still in the process of forming.

a blight of fungus over the ripening grain. The reapers of this new cycle, however, will have a far greater momentum of planetary education to ensure success, allowing them to effect the changes to ensure a bountiful harvest. Shambhalic potency will be directly borne by them to help produce the necessary effects. All forms of pestilence must go.

Morya is 'the Head of all truly esoteric schools'[12] because the first Ray deals with the direction of streams of Life and penetrates deeper into Logoic domains via the atomic (first subplane) substance of the planes of perception. This Ray manifests the highest potency to counter the dark brotherhood, or rather, what is considered 'evil' upon this planet, the solar system and within cosmos. 'Evil' being but primal or darkened substance needing redemption. It incorporates the host of minds that unduly perpetuate the tenure of that substance. The substance in and of itself is not evil, but rather the way that units of mind utilise it to build forms that serve not the evolutionary growth of the whole. When the 2/1-1/2 Ray Ashrams fully form, then the cycle for the dominance of evil upon this planet will have terminated.

In relation to this, the work of the new Mahāchohan and the first Ray department will be closely integrated, for then aspirants will be rightly educated as to what actually constitutes the forces of evil. The first Ray power can then appropriately 'seal the door where evil dwells'. He will become the central dynamo of such esoteric output amongst humanity, as he also plays a role in the Christ's department, which will be closely blended into the service work. Thus the foundation for the oncoming planetary second Ray cycle will be laid. This blend becomes the heart of the new Wisdom Religion broadcast to the world's disciples, and will inaugurate the epoch of the reappearance of the blue Christ.

The upper echelons of the Hierarchy

The interrelation between the upper echelons of Hierarchy and the Ashrams should perhaps be further detailed. First, the major triad of the great Ones at the seventh Initiation level, from which spring the other triadic interrelationships.

---

12 A.A. Bailey, *The Rays and the Initiations* (Lucis Publishing Company, New York, 1993), 373.

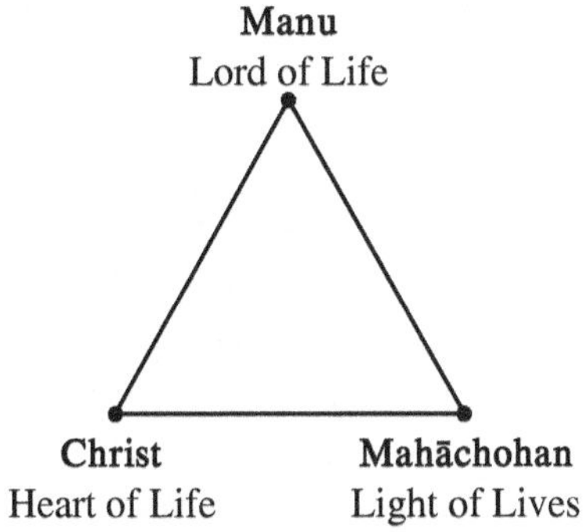

Figure 22. The heads of the major Hierarchical departments

Though the *Manu* (Vaivasvata Manu, for our fifth Aryan Root Race, governing the Element Fire) is denoted part of our Hierarchy, this great first Ray Lord is more truly an integral part of Shambhala. (As effectively are all the Chohans.) His concern is with the evolutionary purpose of the Life aspect of all kingdoms of Nature. This involves their way of abstraction within the *nāḍī* system of the planetary Logos and then their abstraction into cosmos. He thus works directly with the Monadic aspect and angelic Triads of those Lives in the cosmic Landscape that are applicable to our earth evolution. Consequently, very little can be provided concerning the truly esoteric activities of the Manu. Morya is set to take this role in the forthcoming new age for the emerging sixth Root Race humanity.

The Head of the Hierarchy is the *Christ*, as gaining Love-Wisdom is the main purpose of the entire evolutionary pageant on earth. It is the one primordial Ray from which all the others stem. As previously stated, the post of the Christ is presently triune, as this energy manifests in triune form as the Father-Son-Mother. There are thus three entities embodying this role in the present world cycle.

In D.K.'s *The Reappearance of the Christ* under the section entitled 'Christ as the forerunner of the Aquarian Age', the qualities of these three Christs are veiled in the three titles presented:

1. The Point within the Triangle.
2. The Dispenser of the Water of Life.
3. The Nourisher of the Little Ones.

> These are descriptive of his threefold duties to mankind, and of the work which will be distinctive of His world service, throughout the Aquarian Age.[13]

'The Point within the Triangle' refers to the *dharmakāya* attribute, abstracted and working through intermediaries, which is the present form of activity of the past Christ that was the Buddha. He pours down the energies from cosmic sources to our planetary Hierarchy, the blue Christ then distributes this energy according to the demand and spiritual aspiration of humanity. As well as the triad of Buddha, Spirit of Peace and the Avatar of Synthesis mentioned in the next quote, the triangle via which the energy is poured can refer to the above triad of the blue Christ, Hierarchy and humanity. It can also refer to the triad within the second Ray Ashrams of the blue Christ, K.H. and D.K. There is another interpretation involving executive members of Hierarchy that are the lords of the direct second Ray department, namely:

a. The blue Christ, representing the first point or Head of this triad. He manifests the cosmic links of the energy of Love-Wisdom.
b. The second Ray Chohan, K.H., represents the Heart of this triad, the main body for the active dissemination of the second Ray. His arms and hands stretch to all departments within Hierarchy. He is destined to take the role of the blue Christ in the new era.
c. The European Chohan (Tsongkhapa) represents a special dispensation for the fifth Root Race to ensure that the way of Love-Wisdom is properly assimilated by those in the realms of mind. For this reason he has been assigned the role of the regent of Europe wherein the scientific development of mind has produced our modern epoch. Mind must rule the way of the Heart, and not the dark brotherhood way, thus special care has had to be applied in our planetary dispensation to ensure this. Scientific development has therefore evolved to produce much benefit for humanity.

Together they dispense the 'Water of Life' to the entire planetary manifestation under the auspices of the blue Christ, as this Water is from

---

13 Alice A. Bailey, *The Reappearance of the Christ* (Lucis Publishing Company, New York), 83.

the sixth cosmic astral sub-plane and manifests as the magnetic potency of Love upon our planet. It adequately nourishes the evolving principle of Life, pushing forward the streams of sentience and consciousness-attributes to ever higher levels of achievement. The blue Christ represents the subjectively en-Souling *sambhogakāya* aspect, the *anima-mundi* or world-Soul.

'The Nourisher of the Little Ones' refers to the work of the third, or green Christ, the active manifestation, or *nirmaṇakāya* aspect, of this department, an expression of the third Ray quality of the Wisdom aspect of the dual Ray of Love-Wisdom. He also bears the potency of the Will energy projected by the Buddha. He is literally the ambassador for the senior members in this department. He is therefore a focal point for the combined energies of all these great Lords and can bear them for the world disciple. This combined quality thus nourishes 'the little ones', all types of disciples and aspirants with the necessary information, the consciousness-direction they need to enter the ranks of Hierarchy.

In explaining these terms, the Master D.K. states:

> [The Christ] is the first of the great world Teachers to cover two zodiacal cycles—the Piscean and the Aquarian. This is a statement easily made and written down, but again it involves the three modes or techniques of appearance to which I have already referred. His outpouring love and spiritual vitality (augmented by the energies of the Spirit of Peace, the Avatar of Synthesis and the Buddha) were refocussed and channelled into a great stream, pulled through into expression (if I may word it so inadequately) by the words of the Invocation, "Let love stream forth into the hearts of men...Let Light and Love and Power restore the Plan on Earth."
>
> In those three words—light, love and power—the energies of His three Associates (the great Triangle of Force which stands in power behind Him) are described: the energy of the Buddha: Light, for the light ever comes from the East; the energy of the Spirit of Peace: Love, establishing right human relations; the energy of the Avatar of Synthesis; Power, implementing both light and love. At the centre of this Triangle the Christ took His stand; from that point His Aquarian work began, and it will continue for two thousand five hundred years. Thus He inaugurated the new era and, upon the inner spiritual planes, the new world religion began to take form. The word "religion" concerns relationship, and the era of right human relations and of a

> right relation to the Kingdom of God began. Such a statement as this is easily made but its implications are far-reaching and stupendous.
>
> At that time also, the Christ assumed two new functions: one is connected with the second mode of His physical appearance and the other with the mode of overshadowing. Over the masses, light, love and power are being poured forth and the growth of the Christ-consciousness is, therefore, being constantly stimulated. By His physical Presence, He will become the *"Dispenser of the Water of Life"*; through the over-shadowing of those sensitive to His impression and of His focussed Mind, He becomes what is technically known as the *"Nourisher of the little ones."*
>
> As Dispenser of the Water of Life and as Nourisher of the Little Ones, He enters upon His duties in the Aquarian Age, whilst as the centre of the Triangle above mentioned, He influences, enlightens, and produces right relations in the masses of men.[14]

In presenting the above statement, D.K. was limited to what could be revealed at the time, because the role of the new Mahāchohan had to be veiled, to wait for the appropriate time for revelation.[15]

The abovementioned triad of the Avatar of Synthesis, signifying dynamic spiritual Power, the Spirit of Peace, signifying cosmic Love and the Buddha, signifying the Light of Life, projects the principle of Love-Wisdom into our planet. This triad can then be extended, as depicted in Figure 23 showing the power of the Christ.

The Avatar of Synthesis and the Spirit of Peace are exceedingly exalted, representing the first and second points of the planetary triune Logos. They therefore manifest the first and second Ray potencies empowering the office of the Christ, the fused aspects of the Love-Wisdom Ray. The Mother of the World can be included as the actively nurturing Love. Their function is incorporated in the Presence of Sanat Kumāra, who reflects this triune energy into the three Buddhas of Activity as an *iḍā* dispensation.

The three Christs then represent a *piṇgalā* dispensation. Here the *iḍā* represents the Wisdom aspect and the *piṇgalā* the Love aspect of

14 A.A. Bailey, *The Reappearance of the Christ,* 82-83.

15 This consideration is tied in with his Avataric purpose, explained in the doctrine of the Avatars below.

this dual Ray. The *iḍā* is the gain of the past, hence presently more advanced, whilst the *piṇgalā* is the 'present' objective. It is the purpose in the Now of the presiding Logos.

Speaking in terms of the Will, which is ever the attribute of Shambhala, D.K. states:

> There is a definite distinction between Purpose and Will; it is subtle indeed, but quite definite to the advanced initiate, and therefore the dualistic nature of our planetary manifestation and our solar Expression appear even in this. The Members of the Council at Shamballa recognise this distinction and therefore divide Themselves into two groups which are called in the ancient parlance, Registrants of the Purpose and Custodians of the Will. Will is active. Purpose is passive, waiting for the results of the activity of the will. These two groups are reflected in hierarchical circles by the Nirmanakayas or the Planetary Contemplatives, and the Custodians of the Plan. The function of the Registrants of the Purpose is to keep the channel open between our Earth, the planet Venus and the Central Spiritual Sun. The function of the Custodians of the Will is to relate the Council, the Hierarchy and Humanity, thus creating a basic triangle of force between the three major centres of the planetary Life. This is the higher expression (symbolic, if you like) of the six-pointed star, formed of two interlaced triangles. A replica of this fundamental triangle and of this symbol of energy, with its inflow and distribution, is to be found in the relation of the three higher centres in the human being—head, heart and throat—to the three lower centres—solar plexus, sacral centre and the centre at the base of the spine. The Science of Invocation and Evocation is also seen to be symbolically proceeding along evolutionary lines.[16]

The *iḍā* aspect I have described above relates to the 'Custodians of the Will', whilst the *piṇgalā* aspect relates to 'Registrants of the Purpose'. Within the triad of Christs, the blue Christ reflects the function of a 'Registrants of the Purpose' in the form of a Contemplative, and the new Mahāchohan (the green Christ) as a 'Custodians of the Will', in the form of a Custodian of the Plan, actively implementing that Will in the field of strife signified by humanity. The Buddha, the previous

16 A.A. Bailey, *The Rays and the Initiations,* 69.

head of this department, representing comprehensive enlightening Activity, has moved beyond the precincts of Shambhala, nevertheless directly empowers the Will of the new Mahāchohan via the conduit of the Purpose held by the blue Christ. The green Christ represents the activity aspect of the Christ's department.

The power of the Christ's department can be depicted in terms of a Shambhalic pentad. The basic structure allows the qualities of cosmic Love to direct the development of conscious awareness in the five kingdoms (mineral, plant, animal, human and *deva*) via the five planes of perception associated with the expression of mind/Mind. It is an expression of the star of the Logos, of the One Initiator, Sanat Kumāra, who as the Avataric embodiment of the Planetary Logos, takes the place of the Avatar of Synthesis. His influence is all-pervasive, affecting all aspects of our planetary life. This star represents the energies of dynamic, steadfast Love manifesting as Logoic Purpose and all-encompassing Will to drive the Plan forwards.

The Christ's department therefore naturally flows from the second point of the Logoic triad, the Spirit of Peace. His potent, subjective energy is the source of all Love-Wisdom upon our planet. Having said this, two more great Ones need to be added with respect to this department, the one known esoterically as the European Chohan, whom the Tibetans know as Tsongkhapa, and the future blue Christ, K.H. (sGam po pa). Because the Buddha has moved on to cosmic vistas, he plays a subsidiary role, where his energy is abstracted, only affecting high Initiates, rather than being a direct bearer of the Christ energy for humanity. The 'second Buddha', Guru Rinpoche (Padmasambhava), can normally be considered to take the Buddha's place. The present blue Christ manifests the role of the first Christ, K.H. thus takes the role of the second aspect here, whilst the new Mahāchohan retains the position of the third (green-blue) Christ.

In viewing this in terms of the *iḍā* and the *piṅgalā* line mentioned above, where the *iḍā* represents the left side and *piṅgalā* the right side, we see that the blue Christ stands at the centre of this pentad. Above all stands the Spirit of Peace (incorporating also the second Buddha of Activity), signifying Logoic Love expressed in the Heart of the Head centre that is Shambhala. Tsongkhapa manifests as the right hand.

Guru Rinpoche then manifests as the left hand. Koot Humi and the new Mahāchohan stand as the right and left feet. The right and left hands work as a functioning pair, as do the right and left feet, whilst the main lines of energy expression go from right hand to right foot (the Love line) and from left hand to left foot (the Wisdom line). Because the blue Christ is the Heart of this arrangement, as a Registrant of the Purpose, all energies come to and from him. This major pentagram of energy distribution is the central powerhouse of the other *maṇḍalas* of expression of Hierarchy, governing the evolution of consciousness upon the planet.

The qualities of the three Christs are also indicated by the statement of Christ/Jesus in *John 14:6:*

> I am the way, the truth, and the life: no man cometh unto the Father, but by me.

'The way' refers to the quality of expression of the first Christ, the Buddha, where the Will is exemplified because here it represents the door to the cosmic Paths, the way that eventually opens for all Initiates travelling to the Heart of Life. 'The way' thus concerns the process involved in becoming fully enlightened, liberated from *saṃsāra,* via embodying the Love-Wisdom principle as well as developing the Will to overcome all obstacles to liberation. This is the path the Buddha paved for humanity.

'The truth' refers to the qualities of the second Christ. This truth is that of the embodiment of the *dharma*, the law or expressed Word from the domain of the liberated Ones, rightfully directed to all on the path of life and the way of light. It is the potency of the great Teaching department on this earth, and directly opposes the workings of the force of evil, which is 'the father' of all lies.[17]

'The life' refers to the qualities of the third Christ, because the demonstration of wise, enlightened activity manifests the inherent Life of the Love that must succour all who are to travel the way of the *dharma.* Rightly ordained divine activity is the carrier of the 'Blood' that vivifies all lives within the Body of the Lord (the Planetary Logos).

---

17 See *John 8:44.*

This Life manifests as the light that shines on the way, enlightening the fields of darkness that enshroud all lives in *saṃsāra*. It is the light that shines if one is not to lose the way and which one must project if the path to the Father is to be travelled upon.

The above is one way of viewing this trinity, but from another perspective we can reverse the list. Life refers to the first Christ, who controls the demonstration of the Life of the consciousness-principle upon this planet. Truth refers to the second Christ, and 'the Way' to the third Christ, representing the way or open door for the 'little ones' to follow. Thus is the ontology of being/non-being established as a liberating force via a triune methodology.

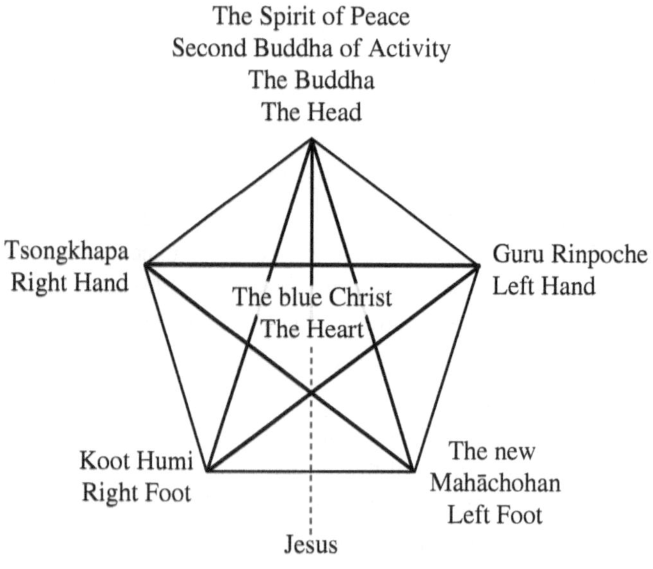

Figure 23. The power of the Christ

1. In Figure 23 the Spirit of Peace (the second Person of the divine trinity of our planetary Logos), the second Buddha of Activity and the Buddha under him can be considered three aspects of the Heart of the planetary Head centre, providing the Breath of Life embodying the Power of Love in our planetary system. Together they represent the mechanism of processing the second Ray purpose

for our planet in accord with its evolution in our solar system and local cosmos. The Spirit of Peace is the source of the *suṣumṇā* line of the dispensation of Love-Wisdom that integrates with the blue Christ's activities. Those of the right hand side of this pentad are specifically receptive to the *piṇgalā* quality of Love directed to them by the second Buddha of Activity. To those on the left hand side are channelled the counterbalancing *iḍā* qualities of Wisdom from the Buddha.

The Spirit of Peace represents the way of approach of the Christ to his 'Father'. As he is, however, normally abstracted, so the second Buddha of Activity can be considered to take his place. Under him is the Buddha.

2. The blue Christ at the heart of this pentad represents the Life of the Way of Truth integrating all of the other points as a unity. The Truth *(dharmakāya)* here represents the forces integrating Hierarchical activity (the Heart centre) with the Heart in the Head of the centre known as Shambhala. This energy becomes 'the Way' when manifesting as the right foot impressing the Hearts of humanity with compassionate activity via the auspices of K.H. and the entire second Ray department. It becomes 'the Light' when impressing humanity's minds with concepts of compassionate service and liberation. This represents the activity of the left foot by the new Mahāchohan and his department.
3. Guru Rinpoche as the left hand. The focus here is broadcasting the Wisdom principle, which demonstrates as Light in our planet. He stands to the left of Tsongkhapa (the right hand) in the Christ's department, because his line of development, like that of the Mahāchohan, is along the Rays of Mind. Both Guru Rinpoche and Tsongkhapa lend helping hands to integrate Shambhalic potencies into the world sphere and to lessen some of the burden of the blue Christ in the immensity of the task of directing the disparaging and separative activities of the human family towards cooperative unity and the spirit of oneness amongst human groups and nations. They also assist in the general work to be accomplished by the Chohans representing the feet of the Christ's department.

4. Tsongkhapa, the right hand of the pentad, represents the active Power of the Truth. He is the point of balance of the dissemination of the energy of Love-Wisdom working to project this quality throughout our planetary manifestation by harmonising disparaging aspects of mind. His quality can best be described as the Light of Love. This power manifests as the mode of dissemination of Love via a fifth Ray methodology. It fosters the love of wisdom within the hearts of the world's intelligentsia. He manifests as the point of balance for the expression of Love-Wisdom in humanity, where the development of their minds are appropriately regulated with thoughts of compassionate service.
5. Koot Humi, the forthcoming blue Christ. His quality here can be described as the empowerment of Truth (the *dharma)*—the Love of Life. He expresses the second Ray dispensation through the light of pure reason, manifesting the purpose of Love by stimulating the vision of compassion-sightedness of the world's disciples. His role can be described above as 'the Nourisher of the little ones'.
6. The new Mahāchohan demonstrates the Way that reveals the Light of Life. As the left foot of this pentad he appropriately demonstrates the way of grounding the purpose of the Christ's department via his *nirmaṇakāyic* (Avataric) appearance for this new (Aquarian) epoch, thereby taking the role of 'Dispenser of the Water of Life'. His role is to offer them the testing ground whereby they can hone their understanding of the nature of compassion in a way that their wisdom is demonstrated. Loving-minded attitudes, where disciples think they know what is right, based upon conventional opinions of what is loving, must be replaced with true Initiate comprehension of the nature of the path. Hence he tests the strength of the comprehension of disciples of the world as to the nature of the Bodhisattva path.
7. Jesus. Because of the attributes of the sixth Ray, Jesus was the bearer of the combined energies of this pentad. Hence he propelled a new religious dispensation that could feed the devotional aspiration of humanity. This came to be known as Christianity, however, the teachings he gave out at the beginning of the Piscean era have been adulterated. This seventh position facilitated his Avataric role 2,000

years ago, in conjunction with there being a direct *suṣumṇā* line of energisation between him, the first Christ, the Spirit of Peace, and the cosmic Christ.

The Great Invocation

The first stanza of the Great Invocation, as I have worded it,[18] refers to the united potency of the triune Logos incorporated within Sanat Kumāra, the Primordial One.

From the point of Light within
The Mind of the Primordial One,
Let Light stream forth into all minds.
Let Light descend on earth.

The 'point of Light' is the blended energies of The Avatar of Synthesis, the Spirit of Peace and the Mother of the World, coupled with the Sirian purpose incorporated within Sanat Kumāra's Mind. This Light is but an expression of dynamic Logoic Wisdom that can descend no further than the higher mental plane whereon human Souls find illumination as to the nature of group purpose. The cosmic vision is implanted in the kingdom of the Sambhogakāya Flower and thereby Light can 'stream forth into all minds'. This Light descends on earth when human units aspire upwards to the domain of their Souls, and thereby receive illumination. As they do so, the testings productive of the third Initiation manifest, and the successful applicants to Light attain the *ālayavijñāna* enlightenment.[19]

The second stanza of the Great Invocation is:

From the point of Love within
The Heart of the Lord of Love,
Let Love stream forth into all Hearts,
May Maitreya issue forth where people dwell.

---

18 See Volume 3, 103. Note that I have changed the wording somewhat from D.K.'s rendering to make the Invocation more universally appealing, especially to Buddhists, who would take offense at the theistic overtones, such as the use of the word 'God'.

19 For general information concerning the *ālayavijñāna* enlightenment see Volume 1, 37, Volume 2, 142-143, 279-289, 301-316, and Volume 3, 129-30, 501.

The 'Lord of Love' is the blue Christ, overshadowed by the cosmic Christ. 'The Heart' represents the sum of Hierarchy, the planetary Heart centre. From this 'point' then let the energy of 'Love stream forth into all Hearts' in the manner described earlier via the twelve petals of this centre and of its overshadowing of Splenic centre I. Through the united activity of all the Ashrams this energy can then affect all of humanity, to teach them the sacrificial ways of Love. Compassionate understanding for all people and the integrated Lives upon this planet and cosmos is then possible. The service arenas of the Ashrams then manifest, as all of Hierarchy find opportunity to incarnate, to appear and wisely begin governing all facets of human affairs. The process of the reappearance of Hierarchy is evoked in the next line of the Invocation. It is 'evoked' because coming forth from within humanity itself they will generate the Love that will manifest as the planetary Maitreya.

Maitreya has always been conceived of as the successor to Gautama, the next Buddha, and indeed it can be so. However, what is here posited is that the advent of Maitreya (meaning 'compassion') is a planetary event. This event signifies a planetary awakening of the principle of compassion as humanity responds to the increased stimulus of the energy of Love from the cosmic Christ overshadowing the planet. This happens as the deeds of compassionate thinking, of concepts of service to others, the communities and nations they are in, and for all in the world, manifests from them. As humanity increasingly think unselfishly and work cooperatively for common goals then the planetary Maitreya manifests and Hierarchy becomes thoroughly externalised.

In terms of being the successor to Gautama, the new Mahāchohan will play the role of Maitreya, as a central conduit for the force from the cosmic Christ. He will principally embody the Wisdom aspect of the Love-Wisdom Ray, as did Gautama before him, in the form of the new teachings to be presented to people everywhere. Some of his activities to help awaken the eyes of humanity in this exceedingly materialistic age may be seen as 'miracles' by the masses. He will stand as part of the testing process for the world's disciples that are preparing to take their first Initiation, and others for their second. In doing so he will be overshadowed by Sanat Kumāra, who will pour the energy for this mass Initiation. This will come after a period of planetary crisis. This process will be productive of the elimination of much of the type of *karma* that was engendered upon the Moon. The key aspects relate to passing testings concerning the fields of sex, money and material plane comforts.

The new Mahāchohan will appear as the forerunner of the blue Christ, who principally embodies the Love aspect of the Love-Wisdom Ray, though of course he utilises both aspects of this Ray. The advent of the blue Christ is signified by D.K.'s version of this line: 'May Christ return to Earth', though as D.K. states in his books, the Christ has never left the earth, he shall simply reappear.[20] He will educate the world's disciples with view of an eventual mass undertaking of the second Initiation, for which he is the Initiator. Great will be the convulsions in the battleground of opinions and desires as the disciples struggle to master their emotions. Much *karma* with former left hand magical practices, the crimes of the mouth, and emotional abuse of others will surface. The true potency of the nine-headed Hydra will rear its head and have to be fought upon a large scale.

Not easy will the task be for the blue Christ to educate humanity, in the light of their massed selfishnesses, self-focus, separative thinking, and often misplaced fervent ardent zeal, idealism and devotion to distorted teachings, especially as there will be an increased energisation from cosmic astral sources. Such energisation is impersonal and will stimulate the Waters generally, and not just the new dispensation of the Christ. This energy will thus intensify the Watery turmoil, but will also be needed to help purify and transform the more murky attributes of the Waters into refined perceptions. The entire world's astral cesspool must thereby be cleansed, as the 'door where evil dwells' will still need sealing. Such work will manifest via group activity and under the ritualistic, organisational and magical auspices of the seventh Ray as the Aquarian age progresses with certainty. This work thus becomes the focus of the Aquarian epoch as the new temples of Initiation spring up in often dormant sacred places to accommodate the influx of new disciples and Initiates. Aquarius is the water bearer, and will pour out the Waters of cosmic Love, via the domain of the Mind, as free-flowing energies that all will have the opportunity to sup.

---

20 See *The Externalisation of the Hierarchy,* 488-91, concerning this Invocation, and pages 591-612 concerning the return of the Christ.

The next stanza is:

> From the centre where the Divine Will is known,
> Let purpose guide the little human wills,
> The purpose which Bodhisattvas know and serve.

'The centre where the Divine Will is known' is Shambhala. There are three principal sub Rays of the first Ray that emanate from Shambhala. As stated by D.K. they are:

4. *The Energy of Purification*: This is the power, innate in the manifested universe, which gradually and steadily adapts the substance aspect to the spiritual by a process which we call purification, where humanity is concerned. It involves the elimination of all that hinders the nature of divinity from full expression, and this again from inherent or latent capacity. This necessitates the leaving behind, stage after stage, cycle after cycle, life after life, and plane after plane, of every tendency in the form nature which veils or hides the glory of God. It is essentially the energy which substitutes good for evil...
5. *The Energy of Destruction*: This is a destruction which removes the forms which are imprisoning the inner spiritual life, and hiding the inner soul light. This energy is therefore one of the major aspects of the purificatory nature of the divine Life, and that is the reason why I have put purification ahead of destruction. It is the destroying aspect of life itself, just as there is a destructive agency in matter itself. Two things must be borne in mind in connection with the destroyer aspect of Deity and with those responsible for its appearance:
   a. The destructive activity is set in motion through the will of Those Who constitute the Council at Shamballa and Who are instrumental in bringing the forms in all the subhuman kingdoms into line with the evolving purpose. Under cyclic law, this destructive energy comes into play and destroys the forms of life which prevent divine expression.
   b. It is also brought into activity through the determinations of humanity itself which—under the Law of Karma—makes man the master of his own destiny, leading him to initiate those causes which are responsible for the cyclic events and consequences in human affairs.

> There is naturally a close connection between the first Ray of Will or Power, the energies concentrated at Shamballa and the Law of Karma, particularly in its planetary potency and in relation to advanced humanity. It will be apparent, therefore, that the more rapidly the individual aspirant approaches the third initiation, the more rapidly and directly will the individual's karma be worked out. Monadic relation, as it becomes established, lets loose the destructive aspect of the basic energy, and all hindrances are destroyed with expedition...
>
> 6. *The Energy of Organisation*: This is the energy which set in motion the activity of the great Ray Lives and started the motivation and impulse of that which produced manifestation. Thus were the seven ray qualities brought into expression. The relation of spirit and matter produced this ordered process which again, cyclically and under law, creates the manifested world as a field for soul development and as an area wherein divine purpose is wrought out through the medium of the plan. Again I call your attention to the distinction existing between purpose and plan. This is the aspect, emanating from Shamballa, and inherent also in form (as are the other two), which eventually relates the human will, through the right use of the mind, to the organised planning of his separate and individual life in the three worlds, and which eventually relates and reorients that will to the Will of God.[21]

Here 'The Energy of Purification' is the second Ray aspect of the Will, 'The Energy of Destruction' is the third Ray application of the Will, hence dealing with the law of Karma. 'The Energy of Organisation' is the seventh Ray aspect of the Will, as directed from Shambhala. The first, second, third and seventh Rays are precisely the energies, as earlier explained, that the new Mahāchohan manifests in his current dispensation. Hence he carries out the purpose of the Planetary Logos into active manifestation. The toned down expression of these Rays, via the mediatorship of the fourth Ray, impregnates 'little human wills' causing them to work to *purify* their thoughts and emotions. In doing so they become receptive to the emanation of the Divine Plan.

---

21 A.A. Bailey, *The Rays and the Initiations,* 84-85.

This purifying process necessitates transforming and transmuting *saṃskāras* into enlightenment vectors. It also relates to zapping away dark brotherhood predations.

Humanity must also *destroy* the old outmoded constructs of political, religious and social forms, as well as the present focus upon scientific materialism, so that the new planned civilisation based upon cooperativeness, unity and esoteric knowledge can replace the old defunct forms. Finally the aspirants, disciples and Initiates must use their will to organise the new evolving civilisation in all of its facets, so that the divine paradigm is externalised in the new garden cities and temples wherein the Mysteries are promulgated.

Here then is the outline of the 'purpose which Bodhisattvas know and serve'. They are the Initiates of the world and many will be aware of much greater detail of what is to be implemented, according to their specific Ray department, Initiation status and appropriate cycle for expression of their part of the manifesting Plan.

The fourth stanza is:

> From the centre which we call humanity,
> Let the Plan of Love and Light work out,
> And may it seal the door where evil dwells.

Nothing can manifest without humanity's active support and willingness to carry out the Plan. They may not know of that Plan individually, but nevertheless will be inspired by the Bodhisattvas working in all seven Ray departments of life; with people in all religions, occupations, and races. The active service of the Bodhisattvas will be to phrase the part of the Plan they are cognisant of in a way that their target audience comprehends and so be inspired to serve. In doing so they learn the ways of Love and Light, which is the custodianship of Hierarchy, and aspire to greater heights of revelation. The testings of Initiation then looms ahead of them. As they pass the crisis via the service arenas they have chosen, so the Door opens behind them and they find they have further vitalised the ranks of Hierarchy.

There will be a continuous movement onwards, outwards to humanity and upwards to Shambhala as aspirants become disciples, disciples Initiates and Initiates take higher Initiations that lead inevitably to the cosmic Paths. The epoch of Love-Wisdom consequently dawns upon human civilisation and as the great majority of humanity gain wisdom, so the 'door where evil dwells' shuts, for the individual and for humanity as a whole.

Evil will not so much be seen in terms of what humanity often presently mistake it to be (often viewed in terms of sexuality, unwanted change, or suffering from the blows of *karma).* Rather, it will be viewed as it truly manifests (from an esoteric perspective), as unregenerate *saṃskāras,* hindering *karma,* lying propaganda, the forceful manipulation of others and theft of their resources[22] for the gain of the separative, self-centred egotist, or by those in power. In the last analysis, evil relates to the predation of the dark brotherhood upon every evolutionary entity, to prevent their journey forwards. Evil relates to the disease bearing factors in a human unit and upon the planet as a whole. What produces physical and mental-emotional sickness and resistance to healthy growth must therefore be conquered, and as humanity does so in their civilisation, so the door where evil dwells will be closed.

The final statement:

> Let Light and Love and Power restore the Plan on earth.
> So let it be and help us do our part.
>
> Oṁ Maṇi Padme Hūṁ

This is a personal affirmation of the individual and of the group of which he/she is a part, to continuously strive to implement the vision of the Plan because of their developing Love. In doing so the disciple evokes the Power to externalise the vision practically to produce effective results. The Light is the demonstration of third Ray purpose, the Love the second Ray purpose, the Power is the materialising potency of the seventh Ray, and the Plan is the first Ray fiat of the Lord of the World manifesting through the hearts and Minds of all serving disciples—the Bodhisattvas that create with their hands the edifice of the new vibrant organism. In doing so they play their part. As spiritual Power increasingly manifests, so Hierarchy will externalise in its effulgent glory, demonstrating the reality of 'the holy city, new Jerusalem',[23] and inevitably the full potency of Shambhala will be revealed upon earth.

22 This includes the resources of our biosphere.

23 *Rev. 21.2.*

The Tibetan mantra Oṁ Maṇi Padme Hūṁ is well known and is an apt seal of approval for the great Invocation. Its meaning has been explained in the earlier volumes of this series.[24] It relates to the liberating work of the Bodhisattva in all 'Six Realms' of human evolution, so that all will eventually be released from the wheel of rebirth.

The doctrine of Avatars

The mystery of Christ-Jesus is explained via the Hindu doctrine of Avatars. It is hinted at in the Buddhist concept of the Tulku, and veiled in the *nirmaṇakāya* of a Buddha or great Bodhisattva. For their Christian brothers such a divine embodiment is regarded as a unique case in Jesus-Christ.

Those greater than the Christ are cosmic beings that have passed through the stage of being a Buddha aeons ago and have superseded the ability to directly incarnate into the substance of the cosmic dense physical plane. The three worlds of human livingness are below their field of normal awareness, therefore they need mediators that can bear their energies and project their purpose into *saṃsāra*.

The Logoi controlling the evolutionary development and Initiation process of all upon our planet are such Avatars. We thus have the triad of the Avatar of Synthesis, the Spirit of Peace and the Mother of the World. They are of such an exalted character that externalisation on the highest three of our seven systemic planes constitutes for them dense physical Incarnation. These planes represent the three *dharmakāyic* levels explained in the earlier volumes. To manifest their purpose upon the lower planes of perception wherein humanity reside, they need intermediaries – enlightened consecrated vehicles through whom they can project their Power, Love, and active Purpose.

Sanat Kumāra manifests as the vehicle of the triune planetary Logos, as explained in chapter two, hence is an exalted Avataric embodiment, a *nirmaṇakāya* incarnate upon the second systemic plane *(anupādaka)*. He esoterically 'walks' via the 'two feet' of Figure 23, however it is the left foot that is firmly planted upon the 'ground' of physical plane activity. Hence the role of the new Mahāchohan is to act as the Incarnation, the Avatar of this great One. The new Mahāchohan is

24 See Volume 3, 296-297, and Volume 5B, 191-192.

the *nirmaṇakāya* that establishes the second Ray purpose into active manifestation via Mind and Will. He will demonstrate the process of divine embodiment by grounding cosmic purpose, not only of Sanat Kumāra but also of the manifesting Ideation of the cosmic Christ via the Avatar of Synthesis, into the lowest plane possible via the Initiates that have incarnated with him for this purpose.

Thus will be established a *maṇḍala* of the dynamic, active, resolute purpose of Love. From this perspective the new Mahāchohan represents the 'personality' incarnation of the planetary Logos. Sanat Kumāra then is the Father and the new Mahāchohan the Mother, who together will manifest a non-dual (yab-yum) union. The awakening new world civilisation will then become the divine Child. Integrated into and producing this new civilisation will be the externalising Hierarchy. To produce this unfolding scenario is the Hierarchical plan for this epoch, being the focal point of cosmic Love for the planet.

The concept of an Avatar therefore must be viewed in its wider group connotation and not be narrowed down to one individual, for out of necessity a cosmic entity, as is an Avatar, must work through a consecrated group capable of bearing His potency to influence the masses. There are always many levels of interpretation to be considered for any esoteric topic.

The magnetic potency of cosmic Love will also be directed via the Spirit of Peace to the blue Christ and the right foot (K.H.) in a manner that it can be rightly used by humanity without the production of undesirable characteristics. (Such as the overstimulation of their desire bodies.) The present objective is thus to awaken the compassionate activity of the Heart centres of humanity, but not to overly stimulate their emotions and devotional attributes, as happened with respect to Jesus's dispensation. A plan will thus manifest to subdue the natural devotional outpouring of the world's aspirants and disciples when the Avatar exoterically appears. When Jesus was earlier overshadowed by the cosmic Christ it affected just one small portion of our planet, now on this higher turn of the spiral the entire world sphere will be involved. This happening will be greatly facilitated by the marvel of modern mass communication.

Peace descends to quieten the astral sea, and power manifests to the extent that Love and light is expressed by those that are incarnate. Such power will overcome the evil that presently prevails everywhere. The major second Ray cycle thus proceeds because a Christ walks again openly amongst us. He, however, will not necessarily be recognised as such by the mass of the common people, or by the intelligentsia, any more than happened 2,000 years ago, when the last great bearer of this principle was crucified. Human minds are blinded through ignorance and reactionary emotions that prevent them seeing the radiance of the Light bearer that has incarnated for their benefit. The lucid teachings promulgated are generally beyond their capacity to comprehend, representing attributes of logic that still lie far in their future. The dark brotherhood thus have ample space to write their scores in people's minds. Nevertheless that future will appear in time and there are always those elevated 'sons of God' incarnate that can and do bear witness to the teachings of the great One, that do comprehend, and will follow that Light to liberation.

The Initiated will see and know and will spread the Truth, Light and Love to an increasingly wider audience, who will listen and whose eyes will open to the compassionate need. Hence the power of the Christ presence will spread with increasing momentum to influence all aspects of civilisation.

From the above preamble the reader can now better comprehend to whom D.K. referred concerning the subject of the appearance of the Avatar.

> Later will come an Avatar Who will achieve neither the full enlightenment of the Buddha nor the full expression of the divine love of the Christ, but Who will have a large measure of wisdom and of love, plus that "materialising power" which will enable Him to found a divine powerhouse upon the physical plane. His task, in many ways, is far more difficult than that of the two preceding Avatars, for He carries in Himself not only the energies of the two divine principles, already "duly anchored" upon the planet by His two great Brothers,[25] but He has also within Himself much of a third divine principle, hitherto not used upon our planet. He carries the Will of God into manifestation, and of that will we, as yet, know really nothing. So difficult is His task that the New Group of World Servers is being

25 The Buddha and the blue Christ.

trained to assist Him. Thus an aspect of the first ray principle will be anchored by Him upon the earth.

All that the student can grasp is that the *Plan* will be the dynamic impulse of this third and vital energy which will pervade the outer court of the Temple, constituting a Temple of Initiation upon the physical plane, thus externalising the activities of the Hierarchy in certain possible respects. The first initiation will then take place upon earth. It will be then no longer a veiled secret. This is the initiation of the outer court, wherein the approach of the soul upon the Way of Descent into manifestation, and the subsequent appropriation of the proffered divine energy by the personality upon the Way of Ascent will take place.

The Holy Place is the place where the second initiation is enacted, and this will some day be given upon the astral plane when illusion there presiding has been somewhat dissipated. Over this second initiation, the Christ presides and, as was said above, it is for us the most difficult and most transforming of the initiations. The acquiescence of the soul to the demands of the personality for spiritual life, and the submission of the personality to the soul, find therein their consummation.

Finally will come the initiation of the Transfiguration,[26] wherein the light breaks forth, the *Touch of Enlightenment* is given, and the soul and the personality stand forth as one. This process requires also the aid of the Buddha and the inspiration of the Christ, and is "occultly guarded" by the Avatar on the physical plane.

In all the above information there is given a hint as to what will take place when human personalities are actively functioning and steadily awakening. The rapid coming of the Avatar Who will found the station of light and power upon the physical plane is dependent upon the rapid unfoldment and appearance of integrated personalities who love and think and seek to serve. There has here been given a new hint upon one of the more esoteric aspects of the work of the New Group of World Servers.[27]

The nature of this Avatar is also explained in *The Externalisation of the Hierarchy*. Section three of that book is entitled 'Forces behind the

---

26 The third Initiation.

27 A.A. Bailey, *Esoteric Psychology II*, (Lucis Publishing House, New York, 1970), 281-282.

Evolutionary Progress of the Race—The Doctrine of Avatars'. Therein an Avatar is defined as a:

> Being Who—having first developed His Own nature, human and divine, and then transcended it—is capable of reflecting some cosmic Principle or divine quality and energy which will produce the desired effect upon humanity, evoking a reaction, producing a needed stimulation and, as it is esoterically called, 'leading to the rending of a veil and the permeation of light.' This energy may be generated within the human family and focussed in a responsive Messenger; it may be generated within the planet itself and produce a planetary Avatar; it may be the expression of the life impulse and energy of the solar system, or of sources outside the solar system and therefore cosmic. But always it is focussed through a manifesting Entity, is called forth by a demand or massed appeal, and evokes response and consequent changes in the life activity, the culture and the civilisation of mankind.
>
> The response or reaction of humanity to the divine Messenger establishes in due time the recognition of something transcendent, something to be desired and striven for, something which indicates a vision which is first a possibility and later an achievement. This is the historically proven process and testifies eventually to a *fact*. This new fact, when added to the facts established by other and earlier Avatars, enriches the spiritual content of the human consciousness, enhances the spiritual life of the race, and stimulates man to move a step forward into the world of reality and out of the world of illusion. Each revelation brings him nearer to the world of causes.[28]

Under the heading *The Appearance of Avatars*, the Master D.K. describes some of the types of Avatars:

1. Racial Avatars
2. Teaching Avatars
3. Ray Avatars
4. Transmitting Avatars
5. Divine Embodiments[29]

Concerning the fifth type of Avatar D.K. states:

---

28 A.A. Bailey, *The Externalisation of the Hierarchy*, 291-292.

29 Ibid., 297-302.

These Avatars appear rarely; when They do, the effectiveness and results of Their work are very great. They issue forth into manifestation via the centre at Shamballa, because They are an expression of the will nature of Deity; They embody divine purpose; the energy pouring through Them and transmitted by Them is focussed through the Lord of the World; They can only be reached by the united voices of the Hierarchy and of humanity speaking in unison; Their service is evoked only by realised need, and only after those who call Them forth have added to their faith strenuous action and have done their utmost, alone and unaided, to overcome evil.

They never descend lower than the mental plane, and the main emphasis and attention of Their work is directed to the Hierarchy; the Hierarchy is Their transmitting agency; They occasionally reach those thinking people, focussed on the mental plane, who have clear vision, potent resolve, directed will and open minds, plus of course, essential purity of form. These Avatars express the Will of God, the energy of Shamballa, and the impulse lying behind divine purpose. When They do come forth, it will be the destroyer aspect of the first ray of power which They will express; They bring about death—the death of all old and limiting forms and of that which houses evil. Their work will, therefore, fall into two categories:

a. They will destroy the forces of evil, using the agency of the Forces of Light.

b. They will reveal as much of the divine purpose as humanity is able to grasp through its best minds and most dedicated aspirants; They will clarify the vision of the world disciples and of all who have the disciplined will-to-know and who are dedicated to and expressive of the will-to-good.[30]

D.K. further states:

When the Avatar comes He will convey to humanity something for which we have as yet no true name. It is neither love nor will as we understand them. Only a phrase of several words can convey something of the significance and then only feebly. This phrase is *"the principle of directed purpose."* This principle involves three factors:

g. Understanding (intuitive and instinctual, but intelligently interpreted) of the plan as it can be worked out in the immediate future.

---

30 Ibid., 301.

h. Focussed intention, based on the above and emphasising an aspect of the will, hitherto undeveloped in man.

i. Capacity to direct energy (through understanding and intent) towards a recognised and desired end, overcoming all obstacles and destroying all that stands in the way. This is not the destruction of forms by force such as is now being imposed on the world, but a destruction brought about by the greatly strengthened life within the form. Only the next one hundred years will reveal the significance of this statement and then only if the massed intent of the people evokes this *Avatar of Synthesis* during the next twelve months. I have called this Being by this name because it expresses the quality and the objective of the force He brings and wields.

Another and lesser Avatar is also awaiting a call from humanity. He is esoterically related to the Avatar of Synthesis, being overshadowed by Him. This Avatar can descend on to the physical plane into outer expression and can thus step down and transmit the stimulation and quality of the force of the greater Avatar Who can come no nearer than the mental plane. Who this Coming One may be is not yet revealed. It may be the Christ, if His other work permits; it may be One chosen by Him to issue forth, overshadowed by the Avatar of Synthesis and directed in His activities by the Christ, the Lord of Love. In this way, the energies of both Shamballa and the Hierarchy will be focussed through the chosen Coming One. Thus a triangle of loving, purposeful energy will be created which may prove a more effective way of releasing energy and a safer way, than the focussed impact of one selected force might be.

I realise the difficulty of this subject and perhaps may simplify the matter by a brief summation:

1. A great cosmic Avatar can come if the Hierarchy and humanity can stand together with massed intent.
    a. He will descend into the three worlds of human endeavour, but no nearer than the mental plane.
    b. He will transmit a cosmic Energy whose quality is *Synthesis.* This will express itself through harmony and unity, producing necessarily understanding, promoting goodwill, and eventually ending the separative, isolating tendencies of mankind.
    c. His note and vibration can be sensed by those whose individual note is also synthesis and whose life objective is the will-to-good. These are consequently the Members of the Hierarchy,

the disciples and aspirants of the world and a few of the men of goodwill.

2. A Messenger or Avatar of equal rank to the Christ in the Hierarchy (or possibly Christ Himself) may come forth as the Representative of the Avatar of Synthesis and as His transmitting Agent.

   a. This lesser Avatar works today as one of the senior Members of the Great White Lodge and is in close touch with the Christ, with the Manu and with the Lord of Civilisation, the Master R—; He will act as the Coordinator between the Hierarchy and Shamballa. He will fuse and blend in Himself, through the quality of His Own life, the three great energies:

      The will-to-spiritual power.
      The will-to-love in its spiritual connotation.
      The will-to-manifest spiritually.

   b. The antiquity of the achievement of this Coming One is to be found in the name applied to Him, which is found in so many of the world Scriptures: The Rider on the White Horse. This refers to the time prior to the phrase so well-known in the Christian fields: "The Lamb slain from the foundation of the world." In the earlier cycle, the then initiates spoke of the "sacrificial horse, slain to all eternity." It conveys the same basic idea.

   c. This Avatar can descend to the physical plane and there appear, to lead His people—as the Prince Who leads through war to peace.

   d. The whole problem before the Hierarchy and humanity today, in connection with the coming Avatar, can be summed up in the following four questions:

      Can He bring the energy of synthesis with Him, thereby bringing about rapid changes?

   This depends upon His being overshadowed by the Avatar of Synthesis and upon That Avatar being evoked through the demand and the massed intent of humanity, aided by the Hierarchy.

      Will the demand of the people be strong enough to evoke the higher potency, or will it be too feeble because

> of the failure of the world disciples and aspirants to focus this massed intent throughout the planet?
>
> Will the higher overshadowing not take place and only the lesser Avatar come to institute a slower method of gradual reform?

> This slower method will be necessitated only if and because humanity will have demonstrated its inability to call forth and receive the higher measure and more potent vibration of divine energy. It is entirely for the decision of the world disciples and aspirants; not poor bewildered, deluded humanity. Will the world disciples and aspirants appreciate the crisis and opportunity? They have not yet, as a whole, done so.[31]

Here some notes should be added:

1. When D.K. speaks of this 'lesser Avatar' as 'of equal rank to the Christ in the Hierarchy (or possibly the Christ Himself)' he is referring to the Christ as a title. The nature of the triune Christ has been explained, where the blue Christ is the 'oldest' member of the Hierarchy, and if we disregard him then the third Christ, who works 'as one of the senior members of the Great White Lodge', becomes the contender here. As a 'Christ' he figuratively is of equal rank and will attain a similar Initiation status in the form of the new Mahāchohan.
2. The Rider on the White Horse will be seen as the new Mahāchohan riding out into incarnation and service work on the steed of the externalising first and second Ray Ashrams, but specifically the entire Mahāchohan's department whilst being overshadowed by Sanat Kumāra and the Avatar of Synthesis. The *horse* here symbolises the body of disciples and Initiates, as well as the mind, which has to be tamed and ridden by the spiritual persona (via the intuition). The head and neck of the 'horse' represents the first, second and third Ray Ashrams. The body represents the sum of the Ashrams along the Rays of Mind. The four feet represent the seventh Ray Ashrams that bear the weight of the above.[32] A Master's

31 Ibid., 302-305.

32 The symbolism of the effects of the riding forth of this Horse is given in *Rev. 19:11ff.*

Ashram is but the extension of the unfoldment of his Mind, it is the symbolic 'horse' ridden into the world service arena.

The second Ray Chohan can then ride out into his service work on the steed of the united second Ray Ashrams, once the preparatory stages of the externalisation process and the necessary world changes have been effected. This will present the testings for him to eventually attain the rank of the blue Christ and will bring into manifestation the complete potency of the major second Ray cycle upon this planet (symbolised by the number 222).

Once all of this has been accomplished then the blue Christ can ride forth on his steed of the entire Hierarchy that have externalised. He will be overshadowed by the Spirit of Peace and his steed will be composed of the integral factors of the second Ray Ashrams and all affiliated Ray lines. His task will not be as exoteric as in the case of the first Rider, thus His true appearance may only be accessible to the relative few, but the effect of his work will be known by all. It will be most widespread and occult, and all kingdoms of Nature will benefit. He will put the millennial seal to the changes brought about by the incoming second Ray cycle. The entire *maṇḍala* of Hierarchy will have moved upwards, onwards and downwards simultaneously.

3. D.K. wrote the above quotations in 1941 during the Second World War when humanity was in the throes of a life-death struggle with the forces of evil. Since then the response to expected possibilities has been only lukewarm, thus the forces of evil in our societies are nowhere near being defeated, and in fact they have again amassed massive forces upon the planet with view of taking complete control over planetary affairs. However, the struggle against their influences continues with generally a much larger number of higher calibre disciples incarnate. The world-wide consciousness-revolution and consequent demand of the people has been strong enough to evoke the appearance of the Rider. His role, however, has mostly been played out quietly behind the scenes of the hubris of human societal activity. Hopefully, that role will eventually manifest in a way so that 'every eye shall see him' *(Rev. 1:7)*.

The manifestation of the major second Ray cycle thus refers to the time of opportunity for the blue Christ to descend from his high place of waiting before outwardly appearing amongst humanity. This appearance signifies the process of undertaking the testings that will eventually make him the Spirit of Peace for the planet. Not much more can be said about the subject than was earlier presented to the public by D.K. in *The Reappearance of the Christ* and *The Externalisation of the Hierarchy*.

It should be obvious that the time of appearance of the blue Christ depends upon whether his forerunner was successful. With respect to this it can be said the 'Secret Place' from where the Rider (the new Mahāchohan, the green Christ) issues forth can be considered to be the high point of the planetary Solar Plexus centre at the door of access to the Heart centre (Hierarchy). From here he helps to protect humanity from the onslaught of cosmic astral plane dark brotherhood. It is a planetary version of what a disciple must do to control the Solar Plexus centre (astralism, emotionality) by means of *manas*. The mind must be used to control the emotions, by utilising the energy of Love, if wisdom is to be obtained.

Here the *manasic* input of the entire Mahāchohan's department is utilised. The focus is upon the work of the Master Jesus, and from him to the world's disciples, devotees and aspirants. The new Mahāchohan also works with Morya's department to help convert the self-will of humanity (developed by Solar Plexus activity) into the Will-to-Good, which is what will finally defeat the forces of evil. The principle of Love governing the entire Hierarchy, specifically developed by K.H.'s department, is here ever-present. However, before aspirants can enter the inner sanctum of this planetary centre they must actively work to transform their own forms of evil *saṃskāras* by passing the tests for Initiation. When viewed on a larger group scale we then see that entire group *saṃskāras* concerning dark brotherhood methodology must be defeated before Hierarchy can accept expansive growth by admittance of new members. Thus we have the effective vigil at the door of entry to Hierarchy by the forces associated with this green Christ.

The blue Christ, on the other hand, is preparing from what D.K. styles 'the High Place', which esoterically refers to the planetary *śūnyatā-saṃsāra* nexus. From here, he who embodies the principle of Love for humanity, defends from the expression of evil emanating from cosmic mental sources. Here he functions as a direct representative of

Shambhala. The European Chohan and Padmasambhava also work as part of a triad with him. Padmasambhava here also specifically manifests as the link between the blue and green Christs.

This thus indicates an aspect of planetary protection from cosmic evil that is the higher correspondence of the Hierarchical Shield explained earlier. Here we have what might be best described as the Shield of 'God', which has the blue Christ in the northern position, the green Christ in the southern position, the European Chohan in the eastern position, Padmasambhava in the western position, and Shambhala as the central activating dynamo.

We can see therefore that when the Rider and the blue Christ after him issue forth into externalised activity, they bring this protection right down to the physical plane, as far as the exigencies of human *karma* will allow. Such protection on the physical plane has existed in the past, however, it was always contingent upon a great One incarnating with his immediate group of servers, and thus was not carried through to a long time period. What is now envisaged is the permanent establishment of the locales for such protection, focused via the new Mystery Schools (temples of Initiation) that will manifest upon the earth.

From the above we effectively see a role reversal between the Mahāchohan's department and that of the Christ, where the new Mahāchohan is here specifically concerned with the Watery aspect of humanity (normally the Christ's forte) and the blue Christ with *manasic* unfoldment (the Mahāchohan's department). The reason for this being that the focus of the new Mahāchohan is upon cleansing the Watery moon Chain *karma* of the humanity that had originated there, whilst the focus of the blue Christ is upon educating earth Chain humanity. They need to rightly use their minds above all in this new cycle. Hence one works from a 'Secret Place', concerned with considerations of the moon, and the other from a 'High Place' for the normal evolution of earth Chain humanity.

D.K. states:

> Thus a great and new movement is proceeding and a tremendously increased interplay and interaction is taking place. This will go on until A.D. 2025. During the years intervening between now and then very great changes will be seen taking place, and at the great General

> Assembly of the Hierarchy—held as usual every century—in 2025 the date in all probability will be set for the first stage of the externalisation of the Hierarchy. The present cycle (from now until that date) is called technically "The Stage of the Forerunner". It is preparatory in nature, testing in its methods, and intended to be revelatory in its techniques and results. You can see therefore that Chohans, Masters, initiates, world disciples, disciples and aspirants affiliated with the Hierarchy are all at this time passing through a cycle of great activity.[33]

Three 75 year cycles (literally the ideal age of a human incarnation) will be traced from the time of the formation of the Theosophical Society in 1875 by Col. Olcott, W.Q. Judge and H.P. Blavatsky, to the actual period of externalisation of the Hierarchy. The first cycle can be considered that of activity and lasted until 1950. Hence it includes the early activity of the Theosophists, the work of A.A. Bailey (who died in 1949) and the Roerichs, as well as the ancillary writings of Rudolf Steiner, who founded the Anthroposophical Society, and others such as Max Heindel of The Rosicrucian Fellowship. The second or Love-Wisdom cycle concerns the process of the popularisation and broadcasting of Hierarchy's teachings to as wide an audience as possible. These are the teachings found in the 'blue books' of the Master D.K. that capitalised on Blavatsky's earlier works. They are supplemented and expanded, including the missing quotient of the Buddhist doctrines, by this present series of writings. The Buddhist foundation of the esoteric lore is largely missing in D.K.'s works,[34] as his focus was the second Ray purpose via the line of dispensation of the blue Christ, whereas my writings relate to a line of dispensation from the Buddha and the green Christ. This cycle will last until the great Hierarchical centennial conclave of 2025 and will signal the appearance of this Avatar upon the world stage. Much will by then have been accomplished to help awaken humanity that the Hierarchy exists.

The final cycle of 75 years, to the year 2,100, will consequently see the externalisation of the Hierarchy, according to the way that the prospective members of the Ashrams have passed the testings

---

33 A.A. Bailey, *The Externalisation of the Hierarchy,* 530.

34 Despite the fact that he was a Rinpoche at Shigatse at the time.

concerning planetary Initiation. It is after all a period of the great awakening of humanity, though much work will still need to be done before Hierarchy will be in a position to govern the main institutions of the then civilisation. This relates to the period when the reappearance of the blue Christ is possible, as prophesised in D.K.'s books, *The Reappearance of the Christ* and *The Externalisation of the Hierarchy.* Each of the 75 year periods are also subdivided into three 25 year periods, hence the blue Christ, the Master of Masters, should be active exoterically around the year 2075, and with him the service activity of the great Ones and their disciples.

In a section entitled 'The Effects of the Externalisation' written in September 1949, D.K. states:

> When, however, the externalisation of the Hierarchy begins to take place (and it will be spread over quite a long period of time), the impact of these substantial energies on matter will be radically altered because they will be—for the first time in history—directed from etheric levels, from the etheric body of the planet in the three worlds; hitherto, these energies have been directed from the buddhic plane which is the lowest of the cosmic etheric levels. Fundamentally, direction will still be from the buddhic plane, but the detailed and focussed direction will be given from within the three worlds and upon the physical plane; this will be the task of the externalised Ashrams, organised to function openly.[35]

From this we see that some members of the externalised Hierarchy will primarily function from the etheric levels and others will be exoterically manifest upon the plane of concrete human affairs. The etheric sub-planes are esoterically considered 'physical', representing the true form of the human persona. This work upon the etheric domain will allow Sanat Kumāra to pour a significantly increased energisation directly upon the physical domain via the Hierarchical force vectors that will then directly empower the *chakras* of humanity. D.K. further states that:

> Earlier I stated that the physical plane areas or localities which constitute the present modern exits for energies, through which directed energies can pass to carry out the creative process, are five in number: New York, London, Geneva, Darjeeling and Tokyo. These

35 A.A. Bailey, *The Externalisation of the Hierarchy,* 673-674.

> five form a five-pointed star of interlocking energies, symbolic of the major divisions of our modern civilisation. I would have you bear in mind that all that I am here giving you anent energy is in relation to the human kingdom and to nothing else; I am not relating these energies to the other kingdoms in nature; I am here concerned with physical plane utilisation of energy through the power of directed thinking and on behalf of the evolution and well-being of mankind. At each one of these five centres one of the Masters will be found present, with His Ashram, and a vortex of spiritual forces will there be organised to hasten and materialise the plans of the Christ for the new and coming world cycle.
>
> The organising of these five centres will be done slowly and gradually. A senior disciple will appear and will work quietly at the foundation work, gathering around him the needed agents, aspirants and assistants. All these workers at any particular centre will be trained to think, and the effort now present in the educational and social world to force men to think for themselves is a general part of this training process.[36]

The process associated with the planned externalisation of certain Masters at these five planetary centres has not yet materialised, mainly owing to the present successful onslaught of the forces of evil upon human civilisation. Plans have had to be adjusted accordingly, and Hierarchy will inevitably be successful in implementing its agenda. The Rays governing this externalisation are: Darjeeling, the first Ray; London, the second Ray; New York, the third Ray; Geneva, the fourth Ray and Tokyo expresses the seventh Ray energy. The effects of a major war may effect the locus of the externalisation of the associated Masters.

The stage of the forerunner of Hierarchical externalisation is well under way, with many Hierarchical members now incarnate and serving. Other great Ones are as children preparing for their time to serve. The Rider has appeared and his work has been successful to date, thus the Avatar of Synthesis has announced His intent to overshadow this One and the *maṇḍala* of serving disciples he works through at the appropriate time.

The exact timing of the appearance of the blue Christ will depend upon the success of the work of K.H., in conjunction with the efforts

36 Ibid., 675.

of the new Mahāchohan, which still lies in the future. The probability is that both the blue Christ and K.H. will appear during the same time sequence to inaugurate the sounding of the major second Ray cycle, symbolised by the number 222.

Look well to clearly discern 'the signs of the times' *(Matt. 16:3)* so that you can assist and play a role to help bring forth the new world civilisation. The Avatar is here, yet unknown by the world's disciples, or the moving masses of people, yet to be seen by All. Come, open your eyes, seek with your hearts and you shall find. Proffer your hearts and minds for the great service, and with his spiritual power help make this world holy. The fanfare of Hierarchy then spreads out the wings of enlightenment for the great awakening of humanity.

Under the heading 'The Needed Steps' for the appearance of the Avatar, D.K. has this to say:

> These steps are various in kind though one in intent. The first step is to realise clearly what are the methods whereby the Avatar can come and so reach humanity. These are the same methods, whether it is the Avatar of Synthesis, working through the Hierarchy, or the Avatar of Coordination (as I might call Him), working through humanity and representing the greater Avatar upon the physical plane.
>
> The methods whereby Avatars reach and influence Their agents or those who respond to Their note, vibration and message are three in number.
>
> 10. *Overshadowing.* Where there is kinship in quality, in objective and in nature, it is possible for the Avatar to overshadow some Member of the Hierarchy (as in the case of the Avatar of Synthesis) or some disciple or aspirant where humanity is concerned (in the case of the lesser Avatar). This is done through meditation, through a directed stream of thought energy, the presentation of a thoughtform and the evocation of the focussed will of the one who is overshadowed. All this proceeds rapidly where there is close cooperation between the latter (the sensitive responding disciple) and the Avatar...
> 11. *Inspiration.* This is more direct than overshadowing and more potent in results. Certain members of the Hierarchy and, above all, the lesser Avatars, are inspired from "on high" by the cosmic Avatar and become at times direct expressions of His mind, His

energy and His plans. This is the spiritual correspondence to obsession. In the case of obsession, a man is taken possession of and inspired by some evil entity; in inspiration, there is no possession but only what is called "identical response"—a very different thing. In the one case, the free will and intelligent understanding of the Master or the disciple is enlisted on the side of the spiritual Agent; the spiritual man, functioning as a soul, becomes the channel for forces, ideas and activities other than his own but to which he gives full intuitive assent. It is all carried forward with full understanding and consciousness of method, process and results. It is an act of free spiritual cooperation, for the good of humanity, in the work of a great spiritual Force or Being. The cooperation of the Master Jesus with the Christ is a case in point. In connection with the coming Avatar, it may involve the cooperation of the Christ or of a "kindred, equal soul" with a cosmic Being or Presence, taking place on still higher spiritual levels of consciousness and producing an incredibly focussed potency.

In the case of obsession, the evil force enslaves the personality which, in the majority of cases, is but a shell. Of this, Hitler is a case in point. This produces greater potency on the physical and on the astral plane; it is quicker and more immediate in results, but the lasting power is less and the effects are relatively temporary.

In the process of inspiration, the lesser Avatar—through His life and contacts in the three worlds—will necessarily influence sensitive, spiritually oriented disciples and aspirants, and thus the inspiration coming from the cosmic Avatar becomes in time a *group inspiration,* and therefore can be more safely handled. This group inspiration can happen today. If it does, there will then be a simultaneous appearing of the cosmic Avatar, the World Saviour in the Person of the lesser Avatar, and—at the same time—a group saviour, composed of responsive disciples and world servers. Ponder again on this.

In this way, if you will note carefully, there is established a direct linked chain from humanity, via the Hierarchy, to Shamballa. The Hierarchy is working at the establishing of this chain, aided by Their disciples. The demand for the cooperation of all aspirants is now going forth, because the times are urgent. If this relationship can be established (and it will be a sad day for humanity if it cannot), then the third method of avataric expression becomes possible.

12. *Appearance or Manifestation.* Every possible step has been taken by the Hierarchy to enable the Avatar, the Coming One, to appear. What these steps are cannot be declared here. Only some questions, suggesting possibility, are permissible.[37]

It should be noted here that the doctrine of Tulkus and to a certain extent of Rinpoches in Tibetan Buddhism is but a distorted conveyance of the teaching of Avataras above. The Tibetans with their usual aplomb took what was useful of the esoteric doctrines and adapted it into their exoteric system for the education of the masses. The teachings then become popularised and distorted, feeding the uncomprehending minds of the laity. The distortions were idolised and handed down as mythologised truth for the successive generations of worshippers. We thus have Tulkus and Rinpoches that have, for instance, been given impossible past lives, really based upon the nature of a past life of the overshadowing great one, and not of the exoteric holder of any Rinpoche's seat. Many of the errors of this philosophy have been adequately explained in Volume 6, hence this subject needs not be repeated here. Problems arise when no enlightened ones are incarnate to properly explain the exoteric teachings, which the great majority now ardently believe and teach as the truth.

The first Ray pentad

Concerning the downpour of the first Ray purpose within Hierarchy we can first consider a triad of the Manu, Padmasambhava (the left hand), and the first Ray Chohan, Morya (the right hand). This then expands into a pentad where Jesus represents the right foot and the new Mahāchohan the left foot. Padmasambhava's relation to the first Ray derives in part from his role in the 2/7 Ashram in Atlantean times. The seventh Ray allows Him to bear the potency of the first Ray energies, especially when coupled to his high spiritual age. In this pentad defining the first Ray power within Hierarchy, Padmasambhava also bears the

37 Ibid., 306-308.

potency of a Buddha, who is abstracted from our planetary life. (As stated, Padmasambhava has been called a second Buddha by Tibetans.)

The left side of the pentad represents the downward flow of the first Ray into the planetary manifestation via *manasic* propensity. The right hand side concerns a *piṇgalā* flow into manifestation via cosmic astral sources. Morya bears the brunt of this first Ray force and organises it so that it can best effect the massed lives evolving on this planet. Jesus adapts the energies, softening or 'toning them down' so that the world's disciples can gain in a positive way. He makes this energy more amenable to people's Watery constitution, helping to mitigate the effects of the intensity of the energies. The relation of Jesus to Morya was brought out exoterically in the Bible story through the baptism of Jesus by John the Baptist, an incarnation of Morya.[38]

Padmasambhava and the new Mahāchohan are closely related. They are part of the special team organised by Sanat Kumāra to help overcome planetary evil by using 'occult' methodology.

The Manu is the head of the first Ray department of Hierarchy, hence is part of the executive Council at Shambhala and directs the streams of Life related to the particular Root Race he oversees. The grand vision and design is carried throughout the planetary life in accordance with cosmic purpose.

Astutely ascertaining exactly what potency is possible for humanity to bear for every fiat of Shambhala (and to the level or extent it must be broadcast) becomes the major part of the work of the first Ray pentad. They must also protect the kingdoms of Nature from the Rays of cosmic evil that may find opportunity to impress our planetary body utilising the destructive potency of the first Ray. This Ray destroys the form as it liberates the imprisoned Life. The first Ray is the expression of the *prāṇic* energisation stemming from the auras of the Lords of Shambhala and via the various *dharmakāya* levels. Normally when directed towards humanity the intensity is too potent for their mental-emotional thought life, hence needs to be adequately toned down via the agency of Hierarchy.

---

38 See *Matt. 3:16, Luke 3:22* and *Mark 1:10.*

Within the confines of the cosmic dense physical plane (to which all of the planes of perception we evolve through are sub-planes) there are forms of sickness and disease manifesting through the Logoic dense form inherited from past cycles. People thus need to be appropriately healed at the appointed time, as the dark brotherhood represent the expressed agents of this disease. The visioning of those working at this scale of planetary rectification is vast, and is facilitated by those that have been Initiated into the first Ray line of service. Our planetary system is still imperfect, hence must bear forms of cosmic *karma* possessed by our planetary Logos. The first Ray department appropriately sees to the effects of this *karma* so that it serves to generate the sanctity of space to make our planet sacred. This is not an easy task, considering the predilection of humanity to forms of evil doing.

Morya (the right hand) and Padmasambhava (the left hand) work in conjunction with each other, carefully monitoring the possible mental-emotional reactions of humanity to the outpouring of any first Ray fiat. Care is needed because this Ray of Will or Power can easily manifest in an aberrant fashion when stimulating the *chakras* conditioning humanity. Padmasambhava works directly with human Minds via Initiates that can bear the power of first Ray injunctions of Mind (Shambhalic directives) so that the appropriate cycles of wilful expression by humanity can be correctly modified. Morya works with the first Ray department and the Hierarchical Shield via human Souls, wisely modifying the intensity of the energies to be borne by them.

The fingers of each *hand* project the complete power of the five types of first Ray *prāṇas* into the planetary manifestation to try to mould the Fiery *manasic* substance of humanity into a more pliable, less concreted form. Therefore, new, vibrant ideals and ideas appear, especially producing beneficent political changes. There is also the more esoteric work associated with psychically countering the dark brother's ploys against the human psyche. The fact that the field of politics is massively corrupted on the planet, where laws favoring powerful interest groups and the super wealthy abound, detrimental to the good of the whole, shows the immaturity of the majority bearing the first Ray. It demonstrates how easily first Ray energies produce venal, etc., distortions in people's thought life. The adage 'power corrupts and absolute power corrupts absolutely', applies well to those who assert political power in our societies.

The first Ray Chohan sets to break the resistance of the reinforced barriers of opinionated mind to the new Hierarchical agendas, so that the second Ray workers can expound their well reasoned teachings. People can thus follow new directions of thought that flow into the mainstream of human society. The biased way people distort things contentious but truthful can then be rectified and new, correct ways of interpretation instigated. Morya also directs the *karma* of the many fields of strife (wars) of the past millennia so that a positive outcome in terms of the development of consciousness of humanity is the eventual outcome.

The *right foot* steps upon the astral plane, thus upon humanity's turbulent emotions, to control the vicissitudes of emotional volatility, and to enflame an aspirational zeal towards divinity and all arenas of service activity. Humanity's Watery tides and surges are thus carefully monitored so that the first Ray flow to the astral sea can be modified with the appropriate level of power and sent out at the correct cycles to produce the most effective results. This then is a major part of the work wielded by the sixth Ray Chohan, Jesus.

The left foot steps upon the dense physical plane and thus directly affects world affairs in all attributes of human civilisation. It works to ensure that all of the attributes of the first Ray agenda seeded into the mind-spaces of humanity actually become properly grounded therein via the activities of the five departments of the Rays of Mind. All aspects of the *karma* that govern the evolution of that civilisation must therefore be carefully seeded.

The sixth Ray function and the Rays of Mind

Jesus' function is interesting, in that as well as bearing the first and sixth Rays, he also bears second Ray Energies, being the vehicle of the cosmic Christ during appointed cycles. His energy represents the conduit for the downpour of the Love of the cosmic Christ from cosmic astral levels to our planetary astral plane. He thus carries through into manifestation the active expression of the cosmic Waters. Consequently, many of the transmutative battles converting the dark brotherhood qualities within humanity are carried out directly within his (astral) field of expression. In many ways therefore, all Ray energies come to a field of mutable Watery expression via his agency. He works with a rainbow coloured potency. The new Mahāchohan works with a similar energy dispensation, however, the difference between the two feet of the first Ray pentad is that Jesus is directly focused upon cleansing the astral murk (massed emotions) upon the planet, whilst the new Mahāchohan is focussed upon the mental constructs governing physical plane livingness. Together they are specialists in rectifying the *kāma-manasic* (desire-mind) potency within humanity. Careful planning and skill in action is needed to help transform this major predilection of humanity, considering how easy it is for the dark brotherhood to feed all aspects of desire-mind in people.

The activity of Jesus can be viewed thus:

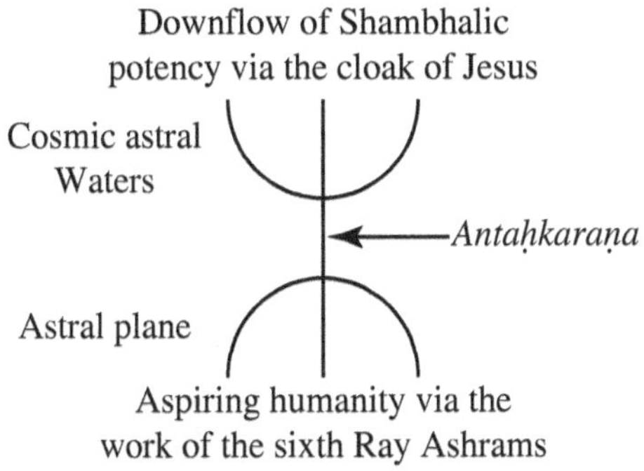

Figure 24. The sixth Ray function

This is but a form of the Pisces symbol, the sign of the World Saviour. The 'cloak of Jesus' refers to his selective, protective ability to gauge the exact potency of the cosmic Waters (the Shambhalic directive at any time) that will properly stimulate the creative imagination and devotional aptitude of disciples, so that they rightly transform Watery *saṃskāras* without manifesting zealous and fanatical attributes. The cloak therefore relates to the efficacy of the cosmic astral sheath he bears for suffering humanity. The sixth Ray Ashrams work within this cloak and upon the matrix of possibilities of the volatile human emotional and desirous fluids.

The world's aspirants and disciples are geared towards attaining the first two Initiations. These disciples must do the bulk of the work of converting the volatile astral substance, as they are also those who originally created many of its fearsome miasmas. Training the large number of aspirants and pledged disciples is the specific task of Jesus' department, whilst educating people as to the need for taking Initiation is the focus of the new Mahāchohan. His department then disseminates the overall purpose according to the internal dynamism of its constitution as a Splenic centre.

The interrelationship between all Ashrams can be viewed in terms of the flow of spiral-cyclic energy. The spirals unfold and continually expand from Shambhala through the sphere of involvement of the Chohans, then that of the Ashrams of the first and second Rays, followed by the Rays of Mind. The purpose then reticulates through the net of the *nāḍīs* of humanity and to the other kingdoms of Nature. This spiral movement through the space-time continuum forms the swastika when extended to the four directions in space, and is the basis to understanding the nature of fifth dimensional motion.[39]

The space-time continuum can be considered the Hierarchical *trumpet* and is the higher correspondence to the trumpet mentioned by Paul in *1Cor. 15:52,* that 'shall sound, and the dead shall be raised incorruptible, and we shall all be changed'. This trumpet relates to the sound of the *prāṇas* exiting at the top of the head. It is the consequence of the first Ray note of the Soul severing its tie to the physical body. The statement also means that the only way to be involved in Hierarchical affairs is to die to one's mortal, corruptible form so as to be born into true immortal spiritual robes. This is accomplished by means of the law of evolution and the Initiation process. The sounding of the trumpet given in *Rev. 1:10-11*[40] provides esoteric information concerning the constitution and qualities of the 'seven churches' that are the seven Ray

39 The fifth, if time is considered a dimension, the fourth if excluded. This motion was explained in my book *Maṇḍalas: Their Nature and Development.*

40 'I was in the Spirit on the Lord's day, and heard behind me a great voice, as of a trumpet. Saying, I am Alpha and Omega, the first and the last: and, What thou seest, write in a book, and send *it* unto the seven churches which are in Asia; unto Ephesus, and unto Smyrna, and unto Pergamos, and unto Thyatira, and unto Sardis, and unto Philadelphia, and unto Laodicea.'

Ashrams. A similar sounding in *Rev. 4:1*[41] presents much information concerning the constitution of Shambhala, when the symbolism of the remainder of the chapter is correctly analysed.

The relationship between the second Ray Ashrams and those of the Mahāchohan was given previously. For the Ashrams of the Rays of Mind we can deduce that the third Ray Chohan's department governs the head of the associated pentagram. The fourth Ray Chohan's department governs the activity of the right hand of the pentad. The fifth Ray Chohan's department governs the activity of the left hand of the pentad. The sixth Ray Chohan's department governs the activity of the right foot of the pentad, and the seventh Ray Chohan's department governs the activity of the left foot of the pentad. The third, fourth and fifth Ray energies together awaken the Mind of humanity that will conform to the qualities needed to attain Initiation. The sixth and seventh Ray energies governing the feet directly feed the locomotive, information-gathering activities of the form, as prompted by the Desire of the Lords of Shambhala to unfold any particular phase of the Plan for the awakening of humanity. These Ashrams walk the Way to every new step of revelation leading to the attainment of Initiation. The sum of such activity is coordinated by the meditation-Mind of the Mahāchohan.

The Hierarchy as a Head lotus

The internal constitution of an Ashram is arranged in a similar fashion to Shambhala, or as the Head Centre (1,000 petalled lotus) of a person. One is but the reflection of the other. The internal structure can be viewed in terms of a lotus blossom unfolding, as depicted in Figure 25.

Notes.

1. Only the major petals are indicated. The Master, or One who sits on the throne, occupies the central point of the diagram.
2. The central square represents the sphere of activity of the four who constitute the seat of power upon which the One sits.[42] When united

41 'After this I looked, and, behold, a door *was* opened in heaven: and it were of a trumpet talking with me; which said, Come up hither, and I will shew thee things which must be hereafter.'

42 The 'four beasts' of *Rev. 4:6 ff.*

with the One they are the custodians of the five *prāṇas*, powers of deity, viewed also in terms of the expression of the five Dhyāni Buddhas.

3. The tier enclosing the triangle and the square represents the sphere of activity of the 'seven spirits of God' that were before the throne.[43] They are the custodians of the seven Ray potencies and are the Ashramic correspondence of the seven sacred petals of the Heart centre. We saw earlier that there are also five non-sacred petals that together make the twelve petals of this tier. When the seven sacred petals are added to the constitution of the throne, they represent the first twelve points of the Ashram.

Figure 25. The Head lotus

4. The next tier circling twenty-four petals represents the sphere of activity of the 'four and twenty elders' that 'fall down before him

43 *Rev. 4:5.*

that sat on the throne'.[44] This represents the beginning of the full awakening of all the petals of the Head lotus (*sahasrāra padma*) governing the manifestation of an incarnate being. This tier represents the qualities of the Heart in the Head explained earlier.

5. We thus have the custodians of the zodiacal potencies and their reflection into the sum of an Ashramic structure, or else of what governs the directive potency of a human unit. These custodians can be considered to exist in two groups, one inwardly focussed to the Heart of the Ashram (and thus to Hierarchy as a unit), from which direct inspiration and energies are drawn. The other is outwardly focussed to the rest of humanity and thus to the world sphere of active service potential. They project the energies, impressions, and Ashramic qualities in a stepped down fashion to humanity, according to the opening gates of the turning wheel as it moves from cycle to cycle. They 'fall down' in that they project themselves downwards into manifestation and corresponding activity with respect to the central twelve, who can be considered quiescent points of dynamic mutability (if it may be so styled). The four and twenty are 'clothed' in an added sheath of substance, of lesser initiatory standing, thus they 'fall'.
6. The remaining outermost tier was explained earlier in terms of being the Solar Plexus in the Head. An explanation of the nature of one of the twelve outermost petals was first provided in the fourth Volume of this Treatise and significantly expanded in Volume 5A. This teaching can also be incorporated here for those that are interested in integrating Tantric Buddhism with esoteric Christianity.
7. The energies of the inner twelve beings radiate out from the first point, the Master of the Ashram, representing the qualities of the sign Aries, to the twelfth point, represented by the qualities of Pisces. As a unit, however, the inner twelve take the functions of the sign Aries, the manifest Will aspect. There are five tiers of expression to the Head lotus, which when expanded from this Aries tier astrologically, would produce the potency of Leo the lion for the outermost tier. Leo represents the king or ruler of the *saṃsāric* jungle of materiality.

44 *Rev. 4:10.*

> The power of the incarnate (Ashramic) Personality is now fully expressed and ready to undergo the trials and tribulations represented by the zodiacal journeying that will eventually produce the complete enlightenment that the awakened Head lotus confers. The outermost tiers then represent the general membership of the Ashram (the Solar Plexus in the Head). The five tiers of expression of this lotus also have a direct reference to the mode of expression of the five Dhyāni Buddhas into manifestation.

The Master of an Ashram should also be viewed as a trinity, constituted of the first three points of the Ashram. They embody the function of the triune Logos for the Ashramic structure as a whole. Around them can be said to stand a pentagram of the next five beings, enclosed in a square of four. This makes the number 3.4.5., the number signifying the sides of a right angled triangle, and of Initiation into the mysteries of being/non-being.

All point positions within any Ashram have direct affinity to similar points in other Ashrams. They become open gates to each other's energies and often play out roles in other Ashrams. Such experience is generally needed to round out the qualities of the individuals concerned. Fluid, mutable exchange and interrelation of energies and personnel is the norm within Hierarchy. Everything is based on the law of Love, the way of unfoldment of cosmic Mind, Divine Reason, ordered *manasic* progression, and ritualised action. All abide by the laws of group evolution.

Note that fully manifesting Ashrams exist on the *buddhic* realm whereon the *chakra* system of deity can be found. These *chakras* are unfolding flowers possessing their own specific colour, number and ordering of petals and perfume. Hierarchy can be considered but one such flower. There is a fluid interrelationship between all the members of Hierarchy dictated by the purpose of the present service need.

An example of fluid mutability in Hierarchy can be found in the process associated with the relatively recent replacement of the earlier Mahāchohan (the Phoenician) by the seventh Ray Chohan. To become Mahāchohan, Rakoczi[45] has had to take on a third Ray flavour:

> When, for instance, the Master R. assumed the task of Mahachohan or

45 Earlier incarnations were the Count St. Germain and Francis Bacon.

> Lord of Civilisation, His Ashram was shifted from the seventh Ray of Ceremonial Order to the third Ray of Active Intelligence; the majority of those who have taken the second and third initiations were transferred with Him under what might be called a "special dispensation."[46]

This is possible because the Monadic Ray of all Initiates within the Mahāchohan's department is that of the third Ray, and Initiates of the third degree or higher necessarily take up the Ray quality of their Monads, to which there is a triad of main hues. The abovementioned move implies that those of *R*'s Ashrams had to move towards further receptivity from the innermost Monadic sphere. This was necessary because Master *R* had to generate much more green Monadic purpose in order to assume the role of Mahāchohan. He, however, is the point of focus of the seventh Ray energy, the mainstay of the Aquarian dispensation. This Ray is needed to adequately ground the first and second Ray energies that will be the basis to the oncoming second Ray cycle and the new civilisation. The seventh Ray is the reflection of the first, but also becomes the vehicle of the second to make the number nine of (planetary) Initiation. This factor necessitates the closest cooperation between Rakoczi and the new Mahāchohan, who helps integrate the energies of the first and second Ray departments into that of the Mahāchohan's. The new Mahāchohan also strongly bears the seventh Ray, but this manifests principally through the three highest Rays, whereas *R*'s forte is the expression via the Rays of Mind. The new Mahāchohan empowers a first and second Ray potency to the seventh Ray previously not possible to be expressed. The great need is for humanity to properly develop the attributes of the second Ray, without stifling the natural efflorescence of the fifth Ray of science in humanity. Proper second Ray development in humanity has however proved elusive because the dark brotherhood found many willing converts to the ways of egotism and material power in humanity.

To ensure the success of the seventh Ray agenda, Master *R* had to abstract for a while to the source of this energy (alpha Centauri) for our planet. Such energy dispensation of the stars can be seen in the Mind's

46 A.A. Bailey, *Discipleship in the New Age,* Vol. II, (Lucis Publishing House, 1980), 383.

Eye of the awakened Initiate. There Master ℛ fine-tuned the processes and rituals needed so that the potency of the violet Ray could better influence the planet via his most advanced disciples. Also for this end D.K. speaks of the appearance of a Ray Avatar:

> These great Beings come forth at relatively long intervals when a ray is coming into manifestation. They embody the quality and force of a particular ray. Next century, when the seventh ray has achieved complete manifestation and the Piscean influence is entirely removed, the *seventh ray* Avatar will appear. His work will demonstrate the law, order and rhythm of the creative process as it works out on the physical plane, blending spirit and matter. And as this ray is called the Ray of Ceremonial Order or Ritual, He will be largely instrumental in producing those conditions which will permit of the reappearance upon Earth of the Mysteries of Initiation, of which the Hierarchy is the custodian.[47]

This Ray Avatar in fact refers to the appearance of the new Mahāchohan at the appropriate time, to promote the higher attributes of the seventh Ray purpose during the new age. Hence he will lay the foundation for the appearance of the new Mystery Schools of Initiation.

By not taking the Mahāchohan's role prior to Rakoczi, for which he was entitled (being actually senior to him), allowed the new Mahāchohan to concentrate on reconverting to the ways of the Hierarchy of Love the large number of disciples that fell victim to dark brotherhood predatory machinations. If he had taken the high office of Mahāchohan, he would have been inordinately burdened by other necessary tasks, preventing proper focusing upon the important arena of reconversion. Master ℛ was certainly adequate to the task of expressing the seventh Ray via the Ray aspects of Mind, which was needed at the time. The potency of the higher two Ray aspects, if expressed too prematurely, could have led to the danger of producing too many black magicians, who would distort the Ceremonial aspect of this Ray for self-focussed agendas. This is an obvious failing of many that bear the seventh Ray power.

Also, as already explained, the time was not yet for a direct influx of the energies of the first three Rays. The new Mahāchohan therefore

---

47 A.A. Bailey, *The Externalisation of the Hierarchy*, 298-299.

took a much more veiled role in Hierarchy until the beginning of the epoch of the major second Ray dispensation, when he could appear as the Avatar on the white horse. Many constituting that steed consist of the reconverted ones, allowing them to apply their forms of expertise in the transition period of converting humanity to the ways of Love-Wisdom. In this way these disciples can also help cleanse some of their *karma* derived from when they were earlier in positions of power amongst humanity and abused their responsibilities. In this way they are tested for high positions within Hierarchy in accordance with the rules of *karmic* cleansing. Many are the shifts of the internal positions within Hierarchy during this transition period.

We see, therefore, that the projection of the seventh Ray into manifestation during the new era is of such potent importance that it takes the care of two great Ones to help direct this Ray energy into manifest power. This is the foundation that will defeat the effects and power of the dark hierarchy upon the physical plane. These Chohans also need to minimise the aberrant misuse of the violet energy by those prematurely wishing occult power.

The higher Ray aspects of the Mahāchohan's department via a seventh Ray hue effectively manifests through a pentad of Ashrams. They ground the ritualistic, enlightening activity that helps prepare general humanity for the oncoming second Ray purpose. We thus have the 3/2-7/2 pair, the 3/7-7/3 pair and the mediating activity of the newly forming 3/4 Ashram. This is assisted by the general shielding activity of the 2/1-1/2-1/7 service, all manifesting via a flux of accommodating fourth Ray disciples. Thus the foundation for the new world civilisation is laid. The three major Rays embodying the qualities of the Father or Shambhalic attributes of Hierarchy are thereby grounded via the seventh Ray upon the seventh or dense physical plane of perception. Thus Hierarchy can externalise. Also, the Will and Love of 'God' (to utilise the theistic terminology of the Bible) manifests amongst humanity, making the new age possible. In this activity lies the hope of the world.

The Occult movement and the Masters

There have been many fanciful and fantastic presentations of the Hierarchy in various occult texts, and promulgated by 'New Age' organisations. They have deluded many into believing that such presentations are actually from Hierarchy. The great majority give insipid, personality biased and illogically presented conceptions of the Masters, even with inclusions of Masters that don't exist. Often pictures are presented of the way they are supposed to look. Such presentations have clouded the teachings concerning the genuine Hierarchical programme for its externalisation. Therefore, perhaps some mention should here be made of the pretensions, such as from the Summit Lighthouse organisation, or from the original 'I AM' teachings, the Elizabeth Claire Prophet, Mark Prophet and Godfrey Ray King propaganda. Such fields of distortion of the nature of the Masters will be obvious to any who would seriously compare the quality of the writings of any such group, with those of A.A. Bailey, the Roerichs, or H.P. Blavatsky, from which the original and authentic pronouncements concerning the Masters came.

Later exponents in the Theosophical movement, such as C.W. Leadbeater, introduced a veil of glamour over the entire subject, especially in relation to purported incarnations of the prominent Theosophical founders, which have only a vague semblance to the truth. Genuine teachings from the Masters feed the mind with high esoteric teachings that often take much meditation and pondering to properly comprehend. They never present teachings that are spiritual platitudes, designed to make one 'feel good', or to feed any other aspect of the emotions. Their teachings are not designed to make devotees, but rather Masters of Wisdom out of humanity. They work to inspire the heart to destroy all aspects of glamour and concepts of personality in their disciples, to produce the *śūnyatā* experience, and later the *dharmakāya* level of identifications. The many forms of glamour must be mastered and left in abeyance to see the higher truths and the way of Initiation into the mysteries of being/non-being.

The true 'akashic records' are not as easy to 'read' as those with astrally based vision seem to think. Many are the deluded occultists who think they see clearly as a consequence of basic psychic faculties, but in fact they view things through a 'glass darkly' in relation to the higher vision. Perceptions gained through the non controlled lower centres, from which the psychic states emanate, serve only to deceive the seer.

Such psychics view things through their own astral substance, which automatically colours perception according to what is inbuilt into its auric sphere. They come under the lure of Māra the ensnarer and flounder in the depths of the great illusion. All emotions and desire will distort the vision, giving the seer what he/she desires, thus the 'untruth', even though the plastic images obtained may seem vividly real. The creative imagination becomes the tool for distortion, and not the base upon which the edifice of the Real can be built. All this provides ample spaces in the minds of such people to be fed images and communications from the ubiquitous Anubis and other members of the dark brotherhood. They smirk with glee for the chances to delude the foolish with contrary teachings to those of the Hierarchy of Light.

The Bailey books have also had their well meaning detractors, as witness the writings of Benjamin Creme, and the books by Douglas Baker.

It should be noted that though an open mind and perusal of all available literature along the esoteric line is useful, nevertheless, much wasted time, fanciful ideas, and erosion of ideals will confront the student, if at the start of the search he/she is swamped with distorted, sensationalised, and erroneous material.

The widespread diarrhoea of published information utilising sensationalised occult and mystical facts is part of the general plan of the forces of darkness. Their aim is to so discredit the genuine teachings by burying them in the morass of pseudo-occultism that it causes the average populace to label one as the other and thus to disregard all teachings as not worthy of genuine consideration. It all becomes categorised under the now ugly phrase, 'the occult'. The aim is to make it exceedingly difficult for the forces of Light to overcome this stumbling block of conditioned, reactionary mind stuff. It also causes the earnest beginner in search of the truth to spend much fruitless time in reading this and that form of lying propaganda that serve only to confuse and confound.

Such teachings do not assist the work relating to preparing for the externalisation of the Hierarchy and building the foundation of the new world religion. It is therefore advisable for all readers to be clear as to the issues, and work hard to ensure that this 'gospel of the kingdom' *(Matt.*

24:14) is rightly promulgated and spread in such a way as to counter all adversity, so that the Plan can proceed without undue delay. No one who dwells in the light should be waylaid upon the quest because of the predominance of so many spiritual impostors on the way.

Perhaps some quotations from the valuable compendium of useful esoteric information, *Letters of Helena Roerich, 1929-38,* Volume I, in relation to erroneous information presented in occult and spiritualistic books, will prove of value to the reader.

> The Great Teachers are grieved because of the predomination of lower psychicism at the expense of true spirituality. Without the understanding and application of the Living Ethics, without spirituality, the lower psychicism can lead to the most grievous results. Therefore, in order to be accepted as disciples it is necessary, first of all, to practice self-perfection, to improve morally and spiritually, and to apply the Teaching in life. This will broaden the consciousness and bring the necessary balance. The Teaching is beautiful and true when it is realized, but no tricks of pseudo-occultism and magic will lead to true discipleship. In order to fill one's vessel from the High Source, one has to establish the corresponding high vibrations. The application in life of the Living Ethics is the quickest way to reach the goal..... And now one more warning: theoretical occultism is most dangerous. Many most harmful books flood the market...[48]
>
> Quite correctly you call spiritualism and all magical practices "spiritual corruption." Spiritualism is a violation; it opens the doors to the disembodied entities who mostly belong to the lower strata of the Subtle World, and of course spiritualism, like magic, cannot be considered evolutionary. It may be observed that many who read occult literature rush to everything which in one way or another deals with psychicism and indicates the possibility of acquiring various psychic powers. But almost nobody thinks, "What is spiritual development?" How to awaken in oneself straight-knowledge, which is the only way to acquire true spiritual enlightenment?...[49]
>
> And now I shall deal with the question about reading other books in general. Apparently this question worries everybody. Of course there

---

48 H. Roerich, *Letters of Helena Roerich, 1929-38,* Volume I, (Agni Yoga Society, New York), 206-207.

49 Ibid., 268-269.

are no objections against reading books concerning various branches of knowledge, art and spirituality, for one should always extend one's knowledge. But it is quite essential to learn to discriminate as regards quality. Thus, I always warn against pseudo-occult books. And when one has the possibility of obtaining all the treasures from the books of the Teaching of Life,[50] which deal with all the problems of life and show new ways of knowledge, and when one has the chance of becoming acquainted with *The Mahatma Letters* (now in a complete edition published in the English language) a well as with not a few works by H.P. Blavatsky, then the reading of lesser books will be a waste of time. With a few exceptions, these other books are often a mere echo—frequently erroneous—of the abovementioned ones....

Of course, there are very many people who, after reading various theories which deal with the foundations of the various Yogas, will compare them with the books of the Teaching of Life and will be disappointed because of various divergencies. That is why the reading of false books dealing with occult subjects is so dangerous for beginners who are not yet firm in their knowledge of the true Teaching. Much sorrow is brought about by spiritual errors. I shall conclude with a paragraph from the Teaching about the evaluation of books:

"The errors in books are equal to a grievous crime. Falsehood in books must be prosecuted as a grave calumny. The falsehood of an orator is prosecuted according to the number of his listeners. The falsehood of an author should be prosecuted according to the number of copies sold of his book. To fill the people's libraries with falsehood is a grave offence...Indeed, one should not impede new views and structures; but incorrect data must not bring one into error because knowledge is the armour of the community and the defence of knowledge is the duty of all the members.

"No more than a year must elapse before books are verified, otherwise the number of victims will be great. It is especially necessary to stand guard over the book when its merit is shaken. The library shelves are full of abscesses of falsehood. It should not be permissible to preserve these parasites...It is indecent and impossible to suggest reading a false book through.

"Why turn over to a lying buffoon the best corner of the fireside?

50 These are the *Agni Yoga* series of books written by the Chohan Morya via Helena Roerich, to which also can be added those by A.A. Bailey, Cyril Scott, and Blavatsky.

... The problem of the book must be dealt with!" ...[51]

Thus, let no one think that the reading of various books is forbidden; this would be absurd. But let people learn to discriminate regarding the quality of books. It is most useful to know about all the latest achievements of science, in order to realize once more how near these recent discoveries approach the affirmations of the Sacred Knowledge...once more I say, let no one think that it is forbidden to nourish one's thought from sources which are more suitable to one's particular type of mind. There are no prohibitions, but only warnings against false information...[52]

Intellect and erudition were never the main factors in the approach to the source of Truth. Often, intellect develops at the expense of the heart and smothers the great fire of straight-knowledge. Disharmony between the intellect and the heart will distort, like a crooked mirror, the reflection of the Great Truth. People reflect every great task *in their own crooked mirrors;* hence, such distortions of the Teachings, such caricatures of the High Images. As it was said, "The purification of consciousness and of the Teachings is the greatest task of our time." There are now so many "initiates," "hierophants" and "great incarnates," etc. But it is not so difficult to recognize the impostors. First of all, they lack *simplicity.* While the true initiates or entrusted ones are entirely simple in their lives, trying not to be different in outward ways and to be silent about their achievements, all the self-deceiving ones are very fond of acting mysteriously and talking about their high initiations, as well as of using high-sounding titles and names, although they themselves do not even know what real initiation means. Real initiations have nothing to do with any kind of ritual invented for the masses; initiation can take place in diverse places and dwellings, and there is only one condition necessary—the readiness of spirit in the disciple. And this readiness is ascertained by the "thermometer" in the hands of the Great Teachers. Initiation consists of the assimilation of the higher rays, of various strengths and qualities...[53]

Finally, it should be noted that high Initiates sent out to serve

51 Footnote in book: *Community.* (One of the Agni Yoga series of books.)

52 H. Roerich, *Letters of Helena Roerich* Volume I, 241-244.

53 Ibid., 271.

humanity by instigating a new Hierarchical or Shambhalic venture (as high Bodhisattvas or Avatars) invariably receive fierce opposition from the forces of darkness. These forces know well how to incarnate into the petty-mindedness, innate selfishness, and ego posturing of many disciples the serving One is trying to help. An example is H.P. Blavatsky, the first of the emissaries to be sent to the world to give birth to the *piṇgalā* stream of the modern esoteric tradition. It was her Charter to anchor the foundational teaching of the new World Religion, preparing humanity for the future externalisation of Hierarchy, and to pioneer the way for the later work of the future Mahāchohan.

As stated by Roerich:

> It is said by the Great Teacher, "Only Blavatsky knew," and it is our duty to rehabilitate the memory of this great woman martyr. If you only knew all the slanderous literature about Mme. Blavatsky, all the betrayals and the perfidity around her, you would be horrified. So much ingratitude, viciousness and ignorance. Of course, all hideousness results from the latter.[54]

She is the 'only one who knew' because she was the only one to have undergone the arduous training necessary to awaken one to such revelation. Such training must be thought of in terms of many seven year cycles, and which necessitated her visiting Tibet to 'sit at the feet' of her Master for direct teaching and awakening.

The Roerich's were also not free from such attacks, as noted by Drayer:

> Roerich was being attacked from all sides. Wallace accused him of spying and "leaked" the stale news that his conduct in Manchukuo and Central Asia had embarrassed America. Horch was trying to oust the Roerichs, Grant, and the Lichtmans so that he could take complete control of the museum and his million-dollar investment...Helena immediately replied that it was imperative to protect the tremendous body of work from any evil intentions. The manuscripts must be recovered because they contained valuable material she had written with the Master from 1923 to 1935...[55]

---

54 Ibid., 207.

55 Ruth A. Drayer, *Nicholas and Helena Roerich,* (Quest Books, Wheaton Illinois, 2005), 316-317.

The entire Inquisitional period in Europe was devised by the scions of the dark brotherhood to oppose the progressive developments instigated by the white brotherhood. History is full of names of the illustrious ones, such as Martin Luther, Galileo, Giordano Bruno, Cagliostro, who were victimised, jailed, tortured, or cruelly put to death to silence them and their work. Calumnious misquotation, malicious slander and evil gossip are other methods used to discredit the workers of light. Christ-Jesus, who was similarly persecuted, had this to say about the religionists of his day:

> O Jerusalem, Jerusalem, *thou* that killest the prophets, and stonest them which are sent unto thee, how often would I have gathered thy children together, even as a hen gathereth her children under *her* wings, but ye would not. Behold, your house is left unto you desolate.[56]

This entire subject esoterically concerns the restoration of the Mysteries, to produce the higher cycle of the teachings promulgated in the ancient Mystery Schools, such as in Delphos, Eleusis, and in ancient Egypt. The teachings from such schools were always highly veiled and given only to their Initiates, who underwent the specialised training to receive them. Revelation of the context of what was once secret can now be broadcast to the world, but the teachings cannot be received if the occult gullibility of aspirants and disciples is fed by a cacophony of misleading 'esoteric' propaganda and pronouncements stemming from the lower psychic domains. The way must be found for them to see past the obscuring glamour, if they are to realise the higher esoteric truths. Their own predilection for the mysterious, the occult and for psychism, however, bars the way for most. Hence the writings provided from genuine Hierarchical sources, such as this Treatise, and those of Alice Bailey, reach only the comparative few, and of them only a handful can undergo the training necessary to pass the higher Initiation testings. In time the new esoteric Schools will be established that will offer succour for the spiritually needy that are truly seeking the higher way. Concerning the restoration of the Mysteries in relation to the externalisation of the Hierarchy, D.K. states:

---

56 *Matthew 23:37-38.*

I have made two affirmations during the past years anent the Hierarchy. One was that as a result of the cleansing of the Earth through the medium of the world war (1914-1945) and through the suffering to which humanity has been subjected (with a consequent purifying effect which will demonstrate later), it will be possible for the Hierarchy to externalise itself and function openly upon the physical plane. This will indicate a return to the situation which existed in Atlantean days when (using the Biblical symbolism) God Himself walked among men—divinity was present in physical form because the Members of the Hierarchy were guiding and directing the affairs of humanity as far as innate freewill permitted. On a higher turn of the spiral, this again will happen. The Masters will walk openly among men. Secondly, the Hierarchy will then restore the ancient Mysteries, the ancient landmarks so earnestly preserved by the Masonic tradition and which have been securely embalmed in the Masonic ritual, awaiting the day of resurrection.

These ancient Mysteries were originally given to humanity by the Hierarchy, and were—in their turn— received by the Hierarchy from the Great White Lodge on Sirius. They contain the clue to the evolutionary process, hidden in numbers and in words; they veil the secret of man's origin and destiny, picturing for him in rite and ritual the long, long path which he must tread. They provide also, when rightly interpreted and correctly presented, the teaching which humanity needs in order to progress from darkness to Light, from the unreal to the Real and from death to Immortality. Any true Mason who understands, even if only to a slight degree, the implications of that in which he participates will recognise this most ancient of Oriental prayers, giving the key to the three degrees of the Blue Lodge. I mention here the Masonic purpose because it is closely related to the restoration of the Mysteries and has held the clue—down the ages—to that long-awaited restoration, to the platform upon which the restored teaching can be based, and the structure which can express, in powerful ritual and in organised detailed rites, the history of man's moving forward upon the Path of Return.

The Mysteries will be restored in other ways also, for they contain much besides that which the Masonic rites can reveal or that religious rituals and ceremonies can disclose; they contain within their teaching and formulas the key to the science which will unlock the mystery of electricity—that mystery of which H.P.B. spoke; though much progress has already been made by science along this line, it is as yet only embryonic in nature, and only when the Hierarchy is present visibly on earth, and the Mysteries of which the Masters are the Custodians are given openly to man, will the true secret and nature of electrical phenomena be revealed.

The Mysteries are, in reality, the true source of revelation, and it can be only when the mind and the will-to-good are closely blended and conditioning human behaviour that the extent of the coming revelation will be grasped, for only then can humanity be trusted with these secrets. They concern those capacities which enable the Members of the Hierarchy to work consciously with the energies of the planet and of the solar system and to control forces within the planet; they will put the ordinary psychic powers (today so stupidly approached and so little understood) in their rightful place and guide man towards their helpful usage.

The Mysteries will restore colour and music as they essentially are to the world and do it in such a manner that the creative art of today will be to this new creative art what a child's building of wooden blocks is to a great cathedral such as Durham or Milan. The Mysteries, when restored, will make real—in a sense incomprehensible to you at present—the nature of religion, the purpose of science and the goal of education. These are not what you think today.[57]

57 A.A. Bailey, *The Rays and the Initiations,* 330-2.

Affirmation of the Initiate

South
In perceiving the field of service
I willingly cast aside the wrath of *māyā*
And thus I stand.

North
In understanding the shade of the tree,
I willingly stand at the door of the spheres
And thus I shield.

West
In hearing the sounds from the Flowers
I willingly shield from the thundering rains
And thus I teach.

East
In listening to the anguish of those wandering
In *saṃsāric* time
I willingly teach, forgetting that I Am
And thus I Am (THAT).

8

Further Esoteric Considerations Concerning Shambhala

The Planetary Head Lotus

In this chapter I shall collate the information found in D.K.'s books concerning the great planetary executives of Shambhala, to elucidate as much as is possible their qualities and functions. This shall allow the presentation of further information hitherto veiled and which now can be revealed. In doing so I shall integrate the information presented throughout this *Treatise on Mind,* especially that concerning the nature of the manifestation of the *chakras,* into a higher synthetic unity. With respect to Shambhala, our focus is upon the nature of the attributes of the planetary Head centre. In considering a Head centre one must take into account that the focus is upon an incarnate personality. In this case the 'Personality' that is the Logos of this planet that is presently incarnate. The concern is thus with the processes of physical plane activity. Here the 'physical plane' is the cosmic physical, constituted of our seven systemic planes: *ādi, anupādaka, ātma, buddhi, mental, astral* and *dense.* Each also have seven sub-planes and other numerical interrelationships.

From the perspective of Shambhala being an incarnate Personality, the Head lotus is overshadowed by a Soul aspect (the Sambhogakāya Flower) which interrelates with it in the manner described in Volume 5A of this series. This 'Soul aspect' here is termed 'The Silent Watcher', as stated by D.K.

> The *"Silent Watcher,"* that great Entity Who is the informing life of the planet, and Who holds the same position to the Lord of the World, Sanat Kumara, as the Ego[1] does to the lower self of man. Some idea of the high stage of evolution of this Great Being may be gathered from the analogous degree of evolutionary difference existing between a human being and a perfected adept. From the standpoint of our planetary scheme, this Great Life has no greater, and He is, as far as we are concerned, a correspondence to the personal God of the Christian. He works through His representative on the physical plane, Sanat Kumara, Who is the focal point for His life and energy. He holds the world within His aura. This great Existence is only contacted directly by the adept who has taken the fifth initiation, and is proceeding to take the other two, the sixth and seventh. Once a year, at the Wesak Festival, the Lord Buddha, sanctioned by the Lord of the World, carries to the assembled humanity a dual stream of force, that emanating from the Silent Watcher, supplemented by the more focalised energy of the Lord of the World. This dual energy He pours out in blessing over the people gathered at the ceremony in the Himalayas, and from them in turn it flows out to all peoples and tongues and races.[2]

Continuing with the information from *Initiation, Human and Solar* we see that the focus of planetary affairs at Shambhala is focussed upon the Lord of the World, who is directly overshadowed by the Silent Watcher.

> At the head of affairs, controlling each unit and directing all evolution, stands the KING, the Lord of the World, Sanat Kumara, the Youth of Endless Summers, and the Fountainhead of the Will, (showing forth as Love) of the Planetary Logos. Co-operating with Him as His advisers are three Personalities called the Pratyeka Buddhas, or the Buddhas of Activity. These four are the embodiment of active intelligent loving will. They are the full flowering of the intelligence, having achieved in an earlier solar system that which man is now striving to perfect. In earlier cycles in this system They began to demonstrate intelligent love, and from the standpoint of the average human being They are perfect love and perfect intelligence, though from the standpoint of that Existence Who embraces even our planetary scheme in His body of manifestation, that love aspect is as yet but in process of developing,

1 The term 'Ego' is sometimes used by D.K. to represent the Sambhogakāya Flower.

2 A.A. Bailey, *Initiation, Human and Solar,* 104-105.

and the will is only embryonic. Another solar system will see the will aspect come to fruition, as love will mature in this.

Standing around the Lord of the World, but withdrawn and esoteric, are three more Kumaras, Who make the seven of planetary manifestation. Their work is to us necessarily obscure. The three exoteric Buddhas, or Kumaras, are the sumtotal of activity or planetary energy, and the three esoteric Kumaras embody types of energy which as yet are not in full demonstration upon our planet. Each of these six Kumaras is a reflection of, and the distributing agent for, the energy and force of one of the six other Planetary Logoi, the remaining six spirits before the Throne. Sanat Kumara alone, in this scheme, is self-sustaining and self-sufficient, being the physical incarnation of one of the Planetary Logoi, which one it is not permissible to state, as this fact is one of the secrets of initiation. Through each of Them passes the life force of one of the six rays, and in considering Them one might sum up Their work and position as follows:—

1. They each embody one of the six types of energy, with the Lord of the World as the synthesiser and the embodier of the perfect seventh type, our planetary type.
2. They are each distinguished by one of the six colours, with the Lord of the World showing forth the full planetary colour, these six being subsidiary.
3. Their work is therefore concerned, not only with force distribution, but with the passing into our scheme from other planetary schemes, of Egos seeking earth experience.
4. Each of Them is in direct communication with one or another of the sacred planets.
5. According to astrological conditions, and according to the turning of the planetary wheel of life, so one or another of these Kumaras will be active. The three Buddhas of Activity change from time to time, and become in turn exoteric or esoteric as the case may be. Only the King persists steadily and watchfully in active physical incarnation.[3]

The Lord of the World, the One Initiator, He Who is called in the Bible "The Ancient of Days," and in the Hindu Scriptures the First Kumara, He, Sanat Kumara it is, Who from His throne at Shamballa in the Gobi desert, presides over the Lodge of Masters, and holds in His

3 Ibid., 38-40.

> hands the reins of government in all the three departments. Called in some Scriptures "the Great Sacrifice," He has chosen to watch over the evolution of men and devas until all have been occultly "saved." He it is Who decides upon the "advancements" in the different departments, and Who settles who shall fill the vacant posts; He it is Who, four times a year, meets in conference with all the Chohans and Masters, and authorises what shall be done to further the ends of evolution.
>
> Occasionally, too, He meets with initiates of lesser degree, but only at times of great crises, when some individual is given the opportunity to bring peace out of strife, and to kindle a blaze whereby rapidly crystallising forms are destroyed and the imprisoned life consequently set free.[4]

A Treatise on Cosmic Fire continues along this vein, speaking in terms of the Lord of the World being an Avatar.

> *An avatar is, but an adept is made,* but frequently the force, energy, purpose or will of a cosmic Entity will utilise the vehicles of an adept in order to contact the physical planes. This method whereby cosmic Existences make Their power felt can be seen working out on all the planes of the cosmic physical plane. A striking instance of this can be seen in the case of the Kumaras, Who, under certain planetary forces, and through the formation of a systemic triangle, gave the impulse to the third kingdom which produced the fourth by bringing it into conjunction with the fifth. These Kumaras, Sanat Kumara and His three pupils, having achieved the highest initiation possible in the last great cycle, but having as yet (from Their standpoint) another step to take, offered Themselves to the planetary Logos of Their Ray as "focal points" for His force, so that thereby He might hasten and perfect His plans on Earth within the cycle of manifestation. They have demonstrated three out of the four methods. They are *overshadowed* by the planetary Logos, and He works directly as the Initiator (in relation to man) through Sanat Kumara, and with the three kingdoms in nature through the three Buddhas of Activity,—Sanat Kumara, being thus concerned directly with the ego on the mental plane, and His three Pupils being concerned with the other three types of consciousness, of which man is the summation. At the moment of initiation (after the second Initiation) Sanat Kumara becomes the direct mouthpiece and

4 Ibid., 106.

agent of the Planetary Logos. That great Entity speaks through Him and for one brief second (if one can use such a term in connection with a plane whereon time, as we understand it, is not) the planetary Logos of a man's Ray consciously—via His etheric brain—turns His thought upon the Initiate, and "calls him by His Name."

Again the Kumaras are *embodied principles,* but in this connection we must remember that this means that the force and energy of one of the principles of the Logos are pouring through Them via that which—to Them—corresponds to the Monad. Through Them, during Their period of incarnation and voluntary sacrifice, the great Prototype of the planetary Logos begins to make His Presence felt, and force from the constellation of the Great Bear faintly vibrates on earth. At initiation, man becomes aware consciously of the Presence of the planetary Logos through self-induced contact with his own divine Spirit. At the fifth Initiation he becomes aware of the full extent of this planetary group influence, and of his part in the great whole. At the sixth and seventh Initiations the influence of the planetary Prototype is sensed, reaching him via the planetary Logos working through the Initiator.

The method of *direct incarnation* was earlier seen when the Kumaras were in physical form. This only applied to some of Them; Sanat Kumara and His Pupils are in physical form, but have not taken dense physical bodies. They work on the vital etheric levels, and dwell in etheric bodies. Shamballa, where They dwell, exists in physical matter as do the Kumaras, but it is matter of the higher ethers of the physical plane, and only when man has developed etheric vision will the mystery lying beyond the Himalayas be revealed. Therefore, *Sanat Kumara is the planetary logos yet He is not.* A reflection of this method of direct incarnation can be seen when a disciple steps out of his body and permits his Guru, or a more advanced chela, to use it.[5]

D.K. also states in *Esoteric Astrology:*

The planetary Logos of this scheme is called 'the First Kumara,' the One Initiator, and the statement is made that he came to this planet from Venus, Venus being 'the Earth's primary.' This needs elucidation somewhat, though it may not be permitted to do more than convey a few hints as to the truth. The fact is one of the most mysterious in the development of our scheme, and in it lies hidden the secret of this

5 A.A. Bailey, *A Treatise on Cosmic Fire,* 751-753.

world cycle. It is not easy to convey the truth and words but seem to veil and cloak.

Perhaps a hint may be given in pointing out that there is an analogy between the coming in of the Ego in full sway and its taking hold at certain periods in the life of a human being. At seven years we are told the Ego "takes hold," and again at adolescence; at twenty-one that hold may be made still firmer. Again, as lives are passed, the Ego (in connection with a human being), grips its vehicles and so sways them to his purpose with more effect and fullness. The same procedure can be seen in relation to a Heavenly Man and His body of manifestation, a scheme. It must be remembered that every scheme has seven chains; that each chain has seven globes, making a totality of forty-nine globes; that each globe is again in turn occupied by the life of the Logos during what we call seven rounds, making literally three hundred and forty-three incarnations, or fresh impulses to manifest. We must add to these major manifestations such lesser ones as those named by us root-races, and sub-races, also branch races, and thus we are faced with a complexity that is enough to stagger the average student. The planetary wheel of life turns on its lesser scale the wheel of life of the little pilgrim we call man; as it turns, it sweeps the life of the evolving planetary Logos into ever new forms and experiences until the fire of Spirit burns up all lesser fires.[6]

Elucidating this statement regarding Venus, D.K. states:

First, it should be borne in mind by the occult student that:

f. This advent signalised the taking of a physical vehicle by the planetary Logos, and was literally the coming of the Avatar.

g. This advent was brought about by a definite systemic alignment which involved:

   The Venus scheme of the system.
   The Venus chain of the Earth scheme.
   The Venus globe of the Earth chain.

h. That the planetary Logos did not come from the Venus scheme but from the Venus chain of His own scheme, the Earth scheme. Owing to systemic alignment logoic kundalini could flow through a certain triangle of which two points were Venus and the Earth.

6 Alice Bailey, *Esoteric Astrology*, 682.

> This caused an acceleration of vibration, and enabled the Heavenly Man of our scheme to take a minor initiation, and to set about His preparations for a major initiation.[7]

The term *kumāra* means 'youthful one', (from *ku,* with difficulty + *māra,* mortal), hence they manifest their mortality (being incarnate on earth) with difficulty. The term is often used for a child or youth, sparks of Divinity not involved with matter. In Hinduism they are the 'mind born' sons of Brahmā, 'virgin youths', who refused to 'procreate' and thus remain *yogins.* There are seven of these, two esoteric and five exoteric. The five Kumāras can be viewed as four manifesting into, or as, the formed realms, and a veiled three manifesting as One: the Trinity of Deity becoming the One. It is the fourth Kumāra, therefore, Who stands midway between the subjective Three and the objective Three (the three Buddhas of Activity), that becomes the 'mirror' or one who bears the weight of the qualities of the abstract Deity for all who are incarnate within the formed realms. He becomes the One and upon our planet is termed Sanat Kumāra, the first Kumāra, from this angle of vision. Sanat Kumāra, plus the three Buddhas of Activity, are the 'beasts' that constitute the Throne of God, upon which the One sits, as related in the fourth chapter of *St. John's Revelation.*

The Kumāras embody the substance of Mind for a planetary Scheme and are thus responsible for the dissemination of the Mind patterns of a creative Logos. They are His representatives for the sum of the Intelligent lives within embodied Space. The Fires of Mind manifest through a patterning associated with the pentagram, of which the five Elements are aspects. Their correspondences in Buddhism are thus the five Dhyāni Buddhas.

In Figure 1 the three *esoteric* Kumāras have been termed the Avatar of Synthesis, the Spirit of Peace, and the Mother of the World. Their mode of interrelation, allowing impress of their Purpose upon humanity via the Manu, was presented in that figure.

It should be noted that D.K. avoids the use of the term 'The Mother of the World' in his books, because, as previously stated, there is no true 'Mother' for our planetary cycle, rather one who holds the office of the feminine principle, and hence specifically governs the activities of the *deva* kingdom for our planet.

---

7 Ibid., 680-681.

The Mother of the World is effectively the fifth Kumāra[8], who is introduced by D.K. in *A Treatise on Cosmic Fire* in relation to our earth Scheme. Her role now comes into esoteric dominance, with the forthcoming epoch of the rule of Mind upon our planet and the outpouring of the fifth Round. She has always played a role, though veiled by the symbolism of the various Mother Goddesses in world mythology, who were subsidiary to masculine deities. The role of the Mother of the World is significant in the history of our planetary Scheme, but has been marred by the happenings upon the moon Chain, which will be explained below. D.K. states:

> We might now consider briefly the subject of the five Kumaras, Who are the sum total of manas on the Earth. I have stated that the Lord of the World, the first Kumara, is the planetary Logos of our scheme in physical incarnation, but nowhere has the impression been conveyed that the three Kumaras, associated with Him, are three other planetary Logoi. This is in no way the case. These three, called the "Buddhas of Activity," are but the vicegerents upon our planet of those three planetary Logoi, Who, with our planetary Logos, make the sum total of the logoic Quaternary. Associated with them are the three esoteric Kumaras, mentioned in the *Secret Doctrine,* Who represent the three other Logoi, and so make focal points for all the logoic forces within our chain. In each chain such representatives are found, six focal points embraced by the seventh, the planetary Logos of the scheme, Who holds them all within His aura.
>
> Their work is threefold:
>
> *First.* They are the centres in the body of the planetary Logos. Each chain corresponds to one centre, and the globes are but the lesser wheels within any particular centre. The life of the Logos in this incarnation on the Earth is flowing through three centres and beginning to stimulate a fourth, hence four globes are involved and the three Kumaras (so called for lack of a better term) are vitally intelligently active; three are in abeyance and one is beginning to function. The globes correspond to the chains. This fourth Kumara[9]

8 A mystery is hidden here, explained in Vol. 2 of my book *Esoteric Astrology for the New Age.*

9 Note that the term 'fourth Kumara' here is not literally 'the fourth' because that position effectively is Sanat Kumāra's, being the fourth of the seven, but rather, one supplementary to the three Buddhas of Activity. This makes this one the fifth,

> is as yet practically unrealised, but as hinted at earlier His day is about to dawn.
>
> *Second. They act as transmitters* of a particular type of force to those units who go to the content of any particular centre. They are, in fact, the agents for the Lords of the Rays to the Monads of any ray in incarnation in any particular chain and on any particular globe.
>
> *Third.* They are the agents for:
>
> *a.* The Lord of a Ray as stated above.
> *b.* The four Maharajahs.
> *c.* The planetary Logos of Their own scheme.
> *d.* The great Deva of the Earth planet.
>
> They work with the law; They are the cognizers of the intelligent purpose of the planetary Logos, and know His plans; They are the vital activity of the planet, and in a subtle sense they are not only the Ray representatives but likewise the link between the chain and the scheme.
>
> It might here be stated that the relative failure that was the fate of the *Moon chain* in our scheme has greatly handicapped Their work, and made it imperative for Them to employ drastic measures in order to offset that failure. Herein lies another clue to the world turmoil.[10]

The significance of the five Kumāras is that the number five allows their integration into the schema of the philosophy of the five Dhyāni Buddhas, as detailed throughout this series. Sanat Kumāra manifests as Akṣobhya, on a *maṇḍala* where Akṣobhya is at the central position. Sanat Kumāra thereby fulfils his role as the Avatar of the principle of Love-Wisdom for our planet as well as the mirror that reflects the impress of the Silent Watcher into manifestation. The Mother of the World then manifests as Vairocana, here embodying the substance of Mind which all of the Kumāras utilise to effect planetary evolution. She literally represents the Womb of mind/Mind of all that must proceed therein, bringing into manifestation the two remaining esoteric Kumāras, the Avatar of Synthesis and the Spirit of Peace. From this perspective the Mother of the World can also be considered the third from above-down,

---

counting from below upwards.

10 A.A. Bailey, *A Treatise on Cosmic Fire,* (Lucis Publishing Company, New York, 1975), 412-413.

however, in terms of the present planetary manifestation, the fifth is appropriate, signifying also that she falls below the three Buddhas of Activity, as they are now appearing into objectivity.

Sanat Kumāra also bears their combined energies into the world play. As a consequence, the energies of the Avatar of Synthesis and the Spirit of Peace will esoterically fall into manifestation during this world period, bringing with them an increased potency of the first and second Ray energies that will herald the new second Ray epoch on earth. Its necessary foundation is the empowerment or awakening of the attributes of Mind into humanity, which is the purpose of the dispensation of the new Mahāchohan coordinating with the Mother of the World.

The Logoi of the sacred planets that these seven are representatives (vicegerents) of, and their generalised areas of speciality can be considered as below. Earth, as a non-sacred planet, veils the attributes of Neptune, the god of the Waters, hence exoterically our planet is a sphere mostly covered by water.

Logoic Being	Planet	Area of Speciality
Avatar of Synthesis	Uranus	first Shambhalic level
Spirit of Peace	Jupiter	second Shambhalic level
Mother of the World	Venus	*deva* kingdom
Sanat Kumāra	Neptune	human kingdom
First Buddha	Saturn	animal kingdom
Second Buddha	Mercury	plant kingdom
Third Buddha	Vulcan	mineral kingdom

Table 5. Logoi of sacred planets and their area of speciality

In terms of the relative spiritual age of the main executives of Shambhala we have the Avatar of Synthesis bearing the Shambhalic first Ray Power, 'the principle of directed Purpose',[11] Sanat Kumāra, the second Ray of synthesis, and the three Buddhas of Activity, the third to the fifth Rays. The Spirit of Peace wields the sixth Ray Shambhalic potency from the cosmic astral, which will be used to equilibrise the turbulence of the systemic astral plane and to baptise those that have mastered the Waters via the development of Love. The Mother of the World then wields the Shambhalic seventh Ray of ritual, hence of the cyclic ebb and flow of the *devas*. With respect to the work with the *devas* She is also an embodiment of the third and fifth Rays within our planetary sphere, hence She commands the *iḍā* line of the third, fifth and seventh Rays for the planetary manifestation. Her role as Vairocana manifests the Divine Will to command the various cycles of manifestation of the *devas* and their various serried ranks and orders of expression. This seventh Ray potency is now coming to the fore in this Aquarian epoch, which promotes the era of the empowerment of the feminine on our planet under the auspices of the great Mother, the fifth Kumāra.

This seventh Ray potency empowers the purpose of the new Mahāchohan as he rides on the steed of the seventh Ray Ashrams to awaken the new. He thereby will sing the songs of the Mother's purpose and empower Her Day. His Avataric purpose will also be overshadowed, hence empowered, by the first Ray potency of the Avatar of Synthesis, combined with the Initiatory Purpose of Sanat Kumāra, who will also overshadow him with the Sirian Lore. The Sirian Lore coupled with the Pleiadian Way of the Mother will potently empower planetary changes that must be manifest upon the physical domain, where the *devas* will also play their roles. They will instate miracles of healing via the acquiescent minds of the world's disciples, who will teach humanity to turn to thoughts of love rather than to self-centred materialism. A purificatory cleansing Fire should then be appropriated by disciples as they rightly organise their minds to bear the unificatory activity of the energies of the Avatar of Synthesis.

This combination of energies and events will pave the Way (prepare humanity) in a way that the Door for the reappearance of the Christ can be opened. He will bring the energies of the Spirit of Peace into

---

11 A.A. Bailey, *The Externalisation of the Hierarchy, 302.*

manifestation, and they will be backed by the triune potency of the three Buddhas of Activity. All kingdoms of Nature will thereby be stimulated as humanity awaken to the purpose of Love because they have opened their eyes to the nature of glamour, and of the murk of the astral domain needing cleansing, to be washed anew with the cosmic Waters. (The saving grace of the second Ray Day.)

The seventh Ray governs the dispensation of the first Initiation, and under the auspices of the new Mahāchohan will produce the onset of undertaking this Initiation upon a mass, planetary scale. There will also be a large number of Initiates that will take their second Initiation, many for the first time, and also a significant number of third degree Initiates. Concerning the effect of this Ray, D.K. states:

> The seventh ray is, par excellence, the medium of relationship. It brings together the two fundamental aspects of spirit and matter. It relates soul and form and, where humanity is concerned, it relates soul and personality. In the first initiation, it makes the initiate aware of that relation; it enables him to take advantage of this "approaching duality" and—by the perfecting of the contact—to produce upon the physical plane the emergence into manifestation of the "new man." At the first initiation, through the stimulation brought about by seventh ray energy, the personality of the initiate and the hovering overshadowing soul are consciously brought together; the initiate then knows that he is—for the first time—a soul-infused personality. His task is now to grow into the likeness of what he essentially is. This development is demonstrated at the third initiation, that of the Transfiguration.
>
> The major function of this seventh ray is to bring together the negative and positive aspects of the natural processes. It consequently governs the sex relationship of all forms; it is the potency underlying the marriage relation, and hence as this ray comes into manifestation in this world cycle, we have the appearance of fundamental sex problems—license, disturbance in the marriage relation, divorce and the setting in motion of those forces which will eventually produce a new attitude to sex and the establishing of those practices, attitudes and moral perceptions which will govern the relation between the sexes during the coming New Age.
>
> The first initiation is therefore closely related to this problem. The seventh ray governs the sacral centre and the sublimation of its energy into the throat or into the higher creative centre; this ray is

therefore setting in motion a period of tremendous creative activity, both on the material plane through the stimulation of the sex life of all peoples and in the three worlds through the stimulation brought about when soul and form are consciously related. The first major proof that humanity (through the medium of the majority of its advanced people) has undergone the first initiation will be the appearance of a cycle of entirely new creative art. This creative urge will take forms which will express the new incoming energies. Just as the period governed by the sixth ray has culminated in a world wherein men work in great workshops and factories to produce the plethora of objects men deem needful for their happiness and well-being, so in the seventh ray cycle we shall see men engaged on an even larger scale in the field of creative art. Devotion to objects will eventually be superseded by the creation of that which will more truly express the Real; ugliness and materiality will give place to beauty and reality. On a large scale, humanity has already been "led from darkness to light" and the light of knowledge fills the land. In the period which lies ahead and under the influencing radiation of the seventh ray, humanity will be "led from the unreal to the Real." This the first initiation makes possible for the individual and will make possible for the mass of men.

Seventh ray energy is the energy needed to bring order out of chaos and rhythm to replace disorder. It is this energy which will bring in the new world order for which all men wait; it will restore the ancient landmarks, indicate the new institutions and forms of civilisation and culture which human progress demands, and nurture the new life and the new states of consciousness which advanced humanity will increasingly register. Nothing can arrest this activity; all that is happening today as men search for the new ways, for organised unity and peaceful security, is being implemented through the incoming Ray of Order or Ceremonial Magic. The white magic of right human relations cannot be stopped; it must inevitably demonstrate effectively, because the energy of this seventh ray is present, and the Lord of the Ray is cooperating with the Lord of the World to bring about the needed "reforming." Soul-infused personalities, acting under this ray influence, will create the new world, express the new qualities and institute those new regimes and organised modes of creative activity which will demonstrate the new livingness and the new techniques of living. It is the distortion of these seventh ray ideals and the prostitution of this incoming energy to serve the unenlightened and selfish ambitions of greedy men which has produced those totalitarian systems which today so terribly imprison the free spirit of men.

To sum up what I have said:

1. The energy of the seventh ray is the potent agent of initiation when taken on the physical plane, that is, during the process of the first initiation.
2. Its effect upon humanity will be:
    a. To bring about the birth of the Christ-consciousness among the masses of intelligently aspiring human beings.
    b. To set in motion certain relatively new evolutionary processes which will transform humanity (the world disciple) into humanity (the world initiate).
    c. To establish in a new and intelligible manner the ever-existent sense of relationship and thus bring about upon the physical plane right human relations. The agent of this is goodwill, a reflection of the will-to-good of the first divine aspect. Of this first Ray of Will or Purpose, goodwill is the reflection.
    d. To readjust negative and positive relationships, and—today—this will be carried forward primarily in connection with the sex relation and marriage.
    e. To intensify human creativity and thus bring in the new art as a basis for the new culture and as a conditioning factor in the new civilisation.
    f. To reorganise world affairs and so initiate the new world order. This is definitely in the realm of ceremonial magic.
3. The stimulation of this seventh ray will, in relation to the individual initiate,
    a. Bring into being upon the mental plane a widespread and recognised relation between the soul and the mind.
    b. Produce a measure of order in the emotional processes of the initiate, thus aiding the preparatory work of the second initiation.
    c. Enable the initiate—upon the physical plane—to establish certain service relationships, to learn the practice of elementary white magic, and to demonstrate the first stage of a truly creative life.

As far as the individual initiate is concerned, the effect of seventh ray energy in his life is potent in the extreme; this is easily realised, owing to the fact that his mind and his brain are conditioned by the seventh ray at the time that the initiatory process is consciously taking place. The effect of this upon the mental plane is similar to that seen—on a much larger scale—in the planet, for it was this ray energy which the planetary Logos utilised when He brought together the major dualities of spirit and matter at the commencement of His creative work. The two aspects of the mind (the lower concrete mind and the soul, the Son of Mind) become more closely related and enter eventually into a conscious, recognised association *on the astral plane*; it is the seventh ray which restores order within the astral consciousness, and (on the mental plane), it is this influence which produces creativity, the organising of the life, and the bringing together "within the head" of the lower and higher energies in such a manner that "the Christ is born." This latter point we shall consider in some detail when we take up the significance of the initiations; we shall then find that the relationship between the pituitary body and the pineal gland is involved.

Finally, it is seventh ray energy which—in the initiatory process between the first and the second initiations—enables the initiate (in his physical plane life) to demonstrate a developing sense of order and of organisation, to express consciously and increasingly a desire to help his fellowmen, and thereby establish relationship with them, and to make his life creative in many ways.

All these factors are embryonic in his nature, but he now begins to consciously lay the foundation for the future initiatory work; the physical disciplines are at this time of great importance, though their value is frequently over-emphasised and their effect is not always good; the relationships established and fostered are sometimes of small value, owing to the disciple being usually self-centered and thus lacking—from ignorance and lack of discrimination—complete purity of motive. Nevertheless, the changes brought about by the influence of this ray become increasingly effective from life to life; the disciple's relation to the Hierarchy, the reorganising of his life on the physical plane, and his growing effort to demonstrate the esoteric sense of white magic will become more and more vital until he is ready for the second initiation.[12]

12 Alice Bailey, *The Rays and the Initiations,* 571-5.

That the seventh Ray 'governs the sex relationship of all forms' is not quite true. D.K. is principally referring to the sex urges emanating from the physical body itself, however, in conjunction with this the main force that empowers the interplay of the sexes, and which produces much of the joy, overriding drive and also the perversions of this energy, is the emotions (and also the creative imagination), which is ruled by the sixth Ray. This Ray combination then, with the waning of the sixth Ray, and the waxing of the seventh Ray, causes the widespread licentiousness of sexuality, the pornography industry, the abortion debate, etc., that specifically affects the western world. The proper resolution of the sexual issue will consequently be one of the main factors that those taking their first Initiations will need to accomplish.

Also, the statement that the seventh Ray governs the Sacral centre needs clarifying because in this case the Sacral and Base of Spine centres must be viewed as a unity and seen from the perspective of the path of discipleship. For average humanity the energy of the sixth Ray dominates, producing the principle of desire-attraction. When this energy is being brought under control by the developed mind then the rhythmic activity of the base of Spine energies via the 7/6 petal of the Sacral centre (see Figure 17) establishes control. It produces the new-found creativity that D.K. speaks of, plus the proper resolution of sexuality, the manifestation of true white magic that supersedes the forms of sex magic so prevalent nowadays. The process of transition between the two types of energy, as is happening presently upon a world-wide scale, produces a period of major turmoil, easily capitalised on by the forces of darkness. Consequently, the dark brotherhood predominantly control all instruments of power in our western societies, plus the main stream media and entertainment channels. For instance, the glorification of war, violence of all types, horror, sexuality, extreme emotionality or inane humour, are the main fare brought to us by our movie industry. Propaganda supporting the evil doing of various nefarious agencies, such as the CIA and the military supremacy of the USA, as well as demonising its current fabricated political 'enemies', manifests as an unceasing torrent for consumption by the world's population. The aim is to keep humanity dumbed-down via useless gratuitous information and accustomed to all forms of brutality aimed against other members of the human race.

With respect to *the Initiation process,* being an important function of Sanat Kumāra, D.K. states:

> The function of the *three Kumaras,* or the three Buddhas of Activity at initiation is interesting. They are three aspects of the one aspect, and the pupils of Sanat Kumara. Though Their functions are many and varied, and concern primarily the forces and energies of nature, and the direction of the building agencies, They have a vital connection with the applicant for initiation, inasmuch as They each embody the force or energy of one or other of the three higher subplanes of the mental plane. Therefore at the third initiation one of these Kumaras transmits to the causal body of the initiate that energy which destroys third subplane matter, and thus brings about part of the destruction of the vehicle; at the fourth initiation another Buddha transmits second plane force, and at the fifth, first subplane force is similarly passed into the remaining atoms of the causal vehicle, producing the final liberation. The work done by the second Kumara, with second subplane force, is in this solar system the most important in connection with the egoic body, and produces its complete dissipation, whereas the final application causes the atoms themselves (which formed that body) to disperse.
>
> During the initiation ceremony, when the initiate stands before the Lord of the World, these three great Beings form a triangle, within whose lines of force the initiate finds himself. At the first two initiations, wherein the Bodhisattva functions as the Hierophant, the Mahachohan, the Manu, and a Chohan who temporarily represents the second department perform a similar office. At the highest two initiations, those three Kumaras who are called "the esoteric Kumaras" form a triangle wherein the initiate stands, when he faces the Planetary Logos.
>
> These facts are imparted to teach two things, first, the unity of the method, second, that the truism "as above so below" is an occult fact in nature.
>
> At the final two initiations many members of the Hierarchy who are, if one might so express it, extra-planetary, and who function outside the dense physical and the etheric globe of our planet, take part, but a stricter enumeration is needless. Sanat Kumara is still the Hierophant, yet in a very esoteric manner it is the Planetary Logos Himself who officiates. They are merged at that time into one Identity, manifesting different aspects.[13]

---

13 A.A. Bailey, *Initiation, Human and Solar,* 107-109.

The Deities of the Bardo Thödol

The constitution of Shambhala in its various levels can be thought of in terms of the Peaceful and Wrathful Deities of the *Bardo Thödol.* They were explained in detail in Volume 5A of this series, *An Esoteric Exposition of the Bardo Thödol.* These Deities were presented in relation to the enlightenment process of a human unit, of what transpired in a *yogin's* or *yoginī's* consciousness in Tibet as the *chakras* were awakened. The related information can be extrapolated and expanded into this new vista of esoteric visioning and phrased in the new terminology, in terms of a similar awakening of all upon the planet. (Taking the sum of humanity as the striving *yogin* or *yoginī.*)

These Deities and their correspondences in Shambhala can be listed thus:

- Ādi Buddha and Consort—Avatar of Synthesis and the Mother of the World.
- The five Dhyāni Buddhas that form the constituency of Her 'Womb'. From this perspective Sanat Kumāra expresses the function of Vairocana, the Spirit of Peace that of Akṣobhya,[14] and the three Buddhas of Activity the remainder of the Dhyāni Buddhas.
- The four Guardians—the four Lipikas, the Mahārājas.
- The six Buddhas of the Bhavacakra—the six Manuśi Buddhas; Osiris, Hercules, the Buddha, Jesus-Christ, the new Mahāchohan, and the future appearance of the Christ.
- The eight Mahābodhisattvas—the seven Ray Chohans and the Mahāchohan.
- The five Vidyadhāras—the Manu, Christ, the new Mahāchohan, the European Chohan and Guru Rinpoche.

To these can be added their Consorts (their *deva* correspondences) within the Womb of the great Mother. We thus have the Consorts of the five Dhyāni Buddhas, the four Guardians, eight Mahābodhisattvas, and the five Vidyadhāras, making 22 in all. These *devas* can here be

14 Note that Vairocana and Akṣobhya are interchangeable as the central point of the *maṇḍala* of the Dhyāni Buddhas, depending upon the emphasis of the *maṇḍala.*

considered as the agents for the twelve zodiacal and ten planetary forces constituting the Womb of Nature. Therefore there are 52 Peaceful Deities altogether. If the Vidyadhāras and Consorts are subtracted then we get the number 42. Also, if the six Buddhas of the Bhavacakra are subtracted then we have the number 36, and when we add the representatives of the twelve signs of the zodiac, which channel energies into the system from cosmos, then we get the number 48 for the number of petals to one lobe of the Ājñā centre, or of the major *chakras* below it.

Note that the six Buddhas of the Bhavacakra represent historical events related to the awakening of the compassionate force in humanity. The Vidyadhāras are a special team related to the awakening of intelligence in humanity. The ten planetary forces represent the potency of the seven *chakras,* plus the outer three tiers of petals of the Head lotus.

From another perspective there is a septenary consisting of the triad of the esoteric Kumāras, Sanat Kumāra, and the three Buddhas of Activity. Then the cosmic gateways are represented by the four Lipikas, followed by the seven Spirits before the Throne[15] and then the 'four and twenty elders'.[16]

The 58 'Wrathful Deities', viewed as planetary transforming agents, are represented by:

- A triad of former planetary executives: the Buddha (the former Christ), the former Mahāchohan (the Phoenician), and the Atlantean Manu. Then there are the present Manu, the blue Christ, and the Mahāchohan (R.). This is coupled to a triad of auxiliary planetary

15 They are the Ray Lords directing energies from the Logoi of the seven sacred planets in accordance with the cycles for the expression for the Rays upon our planet. They are symbolised thus in *Rev: 4:5,* 'And out of the throne proceeded lightnings and thunderings and voices: and *there were* seven lamps of fire burning before the throne, which are the seven Spirits of God'. 'The throne' here represents the energies that emanate from the quaternary of Sanat Kūmara and the three Buddhas of Activity. 'Lightnings and thunderings and voices' represent the energies of the three Buddhas of Activity, and the One who 'sat on the throne' *(Rev: 4:2-3)* represents Sanat Kumāra. Those who manifest as the 'four beasts full of eyes before and behind' *(Rev: 4:6),* symbolise the attributes of the four Mahārājas, who are explained below. See also *The Rays and Initiations,* 206.

16 *Rev: 4:4,* 'round about the throne were four and twenty seats: and upon the seats I saw four and twenty elders sitting, clothed in white raiment; and they had on their heads crowns of gold'.

executives of Guru Rinpoche, the European Chohan, and the new Mahāchohan. Finally, there are the seven Ray Chohans, and the 42 Masters constituting the Ashrams they preside over. (Some of these Ashrams have not yet formed.)

These great Ones, though normally viewed as peaceful by those upon the earth, project wrathful energies from the viewpoint of coming from Shambhala. These energies convert the base *saṃskāras* developed by humanity into the attributes of enlightenment via the Initiation path undertaken by all concerned.

The numbers 42 and 58 produce the 100 Peaceful and Wrathful Deities that are the standard representation of deities to the *Bardo Thödol.* To them are added 17 auxiliary deities, which were explained in Volume 5A, and also incorporated in the arrangement below. The Wrathful Deities, as the protectors of the unfoldment of the various petals of the *chakras,* have already been incorporated in the earlier explanations of the functions of the major *chakras,* as embodied by the constitution of Hierarchy. Hence I shall simply provide a list of the Wrathful Deities as represented in the *Bardo Thödol* here.

- Mahottara and Consort plus Vajrakīla and Consort. They represent the major petals of the Ājñā centre.
- Five Jñāna Ḍākinīs.
- Eight Mātaraḥ, the petals of the Diaphragm centre.
- Eight Piśācī, the petals of Splenic centre II.
- Four Gatekeepers of pristine cognition.

Next can be added the 28 Īśvarī.

- Four Gatekeepers enacting emanation rites, the *iḍā* and *piṇgalā* gates of the Solar Plexus centre, Vairocana, Aether.
- Six Queens of yoga, enacting rites of pacification, remaining six petals of the Solar Plexus centre, Akṣobhya, taste.
- Six Queens of yoga, enacting rites of subjugation, the left Gonad centre, Amitābha, sight.
- Six Queens of yoga, enacting rites of enrichment, right Gonad centre, Ratnasambhava, touch.

- Six Queens of yoga, enacting rites of wrath, Sacral centre, Amoghasiddhi, hearing.

  Excluding Mahottara and Consort, who embody the sum of these deities, there are 55 Wrathful Deities all told. To this total can be added the five Blood-drinking Herukas and their Consorts, making 65 Deities. Next can be added the 42 Peaceful Deities plus the five Vidyadhāras and Consorts, producing the number 117 all told. When Mahottara and Consort are added, then there are 119 deities altogether. When incorporated within the One *maṇḍalic* expression (or Logos), we get the number 120.[17]

The Consorts with respect to Peaceful Deities are:

- Four Guardian Consorts, relating to the zodiacal cardinal cross.
- Eight Mahābodhisattva Consorts, relating to the fixed and mutable crosses of the zodiac. These twelve interrelate the signs of the zodiac into the Womb of space-time.
- Five Dhyāni Buddha Consorts.
- Five Vidyadhāra Consorts.

This grouping are the *laya* centres[18] for the ten planetary Regents for the Womb of space-time. The 10 = 7 + 3 relates to the seven major centres plus the three major tiers of the Head lotus. The *devas* are mostly concerned with Splenic centre II and the cleansing of *prāṇic* substance. Splenic centre I is empowered by the twelve zodiacal potencies and more directly relates to human activity, but all *saṃskāric* cleansing (the major function of the Splenic centres) is enacted via the agency of *deva* substance. The 10 plus 12 makes the number 22.

17 The significance of which has been explained in Volume 5A, page 429.

18 *Laya,* meaning 'melting, dissolution, disappearance, to vanish away'. It is a point of disappearance, a zero-point, or a point in substance where every differentiation has temporarily ceased. It can also represent the ultimate state of quiescence, *śūnyatā*. It is the point where primordial substance differentiates and gives birth to formed space, the *maṇḍala* of things. A *laya* centre then becomes a point where substance is absorbed back to its ineffable source, etheric space, or to be the place of emergence of manifest space. Hence it can be also seen as the dividing point between one dimension of perception and the next. All *chakras* therefore contain at their hearts a *laya* centre.

There are therefore 22 entities and their forces represented. If the Consorts of Ādi Buddha and of Vajrakīla Heruka are added then there are 24.[19]

- The major tiers of petals of the Head centre have Mahottara's Consort at the centre. She therefore acts as the substance embodying the Head lotus.
- The Jina Consorts embody the three Head lotus tiers (the Consorts of Amitābha, Ratnasambhava and Amoghasiddhi), plus the Ājñā centre (the Consort of Vairocana) and the Heart centre (the Consort of Akṣobhya).
- The Vidyadhāra's Consorts embody the Throat centre, Solar Plexus centre, Splenic centre I, Splenic centre II and the Sacral centre.
- Vajrakīla's Consort embodies the Base of Spine centre.

Our concern, therefore, is with the *devas* embodying the substance of the petals of the *chakras* through which the *prāṇas* are channelled and processed.

This information derived from Volume 5A, *An Esoteric Exposition of the Bardo Thödol,* was included here to help the reader to comprehend the significance of numbers, as presented in *A Treatise on Cosmic Fire* with respect to the manifestation of the '105 Kumāras'.

> It has been stated that one hundred and four Kumaras came from Venus to the Earth; literally the figure is one hundred and five, when the synthesising Unit, the Lord of the World Himself, is counted as one. There remain still with Him the three Buddhas of Activity. I would call attention to the dual significance of that name, "Buddha of Activity," bearing out, as it does, the reality of the fact that Entities at Their stage of evolution are active love-wisdom and embody in Themselves the two aspects. The three Buddhas of activity have a correspondence to the three persons of the Trinity.
>
> These Entities are divided into three groups of thirty-five each, and in Themselves embody the three major centres of the planetary Logos, those three groups which we know as the "three departments," for it should be emphasised that each department forms a centre:

19 Explained in Volume 5A, 120-121, 408.

a. The Head centre..............The Ruling Department
b. The Heart centre..............The Teaching Department
c. The Throat centre.............The Mahachohan's Department.

This centre synthesises the lesser four, just as the third Ray synthesises the minor four.

These Kumaras (or Their present substitutes) can also be divided into the seven groups which correspond to the seven Rays, and are in Themselves the life of the centre for which They stand. Fifteen, therefore, of these Entities (again the ten and the five) form a centre in the body of the planetary Logos, and the three Kumaras about Whom we are told (Who in Themselves are fivefold, making the fifteen) are the entifying Lives of the particular centre which is involved in the coming Initiation of the Heavenly Man, and to which the human units at this time, and during this greater cycle, belong.

Another fact that should be noted about these great Beings is, that when viewed in Their seven groups, They form:

d. Focal points for the force or influence emanating from the other solar centres or schemes.
e. The seven divisions of the occult Hierarchy.

They exist, as does the Heavenly Man Himself, in etheric matter, and are literally great Wheels, or centres of living Fire, manasic and electric fire; They vitalise the body of the Heavenly Man and hold all together as an objective whole. They make a planetary triangle within the chain, and each of Them vitalises one globe.[20]

The reason why 105 Kumāras were needed to establish a planetary Head centre upon the physical plane of our earth globe is hid in the nature of the organisation of the Earthy tiers of petals of the Head lotus, as explained in Volume 5A.

Another way of viewing the numbers pertaining to the Earthy tiers is that there are 105 (12 + 33 + 60) petals that correspond to the 'Lords of Flame'.[21] They are a major part of the constituency of Shambhala,

---

20 Ibid., 387-388.

21 See H.P. Blavatsky, *The Secret Doctrine*, (Theosophical Publishing House Madras, 1962, six volume edition), iii, 31, 85-7. Also A.A. Bailey, *A Treatise on Cosmic Fire* (Lucis Publishing, New York, 1977), where they are also called Kumāras (mind-born sons of Brahmā), specifically pages 387-8.

and govern the factors of the evolution of mind/Mind within the sum of *saṃsāra*.[22] This incorporates the three levels of experience of human livingness, denoted above in terms of the three Earthy petals. This leaves twelve major petals governing the activity of the rest (five Watery, four Fiery, two Airy and one Aetheric petal). They can be considered as a unit because their direct concern is with the subjective (peaceful) energies above the diaphragm. The activity associated with the 105 petals involves the development of consciousness within corporeality, hence the (forceful) forces evolved below the diaphragm, plus the transitional processes and factors producing their conversion. The number 105 can also be arranged in terms of 12 + 33 = 45 (3 x 15) and 60 (4 x 15), or 7 x 15 conditioning energies, allowing the seven Ray potencies to govern the manifestation of all the *guṇas* of the five sense-consciousnesses (3 x 5), and of the quaternary of the form (4 x 5). Verily all is hid in the symbolism of numbers.

Of the twelve petals embodying factors or attributes of the Heart centre, five petals can be ascribed to the Herukas. These five relate to the non-sacred petals, dealing with the attributes of the five sense-consciousnesses and the processing of their *saṃskāras*. The remaining seven are sacred petals, hence channel the seven Ray potencies. Together they synthesise all *manasic* factors into the Heart of Life (the entire twelve petals of the Sambhogakāya Flower, or eventually into the Monadic Eye).

The number 105 + 12 = 117 is the number pertaining to the sum of the Peaceful and Wrathful deities of the *Bardo Thödol*, inclusive of the supplementary deities. The twelve synthesising petals of the Head lotus, each incorporating twelve integrating petals, process the *prāṇas* from the foundational petals governing the processes of enrichment, subjugation, wrath and pacification. The result is the pristine cognition that evolves from *manasic* activity. Thus the major sweeps of energy manifest through yogic control, meditation involving the calm abiding *(śamatha)* of the main petals, and the insightful penetration *(vipassana)* needed to accommodate the rest. They represent the *piṅgalā* and *iḍā* of the methodology of the inherent dualities of the petals, to achieve wisdom and compassion and the awakening of the all-seeing Eye of revelation.

---

22 Bodhisattvas of high degree have presently taken their place within Shambhala, freeing them to do other service in cosmos.

> Though other aspects of numerological considerations could be considered, the above suffices for this analysis.
>
> In conclusion, we need to observe another arrangement that these protectors of the *dharma* can generally manifest. This concerns the *prāṇas* coming from the major *chakras*:
>
> - The twenty-eight animal-headed Īśvarī process, help protect and transform the general mix of Earthy *prāṇas* coming from below the diaphragm centre. Twelve come from the Splenic centre, ten via the Solar Plexus centre and six via the Sacral centre.
> - The wrathful, central blood-drinking Herukas protect the Head lotus from any aberrant Watery *prāṇas* that may come via the Heart centre. As stated, seven petals of the Heart centre are sacred, as their (Airy) *prāṇas* are clean, the remaining five need to be converted into pure carriers of undefiled *prāṇas*. The pristine attributes of Mind and the Void Elements pertaining to *śūnyatā* must thereby be wrought.
> - The eight Mātaraḥ and the eight Piśācī protect the Head Lotus from the Watery attributes of the Fiery *prāṇas* coming via the sixteen petals of the Throat Centre.
> - The four animal-headed female Gatekeepers of pristine cognition protect the Head Lotus from defilements within the general Airy *prāṇas* (*iḍā* and *piṇgalā nāḍīs*) originating from the Base of Spine *chakra* onwards.
> - Vajrakīla Heruka, his Consort and the Jñāna Ḍākinīs help protect the Head lotus from all of the above *saṃskāras*.
>
> The Wrathful Deities do not just protect the Head Lotus from the forceful demands from a wilful *yogin* prematurely desirous of obtaining *siddhis*. They also function in the normal course of the awakening of the personal-I to higher states of awareness. They are an integral part of the equipment of the Sambhogakāya Flower, allowing it to control the nature of the *saṃskāras* that it absorbs into its petals, and also to project into the personality what it deems necessary for the mind to learn from.[23]

In this case the *yogin* is the Planetary Logos, and the body of manifestation needing control represents the *prāṇas* that will be

---

23 Volume 5A, 399-401.

developed by the sum of humanity (the kingdom of the Sambhogakāya Flower). In time, by taking all of the kingdoms of Nature into account and the overall evolutionary journey of the planetary Scheme, all of the petals of the Head lotus (as explained in Volume 5A) must be eventually awakened. The relevant information can then be extrapolated in terms of what actually exists in Nature and the interrelated journey of all streams of Lives therein. Such a consideration lies outside the scope of this present volume, but will be a profitable source of meditation for some future Bodhisattva.

Further consideration of the planetary Executives

Here I shall further consider the constitution of what D.K. calls 'the Council Chamber' of the Lord of the World. They are the custodians of the Plan for our planetary evolution, which manifests according to the law of cycles and according to the changing opportunities that present themselves in the kingdoms of Nature. Concerning this 'Plan' D.K. states:

> What you call "the Plan" is the response of the Hierarchy to the inflaming purposeful will of the Lord of the World. Through Sanat Kumara, the Ancient of Days (as He is called in the Bible), flows the unknown energy of which the three divine Aspects are the expression. He is the Custodian of the will of the Great White Lodge on Sirius, and the burden of this "cosmic intention" is shared by the Buddhas of Activity and those Members of the Great Council Who are of so elevated a consciousness and vibration that only once a year (through Their emissary, the Buddha) is it safe for Them to contact the Hierarchy.[24]

When D.K. states 'safe for Them to contact the Hierarchy' he is referring to the general assembly of Initiates constituting Hierarchy (from the third Initiation upwards) where each will receive their impression of what is the unfolding service work for them under the auspices of their Ray Ashram. The executive members of Hierarchy of course are able to contact members of 'the Great Council' at need, but one must eliminate concepts of 'personal attendance'; rather a process of formless telepathy is the mode of communication expressed.

24 A.A. Bailey, *The Rays and the Initiations,* 130.

D.K. later gives a listing of most of these 'Members of the Great Council':

> When the initiate has passed through the three doors, symbolically speaking, he then faces all life, all events, all pre-determinations, all wisdom, all activity and all that the future may hold of service and progress from the angle of the pure reason (infallible and immutable), of true spiritual will (completely identified with the purpose of the planetary Logos), and of the highest possible focussed relation. The mystery of relationship becomes revealed to him. Then the entire scheme of evolution and of the intention of the One in Whom he lives and moves and has his being becomes clear to him; he has no more to learn within this planetary scheme; he has become universal in his attitude to all forms of life, and is also identified with the "isolated unity" of Sanat Kumara. Few of the great Lives Who form the inner group of the Council Chamber at Shamballa are now of greater advancement than he; the "Supernal Three," the "Radiant Seven," the "Lives embodying the forty-nine Fires," the "Buddhas of Activity," and certain "Eternal Spirits" from such centres of dynamic spiritual life as Sirius, or from the constellation which at any one time forms a triangle with our Sun and Sirius and a Representative from Venus are of greater—far greater—advancement. Otherwise, all initiates of the sixth degree, and a few of the Masters Who have undergone specialised training because They are upon the first Ray of Will or Power (the ray conditioning Shamballa itself), form part of the Great Council. Many Masters and Chohans, however, after serving upon the planet in various capacities, working with the Law of Evolution, pass out of our planetary life altogether.[25]

This third door, the *'door of the monadic sense of essential duality'*,[26] is entered at the sixth Initiation. After passing through this Door the Chohan makes his decision as to which of the cosmic Paths to travel, hence the concept of 'essential duality'. The 'duality' represents the Chohan's standing upon the earth and That to which he must travel. 'The Monadic sense' then concerns travelling the higher Way of the cosmic Initiations, which the Monad 'senses' with its transcendental perceptions.

25 Ibid., 141-142.

26 Ibid., 141.

'The Supernal Three' are the three esoteric Kumāras: the Avatar of Synthesis, the Spirit of Peace and the Mother of the World. Then there is Sanat Kumāra and the three Buddhas of Activity. Together they make a septenary. Then there are 'the Radiant Seven', which are the Regents of the seven sacred planets of our Solar system.[27] They are Ray Lords whose purpose is to anchor upon the earth the directives of the energies of their respective planets, according to the Plan related to the possibilities that open up in earth evolution. Next are the 'Lives embodying the forty-nine Fires', who represent the Rāja Lords governing the planes and sub-planes of our planetary system. Omitted in the listing are the four Mahārājas (Lipikas), who are responsible for the expression of the *karma* governing the 'four corners' of the earth. So far 63 entities are represented, and when we add the 'Eternal Spirits' that are effectively 'permanent' residents within the Council Chamber, then we get the number 66 all told. These entities are the representatives of the most important sources of energies to our planetary life. One is the representative from Venus, the earth's 'alter ego', or directive Soul.[28] Another is the representative from Sirius, as Sanat Kumāra is a disciple of the Lord of Sirius, and our Hierarchy similarly is 'the blue Lodge', which takes its instructions from Sirius, the Lord of Love-Wisdom to our planet, as well as to the solar system. Also, the Monads of the earth humanity also esoterically herald from this star system. Finally we have a representative from the Pleiades, who is primarily concerned with the evolution of the feminine principle, the *devas*.

Other representatives from various constellations, planets or stars are often represented at the Council Chamber, who visit for specific purposes, but then return after that purpose has been fulfilled.

The number 66 is important, as it represents the number associated with incarnation into form, as are all of these Great Ones from the cosmic perspective. They have all manifested into the cosmic dense physical plane, which are our seven systemic planes of perception. To this number, one would have to add the constitution of the Hierarchy from the

---

27 See *The Externalisation of the Hierarchy,* 158, where D.K. states: 'the Representatives of the seven sacred planets Who are spoken of in the Christian Bible as the "seven Spirits before the Throne of God"'.

28 Alice Bailey, *Esoteric Astrology,* 683-84.

fifth Initiation up, to make the number 105 explained previously. These planetary executives are concerned with the evolution of consciousness from out of the kingdoms of Nature, rather than the evolution of the sum of the body of manifestation into which all incarnate.

The number 66 is but a shortened version of the number 666 found in chapter 13:18 of the *Revelation of St. John:*

> Here is wisdom. Let him that hath understanding count the number of the beast: for it is the number of a man; and his number *is* Six hundred threescore *and* six.

Being the 'number of a man', implies that this 'beast' represents the sum of humanity incarnating into the material domain via the levels of expression of the *maṇḍala* based upon the hexagram (the Sacral centre). It also refers to the establishment of the astral plane, with its heaven and hell states, which has the power to reflect the attributes of divinity, 'the image of the beast' *(Rev 13:14).* The attributes of the 'beast' in the book of Revelation refers to the symbolism of the reified attributes of a Logos, as such a One manifests via its Rounds and Chains of evolution, hence having 'seven heads and ten horns':

> And I stood upon the sand of the sea, and saw a beast rise up out of the sea, having seven heads and ten horns, and upon his horns ten crowns, and upon his heads the name of blasphemy.[29]

Here the 'sea' is the cosmic astral ocean, from which the earth Scheme arose, which contains seven Chains of evolutionary activity. The 'name of blasphemy' refers to the deviant evolutionary history of moon Chain humanity and its ramifications upon our earth Chain. This process and history is introduced in Blavatsky's *The Secret Doctrine* and expanded somewhat in Bailey's *A Treatise on Cosmic Fire,* from which the pertinent part relating to the above quote is as follows:

> Forget not that the schemes manifest as seven, as ten, as three from the angle of the Eternal Now, or—from the point of view of a Heavenly Man—the manifestation may be written as (3|7).[30]

---

29 *Rev. 13:1.*

30 A.A. Bailey, *A Treatise on Cosmic Fire,* 414.

Concerning the moon Chain

Much conditioning the present planetary situation and the constitution of Shambhala, as well as the higher ordering of Hierarchy, is the result of the disastrous happenings upon the moon Chain. It was a situation that closely involved a wrong decision made by the Mother of the World (the fifth Kumāra), who because of numerical affinity was directly concerned with the evolution of the then humanity. The moon Chain was the third planetary Chain of the earth Scheme and as such its evolution was directly related to the feminine, third Ray dispensation of the past solar system. The journey concerning the process of Individualisation was very slowly achieved as a natural course of the evolution of *manas*. As well as a very large number of third Ray Monads being prepared for Individualisation, there was also a small number of first Ray ones. At a particular cycle, the Mother saw an opportunity to try to hasten the evolutionary process by invoking more first Ray energies. This prematurely precipitated into incarnation the first Ray Monads, whose personalities at that stage could not accommodate the premature stimulation without aberration. They quickly evolved towards the left hand path, reverting to a stage of evolution appropriate in the former solar system's early epochs, but now to be superseded. This activity was also aggravated by a large number of Souls from the former Mars evolution, that were still ensconced in dark brotherhood activity. Consequently, sexual magic became widely prevalent upon the moon.

This subject concerning the genesis of this dark brotherhood in our earth Scheme is also complicated by a decision of the planetary Logos, who prematurely empowered the animal nature that upon the moon Chain was overly identified with the material form of the planetary Entity. This is presented by D.K. via the following terminology:

> The mystery of the moon or of the "divine lunatic" is connected somewhat with the revelation (through the premature compassion of our planetary Logos) of the life of this nature, informing the dense globe of the moon chain. On His high level, pity awoke in the heart of the planetary Logos for certain involutionary existences within the moon chain, and (like the Buddha on a lesser scale and at a much later date) compassionate zeal brought the karmic results with which we are still concerned. The "beast" must be driven back for his own good to

run his cycle, hidden in his den and confined within safe limits until the dawning of a new system brings him conscious opportunity.[31]

Concerning the work of the five Kumāras upon the moon Chain, D.K. states:

> It might here be stated that the relative failure that was the fate of the *Moon chain* in our scheme has greatly handicapped Their work, and made it imperative for Them to employ drastic measures in order to offset that failure. Herein lies another clue to the world turmoil...[32]
>
> The Moon chain with the Earth chain formed two units, or two polarities, negative and positive. The point of merging was reached, and the Earth chain absorbed or synthesised the moon chain in the same sense as certain of the schemes will merge until only three will apparently be left. Therefore the Earth chain is essentially dual in its nature, being the sumtotal of a male and a female chain. This is a mystery impossible to elucidate further, but it is dealt with in certain occult books, and hinted at by H. P. B.
>
> In due course of time another merging in the scheme will eventuate and then Uranus (the chain of that name in our scheme) will flash into objectivity. Forget not that the schemes manifest as seven, as ten, as three from the angle of the Eternal Now, or—from the point of view of a Heavenly Man—the manifestation may be written as (3|7). In time and space the order might be stated to be 7-3-10, and at certain stages 10-7-3. As the opposites merge the ten become the seven and the three, and it is during this process that entire chains and globes, and eventually schemes, will apparently vanish from objectivity, and drop out of sight. They will be simply absorbed. During the twofold process of evolution, it might be numerically expressed as:
>
> During involution the sequence is seen as three, then seven and finally ten.
> During evolution the sequence is ten, then seven and finally three.
>
> The involutionary process is over practically and the evolutionary is approximately midway through. This will be marked by the disappearance or absorption of certain chains as they find their polar opposites, and a simultaneous appearance of the more subtle chains or globes as the manasic principle enables man to see them. The moon

31 Ibid., 846-847.

32 Ibid., 413.

> chain is in process of disappearance, and only a decaying body is left; the life of the second and the first Logos has been withdrawn from it, and only the latent life of matter itself remains. Simultaneously Neptune arose over the horizon, and took its place as one of the seven manifesting chains of the planetary Logos. We are here dealing with the Neptune chain of the earth scheme.[33]

As the earth is 'essentially dual in its nature, being the sum total of a male and a female chain', so the book of Revelation speaks of a 'second beast' (the earth Chain) that arose 'up out of the earth; and he had two horns like a lamb, and he spake as a dragon'.[34] The 'two horns' refers to this dual nature. The concept of a dragon here is but a cosmic extension of a Master of Wisdom being also styled 'a Dragon of Wisdom'. Such a dragon is an extension of the symbolism concerning the evolution of *kuṇḍalinī* (which was somewhat explained in Volume one of this series). We can therefore see from this brief explanation that the phrase 'here is wisdom' in *Rev. 13:18* informs us that if one can properly decipher 'the number of a man' (cosmically as well as systemically) then one is indeed wise, enlightened.

D.K. continues:

> The Moon chain has in itself a curious occult history, not yet to be disclosed. This differentiates it from the other chains in the scheme and even from any other chain in any scheme. An analogous situation or correspondence will be found in another planetary scheme within the solar system. All this is hidden in the history of one of the solar systems which is united to ours within a cosmic ring-pass-not. Hence the impossibility of yet enlarging upon it. Each Heavenly Man of a scheme is a focal point for the force and power and vibratory life of seven stupendous ENTITIES in exactly the same sense as the seven centres in a human being are the focal points for the influence of a corresponding heavenly Prototype. Our Heavenly Man, therefore, is esoterically allied to one of the seven solar systems, and in this mysterious alliance is hidden the mystery of the moon chain.
>
> Certain brief hints may be given for the due consideration of students:

33 Ibid., 414-415.

34 *Rev. 13:11.*

- The Moon chain was a chain wherein a systemic failure was to be seen.
- It is connected with the lower principles, which H.P.B. has stated are now superseded.
- The sexual misery of this planet finds its origin in the moon failure.
- The progress of evolution on the moon was abruptly disturbed and arrested by the timely interference of the solar Logos. The secret of the suffering in the Earth chain, which makes it merit the name of the Sphere of Suffering, and the mystery of the long and painful watch kept by the SILENT WATCHER, has its origin in the events which brought the moon chain to a terrific culmination. Conditions of agony and of distress such as are found on our planet are found in no such degree in any other scheme.
- The misuse of the vibratory power of a certain centre, and the perversion, or distortion of force to certain erroneous ends, not along the line of evolution, account for much of the moon mystery.
- Certain results, such as the finding of its polar opposite, were hastened unduly on the moon chain, and the consequence was an uneven development and a retardation of the evolution of a certain number of deva and human groups.
- The origin of the feud between the Lords of the Dark Face and the Brotherhood of Light, which found scope for activity in Atlantean days, and during the present root race, can be traced back to the moon chain.[35]

Continuing along this vein D.K. states:

The fifth principle of manas is embodied in the five Kumaras, and if the student studies the significance of the first five petals which are unfolded in the egoic lotus, he may touch upon the fringe of the mystery. The fifth Ray, which is the Ray of the fifth Kumara, is potently responsive to the energy flowing through the fifth Hierarchy... His close connection therefore, as a transmitter of force within the Moon chain, the third chain, in connection with the third kingdom, the animal, and with the third round, must be borne in mind. One symbol that may be found in the archaic records in lieu of His Name or description is an inverted five-pointed star, with the luminous Triangle at the centre.[36] It will be noted that the points involved in this symbol

35 A.A. Bailey, *A Treatise on Cosmic Fire,* 415-417.

36 This is also a symbol of Makara (who is explained below), and symbolises the mode of descent of mind into manifestation.

> number eight—a picture of that peculiar state of consciousness brought about when the mind is seen to be the slayer of the Real. The secret of planetary avitchi[37] is hidden here, just as the third major scheme can be viewed as systemic avitchi, and the moon at one time held an analogous position in connection with our scheme. This must be interpreted in terms of consciousness, and not of locality.[38]

The moon Chain evolution never progressed past the Lemurian stage of development (which was carried through into its Atlantean and Aryan phases), with widespread ritualistic and sexual depravity of all types being the norm. There is no need to try to depict the happenings thereon, of which such activities as the Inquisitional period in Europe, the effects of the rapine and pillage in war time and the widespread black magic in Atlantis, are all repercussions of that ancient epoch. The moon was eventually blasted by its voracious appetite and was consequently destroyed prematurely. Its streams of Life were directed to the earth when it was ready to accommodate them, and most of its humanity entered earth evolution during early to mid Atlantean times. This has caused a significant burden upon the Lord of the World and those responsible for the evolution of all Life upon our planet. Special precautions had to be taken to safeguard as much as possible the earth Scheme from the effects of the moon Scheme's failure.

Of particular note is the *karma* of the one we now know as Master Jesus. His failure was significant upon that Chain, as his role was that of the planetary Christ,[39] but abused the post when he was converted into the black path. He then had much power over the deviant and perverse activities of the sexually intoxicated and violent masses. 'Jesus' was

---

37 *Avīci* (from *a* not + *vīci* waves, pleasure), having no waves or movement, happiness or repose. It signifies endless torture, the lowest of the hells. A state of consciousness (not a locality *per se)* seen as virtual uninterrupted hell, but not without hope for final redemption. (The severest of the eight hot hells existing upon the astral domain.) Also a zone or residence for members of the dark brotherhood, the transgressors of the Law, in which they reside awaiting the cycle for when they are again released. The conditionings inside the eighth sphere.

38 A.A. Bailey, *A Treatise on Cosmic Fire*, 704-705.

39 The blue Christ was not incarnate upon the moon Chain at that time. He was preparing to play a role upon the earth, as the conditionings upon the moon were too violent for his further spiritual development.

converted back to the white Hierarchy since Atlantean times, and has consequently undergone a tortuous series of lives to atone for his past misdeeds and to cleanse the related *karma* as fast as he was able.

Reverberations of the activities of that ancient time had to be cyclically cleansed. This is the basis to the *karma* necessitating crucifixion, the symbolism of the crown of thorns, and the scourging with whips that he suffered in the Jesus life. It accounts for the reverberating black magical activities he was later forced to manifest in his life as Milarepa because of the circumstances of his life when he was young and the coercion of his mother.

Having been a planetary Christ on the moon Chain, albeit a failed one, also explains Jesus' special relationship to the present blue Christ, as well as the cosmic Christ, who overshadowed him in the Jesus life to instigate the then new religious dispensation. It is also the basis for Jesus being the sixth Ray Chohan, as upon the moon Chain the sixth Ray stood for the second in our present system. The concept of the 'precarious atonement' of his 'Blood' for the sake of all 'sinners' (those that have karmically transgressed), is hid in this ancient history, and also the symbolism of the sixth Ray energy (cosmic Waters) as 'Blood' *(prāṇa).* Literally, his 'Blood' is now sacrificed, directed to the conversion of all aspirants into Initiates (of the second degree) to help cleanse the *karma* of his past mistakes. Much of this atonement has now been accomplished, and he will be freed from this most ancient duty upon the appearance of the major second Ray cycle on earth. We can also witness his role as the charioteer for Krishna (the Christ) in the Bhagavad Gītā during the battle of Kurukshetra. (Which esoterically also relates to the cleansing of some of this moon Chain *karma* upon the earth.)

It is easy enough to imagine the crisis that would have transpired upon the moon Chain when the then correspondence to our planetary executives had to accommodate the betrayal of the Christ's department (the then correspondence to our present Hierarchy), and their conversion to the black camp. A special team of seven under the leadership of Sanat Kumāra was assembled, who were specialists in the various aspects of the dark brotherhood and their mode of predations. Each were more advanced than would normally have been needed. First, those known as the three Buddhas of Activity were called forth from other duties in our solar system to assist in holding at bay the ferocity of the cosmic forces of darkness who had taken opportunity of the door opened to them by the massed bestial activities of moon Chain humanity. These forces were mental, astral and physical via a ruptured access to the cosmic mental, astral and etheric spheres. The 'tear' in space had to be mended as much as possible by the work of these exalted planetary executives. They are still working at this post, as much cosmic *karma* also needs adjudicating.

Under them was assembled a quaternary of Initiates, whose task concerned bringing some sort of order to the chaotic situation on the planet. This grouping were the early incarnations of the ones presently known as the Buddha, the Phoenician, the new Mahāchohan and Guru Rinpoche. Effectively they governed the expression of the fourth, fifth, sixth and seventh Rays. Their purpose therefore came under the auspices of the third Ray of active Creative Intelligence.[40] They tried to mitigate the general effects of the forces of darkness upon the planet, who prostituted this energy towards all forms of creative depravity. To do so a temple of Initiation was established by the Mother of the World. She oversaw the entire process, with view of the candidates developing the attributes of the third Initiation as they stood then. This was the high goal for moon Chain humanity, taking into account the deplorable conditions of the time.

Under her the Buddha presented the elementary teachings related to the attainment of the second Initiation. Principally, however, he manifested as an energy conduit for the fourth Ray energy (the Ray correspondence for the energy of Love-Wisdom at that time) in order to try to bring order, harmonious interrelationships, out of the martial and sexual strife of those times. The main faculty members that gave instructions concerning the mysteries of the first Initiation as they stood at that time were the then incarnations of the Phoenician, the new Mahāchohan and Guru Rinpoche. The Phoenician taught the development of the mind, hence comprehension of the nature of manifesting phenomena and the mental forces, the mustering of the

40 For average humanity the third Ray manifests in the form of creative intelligent activity, but as the attributes of Mind begin to be awakened, this Ray manifests in the form of mathematically exact activity.

energies needed to control one's activities in the fields of illusion, glamour and *māyā*.[41] The then incarnation of the new Mahāchohan presented the general teachings of the nature of the path, specifically related to the control of sexual energies and some of the attributes of astral plane glamour. He thereby helped to externalise the energy dispensation of the Buddha. Hence he dealt with the major problems of moon Chain humanity, offering solutions in the face of their greatest difficulties. Guru Rinpoche was mainly concerned with physical plane disciplines, the overcoming of material comforts as understood then, the right use of ritual and rhythm in physical activities to control breath and the movement of the *prāṇas* in the body.

Most who are presently the Masters of Wisdom and the Chohans were the attendants of that School, manifesting at the level of aspirants and probationary disciples, as understood now. Sanat Kumāra was also physically incarnate and was the ultimate authority, the directive head, of all activities generated by the School. He clearly saw the future and what needed to be done, coordinating His activities with the three Buddhas of Activity and extra-planetary emissaries. Whilst this quaternary under the auspices of the Mother were working to instate the elements of compassionate thought upon those of the moon Chain's evolution that could respond, the three Buddhas of Activity and Sanat Kumāra were preparing, with help from the Solar Logos and His Council Chamber, to project all streams of Life from the moon (mainly) to the earth. They also instigated the catastrophe that was to ensue on the moon at the end of its fifth Racial cycle (the equivalent of the Aryan epoch on earth), because the cycle that would bring forth the attributes of the sixth Root Race could not manifest. Perversion of the energies of mind, exemplifying its separative and materialistic, self-serving nature, produced the widespread manifestation of dark brotherhood activity. Their momentum could not be averted save by the premature destruction of the planet.

The first Initiation and the associated mysteries was effectively the gain of the few Initiates that passed through the portals of Initiation in those days. Even then, the attributes needed to pass Initiation were significantly milder than needed now. Nevertheless, it was a comparatively

---

41 See Alice Bailey's *Glamour, a World Problem,* for explanation of these terms.

difficult accomplishment for them, considering the fact of the mass (mainly sexual) transgressions of the humanity of those days, coupled with the rapacious abuse of the natural telluric forces of the planet to control all of the forces of Nature (and the corresponding *devas),* and the ruthless enslavement of all people by those that had the power.

The focus of the teaching department thus fell upon the shoulders of the then incarnation of the new Mahāchohan. Effectively he played the role of the planetary Christ, taking over much of the work that should have been accomplished by the fallen 'Christ'. This was by virtue of being the second point of the triad, which dealt with the Watery emotional energies that were much abused in those days of licentious depravity. The way that the Waters could be controlled hence represented the most difficult aspects of the teachings that confronted the prospective Initiates. It is this ancient teaching dispensation that the new Mahāchohan has carried through to the present day as the 'third Christ'. Hence he will also take the role, under Sanat Kumāra who will overshadow him, as the planetary first Initiator, when a significantly large number of the present humanity are ready to take this Initiation. This Initiation undertaken upon a mass scale, plus those that will take their second or third Initiations, will signify the general rectification of the abuses of those that lived on the moon Chain. It will prove the success of the decision to cause the premature termination of that planetary Life. A significant portion of the *karma* from those days will then have been rectified. The new second Ray Day will then awaken. To do so, the present strife, sexual licentiousness and misery of the destructive proceeds of war will have run their course. The dark brotherhood have again played their hand in controlling the nations (focussed via the power of the Zionist controlled USA), and will this time be defeated without the need to destroy the planet. The moon's subjective hold upon the planet will then be largely vanquished.

Concerning the statement 'The fifth Ray, which is the Ray of the fifth Kumāra,[42] is potently responsive to the energy flowing through

---

42 D.K. uses the masculine pronoun 'he' when referring to this Kumāra, which is consistent with the way he designates all great beings, bearers of the (masculine) first Ray energies from Shambhala. In a similar manner he often uses the masculine 'he' or 'his' when referring to H.P. Blavatsky, as in *A Treatise on Cosmic Fire,* 1091.

the fifth Hierarchy', it should be noted that this Kumāra was equated with the Mother of the World above. The 'fifth Hierarchy', counting from above down, of the seven systemic planes (active planetary manifestation), rather than including the liberated Hierarchies, are denoted 'Human Personality, The Crocodiles, Makara, the mystery'.[43] They are the *deva* Hierarchy embodying the mental plane. Hence they manifest in two fundamental divisions:

> Entangled closely with the karma of these two cosmic Entities,[44] was that of the lesser cosmic Entity Who is the Life of our planet, the planetary Logos. It was this triple karma which brought in the "serpent religion" and the "Serpents or Dragons of Wisdom," in Lemurian days. It had to do with solar and planetary Kundalini, or Serpent fire. A hint lies in the fact that the constellation of the Dragon has the same relation to the ONE greater than our Logos as the centre at the base of the spine has to a human being. It concerns stimulation, and vitalisation with a consequent co-ordination of the manifesting fires.
>
> A clue to the mystery lies also in the relation of this fifth group to the two contracting poles. They are the five-fold Links, the "Benign Uniters" and "the Producers of the Atonement." Esoterically, they are the "Saviours of the Race" and from Them emanates that principle which—in conjunction with the highest aspect—lifts the lower aspect up to Heaven.
>
> When these mysteries are carefully studied, and due application made to the lives of the greatest exponents of the at-one-ing principle, it will become apparent how great and all-important is their place in the scheme.
>
> It is for this reason that the units of the fifth Hierarchy are called "The Hearts of Fiery Love"; They save through love, and in Their turn these lives are peculiarly close to the great Heart of Love of the solar Logos. These great redeeming Angels, Who are the Sons of Men on their own true plane, the mental, are ever, therefore, pictured as taking the form of twelve-petalled lotuses—this symbology linking them up with "the Son of Divine Love," the manifested solar system, which is said to be a cosmic twelve-petalled lotus, and with the logoic causal lotus, equally of a twelve-petalled nature.[45]

---

43 A.A. Bailey, *Esoteric Astrology,* 35.

44 The solar Logos and another solar Logos, from whence 'the secret of the Dragon' is derived. Logically, therefore, this other solar Logos exists in the constellation of Draco, the dragon.

45 A.A. Bailey, *Esoteric Astrology,* 45-46.

Part of the mystery related to the fifth Creative Hierarchy is veiled by the nature of the *kuṇḍalinī* Fire. We should realise that all matter is but the externalisation of *manasic* energy. All stems from the mind and all is finally resolved back into it. *Manasic* Fire is thus imbued in the heart of all substance. All atomic spheres (little sentient lives) upon the physical plane are bonded into a coherent form by means of a congealed form of such Fire—pure energy from the point of view of modern physics. The integrated corpus of such atomic lives manifesting a particular form, be it that of a rock, plant, or a human body, are held into unity by a unit of mind. Such a 'unit of mind' then can be considered a tiny *deva* life, the elementals, sylphs, fairies, the greater *devas,* landscape *devas,* the Cherubim, Seraphim, etc., including the human Soul. All are *manasic* in expression. All of this is part of the Mother's department. Consequently, the mystery is intricately bound with a comprehension of the esoteric nature of Motherhood, of the creative principle. As the thinker thinks, so is created the forms of that thought structure. The application of the directive will congeals that thought into reifying, increasingly dense structures, and inevitably the physical plane comes into view (to the mind of another thinker—a perceiver).

At the dawning of time, therefore, the Mind of the 'Creator' caused the units of Fiery Life upon the mental plane to coalesce, congeal and thence to concretise according to a set plan, formula, or idea, (a *maṇḍala* of expression). The Will was utilised to produce a congealing, propulsive motion attracting to it layers of *manasic* substance from earlier cycles of endeavour, until a physical form is produced encasing the seed of the originating Fiery impetus. Each seed of Fiery impulse is but an aspect of the originating thought that moves through time towards its inevitable release from the (temporary) binding encasing it. The nature of that movement is serpentine. The integrated movement of all such seeds is the potency of *kuṇḍalinī.* When a sufficient number of such elemental Fires are liberated at once, then the phenomena of *'kuṇḍalinī* rising' manifests. It can produce an atomic explosion in the field of matter. The inherent Life is released to return to its source.

This fifth Creative Hierarchy are thus the guardians of the mode and timing of the release of the little Fiery lives found as the substance of Nature. They embody the form of it all. They express the *karma* of the substance of the Mother in its union with the Father, veiled by the term 'Makara the mystery'. They direct the growth of the serpentine motion on an elemental as well as a planet-wide scale. The serpents inevitably grow into Dragons of Wisdom (becoming 'the perfect Ones' on the way) by that principle that has mastered the expression of the Fiery Element as an output of all knowledgeable forms. The mysteries of time and space are revealed here. In between is the 'Fiery flying serpent' stage somewhat described in Volume 1 of this Treatise. The appropriate release of the Fiery Life stored at the heart of each atom is the foundation of all alchemy, both the modern form and ancient.

An exposition of the various names of this Creative Hierarchy will elucidate more their nature. There are two pentads of names to consider. The first relates to the Fiery expression of the concrete mind, their extension is found in the five types of sense-perception that concern the mode of ingathering of information for processing by 'the sixth sense', the human intellect. We thus have:

1. 'The Perfect Ones'. D.K. states:

> We now take up for brief consideration two Hierarchies which closely concern ourselves, the human self-conscious entities. These two groups are literally three, as the fifth Hierarchy is a dual one, and it is this which has led to some confusion and is the occult significance behind the ill-omened number thirteen. They are the "Seekers of satisfaction" and the cause of the second fall into generation, the fact behind the taking of a lower nature by the Ego. The fourth and the fifth Hierarchies are the ninth and tenth, or the "Initiates" and the "Perfect Ones." All human beings, or "Imperishable Jivas," are those who evolve through a graded series of initiations, either self-induced or brought about on our planet with extraneous aid. They achieve through a "marriage" with the order next to them, the fifth. They are then completed or perfected, and it is owing to this occult fact that the fourth Hierarchy is regarded as masculine and the fifth as feminine.[46]

'The Perfect Ones' is the general term for the entire grouping of *manasa devas*. (As they are the Mothers of all attributes of mind.) They embody all attributes concerning the concretion of thoughts in such a way that complete comprehension or fluid synthesis is possible to be

46 Ibid., 41-42.

obtained by the fourth (human) Creative Hierarchy and can be projected towards awakening the abstract Mind. They facilitate an alignment with the *dharmakāya* (*ātma*) at a later stage of human evolution, allowing the *yogin* to bypass the Soul and receive direct inspiration from the concreted level of the plane of Logoic causation, as they are the links between cosmic and systemic mind/Mind. They embody the substance of the *antaḥkaraṇas* (of the most refined, wise thoughts) directed to the abstracted Mind. (The three higher mental sub-planes wherein resides the human Soul.) They are the fertile anchoring points of mind for the higher grouping of Mind, such as 'the five-fold Links'. They allow concreted thoughts to manifest flexibility and a mobility that frees *manas* from the constraints of form, producing mental perfection. They are the 'Perfect Ones' because they embody and facilitate the flow of impressions to and from the Sambhogakāya Flower, producing the perfection of mind into Mind.

2. *'The Human Personality'*. This represents an amalgamation between the fifth, sixth and seventh Creative Hierarchies[47] that build the human form, the tangible *māyāvirūpa* that is so well known by us and studied by scientists. The physical domain appears to most people to represent the sum of their universe.

3. *'Makara the Mystery'*. Makara is the goat-fish (*kāma-manas*) that must rise out of the Waters to climb the rocky mount to complete mental mastery. Astrologically it is the fusion between the psychic, Watery attributes of Pisces and the Fiery materialism of Capricorn. The ability of the mind to integrate with all other Elements is exemplified. Inevitably the mind will dominate all within its own Fiery domain, and be able to delve into every direction of its mindscape. The empirical mind controls its domain, yet at the pinnacle of the mountain of mind the attributes of the abstract Mind are perceived. The conversion of mind to Mind is the mystery, and this necessitates the cooperative work and eventual marriage between the fourth and fifth Creative Hierarchies. Love and mind become fused to exemplify great wisdom.

---

47 Also denoted as the tenth, eleventh and twelfth Creative Hierarchies.

4. *'The Crocodiles'* relate to an amalgamation between the fifth Creative Hierarchies and the sixth (the Lunar Lords, or Pitris). This is the basis to the *kāma-manasic saṃskāras* developed by the human kingdom. The term 'crocodiles' is used because they are reptilian, hence expressive of a form of the serpent energy governing the lower form nature. This energy is quite forceful and dangerous, as it stimulates the lower psychic powers, preventing the development of the higher spiritual perceptions, hence the crocodile lives partly on land (the earthy terrain) and in the water (the astral domain of the emotions).

5. *'The Lunar Pitris'*. The term 'Pitris' *(pitṛs)* means 'Fathers' or progenitors. They embody the generalised Watery aspect of the *devas,* which are manipulated by human desires and creative imagination to create their astral heaven and hells, as well as their emotional bodies.

Next to consider are the *manasa devas* that have been incorporated into the Knowledge petals of the Sambhogakāya Flower. Their work is to help rectify the *karma* that has been generated through wilful volitions by the human personalities rayed down into incarnate expression. In doing so they transform the gross volitions generated into more peaceful, enlightened attributes.

1. Knowledge—Knowledge petal, 'the five-fold Links'. They are the general links from the above pentad of *manasa devas* via the brain consciousness (the human personality) to project the knowledgeable *saṃskāras* deemed useful to the Sambhogakāya Flower. These links are those that absorb the experiences derived from the five sense-consciousnesses.

2. Knowledge—Love-Wisdom petal, 'the Benign Uniters'. They manifest gentle but firm action to help transform the *karma* of desire into loving actions. In doing so the Lunar Pitris are eventually controlled, hence strong desire no longer becomes a factor in the person's life. Affection becomes devotion to noble causes and self-focussed desire becomes aspiration to enlightened ideals, divinity. The Love principle developed is the keynote for the evolutionary development of the entire Causal form (the Sambhogakāya Flower).

3. Knowledge—Will petal, the 'Producers of atonement'. Atonement concerns making amends for wrongs or an injury done to others. Such injury or wrong is generally the effect of forceful *manasic* projection, where the often critical separative, empirical mind, as governed by Makara, pronounces critical or even hateful judgement upon the thoughts and opinions of others. This petal of the Sambhogakāya Flower rectifies such attitudes through proper knowledge and the utilisation of the Will-to-Love, hence atones for the misdeeds of the mind. It karmically cleanses the worst of the wilful mentalistic *saṃskāras* formerly developed by an incarnation of the Soul. This ensures that only the most sacrificial attribute of the will of mind can be absorbed by the Sambhogakāya Flower.

4. Love-Wisdom—Knowledge petal, the 'Hearts of Fiery Love'. This grouping of *devas* fan the most compassionate attributes of Mind upon the path of discipleship, which works towards cleansing the human personality from the *saṃskāras* of unloving, selfish, self-centred *kāma-manasic* thoughts. This transformation represents the major battlefield for most people. People must attune to the overtures of their solar Angels (the Sambhogakāya Flower) to do so. In so doing 'the Crocodiles' are transformed into the attributes of their higher brethren, and become 'the Perfect Ones'. The defiling units of the sixth Creative Hierarchy are rejected.

5. Will—Knowledge petal, the 'Saviours of the Race'. This highest grouping of *devas* help to transform all types of concreted thoughts into the most far-reaching and abstracted streams along the lines of the paradigms impressed upon the strata of the higher mental plane from *ātma*. Initiation testings can then be mastered along the path of final elimination of human *karma*. The marriage, or fusion, between the fourth, (human) Hierarchy and the fifth *(deva)* Hierarchy is then possible.

The *devas* integrated into the Causal body are the links (the reflected attributes) to the qualities of the five liberated Hierarchies. The implication is that these liberated Hierarchies manifest a similar role as the *manasa devas* do to our Souls, with respect to the Causal

Body of our Solar Logos. From this perspective the present planetary incarnation is viewed as a personality vehicle whose *manasic* output is in the process of being assimilated into the vast nine petalled Flower governing Solar Incarnation. The *devas* embodying the Sambhogakāya Flower become the receptors to the line of transformative energies from the liberated Hierarchies because of numerical affinity and sympathetic vibration. They are the focal points for the transmutative effect of cosmic Fire (Mahat) that works upon the fourth Creative Hierarchy to convert the dense physical substance into its Aetheric counterpart. The medium is the (cosmic) Watery Love that is the purpose of this solar evolution. When sufficient numbers of the present humanity respond positively to the alchemicalising effect of cosmic Fire then the earth will become 'sacred'.

The epoch of the Mother of the World will then actively demonstrate its dispensation, where the fourth and fifth Creative Hierarchies will work cooperatively in a consciously aware, positive accord. The era of the cooperation between 'angels and men' will have begun, which allows the externalisation of the New Jerusalem to manifest in the image of Shambhala. Humanity will then be able to reject the thrall and misery that their bondage to the lunar Lords (the sixth Creative Hierarchy) has caused for so long.

Planetary *kuṇḍalinī* was prematurely awakened upon the moon and was abused by the developing mind of its humanity by being directed to stimulating violence and deviant sexuality upon a mass scale. The Lunar Pitris were thoroughly, exaggeratedly empowered and crocodilian energies ran amuck, whilst the few humans whose mindset was Makarian controlled the masses. The inability of the planetary Logos to control this energy rampaging through the planet is the cause of its premature death. All that really developed upon the ancient moon was a immense Lemurian-Atlantean epoch. The corresponding Lemurian period upon the earth was thereby burdened by the incarnation of moon Chain souls into them, necessitating very careful monitoring by those in the then Shambhala. The danger was exemplified at the end of the Atlantean epoch when the energy of mind was released into the civilisation causing the overlay of the worst attributes of the Makarian disposition to manifest upon a vast scale. This produced a repeat of moon

Chain turmoil in widespread black magic and witchcraft. Consequently, that civilisation had to be destroyed by the flood, but the planet was spared. The present epoch is reverberating that ancient *karma,* though now the focus is decidedly materialistic rather than psychic. Now the means of destruction of our civilisation is through Fire (mental and physical), however, the Lords of Life in Shambhala are in control of all karmic forces and trends of the planetary situation.

The long quote below further exemplifies the characteristics of the mental plane, as governed by the fifth Kumāra, the Mother. This She does in conjunction with the three Buddhas of Activity. One should note here the dual aspect of mind/Mind. The three Buddhas of Activity primarily rule over the principle of *ahaṃkāra* (see below), hence the evolution of the empirical mind, whilst the Mother is focussed upon the awakening of the abstract Mind. There is an occult connectivity between the two approaches symbolised by the Eye in the triangle[48] and the building of the *antaḥkaraṇa.* The reader should also refer to the earlier information given concerning the role of the fifth Kumāra and the moon Chain.

The mental plane exemplifies both the worst of what presently dominates human civilisation, plus what heralds the dawn of the new era because of the ability of the fifth plane to become the vehicle of the second. The energy of Love-Wisdom can hence be expressed upon a planet-wide scale, supplanting the epoch of desire-mind. Those that can incorporate Love and Wisdom in their minds become light-bearers of the world. Literally, the concern is with the fusion of the energies of the blue Christ (Love) and that of the green Christ (Wisdom) in terms of the manifestation of their respective planetary dispensations. The green Christ bears the forces of the fifth Creative Hierarchy and the blue Christ that of the fourth Creative Hierarchy. Their united efforts amongst humanity produces that divine Marriage, of which the new era of Love-Wisdom, the major planetary second Ray cycle, is the outcome.

> Let me give you some concise definitions of this ray energy, leaving you to make your own individual application, and from your study of these concepts anent the mind, learn to gauge your own mental condition.

48 Note that with respect to the evolution of the *manasic* principle, this Eye is that of the Mother, but with respect to the evolution of humanity it is that of Sanat Kumāra.

6. The energy of what is so peculiarly called "concrete science" is the quality or the conditioning nature of the fifth ray.
7. It is pre-eminently *the substance* of the mental plane. This plane corresponds to the third subplane of the physical plane, and is therefore gaseous in nature—if you care to use its correspondence as a symbol of its nature. It is volatile, easily dispersed, is the receptive agent of illumination, and can be poisonous in its effect, for there are undoubtedly conditions in which "the mind is the slayer of the Real."
8. This energy is characterised by three qualities:
    a. The quality which is the result of relationship with the Spiritual Triad. We call this "abstract mind" and the impact which affects it comes from the atmic level of the Spiritual Triad, that of spiritual will.
    b. The quality which in this solar system is easily responsive to the major ray of the planet, that of love-wisdom. So responsive is it that—in conjunction with emanations from the three worlds—it has produced the one existent form upon the mental plane. This form (in the planetary sense) is that of the Kingdom of God and, in the individual sense, is that of the ego or soul.
    c. The quality which is basically related to the emanations or vibrations arising from the three worlds; these creatively result in the myriads of thoughtforms which are found upon the lower levels of the mental plane. It might therefore be said that these qualities or aspects of the fifth ray of spiritual energy produce:

        Pure thought
        The thinker or the Son of Mind
        Thoughtforms
9. This energy (as far as mankind is concerned) is the thoughtform making energy, and all impressions from the physical, etheric and astral planes force it into activity on the level of concrete knowledge, with a resultant kaleidoscopic presentation of thoughtforms.
10. It is fundamentally the most potent energy at this time in the planet, because it was brought to maturity in the first solar system, that of active intelligence.
11. It is the energy which admits humanity (and particularly the trained disciple or initiate) into the mysteries of the Mind of God Himself. It is the "substantial" key to the Universal Mind.

12. It is profoundly susceptible to the energy of Love-Wisdom, and its fusion with the love aspect is given the name of "wisdom" by us, because all wisdom is knowledge gained by experience and implemented by love.
13. This energy, in its three aspects, is related in a peculiar sense to the three Buddhas of Activity. These great Lives reached Their present state of development in the previous solar system.
14. This energy, in so far as it is considered as the mental energy of a human being—and this is one of its minor limitations though a major one for a human being—is the higher correspondence of the physical brain. It might be said that the brain exists because the mind exists and needs a brain as its focal point upon the physical plane.
15. The quality of this energy of concrete knowledge or science is twofold:
    a. It is extraordinarily responsive to impressions coming from some source or other.
    b. It is rapidly thrown into forms in response to impression.
16. The impressions received come from three sources and are sequentially revealed to man. These three are:
    a. Impressions from the three worlds; these come, first of all, from the individual and then, secondly, from the levels of planetary consciousness.
    b. Impressions from the soul, the Son of Mind, upon the level of mentality itself.
    c. Impressions from the Spiritual Triad, via the antahkarana; these come when the antahkarana is constructed or in process of construction.
17. This energy is essentially a lightbearer. It responds—again sequentially in time and space—to the light of the Logos. It is for this reason that the mind is regarded both as illumined when higher contacts are present and as an illuminator where the lower planes are concerned.
18. This energy is (from the human standpoint) awakened and brought into activity through the action of the five senses which are the conveyors of information from the three worlds to the mental plane. It might be said that
    a. Five streams of informative energy, therefore, make their impact upon the concrete mind and emanate from the physico-astral plane.

b. Three streams of energy, coming from the soul, also make an impression upon the concrete mind.
c. One stream of energy—during the initiatory process—contacts the mind. This comes from the Spiritual Triad and utilises the antahkarana.

19. The energy of this fifth ray might be regarded as the *commonsense*, because it receives all these impacts of varying energies, synthesises them, produces order out of the many ceaseless impacts and interprets them, thus creating the multiplicity of forms to which we give the name of "world thought".

1. This energy transforms the divine ideas into human ideals, relating the knowledges and sciences of humanity to these ideals, thus making them workable factors in human evolution, its cultures and civilisations.[49]

The Lipika Lords (Mahārājas)

The term Lipika is a Sanskrit term meaning 'scribes' or 'recorders' (from the root *'lip'*, 'to record'), thus they are agents of *karma,* impressing, 'recording' every act or thought instigated by those that manifest volitions in space. But they are more than mere recorders, as they are esoterically the geometricians of any formed space, such as that occupied by a planetary Logos. They circumscribe the *maṇḍalic* patterns that become the blueprint of *manvantaric* space through which the Word of the Logos can sound out and attract the Builders that build the substance of the forms. They are effectively instruments of the Mind of the Creative Logos generating the Plan of what is to be. They are the vehicles of the divine Ideation and express the karmic law from a former cycle of expression into the new paradigm. Hence they work from outside the manifest system, and yet their Ideation is also incorporated within it. They produce the ring-pass-not or sphere of (karmic) limitation of any manifest form, and stand as the 'four corners' of the circumscribed space, which also represent the doorways of escape from that space. Hence there are said to be four (embodying the substance of the Throne of Deity).

In the *Bardo Thödol* they are called the Guardians, or alternatively they are the four Mahārājas, the four great Deva Lords that embody the

49 A.A. Bailey, *The Rays and the Initiations,* 589-592.

substance of the Throne of Deity. These are the four great Rāja (kingly) Lords that embody the four directions in space, the four continents or Elements in Buddhist and Hindu philosophy. They are sometimes equated with the four Kumāras, but more correctly are their Deva compliments. Their technical names in Hinduism[50] are Vessāvana (or Kuvera, north), Virūdhaka (south), Dhataraṭṭha (east), and Virupākśa (west). They are the regents and protectors of the four directions of space; north, south, east, and west, hence are Lipikas that circumscribe the activities of that space and are agents of the related *karma.*

In the book of Revelation the Lipikas are depicted as the 'four beasts full of eyes before and behind' that were 'in the midst of the throne, and round about the throne'.[51] This phrase implies that they are within the body of manifestation, symbolised by the throne, and also 'round about', outside of it, hence outside of formed space. They embody the substance of the *antaḥkaraṇa* from the Mind of the Creative Logos to that which is 'created'. Their 'eyes' *(chakras)* see in all directions of space at once. The description of them is as follows:

> And the first *was* like a lion, and the second beast like a calf, and the third beast had a face as a man, and the fourth beast *was* like a flying eagle.
>
> And the four beasts had each of them six wings about *him;* and they were full of eyes within: and they rest not day and night, saying, Holy, holy, holy, Lord God Almighty, which was, and is, and is to come.[52]

Being 'like a lion' refers to the sign Leo the lion, 'a calf' to Taurus the bull, having a 'face as a man' to Aquarius the water bearer, and 'a flying eagle' to Scorpio the scorpion. They symbolise the fixed cross of the heavens, where Aquarius is north, Leo is south, Taurus is east and Scorpio is west. This is representative of the four quadrants of space ruled by the Mahārājas. Being a fixed cross, we have the energy of consciousness (Love-Wisdom) exemplified, for which they weave the *karma,* not just for humanity but the lower kingdoms of Nature as well.

---

50 For the Buddhist names and qualities of the Guardians, see Volume 5A, 79.

51 *Rev: 4:6.*

52 *Rev: 4:7-8.*

The 'six wings' refer to the substance of the sub-planes of perception embodying the quaternary of deity, where 'wings' are the attributes of the *devas* which they control. The 'eyes' *(chakras)* govern multidimensional space via which they work. Their mantric sound, to make 'holy', refers to the redemption of substance (upon the three planes of *saṃsāra,* hence repeated three times). This process persists throughout the three times: past, present and the future, 'which was, and is, and is to come'.

D.K. states:

> Besides these main presiding Personalities in the Council Chamber at Shamballa, there is a group of four Beings Who are the representatives upon the planet of the four Maharajas, or the four Lords of Karma in the solar system, who are specifically concerned with the evolution at the present time of the human kingdom. These four are connected with:—
>
> 20. The distribution of karma, or human destiny, as it affects individuals, and through the individuals, the groups.
> 21. The care and tabulation of the akashic records. They are concerned with the Halls of Records, or with the "keeping of the book," as it is called in the Christian Bible; They are known in the Christian world as the recording angels.
> 22. The participation in solar councils. They alone have the right during the world cycle to pass beyond the periphery of the planetary scheme, and participate in the councils of the Solar Logos. Thus They are literally planetary mediators, representing our Planetary Logos and all that concerns Him in the greater scheme of which He is but a part.
>
> Co-operating with these karmic Lords are the large groups of initiates and devas who occupy themselves with the right adjustment of:—
>
> a. World karma,
> b. Racial karma,
> c. National karma,
> d. Group karma,
> e. Individual karma,
>
> and who are responsible to the Planetary Logos for the correct manipulation of those forces and building agencies which bring in the right Egos on the different rays at the correct times and seasons.[53]

53 A.A. Bailey, *Initiation, Human and Solar,* 40-41.

We can see from this that they are also an integral part of the Mother's department, essentially directing Wills that coordinate the *devas,* in whose forms the karmic imprint is registered. They direct what has been registered in accordance to the Plan of the presiding Logos in conjunction with the part that the Logos plays within the general solar evolution. The interrelated *karma* must be coordinated also with cosmic *karma,* so that all can move forward as One grand harmonious Scheme. Nothing can be left to chance. Hence all evolve together within One spiral dance of Life. From this perspective Love is the coordinating directive fusion of all separating action *(karma)* into one overall schema of expression. Will is the direction of that expression towards one envisioned goal. Wisdom is the means that determines the right pathways that each disparaging unit must be accommodated in order to produce the envisioned outcome. Tension is produced in the meditative Mind of a Logos as all of these forces are held *in situ* so that the Plan can unfold.

The Lipikas represent the binding forces that weld the activities of the evolving Thought into unity, integrating it as part of a greater expansive Inclusiveness. They move from the great Thought to the lesser ones it incorporates with mathematical precision, projecting the exact coordinates of what is to be, according to a prearranged formula. Hence they are the active Intelligent units of expression Logoically considered. They are the forces of Mahat, the embodiers of the third Ray methodology throughout the aeons of time. They are the Aūṁ of evolutionary being, from whence the septenary of Life's expression rebounds in cyclic reverberation as it converts into the Oṁ of consciousness, cosmic Awareness. Here there is a cross integration with the activity of the three Buddhas of Activity. The Lipikas are the recording agents and the Buddhas the directive Wills. Together they manifest the functions of the 4 + 3, where the Lipikas are focussed via the four cosmic ethers and the building forces of Nature, whilst the Buddhas of Activity control the Lives evolving through the three planes of *saṃsāra.*

The Buddhas of Activity are the directive agents for the *prāṇas* (the lives) that must play a karmic role in what is to be, hence they and their representatives work as transformative agents in the scheme of things. The Lipikas abstract the Lives towards the correct cosmic centres once their purpose in the NOW has been exhausted.

The Lipikas govern the *ākāśic* records, which are the 'records' that are the effect of all actions in thought, word or deed (subtle or gross) of former actions (of past lives) impressed upon the four ethers. They are reflected into manifestation via the sheath of *ākāśic* substance (the third plane of perception) that surrounds all manifest beings. (This sheath manifests as a ring-pass-not for all such actions committed by an evolving entity.) This produces the records of karmic interrelations, as all *karma* is either originally projected from or resolves into *ākāśa*. The *karma* created in the lower planes is thus eventually absorbed into *ākāśa*. All happenings of the past, plus their tendencies in the future, can be instantly contacted by the enlightened one and seen and experienced exactly as they eventuated.

The 'akashic records' that most seers, mediums, and clairvoyants contact is the astral plane reflection of the impression discernable from the higher mental plane. This is accordingly distorted by the state of agitation and colouring of the Waters (emotions/subtle desires), both of the person's own astral body, and upon the sub-plane of the astral from where such impressions are derived. They generally 'see' only fleeting images through veils of glamour, and their desire bodies add the missing portions, thus we have the many erroneous pronouncements and cryptic impressions from such sources.

D.K. states:

> At this point in the treatise we are confining our attention to the Ray of Active Matter, or to that latent heat in substance which underlies its activity and is the cause of its motion. If we think with sincerity and with clarity we will see how closely therefore the Lipika Lords or the Lords of Karma are associated with this work. Three of Them are closely connected with Karma as it concerns one or other of the three great Rays, or the three FIRES, while the fourth Lipika Lord synthesizes the work of his three Brothers and attends to the uniform blending and merging of the three fires. On our planet, the Earth, They find Their points of contact through the three "Buddhas of Activity," (the correspondence should be noted here) and the fourth Kumara, the Lord of the World.[54]

In considering these Fires it should be noted that they are the internal heat *(kuṇḍalinī)* sustaining the three planes of perception wherein

54 A.A. Bailey, *A Treatise on Cosmic Fire,* 74.

humans find their place of experiential attainment, hence wherein the *karma* that is experienced and created by them is sustained. The objective of human evolution is to free itself from such self-conditioned imprisonment, hence the need for mastery of these creative Fires. In doing so people enter *śūnyatā,* the foundation of the training ground that will inevitably lead them out of the conditionings of experience of life on earth and into a field of expression conditioned by cosmic *karma,* as directed by the extra-systemic Lipika. Taking this level of Lipika Lords into account, D.K. states:

> Another series of files in the records give—under a different formula—information as to what is esoterically called "the heat content" of any unit, "the radiating light" of any form, and the "magnetic force" of every life. It is through this knowledge that the Lipikas control the bringing in, and the passing out, of every Life, divine, superhuman, solar and human, and it is through a consideration of that formula which is the basic formula for a solar system that the physical plane appearance of a solar Logos is controlled, and the length of a cosmic pralaya settled...[55] The Lipika Lords, controlling the periodical manifestation of life are, roughly speaking, divided into the following groups, which it might be of interest to note:
>
> 1. Three extra-systemic or cosmic Lords of Karma, Who work from a centre in Sirius through the medium of three representatives. These form a group around the solar Logos, and hold to Him a position analogous to the three Buddhas of Activity Who stand around Sanat Kumara.
> 2. Three Lipika Lords Who are the karmic agents working through the three aspects.
> 3. Nine Lipikas Who are the sumtotal of the agents for the Law working through what the *Qabbalah* calls the nine Sephiroth.
> 4. Seven presiding agents of karma for each one of the seven schemes.
>
> These four groups correspond in manifestation to the Unmanifested, manifesting through the triple Aspects, and under Them work an infinity of lesser agents. These lesser agents might again be somewhat differentiated, each of the following groups being found in every scheme and on every ray-emanation.

55 Ibid., 1142.

1. The Lipika Lords of a scheme Who, through the manipulation of forces, make it possible for a planetary Logos to incarnate under the Law, and work out His cyclic problem.
2. Those who (under the first group) control the destiny of a chain.
3. Those who are the energy-directors of a globe.
4. Agents of every kind Who are concerned with the karmic adjustments, incident upon the periodical manifestation of such forms as:
    a. A round, seven in all.
    b. A kingdom in nature, seven in all.
    c. The human kingdom.
    d. A rootrace, subrace and branch race.
    e. A nation, a family, a group, and their correspondences in all the kingdoms.
    f. A plane.
    g. The reptile and insect world.
    h. The bird evolution.
    i. The devas.
    j. Human units, egoic groups, monadic lives, and myriads of other forms, objective and subjective, planetary and interplanetary, in connection with the Sun, and in connection with the planetoids.[56]

By 'nine Sephiroth' one presumes that D.K. is referring to the nine that are supported by Malkuth, relating to the kingdom of the physical world, as the Sefer Yetzirah designates ten Sephiroth altogether. In the familiar Kabbalistic Tree of Life there are 22 paths leading to Keter, the crown (signifying the Head centre). Interestingly, when we count the 'Three extra-systemic or cosmic Lords of Karma', the 'Three Lipika Lords Who are the karmic agents', the 'Nine Lipikas Who are the sumtotal of the agents for the Law' and the 'Seven presiding agents of karma' then the 22 Lipikas are represented, which one can presume manifest a similar pattern to the interrelation between the triads and squares forming the ladder formation of the Tree of Life. The 3-4 interrelationship also presents the concept of the three falling into the four, where the third point interrelates with the fourth, but not quite completing a square, hence the appearance of the interlaced triangles

56 Ibid., 1142-1144.

making the hexagram of the Seal of Solomon. These 22 energies then bear upon the 'Lipika Lords of a scheme', which takes the role of Malkuth. It is interesting to note that the number 22 also relates to the ten planetary and twelve zodiacal energies that must be similarly borne by a planetary Logos. From this perspective it is a number that relates to an adept, one who has mastered these energies.

It is tempting to associate each of the *yugas,* a great age or era of the evolutionary journeying, a divine year, to the jurisdiction of one or other of the Mahārājas, as a *yuga* is one of the four ages of the world. They are the *kṛta, tretā, dvārpara,* and the *kali yuga,* signifying the golden, silver, brass and iron ages respectively. The series is proceeded in succession during the *manvantaric* cycle. Each *yuga* is preceded by a period called *sandhya* (twilight) or transition period, and is followed by another period of like duration called *sandhyāsana,* 'portion of twilight'. Each *sandhyāsana* is equal to one-tenth of the *yuga.* A group of four *yugas* are expressions based on the *divine* years. Each such year being equal to 360 human years. Thus we have, in *divine years:*

1.	Krita or Satya Yuga	4,000
	Sandhyā	400
	Sandhyāsana	400
		4,800
2.	Tretā Yuga	3,000
	Sandhyā	300
	Sandhyāsana	300
		3,600
3.	Dvāpara Yuga	2,000
	Sandhyā	200
	Sandhyāsana	200
		2,400
4.	Kali Yuga	1,000
	Sandhyā	100
	Sandhyāsana	100
		1,200
	Total	12,000

12,000 divine years multiplied by 360 such days makes the complete period of these four ages. This rendered in years of mortals equals:

4,800 x 360	=	1,728,000
3,600 x 360	=	1,296,000
2,400 x 360	=	864,000
1,200 x 360	=	432,000
Total		4,320,000

The above is called a *mahāyuga* or *manvantara.* 2,000 such *manvantaras,* or a period of 8,640,000,000 years, make a *kalpa;* the latter being only a day and night, or twenty-four hours, of Brahmā. Thus an age of Brahmā, or one hundred years of his divine years, equals 311,040,000,000,000 of our mortal years. A *yuga* is a 1,000th part of a *kalpa.*

These four *yugas* represent the stages of descent of mind into complete incarnation into the physical vehicle *(kali yuga)* wherein the most evil *karma* is generated. This takes the reverberation of many cycles of incarnations to cleanse. It is mind, fused with the emotions, that produces the intensity of the personal *karma* that most people bear. However, the foundations for the world, racial, national and group *karma* is set in the earlier *yugas.* They establish the background for the expression for individual *karma* that finds its apogee in the *kali yuga.*

In terms of the trinities mentioned above we can see that *satya yuga,* as part of the accounting, being 'golden', literally relates to a sub-period of *pralaya* (after-death state) within a *manvantaric* cycle, or periods of rest (disincarnation) for the evolving *jīvas.* After this they find opportunity to incarnate again. It can also refer to the childhood stage to adolescence of an evolutionary period, such as the first two Root Races of humanity. The mind is not developed, hence the karmic volition associated with its expression is practically non-existent. The Lipika presiding over this period can be considered the Lord of the *karma* that synthesises the fruits of the remaining three, i.e., the period of incarnatory expression.

The Lipikas integrate the *karma* of the kingdoms of Nature with extra-systemic *karma.* The Buddhas of Activity integrate the *karma* of the earth sphere for the three kingdoms of Nature. Sanat Kumāra at the centre holds the entire planetary construct into a unity. The first Lipika embodies the substance of the ring-pass-not of the planetary sphere and integrates it with all similar spheres in the solar system, so that they all share the same karmic interrelationships within the solar *mahāmanvantara*. The Mother of the World controls the *deva* substance within this sphere wherein all of this activity occurs, and within whose bodies of manifestation the karmic imprint manifests. Hence She represents the central coordinating factor of *karma*, via which the Buddhas of Activity manifest their purpose.

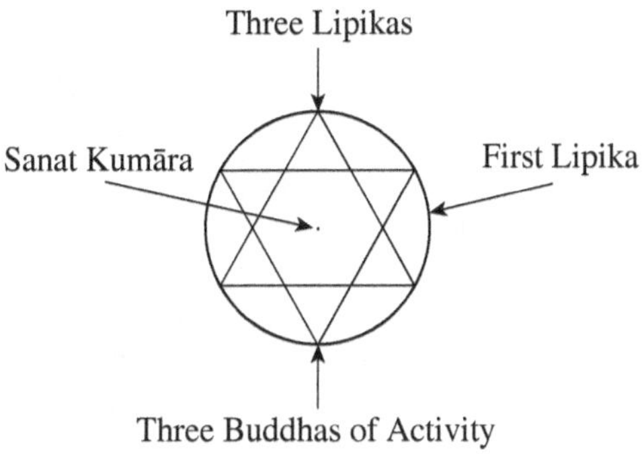

Figure 26. The Lipikas and the Buddhas of Activity

In relation to the factor of the *devas* in this respect D.K. states:

> The devas are the agents of the divine will because they are a consequence of the point of attainment of our planetary Logos as He exists outside the seven planes of our sphere of existence, the cosmic physical plane. They are conditioned by His cosmic astral and mental vehicles. In a definite sense, they *are* the agents of the Universal Mind, even though they are *not* mental *as we understand that term.* They are sometimes regarded as blind forces, but that is only because they get their inspiration from levels of divine awareness outside the range of the human consciousness, no matter how high, or when used in its widest connotation.
>
> Their controlling Agent in manifestation is the Triangle of Energy to which we give the name the "Three Buddhas of Activity." They are therefore closely connected with the third aspect of divinity. They are essentially the "eye within the Triangle"—a most familiar symbol to

many today. They are the expression, in activity, of the All-See-ing Eye"; through their agency God *sees*, and through them and the energy directed through them, He directs the creative process. They are under the complete control of the three Buddhas of Activity, Who are the cosmic Prototypes of the Lords of the three major rays, but not in the sense usually understood when the rays are considered in their relation to man. They are the correspondence of these three rays and are responsible for the entire manifested universe, but only within the orbit of the third aspect, the expression of the Universal Mind.

They come from the cosmic mental plane, just as the energy—distinctive of the second aspect—comes from the cosmic astral plane. God is mind. God is intelligent functioning. God is creative activity. *These are the qualities of the deva evolution.* God is love. God is relationship. God is consciousness. These are *the three qualities of the Christ evolution.* This latter evolution is carried on within the created sphere of influence of the third aspect. God is life. God is fire. God is pure being. *These are the qualities of the spirit aspect, the omnipotent aspect of Deity.* All these three aspects focus themselves and find an outlet for expression upon the levels of the cosmic etheric planes and upon the levels of the etheric planes known to humanity in the three worlds. The Law of Correspondences is infallible, if rightly approached and applied.[57]

Detailing further the role of the Buddhas of Activity D.K. states:

It might here be pointed out that:

a. The work of the deva evolution comes under the ray energy of the third Buddha of Activity.
b. The work with humanity comes under the influence of the ray energy of the second Buddha of Activity, Who embodies in a most peculiar sense the conditioning energy of the Hierarchy.
c. The work with the subhuman kingdoms of nature is under the energy stimulation of the first Buddha of Activity.

Each of these great energising Lives works through certain Masters and Initiates of the sixth initiation; these Masters work in full consciousness upon the atmic plane, the plane of the spiritual will; from that high

57 A.A. Bailey, *The Rays and the Initiations,* 179-180.

> level, They function as transmitting agents for the energy of one of the three Buddhas of Activity. These three Buddhas are the creative Agents of the planetary Logos and are Wielders of the Law of Evolution.[58]

Effectively, the Mother, as the fifth Kumāra, is the 'eye within the Triangle' controlling the function of the *devas,* through whose agency the planetary Logos can See into manifest space. Hence the Mother represents the *iḍā* aspect of the Eye of Logoic Vision (the Ājñā centre) via embodying the mental substance of the fifth plane of perception. By incorporating the substance of the minds/Minds of humanity via the *devas,* all of the three planes of *saṃsāra* are thus open to Logoic Vision. (One must remember here that the mental plane represents cosmic dense physical substance for the Lords of Shambhala, hence would otherwise be inaccessible.)

The Buddhas of Activity are extremely exalted entities, Lords of Sacrifice that have incarnated into our planetary sphere because of the disastrous happenings upon the moon Chain. Because of the success of the dark brotherhood upon that Chain the cosmic Door of entry to our planetary Scheme was opened wide, with many black adepts of that past cycle having gained far greater power, Initiations, along the line of Mahat (cosmic lower Mind). The process concerning the closing of that Door has consequently to be carefully regulated by the Buddhas of Activity working in conjunction with the Lipikas. Hence a fundamental aspect of their Service is to help the Mother of the World to rectify the mistakes made in that Chain, by carefully regulating cosmic *karma* via the *deva* evolution. In doing so they work through the great Mother via the plane *ātma* and its reflection upon the mental plane (the Fires of Mind) the creative principle commonly accessed by both *devas* and humans. We can see from above, this interrelationship is fundamentally between the Mother and the third Buddha of Activity.

Because of the moon Chain failure, the Mother of the World has played a passive, subsidiary role under the directive of this third Buddha of Activity and Sanat Kumāra, but will now manifest a more proactive, forthright function in planetary affairs, as the cycle has appeared for a significant portion of that ancient *karma* to be cleansed. For this reason

58 Ibid., 587.

there has been a ferocious attempt by the dark brotherhood to offset the planned beauty of the coming era concerning the cooperation between three kingdoms - the human, the *deva,* and the Kingdom of 'God'.

We can see that the main effect of the forces of evil upon the planet is obtained by controlling the agenda of the ideas and ideologies fed to humanity by the mass media and the psychopaths in power over all branches of our governments, principally in the Western world. The ideologies and incessant lies bleated out by the propaganda machines that are antagonistic to what benefits humanity in general, must be adamantly countered by the disciples of the world. Here the main battle lines are drawn. The main weapon nowadays for the forces of light to overcome the massed disinformation against the world's population is the internet. Many bloggers and conscientious journalists have appeared, largely unfunded, that have taken up the challenge of the good fight, whilst many whistleblowers have been incarcerated. They are attacked by the mainstream media with their vast resources, assisted by government agencies. Western governments are increasingly creating fascist laws (such as Germany with respect to the Holocaust issue) denying freedom of speech to their citizens. Myriad are the methods that the incarnate forces of darkness have at their disposal to prevent truths on many subjects to appear, so that their agenda for total planetary control can be gained. Their power upon the physical domain is at present overwhelmingly vast, but there is a Hierarchical agenda currently in swing to overcome this.

The Buddhas of Activity further explained

In the book *The Rays and the Initiations,* D.K. gives his final detailed presentation concerning the role of the Buddhas of Activity, which I shall quote in full.

> First, let me make reference to the words "the Higher Three"; let me see if I cannot somewhat clarify the entire complex idea. The words "Higher Three" refer to the three Buddhas of Activity Who still remain actively cooperating with the Lord of the World. They are, as you have been told, close to Sanat Kumara and came with Him when He decided to take incarnation through the medium of our planet, Earth. It is difficult to understand Their mysterious and peculiar

functions. They do not belong to this solar system at all; They have passed through the human stage in such far distant and remote world cycles that the experience is no longer a part of Their consciousness; They act as advisors to Sanat Kumara where His initial purpose is concerned, and that is why the words "the will of God holds sway" occur in this rule. It is Their supreme task to see that, in the Council Chamber of Shamballa, that purpose is ever held steadily within the "area of preparation" (I know not how else to word it) of that Council. They function, in a peculiar sense, as linking intermediaries between the Logos of our solar system and the informing Life of the constellation Libra; They relate these two great centres of energy to our planetary Logos.

In the last solar system They were the planetary Logoi of three planets in which the mind principle reached its highest stage of development; They embody in Themselves in a most peculiar manner the wisdom aspect of the second ray, as it expresses itself primarily through what has been called in the Bhagavad Gita "skill in action." Hence Their name, the Buddhas of Activity.

Sanat Kumara has now moved one step ahead of Them upon the great cosmic ladder of evolution, for an aspect of the Law of Sacrifice has conditioned Them. However, within the planetary consciousness and among Those Who work out the divine purposes, there are none Who approach the Eternal Youth and these three Buddhas in point of Evolution. They work out Their plans—these four Great Lives—through the medium of the Lords of the Seven Rays. Under the Law of Analogy, They are to Sanat Kumara what the three mind aspects upon the mental plane are to the disciple and the initiate. They represent in action:

The concrete or lower mind of the planetary Logos,
That energy which we call the soul and which the disciple calls "the Son of Mind,"
The higher or abstract mind,

but all this from cosmic levels and with cosmic implications. It was Their activity which (after evolution had run a long course) brought about the act of individualisation and thus brought the human kingdom into existence. In a mysterious sense, therefore, it might be said that the three Buddhas of Activity are responsible for:

4. *The Act of Individualisation.* The work of the particular Buddha responsible at the time for this major activity, has been temporarily

quiescent since Lemurian days. He works, when active, through the seventh ray and draws the needed energy from two constellations: Cancer and Gemini.

5. *The Act of Initiation.* I would call your attention to the word *act*; I am not here referring to process. His work only begins at the third initiation when the planetary Logos is the Initiator. At that initiation, the will aspect begins to function. The Buddha behind the initiatory process is extremely active at this time; He works through the Christ and the Lord of the second ray, drawing the needed energy from the constellations Capricorn and Aquarius.
6. *The Act of Identification.* This involves what has been called a "moment of opening-up," during which the initiate sees that which lies within the cosmic intent and begins to function not only as a planetary unit but as a cosmic focal point. The Buddha of Activity, responsible for this type of planetary activity, works with the Lord of the first ray and functions as an outpost of the consciousness of the informing life of Aries and of Leo. His work is only now beginning to assume importance.

I realise that this information has little meaning to you and lies beyond your understanding, but so was much that I gave you in *A Treatise on Cosmic Fire.* Its sole value for you lies in the revelation of the linking up and the interplay between all parts of our solar system, our universe and the zodiac. Through these three great Buddhas there is a basic relation, established aeons ago and steadfastly held, between our planet, three of the seven sacred planets, and six of the major constellations—the three and the six which most uniquely concern the fourth kingdom in nature. Other planets and other constellations are also related to the human family, but their relation is more aggressively (if I might use that word) related to the three subhuman kingdoms; with these we shall not here deal. Their relation to the human kingdom has been covered by me in the astrological section of this Treatise: *A Treatise on the Seven Rays*, Vol. III (*Esoteric Astrology*).

You will note that I have here indicated the existence of five triangles:

1. That existing in the interplay of the energies of the three Buddhas of Activity Who create a triangle, closely related to the planet Saturn.

2. The triangle of the three rays through whom the three Buddhas work.
3. The three planets which are connected with the three Lords of the three rays and by means of which They express Their impelling energy.

4 - 5. Two interlaced triangles, created by the six constellations from which the three Buddhas of Activity draw Their needed energy and to which They are uniquely related through Their individual karma. These two interlaced triangles are the cause of the six-pointed star, so familiar among the many occult symbols.

From the Law of Analogy, another exceedingly important triangle is found in the human body and (esoterically considered) is related to the subject under consideration:

7. *The ajna centre*, embodying the directing energy of that body of activity which we call the personality.
8. *The throat centre*, which is peculiarly active today in all human beings; this testifies to the success of the creative work of the Buddhas of Activity. This, in its turn, has a small symbolic triangle of its own, to which I would call attention: the thyroid gland and the para-thyroids.
9. *The centre at the base of the spine*. This is galvanised into activity at a certain stage of the evolutionary process, by energy emanating from the Buddhas of Activity Who are the least active at this particular time. It is an energy pouring towards the fourth kingdom but *not* directed towards any individual. These great Lives work through major groups. Their potency is such that it would otherwise prove destructive.

The purpose of Deity is necessarily embodied in a mental proposition; it is through this mental proposition that the three Buddhas of Activity implement Their work. I can put it no clearer. There will come a time in the experience of all initiates when—each for himself—a formulation of this mental proposition will be absolutely necessary. By means of this, each initiate will embody his individual understanding of the divine purpose as the Plan has been revealed to him.

This he can do only through the means of group experience, in cooperation with his group and when the group—as a whole—has reached a similar point of realisation and has *together* touched the fringes of this highest of all revelations for humanity. When, for the first time, they succeed in doing this, they will come—as a group—under the direct emanation of the Higher Three and under an aspect of the Council Chamber at Shamballa which has been hitherto unknown and unrealised. This will connote a high stage of initiation of the group and is, in effect, connected with inter-hierarchical activity. It is a working out into the consciousness of the group members of an event which has taken place within the Ashram of Sanat Kumara, the Hierarchy itself; this takes place through the stimulation of all the Ashrams at a certain Full Moon, and concerns the relation of the Ashrams as a whole to Shamballa, and not to Humanity.

Can you grasp something of what I am endeavouring somewhat unsuccessfully to convey? There is an ashramic activity of which disciples know nothing in their brain consciousness until such time as the third initiation has been taken and the results of it are then dimly but increasingly sensed. It is related to the interplay between Shamballa and the Hierarchy, but not between the Hierarchy and Humanity. It concerns the purpose and the plan as the latter is the instrument of the former. The event of realisation takes place via the triad formed by a Master and His two senior disciples, or it is formed by three Masters all upon the same ray, as for instance, the Master K.H. and his Ashram, myself and my Ashram and another affiliated Ashram.

It is for this reason that in all exoteric groups connected with an Ashram, there is always a group leader and two others who are the reflection or the correspondence to the higher triad. This is part of the externalisation of the Hierarchy which is proceeding rapidly at this time.

The importance of understanding the function of triangles is a prime necessity. A hint lies here for students in the political realm, where every country, under differing names, has its chosen ruler, and its ministers responsible for home affairs (or interior relations), and its foreign secretary, responsible for exoteric relationships.

One further point anent the Buddhas of Activity might here be of interest. Each of Them has a special relation to the three races which have been or are strictly human: these are the third, the fourth and the fifth rootraces which we call the Lemurian, the Atlantean and the present Aryan race (I do *not* use the word "Aryan" in the manner of the German race). In some peculiar manner, They represent in Shamballa the soul of each of these three races. One thing complicates this question for you, but it is in reality quite simple. The same souls re-incarnate in each race, and each soul therefore comes in turn under the influence of each of the three Buddhas, each of Whom is of a quality different to that of his two Associates. They represent—in Their lowest aspect—the three aspects of the mind, as I earlier said. There is:

10. The instinctual nature as it develops into the mind nature and makes a transition into an automatic, subconscious character and—at the same time—assumes some of its paralleling higher qualities.

11. The lower concrete mind in its more developed stage, as it gradually assumes control and supersedes instinct in the consciousness of man. The Buddhas of Activity preside over what might be called (using a technical, occult term) the ahamkara principle—the mind as it serves the selfish interests of man and enables man thereby to achieve a sense of proportion and a finer estimate of values. Forget not that selfishness is a stage of unfoldment, and that it is a necessary stage whereby humanity learns the price of self-interest.

12. The personality mind. This assumes control over the man and leads him to prove the nature of power and of success and—above all else—of integration. This too is a necessary phase and precedes a stage of awakening.

These three great Lives Who have associated Themselves with the Lord of the World might be regarded as constituting aspects of His personality, though this is *not* technically so. The name Sanat Kumara is not His true name; it is only the first letter of that name which is known only to the Masters, whilst the second letter is known only to the Chohans. The first syllable of His name is known in the Council Chamber at Shamballa, but the rest of His name remains unknown as yet. The three Buddhas of Activity are to the planetary Logos (to give you another definition) what the Spiritual Triad is to the dedicated personality of the initiated disciple, for such is the spiritual status of the planetary Logos; the one of the three Buddhas now coming into activity is the one Who works through the spiritual will.

Within the body of the planetary Logos humanity is slowly building that which they call the antahkarana; this is, in reality, the linking thread between the head centre of Sanat Kumara and His heart centre. Ponder on these words. There is a mystery involved here and it is little that I can do to make it clearer. As humanity builds or creates the triangles of light and of goodwill, they are in reality invoking a response activity from two of the Buddhas of Activity—the One Who works through the medium of the will aspect, and the One Who works through love in humanity, *intelligently* applied. Forget not that these three great Buddhas summarise in a peculiar sense the transmuted essence of the previous solar system in which intelligent activity was the goal. Today, that essence underlies all the activity of this solar system but is motivated by love, which was not the case in the earlier manifestation. The Buddhas Themselves form a deeply esoteric Triangle.

The two types of triangles now being created by a mere handful of people are related to that basic triangle. A third type of triangle will at some much later date be constructed but only when these two earlier types are well established in the consciousness of humanity. Then the activity of all the three Buddhas will be involved and present, and a major planetary integration will take place. This is symbolised in man when the three centres in the head (the ajna centre, the brahmarandra centre, and the alta major centre) are all functioning and unshakably related, thereby constituting a triangle of light within the head.

From the triangles now being created and those later to be assembled, the Buddhas of Activity will extract that essential quality (at present very rarely to be found) which will go to the building of this aspect of the planetary antahkarana.

The triangles of light and of goodwill are essentially invocative. They constitute the a.b.c. of the coming Science of Invocation. Their strength is dependent upon the depth of feeling in the one case, and the strength of the will in the other, with which they are created. I have here given those disciples who are launching this new project which is so close to my heart a new and useful hint. This work *must* go on. It is because the entire concept is so new and different to anything hitherto projected that it seems so impossible of achievement; the triangles project has its incentive in such highly esoteric sources that some disciples regard the work as exceedingly difficult and thus complicate, by their thinking, its essential simplicity; others regard it as the simplest thing in the world, and by an emphasis upon the exoteric and the organisational angle, they again hinder the true type of triangle being created. Disciples need to be aware of the true proposed plan and find ways to make clear the middle position between the difficulties brought forward and the simplicities which distort.[59]

---

59 A.A. Bailey, *The Rays and the Initiations*, 267-274.

First, with respect to the statement that the Buddhas of Activity act 'as linking intermediaries between the Logos of our solar system and the informing Life of the constellation Libra', it can be said that Libra controls the manifestation of the law of Karma and of the appearance of cycles. Regulation of cosmic *karma* is necessary if the flow of the activities of the cosmic dark forces are to manifest in relation to the doors of opportunity for the appearance of their activities upon earth. Cosmic *karma* must be rightly coordinated throughout our solar system so only that which is appropriate under the law can manifest. This is also determined by the invocative appeal of humanity reaching out into cosmic space that will call into manifestation such forces and entities. The Buddhas of Activity act as conditioning agents for the encroachment of the forces of evil, sieving out what is impermissible from the available forces, hence the cycles allowing the dark brotherhood to appear are rightly monitored. Such activity comes under the jurisdiction of cosmic Intelligence and has its roots in the activity of the past solar system, wherein the dark brotherhood were spawned. They therefore represent the karmic heirloom of the Buddhas of Activity, the unregenerate aspect of that evolution which still needs conversion.

The happening upon the moon Chain empowered the dark brotherhood that had evolved in the previous solar system and generated the karmic duty (coming under the auspices of the Lord of Saturn) of the Buddhas of Activity. Their own evolution was set back somewhat whilst they tackled the problem under the law of Sacrifice. The earth has inherited this problematic *karma,* causing the necessity for the close involvement of the three Buddhas of Activity with our planet. Aspects of mind (mental-emotional *saṃskāras),* cosmically considered, still need to be resolved via this relationship.

In relation to the statement that 'In the last solar system They were the planetary Logoi of three planets in which the mind principle reached its highest stage of development', it can be imputed that D.K. is here referring to the Soul aspect of what he depicts elsewhere in his writings, who therefore are Avatars, the embodied 'Personality expression', of these former planetary Logoi. The Avatars therefore limit, 'tone down', the Potency of what would otherwise be expressed. Here there appears to be a conflict with D.K.'s earlier statement:

> The Lord of the World, the first Kumara, is the planetary Logos of our scheme in physical incarnation, but nowhere has the impression been conveyed that the three Kumaras, associated with Him, are three other planetary Logoi. This is in no way the case. These three, called the "Buddhas of Activity," are but the vicegerents upon our planet of those three planetary Logoi, Who, with our planetary Logos, make the sum total of the logoic Quaternary.

One can reconcile the apparent discrepancy in that the first statement refers to their actual role in the last solar system, where all have since moved on to other cosmic roles, whereas the second statement refers to the *present* solar system. Here they do not manifest as planetary Logoi, but rather are 'vicegerents', delegators of the power of any planetary or solar Logos to which they are affiliated to our earth.

The statement that 'Sanat Kumara has now moved one step ahead of Them upon the great cosmic ladder of evolution, for an aspect of the law of Sacrifice has conditioned Them' can be considered in the light of the work still needing to be accomplished by the Sacrifice of the Buddhas of Activity. The law of Sacrifice is the law of limitation that binds one to a form until a certain chore has been completed. Sanat Kumāra's prime 'chore' is the liberation of the humanity upon the earth, whereas the work of the three Buddhas of Activity is the conversion of the dark forces, the solar *saṃskāras,* the principle of *ahaṃkāra,*[60] that remained from past Incarnations of planetary Logoi. (This principle relates to the substance of the three lowest planes of perception.) Such forces have preyed upon the present humanity, continuing a most ancient

---

60 *Ahaṃkāra* (from *aham* ego, the 'I', plus *kāra, a* maker, that which acts) is the force that generates the self-focussed ego, the I-concept born of *avidya* (ignorance), and which differentiates itself from the universal self. I-am-ness, the principle of individuality, self-sense, the tendency towards definiteness, origin of all manifestation. It is the thought of selfhood, that the individual contains some immortal and unchanging faculty of the Soul, when in reality there is no such phenomenal thing, for everything is in perpetual flux and changes in relation to everything else around it. There is, however, a higher version of this concept of 'selfhood'. This concerns the drawing down of the qualities of the highest principle within the person, the Father or Monadic aspect (the Buddha within, or else the *tathāgatagarbha*), for the purpose of awakening the highest spiritual possibilities, making the divine 'individuality' of the Master, Arhat, or Adept possible.

pattern of expression, which would regress the all back to the past, hence destroying present Logoic purpose.

The significance of the manifestation of *ahaṃkāra* in relation to the three Buddhas of Activity upon a planetary scale is hid in the statement:

> The Buddhas of Activity, Who embody within Themselves the essence of the third Ray of Active Intelligence, through which the third aspect can successfully project and express itself. It is these three Buddhas Who were instrumental in the amazing and occult process of implementing the mental principle upon our planet, and Who—through Their creative meditation—brought our planet, the Earth, and the planet Venus into direct alignment. This made possible the comings of the Sons of Mind and the formation of the fourth kingdom in nature, Humanity. They are Embodiments of the intuition, and control the inflow of intuitional energy into the minds of men.[61]

From the definition of *ahaṃkāra* we see that it is a necessary principle in evolution because it allows the development of the intellect, the principle that distinguishes the one from the other. However, this principle also needs to be superseded by that which integrates the one into the all, and this conversion process concerns the development of Love-Wisdom and the making of a Dragon of Wisdom. What does not convert must be recycled until it can do so. The mystery of Makara relates to this process. The incarnating *jīva* (individual life force, a human unit) must undergo the conversion according to its own inherent will to overcome mental-emotional *saṃskāras* (which collectively can be considered Makara). The process produces the attainment of Initiation. The Buddhas of Activity preside over the act of Initiation, which seals the accomplishment achieved by the *jīva,* liberating the being to a higher level of freedom to act. The energies of the two signs Capricorn and Aquarius are drawn upon in this liberating act. Capricorn is the mount of mind, whose substance is being transformed into Mind, whilst the Fiery Waters of Aquarius are used to transform the hardened substance of mind into an Airy universality of expression.

Concerning the 'Two interlaced triangles, created by the six constellations' we see that the upright triangle consists of Aries, Gemini

61 A.A. Bailey, *Discipleship in the New Age,* Vol. II, 200.

(the right side) and Cancer (the left side), and an inverted triangle with Leo at the bottom, Aquarius at the right side and Capricorn at the left. The inverted triangle refers to the triangle of Initiation for humanity, wherein they need to overcome egotistic pursuits (Leo), thus becoming the selfless world server (Aquarius) whilst climbing the mount of Initiation (Capricorn). Upon the mount one ascends to experience the attributes of cosmic Mind. The upright triangle concerns the way of ascending towards attaining cosmic Individualisation by way of mastering cosmic Mind. Planetary Individualisation has been left behind, but the Initiate now walks the way of the Christ in Gemini, administering to the needs of both human and *deva* evolution in the adytum of Life.[62] In doing so the Door to the cosmic astral plane opens wide and the respective chosen cosmic Path can be trod (Cancer). This eventually leads to that higher cycle of expression of cosmic Will and projection of the *antaḥkaraṇa* (Aries) after the attainment of the ninth Initiation (Capricorn) that leads to the higher cosmic Mental domains (and the appropriation of a Causal Form) in preparation to become a Logos of a planetary sphere. (If that is the direction of the associated Initiate's Decision.) Such is the task eventually confronting all of us.

The statement that each of the Buddhas of Activity 'has a special relation to the three races which have been or are strictly human: these are the third, the fourth and the fifth rootraces which we call the Lemurian, the Atlantean and the present Aryan race' implies that as we enter into a new era with the emergence of the sixth Root Race, then the main work of the three Buddhas will cease. The epoch of the fifth Kumāra will then commence, who will oversee the expression of the abstract Mind that will be the forte of this Root Race, whereas the evolution of the empirical mind and then overcoming the negative attributes of *ahaṃkāra* was the objective of the former three. The awakening of Mind necessitates the marriage between human and *deva* forces (the *iḍā* and *piṅgalā nāḍīs)* in consciousness. The epoch of the Mother of the World commences as this happens upon a large scale. The process also converts those *devas* whose bodies of expression were grossly distorted and their functions stifled, malformed by the energies of the wielders of *ahaṃkāra*. Beauty, harmony and peaceful coexistence

62 In this case these evolutions become the pillars of the temple ruled by Gemini.

will descend upon the nations of the world, producing transcendental scientific achievements, as the gnosis of the higher Mind begins to produce the forthcoming civilisation.

It should be noted that there are held 'great Councils' once a century whereby the great Lives supporting Sanat Kumāra are contacted and the Plan for the forthcoming century and even millennia are discussed. This is necessary in order to fine tune developments upon the earth, and to ensure that all that are to play a role in the external affairs of the planet manifest in accord to the Divine Ideation, and the necessary *karma* is appropriately adjudicated. As D.K. states:

> The major characteristic of these Lives is Will or Purpose. They embody and consciously know and intelligently appreciate what is the motivating idea which the Planetary Logos—working consciously on His own high level—seeks to work out and achieve in His planned incarnation through a planet. He functions when in incarnation on the cosmic physical plane, and embodies the seven principles of which we know, and all is focussed in and through the Individuality of Sanat Kumara, implemented and energised through the seven planetary centres. The three Buddhas of Activity (Who are also Members of the Great Council) are expressions of the counterparts on cosmic levels of the energies latent in the three permanent atoms in the three worlds of human endeavour. This is again a dangerous parallel to propose for—as a symbol—it lacks any true analogy.
>
> The Seven Spirits before the Throne of God are also Members of the Council, and each of Them is in close rapport and contact with one or other of the seven sacred planets in our solar system, and can thus draw upon the energies which they embody.
>
> It will therefore be apparent to you inferentially, how comparatively few of the Members of our Hierarchy have yet been able to reach the state or condition of development which would warrant Their forming a part of the great Council, or which would enable them to respond to the O, sounded out at intervals of one hundred years by Sanat Kumara. It is this sound which gathers together the responsive Units into the Council. This Council is held at one hundred year intervals, and as far as our modern humanity is concerned, these Councils have been held—under our arbitrary dates—in 1725, 1825, 1925.
>
> At these Councils, Those Who are responsible for the planetary development, along certain predetermined lines, make Their reports;

> decision is made as to new unfoldments; certain types of energy, cosmic and solar, are made available for the carrying forward of the Plans which implement the Purpose; the evolution of consciousness in the three worlds receives, necessarily, major attention.
>
> I would have you remember that this refers not only to the human kingdom and its unfoldment, but to the three subhuman kingdoms also which are—from many points of view—of equal importance to the human. This is a hard saying for humanity to accept.[63]

D.K. makes the comparison of the three Buddhas of Activity to the three permanent atoms because in those atoms is stored the *karma* of the reincarnating *jīvas,* those that must access the three vehicles of their personality expression. Similarly, upon a Logoic scale the three Buddhas regulate the sum of the *karma* of the physical manifestation of our planetary Logos.

During the 2025 Gemini full moon the great Hierarchical centennial Council fine-tuned the final stages of the reappearance process of Hierarchy. This will involve the planned happenings concerning the prophesied Avatar, plus other activities to manifest over the next hundred years, and on, so as to produce the advent of the new Aquarian epoch, and the making of the earth a sacred planet. This mainly involves the mode of the rectification of the *karma* from the moon Chain. The reverberations of this activity will carry through into the next globe of the earth Scheme that will bear human life. Far-sighted are all such plans by Hierarchy.

---

63 A.A. Bailey, *The Rays and the Initiations,* 206-207.

Bibliography

Alford, Alan F. *Gods of the New Millennium.* London: New English Library, 1994.

Bailey, Alice A. *A Treatise on Cosmic Fire.* New York: Lucis Publishing Company, 1973.

——. *A Treatise on White Magic.* London: Lucis Publishing Company, 1934.

——. *Destiny of the Nations.* London: Lucis Publishing Company, 1949.

——. *Discipleship in the New Age, Volume II.* London: Lucis Publishing Company, 1979.

——. *Esoteric Astrology.* London: Lucis Publishing Company, 1968.

——. *Esoteric Healing,* London: Lucis Publishing Company, 1953.

——. *Esoteric Psychology, Volumes 1 and II.* London: Lucis Publishing Company, 1977.

——. *Glamour, a World Problem.* London: Lucis Publishing Company, 1950.

——. *Initiation, Human and Solar.* New York: Lucis Publishing Company, 1972.

——. *The Externalisation of the Hierarchy.* New York: Lucis Publishing Company, 1988.

——. *The Labours of Hercules.* New York: Lucis Publishing Company, 1974.

——. *The Rays and the Initiations.* New York: Lucis Publishing Company, 1960.

——. *The Reappearance of the Christ.* New York: Lucis Publishing Company, 1947.

——. *The Unfinished Autobiography.* New York: Lucis Publishing Company, 1951.

Balsys, Bodo. *Ahimsā: Buddism and the Vegetarian Ideal.* New Delhi: Munishram Manoharlal, 2004.

——. *A Treatise on Mind, Volume 1* Sydney: Universal Dharma Publishing, 2016.

——. *A Treatise on Mind, Volume 2* Sydney: Universal Dharma Publishing, 2016.

——. *A Treatise on Mind, Volume 3* Sydney: Universal Dharma Publishing, 2016.

——. *A Treatise on Mind, Volume 4* Sydney: Universal Dharma Publishing, 2015.

——. *A Treatise on Mind, Volume 5A* Sydney: Universal Dharma Publishing, 2015.

——. *A Treatise on Mind, Volume 5B* Sydney: Universal Dharma Publishing, 2015.

——. *A Treatise on Mind, Volume 6* Sydney: Universal Dharma Publishing, 2014.

——. *Karma and the Rebirth of Consciousness.* Delhi: Munshiram Manoharlal, 2006.

Bauval, Robert and Gilbert, Adrian. *The Orion Mystery.* London: Mandarin, 1994.

Balyoz, Harold. *Three Remarkable Women.* Flagstaff, Arizona: Altai Publishers, 1986.

Bernbaum, Edwin. *The Way to Shambhala.* New York: Anchor Books, 1980.

Besant, Annie and Das, Bhagavan. *The Bhagavad Gītā.* Adyar: Theosophical Publishing House, 1926.

Blavatsky, H.P. *The Secret Doctrine. Vol. 3.* Adyar: Theosophical Publishing House, 1962.

Chang, Garma C.C. *The Hundred Thousand Songs of Milarepa.* University Books, 1962.

Cowell, E. B. *Buddhist Mahāhyāna Texts.* Delhi: Motilal Banarsidass, 1997.

Drayer, Ruth A. *Nicholas and Helena Roerich.* Illinois: Wheaton, 2005.

Evans-Wentz, W.Y. *Tibetan Yoga and Secret Doctrines.* London: Oxford University Press, 1958.

——. *Tibet's Great Yogi, Milarepa.* London: Oxford University Press, 1972.

Gilbert, Adrian. *Signs in the Sky.* New York: Three Rivers Press, 2000.

Guirand, Felix. *The New Larousse Encyclopedia of Mythology.* London: Hamlyn, 1983.

Graves, Robert. *The Greek Myths, Complete Edition.* London: Penguin, 1992.

Gyatso, Khedrup Norsang. *Ornament of Stainless Light. An Exposition of the Kālacakra Tantra.* Boston: Wisdom Publications, 2004.

Gyatso, Tenzin and Hopkins, Jeffrey. *Kālachakra Tantra: Rite of Initiation.* Boston: Wisdom Publications, 1991.

Hancock, Graham. *Fingerprints of the Gods.* London: Mandarin, 1994.

——. *Underworld.* Penguin Books, 2003.

Henning, Edward. *Kālacakra and the Tibetan Calendar.* New York: American Institute of Buddhist Studies, 2007.

LePage, Victoria. *Shambhala; The Fascinating Truth Behind the Myth of Shangri-la.* Kathmandu: Pilgrims Publishing, 1996.

Muck, Otto. *The Secrets of Atlantis.* London: William Collins, 1976.

Oakes, Lorna and Gahlin, Lucia. *The Mysteries of Ancient Egypt.* London: Hermes House, 2005.

Richelieu, Peter. *A Soul's Journey.* London: Thorsons, 1958.

Roerich, Helena. *Agni Yoga.* New York: Agni Yoga Society, 1944.

——. *Aum.* New York: Agni Yoga Society, 1944.

——. *Brotherhood.* New York: Agni Yoga Society, 1944.

——. *Community.* New York: Agni Yoga Society, 1952.

——. *Fiery World Vols I, II and III.* New York: Agni Yoga Society, 1944.

——. *Heart.* New York: Agni Yoga Society, 1944.

——. *Hierarchy.* New York: Agni Yoga Society, 1944.

——. *Infinity Vols I, II and III.* New York: Agni Yoga Society, 1944.

——. *Leaves of Morya's Garden Vols I and II.* New York: Agni Yoga Society, 1944.

——. *Letters of Helena Roerich, Volumes I and II.* New York: Agni Yoga Society, 1946.

——. *New Era Community.* New York: Agni Yoga Society, 1944.

Roerich, Nicholas. *Shambhala.* New Delhi: VEDAMS, 2003.

Schoch, Robert. *Voices of the Rocks.* Harmony, 1999.

——. *Voyages of the Pyramid Builders.* Tarcher/Penguin, 2004.

Scott, Cyril. *The Initiate.* Maine: Samuel Weiser, 1977.

——. *The Initiate in the New World.* Maine: Samuel Weiser, 1991.

——. *The Initiate in the Dark Cycle.* Maine: Samuel Weiser, 1991.

The King James Version Bible. London: Oxford University Press, 1922.

Tompkins, Peter. *Secrets of the Great Pyramid.* New York: Harper Colophon Books, 1978.

Index

A

orchestra of sound, 366–367
overcoming, 368
understanding of, 366
Aquarian dispensation, 176, 379, 421
Aquarian era, 54, 110, 126, 153, 156, 162, 168, 171, 175, 202, 294, 371, 377, 378, 380, 386, 389, 444
Aquarian gate, 162
Archangels, 266
Argos, 258
Arhant, 502
Arhat path, 42
Arian controversy, 154
Arjuna, 20
Armour of the Lord, 201
Arūpa, 206
Aryan. *See* Root Race, 5th (Aryan)
epoch, 225, 251, 252, 262, 275, 276
explained, 26
Hierarchy, 260
Ascended Masters, 330
Ashram/s, 2. *See also* Ray Ashram/s
formation of, 107
'holding', 106
on buddhic plane, 107
service work, 94
Aśoka, 49
Aspiration, 134
Aspirational idealism, 316
Aṣṭadiśas, 7
Astral body, 486
Astral sea, 366
Asuras, 15, 72
Athene, 249, 253, 254
Atiśa, 158
Atlantean
behaviour, 332
clairvoyance, 186
era, 252, 253, 257, 266, 323, 411, 431, 466, 468, 478
Hierarchy, 253, 255, 256, 259, 260
Initiates, 258
people, 171, 255, 256, 259, 262
psychic wars, 279
wisdom, 276
Atlantis, 18, 31, 40, 51, 91, 108, 127, 140, 149, 185, 266, 322
black magic in, 467
fall of, 149, 261, 275
Atonement, explained, 477
Aūṁ, 348, 485
Auxiliary deities, seventeen, 453
Avalokiteśvara, 5, 11, 12, 57
Avatāra. *See* Avatar/s
Avatar of Coordination, 409
Avatar of Synthesis, 24, 32, 34, 35, 36, 378, 379, 380, 382, 387, 394, 395, 400, 401, 402, 408, 409, 440, 442, 443–444, 451, 461
Avatar on the white horse, 423
Avatar/s, 19–20, 224, 236, 237, 386, 501
and fierce opposition, 429
appearance of, 396–406, 409–411
coming, 233–234, 399–400, 410, 439
cosmic, 409, 410
definition, 398
doctrine of, 394–411
explained, 395
great cosmic, 400
in contrast to Adept, 437
lesser, 400–401, 402, 409, 410
Ray, 422
types of, 398–399
Avīci, explained, 467
Avidya, 502

B

Baha'i, 155
Bankers, 339
Banner of Peace, 92
Bardo Thödol, 4, 72, 364, 451, 453, 457
Beast/s, 440, 462, 463
four, 417, 483
Beatitude, 369
Beauty, explained, 300

Beethoven, 96
Benign Uniters, 472, 476
Benjamin Creme, 425
Bhagavad Gītā, 20, 260, 468, 495
Bīja/s, 32
Black magic, 467, 479
Black magicians, 15, 226, 422
power of, 71
Bliss, 353
Blood, 212, 468
Cosmic, 233
symbolism, 126, 192–193, 196, 200
Blue Lodge, 431, 461
Boar, 251
Bodhicitta, 35, 37, 45, 54, 64, 86, 99, 106, 117, 123, 126, 129, 140, 180, 191, 192, 210, 235, 287, 338, 351
and Hierarchy, 124
Bodhisattva/s, 357
11th level, 24
bhūmis, 3, 8, 19, 22, 148, 193
challenge of, 69
Council of, 2–3, 18, 23, 41, 46, 57, 74, 75, 82, 124, 135
fierce opposition to, 429
path, 69, 115, 127, 326, 356
purpose, 392
Bodhi tree, 106, 115
Books, errors in, 427–428
Brahmā, 12, 16, 35, 265, 456
age of, 490
'mind born' sons of, 440
Breastplates explained, 228
Bridles, symbolism, 193
Brotherhood of Light, 466
Buddhadharma, 18, 42, 83, 363
Buddha-fields, 135, 338, 351
Buddha, Gautama, 40, 64, 66, 243, 356, 388
3rd Initiation, 115
demise of, 13
Buddhahood, 359
Buddha/s, 4, 16, 57, 58, 62, 63, 64, 87, 104, 261, 262, 378, 379, 380, 381–382, 383, 384, 397, 451, 452, 459
and 4th Ray, 42, 67
and the moon, 469–470
constitution of, 2–3
early history, 39–41
endowments of, 84
Manuśi, 451
nirmaṇakāya aspect, 394
of meditation, 32
Pratyeka, 435
second, 412
six of the Bhavacakra, 451, 452
three, 262
Buddhas of Activity, 24–25, 31, 32, 35–36, 37, 40, 78, 271, 380, 435–436, 437, 440, 441, 443, 445, 452, 455, 459, 460, 461, 468, 470, 479, 481, 485, 487, 490, 491, 503, 505
1st, 29
2nd, 25, 382, 384–385
3rd, 28, 121
and Initiation, 450
and Libra, 501
and permanent atoms, 506
and planetary Logos, 499, 502
and Saturn, 496
and the Root Races, 498
further explained, 494–506
role of, 492–493
Buddhi, 369
Buddhic energy, 228
Buddhic perception, 74
Buddhism, 63–64
and compassion, 160
as heir to Egypt, 364
doctrines, 406
esoteric doctrine, 83
esoteric history, 68
Tibetan, 411
Builders, 229, 482

C

Caduceus staff, 190–191, 253
Cagliostro, 430

Cakrī, explained, 16
Capitalism, 339, 346
Cardinal directions, 8
Cassiopeia, 258
Causal body, 476, 477, 504
Cavernous spaces, symbolism, 225
Cepheus, 258
Ceremonial Magic, 446
Chain/s
  Earth, 439, 462, 464, 465
    humanity, 405
  Moon, 31, 36, 148, 268, 441, 462, 463–472, 501
    and Jesus, 468
    Aryan stage, 467
    Atlantean stage, 467
    failure of, 140, 466, 493
    fate of, 442
    humanity, 264, 267, 469, 470
    karma, 405, 468
    Lemurian stage, 467
    souls, 478
    special team, 468–469
    turmoil, 479–480
  Neptune, 465
  third planetary, 463
Chakra/s, 1, 3, 4, 193, 225, 251
  Ājñā centre, 5, 48, 185, 186, 188, 194, 257, 453, 455, 493, 497, 500
  Alta major centre, 500
  as eyes, 483, 484
  Base of Spine centre, 47, 49, 190, 204, 286, 287, 288, 289, 294, 297, 299, 300, 301, 310, 328, 366, 449, 455, 458, 497
    Ashrams, 302
  below the diaphragm, 206, 347
  Brahmarandhra centre, 500
  Diaphragm centre, 7, 126, 181, 187, 254, 257, 453
  Gonad centre, left, 208, 310, 312, 453
  Gonad centre, right, 204, 205, 303, 453
  Gonad centres, 204–205, 212, 213
  Head centre, 2, 3, 4, 7, 8, 9, 14, 15, 16, 17, 19, 23, 24, 34, 37, 98, 120, 135, 191, 193, 195, 216, 222, 257, 313, 333, 384, 417, 419, 434, 454, 455, 456, 457, 458, 459, 488
    1200 petals, 9
    and Shambhala, 17, 23, 238, 294
    maṇḍala of, 188
  Heart centre, 2, 7, 9, 15, 23, 26, 29, 48, 70, 123, 132, 133, 181, 210, 228, 236, 254, 257, 258, 286, 288, 291, 301, 306, 310, 315, 318, 325, 326, 327, 328, 348, 364, 365, 388, 395, 455, 456, 457, 458
    cosmic, 350
    in the Head, 26, 180, 182, 188, 385, 419
    Logoic, 110
    non-sacred petals, 310, 418
    of humanity, 182
    sacred petals, 418
  Hierarchical Heart centre, 136, 141, 145, 155, 178, 180, 181, 185, 187, 246–247, 261, 404
    Sagittarian petal, 133–134
    suṣumṇā petal, 123, 127, 129
    Taurean petal, 123–125
  Liver centre, 161, 287, 318, 330, 331, 333, 334
  Lung centres, 130, 133, 137
  of humanity, 111, 407
  Sacral and Base of Spine centre interrelation, 293–314
  Sacral centre, 9, 49, 100, 101, 187, 190, 194, 204–205, 212, 215, 227, 250, 286, 287, 289, 291, 303, 308, 309, 310, 316, 326, 327, 328, 454, 455, 458, 462
    and 7/6 petal, 449
    and the 7th Ray, 449
    explained, 290–314
    Hierarchical, 293

Sahasrāra padma. *See* Head centre
Solar Plexus centre, 3, 30, 34, 48, 70, 100, 101, 110, 128, 133, 187, 203, 227, 250, 254, 256, 257, 258, 286, 287, 306, 310, 314, 316, 317, 318, 319–334, 364, 366, 404, 453, 455, 458
activity, 290, 367
and 1st Ray Ashrams, 180
and Shambhala, 180
cosmic, 135
Hierarchical, 314–337
in the Head, 180, 419, 420
of humanity, 126, 146, 181, 288, 321, 334
Splenic centre I, 100, 128, 140, 144–145, 147, 162, 178, 185, 187–188, 206, 208, 209, 211, 212, 213, 215, 216, 250, 260, 286, 300, 303, 319, 331, 348, 388, 416, 454, 455, 458
Zodiacal petals, 148, 150, 152, 153, 156, 157, 158, 160, 161, 163, 167, 168, 174, 296, 303, 317–318, 325
Splenic centre II, 100, 101, 145, 147, 150, 161, 164, 165, 168, 209, 250, 297, 308, 309, 316, 319, 347, 453, 454, 455
function, 203–218
Splenic centres, 151, 187, 211, 250, 254, 255, 256, 287, 314
Hierarchical, 247
Stomach centre, 165, 168, 287, 318, 321, 323, 334
of humanity, 320
symbolism, 7
the Inner Round, 6, 205, 210, 212, 213, 215, 250, 253, 286, 287, 300, 302, 303, 311, 312, 315, 318, 335
Throat centre, 34, 48, 135, 180, 187, 194, 210, 253, 254, 286, 298, 326, 455, 456, 458, 497
and Ashrams, 182
awakening, 134
of humanity, 185
Viśuddha. *See* Throat centre
Cheops, 275
Cherubim, 266, 473
Chohan/s, 23–24, 75, 89, 451, 453
1st Ray, 45, 49, 92, 112, 129, 130, 138–139, 151, 169, 203, 240, 246, 374, 411, 414
2nd Ray, 43, 62, 76, 112, 126, 164, 245, 246, 318, 374, 378, 403
3rd Ray, 49, 93, 128, 135, 138–139, 148, 157–158, 169, 171, 278–279, 320, 417
4th Ray, 49, 133, 148, 158–159, 161, 238, 348, 417
5th Ray, 49, 135, 148, 156, 165, 238, 417
6th Ray, 49, 132, 148, 153, 159–160, 161, 238, 239, 292, 374, 414, 417, 468
7th Ray, 49, 53, 136, 148, 150, 151, 156, 169, 174, 277, 417, 420
and Dhyāni Buddhas, 125–128
and Shambhala, 77
European, 38, 39, 47, 51, 112–113, 123, 237, 351, 378, 382, 405, 451, 453
Christ, 20, 38, 42, 46, 87, 104, 112, 129, 137, 140, 141, 169, 260, 281, 352, 353, 370, 377, 380, 389, 400, 401, 402, 451, 467
and 2nd Initiation, 397
and Jesus, 410
and Perseus, 252
and Spirit of Peace, 444
blue, 37, 56–57, 62, 65, 120, 123, 130, 164, 170, 237, 238, 246, 264, 376, 378, 379, 381, 382, 383, 385, 388, 389, 402, 403, 405, 406–407, 408, 452, 468, 479
and K.H., 409
and moon Chain, 467
time of appearance, 404
blue and green link, 405
explained, 41, 56–67

first, 57, 62, 64, 259
The Life, 384
The Way, 383
green, 65, 379, 381–382, 404, 405, 406, 479
in Gemini, 504
nirmaṇakāya aspect, 379, 386
past, 378
planetary (moon), 471
sambhogakāya aspect, 379
second, 57, 58, 62–63, 65
The Truth, 383
third, 57–58, 62, 63, 64–65, 66, 236, 402, 471
The Life, 383–384
The Way, 384
unrecognised, 396
Christ-child, 167
Christ-consciousness, 380, 447
Christian era, 153–155
Christ-Jesus, 58, 65, 66, 246, 261, 263, 394
persecution of, 430
Christ-Light, 221
Christ principle, 27, 194, 257
Christ's Church, 116, 245
Christ's department, 159, 374, 382, 468
Christs, three, 259, 262, 377, 380, 383, 402
City of God, 179, 244
City, symbolism, 193–194
Civilisation, new world, 62, 198
Civilisations and chakras, 131–132
Clairaudience, 316
Clairvoyance, 316
Claws of bronze, symbolism, 251
Clear Light, 7, 47, 222, 223, 224, 356, 365
Col. Olcott, 406
Colour and Devas, 329
Coming One, 400, 401
Commonsense and 5th Ray, 482
Compassion and Hierarchy, 66
Contemplatives, 40, 186
Copernicus, 154
Copyright laws, 344–345
Corporate CEOs, larceny of, 339
Cosmic astral energy, 138, 159, 188, 193
Cosmic astral plane, 45, 289, 351, 362, 412, 444, 491, 492, 504
Cosmic astral sub-plane, 135, 233, 235, 351, 379
Cosmic astral Waters, 287, 302, 305, 315, 414, 445, 462, 468
Cosmic Christ, 83, 123, 159, 172, 195, 388, 395, 468
and Jesus, 414
Cosmic Cow, 124, 170
Cosmic etheric space, 274, 485, 486
Cosmic evil, 32, 37, 412
Cosmic evolution, 357
Cosmic law, 369
Cosmic Love, 40, 41, 45, 127, 135, 137, 273, 380, 382, 389, 395
Cosmic Mind, 40, 135, 138, 361, 420, 504
Cosmic Paths, 392, 460
Cosmic physical plane, 45, 413, 437
Council at Nicaea, 82
Count St. Germain, 38, 50, 53–54, 277–278, 420
Creative Hierarchy
4th, 474, 475, 478, 479
5th, 472–473, 476, 478, 479
names of, 474–476
6th, 476, 477, 478
three higher, 475
Creative imagination, 425
Creative urge, 446
Creator, Mind of, 473
Crescent moon, symbolism, 8
Critical mind, 369
Crocodiles, 472, 476, 477
Crop circles, 185, 277
Cross
cardinal, 119, 128, 151, 198, 454
fixed, 119, 151, 198, 211, 454, 483
mutable, 119, 151, 207, 211, 454
Crown of thorns, 468

Crow, symbolism, 216, 217
Crucifixion, 87, 118
    of Jesus, 468
Cuba, 60
C.W. Leadbeater, 424
Cyclopes, 255, 258, 259
Cyril Scott, 337, 427

D

Ḍākinī/s, 33, 37, 73, 124
    explanation, 3
    Jñāna, 453, 458
Dalai Lama, 57
    13th, 82
Ḍamaru, 151, 152
Danaë, 255
Darjeeling, 407, 408
Dark brotherhood, 30, 39, 52, 71, 85, 92, 111, 132, 135, 139, 147, 149, 150, 168, 173, 179, 192, 195, 198, 202, 203, 204, 207, 210, 214, 221, 225, 229, 230, 238, 241, 246, 248, 252, 254, 268, 274, 278, 279, 291, 301, 310, 314, 330, 336–337, 354, 357, 361, 362, 376, 393, 396, 404, 413, 421, 425, 449, 466, 467, 468, 470, 494, 501
    activity, 363
    and meditation, 356
    and moon Chain, 493
    and the inquisition, 430
    conversion of, 414, 415, 422
    defeat of, 358–359
    grey, 363
    hierarchy, 423
    saṃskāras, 214
Dark One, 230
Dead, symbolism, 302
Death, explained, 248
Debt-slavery, 61
Deity
    destroyer aspect, 390
    purpose of, 497
    revelation of, 336
Delphi, 104
Delphos, 430
Demagogy of nations, 346
Demeter, 32
Demons, 219, 221
Dependent Origination, 64
Desire
    dual aspects of, 326
    effects of, 206–207, 217
    mind, 360
Destruction, energy of, 390–391
Deva and human interrelationships, 297, 329
Deva compliments
    of four Kumāras, 483
Deva Lord/s, 189, 265
    four great, 482–483
Deva of the Earth, 442
Deva/s, 2, 16, 18, 34, 111, 121, 129, 156, 159–160, 167, 173, 190, 249, 265, 274, 277, 278, 293, 298, 301, 313, 321–322, 333, 382, 455, 466, 471, 473, 476, 477, 484, 485, 504
    activity, 134
    and evil forces, 362
    and karma, 34, 270
    and magic, 131
    and Mother of the World, 444
    builders, 301
    compliments, 23, 120
    evolution, 3, 170, 492, 493, 504
    feminine forces, 129
    Fire, 269
    Hierarchy, 2, 33, 158, 259, 276, 472, 477
    higher, 269
    lore, 124
    manasa, 474, 476, 477
    of the Shadows, 278, 371
    role of, 136, 271, 336
    Solar, 348
    substance, 267, 491
    work of, 324, 493
Devil, 226, 307
Devotion, 160, 357–358
Dharmakāya, 23, 24, 34, 40, 63, 74, 77, 81, 85, 117, 134, 169, 234, 239, 262, 264, 369, 378, 385, 424, 475

levels, 412
lowest level, 348
second level, 350
sword of, 201
Dharmakāya Flower, 2, 10, 17
Dharmakāya Way, 18, 67–70, 167, 338
Dharmakāyic aspect, 360
Dharmatā, 316
Dharma, white, 14, 15
Dhataraṭṭha, 483
Dhītika, 48, 49
Dhritarashtra, 33
Dhyāni Buddhas, 10, 35, 40, 61, 75, 76, 118, 125, 152, 192, 222, 263, 266, 418, 420, 440, 442, 451
Akṣobhya, 24, 35, 37, 46, 62, 148, 159, 161, 263, 442, 451, 453
Amitābha, 23, 35, 46, 77, 110, 148, 157, 165, 263, 288, 453
Amoghasiddhi, 24, 35, 47, 62, 74, 110, 148, 156, 168, 209, 263, 288, 454
and Splenic centre I, 148
Consorts, 190, 269, 270, 272, 273, 451, 454, 455
Ratnasambhava, 35, 47, 62, 76, 110, 148, 161, 263, 287, 453
Vairocana, 24, 35, 46, 61, 148, 158, 164, 263, 442, 444, 451
Diplomatic immunity, 345
Dispenser of Water of Life, 377, 386
Divine Embodiments, 398–399
Divine Ideation, 505
Divine Love, 472
Divine lunatic, 463
Divine Messenger, 398
Divine Plan, 391
Divine Reason, 420
Divine Will, 65, 180, 390, 444
Divine years, 489
Djed column, 29
Djwhal Khul (D.K.), 81, 93, 102–103, 105, 116, 170, 320, 378, 380, 389, 396, 403, 406, 440, 449, 459
as 2/3 Master, 93, 163–164, 169
Door where evil dwells, 173, 389, 392, 393
Douglas Baker, 425
Dove, 219, 281
explained, 308
of peace, 202, 246
Draco, 472
Dragons, 19, 465
Dragons of Wisdom, 465, 472, 474, 503
Dusum Khyenpa, 76
Dweller on the threshold, 358

E

Earth's primary - Venus, 438–440
Earth, the, 139
Easter Island statues, 91
Economic sanctions, 342
Economic slavery, 343
Edison, 96
Ego, explained, 435
Egypt, 29, 430
Egyptian Book of the Dead, 363
Egyptian heritage, 369
Egyptian magic, 30
Egyptian religion, 364
Eight hot hells, 467
Eighth sphere, 214, 248, 250, 252, 303, 467
for Hierarchy, 247
Einstein, 96
Electricity, mystery of, 431
Electronic magic, 323
Elemental Fires, 473
Elemental lives, 316
Elements
Aether, 46, 136, 213
Air, 8, 114, 157, 215, 300, 325
and swastika, 370
Earth, 8, 209, 215, 216, 255, 314
Fire, 8, 31, 36, 46, 189, 244, 251, 272, 444, 474, 487
downpour of, 136
transforming, 190
five, 35, 102, 370, 440

Void, 458
Water, 259, 308, 326, 332, 360
Eleusis, 104, 262, 430
Elite, moneyed, 59
Elizabeth Claire Prophet, 330, 424
Emanations
black, 355
evil, 355
grey, 355, 363
Emerald Tablet, 28
Emotional body as glue, 360–361
Emotional tide, 309
Emotions
control of, 307
Watery, 312
Endurance, explained, 306
English Master J.M. Haig, 91, 337
Enlightenment
explained, 357
realms of, 73
wings of, 409
Ephesians, extract from, 226–232
Ephesus, 104
Esoteric astrology, 122
Esoteric chemistry, 366
Esoteric schools, 376
Eternal Spirits, 460
Eternal Youth, 34, 495
Etheric
body of the planet, 407
grid, 370
miasma, 216
space, 454
vehicle, 371
vision, 371, 438
Euryale, 249, 250
Eurystheus of Argos, 26
Evil, 109, 185, 199, 226–227, 354–355, 359–370, 376, 393, 399, 403, 408, 410, 494
and the mind, 359
doing, 333
one, 219
predatory, 303
sources of, 360–362
weeds, 222
Externalisation, effects of, 407
Eye, 177–178, 210
all-seeing, 22, 24, 32, 40, 124, 182, 194, 230, 303, 457
Hierarchical, 188, 371
in the triangle, 479
Logoic, 188
Monadic, 360, 457
of Deity, 178

F

Faithful, explained, 234, 237, 238
Fall down, symbolism, 419
Fathers, 476
Fiat money system, 60–61, 346
Fiery flying serpent, 474
Fiery impetus, 473
Fiery lives, 473
Fiery power, 314
Fiery Waters, 503
Fifth dimensional motion, 416
Five fingers and prāṇas, 218
Five-fold Links, 472, 475, 476
Flight, symbolism, 214
Flowers, as chakras, 327
Fohat, 242
Forty-nine Fires, 460, 461
Four and twenty elders, 418, 452
Fox, symbolism, 208, 209
Francis Bacon, 38, 277, 420
French Revolution, 154
Fungi, 269
Furlong, explained, 194
1000 furlongs, 195

G

Galileo, 154, 430
Gandharvas, explained, 33
Garibaldi, 93
Garuda, 269
Gatekeepers
enacting rites, 7, 453
of pristine cognition, 453, 458
Geb, 29
Geneva, 407, 408
Ghengis Khan, 241

Gilgamesh, 40
Giordano Bruno, 430
Giza, 30, 259
Glamour, 424, 470
Glaring eyes, symbolism, 251
Glastonbury, 104
Glory, greater, 353
Gnostics, 154
Goat-fish, 475
Gobekli Tepi, 91
Gobi desert, 28, 436
'God', 58, 237, 312, 373, 492
  and His Angels, 333
  armour of, 227
  City of, 192
  glory of, 390
  Heart of, 41
  Kingdom of, 58, 94, 122, 134, 380, 480
  Mind of, 135, 296, 299, 480
  mysteries of, 22
  of the Christian, 435
  sons-of, 58
  temple of, 229, 301
  Will of, 391
  word of, 231–233, 236–237
  wrath of, 189, 192, 195, 196
Godfrey Ray King, 424
Goethe, 96
Golden fleece, 27
Golden wings, symbolism, 251
Goodwill, 133, 271, 347
Gorgon/s, 249, 254
  Medusa, 249, 250, 251, 252, 254, 256, 257, 258, 259–260, 261
Gospel of peace, explained, 228
Graeae, 256
Grapes, explained, 190–191, 192, 194, 235
Great awakening, 225, 409
Great Bear, 438
Great flood, the, 40
Great game, 60
Great Invocation, 387–394
Great King, 281
Great Mother, 236
Great Ones, 376
  impersonators of, 330
Great Sacrifice, 34, 437
Great White Lodge, 401, 402, 459
Greed, doctrine of, 336
Grey energies, 365
Grindstone, explained, 191–192
Guardians, four, 451
  Consorts, 454
Guṇas, 457
Guruparamparā, 3, 76, 123
Guru Rinpoche, 39, 44, 50, 58, 112, 115, 120, 125, 127–128, 138, 140, 141, 149, 174, 382–383, 385, 451, 453
  and the moon, 469–470
  and Tibet, 53, 128

H

Half moon, symbolism, 8
Halls of Records, 484
Hand of deity, 239
Hand of 'God', 217
Hands, symbolism, 206
Harvest, golden, 375
Hathor, 265
Head, symbolism, 118
Health, 207
Heart, and blood, 168
Heart-born sons, 107
Heart of Life, 152, 297
Heart of Love, 350
Heart of the Sun, 159, 327
Heart's Mind, 365
Hearts of Fiery Love, 477
Heart, way of the, 353
Heat content, 487
Heavenly City, 165
Heavenly Man, 439
Helena Blavatsky, 3, 92, 105, 150, 330, 406, 424, 427
  mystery of, 93
  opposition to, 429
Helena Roerich, 2, 83, 92, 197, 330, 406, 424, 427

opposition to, 429
Helmet of invisibility, 254, 256
Helmet, symbolism, 230–231
Hephaestus, 253
Hercules, 25–27, 260–261, 451
3rd Initiation, 27
12 labours, 26
and Hierarchy, 26
as Christ, 61
Hermes, 253, 256
Hermes Trismegistus, 28, 275–276
Herukas, 121, 147–148, 151, 156, 157, 158, 159, 160, 161, 165, 192, 453, 457
Blood-drinking, 454, 458
Consort/s, 164, 168, 453, 455
Hexagram, 39, 462
Hierarchical
hand, 153
life, 159
maṇḍala, 161, 351
power, 329
shield, 199, 201, 303, 405, 413
sun, 326
swastika, 374
twelve-petalled lotus, 119–137, 178. *See also* Chakra, Hierarchical Heart centre
Hierarchy, black, 149. *See also* Dark brotherhood
Hierarchy of Light, 23, 66, 86, 110, 172, 219, 291, 302, 315, 317, 321, 400, 498, 505. *See also* White brotherhood
and astral plane, 288–289, 292
and Hercules, 26
and New Group of World Servers, 183–185
and new United Nations, 346
and Shambhala, 410
and the Mysteries, 432
and wolves, 366
as Heart centre, 120, 121–137
iḍā and piṅgalā flow, 123, 140
suṣumṇā flow, 137
birth of, 255
Council, 242
esoteric doctrines, 320
externalisation, 62, 132, 189, 234, 236, 265, 266, 347, 388, 406, 408, 425, 431
Eye of, 177–182, 371
general assembly of, 406–407
Head of, 57, 377
Heart in the Head, 120
infant, 261
Plan, 158, 162, 340, 349, 351, 368, 395
purpose, 334
rearrangement of, 67
Solar Plexus in the Head, 120
teachings contrary to, 425
thought-streams, 332
Throat in the Head, 120
upper echelons, 376–387
High Place, 404, 405
Hilarion, 49, 135–136, 156–157, 169, 171, 236, 239
Hippodameia, 256
Hitler, 185, 410
Holy Ghost, 164
Holy Place, 397
Horses, symbolism, 192, 402–403
Horus, 29
Hosts, Lord of, 143
Hourglass, 219
Huge teeth, symbolism, 251
Human corpse, symbolism, 205, 210, 213
Humanity, two levels, 58–59
Human Personality, 475
Humbleness, 165, 365
Hydra, nine-headed, 132, 212, 252, 260, 261, 334, 389
swamp of, 161
Hyperboreans, 256

I

I AM movement, 330
I-concept, 502
Identification, 496

Ignorance, 334
Illusion, 470
Impressionists, 154
Incarnations (777), 360
Indigo blue Light, 219
Individualisation, 36, 463, 495, 504
Indra, 12, 16
Industrial Revolution, 154, 277
Initiated, the, 396
Initiate, explained, 373
Initiates, 392, 474
 3rd degree, 22, 77, 358
 4th degree, 22, 77
 5th degree, 23, 358
Initiation, 93, 105, 120, 416, 424, 428, 436, 496
 1st, 261, 313, 323, 388, 397, 445, 446
  and the moon, 470
 1st Ray method, 117
 2nd, 17, 212, 259–260, 261, 315, 333, 397, 437, 445
 2nd Ray method, 117–118
 3rd, 87, 114, 115, 196, 260, 261, 263, 274, 298, 387, 445, 450, 459, 469
 3rd Ray method, 118
 3 ways to attain, 117–118
 4th, 47, 87, 97, 170, 239, 262, 263, 450
  Ray methods, 114
 5th, 108, 115, 438, 450, 462
  testings, 109
 6th, 24, 67, 438, 460
 7th, 376, 438
 9th, 504
 and Shambhala, 2
 ceremony, 450
 Crucifixion, 87
 first two and astral substance, 416
 group, 191
 level, 95, 298
 mount of, 138, 191
 of Christ and Buddha, 87
 of Hercules, 27
 path of, 203, 241, 296, 338, 339, 357
 planetary, 37, 189, 197, 271, 407
 schools, new, 126, 137, 422
 temples of, 301, 397, 405, 469
 testings, 70, 192, 247, 367, 392
 to the Mysteries, 275
 tree, 168, 190, 274
Initiator, first, 471
Inner realms, 72
Inquisitional period, 430, 467
Inspiration, 409, 410
International Court of Justice, new, 342
International Monetary Fund, new, 346
Invocation, science of, 500
Involutionary process, 464
Iraq, 60
Ishtar, 266
Isis, 29, 32, 266
Isis Unveiled, 92
Israel, twelve tribes, 195
Īśvarī, 293, 453, 458

J

Jackel-headed deity, 363. *See also* Anubis
Jail, symbolism, 248
Jambudvīpa, 11, 14
Jason and the Argonauts, 27
Jataka Tales, 64, 68
Jerusalem, new, 62
Jesus, 37, 49, 66, 116, 130, 132–133, 159–160, 161, 169, 170, 233, 235, 239, 263, 292, 374, 386, 404, 410, 412, 414, 415
 and crucifixion, 87, 114
 and piṇgalā flow, 132
 cloak of, 415
 dispensation, 395
 karma of, 467–468
 teachings of, 82–83

Jesus' Baptism, 246
Jesus-Christ, 451
Jigme Lingpa, 157
Jina Wisdoms. *See* Wisdoms
Jīvas, 490, 503, 506
imperishable, 474
John the Baptist, 114, 246
Judgement, explained, 238
Jungian psychology, 333–334
Jungle, symbolism, 206
Jupiter (Master), 38, 39, 98, 112, 139, 149, 156, 174

K

Kaballah, 94
Kālachakra Tantra, 4, 12, 18, 70
deity, 17
Mūlatantra, 5
system, 2
teachings of, 5
Kāla, defined, 4
Kalapa, 6
Kali, 266
Kalkī Avatar, 11, 20
Kalkī kings, 5, 9–11
Aja, 5, 10
Harivikrama, 9
Kulika, 12
Mañushrīkīrti, 10
Puṇḍarīka, 5
Puṇḍarīka, 11
Rudracakrī, 9, 11, 12, 13, 16, 19
Samudravijaya, 10
Sucandra, 4
Sucrenda, 10
Sūrya, 10
Yaśas, 5, 10
Kāma-manas, 101, 110, 208, 309, 312, 415, 475
Kāma-manasic thoughts, 477
Kapāla, 152
Kargupta order, 115
Karma, 19, 32, 71, 72, 121, 129, 130, 131, 138, 191, 207, 210, 229, 234, 236, 237, 242, 243, 247, 252, 253, 256, 257, 264, 265, 268, 280, 315, 318, 339, 355, 359, 362, 389, 390, 393, 413, 423, 476, 477, 479, 490, 505, 506
ancient Egyptian, 363
and Ākāśa, 486
and Libra, 501
cosmic, 469, 485, 493, 501
distribution of, 484
external, 266
interwoven, 111
minutiae of, 357
moon Chain, 468
of group-Souls, 322
of Jesus, 467–468
of strife, 414
psychic, 356
weaving of, 483
Karmapa, 76
Karma Pakshi, 76
Karmic agents, 487
Karmic law and the Lipikas, 482
Keter, 488
Khaṭvāṅga, 113–114, 125, 138, 151, 152
King of Kings, 233
King's Chamber, 275
Kites, symbolism, 213
Kleśa/s, 14
Kliṣṭamanas, 209, 210
Knowledge, concrete, 481
Koot Hoomi. *See* Koot Humi (K.H.)
Koot Humi (K.H.), 42, 49, 52, 61, 62, 63, 65, 112, 125, 126, 137, 140, 146, 148, 151, 152, 169, 170, 173, 174, 236–237, 238, 264, 320, 331, 374, 378, 382, 383, 385, 386, 395, 498
work of, 408–409
Koot Humi's department, 404
Krishna, 20, 48, 49, 64, 65, 104, 260, 468
Krodheśvarī, 148
Kublai Khan, 76
Kumāra/s, 456

1st, 436, 438, 440, 441
4th, 440, 441–442
5th, 31, 441, 444, 463, 466, 471, 479–482, 493, 504
and moon Chain, 464–465
defined, 440
esoteric, 24, 32, 450, 452
explained, 35–36, 438
five, 440, 441–442, 466
four, 483
one hundred and five, 455–456
Sanat, 24, 31–32, 37, 40, 46, 53, 88, 123, 148, 253, 271, 274, 380, 382, 387, 388, 394–395, 402, 407, 412, 435, 436, 437, 442, 443, 444, 450, 451, 452, 459, 460, 461, 468, 470, 471, 479, 493, 498, 499, 502, 505
and Buddhas of Activity, 494–495
explained, 34–36
seven, 36, 436
subjective, 31
three esoteric, 440, 442, 461
threefold work, 441–442
Kuṇḍalinī, 294, 322, 465, 473, 486
planetary, 303, 472, 478
rising, 473
Kurukshetra, 260
Kuvera, 483

L

Labour, and 3/7 Ashram, 335
Labour, true value of, 343
Lady Dembu, 116
Laghutantra, 5
Lamb, the, 401
Lao-tzu, 104
Law of Analogy, 495, 497
Law of Attraction, 290
Law of Correspondences, 492
Law of Cycles, 131
Law of Magnetic Work, 290
Law of Sacrifice, 495, 501, 502
Law of Synthesis, 290
Laya centres, defined, 454
Lazarus, 114, 116
League of Nations, 92, 298
Left hand path, 368, 463
Left hand practices, 230
Lemurian-Atlantean epoch, 478
Lemurian cycle, 255, 472, 496. *See also* Root Races, 3rd (Lemurian)
Lemurian Initiates, 255, 258
Leonardo da Vinci, 51, 124
Levitation, 371
Libya, 60
Life, building blocks of, 367
Life, Waters of, 163
Light, 385, 393
army of, 220
forces of, 399
Light of Life, 380, 386
Light of Love, 386
Lion of the Lord, 157
Lion, symbolism, 261, 326, 331
Lipika Lords, 451, 452, 482–495
and evolving Thought, 485
and the akashic records, 486
four groups, 487
lesser, 488
of a scheme, 489
three, 488
Lipika/s
1st, 491
and integration of karma, 490–491
defined, 482
extra-systemic, 487
nine, 488
twenty two, 488
Living Ethics, 426
Logoi
as Avatars, 394
of sacred planets, 443, 452
solar, 135
Logoic kuṇḍalinī, 439
Logoic Mind, 134, 193, 195
Logoic Purpose, 348
Logoic Quaternary, 441
Logoic triad, 382
Logoic Vision, 493

Logoic Wisdom, 387
Logos, 268
343 incarnations, 439
abstract, 36
and the Lipikas, 485
and war, 248–249
appearance of, 362
chakras in, 191
Creative, 482, 483
Desire-Mind, 124
planetary, 36, 41, 78, 189, 243, 382, 434, 435, 438, 439, 450, 458, 460, 463, 484, 489, 491, 493, 505
centres in, 441
Head centre of, 190
Solar, 470, 478, 484, 487
London, 407, 408
Lord of Civilisation, 151, 171–174, 401. *See also* Mahāchohan
Lord of form, 335
Lord of Liberation, 171–172
Lord of Lords, 233
Lord of Love, 246, 388, 400
Lord of Saturn, 501
Lord of the World, 1, 87, 271, 393, 399, 435–436, 437, 441, 446, 450, 455, 459, 486, 499
Lord, Power of the, 190
Lords of Dark Face. *See* Dark brotherhood
Lords of Fire, 190
Lords of Flame, 36, 37, 456
Lords of Karma, 256, 354, 484, 486, 487, 488
Lords of Liberation, 142
Lords of Life, 3, 40, 237, 299
Lords of Light, 150
Lords of Sacrifice, 493
Lord, warriors of, 200, 201
Loud cry, explained, 190
Love, 393
and evil, 219
blood of, 152
cosmic, 40, 45, 127, 135, 137, 380, 382, 389, 395, 478
explained, 54–55, 357–358
Fiery, 165
flames of, 369
mental, 369
ocean of, 134
piṇgalā line, 369
power of, 218
resolute purpose of, 395
sacrificial ways of, 388
zephyr of, 370
Love of Life, 386
Love-Wisdom, 32, 41, 45, 46, 56, 58, 62, 96, 108, 124–125, 131, 140, 141, 148, 151, 181, 182, 191, 196, 198, 202, 203, 210, 229, 233, 237, 245, 246, 248, 257, 263, 264, 271, 277, 318, 348, 377, 379, 380, 383, 385, 388, 389, 423, 479, 481, 483, 503
and humanity, 115
cycle, 276, 392, 406
Lords of, 183
Lunar lords, 361, 476, 478
Lying propaganda, 425

M

Ma'at, 160
Madhyamaka pratipad, 49
Magic, 366, 426
Magic wallet, 256
Magnetic force, 487
Magnetic healing, 291
Mahābodhisattvas, 10, 23, 236
Consorts, 454
eight, 74, 107, 120, 122, 451
maṇḍala of, 65
Mahāchohan, 23, 24, 38, 40, 65, 265, 279, 371, 450, 452
final, 280
new, 38, 43, 46, 49, 50, 52–54, 62, 93, 116, 120, 129, 130, 131, 137, 140, 141, 148, 149, 151, 160, 169, 170, 171, 174, 175, 177, 198, 209, 236–237, 238, 245, 263–264, 274, 277, 278, 351, 372, 373, 374, 376,

380, 381–382, 385, 386, 391, 402, 404, 411, 415, 416, 421, 422–423, 443, 445, 451, 453
and 7th Ray Ashrams, 444
and K.H., 408–409
and Padmasambhava, 412
and the moon, 469–470
and Throat centre, 187
as Arian position, 145–146, 147
as Avatar, 394–395
as Maitreya, 388–389
relation to Master ℛ, 172–174
rise of, 148
weapons of, 151
role of, 421
Mahāchohan's department, 29, 54, 165, 264–280, 286, 314, 338, 347, 370, 374, 402, 405, 421, 456
and swastikas, 371–373
future work of, 345
Mahāchohan's trident, 130
Mahākaśyapa, 38, 42, 43, 45, 46, 47, 48, 58
Mahāmanvantara, 491
Mahāmudrā, 64
Mahārājas, four, 25, 442, 451, 452, 461, 482–495
Mahāsiddha/s, 50, 68, 71, 357
Mahāsudarśana, 48, 49
Mahat, 135, 138, 160, 268, 478
and the Lipikas, 485
Mahāyāna Buddhism, 104
Mahāyuga, 490
Maitreya, 13, 52, 58, 63, 65, 233, 370, 387, 388
and 5th Initiation, 115
epoch of, 53
meaning of, 66
purpose, 96
Makara, 466, 472, 474, 475, 477, 503
Makarian, 478
Malkuth, 488, 489
Manas, 309, 466
effect of, 348
evolution of, 463
sum total of, 441
Manasic Fire, 134, 413, 473
Manaskāras, explained, 337
Maṇḍala, 1
Mañjuśrī, 5, 10, 11, 12
Man-plant (Mānasaputra), 162, 361
Mantra, secret, 16
Mantric cry, 189–190
Manu, 37, 38, 40, 112, 120, 264, 377, 401, 411, 412, 450, 451
Aryan, 30
Atlantean, 30, 452
explained, 30–31
Vaivasvata, 31
Manu's department, 29, 129, 200
Manvantara, 191, 268, 482, 489, 490
Māra, 57, 243, 356, 425
Mark Prophet, 424
Marpa, 115, 116
Marriage, divine, 479
Mars, 100, 137, 139, 141
evolution, 463
god of war, 349
Martin Luther, 430
Marx, 96
Masonic art, 214
Masonic tradition, 154, 229, 299, 431
Masses, the, 60
Master of an Ashram, 420
Master of Masters, 264, 407
Master ℛ, 84, 136, 150, 171, 236, 277–278, 401, 420–421
and violet energy, 131
relation to new Mahāchohan, 172–174
Master, ritual of, 244
Masters, forty two, 453
Masters of Wisdom, 75–76, 77, 247, 330, 357, 358, 424, 465
and the moon, 470
Ashrams of, 22–25, 81, 89, 107

Mātaraḥ, eight, 7, 453, 458
Materialistic scientists, 91
Maudgalyāyana, 39, 41, 44, 45, 47, 50, 58
Max Heindel, 406
Māyā, 69, 125, 152, 470
Māyāvirūpa, 475
Meditation
  and enlightened beings, 357
  explained, 355
  objectives of, 69–70
Meditation-Mind, 1–2, 19
Meekness, explained, 230
Melchisedec, 34
Mercury, 99, 137, 139, 141
Middle East conflict, 59
Milarepa, 82, 115–116, 159, 239, 468
Militarism, 341
mind
  and evil, 359–360
  critical, 369
  empty, 355–356
  Fires of, 3, 333
  laws of, 72
Mind, 167, 193, 309, 395
  abstract, 42, 47, 70, 93, 140, 144, 234, 475
  and the 6th Ray, 305
  ascendency of, 279
  Clear Light of, 7, 47, 222, 223, 224, 365, 368
  cosmic, 40, 135, 138, 141, 361, 420, 504
  dharmakāyic, 7, 74
  epoch of, 177
  Fires of, 146, 440
  laws of, 180
  Logoic, 134, 193, 195
  Logoic Desire, 124, 135
  meditation, 1–2, 19
  nāḍīs of, 222
  prāṇas of, 135
  rule of, 441
  Shambhalic, 74–75, 120
mind/Mind as all, 360
Monadic aspect, 233, 377
Monadic domain, 350
Monadic evolution, 361
Monadic Eye, 360, 457
Monadic sense, 460
Monad/s, 117, 360, 442, 461
  1st Ray, 463
  3rd Ray, 264
Monera, 269
Money, power of, 335
Moon, 138, 139, 141, 267, 362, 389
  and kuṇḍalinī, 478
  mystery of, 58, 251, 463
  phases of, 190
Moon-goddess, 250, 255
Morya, 45, 49, 52, 83, 92, 93, 112, 114, 129, 130, 137, 139, 149, 150, 170, 174, 198, 203, 231, 236, 237, 240, 241, 331, 374, 376, 377, 411, 412, 413, 414, 427
Morya's department, 404
Mother, 493
Mother aspect, 102
Mother Goddesses, 441
Motherhood, esoteric nature of, 473
Mother of the World, 24, 29, 31, 32–34, 35, 36, 141, 197, 264–280, 380, 387, 394, 440–441, 442, 451, 461, 463, 469, 493
  5 individuals, 266–280
  and 5th creative Hierarchy, 472–475
  and karma, 491
  and the 7th Ray, 444
  definition, 268–269
  department, 92
  epoch of, 109, 478, 504
  first, 269
  meanings of, 267–268
  role of, 441–445
  temples of, 301
Mother's breath, 321
Mother's department, 322
  and the Lipikas, 485

domain, 319, 354
garden, 222, 223, 296, 327
Mountains, symbolism, 7
Mount Olympus, 18, 254, 257, 261
Mouth, 205
Mozart, 96
Mūlatantra, 9
Muslim faith, 154
Mycenae, 262
Mysteries, 25, 392, 431
restoration of, 430, 430–432
Mystery Schools, 105, 156, 405, 430
Myths, explained, 27

N

Nāḍīs, 158
iḍā, 8, 9, 38, 94, 113, 128, 129, 156, 168, 169, 190, 208, 312, 313, 314, 320, 326, 327, 334, 371
and first Christ, 64
function, 260
manasic, 135
of humanity, 348
piṇgalā, 8, 9, 94, 113, 126, 152, 159, 161, 169, 190, 306, 325, 326, 328, 371, 412
and second Christ, 64–65
attributes, 133
suṣumṇā, 94, 113, 134, 164, 169, 190, 232–233, 314, 385
three major, 169
Nāḍī system, 1, 9, 16, 107, 175, 187, 190, 206, 272, 310, 377
feminine, 322
iḍā, 135
Nāgārjuna, 38
Nature
building forces of, 485
kingdoms of, 269, 348
Nazca lines, 91
Neptune, 100, 113, 138, 139, 141, 443
Neptune's trident, 113–114
Nereids, 258
New Age Community, 352
New Age organisations, 423–432
New era, 62, 144, 201, 202, 218, 271, 317, 370–371, 422
New era civilisation, 237, 241, 338, 395, 423, 445
New Group of World Servers, 164, 180, 183–185, 186–187, 396–397
New Jerusalem, 165, 179, 201, 244, 297, 317, 322, 332, 393
New planet, 280
Newton, 96, 154
New World Order, 339, 369
and the 7th Ray, 446
New York, 407, 408
Nexus
śūnyatā-saṃsāra, 70, 118, 134, 228, 404
Nicholas Roerich, 2, 92, 298, 330, 406, 424
opposition to, 429
Nile river symbolism, 29
Nirmaṇakāya/s, 186, 381, 395
Noah, 31
Nourisher of the little ones, 377, 379–380, 386
Nuclear energy, 197
Numbers explained
2 to the power of 7, 194
3x9, 196
6, 9
8, 194
10, 8
12, 9
16, 194
18, 16–17
22, 454, 489
24, 9, 194
30, 196
42, 452, 453
48, 195
58, 453
66, 461–462
72, 5
96, 5
105, 36, 457–458, 462
108, 36
117, 454

120, 454
156, 187–188
168, 187
180, 188
192, 188
220, 194
222, 403, 409
600, 194, 195
666, 462
800, 16
960 million, 4–5
1000, 6, 41, 194
1200, 9
1600, 194
1800, 16
12000, 9
60000, 9
144000, 195
symbolism, 17
Nut, 29
Nyingma tradition, 115

O

Obsession, explained, 410
Occult sensationalism, 425
Odyssey, the, 27
Olympus, 27, 253
Oṁ, 485
Oṁ Maṇi Padme Hūṁ, 394
One Initiator, 34, 87, 123, 382, 436, 437, 438
Order of the Golden Dawn, 94
Organisation, energy of, 391
Ormazd, 359
Orpheus, 64, 68
Osiris, 29–30, 451
Overshadowing, 409
Owl, symbolism, 214

P

Padmasambhava, 39, 40, 41, 47, 50, 112–114, 115, 236, 237, 351, 382, 405, 411–412, 413
and the new Mahāchohan, 412
Pagodas, symbolism, 8
Panama, 60
Panchen Lama, 82
Pancreas, 335
Paracelsus, 154
Para-thyroids, 497
Parinirvāṇa, 263
Pasteur, 96
Path of Magnetic Work, 289
Patience, 209
Patriarchs of Buddhism, 42–50
Peace, 395
Peaceful and Wrathful Deities, 453, 457
Peaceful Deities, 451, 452, 454
Peacock, symbolism, 272
Pegasus, 257
Pelops, 256
Pentagram, 244
Perfect Ones, 474, 475, 477
Perseus, 249–264
Pestilence, 376
Peter, 82, 116, 245
Philosopher's gold, 223
Philosopher's stone, 155, 168
Phoenician, the, 38, 40, 42, 46, 53, 67, 120, 125, 134–135, 141, 276–277, 420, 452, 469–470
as new Mother, 272–273
Piśācī, 203, 453, 458
Gṛdhamukhī, 211, 213
Kākamukhī, 216
Kaṅkamukhī, 213
Siṃhamukhī, 204, 205
Śṛgālamukhī, 207
Śvānamukhī, 209
Ulūkamukhī, 214
Vyāghrīmukhī, 206
Piscean era, 89, 156, 176, 386
five subdivisions, 153
significance, 152–154
Pitris, lunar, 476, 478
Planes of perception
ādi, 98, 351, 434
anupāḍaka, 45, 98, 350, 360, 394, 434
astral, 72, 100, 127, 133, 168, 202, 217, 236, 252, 256, 273,

278, 288, 289, 291–292, 308, 349, 397, 414, 434, 448, 480, 486
ātma, 23, 45, 56, 99, 144, 178, 348, 434, 475, 477, 492, 493
buddhi, 45, 74, 99, 144, 178, 191, 348, 407, 420, 434
etheric Devas, 278
mental, 360, 434, 479–482, 493
physical, 434
etherealisation of, 279
Planetary
centres, 408–409
Contemplatives, 381
evil, 337–347
forces, ten, 452
Regents, 454
transformation, 359
woe, 61
Plantae, 269
Plan, the, 352, 379, 392, 393, 397, 459, 461, 505
blueprint of, 330–331
Custodians of, 381
Plato, 91, 104
Pleiades, 33, 50, 124, 265, 272, 276
Mind, 124
representative from, 461
Pleiadian Way, 444
Plight of women, 347
Pluto, 98, 139, 156, 176
Point within the Triangle, 377, 378
Policemen, esoteric, 247
Politics, 242
Polydectes, 255–256, 258
Poseidon, 249, 253, 258
Power, 379
materialising, 393, 396
Power of Love, 384
Power of the Truth, 386
Power to detach, 311
Prajñā, 269
Prajñāpāramitā, 10, 114, 222
Pralaya, 193, 195, 274, 487, 490
Prāṇa/s, 1, 7, 152, 468
1st Ray, 413
aberrant, 248
Airy, 216
concretising, 214
Cosmic, 237
darkened, 315, 356, 362
Earthy, 211, 215, 297, 301, 458
of Hierarchy, 296
Fiery, 332, 458
five types of, 155, 218, 291, 370, 418
iḍā, 328
manasic, 312, 334
piṅgalā, 307, 331
solar, 157
to be discovered, 324
undefiled, 458
Watery, 207, 287, 303, 315, 458
Prāṇic vitality, 348
Pratikyekabuddhas, 67
Pratītyasamutpāda. *See* Dependent Origination
Pratyakṣa, 22
Pretas, 72
Primordial One, 387
Princes, ninety-six, 6, 7
Privatisation, 343
Producers of atonement, 477
Profiteering, undue, 345
Prometheus, 253
Proteus, 255
Protista, 269
Protruding tongue, symbolism, 251
Pseudo-occultism, 425, 426, 427
Psyche, manipulation of, 355
Psychic attack, 361
Psychic domains, 430
Psychicism, 426, 430
Psychic powers. *See* Siddhis
Psychics and astral substance, 425
Psychometry, 316
Public money, 344
Pure reason, 88
Purification, energy of, 390
Purpose, 381, 391, 505
directed, 399–400
principle of, 444

Pyramid, great, 90, 275
Pythagoras, 104

Q

Qabbalah, 487
Quantum chromodynamics, 73
Quarks, 73
Queens of yoga, 453–454

R

Radiant Seven, 78, 460, 461
Radiating light, 487
Radiatory Activity, 295
Rāja Lord/s, 461, 483
Rāja yoga, 324
Rakoczi, 38, 49, 150, 171, 174–175, 277–278, 371–372, 401, 420, 422
Raven, explained, 308
Ray Ashram/s, 76
  1/1, 232
  1/2, 104–105, 110, 198, 200, 201, 202–203, 204, 209, 231, 240, 374
    Master, 241, 243
  1/3, 232
  1/3 - 2/3, 231
  1/4, 198, 201–202, 203, 207, 214–216, 240
  1/4 - 2/4, 228
  1/5, 178, 231
  1/5 - 2/5, 230
  1/6, 198, 200–201, 202, 203, 216–218, 240
  1/7, 198, 201, 202, 207–209, 240
  1/7 - 2/7, 228
  1/7 - 7/1, 188
  1st and 2nd united, 229, 350
  1st Ray, 147, 149, 177, 178, 183, 196, 200, 227, 231, 241, 243, 247, 303, 351
    and the sword, 240
    pentad, 202
  2/1, 52, 85–86, 104–105, 148–149, 173, 178, 198, 202–203, 209–211, 229–230, 231, 240, 245, 246, 351, 370
    Master, 373
    statement, 218
  2/1 - 1/2, 169, 177, 179, 188, 232, 235, 241, 248, 375, 376
  2/1 - 1/2 - 1/7 service, 423
  2/2, 179, 245, 247
    statement, 219
  2/3, 103, 163–165, 178, 179, 245, 246, 247, 320
    outpouring, 164
    statement, 219
  2/3 - 3/2, 153, 163, 164, 321
  2/3 Master, 93, 245
  2/4, 325
    statement, 219–220
  2/4 - 4/2, 153, 161
  2/5 - 5/2, 153, 162, 165–166
  2/5 statement, 220
  2/6 - 6/2, 160, 161
  2/6 statement, 220–221
  2/7, 175, 411
    statement, 221
  2/7 - 7/2, 153, 167
  2nd Ray, 103–104, 151, 155, 169, 173, 180, 218–222, 227, 296, 337, 338, 348, 370, 378, 402, 403, 417
    planners, 350
  2nd sub-Ray, 155, 297
  3/1, 181
  3/2, 317–321
  3/2 - 7/2, 423
  3/3, 180
  3/4, 173, 183, 320, 351
  3/4 - 4/3, 188, 196
  3/5, 181
  3/6, 181
  3/7, 91, 93, 335–337
  3/7 - 7/3, 423
  3rd Ray, 153, 155, 169, 173, 177, 179, 180, 185, 231, 347, 348, 402
    activity of, 92–94
  4/1, 179, 206, 207, 210
  4/2, 325–326
  4/3, 183

4/5, 90, 326, 334
4/6, 326, 327–328
4/7, 328–331
4th Ray, 87, 153, 162–163, 169, 179, 228, 325, 337, 347–348
purpose, 338
5/2, 331–333, 334
5/4, 333–335
5/6, 90, 312–314
5/7, 320, 323–325
5th Ray, 169, 331, 332, 348–349
6/1, 179, 211–213, 217
6/2, 303–306
6/4, 306–308
6/5, 90, 310–312, 313
6/5 - 5/6, 312
6/7, 308–310
6th Ray, 152, 159, 161, 169, 227–228, 291, 307, 309, 349, 415
and sacral centre, 289
disciples, 292, 306
7/1, 92, 180, 181, 183, 197, 213, 215, 240
7/2, 174–175, 180, 295–297, 371
7/2 - 2/7, 165
7/3, 91, 92, 93, 110, 180, 181, 297–298, 303
7/3 Master, 298
7/4, 300–301
7/5, 298, 299–300
7/6, 301–303, 308
workers, 303
7/6 - 7/2 interrelation, 294, 302
7th Ray, 153, 156, 169, 173, 179, 180, 183, 227, 228, 242, 287, 288, 289, 294, 297, 298, 299, 301, 314, 329, 349–350, 370, 444
disciple, 295
formation of, 84–96, 188, 196
holding, 179
number of, 182
order of formation, 86–89
seven, 152, 417
Ray aspects/qualities
1/2, 179
1-4-7 relation, 113
1/6 - 2/6, 227
1/6 warrior, 217
1-7 relation, 190, 192
1st ray, 11, 30, 43, 45, 49, 54, 57, 62, 67, 88, 98, 109, 115, 144, 167, 168, 170, 173, 175, 176, 179, 180, 181, 186, 188, 189, 193, 195, 197, 208, 214, 215, 216, 217, 218, 239, 247, 252, 264, 269, 273, 279, 295, 316, 337, 350, 373, 374, 391, 393, 408, 412, 447, 460, 496
agenda, 414
and the sword, 233
builders, 201
department, 203, 205, 339, 412, 413
energies, 234, 235, 463
fiat, 413
Lord, 377
note, 416
power, 241–243, 246, 316–317, 375, 376, 444
purpose, 150, 237, 397, 411
Ray line, 197–203, 232
shield, 374
virtue, 234
1st ray pentad, 411–414, 415
2/1, 246, 370–371, 373
2/3, 178
2nd ray, 11, 41, 43–44, 48, 50, 57, 63, 65, 84, 86, 87, 88, 96, 98–99, 120, 144, 146, 147, 148–149, 150, 156, 164, 167, 168, 175, 176, 177, 186, 209, 235, 239, 240, 247, 251, 264, 268, 304, 315, 316, 317, 325, 338, 350, 368, 408, 421, 496
aberrant, 330
and Initiation Schools, 126
and Jesus, 414
and Sanat Kumāra, 444
as blue, 278
cycle, 181, 193, 195, 197,

218, 225, 396, 403, 409, 479
dispensation, 423
epoch, 222, 243, 274
explained, 54–55
outpouring, 109, 288
purpose, 115, 132, 140, 152, 192, 237, 320, 374, 393, 395
Ray line, 234, 245, 246, 280, 351
workers, 414
3rd ray, 11, 42, 44, 48, 50, 54, 88, 99, 102, 114, 141, 144, 147, 167, 168, 169, 172, 174, 175, 177, 188, 190, 192, 222, 225, 251, 268, 269, 270, 271, 278, 279, 316, 318, 319, 320, 321, 322, 338, 372, 408, 420, 463, 469, 485
as emerald, 265, 275
as midwife, 96
department, 128
explained, 55–56
Monadic, 421
outpouring, 109
purpose, 158, 393
Ray line, 234
statement, 222
virtue, 234
4th ray, 43, 45, 48, 50–51, 67, 87, 99–100, 134, 137, 141, 144, 155, 161, 168, 170, 175, 188, 215, 238, 253, 270, 306, 316, 321, 325, 337, 391, 408
and the Buddha, 469
explained, 55–56
flux, 321
purpose, 154, 159
Ray line, 330, 351
statement, 224
virtue, 234
5/2, 333
5/7, 321
5th ray, 42, 43, 45, 48, 56, 90, 100, 108–109, 138, 141, 166–167, 168, 230, 250, 270, 298, 316, 326, 337, 421, 466, 471, 480, 482
function, 239, 338
Ray line, 313
6/2, 304–305
6-7 unity, 175–177, 309
6th ray, 43–44, 45, 48, 49, 89, 90, 100–101, 115, 133, 141, 153–154, 155, 156, 161, 168, 194, 200, 216, 217, 234, 252, 270, 288, 291, 302, 304–305, 306, 307, 316, 337, 386, 446
and desire-attraction, 449
and Milarepa, 116
and moon Chain, 468
and the sex function, 449
department, 160
force, 349
function, 414–417
purpose, 159
Ray line, 330
7/2 Ray line, 371
7th ray, 41, 44, 45, 47, 48, 50, 52–53, 55, 65, 67, 94, 101, 115, 126, 136, 137, 141, 144, 151, 154, 156, 167, 168, 172, 175, 181, 188, 197, 202, 208, 213, 214, 225, 228–229, 233, 247, 252, 269, 270, 278, 289, 294–295, 298, 301, 314, 316, 317, 321, 323, 337, 371, 374, 389, 391, 393, 422
and 2nd Initiation, 448
and the Initiate, 448
department, 296, 300
dispensation, 445–452
function, 235, 444, 457
purpose, 171, 189, 223, 338, 408, 422, 423
Ray line, 300, 335, 351, 372
colours, 188
Monadic, 97
of Mind, 44
personality, 97
primordial, 377
seven Ray Lords, 121, 418, 456, 461, 495

Soul, 97
Ray representatives, 442
Rays of Mind, 104, 177, 179, 190, 196, 264, 286, 287, 348, 369, 371, 375, 385, 414, 416
five, 102, 125
rapid advancement, 108
Reapers of new cycle, 376
Rechungpa, 82, 116
Recorders, 482
Recording angels, 484
Red wine, symbolism, 233
Registrant of the Purpose, 383
Regulus, 39
Renaissance, 154, 277
Renunciation, need for, 366
Resource sharing, 340
Rider on the white horse, 19, 171–175, 244, 401–402
Rider, the, 150, 403, 405, 408
Right angled triangle, 420
Righteousness, explained, 228, 234, 238
Right hand path, 366
Rinpoches, 33, 68–69, 76, 411
Ritualistic activity, 300
Rock, symbolism, 82, 245
Rod of power, 314
Roman Catholic Church, 82
Root Race
3rd (Lemurian), 251, 255, 498, 504
4th (Atlantean), 26, 255, 498, 504
5th (Aryan), 25, 26, 31, 253, 259, 276, 377, 378, 498, 504
6th, 112, 253, 273, 278, 279, 377, 470, 504
7th, 232
Rosicrucians, 154, 406
Rounds, 439
Ṛṣis (Rishis), 5, 10, 171, 276
Brahmin, 5
of the great Bear, 272
Rudolf Steiner, 155, 406

S

Sacrificial horse, 401
Śākyamuni, 63
Sakya Paṇḍita, 156
Salvation, 231
Samantabhadra, 34–35
Samantabhadrī, 34
Śamatha, 457
Sambhogakāya Flower, 2, 10, 23, 36, 38, 144, 157, 191, 259, 273, 315, 331–332, 348, 387, 434, 435, 457, 458, 459, 475, 478
and Ashrams, 96–98
and Initiation path, 95
discovery of, 166
Knowledge - Knowledge petal, 476
Knowledge - Love-Wisdom petal, 476
Knowledge petals, 476–477
Knowledge - Will petal, 477
Love-Wisdom - Knowledge petal, 477
Will - Knowledge petal, 477
Samos, 249
Saṃsāra, 77–78, 122, 152, 191
and evil, 360
Saṃskāras, 392
battles over, 133
conversion of, 14, 121, 149, 207
countering of, 355
gross, 316
kāma-manasic, 338, 476
mastering of, 339
mentalistic, 477
of dark brother, 214, 248
of desire-mind, 250
of humanity, 319–320
of illogic, 368–369
planetary, 32
Watery, 216, 311, 415
Śāṇavāsika, 42–43, 44, 45, 48
Sandalwood tree, symbolism, 8
Sandhya, 489
Sandhyāsana, 489

Saṇgha, 42, 47–50
Sanhedrin, 66
Śāriputra, 37, 41–42, 43, 45, 46, 57
Satan, 226
Saturn, 99, 138, 139, 141, 190, 191, 219, 256, 274, 496
  globe, 274
Saviours of the Race, 472, 477
Scheme/s, 439
  Earth, 274, 439, 441, 462, 463
  planetary, 274, 440
  Venus, 439
Scientific activity, 323–324
Scientific materialism, 313
  ending of, 166
Scientific methodology, 332, 349
Scribes, 482
Seal of Solomon, 489
Sea, symbolism, 236, 462
Secret Place, 174, 404, 405
Seekers of satisfaction, 474
Sefer Yetzirah, 488
Sense-consciousnesses, 457
Sense perceptions
  hearing, 211, 324
  sight, 206
  smell, 213
  taste, 215
Sephiroth, 487, 488
Seraphim, 266, 473
Serapis, 49, 133, 134, 158–159, 169, 170, 236, 238, 348
Seriphos, 256
Serpent
  energy, 476
  fire, 472
  symbolism, 230
Serpent locks, symbolism, 252
Service, explained, 161
Seth, 29, 30
Seven churches, 416–417
Seven sacred planets, 496
  Regents of, 461
Seven Spirits of God, 418, 452, 505
Seventy five year cycles, 406
Sewer system, 205
Sex magic, 308, 309–310, 449
Sex relationship, 445–447
Sexual misery, 466
sGam po pa, 42, 65, 76, 77, 116
Shades, explained, 329–330
Shambhala, 2–3, 7, 58, 67, 72, 81, 106, 113, 145, 146, 151, 162, 163, 167, 170, 172, 177, 180, 181, 186, 189, 191, 192, 193, 198, 199, 200, 205, 230, 253, 254, 257, 259, 266, 274, 278, 289, 298, 299, 303, 317, 322, 328, 334, 357, 369, 377, 385, 390, 391, 392, 393, 399, 410, 438, 460, 463, 478, 479
  8 regions of, 16
  and Atlantis, 18
  and Bodhisattvas, 19
  and crisis of Initiation, 87
  and Dharmakāya Way, 70–71
  and Head centre, 17, 34
  and Hierarchy, 86
  and Manu, 120
  and myths, 2, 6
  and suṣumṇā nāḍī, 94
  and will-to-good, 85
  and young Hierarchy, 27–28
  as chakra, 1, 4
  as shield of ‘God’, 405
  constitution of, 451, 456
  Council Chamber, 25, 78, 87, 188, 381, 459–460, 461, 470, 484, 495, 498, 499
  executive Council, 24, 505, 506
  externalisation of, 272
  in texts, 4–20
  king/s of, 6, 8, 14, 34, 234
  levels of, 22–79
  Lords of, 18, 23, 40, 53, 77, 108, 169, 192, 201, 202, 231, 242, 265, 271, 323, 373, 412, 417, 493
  planetary executuves, 434
Shambhalic
  level
    1st, 24–37, 46, 135
    2nd, 37–50, 122, 125, 126
    3rd, 74, 122

4th, 75–76
5th, 77
maṇḍala, 112
Mind, 74–75, 120
pentad, 382
inverted, 351
potency, 376
purpose, 150, 350
Will, 241
Shangri-la, 2, 4
Sharia law, 347
Shekinah, 103, 106
Shield, 219, 254
Hierarchical, 254, 405, 413
of faith, 229
of God, 350, 405
Shigatse, 81, 406
Shiwa Aui, 116
Sickle, explained, 190, 191
Siddhis, 39, 44, 66, 115, 357, 364
awakening of, 123
development of, 127, 356
higher, 136
minor, 315–316, 323
modern, 131
Signs of the times, 409
Silent Watcher, 271, 442, 466
Sirian blue, 272
Sirian Logos, 235, 236
Sirian Lore, 444
Sirian purpose, 124, 387
Sirius, 78, 123, 276, 431, 459, 460, 487
representative from, 461
Śītā River, 4, 11, 12, 14, 16
Śiva, 265
Six Realms, 394
Six spirits before the Throne, 436
Sixth great sphere, 308, 309
Six wings, symbolism, 484
Six Yogas of Naropa, 116
Skull cup, 201
Skull, symbolism, 216
S.L. MacGregor Mathers, 94
Socialism, new form of, 347
Solar Incarnation, 478
Solar system
1st, 480
previous, 495, 500, 501
Sorcerers, 226, 362
cosmic, 361
Soul, 475
Soul groups, 190
Sound and true law, 367
Sound, explained, 329
Space craft, 180
Space-time continuum, 416
Sphinx, 90, 259, 276
Spica, 265
Spinoza, 96
Spiral-cyclic energy, 416
Spirit of Peace, 24, 32, 34, 35, 36, 253, 378, 379, 380, 382, 384, 385, 387, 394, 404, 440, 442, 443, 451, 461
and the 6th Ray, 444
Spiritual age, explained, 372–373
Spiritualism, 426
Spiritual Power, 366, 380
Spiritual Triad, 480, 481, 482
Spiritual University, 352
Square, symbolism, 119
Srota-āpannas, 13
Stage of the forerunner, 237, 406
Stalin, 185
Stheino, 249, 250
Stone, turning to, 252
Straight-knowledge, 426, 428
Stygnian Nymphs, 256
Subhūti, 39, 43, 45, 47
Subtle World, 426
Summit Lighthouse, 424
Sun, 139
Heart of, 30
spiritual, 353
Sun-moon relationship, 190
Śūnyatā, 34, 44, 45, 47, 81, 114–115, 239, 241, 263, 270, 360, 454, 458, 487
experience, 424
goal of, 69–70
Supernal Three, 460, 461

Survival of the fittest, 90
Surya, 31
Suṣumṇā
and third Christ, 64–65
energy, 128
of Hierarchy, 298
Swastika, 151, 152, 198, 370–373, 416
Sword, 254
of Light, 203
of righteousness, 200
symbolism, 118–119, 231, 232, 233
two-edged, 239–241
Synthesis, 400
Syria, 60

T

Tarā, 32
Tāranātha, 4
Tashi Lungpo Monastery, 81
Tathāgatagarbha, 30, 146, 360, 361, 502. *See also* Sambhogakāya Flower
Teleportation, 371
Tell-el-Amarna, 30
Temple Hierophants, 221
Temple of Love, 159
Temple of the Lord, 161
Temple of the Mysteries, 106, 126
Temples of Deity, 296
Temples of liberation, 196
Tension, explained, 355–356
Teotihicán, 91
Tesla, 96
The Great Invocation, 217
The Mahatma Letters, 427
Theory of Relativity, 73
Theosophical Society, 92–93, 155, 406
Theosophists, 406, 424
Theriomorphic deities, 121
The Secret Doctrine, 83, 93
The Silent Watcher, 434–436
Thoth, 28
Throne of God, 119, 440
Throne of Service, 183
Thusness, error-free, 134
Thymus gland, 129
Thyroid gland, 497
Tiger, symbolism, 206
Time, concept of, 12
Toiling masses, education of, 336
Tokyo, 407, 408
Tomb, and Initiation, 114, 118
Tooth of prophecy, 257
Touch of Enlightenment, 397
Transfiguration initiation, 397, 445
Tree of knowledge, 190
Tree of Life, 488
Triangle, eye within, 491, 493
Triangles, function of, 498
Trident, 222
Trimūrti, 265
Trinity of Deity, 440
Tripiṭaka, 48
True, explained, 234
Trumpet, explained, 416
Truth, 240
distortions of, 227
'ear-whispered', 22
empowerment of, 386
Tsongkhapa, 39, 45, 47, 50–51, 77, 112–113, 120, 122, 123–124, 125, 126, 132, 140, 378, 382, 385–386
Tulku/s, 394, 411
Tum-mo, 314, 316
Twelve labours, 260, 261

U

Unicorns, 19
United Nations, 163
new, 338–347, 347
transforming of, 297
Unit of mind, 473
Upagupta, 48, 49
Upāli, 43, 45–46, 49–50
Uranus, 101, 137, 139, 156, 371, 464
Urusvati, 32
USA, 176, 449, 471

V

Vaiśālī, 48
Vajra (dorje), 10, 16, 35, 106, 113, 151, 152, 214–215, 222, 370
Vajrapāṇi, 4, 10, 11, 120
Vajrasattva, 35
Vajra Vehicle, 11–12, 14
Vajrayāna, 5
Vasubandu, 65
Vāyus, 102, 121
Venetian, the, 49, 128, 157–158, 320
Venus, 78, 100, 137, 138, 139, 438, 455, 460, 503
    representative from, 461
Vessāvana, 483
Veto power, 340
Vibhūticandra, 9
Vidyadhāras, five, 451, 452, 454
    Consorts, 454, 455
Vietnam, 60
Vinayapiṭaka, 45
Vincent Van Gogh, 96
Vine of the earth, 190, 191
Violet devas of the shadows, 33
Vipassana, 457
Virgin Mary, 32, 267
Virgoan, woman's head, 259
Virūdhaka, 483
Virupākśa, 483
Vishnu, 11, 20, 31, 104, 265
Voice of Silence, 325, 367
Void, doctrine of, 114
Void Elements, 458
Vulcan, 98, 139
Vulture, symbolism, 211

W

War between dark and white forces, 356–359
Warlocks, 362
War machines, 341
War on drugs, 344
Wars, explained, 182
Water of Life, 377
Waters, 471, 486
Watery turmoil, 389
Way of Truth, 385
Weapons of mass destruction, 341
Wesak festival, 84–85, 435
White brotherhood, 149, 230, 254, 359, 364, 430. *See also* Hierarchy of Light
White dharma, 53
White horse, 11, 172, 233
White magic, 367, 448
Will, 182, 206, 239, 247, 257, 297, 373, 395, 505
    2nd Ray aspect, 391
    and tension, 356
    cosmic, 39
    direction of, 485
    Divine, 65, 180, 390, 444
    energy, 379
    personal, 316
    to transform, 328
Will-Love-Activity, 347
Will of God, 188
Will-of-Love, 63, 86, 106, 130, 131, 133, 134, 139, 149, 169, 180, 210, 357
Will-of-mind, 139, 141
Will-to-good, 85, 399, 404
Will-to-know, 399
Will-to-Love, 63, 104, 127, 134, 325, 357, 401
Will-to-manifest, 401
Will-to-spiritual power, 401
Will vs Purpose, 381
Wine, explained, 235
Winepress, great, 189, 191, 193, 195, 196, 233, 234, 235, 237
Wisdom
    All-accomplishing, 47, 62, 74, 168, 209, 263, 288
    Dharmadhātu, 24, 46, 62, 164, 263
    Discriminating Inner, 77,165, 263
    Equalising, 47, 55, 62, 76, 161, 263, 287
    Hierarchical, 319
    Mirror-like, 46, 62, 263

Wisdom Religion, new, 376
Witchcraft, 71, 479
Witches, 362, 368
Wolf, symbolism, 209–210
Wolves, 363–370
Womb, 268
  of Life, 319
  of mind/Mind, 442
  of Nature, 452
  of space-time, 194, 454
Word, 238
World egg, 319
World Saviour, 410, 415
World-Soul, 154, 164, 261, 379
World spheres, 3
World Teacher, 379
World War II, 403
World War III, 341
W.Q. Judge, 406
Wrath, 237
Wrathful Deities, 9, 70, 193, 200, 235, 364, 451, 452–454, 458

Y

Yakṣinī Hiṅgalācī, 48
Year 2025 and Hierarchy, 406
Yogācāra tradition, 360
Yogin, 451
Yoginī, 451
Yuga/s, 489–490
  Dvāpara, 489
  Kali, 12, 20, 52, 363, 489, 490
  Krita, 489
  Satya, 489, 490
  Tretā, 489

Z

Zapping, explained, 355
Zeus, 25, 26, 249, 253
Zodiac, 122
  and Splenic centre I, 148
  Aquarius the water bearer, 83, 135, 139, 157, 165, 483, 496, 503, 504
    keynote, 156
  Aries the ram, 123–125, 137, 139, 146, 275, 419, 496, 503, 504
  Cancer the crab, 14, 127, 138, 139, 152, 195, 261, 496, 504
    keynote, 163
  Capricorn the goat, 93, 134–135, 138, 139, 191, 475, 496, 503, 504
    keynote, 158
  Gemini the twins, 29, 125, 126, 139, 158, 161–163, 496, 503, 504
    keynote, 161
  Leonine activity, 110
  Leo the lion, 26–27, 39, 128, 129, 259, 261, 331, 419, 483, 496, 504
    keynote, 165
  Leo-Virgo relationship, 138
  Libra the balances, 130, 131, 137, 139, 140, 147, 151, 495, 501
  Pisces the fishes, 136, 139, 161, 195, 419, 475
    extreme aspects, 153
    key phrase, 156
    symbol, 415
  potencies of, 419
  Sagittarius the archer, 139, 158, 173
    keynote, 134, 159
  Scorpio the scorpion, 132, 139, 152, 160, 161, 261, 328, 483
    keynote, 159
  signs, three rulers, 139
  Taurus-Gemini relationship, 139
  Taurus-Scorpio relationship, 153
  Taurus the bull, 139, 160–161, 194, 260, 265, 275, 303, 483
    keynote, 160
  Virgo the virgin, 29, 129, 259, 265, 296
    keynote, 167
Zoroastrian religion, 276
  mythology, 359

About the Author

BODO BALSYS is the founder of The School of Esoteric Sciences. He is an author of many books on subjects centred on Buddhism and the Esoteric Sciences, a meditation teacher, poet, artist, spiritual scientist and healer. He has studied extensively across multiple traditions including Esoteric Science, Buddhism, Christianity, Esoteric Healing, Western Science, Art, Politics and History. His advanced esoteric insights, gained through decades of meditative contemplation, enable him to provide a rich understanding of the spiritual pathway toward enlightenment, healing and service.

Bodo's teachings can be accessed via the School of Esoteric Science's website:
http://universaldharma.com

For any other enquiries, please email
sangha@universaldharma.com

About Universal Dharma Publishing

Universal Dharma Publishing is a not for profit publisher. Our aim is make innovative, original and esoteric spiritual teachings accessible to all who genuinely aspire to awaken and serve humanity. The books published aim in part to provide an esoteric interpretation of the meaning of Buddhist *dharma* with view of reformation of the way people perceive the meaning of the related teachings. Hopefully then Buddhism can more effectively serve its principal function as a vehicle for enlightenment, and further prosper into the future. A further aim is to provide the next level of exposition of the esoteric doctrines to be revealed to humanity following on the wisdom tradition pioneered by H.P. Blavatsky and A.A. Bailey.

Cover Design by
Angie O'Sullivan & Kylie Smith

www.ingramcontent.com/pod-product-compliance
Lightning Source LLC
Chambersburg PA
CBHW020631300426
44112CB00007B/85